Lecture Notes in Computer Science   8366

Commenced Publication in 1973
Founding and Former Series Editors:
Gerhard Goos, Juris Hartmanis, and Jan van Leeuwen

Lecture Notes in Computer Science 8566

Commenced Publication in 1973

Founding and Former Series Editors:
Gerhard Goos, Juris Hartmanis, and Jan van Leeuwen

Editorial Board

David Hutchison
  Lancaster University, UK
Takeo Kanade
  Carnegie Mellon University, Pittsburgh, PA, USA
Josef Kittler
  University of Surrey, Guildford, UK
Jon M. Kleinberg
  Cornell University, Ithaca, NY, USA
Alfred Kobsa
  University of California, Irvine, CA, USA
Friedemann Mattern
  ETH Zurich, Switzerland
John C. Mitchell
  Stanford University, CA, USA
Moni Naor
  Weizmann Institute of Science, Rehovot, Israel
Oscar Nierstrasz
  University of Bern, Switzerland
C. Pandu Rangan
  Indian Institute of Technology, Madras, India
Bernhard Steffen
  TU Dortmund University, Germany
Madhu Sudan
  Microsoft Research, Cambridge, MA, USA
Demetri Terzopoulos
  University of California, Los Angeles, CA, USA
Doug Tygar
  University of California, Berkeley, CA, USA
Gerhard Weikum
  Max Planck Institute for Informatics, Saarbruecken, Germany

Josh Benaloh (Ed.)

Topics in Cryptology – CT-RSA 2014

The Cryptographer's Track at the RSA Conference 2014
San Francisco, CA, USA, February 25-28, 2014
Proceedings

 Springer

Volume Editor

Josh Benaloh
Microsoft Research
Redmond, WA, USA
E-mail: benaloh@microsoft.com

ISSN 0302-9743   ISSN 1611-3349 (electronic)
ISBN 978-3-319-04851-2   ISBN 978-3-319-04852-9 (eBook)
DOI 10.1007/978-3-319-04852-9
Springer Cham Heidelberg New York Dordrecht London

Library of Congress Control Number: 2014930761

LNCS Sublibrary: SL 4 – Security and Cryptology

Typesetting: Camera-ready by author, data conversion by Scientific Publishing Services, Chennai, India

Printed on acid-free paper

Springer is part of Springer Science+Business Media (www.springer.com)

Preface

The RSA conference has been a major international event for information security experts since its inception in 1991. It is an annual event that attracts hundreds of vendors and thousands of participants from industry, government, and academia. Since 2001, the RSA conference has included the Cryptographers' Track (CT-RSA), which provides a forum for current research in cryptography. CT-RSA has become a major publication venue for cryptographers.

This volume represents the proceedings of the 2014 RSA Conference Cryptographers' Track which was held in San Francisco, California, February 25–28, 2014. A total of 66 submissions were received out of which 25 papers were selected. As Chair of the Program Committee, I heartily thank all of the authors who contributed their innovative ideas and all of the Program Committee members and their designated assistants who carefully reviewed the submissions. The evaluation process was thorough with each submission receiving at least three independent reviews (four if the submitted paper included a Program Committee member as an author) and extensive discussion to complete the selection process.

Antione Joux of the University of Versailles delivered an invited address on *Discrete Logarithms: Recent Progress (and Open Problems)* and Bart Preneel moderated a panel discussion on pseudo-random number generators featuring Dan Boneh, Paul Kocher, Adi Shamir, and Dan Shumow.

December 2013   Josh Benaloh

Organization

The RSA Cryptographers' Track is an independently managed component of the annual RSA Conference.

Steering Committee

Josh Benaloh	Microsoft Research, USA
Ed Dawson	Queensland University of Technology, Australia
Orr Dunkelman	University of Haifa, Israel
Ari Juels	Roving Chief Scientist, USA
Ron Rivest	Massachusetts Institute of Technology, USA
Moti Yung	Google, USA

Program Chair

Josh Benaloh	Microsoft Research, USA

Program Committee

Josh Benaloh (Chair)	Microsoft Research, USA
Tom Berson	Anagram Laboratories, USA
Alex Biryukov	University of Luxembourg, Luxembourg
John Black	University of Colorado, USA
Xavier Boyen	Queensland University of Technology, Australia
Christian Cachin	IBM Research, Switzerland
Orr Dunkelman	University of Haifa, Israel
Steven D. Galbraith	University of Auckland, New Zealand
Jens Groth	University College London, UK
Helena Handschuh	Cryptography Research, Inc., USA
Marc Joye	Technicolor, France
John Kelsey	National Institute of Standards and Technology, USA
Kwangjo Kim	Korea Advanced Institute of Science and Technology, South Korea
Lars Knudsen	Technical University of Denmark, Denmark
Alptekin Küpçü	Koç University, Turkey
Susan Langford	Hewlett-Packard, USA
Anna Lysyanskaya	Brown University, USA

Mitsuru Matsui	Mitsubishi Electric, Japan
Sarah Meiklejohn	University of California, San Diego, USA
Daniele Micciancio	University of California, San Diego, USA
Tal Moran	Interdisciplinary Center Herzliya, Israel
Bart Preneel	KU Leuven, Belgium
Christian Rechberger	Technical University of Denmark, Denmark
Matt Robshaw	Impinj, USA
Rei Safavi-Naini	University of Calgary, Canada
Nigel Smart	University of Bristol, UK
Vanessa Teague	University of Melbourne, Australia
Eran Tromer	Tel Aviv University, Israel
Serge Vaudenay	École Polytechnique Fédérale de Lausanne, Switzerland
Hoeteck Wee	George Washington University, USA
Yiqun Lisa Yin	Independent Security Consultant, USA

External Reviewers

Table of Contents

Symmetric Encryption and Cryptanalysis

Digital Signatures

Protocols

Hash Function Cryptanalysis

Applications of Cryptographic Primitives

Efficient and Secure Algorithms for GLV-Based Scalar Multiplication and Their Implementation on GLV-GLS Curves

Armando Faz-Hernández[1,*], Patrick Longa[2], and Ana H. Sánchez[3]

[1] Institute of Computing,
University of Campinas, Brazil
armfazh@ic.unicamp.br
[2] Microsoft Research,
One Microsoft Way, Redmond, USA
plonga@microsoft.com
[3] Computer Science Department, CINVESTAV-IPN, México
asanchez@computacion.cs.cinvestav.mx

Abstract. We propose efficient algorithms and formulas that improve the performance of *side-channel protected* scalar multiplication exploiting the Gallant-Lambert-Vanstone (CRYPTO 2001) and Galbraith-Lin-Scott (EUROCRYPT 2009) methods. Firstly, by adapting Feng et al.'s recoding to the GLV setting, we derive new regular algorithms for variable-base scalar multiplication that offer protection against simple side-channel and timing attacks. Secondly, we propose an efficient technique that interleaves ARM-based and NEON-based multiprecision operations over an extension field, as typically found on GLS curves and pairing computations, to improve performance on modern ARM processors. Finally, we showcase the efficiency of the proposed techniques by implementing a state-of-the-art GLV-GLS curve in twisted Edwards form defined over $\mathbb{F}_{p^2}$, which supports a four dimensional decomposition of the scalar and runs in constant time, i.e., it is fully protected against timing attacks. For instance, using a precomputed table of only 512 bytes, we compute a variable-base scalar multiplication in 92,000 cycles on an Intel Ivy Bridge processor and in 244,000 cycles on an ARM Cortex-A15 processor. Our benchmark results and the proposed techniques contribute to the improvement of the state-of-the-art performance of elliptic curve computations. Most notably, our techniques allow us to reduce the cost of adding protection against timing attacks in the GLV-based variable-base scalar multiplication computation to below 10%.

Keywords: Elliptic curves, scalar multiplication, side-channel protection, constant-time computation, GLV method, GLS method, GLV-GLS curve, x64 processor, ARM processor, NEON instructions.

---

* Author became affiliated to University of Campinas at the time of publication.

J. Benaloh (Ed.): CT-RSA 2014, LNCS 8366, pp. 1–27, 2014.
© Springer International Publishing Switzerland 2014

1 Introduction

Let P be a point of prime order r on an elliptic curve over $\mathbb{F}_p$ containing a degree-2 endomorphism ϕ. The Gallant-Lambert-Vanstone (GLV) method computes the scalar multiplication kP as $k_1 P + k_2 \phi(P)$ [15]. If k_1, k_2 have approximately half the bitlength of the original scalar k, one should expect an elimination of half the number of doublings by using the Straus-Shamir simultaneous multi-scalar multiplication technique. Thus, the method is especially useful for speeding up the case in which the base point P is variable, known as variable-base scalar multiplication. Later, Galbraith et al. [14] showed how to exploit the Frobenius endomorphism to enable the use of the GLV approach on a wider set of curves defined over the quadratic extension field $\mathbb{F}_{p^2}$. Since then, significant research has been performed to improve the performance [29,23] and to explore the applicability to other settings [19,34] or to higher dimensions on genus one curves [23,30] and genus two curves [7,8]. Unfortunately, most of the work and comparisons with other approaches have been carried out with *unprotected* algorithms and implementations. In fact, little effort has been done to investigate methods for protecting GLV-based implementations against side-channel attacks. Just recently, Longa and Sica [30] used the regular windowed recoding by Okeya and Takagi [33] in combination with interleaving [15,32] to make their four-dimensional implementation constant time. However, the use of this standard approach in the GLV paradigm incurs in a high cost in terms of storage and computing performance because of the high number of required precomputations. This issue worsens for higher dimensions [8].

In this work, we propose a new signed representation, called GLV-based Sign-Aligned Column (GLV-SAC), that gives rise to a new method for scalar multiplication using the GLV method. We depart from the traditional approach based on interleaving or joint sparse form and adapt the recoding by Feng et al. [11], originally intended for standard comb-based fixed-base scalar multiplication, to the computation of GLV-based variable-base scalar multiplication. The method supports a regular execution and thus provides a first layer of protection against some simple side-channel (SSCA) attacks such as simple power analysis (SPA) [26]. Moreover, it does not require dummy operations, making it resilient to safe-error attacks [40,41], and can be used as a basis for constant-time implementations secure against timing attacks [25,9,2,35]. In comparison with the best previous approaches, the method improves the computing performance, especially during the potentially expensive precomputation stage, and allows us to save *at least* half of the storage requirement for precomputed values without impacting performance. For instance, the method injects a 17% speedup in the overall computation and a 78% reduction in the memory consumption for a GLV-GLS curve using a 4-GLV decomposition (see §5). The savings in memory without impacting performance are especially relevant for the deployment of GLV-based implementations in constrained devices. Depending on the cost of endomorphisms, the improvement provided by the method is expected to increase for higher-degree decompositions.

Processors based on the ARM architecture are widely used in modern smartphones and tablets due to their low power consumption. The ARM architecture comes equipped with 16 32-bit registers and an instruction set including 32-bit operations, which in most cases can be executed in one cycle. To boost performance in certain applications, some ARM processors include a powerful set of vector instructions known as NEON. This consists of a 128-bit Single Instruction Multiple Data (SIMD) engine that includes 16 128-bit registers. Recent research has exploited NEON to accelerate cryptographic operations [6,18,36]. On one hand, the interleaving of ARM and NEON instructions is a well-known technique (with increasing potential on modern processors) that can be exploited in cryptography; e.g., see [6]. On the other hand, the vectorized computation using NEON can be advantageously exploited to compute independent multiplications, as found in operations over $\mathbb{F}_{p^2}$; e.g., see [36]. In this work, we take these optimizations further and propose a technique that interleaves ARM-based and NEON-based multiprecision operations, such as multiplication, squaring and modular reduction, in extension field operations in order to maximize the inherent parallelism and hide the execution latency. The technique is especially relevant for implementing the quadratic extension field layer, as found in GLS curves [14] and pairing computations [1]. For instance, it injects a significant speedup in the range 17%-34% in the scalar multiplication execution on the targeted GLV-GLS curve (see §4 and §5).

To demonstrate the efficiency of our techniques, we implement the state-of-the-art twisted Edwards GLV-GLS curve over $\mathbb{F}_{p^2}$ with $p = 2^{127} - 5997$, recently proposed by Longa and Sica [30]. This curve, referred to as Ted127-glv4, supports a 4-GLV decomposition. Moreover, we also present efficient algorithms for implementing field and quadratic extension field operations targeting our 127-bit prime on x64 and ARM platforms. We combine and exploit incomplete reduction [39] and lazy reduction [38], expanding techniques by [29]. These optimized operations are then applied to state-of-the-art twisted Edwards formulas [3,22] to speed up computations in the setting of curves over $\mathbb{F}_{p^2}$. Our implementations of variable-base scalar multiplication target modern x64 and ARM processors, and include *full* protection against timing attacks: the scalar is decomposed and recoded (in constant time) in a regular pattern using the proposed GLV-SAC representation, secret-data conditional branches are avoided and memory accesses (over precomputed points) are performed in constant time.

Notably, we show that the proposed algorithms and formulas reduce dramatically the cost of protecting against timing attacks and the storage for precomputations, and set a new speed record for protected software. For instance, a protected variable-based elliptic curve scalar multiplication on curve Ted127-glv4 runs in 96,000 cycles on an Intel Sandy Bridge, using only 512 bytes of memory for precomputed values. This is 30% faster, using almost 1/5 of the storage, than a previous implementation by Longa and Sica [30] also based on curve Ted127-glv4 that computes the same operation in 137,000 cycles using 2.25KB of memory for precomputations. Moreover, this result is only 5% slower, using 1/2 of the storage, than the *unprotected* computation by the same authors, which runs in 91,000 cycles and uses 1KB of memory. This not only represents a new speed record for protected software but also marks the first time that a constant-time variable-base scalar multiplication computation is performed under 100K cycles on an Intel processor. Similar results are obtained for ARM processors exploiting the technique that interleaves NEON and ARM-based operations.

This paper is organized as follows. In §2, we give some preliminaries about the GLV and GLS methods, and side-channel attacks. In §3, we present the new GLV-based representation and the corresponding scalar multiplication method. We describe the implementation of curve `Ted127-glv4` as well as optimized algorithms for field, extension field and point operations targeting x64 and ARM platforms in §4. In this section, we also discuss the interleaving technique for ARM. Finally, in §5, we perform an analysis of the proposed methods and present benchmark results of scalar multiplication on several x64 and ARM processors.

2   Preliminaries

2.1   The GLV and GLS Methods

In this section, we briefly describe the GLV and GLS methods in a generic, m dimensional framework. Let C be a curve defined over a finite field $\mathbb{F}_p$ equipped with an efficiently computable endomorphism ϕ. The GLV method to compute scalar multiplication [15] consists of first decomposing the scalar k into sub-scalars k_i for $0 \leq i < m$ and then computing $\sum_{i=0}^{m-1} k_i D_i$ using the Straus-Shamir trick for simultaneous multi-scalar multiplication, where D_0 is the input divisor from the divisor class group of the curve and $D_i = \phi^i(D_0)$. If all of the sub-scalars have approximately the same bitlength, the number of required doublings is reduced to approximately $\log_2 r/m$, where r is the prime order of the curve subgroup. Special curves equipped with endomorphisms which are different to the Frobenius endomorphism are known as GLV curves.

The GLS method [14,13] lifts the restriction to special curves and exploits an endomorphism ψ arising from the p-power Frobenius endomorphism on a wider set of curves C' defined over a extension field $\mathbb{F}_{p^k}$ that are $\mathbb{F}_{p^n}$-isogenous to curves $C/\mathbb{F}_p$, where $k|n$. Equipped with ψ to perform the scalar decomposition, one then proceeds to apply the GLV method as above. More complex decompositions arise by applying the GLS paradigm to GLV curves (a.k.a. GLV-GLS curves [14,30]).

These techniques have received lots of attention recently, given their significant impact in the performance of curve-based systems. Longa and Gebotys [29] report efficient implementations of GLS curves over $\mathbb{F}_{p^2}$ using two-dimensional decompositions. In [23], Hu, Longa and Xu explore a GLV-GLS curve over $\mathbb{F}_{p^2}$ supporting a four-dimensional decomposition. In [7], Bos et al. study two and four-dimensional decompositions on genus 2 curves over $\mathbb{F}_p$. Bos et al. [8] explore the combined GLV-GLS approach over genus 2 curves defined over $\mathbb{F}_{p^2}$, which supports an 8-GLV decomposition. In the case of binary GLS elliptic curves, Oliveira et al. [34] report the implementation of a curve exploiting the 2-GLV method. More recently, Guillevic and Ionica [17] show how to exploit the 4-GLV method on certain genus one curves defined over $\mathbb{F}_{p^2}$ and genus two curves defined over $\mathbb{F}_p$; and Smith [37] proposes a new family of elliptic curves that support 2-GLV decompositions.

From all these works, only [30] and [34] include side-channel protection in their GLV-based implementations.

2.2 Side-Channel Attacks and Countermeasures

Side-channel attacks [25] exploit leakage information obtained from the physical implementation of a cryptosystem to get access to private key material. Examples of physical information that can be exploited are power, time, electromagnetic emanations, among others. In particular, much attention has been put on timing [25,9] and simple power attacks (SPA) [26], given their broad applicability and relatively low costs to be realized in practice. Traditionally, the different attacks can also be distinguished by the number of traces that are exploited in the analysis: simple side-channel attacks (SSCA) require only one trace (or very few traces) to observe the leakage that directly reveals the secret bits, whereas differential side-channel attacks (DSCA) require many traces to perform a statistical analysis on the data. The feasibility of these attacks depends on the targeted application, but it is clear that SSCA attacks are feasible in a wider range of scenarios. In this work, we focus on methods that minimize the risk posed by SSCA attacks such as SPA, and timing attacks.

In curve-based cryptosystems, the first step to achieve protection against these attacks is to use regular algorithms for performing scalar multiplication (other methods involve the use of unified formulas, but these are generally expensive). One efficient approach in this direction is to recode the scalar to a representation exhibiting a regular pattern. In particular, for the case of variable-base scalar multiplication, the regular windowed recoding proposed by Okeya and Takagi [33] and further analyzed by Joye and Tunstall [24] represents one of the most efficient alternatives. Nevertheless, in comparison with the standard width-w non-adjacent form (wNAF) [20] used in unprotected implementations, the Okeya-Takagi recoding increases the nonzero density from $1/(w+1)$ to $1/(w-1)$. In contrast, side-channel protected methods for scalar multiplication exploiting the GLV method have not been fully studied. Furthermore, we note that methods typically efficient in the standard case are not necessarily efficient in the GLV paradigm. For example, in [30], Longa and Sica apply the Okeya-Takagi recoding to protect scalar multiplication on a GLV-GLS curve using a four-dimensional GLV decomposition against timing attacks. The resulting protected implementation is about 30% more expensive than the unprotected version. In this work, we aim at reducing that gap, providing efficient methods that can be exploited to improve and protect GLV and GLS-based implementations.

The comb method [27] is an efficient approach for the case of fixed-base scalar multiplication. However, in its original form, the method is unprotected against SSCA and timing attacks. An efficient approach to achieve a regular execution is to recode the scalar using signed nonzero representations such as LSB-set [11], MSB-set [12] or SAB-set [21]. A key observation in this work is that the basic version of the fixed-base comb execution (i.e., without exploiting multiple tables) has several similarities with a GLV-based variable-base execution. So it is therefore natural to adapt these techniques to the GLV setting to achieve side-channel protection. In particular, the LSB-set representation is a good candidate, given that an analogue of this method in the GLV setting minimizes the cost of precomputation.

2.3   The Least Significant Bit - Set (LSB-Set) Representation

Feng et al. [11] proposed a clever signed representation, called LSB-set, that is based on the equivalence $1 \equiv 1\bar{1}\ldots\bar{1}$ (assuming the notation $-1 \equiv \bar{1}$), and used it to protect the comb method [27] in the computation of fixed-base scalar multiplication (we refer to this method as LSB-set comb scalar multiplication). Next, we briefly describe the LSB-set recoding and its application to fixed-base scalar multiplication. The reader is referred to [27] and [11] for complete details about the original comb method and the LSB-set comb method, respectively.

Let t be the bitlength of a given scalar k. Assume that k is partitioned in w consecutive parts of $d = \lceil l/w \rceil$ bits each, padding k with $(dw - t)$ zeros to the left. Let the updated binary representation of k be $(k_{l-1}, k_{l-2}, \ldots, k_0)$, where $l = dw$. One can visualize the bits of k in matrix form by considering the w pieces as the rows and arranging them from top to bottom. The LSB-set recoding consists of first applying the transformation $1 \mapsto 1\bar{1}\ldots\bar{1}$ to the least significant d bits of the scalar (i.e., the first row in the matrix) and, then, converting every bit k_i in the remaining rows in such a way that output digits b_i for $d \leq i \leq (l-1)$ are in the digit set $\{0, b_{i \bmod d}\}$. That is, digits in the same column are 0 or share the same sign. Then, for computing a comb fixed-base scalar multiplication, one scans the "digit-columns" in the matrix from left to right. Since every digit-column is nonzero by definition, the execution consists of a doubling-addition computation at every iteration, which provides protection against certain SSCA attacks such as SPA.

3   The GLV-Based Sign-Aligned Column (GLV-SAC) Representation

In this section, we introduce a variant of the LSB-set recoding that is amenable for the computation of side-channel protected variable-base scalar multiplication in the GLV setting. The new recoding is called GLV-Based Sign-Aligned Column (GLV-SAC). Also, we present a new method for GLV-based scalar multiplication exploiting the proposed representation.

In the following, we first discuss the GLV-SAC representation in a generic setting. In Section 3.2, we discuss variants that are expected to be more efficient when $m = 2$ and $m \geq 8$. To simplify the descriptions, we assume in the remainder that we are working on an elliptic curve. The techniques and algorithms can be easily extended to other settings such as genus 2 curves.

Let $\{k_0, k_1, \ldots, k_j, \ldots, k_{m-1}\}$ be a set of positive sub-scalars in the setting of GLV with dimension m. The basic idea of the new recoding is to have one of the sub-scalars of the m-GLV decomposition, say k_J, represented in signed nonzero form and acting as a "sign-aligner". The latter means that k_J determines the sign of all the digits of remaining sub-scalars according to their relative position.

The GLV-SAC representation has the following properties:

(i) The length of the digit representation of every sub-scalar k_j is fixed and given by $l = \lceil \log_2 r/m \rceil + 1$, where r is the prime subgroup order.

(ii) Exactly one sub-scalar, which should be odd, is expressed by a signed nonzero representation $k_J = (b_{l-1}^J, \ldots, b_0^J)$, where all digits $b_i^J \in \{1, -1\}$ for $0 \leq i < l$.

(iii) All the sub-scalars k_j, with exception of k_J from (ii), are expressed by signed representations $(b_{l-1}^j, \ldots, b_0^j)$ such that $b_i^j \in \{0, b_i^J\}$ for $0 \leq i < l$.

In the targeted setting, (i) and (ii) guarantee a constant-time execution regardless of the value of the scalar k and without having to appeal to masking for dealing with the identity element. Item (iii) allows us to reduce the size of the precomputed table by a factor of 2, while minimizing the cost of precomputation.

Note that we do not impose any restriction on which sub-scalar should be designated as k_J. In some settings, choosing any of the k_j (with the exception of the one corresponding to the base point, i.e., k_0) could lead to the same performance in the precomputation phase and be slightly faster than $k_J = k_0$, if one takes into consideration the use of mixed point additions. The condition that k_J should be odd enables the conversion of any integer to a full signed nonzero representation using the equivalence $1 \equiv 1\bar{1}\ldots\bar{1}$. To deal with this restriction during the scalar multiplication, we first convert the selected sub-scalar k_J to odd (if even), and then make the corresponding correction at the end (more details can be found in Section 3.1). Finally, the reader should note that the GLV-SAC representation, in the way we describe it above, assumes that the sub-scalars are all positive. This restriction is imposed in order to achieve the minimum length $l = \lceil \log_2 r/m \rceil + 1$ in the representation. Note that it is possible to lift this restriction if needed in a certain setting (the analysis of this case is included in the extended paper version [10]).

An efficient algorithm to recode the sub-scalars to GLV-SAC proceeds as follows. Assume that each sub-scalar k_j is padded with zeros to the left until reaching the fixed length $l = \lceil \log_2 r/m \rceil + 1$, where r is the prime order of the curve subgroup. After choosing a suitable k_J to act as the "sign-aligner", the sub-scalar k_J is recoded to signed nonzero digits b_i^J using the equivalence $1 \equiv 1\bar{1}\ldots\bar{1}$. Remaining sub-scalars are then recoded in such a way that output digits at position i are in the set $\{0, b_i^J\}$, i.e., nonzero digits at the same relative position share the same sign. This is shown as Algorithm 1.

We highlight that, in contrast to [11, Alg. 4] and [12, Alg. 2], our recoding algorithm is simpler and exhibits a regular and constant time execution, making it resilient to timing attacks. Moreover, Algorithm 1 can be implemented very efficiently by exploiting the fact that the only purpose of the recoded digits from the sub-scalar k_J is, by definition, to determine the sign of their corresponding digit-columns (see details in Alg. 2 below). Since $k_{i+1}^J = 0$ and $k_{i+1}^J = 1$

Algorithm 1. Protected Recoding Algorithm for the GLV-SAC Representation.

Input: m l-bit positive integers $k_j = (k_{l-1}^j, \ldots, k_0^j)_2$ for $0 \leq j < m$, an odd "sign-aligner" $k_J \in \{k_j\}^m$, where $l = \lceil \log_2 r/m \rceil + 1$, m is the GLV dimension and r is the prime group order.
Output: $(b_{l-1}^j, \ldots, b_0^j)_{\text{GLV-SAC}}$ for $0 \leq j < m$, where $b_i^J \in \{1, -1\}$, and $b_i^j \in \{0, b_i^j\}$ for $0 \leq j < m$ and $j \neq J$.

1: $b_{l-1}^J = 1$
2: **for** $i = 0$ to $(l-2)$ **do**
3:      $b_i^J = 2k_{i+1}^J - 1$
4: **for** $j = 0$ to $(m-1), j \neq J$ **do**
5:      **for** $i = 0$ to $(l-1)$ **do**
6:          $b_i^j = b_i^J \cdot k_0^j$
7:          $k_j = \lfloor k_j/2 \rfloor - \lfloor b_i^j/2 \rfloor$
8: **return** $(b_{l-1}^j, \ldots, b_0^j)_{\text{GLV-SAC}}$ for $0 \leq j < m$.

---

indicate that the corresponding output digit-column i will be negative and positive, respectively, Step 3 of Algorithm 1 can be reduced to $b_i^J = k_{i+1}^J$ by assuming the convention $b_i^J = 0$ to indicate negative and $b_i^J = 1$ to indicate positive, for $0 \leq i < l$. Following this convention, further efficient simplifications are possible for Steps 6 and 7.

3.1 GLV-Based Scalar Multiplication Using GLV-SAC

We now present a new method for computing variable-base scalar multiplication using the GLV method and the GLV-SAC representation (see Algorithm 2). To simplify the description, we assume that k_0 is fixed as the "sign-aligner" k_J (it is easy to modify the algorithm to set any other sub-scalar to k_J). The basic idea is to arrange the sub-scalars, after being converted to their GLV-SAC representation, in matrix form from top to bottom, with sub-scalar $k_J = k_0$ at the top, and then run a simultaneous multi-scalar multiplication execution scanning digit-columns from left to right. By using the GLV-SAC recoding, every digit-column i is expected to be nonzero and have any of the possible combinations $[b_i^{m-1}, \ldots, b_i^2, b_i^1, b_i^0]$, where $b_i^0 \in \{1, -1\}$, and $b_i^j \in \{0, b_i^0\}$ for $1 \leq j < m$. Since nonzero digits in the same column have the same sign, one only needs to precompute all the positive combinations $P_0 + u_1 P_1 + \ldots + u_{m-1} P_{m-1}$ with $u_j \in \{0, 1\}$, where P_j are the base points of the sub-scalars. Assuming that negation of group elements is inexpensive in a given curve subgroup, negative values can be computed on-the-fly during the evaluation stage.

Since the GLV-SAC recoding requires that the "sign-aligner" k_J (in this case, k_0) be odd, k_0 is subtracted by one if it is even in Step 3 of Algorithm 2. The correction is then performed at the end of the evaluation stage at Step 9. These computations, as well as the accesses to the precomputed table, should be performed in constant time to guarantee protection against timing attacks. For example, in the implementation discussed in Section 5, the value $P[\mathbb{K}_i]$ required

---

Algorithm 2. Protected m-GLV Variable-Base Scalar Multiplication using the GLV-SAC Representation.

Input: Base point P_0 of order r and $(m-1)$ points P_j for $1 \leq j < m$ corresponding to the endomorphisms, m scalars $k_j = (k_{t_j-1}^j, \ldots, k_0^j)_2$ for $0 \leq j < m$, $l = \lceil \frac{\log_2 r}{m} \rceil + 1$ and $\max(t_j) = \lceil \frac{\log_2 r}{m} \rceil$.

Output: kP.

Precomputation stage:

1: Compute $P[u] = P_0 + u_0 P_1 + \ldots + u_{m-2} P_{m-1}$ for all $0 \leq u < 2^{m-1}$, where $u = (u_{m-2}, \ldots, u_0)_2$.

Recoding stage:

2: even $= k_0 \bmod 2$

3: **if** even $= 0$ **then** $k_0 = k_0 - 1$

4: Pad each k_j with $(l - t_j)$ zeros to the left for $0 \leq j < m$ and convert them to the GLV-SAC representation using Algorithm 1 s.t. $k_j = (b_{l-1}^j, \ldots, b_0^j)_{\text{GLV-SAC}}$. Set digit-columns $\mathbb{K}_i = [b_i^{m-1}, \ldots, b_i^2, b_i^1] \equiv |b_i^{m-1} 2^{m-2} + \ldots + b_i^2 2 + b_i^1|$ and digit-column signs $s_i = b_i^0$ for $0 \leq i \leq l - 1$.

Evaluation stage:

5: $Q = s_{l-1} P[\mathbb{K}_{l-1}]$

6: **for** $i = l - 2$ **to** 0 **do**

7:      $Q = 2Q$

8:      $Q = Q + s_i P[\mathbb{K}_i]$

9: **if** even $= 0$ **then** $Q = Q + P_0$

10: **return** Q

---

at Step 8 is retrieved from memory by performing a linear pass over the whole precomputed table using conditional move instructions. The final value $s_i P[\mathbb{K}_i]$ is then obtained by performing a second linear pass over the points $P[\mathbb{K}_i]$ and $-P[\mathbb{K}_i]$. Similarly, to realize Step 9, we always carry out the computation $Q' = Q + P_0$ and then perform a linear pass over the points Q and Q' using conditional move instructions to transfer the correct value to the final destination.

Note that Algorithm 2 assumes a decomposed scalar as input. This is sufficient in some settings, in which randomly generated sub-scalars could be provided. However, in others settings, one requires to calculate the sub-scalars in a decomposition phase. We remark that this computation should also be computed in constant time for protecting against timing attacks (e.g., see the details for Ted127-glv4 in §5).

Example 1. Let $m = 4$, $\log_2 r = 16$ and $kP = 11P_0 + 6P_1 + 14P_2 + 3P_3$. Using Algorithm 1, the corresponding GLV-SAC representation with fixed length $l = \lceil 16/4 \rceil + 1 = 5$ is given by (arranged in matrix form from top to bottom as required in Alg. 2)

$$
\begin{bmatrix} k_0 \\ k_1 \\ k_2 \\ k_3 \end{bmatrix} \equiv \begin{bmatrix} 0 & 1 & 0 & 1 & 1 \\ 0 & 0 & 1 & 1 & 0 \\ 0 & 1 & 1 & 1 & 0 \\ 0 & 0 & 0 & 1 & 1 \end{bmatrix} \equiv \begin{bmatrix} 1 & \bar{1} & 1 & \bar{1} & 1 \\ 1 & \bar{1} & 0 & \bar{1} & 0 \\ 1 & 0 & 0 & \bar{1} & 0 \\ 0 & 0 & 1 & \bar{1} & 1 \end{bmatrix}
$$

According to Algorithm 2, digit columns are given by $\mathbb{K}_0 = [100] = 4, \mathbb{K}_1 = [\bar{1}\bar{1}\bar{1}] = 7, \mathbb{K}_2 = [100] = 4, \mathbb{K}_3 = [00\bar{1}] = 1$ and $\mathbb{K}_4 = [011] = 3$, and their corresponding s_i are $s_0 = 1, s_1 = -1, s_2 = 1, s_3 = -1$ and $s_4 = 1$. Precomputed values $P[u]$ are given by $P[0] = P_0, P[1] = P_0 + P_1, P[2] = P_0 + P_2, P[3] = P_0 + P_1 + P_2, P[4] = P_0 + P_3, P[5] = P_0 + P_1 + P_3, P[6] = P_0 + P_2 + P_3$ and $P[7] = P_0 + P_1 + P_2 + P_3$. At Step 5 of Alg. 2, we compute $Q = s_4 P[\mathbb{K}_4] = P[3] = P_0 + P_1 + P_2$. The main loop in the evaluation stage is then executed as follows

i	3	2	1	0
$2Q$	$2P_0 + 2P_1 + 2P_2$	$2P_0 + 2P_1 + 4P_2$	$6P_0 + 4P_1 + 8P_2 + 2P_3$	$10P_0 + 6P_1 + 14P_2 + 2P_3$
$Q + s_i P[\mathbb{K}_i]$	$P_0 + P_1 + 2P_2$	$3P_0 + 2P_1 + 4P_2 + P_3$	$5P_0 + 3P_1 + 7P_2 + P_3$	$11P_0 + 6P_1 + 14P_2 + 3P_3$

Cost Analysis. To simplify comparisons, we will only consider a setting in which precomputed points are left in some projective system. When converting points to affine is convenient, one should include the cost of this conversion. Also, we do not consider optimizations exploiting cheap endomorphism mappings during precomputation, since this is dependent on a specific application. The reader is referred to Section 5 for a more precise comparison in a practical implementation using a GLV-GLS twisted Edwards curve.

The cost of the proposed m-GLV variable-base scalar multiplication using the GLV-SAC representation (Alg. 2) is given by $(l-1)$ doublings and l additions during the evaluation stage using 2^{m-1} points, where $l = \lceil \frac{\log_2 r}{m} \rceil + 1$. Naively, precomputation costs $2^{m-1} - 1$ additions (in practice, several of these additions might be performed using cheaper mixed additions). So the total cost is given by $(l-1)$ doublings and $(l + 2^{m-1} - 1)$ additions.

In contrast, the method based on the regular windowed recoding [33] used in [30] requires $(l-1)$ doublings and $m \cdot (l-1)/(w-1) + 2m - 1$ additions during the evaluation stage and m doublings with $m \cdot (2^{w-2} - 1)$ additions during the precomputation stage, using $m \cdot (2^{w-2} + 1)$ points (naive approach without exploiting endomorphisms). If, for example, $r = 256, m = 4$ and $w = 5$ (typical parameters to achieve 128-bit security on a curve similar to Ted127-glv4), the new method costs 64 doublings and 72 additions using 8 points, whereas the regular windowed method costs 68 doublings and 99 additions using 36 points. Thus, the new method improves performance while reduces dramatically the number of precomputations (in this case, to almost $1/5$ of the storage). Assuming that one addition costs 1.3 doublings, the expected speedup is 20%.

Certainly, one can reduce the number of precomputations when using the regular windowed recoding by only precomputing multiples corresponding to one or some of the sub-scalars. However, these savings in memory come at the expense of computing endomorphisms during the evaluation stage, which can cost from several multiplications [7] to approximately one full point addition each (see Appendix A). The proposed method always requires the minimum storage without impacting performance.

The basic GLV-SAC representation and its corresponding scalar multiplication are particularly efficient for four-dimensional GLV. In the following section, we discuss variants that are efficient for $m = 2$ and $m \geq 8$.

3.2 Windowed and Partitioned GLV-SAC: Case of Dimension 2 and ≥ 8

In some cases, the performance of the proposed scalar multiplication can be improved further by combining windowed techniques with the GLV-SAC recoding. Given a window width w, assume that a set of sub-scalars k_j has been padded with enough zeros to the left to guarantee that $w|l$, where l is the expected length of an extended GLV-SAC representation that we refer to as wGLV-SAC. The basic idea is to join every w consecutive digits in the wGLV-SAC representation, and precompute all possible values $P[u] = u'P_0 + u_0P_1 + \ldots + u_{m-2}P_{m-1}$ for $0 \leq u < 2^{wm-1}$ and $u' \in \{1, 3, \ldots, 2^w - 1\}$ (again, points corresponding to negative values of u' can be computed on-the-fly). Scalar multiplication then proceeds by scanning w-digit columns from left to right.

Conveniently, Algorithm 1 can also be used to obtain wGLV-SAC(k_j), with the only change in the fixed length to $l = (\lceil \log_2 r/w \rceil + 1) + (\lceil \log_2 r/w \rceil + 1) \bmod w$.

Example 2. Let $m = 2, \log_2 r = 8, w = 2$ and $kP = 11P_0 + 14P_1$. Using Algorithm 1, the corresponding wGLV-SAC representation with fixed length $l = \lceil 8/2 \rceil + 1 + (\lceil 8/2 \rceil + 1) \bmod 2 = 6$, arranged in matrix form from top to bottom, is given by

$$\begin{bmatrix} k_0 \\ k_1 \end{bmatrix} \equiv \begin{bmatrix} 0 & 0 & 1 & 0 & 1 & 1 \\ 0 & 0 & 1 & 1 & 1 & 0 \end{bmatrix} \equiv \begin{bmatrix} 1 & \bar{1} & \bar{1} & 1 & \bar{1} & 1 \\ 1 & \bar{1} & 0 & 0 & \bar{1} & 0 \end{bmatrix} \qquad (1)$$

The 2-digit columns are given by $\mathbb{K}_0 = [\bar{2}\bar{1}] = 3, \mathbb{K}_1 = [0\bar{1}] = 1$ and $\mathbb{K}_2 = [11] = 2$, and their corresponding s_i are $s_0 = -1, s_1 = -1$ and $s_2 = 1$. Precomputed values $P[u]$ are given by $P[0] = P_0 - P_1, P[1] = P_0, P[2] = P_0 + P_1, P[3] = P_0 + 2P_1, P[4] = 3P_0, P[5] = 3P_0 + P_1, P[6] = 3P_0 + 2P_1$ and $P[7] = 3P_0 + 3P_1$. In the evaluation stage we first compute $Q = s_2P[\mathbb{K}_2] = P[2] = P_0 + P_1$ and then execute

i	1	0
2^wQ	$4P_0 + 4P_1$	$12P_0 + 16P_1$
$Q + s_iP[\mathbb{K}_i]$	$3P_0 + 4P_1$	$11P_0 + 14P_1$

Since the requirement of precomputations, given by 2^{wm-1}, increases rapidly as w and m grow, windowed GLV-SAC is especially attractive for 2-GLV implementations. In this case, by fixing $w = 2$ the number of precomputed points is only 8. At the same performance level (in the evaluation stage), this is approximately half the memory requirement of a method based on the regular windowed recoding [33] [1].

Whereas joining columns in the representation matrix is amenable for small m using windowing, for large m it is recommended to join rows instead. We illustrate the approach with $m = 8$. Given a set of sub-scalars k_j for $0 \le j < 8$, we first partition it in c consecutive sub-sets k_i' such that $c|8$, and then convert every sub-set to the GLV-SAC representation (using Alg. 1). In this case, every column in the matrix consists of c sub-columns, each one corresponding to a sub-set k_i'. Scalar multiplication then proceeds by scanning c sub-columns per iteration from right to left. Thus, with this "partitioned" GLV-SAC approach, one increases the number of point additions per iteration in the main loop of Alg. 2 from one to c. However, the number of required precomputations is reduced from 2^{m-1} to $c \cdot 2^{\frac{m}{c}-1}$. For example, for $m = 8$, this approach reduces the number of points from 128 to only 16 if c is fixed to 2 (each sub-table corresponding to a sub-set of scalars contains 8 points). At the same performance level (in the evaluation stage), this is approximately half the memory requirement of a method based on the regular windowed recoding [33], as discussed by the recent work by Bos et al. [8]. Performance is also expected to improve since the number of point operations for precomputation is significantly reduced. Note that, if one only considers positive sub-scalars and the endomorphism mapping is inexpensive in comparison to point addition, then sub-tables can be computed by simply applying the endomorphism to the first sub-table arising from the base point P_0. In some instances, such as the 8-GLV in [8], this approach is expected to reduce further the cost of precomputation. Although an issue arises when sub-scalars can also be negative, this can be dealt with by adding one extra bit containing the sign to the representation. We give the full details in the extended paper version [10].

4   High-Speed Implementation on GLV-GLS Curves

In this section, we describe implementation aspects of the GLV-GLS curve Ted127-glv4. We present optimized algorithms for prime field, extension field and point arithmetic. We also present the technique of interleaving NEON and ARM-based multiprecision operations over $\mathbb{F}_{p^2}$. Although our techniques are especially tuned for the targeted curve, we remark that they can be adapted and exploited in other scenarios.

4.1   The Curve

For complete details about the four-dimensional method using GLV-GLS curves, the reader is referred to [14] and [31]. We use the following GLV-GLS curve in twisted Edwards form [30], referred to as Ted127-glv4:

---

[1] However, in some cases one can afford the reduction of precomputations from 16 to 8 when using the windowed recoding if endomorphisms are cheap and can be computed on-the-fly during the evaluation stage; e.g., see [34].

$$E'_{TE}/\mathbb{F}_{p^2} : -x^2 + y^2 = 1 + dx^2y^2, \tag{2}$$

where $\mathbb{F}_{p^2}$ is defined as $\mathbb{F}_p[i]/(i^2 - \beta)$, $\beta = -1$ is a quadratic non-residue in $\mathbb{F}_p$ and $u = 1 + i$ is a quadratic non-residue in $\mathbb{F}_{p^2}$. Also, $p = 2^{127} - 5997$, $d = 170141183460469231731687303715884099728 + 116829086847165810221872975542241037773i$ and $\#E'_{TE}(\mathbb{F}_{p^2}) = 8r$, where r is the 251-bit prime $2^{251} - 255108063403607336678531921577909824432295$. E'_{TE} is isomorphic to the Weierstrass curve $E'_W/\mathbb{F}_{p^2} : y^2 = x^3 - 15/2 \ u^2x - 7u^3$, which is the quadratic twist of a curve isomorphic to the GLV curve $E_W/\mathbb{F}_p : y^2 = 4x^3 - 30x - 28$ (see [30, Section 5]). $E'_{TE}/\mathbb{F}_{p^2}$ is equipped with two efficiently computable endomorphisms Φ and Ψ defined over $\mathbb{F}_{p^2}$, which enable a four-dimensional decomposition for any scalar $k \in [1, r - 1]$ in the subgroup generated by a point P of order r and, consequently, enable a four-dimensional scalar multiplication given by

$$kP = k_1P + k_2\Phi(P) + k_3\Psi(P) + k_4\Psi\Phi(P), \quad \text{with } \max_i(|k_i|) < C\,r^{1/4}$$

where $C = 179$ [30]. Let $\zeta_8 = u/\sqrt{2}$ be a primitive 8th root of unity. The affine formulas for $\Phi(x, y)$ and $\Psi(x, y)$ are given by

$$\Phi(x,y) = \left(-\frac{(\zeta_8^3 + 2\zeta_8^2 + \zeta_8)xy^2 + (\zeta_8^3 - 2\zeta_8^2 + \zeta_8)x}{2y}, \frac{(\zeta_8^2 - 1)y^2 + 2\zeta_8^3 - \zeta_8^2 + 1}{(2\zeta_8^3 + \zeta_8^2 - 1)y^2 - \zeta_8^2 + 1} \right) \text{ and } \Psi(x,y) = \left(\zeta_8 x^p, \frac{1}{y^p} \right),$$

respectively. It can be verified that $\Phi^2 + 2 = 0$ and $\Psi^2 + 1 = 0$. The formulas in homogeneous projective coordinates can be found in Appendix A.

Note that Ted127-glv4 has $a = -1$ (in the twisted Edwards equation; see [3]), corresponding to the most efficient set of formulas proposed by Hisil et al. [22]. Although GLV-GLS curves with suitably chosen parameters when transformed to twisted Edwards form offer roughly the same performance, as discussed in [30], there are certain differences in the cost of formulas for computing the endomorphisms Φ and Ψ. Curve Ted127-glv4 exhibits relatively efficient formulas for computing the endomorphisms in comparison with other GLV-GLS curves from [30]. On the other hand, our selection of the pseudo-Mersenne prime $p = 2^{127} - 5997$ enables efficient field arithmetic by exploiting lazy and incomplete reduction techniques (see the next section for details). Also, since $p \equiv 3 \pmod 4$, -1 is a quadratic non-residue in $\mathbb{F}_p$, which minimizes the cost of multiplication over $\mathbb{F}_{p^2}$ by transforming multiplications by β to inexpensive subtractions.

4.2 Field Arithmetic

For field inversion, we use the modular exponentiation $a^{p-2} \pmod p \equiv a^{-1}$ using a fixed and short addition chain. This method is simple to implement and is naturally protected against timing attacks.

In the case of a pseudo-Mersenne prime of the form $p = 2^m - c$, with c small, field multiplication can be efficiently performed by computing an integer multiplication followed by a modular reduction exploiting the special form of the prime. This separation of operations also enables the use of lazy reduction in the extension field arithmetic. For x64, integer multiplication is implemented in product scanning form (a.k.a Comba's method), mainly exploiting the powerful 64-bit unsigned multiplier instruction. Let $0 \leq a, b < 2^{m+1}$. To exploit the extra room of one bit in our targeted prime $2^{127} - 5997$, we first compute $M = a \cdot b = 2^{m+1}M_H + M_L$ followed by the reduction step $R = M_L + 2c\,M_H \leq 2^{m+1}(2c + 1) - 2$. Then, given $R = 2^m R_H + R_L$, we compute $R_L + c\,R_H \pmod{p}$, where $R_L, c\,R_H < 2^m$. This final operation can be efficiently carried out by employing the modular addition proposed by Bos et al. [7] to get the final result in the range $[0, p-1]$. Note that the computation of field multiplication above naturally accepts inputs in unreduced form without incurring in extra costs, enabling the use of additions without correction or operations with incomplete reduction (see below for more details). We follow a similar procedure for computing field squaring. For ARM, we implement the integer multiplication using the schoolbook method. In this case, and also for modular reduction, we extensively exploit the parallelism of ARM and NEON instructions. The details are discussed in Section 4.4.

Let $0 \leq a, b < 2^m - c$. Field subtraction is computed as $(a - b) + borrow \cdot 2^m - borrow \cdot c$, where $borrow = 0$ if $a \geq b$, otherwise $borrow = 1$. Notice that in practice the addition with $borrow \cdot 2^m$ can be efficiently implemented by clearing the $(m + 1)$-th bit of $a - b$.

Incomplete Reduction. Similar to [29], we exploit the form of the pseudo-Mersenne prime in combination with the incomplete reduction technique to speedup computations. We also mix incompletely reduced and completely reduced operands in novel ways.

Let $0 \leq a < 2^m - c$ and $0 \leq b < 2^m$. Field addition with incomplete reduction is computed as $(a + b) - carry \cdot 2^m + carry \cdot c$, where $carry = 0$ if $a + b < 2^m$, otherwise $carry = 1$. Again, in practice the subtraction with $carry \cdot 2^m$ can be efficiently implemented by clearing the $(m+1)$-th bit of $a+b$. The result is correct modulo p, but falls in the range $[0, 2^m - 1]$. Thus, this addition operation with incomplete reduction works with both operands in completely reduced form or with one operand in completely reduced form and one in incompletely reduced form. A similar observation applies to subtraction. Consider two operands a and b, such that $0 \leq a < 2^m$ and $0 \leq b < 2^m - c$. The standard field subtraction $(a - b) \bmod (2^m - c)$ described above will then produce an incompletely reduced result in the range $[0, 2^m - 1]$, since $a - b$ with $borrow = 0$ produces a result in the range $[0, 2^m - 1]$ and $a - b$ with $borrow = 1$ produces a result in the range $[-2^m + c+1, -1]$, which is then fully reduced by adding $2^m - c$. Thus, performance can be improved by using incomplete reduction for an addition preceding a subtraction. For example, this technique is exploited in the point doubling computation (see Steps 7-8 of Algorithm 8). Note that, in contrast to addition, only the first operand is allowed to be in incompletely reduced form for subtraction.

To guarantee correctness in our software, and following the previous description, incompletely reduced results are always fed to one of the following: one of the operands of an incompletely reduced addition, the first operand of a field subtraction, a field multiplication or squaring (which ultimately produces a completely reduced output), or a field addition without correction preceding a field multiplication or squaring.

In the targeted setting, there are only a limited number of spots in the curve arithmetic in which incompletely reduced numbers cannot be efficiently exploited. For these few cases, we require a standard field addition. We use the efficient implementation proposed by Bos et al. [7]. Again, let $0 \leq a, b < 2^m - c$. Field addition is then computed as $((a + c) + b) - carry \cdot 2^m - (1 - carry) \cdot c$, where $carry = 0$ if $a + b + c < 2^m$, otherwise $carry = 1$. Similar to previous cases, the subtraction with $carry \cdot 2^m$ can be efficiently carried out by clearing the $(m + 1)$-th bit in $(a + c) + b$. As discussed above, this efficient computation is also advantageously exploited in the modular reduction for multiplication and squaring.

4.3   Quadratic Extension Field Arithmetic

For the remainder, we use the following notation: (i) I, M, S, A and R represent inversion, multiplication, squaring, addition and modular reduction over $\mathbb{F}_p$, respectively, (ii) M_i and A_i represent integer multiplication and integer addition, respectively, and (iii) i, m, s, a and r represent analogous operations over $\mathbb{F}_{p^2}$. When representing registers in algorithms, capital letters are used to allocate operands with "double precision" (in our case, 256 bits). For simplification purposes, in the operation counting an integer operation with double-precision is considered equivalent to two integer operations with single precision. We assume that addition, subtraction, multiplication by two and negation have roughly the same cost.

Let $a = a_0 + a_1 i \in \mathbb{F}_{p^2}$ and $b = b_0 + b_1 i \in \mathbb{F}_{p^2}$. Inversion over $\mathbb{F}_{p^2}$ is computed as $a^{-1} = (a_0 - a_1 i)/(a_0^2 + a_1^2)$. Addition and subtraction over $\mathbb{F}_{p^2}$ consist in computing $(a_0 + b_0) + (a_1 + b_1)i$ and $(a_0 - b_0) + (a_1 - b_1)i$, respectively. We compute multiplication over $\mathbb{F}_{p^2}$ using the Karatsuba method. In this case, we fully exploit lazy reduction and the room of one bit that is gained by using a prime of 127 bits. The details for the x64 implementation are shown in Algorithm 3. Remarkably, note that only the subtraction in Step 3 requires a correction to produce a positive result. No other addition or subtraction requires correction to positive or to modulo p. That is, $\times$, $+$ and $-$ represent operations over the integers. In addition, the algorithm accepts inputs in completely or incompletely reduced form and always produces a result in completely reduced form. Optionally, one may "delay" the computation of the final modular reductions (by setting $reduction = FALSE$ in Alg. 3) if lazy reduction could be exploited in the curve arithmetic. This has been proven to be useful to formulas for the Weierstrass form [1], but unfortunately the technique cannot be advantageously exploited in the most efficient formulas for twisted Edwards (in this case, one should set $reduction = TRUE$). Squaring over $\mathbb{F}_{p^2}$ is computed using the complex method. The details for the x64 implementation are shown in Algorithm 4. In this case, all the additions are computed as integer operations since, again, results can be let to grow up to 128 bits, letting subsequent multiplications take care of the reduction step.

Algorithm 3. Multiplication in $\mathbb{F}_{p^2}$ with reduction $(m = 3M_i + 9A_i + 2R)$ and without reduction $(m_u = 3M_i + 9A_i)$, using completely or incompletely reduced inputs (x64 platform).

Input: $a = (a_0 + a_1 i)$ and $b = (b_0 + b_1 i) \in \mathbb{F}_{p^2}$, where $0 \le a_0, a_1, b_0, b_1 \le 2^{127} - 1, p = 2^{127} - c, c$ small.
Output: $a \cdot b \pmod{p} \in \mathbb{F}_{p^2}$

1: $T_0 \leftarrow a_0 \times b_0$	$[0, 2^{254} >$
2: $T_1 \leftarrow a_1 \times b_1$	$[0, 2^{254} >$
3: $C_0 \leftarrow T_0 - T_1$	$< -2^{254}, 2^{254} >$
4: **if** $C_0 < 0$, **then** $C_0 \leftarrow C_0 + 2^{128} \cdot p$	$[0, 2^{255} >$
5: **if** $reduction = TRUE$, **then** $c_0 \leftarrow C_0 \bmod p$	$[0, p >$
6: $t_0 \leftarrow a_0 + a_1$	$[0, 2^{128} >$
7: $t_1 \leftarrow b_0 + b_1$	$[0, 2^{128} >$
8: $T_2 \leftarrow t_0 \times t_1$	$[0, 2^{256} >$
9: $T_2 \leftarrow T_2 - T_0$	$[0, 2^{256} >$
10: $C_1 \leftarrow T_2 - T_1$	$[0, 2^{256} >$
11: **if** $reduction = TRUE$, **then** $c_1 \leftarrow C_1 \bmod p$	$[0, p >$
12: **return** if $reduction = TRUE$ then $a \cdot b = (c_0 + c_1 i)$, else $a \cdot b = (C_0 + C_1 i)$.	

Algorithm 4. Squaring in $\mathbb{F}_{p^2}(s = 2M + 1A + 2A_i)$, using completely reduced inputs (x64 platform).

Input: $a = (a_0 + a_1 i) \in \mathbb{F}_{p^2}$, where $0 \le a_0, a_1 \le p - 1, p = 2^{127} - c, c$ small.
Output: $a^2 \pmod{p} \in \mathbb{F}_{p^2}$

1: $t_0 \leftarrow a_0 + a_1$	$[0, 2^{128} >$
2: $t_1 \leftarrow a_0 - a_1 \bmod p$	$[0, p >$
3: $c_0 \leftarrow t_0 \times t_1 \bmod p$	$[0, p >$
4: $t_0 \leftarrow a_0 + a_0$	$[0, 2^{128} >$
5: $c_1 \leftarrow t_0 \times a_1 \bmod p$	$[0, p >$
6: **return** $a^2 = (c_0 + c_1 i)$.	

4.4   Extension Field Arithmetic on ARM: Efficient Interleaving of ARM-Based and NEON-Based Multiprecision Operations

The potential performance gain when interleaving ARM and NEON operations is well-known. This feature was exploited in [6] to speed up the Salsa20 stream cipher. On the other hand, Sánchez and Rodríguez-Henríquez [36] showed how to take advantage of NEON instructions to perform independent multiplications in operations over $\mathbb{F}_{p^2}$. In the following, we go a step further and show how to exploit the increasingly efficient capacity of modern ARM processors for executing ARM and NEON instructions "simultaneously" to implement multiprecision

Algorithm 5. Double 128-bit integer product with ARM and NEON interleaved (`double_mul_neonarm`)

Input: $a = \{a_i\}, b = \{b_i\}, c = \{c_i\}, d = \{d_i\}, i \in \{0, \ldots, 3\}$.
Output: $(F, G) \leftarrow (a \times b, c \times d)$.

1: $(F, G) \leftarrow (0, 0)$
2: **for** $i = 0$ **to** 1 **do**
3:   $(C_0, C_1, C_2) \leftarrow (0, 0, 0)$
4:   **for** $j = 0$ **to** 3 **do**
5:     $(C_0, F_{i+j}, C_1, F_{i+j+2}) \leftarrow (F_{i+j} + a_i b_j + C_0, F_{i+j+2} + a_{i+2} b_j + C_1)$ {done by NEON}
6:   **for** $j = 0$ **to** 3 **do**
7:     $(C_2, G_{i+j}) \leftarrow G_{i+j} + c_j d_i + C_2$ {done by ARM}
8:   $(F_{i+4}, F_{i+6}, G_{i+4}) \leftarrow (F_{i+4} + C_0, C_1, C_2)$
9: **for** $i = 2$ **to** 3 **do**
10:    **for** $j = 0$ **to** 3 **do**
11:      $(C_2, G_{i+j}) \leftarrow G_{i+j} + c_j d_i + C_2$ {done by ARM}
12:    $G_{i+4} \leftarrow C_2$
13: **return** (F, G)

Algorithm 6. Triple 128-bit integer product with ARM and NEON interleaved (`triple_mul_neonarm`)

Input: $a = \{a_i\}, b = \{b_i\}, c = \{c_i\}, d = \{d_i\}, e = \{e_i\}, f = \{f_i\}, i \in \{0, \ldots, 3\}$.
Output: $(F, G, H) \leftarrow (a \times b, c \times d, e \times f)$.

1: $(F, G, H) \leftarrow (0, 0, 0)$
2: **for** $i = 0$ **to** 3 **do**
3:   $(C_0, C_1, C_2) \leftarrow (0, 0, 0)$
4:   **for** $j = 0$ **to** 3 **do**
5:     $(C_0, F_{i+j}, C_1, G_{i+j}) \leftarrow (F_{i+j} + a_j b_i + C_0, G_{i+j} + c_j d_i + C_1)$ {done by NEON}
6:   **for** $j = 0$ **to** 3 **do**
7:     $(C_2, H_{i+j}) \leftarrow H_{i+j} + e_j f_i + C_2$ {done by ARM}
8:   $(F_{i+4}, G_{i+4}, H_{i+4}) \leftarrow (C_0, C_1, C_2)$
9: **return** (F, G, H)

operations, such as multiplication, squaring and modular reduction, over $\mathbb{F}_{p^2}$. In other words, we exploit the fact that when ARM code produces a data hazard in the pipeline, the NEON unit may be ready to execute vector instructions, and vice versa. Note that loading/storing values from ARM to NEON registers still remains relatively expensive, so in order to achieve an effective performance improvement, one should carefully interleave *independent* operations while minimizing the loads and stores from one unit to the other. Hence, operations such as multiplication and squaring over $\mathbb{F}_{p^2}$ are particularly friendly to this technique, given the availability of internal independent multiplications in their formulas. Thus, using this approach, we implemented:

Algorithm 7. Double modular reduction with ARM and NEON interleaved (`double_red_neonarm`)

Input: A prime $p = 2^{127} - c$, $a = \{a_i\}, b = \{b_i\}$, $i \in \{0, \ldots, 7\}$.
Output: $(F, G) \leftarrow (a \bmod p, \, b \bmod p)$.

1: $(F_i, G_i) \leftarrow (a_i, b_i)_{i \in \{0, \ldots, 3\}}$
2: $(C_0, C_1, C_2) \leftarrow (0, 0, 0)$
3: **for** $j = 0$ **to** 1 **do**
4:    $(C_0, F_j, C_1, F_{j+2}) \leftarrow (F_j + a_{j+4}c + C_0, F_{j+2} + a_{j+6}c + C_1)$ {done by NEON}
5: **for** $j = 0$ **to** 3 **do**
6:    $(C_2, G_j) \leftarrow G_j + b_{j+4}c + C_2$ {done by ARM}
7: $(F_2, F_4, G_4) \leftarrow (F_2 + C_0, C_1, C_2)$
8: $(F_0, G_0) \leftarrow (F_4c + F_0, G_4c + G_0)$
9: **return** (F, G)

- a double integer multiplier (`double_mul_neonarm`) detailed in Algorithm 5, which interleaves a single 128-bit multiplication using NEON and a single 128-bit multiplication using ARM,
- a triple integer multiplier (`triple_mul_neonarm`) detailed in Algorithm 6, which interleaves two single 128-bit multiplication using NEON and one single 128-bit multiplication using ARM, and
- a double reduction algorithm (`double_red_neonarm`) detailed in Algorithm 7, that interleaves a single modular reduction using NEON and a single modular reduction using ARM.

Note that integer multiplication is implemented using the schoolbook method, which requires one multiplication, two additions, one shift and one bit-wise AND per iteration. These operations were implemented using efficient fused instructions such as UMLAL, UMAAL, VMLAL and VSRA [28], which add the result of a multiplication or shift to the destination register in one single operation, reducing code size.

To validate the efficiency of our approach, we compared the interleaved algorithms above with standard implementations using only NEON or ARM. In all the cases, we observed a reduction of costs in favor of our novel interleaved ARM/NEON implementations (see Section 5 for benchmark results).

`Triple_mul_neonarm` is nicely adapted to the computation of multiplication over $\mathbb{F}_{p^2}$, since this operation requires three integer multiplications of 128 bits (Steps 1, 2 and 8 of Algorithm 3). For the case of squaring over $\mathbb{F}_{p^2}$, we use `double_mul_neonarm` to compute the two independent integer multiplications (Steps 3 and 5 of Algorithm 4). Finally, for each case we can efficiently use a `double_red_neonarm`. The final algorithms for ARM are shown as Algorithms 10 and 11 in Appendix B.

4.5   Point Arithmetic

In this section, we describe implementation details and our optimized formulas for the point arithmetic. We use as basis the most efficient set of formulas proposed by Hisil et al. [22], corresponding to the case $a = -1$, that uses a combination of homogeneous projective coordinates $(X : Y : Z)$ and extended homogeneous coordinates of the form $(X : Y : Z : T)$, where $T = XY/Z$.

The basic algorithms for computing point doubling and addition are shown in Algorithms 8 and 9, respectively. In these algorithms, we extensively exploit incomplete reduction (denoted by with $\oplus, \ominus$), following the details given in Section 4.2. To ease coupling of doubling and addition in the main loop of the scalar multiplication computation, we make use of Hamburg's "extensible" strategy and output values $\{T_a, T_b\}$, where $T = T_a \cdot T_b$, at every point operation, so that a subsequent operation may compute coordinate T if required. Note that the cost of doubling is given by $4m + 3s + 5a$. We do not apply the usual transformation $2XY = (X + Y)^2 - (X^2 + Y^2)$ because in our case it is faster to compute one multiplication and one incomplete addition than one squaring, one subtraction and one addition. In the setting of variable-base scalar multiplication (see Alg. 2), the main loop of the evaluation stage consists of a doubling-addition computation, which corresponds to the successive execution of Algorithms 8 and 9. For this case, precomputed points are more efficiently represented as $(X + Y, Y - X, 2Z, 2T)$ (corresponding to setting $EXT\_COORD = TRUE$ in Alg. 9), so the cost of addition is given by $8m + 6a$.

Algorithm 8. Twisted Edwards point doubling over $\mathbb{F}_{p^2}$ (DBL $= 4m + 3s + 5a$)

Input: $P = (X_1, Y_1, Z_1)$.
Output: $2P = (X_2, Y_2, Z_2)$ and $\{T_a, T_b\}$ such that $T_2 = T_a \cdot T_b$.

1: $T_a \leftarrow X_1^2$	(X_1^2)
2: $t_1 \leftarrow Y_1^2$	(Y_1^2)
3: $T_b \leftarrow T_a \oplus t_1$	$(X_1^2 + Y_1^2)$
4: $T_a \leftarrow t_1 - T_a$	$(Y_1^2 - X_1^2)$
5: $Y_2 \leftarrow T_b \times T_a$	$(Y_2 = (X_1^2 + Y_1^2)(Y_1^2 - X_1^2))$
6: $t_1 \leftarrow Z_1^2$	(Z_1^2)
7: $t_1 \leftarrow t_1 \oplus t_1$	$(2Z_1^2)$
8: $t_1 \leftarrow t_1 \ominus T_a$	$(2Z_1^2 - (Y_1^2 - X_1^2))$
9: $Z_2 \leftarrow T_a \times t_1$	$(Z_2 = (Y_1^2 - X_1^2)[2Z_1^2 - (Y_1^2 - X_1^2)])$
10: $T_a \leftarrow X_1 \oplus X_1$	$(2X_1)$
11: $T_a \leftarrow T_a \times Y_1$	$(2X_1Y_1)$
12: $X_2 \leftarrow T_a \times t_1$	$(X_2 = 2X_1Y_1[2Z_1^2 - (Y_1^2 - X_1^2)])$
13: **return** $2P = (X_2, Y_2, Z_2)$ and $\{T_a, T_b\}$ such that $T_2 = T_a \cdot T_b$.	

---

5   Performance Analysis and Experimental Results

In this section, we carry out the performance analysis of the proposed GLV-based scalar multiplication method using the GLV-SAC representation, and present

Algorithm 9. Twisted Edwards point addition over $\mathbb{F}_{p^2}$ (ADD $= 8m + 6a$, mADD $= 7m + 7a$ or $8m + 10a$)

Input: $P = (X_1, Y_1, Z_1)$ and $\{T_a, T_b\}$ such that $T_1 = T_a \cdot T_b$. If $EXT\_COORD = FALSE$ then $Q = (x_2, y_2)$, else $Q = (X_2 + Y_2, Y_2 - X_2, 2Z_2, 2T_2)$.
Output: $P + Q = (X_3, Y_3, Z_3)$ and $\{T_a, T_b\}$ such that $T_3 = T_a \cdot T_b$.

1: $T_1 \leftarrow T_a \times T_b$ $\hfill (T_1)$
2: **if** $EXT\_COORD = FALSE$ **then** $T_2 = x_2 \oplus x_2$, $T_2 = T_2 \times y_2$ $\hfill (2T_2)$
3: $t_1 \leftarrow T_2 \times Z_1$ $\hfill (2T_2Z_1)$
4: **if** $Z_2 = 1$ **then** $t_2 \leftarrow T_1 \oplus T_1$ **else** $t_2 \leftarrow T_1 \times 2Z_2$ $\hfill (2T_1Z_2)$
5: $T_a \leftarrow t_2 - t_1$ $\hfill (T_a = \alpha = 2T_1Z_2 - 2T_2Z_1)$
6: $T_b \leftarrow t_1 \oplus t_2$ $\hfill (T_b = \theta = 2T_1Z_2 + 2T_2Z_1)$
7: $t_2 \leftarrow X_1 \oplus Y_1$ $\hfill (X_1 + Y_1)$
8: **if** $EXT\_COORD = TRUE$ **then** $Y_3 = Y_2 - X_2$, **else** $Y_3 = y_2 - x_2$ $\hfill (Y_2 - X_2)$
9: $t_2 \leftarrow Y_3 \times t_2$ $\hfill (X_1 + Y_1)(Y_2 - X_2)$
10: $t_1 \leftarrow Y_1 - X_1$ $\hfill (Y_1 - X_1)$
11: **if** $EXT\_COORD = TRUE$ **then** $X_3 = X_2 + Y_2$, **else** $X_3 = x_2 \oplus y_2$ $\hfill (X_2 + Y_2)$
12: $t_1 \leftarrow X_3 \times t_1$ $\hfill (X_2 + Y_2)(Y_1 - X_1)$
13: $Z_3 \leftarrow t_2 - t_1$ $\hfill \beta = (X_1 + Y_1)(Y_2 - X_2) - (X_2 + Y_2)(Y_1 - X_1)$
14: $t_1 \leftarrow t_1 \oplus t_2$ $\hfill \omega = (X_1 + Y_1)(Y_2 - X_2) + (X_2 + Y_2)(Y_1 - X_1)$
15: $X_3 \leftarrow T_b \times Z_3$ $\hfill (X_3 = \beta\theta)$
16: $Z_3 \leftarrow t_1 \times Z_3$ $\hfill (Z_3 = \beta\omega)$
17: $Y_3 \leftarrow T_a \times t_1$ $\hfill (Y_3 = \alpha\omega)$
18: **return** $P + Q = (X_3, Y_3, Z_3)$ and $\{T_a, T_b\}$ such that $T_3 = T_a \cdot T_b$.

---

benchmark results of our constant-time implementations of curve `Ted127-glv4` on x64 and ARM platforms. We also assess the performance improvement obtained with the proposed ARM/NEON interleaving technique. For our experiments, we targeted a 3.4GHz Intel Core i7-2600 Sandy Bridge processor and a 3.4GHz Intel Core i7-3770 Ivy Bridge processor, from the Intel family, and a Samsung Galaxy Note with a 1.4GHz Exynos 4 Cortex-A9 processor and an Arndale Board with a 1.7GHz Exynos 5 Cortex-A15 processor, from the ARM family, both equipped with the NEON vector unit. The x64 implementation was compiled with Microsoft Visual Studio 2012 and ran on 64-bit Windows (Microsoft Windows 8 OS). In our experiments, we turned off Intel's hyperthreading and Turbo Boost technologies; we averaged the cost of 10^4 operations which were measured with the timestamp counter instruction `rdtsc`. The ARM implementation was developed and compiled with the Android NDK (ndk8d) toolkit. In this case, we averaged the cost of 10^4 operations which were measured with the `clock_gettime()` function and scaled to clock cycles using the processor frequency.

First, we present timings for all the fundamental operations of scalar multiplication in Table 1. Implementation details for quadratic extension field operations and point operations over $\mathbb{F}_{p^2}$ can be found in Section 4. "IR" stands for incomplete reduction and "extended" represents the use of the extended coordinates

$(X + Y, Y - X, 2Z, 2T)$ to represent precomputed points. The four-dimensional decomposition of the scalar follows [30]. In particular, a scalar k is decomposed in smaller k_i s.t. $\max(|k_i|) < C\,r^{1/4}$ for $0 \leq i \leq 3$, where r is the 251-bit prime order and $C = 179$ for our case (see §4.1). In practice, however, we have found that the bitlength of k_i is at most 63 bits for our targeted curve. The decomposition can be performed as a linear transformation by computing $k_i = \sum_{j=0}^{3} \mathrm{round}(S_j k) \cdot M_{i,j}$ for $0 \leq i < 4$, where $M_{i,j}$ and S_j are integer constants. We truncate operands in the $\mathrm{round}()$ operation, adding enough precision to avoid loss of data. Thus, the computation involves a few multi-precision integer operations exhibiting constant-time execution.

Table 1. Cost (in cycles) of basic operations on curve `Ted127-glv4`

Operation		ARM Cortex-A9	ARM Cortex-A15	Intel Sandy Bridge	Intel Ivy Bridge
$\mathbb{F}_{p^2}$	ADD with IR	20	19	12	12
	ADD	39	37	15	15
	SUB	39	37	12	12
	SQR	223	141	59	56
	MUL	339	185	78	75
	INV	13,390	9,675	6,060	5,890
ECC	DBL	2,202	1,295	545	525
	ADD	3,098	1,831	690	665
	mADD ($Z_1 = 1$)	2,943	1,687	622	606
	Φ endomorphism ($Z_1 = 1$)	3,118	1,724	745	712
	Ψ endomorphism ($Z_1 = 1$)	1,644	983	125	119
Misc	8-point LUT (extended)	291	179	83	79
	GLV-based LSB-set recoding	1,236	873	482	482
	4-GLV decomposition	756	430	305	290

Next, we analyze the cost of GLV-based variable-base scalar multiplication on curve `Ted127-glv4`. Based on Algorithm 2, this operation involves the computation of one Φ endomorphism, 2 Ψ endomorphisms, 3 additions and 4 mixed additions in the precomputation stage; 63 doublings, 63 additions, one mixed addition and 64 protected table lookups in the evaluation stage; and one inversion and 2 multiplications over $\mathbb{F}_{p^2}$ for converting the final result to affine. In total, the cost is given by $1i + 833m + 191s + 769a + 64LUT8 + 4M + 9A$. This operation count does not include other additional computations, such as the recoding to the GLV-SAC representation or the decomposition to 4-GLV, which are relatively inexpensive (see Table 1).

Compared to [30], which uses a method based on the regular windowed recoding [33], the optimized GLV-SAC method for variable-base scalar multiplication allows us to save 181 multiplications, 26 squarings and 228 additions over $\mathbb{F}_{p^2}$. Additionally, it only requires 8 precomputed points, which involve 64 protected table lookups over 8 points (denoted by $LUT8$) during scalar multiplication, whereas the method in [30] requires 36 precomputed points, which involve 68 protected table lookups over 9 points. For example, this represents in practice a

17% speedup in the computation and a 78% reduction in the memory consumption of precomputation on curve `Ted127-glv4`.

Finally, in Table 2 we summarize our benchmark results for scalar multiplication and compare them with other constant-time implementations in the literature. The results for the representative variable-base scenario set a new speed record for protected curve-based scalar multiplication on x64 and ARM processors. In comparison with the previously fastest genus one implementation on x64 by Longa and Sica [30], which runs in 137,000 cycles, the presented result injects a cost reduction of 30% on a Sandy Bridge machine. Likewise, in comparison with the state-of-the-art genus 2 implementation by Bos et al. [7], our results are between 21%-24% faster on x64 processors. It is also between 17%-19% faster than the very recent implementation by Oliveira et al. [34] based on a binary GLS curve using the 2-GLV method[1], and about 2 times faster than Bernstein et al.'s implementation using a Montgomery curve over $\mathbb{F}_p$ [4]. Moreover, our results also demonstrate that the proposed techniques bring a dramatic reduction in the overhead for protecting against timing attacks. An unprotected version of our implementation computes a scalar multiplication in 87,000 cycles on the Sandy Bridge processor, which is only 9% faster than our protected version. In the case of ARM, our implementation of variable-base scalar multiplication on curve `Ted127-glv4` is 27% and 32% faster than Bernstein and Schwabe's [6] and Hamburg's [18] implementation (respect.) of `curve25519` on a Cortex-A9 processor. Note, however, that comparisons on ARM are particularly difficult. The implementation of [6] was originally optimized for Cortex-A8, and [18] does not exploit NEON.

Table 2. Cost (in 10^3 cycles) of implementations of variable-base scalar multiplication with protection against timing-type side-channel attacks at approximately 128-bit security level. Results are approximated to the nearest 10^3 cycles.

Work		ARM	ARM	Intel	Intel
Curve	Precomputations	Cortex-A9	Cortex-A15	Sandy Bridge	Ivy Bridge
Ted127-glv4 (this work)	512 bytes (8 points)	417	244	96	92
Ted127-glv4, Longa-Sica [30]	2.25 KB (36 points)	-	-	137	-
Binary GLS $E/\mathbb{F}_{2^{254}}$, Oliveira et al. [34]	512 bytes (8 points)	-	-	115	113
Genus 2 Kummer $C/\mathbb{F}_p$, Bos et al. [7]	0	-	-	126 (*)	117
Curve25519, Bernstein et al. [4]	0	-	-	194 (*)	183 (*)
Curve25519, Bernstein et al. [6]	0	568 (*)	-	-	-
Curve25519, Hamburg [18]	0	616	-	153	-

(*) Source: eBACS [5].

To put our results in perspective, note that the original GLS paper [14] reported a scalar multiplication that ran in 0.76 the time of the best available implementation on x64 (Core 2 Duo) at that time, namely a Montgomery curve

---

[1] In the case of *unprotected* software on x64, Oliveira et al. [34] hold the current speed record with 72,000 cycles on an Intel Sandy Bridge. Their protected version is significantly more costly and runs in about 115,000 cycles.

over $\mathbb{F}_p$ [16]. However, the former implementation is not protected against timing attacks whereas the latter is protected. If, optimistically, one assumes a 10% overhead to protect [14], the ratio above would increase to at least 0.83. Our software, on the other hand, runs in only 0.63 and 0.49 the time of two contemporary implementations also based on the same Montgomery curve, namely [18] and [4], respectively, on another x64 processor (Sandy Bridge). Although a precise comparison is difficult (ratios are obtained on different x64 architectures, GLS implementation [14] and ours exploit different prime forms, have different endomorphism and precomputation costs, etc.) and part of the increase in the speedup can be attributed to moving from 2 to 4-GLV decomposition, there is a wide margin that makes clear the improvement obtained by using the proposed techniques. A similar experimental comparison for ARM is not available in the literature. To our knowledge, we report the first implementation of a GLV-based GLS curve on an ARM processor.

Finally, in our experiments to assess the improvement obtained with the proposed ARM/NEON interleaving technique on the Cortex-A9 processor, we observed speedups close to 17% and 24% in comparison with implementations exploiting only ARM or NEON instructions, respectively. Remarkably, for the same figures on the Cortex-A15, we observed speedups in the order of 34% and 35%, respectively. These experimental results confirm the significant performance improvement enabled by the proposed technique, which exploits the increasing capacity of the latest ARM processors for parallelizing ARM and NEON instructions.

Acknowledgements. We would like to thank Joppe Bos, Craig Costello, Francisco Rodríguez-Henríquez and the reviewers for their useful comments that helped us improve the quality of this work. Also, we would like to thank Francisco Rodríguez-Henríquez for giving us access to the Arndale board for the development of the ARM implementation.

References

1. Aranha, D.F., Karabina, K., Longa, P., Gebotys, C., López, J.: Faster explicit formulas for computing pairings over ordinary curves. In: EUROCRYPT 2011. LNCS, vol. 6632, pp. 48–68. Springer, Heidelberg (2011)
2. Bernstein, D.: Cache-timing attacks on AES (2005),
   http://cr.yp.to/antiforgery/cachetiming-20050414.pdf
3. Bernstein, D.J., Birkner, P., Joye, M., Lange, T., Peters, C.: Twisted Edwards curves. In: Vaudenay, S. (ed.) AFRICACRYPT 2008. LNCS, vol. 5023, pp. 389–405. Springer, Heidelberg (2008)
4. Bernstein, D.J., Duif, N., Lange, T., Schwabe, P., Yang, B.-Y.: High-speed high-security signatures. In: Preneel, B., Takagi, T. (eds.) CHES 2011. LNCS, vol. 6917, pp. 124–142. Springer, Heidelberg (2011)
5. Bernstein, D., Lange, T.: eBACS: ECRYPT Benchmarking of Cryptographic Systems, http://bench.cr.yp.to/results-dh.html (accessed on December 12, 2013)

6. Bernstein, D.J., Schwabe, P.: NEON crypto. In: Prouff, E., Schaumont, P. (eds.) CHES 2012. LNCS, vol. 7428, pp. 320–339. Springer, Heidelberg (2012)
7. Bos, J.W., Costello, C., Hisil, H., Lauter, K.: Fast cryptography in genus 2. In: Johansson, T., Nguyen, P.Q. (eds.) EUROCRYPT 2013. LNCS, vol. 7881, pp. 194–210. Springer, Heidelberg (2013)
8. Bos, J.W., Costello, C., Hisil, H., Lauter, K.: High-performance scalar multiplication using 8-dimensional GLV/GLS decomposition. In: Bertoni, G., Coron, J.-S. (eds.) CHES 2013. LNCS, vol. 8086, pp. 331–348. Springer, Heidelberg (2013)
9. Brumley, D., Boneh, D.: Remote timing attacks are practical. In: Mangard, S., Standaert, F.-X. (eds.) Proceedings of the 12th USENIX Security Symposium. LNCS, vol. 6225, pp. 80–94. Springer (2003)
10. Faz-Hernández, A., Longa, P., Sánchez, A.H.: Efficient and secure algorithms for GLV-based scalar multiplication and their implementation on GLV-GLS curves (extended version). Cryptology ePrint Archive, Report 2013/158 (2013), http://eprint.iacr.org/2013/158
11. Feng, M., Zhu, B.B., Xu, M., Li, S.: Efficient comb elliptic curve multiplication methods resistant to power analysis. Cryptology ePrint Archive, Report 2005/222 (2005), http://eprint.iacr.org/2005/222
12. Feng, M., Zhu, B.B., Zhao, C., Li, S.: Signed MSB-set comb method for elliptic curve point multiplication. In: Chen, K., Deng, R., Lai, X., Zhou, J. (eds.) ISPEC 2006. LNCS, vol. 3903, pp. 13–24. Springer, Heidelberg (2006)
13. Galbraith, S.D., Lin, X., Scott, M.: Endomorphisms for faster elliptic curve cryptography on a large class of curves. J. Cryptology 24(3), 446–469 (2011)
14. Galbraith, S.D., Lin, X., Scott, M.: Endomorphisms for faster elliptic curve cryptography on a large class of curves. In: Joux, A. (ed.) EUROCRYPT 2009. LNCS, vol. 5479, pp. 518–535. Springer, Heidelberg (2009)
15. Gallant, R.P., Lambert, R.J., Vanstone, S.A.: Faster Point Multiplication on Elliptic Curves with Efficient Endomorphisms. In: Kilian, J. (ed.) CRYPTO 2001. LNCS, vol. 2139, pp. 190–200. Springer, Heidelberg (2001)
16. Thomé, E., Gaudry, P.: The mpFq library and implementing curve-based key exchanges. In: SPEED 2007, pp. 49–64 (2007)
17. Guillevic, A., Ionica, S.: Four dimensional GLV via the Weil restriction. In: Sako, K., Sarkar, P. (eds.) ASIACRYPT 2013, Part I. LNCS, vol. 8269, pp. 79–96. Springer, Heidelberg (2013)
18. Hamburg, M.: Fast and compact elliptic-curve cryptography. In: Cryptology ePrint Archive, Report 2012/309 (2012), http://eprint.iacr.org/2012/309
19. Hankerson, D., Karabina, K., Menezes, A.: Analyzing the Galbraith-Lin-Scott point multiplication method for elliptic curves over binary fields. IEEE Trans. Computers 58(10), 1411–1420 (2009)
20. Hankerson, D., Menezes, A., Vanstone, S.: Guide to elliptic curve cryptography. Springer (2004)
21. Hedabou, M., Pinel, P., Bénéteau, L.: Countermeasures for preventing comb method against SCA attacks. In: Deng, R.H., Bao, F., Pang, H., Zhou, J. (eds.) ISPEC 2005. LNCS, vol. 3439, pp. 85–96. Springer, Heidelberg (2005)
22. Hisil, H., Wong, K.K.-H., Carter, G., Dawson, E.: Twisted Edwards curves revisited. In: Pieprzyk, J. (ed.) ASIACRYPT 2008. LNCS, vol. 5350, pp. 326–343. Springer, Heidelberg (2008)
23. Hu, Z., Longa, P., Xu, M.: Implementing 4-dimensional GLV method on GLS elliptic curves with j-invariant 0. Designs, Codes and Cryptography 63(3), 331–343 (2012), http://eprint.iacr.org/2011/315

24. Joye, M., Tunstall, M.: Exponent recoding and regular exponentiation algorithms. In: Preneel, B. (ed.) AFRICACRYPT 2009. LNCS, vol. 5580, pp. 334–349. Springer, Heidelberg (2009)
25. Kocher, P.C.: Timing Attacks on Implementations of Diffie-Hellman, RSA, DSS, and Other Systems. In: Koblitz, N. (ed.) CRYPTO 1996. LNCS, vol. 1109, pp. 104–113. Springer, Heidelberg (1996)
26. Kocher, P.C., Jaffe, J., Jun, B.: Differential Power Analysis. In: Wiener, M. (ed.) CRYPTO 1999. LNCS, vol. 1666, pp. 388–397. Springer, Heidelberg (1999)
27. Lim, C.H., Lee, P.J.: More flexible exponentiation with precomputation. In: Desmedt, Y.G. (ed.) CRYPTO 1994. LNCS, vol. 839, pp. 95–107. Springer, Heidelberg (1994)
28. ARM Limited. ARM Architecture Reference Manual: ARMv7-A and ARMv7-R edition (2012)
29. Longa, P., Gebotys, C.: Efficient techniques for high-speed elliptic curve cryptography. In: Mangard, S., Standaert, F.-X. (eds.) CHES 2010. LNCS, vol. 6225, pp. 80–94. Springer, Heidelberg (2010)
30. Longa, P., Sica, F.: Four-dimensional Gallant-Lambert-Vanstone scalar multiplication. In: Wang, X., Sako, K. (eds.) ASIACRYPT 2012. LNCS, vol. 7658, pp. 718–739. Springer, Heidelberg (2012)
31. Longa, P., Sica, F.: Four-dimensional Gallant-Lambert-Vanstone scalar multiplication. Journal of Cryptology (to appear, 2013)
32. Möller, B.: Algorithms for multi-exponentiation. In: Vaudenay, S., Youssef, A.M. (eds.) SAC 2001. LNCS, vol. 2259, pp. 165–180. Springer, Heidelberg (2001)
33. Okeya, K., Takagi, T.: The width-w NAF method provides small memory and fast elliptic curve scalars multiplications against side-channel attacks. In: Joye, M. (ed.) CT-RSA 2003. LNCS, vol. 2612, pp. 328–342. Springer, Heidelberg (2003)
34. Oliveira, T., López, J., Aranha, D.F., Rodríguez-Henríquez, F.: Lambda coordinates for binary elliptic curves. In: Bertoni, G., Coron, J.-S. (eds.) CHES 2013. LNCS, vol. 8086, pp. 311–330. Springer, Heidelberg (2013)
35. Osvik, D.A., Shamir, A., Tromer, E.: Cache attacks and countermeasures: the case of AES. In: Pointcheval, D. (ed.) CT-RSA 2006. LNCS, vol. 3860, pp. 1–20. Springer, Heidelberg (2006)
36. Sánchez, A.H., Rodríguez-Henríquez, F.: NEON implementation of an attribute-based encryption scheme. In: Jacobson, M., Locasto, M., Mohassel, P., Safavi-Naini, R. (eds.) ACNS 2013. LNCS, vol. 7954, pp. 322–338. Springer, Heidelberg (2013)
37. Smith, B.: Families of fast elliptic curves from $\mathbb{Q}$-curves. In: Sako, K., Sarkar, P. (eds.) ASIACRYPT 2013, Part I. LNCS, vol. 8269, pp. 61–78. Springer, Heidelberg (2013)
38. Weber, D., Denny, T.: The solution of McCurley's discrete log challenge. In: Krawczyk, H. (ed.) CRYPTO 1998. LNCS, vol. 1462, pp. 458–471. Springer, Heidelberg (1998)
39. Yanik, T., Savaş, E., Koç, Ç.K.: Incomplete reduction in modular arithmetic. IEE Proc. of Computers and Digital Techniques 149(2), 46–52 (2002)
40. Yen, S.-M., Joye, M.: Checking before output not be enough against fault- based cryptanalysis. IEEE Trans. Computers 49(9), 967–970 (2000)
41. Yen, S.-M., Kim, S., Lim, S., Moon, S.-J.: A countermeasure against one physical cryptanalysis may benefit another attack. In: Kim, K.-c. (ed.) ICISC 2001. LNCS, vol. 2288, pp. 414–427. Springer, Heidelberg (2002)

A   Formulas for Endomorphisms Φ and Ψ on Curve Ted127-glv4

Let $P = (X_1, Y_1, Z_1)$ be a point in homogeneous projective coordinates on a twisted Edwards curve with eq. (2), $u = 1 + i$ be a quadratic non-residue in $\mathbb{F}_{p^2}$, and $\zeta_8 = u/\sqrt{2}$ be a primitive 8th root of unity. Then, we can compute $\Phi(P) = (X_2, Y_2, Z_2, T_2)$ as follows

$$X_2 = -X_1 \left(\alpha Y_1^2 + \theta Z_1^2 \right) \left[\mu Y_1^2 - \phi Z_1^2 \right], \quad Y_2 = 2Y_1 Z_1^2 \left[\phi Y_1^2 + \gamma Z_1^2 \right],$$
$$Z_2 = 2Y_1 Z_1^2 \left[\mu Y_1^2 - \phi Z_1^2 \right], \quad T_2 = -X_1 \left(\alpha Y_1^2 + \theta Z_1^2 \right) \left[\phi Y_1^2 + \gamma Z_1^2 \right],$$

where $\alpha = \zeta_8^3 + 2\zeta_8^2 + \zeta_8$, $\theta = \zeta_8^3 - 2\zeta_8^2 + \zeta_8$, $\mu = 2\zeta_8^3 + \zeta_8^2 - 1$, $\gamma = 2\zeta_8^3 - \zeta_8^2 + 1$ and $\phi = \zeta_8^2 - 1$.

For curve Ted127-glv4, we have the fixed values

$$\zeta_8 = 1 + Ai, \qquad \alpha = A + 2i, \qquad \theta = A + Bi,$$
$$\mu = (A-1) + (A+1)i, \quad \gamma = (A+1) + (A-1)i, \quad \phi = (B+1) + i,$$

where $A = 143485135153817520976780139629062568752$, $B = 170141183460469231731687303715884099729$.

Computing an endomorphism Φ with the formula above costs $12m + 2s + 5a$ or only $8m + 1s + 5a$ if $Z_1 = 1$. Similarly, we can compute $\Psi(P) = (X_2, Y_2, Z_2, T_2)$ as follows

$$X_2 = \zeta_8 X_1^p Y_1^p, \quad Y_2 = Z_1^{p^2}, \quad Z_2 = Y_1^p Z_1^p, \quad T_2 = \zeta_8 X_1^p Z_1^p.$$

Given the value for ζ_8 on curve Ted127-glv4 computing an endomorphism Ψ with the formula above costs approximately $3m + 1s + 2M + 5A$ or only $1m + 2M + 4A$ if $Z_1 = 1$.

B   Algorithms for Quadratic Extension Field Operations Exploiting Interleaved ARM/NEON Multiprecision Operations

Below are the algorithms for multiplication and squaring over $\mathbb{F}_{p^2}$, with $p = 2^{127} - c$, for ARM platforms. They exploit functions interleaving ARM/NEON-based operations, namely double_mul_neonarm, triple_mul_neonarm and double_red_neonarm, detailed in Algorithms 5, 6 and 7, respectively.

Algorithm 10. Multiplication in $\mathbb{F}_{p^2}$ using completely or incompletely reduced inputs, $m = 3M_i + 9A_i + 2R$ (ARM platform)

Input: $a = (a_0 + a_1 i)$ and $b = (b_0 + b_1 i) \in \mathbb{F}_{p^2}$, where $0 \leq a_0, a_1, b_0, b_1 \leq 2^{127} - 1, p = 2^{127} - c, c$ small.
Output: $a \cdot b \in \mathbb{F}_{p^2}$.

1: $t_0 \leftarrow a_0 + a_1$ $[0, 2^{128} >$
2: $t_1 \leftarrow b_0 + b_1$ $[0, 2^{128} >$
3: $(T_0, T_1, T_2) \leftarrow \texttt{triple\_mul\_neonarm}(a_0, b_0, a_1, b_1, t_0, t_1)$ $[0, 2^{256} >$
4: $C_0 \leftarrow T_0 - T_1$ $< -2^{254}, 2^{254} >$
5: **if** $C_0 < 0$, **then** $C_0 \leftarrow C_0 + 2^{128} \cdot p$ $[0, 2^{255} >$
6: $T_2 \leftarrow T_2 - T_0$ $[0, 2^{256} >$
7: $C_1 \leftarrow T_2 - T_1$ $[0, 2^{256} >$
8: **return** $(c_0, c_1) \leftarrow \texttt{double\_red\_neonarm}(C_0, C_1)$ $[0, p >$

Algorithm 11. Squaring in $\mathbb{F}_{p^2}$ using completely reduced inputs, $s = 2M + 1A + 2A_i$ (ARM platform)

Input: $a = (a_0 + a_1 i) \in \mathbb{F}_{p^2}$, where $0 \leq a_0, a_1 \leq p - 1, p = 2^{127} - c, c$ small.
Output: $a^2 \in \mathbb{F}_{p^2}$.

1: $t_0 \leftarrow a_0 + a_1$ $[0, 2^{128} >$
2: $t_1 \leftarrow a_0 - a_1 \bmod p$ $[0, p >$
3: $t_2 \leftarrow a_0 + a_0$ $[0, 2^{128} >$
4: $(C_0, C_1) \leftarrow \texttt{double\_mul\_neonarm}(t_0, t_1, t_2, a_1)$ $[0, p^2 >$
5: **return** $a^2 = \texttt{double\_red\_neonarm}(C_0, C_1)$ $[0, p >$

An Improved Compression Technique for Signatures Based on Learning with Errors

Shi Bai and Steven D. Galbraith

Department of Mathematics,
University of Auckland,
New Zealand
S.Bai@auckland.ac.nz,
S.Galbraith@math.auckland.ac.nz

Abstract. We present a new approach to the compression technique of Lyubashevsky et al. [17,13] for lattice-based signatures based on learning with errors (LWE). Our ideas seem to be particularly suitable for signature schemes whose security, in the random oracle model, is based on standard worst-case computational assumptions. Our signatures are shorter than any previous proposal for provably-secure signatures based on standard lattice problems: at the 128-bit level we improve signature size from (more than) 16500 bits to around 9000 to 12000 bits.

Keywords: Lattice-based signatures, learning with errors.

1 Introduction

An important problem is to obtain practical and provably secure public key signature schemes based on lattice assumptions. One approach is to use trapdoor functions and the hash-and-sign methodology (see Gentry, Peikert and Vaikuntanathan [12], Stehlé and Steinfeld [22]). However, the most promising avenue for practical signatures (with security in the random oracle model) has long been the use of the Fiat-Shamir paradigm; this is the approach used for all currently deployed discrete-logarithm-based digital signature schemes. (For signatures that are proven secure in the standard model, we refer to Boyen [6] and Böhl et al. [5].)

A series of works by Lyubashevsky and others [15,17,13,9] have developed schemes based on the Fiat-Shamir paradigm that are secure in the random oracle model. There are several challenges when implementing lattice-based signature schemes, including the size of the public key, the size of the signature and the requirement to sample from discrete Gaussians during the signing process. Our main focus in this paper is to reduce the size of signatures.

The basic idea of Lyubashevsky's signatures in the case of LWE is to have a public key of the form $(\mathbf{A}, \mathbf{T} = \mathbf{AS} + \mathbf{E} \pmod{q})$ where $\mathbf{A}$ is an $m \times n$ matrix and $m \approx n$. The signing procedure starts by choosing vectors $\mathbf{y}_1, \mathbf{y}_2$ of small norm and computing $\mathbf{v} = \mathbf{Ay}_1 + \mathbf{y}_2 \pmod{q}$. Then, using the Fiat-Shamir paradigm, the signer computes $\mathbf{c} = H(\mathbf{v}, \mu)$ where μ is the message and H is a

J. Benaloh (Ed.): CT-RSA 2014, LNCS 8366, pp. 28–47, 2014.
© Springer International Publishing Switzerland 2014

hash function. Finally, the signer computes $\mathbf{z}_1 = \mathbf{y}_1 + \mathbf{Sc}$ and $\mathbf{z}_2 = \mathbf{y}_2 + \mathbf{Ec}$. The signature is $(\mathbf{z}_1, \mathbf{z}_2, \mathbf{c})$. The verifier checks that $\|\mathbf{z}_1\|$ and $\|\mathbf{z}_2\|$ are small enough and that $H(\mathbf{Az}_1 + \mathbf{z}_2 - \mathbf{Tc} \pmod{q}, \mu)$ is equal to $\mathbf{c}$. A significant obstacle to short signatures is the need to send the length m vector $\mathbf{z}_2$. Recent work [13,9] has introduced compression techniques that greatly reduce the amount of data to be sent for the vector $\mathbf{z}_2$. The main contribution of our paper is to give a variant of the signature scheme with the feature that $\mathbf{z}_2$ can be omitted entirely.

1.1   Related Work

At Eurocrypt 2012, Lyubashevsky [17] gave a signature scheme whose security (at around the 100-bit security level) relies on SIS and LWE, and for which signatures are 16500 bits. To our knowledge, this is the current record in the literature for signatures whose security is reduced to worst-case assumptions in general lattices. The signing algorithm for that scheme requires sampling from discrete Gaussians. At the 128-bit security level, signatures for this scheme would be around 20000 bits.

Güneysu, Lyubashevsky and Pöppelmann [13] introduced an important compression technique and gave a signature scheme that does not require sampling from Gaussians. The security depends on the Ring-SIS and DCK (an NTRU-like variant of Ring-LWE with small parameters) assumptions, however a full security analysis is not given in their paper. The signatures are around 9000 bits. The compression technique can be modified to shorten the signatures from [17] (changing the rejection sampling to a Gaussian distribution).

Recently Ducas, Durmus, Lepoint and Lyubashevsky [9] have given a new scheme with several further tricks to reduce the signature size. For security based on SIS (and hence on standard worst-case lattice problems) their scheme has signatures of size more than 20000 bits[1]. They also give a variant, based on a non-standard computational assumption related to NTRU, that has signatures of around 5000 bits.

1.2   Our Contribution

As mentioned already, our main contribution is to present a variant of the Lyubashevsky signature scheme based on LWE that does not require sending any information about the $\mathbf{z}_2$ vector. At a high level, Lyubashevsky's scheme [13,17] based on LWE has public key $(\mathbf{A}, \mathbf{b} = \mathbf{As} + \mathbf{e} \pmod{q})$ and a signature is like a proof of knowledge of the pair $(\mathbf{s}, \mathbf{e})$. The key feature of our scheme is to prove knowledge of only $\mathbf{s}$. The smallness of $\mathbf{e}$ becomes implicit in the verification equation, so we no longer need to send any information about $\mathbf{e}$. Since $\mathbf{s}$ has length n and $\mathbf{e}$ has length $m \approx n$, not needing to prove knowledge of $\mathbf{e}$ has the potential to provide a significant reduction in signature size.

---

[1] It may seem paradoxical that the improved techniques of [9] lead to larger signatures than [17]. This is due to the requirement that the matrix $\mathbf{A}$ in the public key be indistinguishable from a uniformly chosen matrix, which makes m larger where $m = O(\frac{n \log q}{\log n})$.

Briefly, the public key for our scheme is an LWE instance $(\mathbf{A}, \mathbf{T} = \mathbf{AS} + \mathbf{E}$ (mod q)) where all terms are matrices, and $\mathbf{S}, \mathbf{E}$ have small entries. A signature is formed by first choosing a vector $\mathbf{y}$ and computing $\mathbf{v} = \mathbf{Ay}$ (mod q). One then throws away the least significant bits of $\mathbf{v}$ and hashes the remaining bits together with the message μ to get a hash value c. The value c is used to create a low weight vector $\mathbf{c}$ and the signature is the pair $(\mathbf{z} = \mathbf{y} + \mathbf{Sc}, c)$. As in [9,13,17], we use rejection sampling to ensure that the distribution of $\mathbf{z}$ is independent of the secret. To verify the signature one computes $\mathbf{w} = \mathbf{Az} - \mathbf{Tc} \equiv \mathbf{Ay} - \mathbf{Ec}$ (mod q). Assuming that $\mathbf{Ec}$ is small enough then the most significant bits of $\mathbf{w}$ will match those of $\mathbf{v}$ and so the hash value computed using the most significant bits of $\mathbf{w}$ equals c.

Our work employs several ideas from [9,13,17]. We prove the security of our scheme using the proof methodology from [17].

For signatures based on worst-case lattice assumptions we improve signature size from more than 16500 bits to around 9000 bits. The security level (at the 128 bits-level) of our signatures is supported by Regev's reduction for LWE and also arguments about BKZ 2.0 lattice reduction due to Chen and Nguyen [8]. Hence, we match the signature size of [13], and still with the beneficial feature of using uniform distributions, but with security based on standard assumptions. Relaxing the conditions of Regev's theorem also allows signatures of size under 10000 bits (see Section B.2). We also give signatures of under 8000 bits with security based on a non-standard matrix-NTRU-like problem (see Section B.3).

Another aspect of our result is that we use standard LWE rather than Ring-LWE. Previous work on lattice signatures assumed that using Ring-LWE or NTRU would give more practical signatures. While there are certainly significant practical benefits from using Ring-LWE (such as smaller public keys), there are also some constraints (such as preferring n to be a power of 2).

2   Preliminaries

2.1   Basic Notation and Gaussians

Let $q \in \mathbb{N}$ be a prime. We write $\mathbb{Z}_q$ for the integers modulo q and represent this set by integers in the range $(-q/2, q/2]$. We write (column) vectors in bold face as $\mathbf{v} = (v_1, \ldots, v_n)^T$, where $\mathbf{v}^T$ denotes the transpose of the vector, and matrices in bold face as $\mathbf{A}$. The $n \times n$ identity matrix is denoted $\mathbf{I}_n$. The Euclidean norm is $\|\mathbf{v}\| = \|\mathbf{v}\|_2 = \sqrt{\sum_{i=1}^{n} v_i^2}$ and the infinity norm (or sup norm) is $\|\mathbf{v}\|_\infty = \max_{1 \le i \le n} |v_i|$.

For $a \in \mathbb{Z}$ and $d \in \mathbb{N}$, define $[a]_{2^d}$ to be the unique integer in the set $(-2^{d-1}, 2^{d-1}]$ such that $a \equiv [a]_{2^d}$ (mod 2^d). For $a \in \mathbb{Z}$, we define $\lfloor a \rfloor_d = (a - [a]_{2^d})/2^d$ (dropping the d-least significant bits). Note that it satisfies $\lfloor 2^{d-1} \rfloor_d = \lfloor -2^{d-1} + 1 \rfloor_d = 0$ and $\lfloor 2^{d-1} + 1 \rfloor_d = -\lfloor -2^{d-1} \rfloor_d = 1$. We extend this function to vectors: on input a length m vector $\mathbf{v} = (v_1, \ldots, v_m)^T \in \mathbb{Z}^m$ the function $\lfloor \mathbf{v} \rfloor_d$ is the length m vector with entries $\lfloor v_i \rfloor_d$. A lattice in $\mathbb{Z}^m$ is a subgroup of $\mathbb{Z}^m$; for background see [18,19].

Let A be a finite set. We write $a \leftarrow A$ to denote that a is sampled uniformly from A. We write $\mathbf{A} \leftarrow \mathbb{Z}_q^{m \times n}$ to denote that $\mathbf{A}$ is an $m \times n$ matrix with entries uniformly and independently sampled from $\mathbb{Z}_q$. Let $\sigma \in \mathbb{R}_{>0}$. Define $\rho_\sigma(x) = \exp(-x^2/(2\sigma^2))$ and $\rho_\sigma(\mathbb{Z}) = 1 + 2\sum_{x=1}^\infty \rho_\sigma(x)$. The discrete Gaussian distribution on $\mathbb{Z}$ with standard deviation σ is the distribution that associates to $x \in \mathbb{Z}$ the probability $\rho_\sigma(x)/\rho_\sigma(\mathbb{Z})$. We denote this distribution D_σ. Some authors write $s = \sqrt{2\pi}\sigma$ and define $\rho_s(x) = \exp(-\pi x^2/s^2)$ and denote the distribution D_s. The tail of a discrete Gaussian variable can be bounded by the following result.

Lemma 1. *(Lemma 4.4, full version of [17]) For any $k > 0$,*

$$Pr_{x \leftarrow D_\sigma}(|x| > k\sigma) \le 2e^{-k^2/2}. \tag{1}$$

Taking $k = 13$ gives tail probability approximately 2^{-121}, taking $k = 13.5$ gives 2^{-130} and $k = 14$ gives 2^{-140}.

One can also define discrete Gaussian distributions on vectors. We write $\mathbf{y} \leftarrow D_\sigma^n$ to mean that the vector $\mathbf{y} = (y_1, \dots, y_n)^T \in \mathbb{Z}^n$ is sampled such that each entry y_i is independently sampled according to the distribution D_σ.

2.2   Learning with Errors

The learning with errors problem (LWE) was introduced by Regev [23]. It is parameterised by integers $n, q \in \mathbb{N}$ and distributions χ and ϕ on $\mathbb{Z}$ (typically χ is the uniform distribution on $\mathbb{Z}_q$ and $\phi = D_{\alpha q}$ for some fixed real number $0 < \alpha < 1$).

Definition 1. *Let $n, q \in \mathbb{N}$ and let χ and ϕ be distributions on $\mathbb{Z}$. The LWE distribution for a given vector $\mathbf{s} \in \mathbb{Z}_q^n$ is the set of pairs $(\mathbf{a}, \mathbf{a} \cdot \mathbf{s} + e \pmod{q})$ where $\mathbf{a} \in \mathbb{Z}_q^n$ is sampled uniformly and where e is sampled from ϕ.*

- *The computational-LWE problem is: For a vector $\mathbf{s} \leftarrow \chi^n$ and given arbitrarily many samples from the LWE distribution for $\mathbf{s}$, to compute $\mathbf{s}$.*
- *The decisional-LWE problem is: Given arbitrarily many samples from $\mathbb{Z}_q^{n+1}$ to distinguish whether the samples are distributed uniformly or whether they are distributed as the LWE distribution for some fixed vector $\mathbf{s} \leftarrow \chi^n$.*

We sometimes use notation like (n, q, ϕ)-LWE to mean the computational LWE problem with these parameters. We also write (n, q, α)-LWE to mean LWE where $\phi = D_{\alpha q}$.

If the error distribution is small enough compared with q and if one has enough samples from the LWE-distribution then it can be shown that these computational problems are well-defined. Well-defined for decisional-LWE means that the LWE-distribution, for all vectors likely to be sampled as $\mathbf{s} \leftarrow \chi^n$, is not statistically close to the uniform distribution. Well-defined for computational-LWE means that there is a unique solution $\mathbf{s}$ that is most likely to be the one used to generate the samples from the LWE distribution (in other words, computational-LWE is well-defined as a maximum likelihood problem). There is a reduction (Lemma 4.2 of Regev [24]) from the computational-LWE problem to the decisional-LWE problem. So if one problem is hard then so is the other.

Regev's main theorem is that the LWE problems are as hard as worst-case assumptions in general lattices when χ is the uniform distribution and when ϕ is a discrete Gaussian with standard deviation $\sigma = \alpha q$ for some fixed real number $0 < \alpha < 1$.

Theorem 1. *(Regev) Let $n, q \in \mathbb{N}$ and $0 < \alpha < 1$ be such that $\alpha q \geq 2\sqrt{n}$. Then there exists a quantum reduction from worst-case $GapSVP_{\tilde{O}(n/\alpha)}$ to (n, q, α)-LWE.*

One can also fix an integer m and consider the case of *LWE with a bounded number of samples*. We often write the LWE instance in this case as $(\mathbf{A}, \mathbf{b} \equiv \mathbf{As} + \mathbf{e} \pmod{q})$ where $\mathbf{A}$ is an $m \times n$ matrix over $\mathbb{Z}_q$, $\mathbf{s}$ is a length n column vector, and $\mathbf{e}$ is a length m vector with entries sampled independently from ϕ. As long as the bounded LWE instance is well-defined then this problem cannot be easier than the general LWE instance. Consider the bounded samples LWE problem when χ is the uniform distribution on $\mathbb{Z}_q$ and when ϕ is such that error values satisfy $|e| \leq E$ with overwhelming probability (in our application we will have $E = 2^{d-1}$ or $E = 2^d$). Then there are at most $q^n(2E+1)^m$ choices for $(\mathbf{s}, \mathbf{e})$ compared with q^m choices for $\mathbf{b}$. Hence, as a rule of thumb, we need $q^m > q^n(2E+1)^m$ for the bounded samples LWE problem to be well-defined.

Another well-known fact (see [2]) is that one may reduce LWE to the case where $\chi = \phi$. Suppose we have m samples, where m is significantly larger than n, and write the LWE instance as $(\mathbf{A}, \mathbf{b} \equiv \mathbf{As} + \mathbf{e} \pmod{q})$. With overwhelming probability, $\mathbf{A}$ has rank n and (swapping rows of $\mathbf{A}$ if necessary) we may write

$$\mathbf{A} = \begin{pmatrix} \mathbf{A}_1 \\ \mathbf{A}_2 \end{pmatrix}$$

where $\mathbf{A}_1$ is an invertible $n \times n$ matrix and $\mathbf{A}_2$ is an $(m-n) \times n$ matrix. Write $\mathbf{b} = \begin{pmatrix} \mathbf{b}_1 \\ \mathbf{b}_2 \end{pmatrix}$ and $\mathbf{e} = \begin{pmatrix} \mathbf{e}_1 \\ \mathbf{e}_2 \end{pmatrix}$ where $\mathbf{b}_1$ and $\mathbf{e}_1$ have length n and we have $\mathbf{b}_1 = \mathbf{A}_1\mathbf{s} + \mathbf{e}_1$ and $\mathbf{b}_2 = \mathbf{A}_2\mathbf{s} + \mathbf{e}_2$. It follows that

$$\mathbf{b}_2 - \mathbf{A}_2\mathbf{A}_1^{-1}\mathbf{b}_1 = (-\mathbf{A}_2\mathbf{A}_1^{-1})\mathbf{e}_1 + \mathbf{e}_2 \pmod{q}$$

which gives an LWE instance where the solution $(\mathbf{e}_1, \mathbf{e}_2)$ is sampled from the error distribution. We call this problem *LWE with short secrets*.

It follows that LWE with short secrets is not easier than the general case. We can also consider the LWE problem with short secrets *and* with a bounded number of samples. As long as this problem is well defined then it is also not easier than the general case. Furthermore, fewer samples are required for the LWE with short secrets problem to be well-defined: If we again assume the distribution ϕ is such that error values satisfy $|e| \leq E$ with overwhelming probability, then we need, as a rule of thumb, $q^m > (2E+1)^{n+m}$ for the LWE problem to be well-defined. To get very short signatures one can push this further and have the distribution χ having smaller support than the error distribution ϕ (cf. Appendix B.2).

In our work we will consider a matrix variant of LWE. The LWE distribution is on pairs $(\mathbf{A}, \mathbf{AS} + \mathbf{E} \pmod{q})$ where $\mathbf{S}$ and $\mathbf{E}$ are matrices. Each of the columns of $\mathbf{S}$ and $\mathbf{E}$ corresponds to an LWE instance $(\mathbf{A}, \mathbf{As} + \mathbf{e} \pmod{q})$, so this is just a collection of individual LWE instances. However, note that the matrix $\mathbf{A}$ is shared across all instances; we call them *semi-independent instances of LWE*. In any case, it is clear that this matrix variant of LWE cannot be easier than LWE with a single vector $\mathbf{b} \equiv \mathbf{As} + \mathbf{e} \pmod{q}$.

To summarise, we may choose (n, q, α) such that $\alpha q > 2\sqrt{n}$ and set $\chi = \phi = D_{\alpha q}$. We should choose m such that $q^m > (28\alpha q)^{n+m}$ so that the problem is well-defined with overwhelming probability. Consider the computational LWE problem $(\mathbf{A}, \mathbf{AS} + \mathbf{E} \pmod{q})$ where $\mathbf{A}$ is an $m \times n$ matrix uniformly chosen from $\mathbb{Z}_q^{m \times n}$ and where $\mathbf{S}$ and $\mathbf{E}$ are chosen to have entries sampled independently from $D_{\alpha q}$. Then this problem is not easier than $\text{GapSVP}_{\tilde{O}(n/\alpha)}$ in n-dimensional lattices.

2.3 Rejection Sampling

For security we will need to ensure that the signatures do not leak the private key. We use a variant of the general rejection sampling lemma of [17] (also see Chapter 2 of Devroye [10]).

Lemma 2. *Let $f : \mathbb{Z}^n \to \mathbb{R}$ be a probability distribution. Given a subset $V \subseteq \mathbb{Z}^n$, let $h : V \to \mathbb{R}$ be a probability distribution defined on V. Let $g_v : \mathbb{Z}^n \to \mathbb{R}$ be a family of probability distributions indexed by $v \in V$ such that for almost all v's from h there exists a universal upper bound $M \in \mathbb{R}$ such that*

$$Pr[Mg_v(z) \geq f(z); \ z \leftarrow f] \geq 1 - negligible.$$

Then the output distributions of the following two algorithms have negligible statistical difference:

1. *$v \leftarrow h$, $z \leftarrow g_v$, output (z, v) with probability $\min\left(\frac{f(z)}{Mg_v(z)}, 1\right)$, else fail.*
2. *$v \leftarrow h, z \leftarrow f$, output (z, v) with probability $\frac{1}{M}$.*

In the signature (and the security proof), distribution f is a uniform distribution over $[-B + U, B - U]^n$ where $U = 14\sigma_{\mathbf{Sc}}$. Each $\mathbf{v} = \mathbf{Sc}$ is a vector with entries in a close-to-Gaussian distribution with standard deviation $\sigma_{\mathbf{Sc}}$. With high probability, the coefficients in $\mathbf{v}$ are bounded by $14\sigma_{\mathbf{Sc}}$. This accounts for the "almost all" argument in above lemma. In the signature $\mathbf{z} = \mathbf{Sc} + \mathbf{y}$, vector $\mathbf{y}$ is generated from a uniform distribution over $[-B, B]^n$ (so each entry is set for 2^{-140} error). For success probability of roughly $1/e$, we can set $B = 14\sigma_{\mathbf{Sc}}n$.

3   Our Signature Scheme

In Appendix A, we recall some standard background on signature schemes. We will focus on our signature scheme (Figure 1) in this section.

The scheme depends on parameters $n, m, k, \kappa, w, q, \alpha, d, B$ and distributions D_E, D_S, D_y and D_z. The distributions D_S and D_E are the distributions for the secret and error respectively in the LWE assumption. As in [9,17], the distribution $D^n_{y,\mathbf{Sc}}(\mathbf{z})$ is the distribution coming from the shift of the distribution D^n_y by an offset vector $\mathbf{Sc}$. Various constraints on the parameters will be given later, but we typically have $m > n = k$ and $q > 2^d \geq B$. The main security parameters are n (the security of our scheme will depend on (n, q, α)-LWE) and κ (which controls the probability of breaking the hash function).

The scheme requires a hash function H to binary strings of fixed length κ, and an encoding function F that maps binary strings of length κ to elements of the set $\mathcal{B}_{k,w}$ of length k vectors of weight w with coefficients in $\{-1, 0, 1\}$. We require F to be close to an injection in the sense that

$$\mathrm{Pr}_{s_1,s_2 \leftarrow \{0,1\}^\kappa}(F(s_1) = F(s_2)) \leq \frac{c_1}{2^\kappa} \tag{2}$$

for some constant c_1. We also typically choose parameters so that $2^\kappa \approx \#\mathcal{B}_{k,w} = 2^w \binom{k}{w}$. There are several ways to construct a suitable function F. One method is given in Section 4.4 of [9] and some other approaches are discussed in Appendix C (and the references) of Biswas and Sendrier [4].

The verifier wants to test that signature vectors $\mathbf{z}$ have come from the correct distribution D^n_z. This could be done in many ways, depending on D_z and how much statistical analysis the verifier wishes to perform. If D_z is a uniform distribution on $[-B, B]$ then the natural test is that $\|\mathbf{z}\|_\infty \leq B$; this could be entirely implicit if the interval is of the form $[-2^{a-1}+1, 2^{a-1}]$ and entries of $\mathbf{z}$ are represented by a bits. If D_z is a Gaussian or Gaussian-like distribution with mean 0 and standard deviation σ_z then a a cheap test is to have a bound B (e.g., $B = 2\sqrt{n}\sigma_z$; see Lemma 4.4 of the full version of [17]) such that $\mathbf{z} \leftarrow D^n_z$ implies $\|\mathbf{z}\|_2 \leq B$ with high probability. Hence, in Line 4 of Algorithm 3 we write this as $\|\mathbf{z}\|_\ell \leq B$ where typically $\ell \in \{2, \infty\}$.

The scheme is given by Algorithms 1, 2 and 3 in Figure 1. While reading the protocol the reader may keep in mind the following set of parameters:

$$(n, m, k, \kappa, q, d, B) = (512, 945, 512, 132, \approx 2^{30.84}, 24, \approx 2^{20.97}).$$

The distributions $D_E = D_S$ used here are discrete Gaussians with standard deviation $\sigma_E = \sigma_S \geq 2\sqrt{n}$. We will choose the distributions D_y and D_z to be uniform distributions, like $[-B, B]$. A minor subtlety is that D_y must cover D_z with a little slack on each side, so to keep the notation simple we choose D_y to be the uniform distribution on $[-B, B]$ and D_z to be the uniform distribution on $[-(B-U), B-U]$ where $U = 14\sqrt{w}\sigma_E \geq 28\sqrt{wn}$. If one wanted to be pedantic would one could modify line 4 of Algorithm 3 to $\|\mathbf{z}\|_\ell \leq B - U$.

The message is denoted μ. Recall that, for $a \in \mathbb{Z}$, $\lfloor a \rceil_d = (a - [a]_{2^d})/2^d$ is essentially the integer a with its d least significant bits removed. The value M used in the rejection sampling in Line 10 of Algorithm 2 is a bound for the expected number of trials until rejection sampling succeeds, as in Lemma 2. The rejection in Line 4 of Algorithm 1 occurs with probability less than $1/30$ for our parameters, and since LWE with bounded number of samples is not easier than general LWE (see Section 2.2), it follows that the outputs of the key generation algorithm are hard LWE instances.

Algorithm 1. Key generation

INPUT: $n, m, k, q, \sigma_S, \sigma_E$
OUTPUT: $\mathbf{A}, \mathbf{T}$
1: $\mathbf{A} \leftarrow \mathbb{Z}_q^{m \times n}$
2: $\mathbf{S} \leftarrow D_S^{n \times k}$
3: $\mathbf{E} \leftarrow D_E^{m \times k}$
4: **if** $|\mathbf{E}_{i,j}| > 7\sigma_E$ for any (i, j) **then**
5:     Restart
6: **end if**
7: $\mathbf{T} \equiv \mathbf{AS} + \mathbf{E} \pmod{q}$
8: **return** $\mathbf{A}, \mathbf{T}$

Algorithm 2. Signing

INPUT:
    $\mu, \mathbf{A}, \mathbf{T}, \mathbf{S}, D_y, D_z, d, w, \sigma_E, H, F, M$
OUTPUT: $(\mathbf{z}, c)$
1: $\mathbf{y} \leftarrow D_y^n$
2: $\mathbf{v} \equiv \mathbf{Ay} \pmod{q}$
3: $c = H(\lfloor \mathbf{v} \rceil_d, \mu)$
4: $\mathbf{c} = F(c)$
5: $\mathbf{z} = \mathbf{y} + \mathbf{Sc}$
6: $\mathbf{w} \equiv \mathbf{Az} - \mathbf{Tc} \pmod{q}$
7: **if** $|[\mathbf{w}_i]_{2^d}| > 2^{d-1} - 7w\sigma_E$ **then**
8:     Restart
9: **end if**
10: **return** $(\mathbf{z}, c)$ with probability
    $\min \left(D_z^n(\mathbf{z}) / (M \cdot D_{y,\mathbf{Sc}}^n(\mathbf{z})), 1 \right)$

Algorithm 3. Verifying

INPUT: $\mu, \mathbf{z}, c, \mathbf{A}, \mathbf{T}, \ell, B, d, H, F$
OUTPUT: Accept or Reject
1: $\mathbf{c} = F(c)$
2: $\mathbf{w} \equiv \mathbf{Az} - \mathbf{Tc} \pmod{q}$
3: $c' = H(\lfloor \mathbf{w} \rceil_d, \mu)$
4: **if** $c' = c$ and $\|\mathbf{z}\|_\ell \leq B$ **then**
5:     **return** "Accept"
6: **else**
7:     **return** "Reject"
8: **end if**

Fig. 1. The LWE Signature Scheme

The test in Line 7 of Algorithm 2 ensures that $\lfloor \mathbf{v} \rceil_d = \lfloor \mathbf{v} - \mathbf{Ec} \rceil_d = \lfloor \mathbf{w} \rceil_d$, and so the signatures do verify. The bound $7w\sigma_E$ comes from the fact that entries of $\mathbf{E}$ are bounded by $7\sigma_E$ and that the weight of $\mathbf{c}$ is w. Assuming that $\mathbf{w}$ is distributed close to uniformly, then this condition will hold with probability $(1 - 14w\sigma_E / 2^d)^m$ and so we require

$$2^d \gtrsim 7wm\sigma_E. \tag{3}$$

The probability of acceptance is targeted between $1/3$ and $1/2$ for our parameters (see Table 1 for details).

Remark 1. The signature size essentially depends on n and the distribution D_z. Due to the rejection sampling, the distribution D_z depends on the size of $\mathbf{Sc}$, which depends on D_S (i.e., σ_S) and the weight w of $\mathbf{c}$. Hence, the signature size is driven by n, w and D_S. A surprising fact is that the signature size does not depend on m or d. In fact, it seems to be quite possible to choose 2^d rather large and q quite a bit larger than 2^d (as a minimum we need $\lfloor \mathbf{A}\mathbf{y} \pmod{q} \rceil_d$ to provide more than κ-bits of entropy into the hash function.

4 Security Proofs

There are several ways to prove security of our signature scheme in the random oracle model. Each requires different conditions on the parameters. Theorem 2 follows Lyubashevsky's blueprint and seems to be the most useful for short signatures.

Theorem 2. *Let q be prime. Let parameters n, m, d, κ, B be such that*

$$(2B)^n q^{m-n} \geq (2^{d+1})^m 2^\kappa. \tag{4}$$

and suppose equation (2) holds. Let $D_y = [-B, B]$ with the uniform distribution and let $\mathbf{S}, \mathbf{E}$ have entries chosen from discrete Gaussian distributions with standard deviation $\sigma_S = \sigma_E = \alpha q$. Let A be a forger against the signature scheme in the random oracle model that makes h hash queries, s sign queries, runs in time t and succeeds with probability δ. Then there is a negligible ε and some $0 \leq \delta' \leq \delta$ such that A can be turned into either of the following two algorithms:

1. *an algorithm, running in time approximately t and with advantage $\delta - \delta' - \varepsilon$, that solves the (n, m, q, α)-decisional-LWE problem.*
2. *an algorithm, running in time approximately $2t$ and with success probability $\delta' \left(\frac{\delta'}{h} - \frac{1}{2^\kappa} \right)$, that solves the unbalanced $(m + n, m, q)$-search-SIS problem: Given an $m \times (n+m)$ matrix $\mathbf{A}'$ to find a length n vector $\mathbf{y}_1$ and a length m vector $\mathbf{y}_2$ such that $\|\mathbf{y}_1\|_\infty, \|\mathbf{y}_2\|_\infty \leq \max(2B, 2^{d-1}) + 2E'w$ and $\mathbf{A}'\binom{\mathbf{y}_1}{\mathbf{y}_2} \equiv 0 \pmod{q}$ where E' satisfies*

$$(2E')^{m+n} \geq q^m 2^\kappa. \tag{5}$$

The proof of Theorem 2 is given in Subsection 4.2. We sketch the main idea here. We first replace the signing oracle with a simulation in the random oracle model. We then replace the public key $(\mathbf{A}, \mathbf{T})$ with a different value; the decisional-LWE assumption appears at this point. The forking lemma is then used to transform a forger into an algorithm that solves SIS.

Here, we first show that there is enough entropy going into the hash function. In Algorithm 2 the vector $\mathbf{y}$ is sampled from D_y^n, and when D_y is the uniform distribution on $[-B, B]$ this means there are $(2B + 1)^n$ choices for $\mathbf{y}$. There are at most $(q/2^d)^m$ choices for $\lfloor \mathbf{A}\mathbf{y} \rceil_d$, and these values are hashed to κ-bit strings, giving at most 2^κ possible values for c. It is necessary that the hash outputs are uniformly distributed, which requires that there is sufficient entropy in the distribution of values $\lfloor \mathbf{A}\mathbf{y} \rceil_d$ being hashed. Since $(2B + 1)^n$ will be much greater than 2^κ (this condition is required for the computational assumptions to be reasonable), it suffices to ensure that there is a sufficiently large supply of possible values for $\lfloor \mathbf{A}\mathbf{y} \rceil_d$. This is the content of Lemma 3.

Lemma 3. *Let $q > 4B > 4$ and $m > n > \kappa$ and other notation be as above. Let D_y be the uniform distribution on $[-B, B]$ and suppose the condition in Equation (4) holds. Then the number of values for $\lfloor \mathbf{A}\mathbf{y} \pmod{q}\rceil_d$ is at least 2^κ, and the probability that two values $\mathbf{y}_1, \mathbf{y}_2$ sampled uniformly from $[-B, B]^n$ give the same value is at most $1/2^\kappa$.*

Proof. Let $\mathbf{A}$ be a randomly chosen matrix. We can assume the rank of $\mathbf{A}$ is n provided that $m \geq n$ (if not then we can re-generate $\mathbf{A}$ in the key generation). Hence $\mathbf{A}$ defines an injective linear map from $\mathbb{Z}^n$ to $\mathbb{Z}^m$.

Let $\mathbf{y}_1 \in D_y^n$ and set $u = \lfloor \mathbf{A}\mathbf{y}_1 \pmod{q}\rceil_d$. Define

$$S_u = \{\mathbf{y}_2 \in D_y^n : \lfloor \mathbf{A}\mathbf{y}_2 \pmod{q}\rceil_d = u\}.$$

It suffices to bound $\#S_u$. Note that if $\mathbf{y}_2 \in S_u$ then $\mathbf{y} = \mathbf{y}_1 - \mathbf{y}_2$ satisfies $\|\mathbf{y}\|_\infty \leq 2B$ and

$$\mathbf{A}\mathbf{y} \pmod{q} \in [-2^d, 2^d]^m.$$

Hence, to bound $\#S_u$ it suffices to bound the number of such vectors $\mathbf{y}$.

A randomly chosen matrix $\mathbf{A}$ defines a random lattice $L = \{\mathbf{v} \in \mathbb{Z}^m : \mathbf{v} \equiv \mathbf{A}\mathbf{y} \pmod{q}$ for some $\mathbf{y} \in \mathbb{Z}^n\}$. The volume of L is q^{m-n}. By the Gaussian heuristic, the number of elements in $L \cap [-2^d, 2^d]^m$ is expected to be $2^{(d+1)m}/q^{m-n}$. Finally, suppose $\mathbf{y}, \mathbf{y}' \in [-2B, 2B]^n$ are such that $\mathbf{A}\mathbf{y} \equiv \mathbf{A}\mathbf{y}' \pmod{q}$. Then $\mathbf{A}(\mathbf{y} - \mathbf{y}') \equiv 0 \pmod{q}$, which implies $\mathbf{y} \equiv \mathbf{y}' \pmod{q}$ which, due to the size constraints and the condition $q > 4B$, implies $\mathbf{y} = \mathbf{y}'$. Hence, $\#S_u$ is upper bounded by $2^{(d+1)m}/q^{m-n}$ for all u.

There are $(2B + 1)^n$ choices for $\mathbf{y}_1$, so if we choose two of uniformly, the probability of a collision is bounded by

$$\frac{2^{(d+1)m}/q^{m-n}}{(2B+1)^n} \leq \frac{1}{2^\kappa}. \tag{6}$$

$\square$

4.1   Simulation in the Random Oracle Model

Let A be a forger for the signature scheme. The forger takes as input a public key for the signature scheme, makes h random oracle queries and s sign queries, runs in time t, and outputs a valid signature with probability δ. Note that sign queries contain implicit hash queries, but we count those separately. So the total number of calls to the random oracle is actually $s + h$. We want to use A to solve LWE or SIS.

Game 0 is running the forger A on the real cryptosystem. Game 1 is the same as Game 0, except that the sign queries are replaced by a simulation in the random oracle model (see Algorithm 4 below) and hash queries are handled by answering with random values (as usual we use a list to ensure that the hash function responses are consistent). Our goal in this section is to show that Game 0 and Game 1 are indistinguishable.

Algorithm 4. Game 1 sign query handler

INPUT: $\mu, \mathbf{A}, \mathbf{T}, D_y, D_z, d, w, \sigma_E, H, F, M$
OUTPUT: $(\mathbf{z}, c)$
1: choose uniformly a κ-bit binary string c
2: $\mathbf{c} = F(c)$
3: $\mathbf{z} \leftarrow D_z^n$
4: $\mathbf{w} \equiv \mathbf{Az} - \mathbf{Tc} \pmod{q}$
5: **if** $|[\mathbf{w}_i]_{2^d}| > 2^{d-1} - 7w\sigma_E$ **then**
6:     Restart
7: **end if**
8: **if** H has already been defined on $(\lfloor \mathbf{w} \rceil_d, \mu)$ **then**
9:     Abort game
10: **else**
11:     Program $H(\lfloor \mathbf{w} \rceil_d, \mu) = c$
12: **end if**
13: **return** $(\mathbf{z}, c)$ with probability $1/M$

Lemma 4. *Let notation be as above and suppose the conditions of Lemma 3 hold. Then Game 0 and Game 1 are indistinguishable.*

Proof. As with Lemma 5.3 of [17] the indistinguishability can be shown in several steps. We sketch the main ideas.

The first step is to show that, in the random oracle model, one can consider $\mathbf{c}$ as being independent of $\mathbf{y}$. We decouple $\mathbf{c}$ from $\mathbf{y}$ and show that the changes (Lines 1-2, 8-9) are statistically negligible. First, by Lemma 3 the distribution of values $\lfloor \mathbf{Ay} \pmod{q} \rceil_d$ has sufficient entropy that c is uniformly distributed on κ-bit strings. Hence the real signing algorithm is consistent with line 1 of the simulation.

Lemma 3 can be used to show that the values $\lfloor \mathbf{w} \rceil_d$ are well-distributed. Hence, the probability that the game aborts in line 9 of Algorithm 4 is negligible (the danger is that two values of $\lfloor \mathbf{w} \rceil_d$ might arise from different choices of c, and this cannot happen in Algorithm 2). This follows by an argument similar to that in [17]. The probability is bounded by $s(s+h) \max \left((2^{d+1}/q)^m, 2^{-\kappa} \right)$ using a hybrid argument (this term contributes to the ε in the statement of Theorem 2).

The next step of the proof is to note that the output distributions have negligible statistical difference, due to the rejection sampling (*cf.* Lemma 2) in two places in the sign algorithm. Hence, the success of any distinguisher between these two games is negligible. □

4.2 Completing the Proof of Theorem 2

We want to show that a forger A can be used to solve SIS. We could apply the forking lemma to Game 1, showing that an adversary who can win Game 1 can be used to solve search-SIS. This approach is analogous to Lemma 5.4 of Lyubashevsky [17]. The argument requires there to be more than one private key for the given public key $(\mathbf{A}, \mathbf{T})$. Precisely, we need there to exist at least two pairs $(\mathbf{S}, \mathbf{E}), (\mathbf{S}', \mathbf{E}')$ such that $\mathbf{T} \equiv \mathbf{AS} + \mathbf{E} \equiv \mathbf{AS}' + \mathbf{E}' \pmod{q}$ and where both pairs are roughly equally likely with respect to the output distribution of the key generation algorithm. This is achieved in Lemma 5.2 of [17] in the case of SIS by taking m to be sufficiently large. This approach would require taking n large and the signature size is increased.

Instead we employ an alternative proof technique given in Section 6 of Lyubashevsky [17]. The idea is to introduce Game 2, which is Game 1 but with the public key replaced by a pair $(\mathbf{A}, \mathbf{T} \equiv \mathbf{AS}' + \mathbf{E}' \pmod{q})$ of matrices over $\mathbb{Z}_q$, where $\mathbf{S}'$ and $\mathbf{E}'$ have larger entries than $\mathbf{S}$ and $\mathbf{E}$ do. The decisional-LWE assumption is that Game 1 and Game 2 are computationally indistinguishable: the only change happens in the public keys which the adversary can not distinguish.

More precisely, the key generation in Game 2 is to choose a random $n \times k$ matrix $\mathbf{S}'$ with entries in $[-E', E']$ and a random $m \times k$ matrix $\mathbf{E}'$ with entries in $[-E', E']$. The inequality in Equation (5) implies that the LWE instance has non-unique solutions with overwhelming probability. We set $\mathbf{T} \equiv \mathbf{AS}' + \mathbf{E}' \pmod{q}$. We do not claim that $(\mathbf{A}, \mathbf{T})$ are uniformly distributed, but an argument analogous to Lemma 3.6 of [17] together with a hybrid argument shows that the decisional LWE assumption implies it is hard to distinguish such a pair $(\mathbf{A}, \mathbf{T})$ from a pair $(\mathbf{A}, \mathbf{T})$ output by Algorithm 1.

We write δ' for the success probability of the forger when running Game 2. If the decisional-LWE assumption holds then $\delta - \delta'$ is negligible. Finally, we apply the forking lemma to Game 2; this is the content of Lemma 5. Theorem 2 follows from Lemma 5.

Lemma 5. *Suppose the forger A plays Game 2, makes h hash function queries and s sign queries, runs in time t, and succeeds with probability δ'. Suppose the parameters satisfy the conditions in Theorem 2. Then there exists an algorithm running in time approx $2t$ and with success probability $\frac{\delta'}{h}\left(\frac{\delta'}{h} - \frac{1}{2^k}\right) + O(\frac{s^2}{2^\kappa} + \frac{n+m}{2^{140}})$ that solves the unbalanced search-SIS problem defined in Theorem 2.*

Proof. Let $\mathbf{A}'$ be the $m \times (n+m)$ matrix giving the input SIS instance. Taking the Hermite normal form we can write $\mathbf{A}' = (\mathbf{A}|\mathbf{I}_m)$, where $\mathbf{A}$ is an $m \times n$ matrix. The goal of the proof is to compute short non-zero vectors $\mathbf{y}_1, \mathbf{y}_2$ such that $\mathbf{A}\mathbf{y}_1 + \mathbf{y}_2 \equiv 0 \pmod{q}$.

As mentioned, we choose a random $n \times k$ matrix $\mathbf{S}'$ with entries in $[-E', E']$ and a random $m \times k$ matrix $\mathbf{E}'$ with entries in $[-E', E']$. Set $\mathbf{T} \equiv \mathbf{AS}' + \mathbf{E}' \pmod{q}$. The inequality in Equation (5) implies that the LWE instance has non-unique solutions with overwhelming probability. Game 2 is to run the forger A on $(\mathbf{A}, \mathbf{T})$.

The forger makes hash and sign queries that are simulated in the random oracle model as usual. Eventually A outputs a valid signature $(\mathbf{z}, c)$ on message μ. We know that the random oracle has been queried in order for the verification equation $c = H(\lfloor \mathbf{w} \rfloor_d, \mu)$ to hold for $\mathbf{w} = \mathbf{Az} - \mathbf{Tc} \pmod{q}$.

We will now reduce to the case where c arises from a hash query, rather than a sign query. Suppose not: then there is a sign query on a message μ' with output equal to $(\mathbf{z}', c)$, and so

$$c = H(\lfloor \mathbf{Az} - \mathbf{Tc} \pmod{q} \rfloor_d, \mu) = H(\lfloor \mathbf{Az}' - \mathbf{Tc} \pmod{q} \rfloor_d, \mu').$$

If $\mu' \neq \mu$ or $\lfloor \mathbf{Az} - \mathbf{Tc} \pmod{q} \rfloor_d \neq \lfloor \mathbf{Az}' - \mathbf{Tc} \pmod{q} \rfloor_d$ then we have a collision in H, so this event occurs with probability $1/2^\kappa$. Therefore we may assume that $\mu' = \mu$ and that $\mathbf{A}(\mathbf{z} - \mathbf{z}') \pmod{q}$ has entries in $[-2^d, 2^d]$. If $\mathbf{z} \neq \mathbf{z}'$ then we have a non-zero solution to $\mathbf{Ay}_1 + \mathbf{y}_2 \equiv 0 \pmod{q}$ with $\|\mathbf{y}_1\|_\infty \leq 2B$ and $\|\mathbf{y}_2\|_\infty \leq 2^d$ and we have solved the SIS instance and we are done. Finally, if $\mathbf{z} = \mathbf{z}'$ then $(\mu', \mathbf{z}', c)$ is equal to $(\mu, \mathbf{z}, c)$ and so it is not a forgery. Hence, for the remainder of the proof we may assume that the forgery $(\mathbf{z}, c)$ has c an output of a random oracle query (on some index I) that was not made as part of a sign query.

Now we apply the Bellare-Neven [3] version of the forking lemma. In other words, we re-wind the attack, so that $\mathbf{v}$ is the same but the I-th random oracle output is taken to be a different binary string c'. One can verify that our signature scheme is a generic signature scheme with security parameter κ. With probability $\delta'(\frac{\delta'}{h} - \frac{1}{2^\kappa})$ we obtain a valid signature $(\mathbf{z}', c')$ on the same message μ. Let $\mathbf{c} = F(c)$ and $\mathbf{c}' = F(c')$. With overwhelming probability we have $\mathbf{c} \neq \mathbf{c}'$.

Now, we have $\lfloor \mathbf{Az} - \mathbf{Tc} \pmod{q} \rfloor_d = \lfloor \mathbf{Az}' - \mathbf{Tc}' \pmod{q} \rfloor_d$ and so $\mathbf{Az} - \mathbf{Tc} + \mathbf{e} \equiv \mathbf{Az}' - \mathbf{Tc}' \pmod{q}$ for some vector $\mathbf{e}$ satisfying $\|\mathbf{e}\|_\infty \leq 2^{d-1}$ coming from the rounding. Hence, putting $\mathbf{T} \equiv \mathbf{AS}' + \mathbf{E}' \pmod{q}$, we see

$$\mathbf{A}(\mathbf{z} - \mathbf{z}' + \mathbf{S}'(\mathbf{c}' - \mathbf{c})) + \mathbf{e} + \mathbf{E}'(\mathbf{c}' - \mathbf{c}) \equiv 0 \pmod{q}. \tag{7}$$

Writing $\mathbf{y}_1 = \mathbf{z} - \mathbf{z}' + \mathbf{S}'(\mathbf{c}' - \mathbf{c})$ and $\mathbf{y}_2 = \mathbf{e} + \mathbf{E}'(\mathbf{c}' - \mathbf{c})$ we have $\|\mathbf{y}_1\|_\infty \leq 2B + 2E'w$ and $\|\mathbf{y}_2\|_\infty \leq 2^{d-1} + 2E'w$. Hence, as long as $(\mathbf{y}_1, \mathbf{y}_2) \neq (0, 0)$, we have a solution to the input SIS instance. Finally, since the matrices $(\mathbf{S}', \mathbf{E}')$ are not uniquely defined with high probability, the adversary does not know which pair $(\mathbf{S}', \mathbf{E}')$ is being used to construct the vectors $\mathbf{y}_1$ and $\mathbf{y}_2$. Hence, with probability at least $\frac{1}{2}$, we deduce that $(\mathbf{y}_1, \mathbf{y}_2) \neq (0, 0)$. $\square$

5   Parameter Selection

In Table 1, we give some concrete parameters for our signature scheme in Figure 1. The parameters are provably secure (*cf.* Theorem 2) and reduce to worst-case computational problems in general lattices. In Appendix B.2, we also give some shorter signatures that are based on non-standard LWE assumptions.

We discuss how the signature parameters in Table 1 are chosen. Given the security parameter n, the weight w is chosen such that $1/(2^w \cdot \binom{n}{w}) < 2^{-\kappa}$. Standard estimates show that $w \approx \kappa / \log(n)$. The standard deviation of Gaussian entries $\mathbf{S}$ and $\mathbf{E}$ are chosen such that the LWE problem for the key is secure. In the signature, one computes $\mathbf{z} = \mathbf{y} + \mathbf{Sc}$. By the central limit theorem the entries of $\mathbf{Sc}$ are Gaussian with mean 0 and standard deviation $\sigma_{\mathbf{Sc}} = \sqrt{w}\sigma_{\mathbf{S}}$. We bound the entries of $\mathbf{Sc}$ by $14\sigma_{\mathbf{Sc}}$, which is true with probability 2^{-140}. Let D_z and D_y be the uniform distribution on $[-B + U, B - U]$ and $[-B, B]$ respectively. The probability of acceptance in line 7 of Algorithm 2 is $(1 - 14\sigma_{\mathbf{E}}w/2^d)^m$; hence we need $q > 2^d \geq 14m\sigma_{\mathbf{E}}w$. We also need the parameters to satisfy the conditions in the statement of Theorem 2. The signature size is given by $n\lceil \log_2(2(B - U)) \rceil + \kappa \approx \lceil \log_2(2B) \rceil + \kappa$. Note that the public key size can be effectively halved by generating $\mathbf{A}$ using a pseudo-random generator and by publishing only the seed for the generator as part of the public key (*cf.* [11]).

Table 1. Parameters for LWE Signatures using Uniform Distributions

		I	II	III	IV	V
n		640	576	512	512	400
m		1137	969	945	1014	790
w	$2^w \cdot \binom{n}{w} \geq 2^{128}$	18	18	19	19	20
Approx. $\log_2(q)$		34.34	33.10	30.84	32.66	28.71
κ		132	132	132	132	132
$\sigma_{\mathbf{E}}$		58	68	66	224	70
$\sigma_{\mathbf{S}}$		58	68	66	224	70
$\sigma_{\mathbf{Sc}}$	$\sqrt{w}\sigma_{\mathbf{S}}$	246.07	288.50	287.69	976.39	313.05
B	$14\sigma_{\mathbf{Sc}}(n-1)$	2201370	2322422	2058115	6985118	1748695
2^d		2^{24}	2^{24}	2^{24}	2^{26}	2^{24}
Prob. acceptance in line 7 of Alg 2.	$\left(1 - 14\sigma_{\mathbf{E}}w/2^d\right)^m$	0.371	0.371	0.372	0.406	0.397
Hermite factor	(for breaking the key)	1.0056	1.0057	1.0057	1.0055	1.0064
Hermite factor	(for forging signature)	1.0038	1.0044	1.0048	1.0047	1.0061
Signature (bits)	$n\lceil \log_2(2B) \rceil + \kappa$	14852	13380	11396	12420	8932
Public key (Mb)	$2mn \log_2(q)$	6.0	4.4	3.6	4.0	2.2
Signing key (Mb)	$2mn \log_2(4\sigma_S)$	1.4	1.0	0.9	1.2	0.6

To evaluate the security of our parameters against practical lattice attacks we consider the LWE problem for the secret key and the SIS problem for the forgery. The security can be estimated by computing the (root) Hermite factor γ of the lattices (based on the BKZ 2.0 estimates of Chen and Nguyen [8]). Tables 2 and 3 of [8] suggest that instances with $\gamma \leq 1.0065$ should require around 2^{128} operations to solve using BKZ lattice reduction. These security estimations are standard in the field so we only sketch the details.

Solving an LWE instance $(\mathbf{A}, \mathbf{b} \equiv \mathbf{As} + \mathbf{e} \pmod{q})$ corresponds to solving the closest vector problem (CVP) with target $\mathbf{b}$ in the image lattice $\{\mathbf{v} \in \mathbb{Z}^m : \mathbf{v} \equiv \mathbf{As} \pmod{q}\} \subseteq \mathbb{Z}^m$. It is known that the optimal dimension m, when using a lattice reduction algorithm with root Hermite factor δ, is around $\sqrt{n \log(q)/\log(\delta)}$. To get closer to the optimal dimension (which is often larger than m) one can consider the inhomogeneous SIS (ISIS) problem $\mathbf{b} = (\mathbf{A}|\mathbf{I}_m)(\mathbf{s}^T, \mathbf{e}^T)^T \pmod{q}$. Let $\mathbf{v}' \in \mathbb{Z}^{n+m}$ be any solution (not necessarily small) to the equation $\mathbf{b} = (\mathbf{A}|\mathbf{I}_m)\mathbf{v}'$ $\pmod{q}$. One can solve the ISIS problem by solving the CVP (with target $\mathbf{v}'$) in the kernel lattice $\{\mathbf{v} \in \mathbb{Z}^{n+m} : \mathbf{b} \equiv (\mathbf{A}|\mathbf{I}_m)\mathbf{v} \pmod{q}\} \subseteq \mathbb{Z}^m$.

The CVP problem can be solved use the embedding technique. It is plausible to turn the CVP problem into an Unique-SVP problem in the embedded lattice. For instance, using the embedding technique, the above ISIS problem gives $(\mathbf{A}|\mathbf{I}_m|\mathbf{b})(\mathbf{s}^T, \mathbf{e}^T, -1)^T \equiv 0 \pmod{q}$ and so one can solve the problem by finding a short vector in this lattice. Since the short vector $(\mathbf{s}^T, \mathbf{e}^T, -1)^T$ is often very small, the standard approach is to estimate the lattice gap $\gamma = \lambda_2(L)/\lambda_1(L)$ (see [16,1]). We let $\lambda_1(L)$ be the length of the target vector and $\lambda_2(L)$ be the Gaussian expected shortest vector of the q-ary lattice. In the ISIS case, the target vector has norm $\sqrt{n+m+1}\,\sigma_E$ in the case $\sigma_S = \sigma_E$. The root Hermite factor δ (needed for the attack) is $\gamma^{1/(n+m+1)} = \left(\dfrac{q^{m/(n+m+1)}}{\sigma_E\sqrt{2\pi e}}\right)^{1/(n+m+1)}$.

We also want the SIS problem in the forgery to be hard. In the proof of Lemma 5, we choose random matrices $\mathbf{S}'$ and $\mathbf{E}'$ with entries in $[-E', E']$ for large enough E' such the there exists alternative keys. The short vectors in the forgery (cf. Equation (7)) have entries bounded by $\max(2B, 2^{d-1}) + 2E'w$. The short vectors $\mathbf{v}$ in the forging problem $\mathbf{Av} \equiv 0 \pmod{q}$ have length $\|\mathbf{v}\|_2 \leq \left(\max(2B, 2^{d-1}) + 2E'w\right)\sqrt{m+n}$. Following Section 3 and equation (1) of [19], an estimate for the length of the shortest vector that we can find is $q^{m/(n+m)}\delta^{m+n}$ (where $\delta \approx 1.0065$), and for the forgery security we need this to be larger than $D = \left(\max(2B, 2^{d-1}) + 2E'w\right)\sqrt{m+n}$. In Table 1 we estimate the Hermite factor required to solve the problem by $\delta = (D/q^{m/(m+n)})^{1/(n+m)}$.

6   Conclusion

We described a new method for compressing lattice-based signatures in Lyubashevsky's framework. The new signature scheme, together with the compression method, is based on the standard worst-case hardness of LWE and SIS in general modular lattices. Our signature size for 128-bit security is about 12000 bits, which is shorter than the previous signatures (≥ 16500 bits) whose security are based on hard problems in general lattices.

Acknowledgements. The authors are grateful to Vadim Lyubashevsky, Chris Peikert and anonymous referees for helpful comments and discussions on drafts of this paper. The authors wish to acknowledge NeSI (New Zealand eScience Infrastructure) and the Centre for eResearch at the University of Auckland for providing CPU hours (for searching the parameters in Table 1) and support.

References

1. Albrecht, M.R., Fitzpatrick, R., Göpfert, F.: On the Efficacy of Solving LWE by Reduction to Unique-SVP. To appear Proceedings of International Conference on Information Security and Cryptology (2013)
2. Applebaum, B., Cash, D., Peikert, C., Sahai, A.: Fast Cryptographic Primitives and Circular-Secure Encryption Based on Hard Learning Problems. In: Halevi, S. (ed.) CRYPTO 2009. LNCS, vol. 5677, pp. 595–618. Springer, Heidelberg (2009)
3. Bellare, M., Neven, G.: Multi-Signatures in the Plain Public-Key Model and a General Forking Lemma. In: Juels, A., Wright, R.N., De Capitani di Vimercati, S. (eds.) ACM CCS 2006, pp. 390–399. ACM (2006)
4. Biswas, B., Sendrier, N.: McEliece Cryptosystem Implementation: Theory and Practice. In: Buchmann, J., Ding, J. (eds.) PQCrypto 2008. LNCS, vol. 5299, pp. 47–62. Springer, Heidelberg (2008)
5. Böhl, F., Hofheinz, D., Jager, T., Koch, J., Seo, J.H., Striecks, C.: Practical Signatures From Standard Assumptions. In: Johansson, T., Nguyen, P.Q. (eds.) EUROCRYPT 2013. LNCS, vol. 7881, pp. 461–485. Springer, Heidelberg (2013)
6. Boyen, X.: Lattice Mixing and Vanishing Trapdoors – A Framework for Fully Secure Short Signatures and More. In: Nguyen, P.Q., Pointcheval, D. (eds.) PKC 2010. LNCS, vol. 6056, pp. 499–517. Springer, Heidelberg (2010)
7. Brakerski, Z., Langlois, A., Peikert, C., Regev, O., Stehlé, D.: Classical Hardness of Learning with Errors. In: Boneh, D., Roughgarden, T., Feigenbaum, J. (eds.) STOC 2013, pp. 575–584. ACM (2013)
8. Chen, Y., Nguyen, P.Q.: BKZ 2.0: Better Lattice Security Estimates. In: Lee, D.H., Wang, X. (eds.) ASIACRYPT 2011. LNCS, vol. 7073, pp. 1–20. Springer, Heidelberg (2011)
9. Ducas, L., Durmus, A., Lepoint, T., Lyubashevsky, V.: Lattice Signatures and Bimodal Gaussians. In: Canetti, R., Garay, J.A. (eds.) CRYPTO 2013, Part I. LNCS, vol. 8042, pp. 40–56. Springer, Heidelberg (2013)
10. Devroye, L.: Non-Uniform Random Variate Generation. Springer, New York (1986)
11. Galbraith, S.D.: Space-efficient variants of cryptosystems based on learning with errors (2013) (preprint)
12. Gentry, C., Peikert, C., Vaikuntanathan, V.: Trapdoors for Hard Lattices and New Cryptographic Constructions. In: Dwork, C. (ed.) STOC 2008, pp. 197–206. ACM (2008)
13. Güneysu, T., Lyubashevsky, V., Pöppelmann, T.: Practical Lattice-Based Cryptography: A Signature Scheme for Embedded Systems. In: Prouff, E., Schaumont, P. (eds.) CHES 2012. LNCS, vol. 7428, pp. 530–547. Springer, Heidelberg (2012)
14. Liu, M., Nguyen, P.Q.: Solving BDD by Enumeration, An Update. In: Dawson, E. (ed.) CT-RSA 2013. LNCS, vol. 7779, pp. 293–309. Springer, Heidelberg (2013)
15. Lyubashevsky, V.: Fiat-Shamir with Aborts: Applications to Lattice and Factoring-Based Signatures. In: Matsui, M. (ed.) ASIACRYPT 2009. LNCS, vol. 5912, pp. 598–616. Springer, Heidelberg (2009)
16. Lyubashevsky, V., Micciancio, D.: On Bounded Distance Decoding, Unique Shortest Vectors, and the Minimum Distance Problem. In: Halevi, S. (ed.) CRYPTO 2009. LNCS, vol. 5677, pp. 577–594. Springer, Heidelberg (2009)
17. Lyubashevsky, V.: Lattice Signatures without Trapdoors. In: Pointcheval, D., Johansson, T. (eds.) EUROCRYPT 2012. LNCS, vol. 7237, pp. 738–755. Springer, Heidelberg (2012)

18. Micciancio, D., Goldwasser, S.: Complexity of Lattice Problems: A cryptographic Perspective. Kluwer (2002)
19. Micciancio, D., Regev, O.: Lattice-Based Cryptography. In: Bernstein, D.J., Buchmann, J., Dahmen, E. (eds.) Post Quantum Cryptography, pp. 147–191. Springer (2009)
20. Micciancio, D., Peikert, C.: Hardness of SIS and LWE with Small Parameters. In: Canetti, R., Garay, J.A. (eds.) CRYPTO 2013, Part I. LNCS, vol. 8042, pp. 21–39. Springer, Heidelberg (2013)
21. Pointcheval, D., Stern, J.: Security Arguments for Digital Signatures and Blind Signatures. J. Cryptology 13, 361–396 (2000)
22. Stehlé, D., Steinfeld, R.: Making NTRUEncrypt and NTRUSign as Secure as Standard Worst-Case Problems over Ideal Lattices, Cryptology ePrint Archive: Report 2013/004 (2013)
23. Regev, O.: On Lattices, Learning with Errors, Random Linear Codes, and Cryptography. In: Gabow, H.N., Fagin, R. (eds.) STOC 2005, pp. 84–93. ACM (2005)
24. Regev, O.: On Lattices, Learning with Errors, Random Linear Codes, and Cryptography. Journal of the ACM 56(6), article 34 (2009)

A   Signatures

A signature scheme comprises three randomized algorithms: KeyGen, Sign, Verify. KeyGen takes as input a security parameter and outputs a public/private key pair (pk, sk). Sign takes as input a message μ and a private key sk, and outputs a signature Σ. Verify takes as input a message μ, signature Σ and public key pk, and outputs "valid" or "invalid". We require that, at least with overwhelming probability, Verify(μ, Sign(μ, sk), pk) = "valid".

Adaptive security for signatures is defined using a game between a forgery algorithm F and a challenger. The challenger generates a public key pk for the signature scheme at a given security level and runs the forger. The forger takes as input the public key for the signature scheme, makes h random oracle queries and s sign queries, runs in time t, and outputs (μ, Σ). The forger wins if Verify(μ, Σ, pk) = "valid". The success probability (taken over all public keys generated by the challenger, all responses to the hash and sign queries, and over the random choices made by F) is denoted ϵ. The signature scheme is *secure* if there is no polynomial-time (in terms of the security parameter) algorithm F whose success probability in the above game is non-negligible.

An important tool for analysing signatures in the random oracle model is the Forking Lemma of Pointcheval and Stern [21]. We need the signature scheme to be a generic signature scheme (the scheme in this paper does satisfy that requirement) with security parameter κ and hash output of size 2^κ. Note that a sign query involves an implicit hash query, but that this is to a random value that is chosen by the challenger. Hence, when we say that F makes h hash queries we are only counting the actual queries to the random oracle, and not the additional s hash queries implicit in the signing algorithm.

The basic principle is to run a forger for the signature scheme, interacting with a specific instance of the random oracle, to get a forgery. The forgery corresponds to specific hash value corresponding to the I-th random oracle query. One then replays or rewinds the forger, with the same random tape, and answering the first $I - 1$ queries to the random oracle with the same values as before, but answering the subsequent queries with freshly chosen random values. With a certain probability, the forger outputs a new forgery that corresponds once again to the I-th hash query.

Theorem 13 of [21] considers a forger F that runs in time t, makes h queries to the random oracle (including those performed by the sign oracle), s sign queries, and outputs a forgery with probability $\epsilon > 10(s + 1)(s + h)/2^\kappa$. Then the re-winding process produces, with probability one, two valid signatures with the same "y-value" but different hash values in time $t' \leq 120686\,th/\epsilon$.

An alternative formulation was given by Bellare and Neven [3]. The two main differences are a cleaner and more general presentation, and an analysis in the case where the forking lemma just runs F twice (rather than $120686\,th/\epsilon$ times). Bellare and Neven consider a forger F that outputs a valid forgery in time t with probability ϵ making h random oracle queries and s sign queries. Then the rewinding algorithm outputs two valid signatures in time approximately $2t$ and with probability at least (Lemma 1 of [3])

$$\epsilon \left(\frac{\epsilon}{h} - \frac{1}{2^\kappa} \right).$$

We use a slight variant of the forking lemma. In our case, we must guess in advance the index I of the hash query that corresponds to a successful forgery (as we need to program this hash value to be a specific element corresponding to the problem instance). Hence, we need to guess the index I from among the h possible values. We then answer the I-th hash query with a specific value c^* and then, in the re-winding, answer the I-th hash query with another specific value $c^\dagger$. Both values c^* and $c^\dagger$ are chosen uniformly at random. Hence, the probability the rewinding algorithm outputs two valid signatures in time approximately $2t$ is

$$\frac{\epsilon}{h} \left(\frac{\epsilon}{h} - \frac{1}{2^\kappa} \right). \tag{8}$$

B   Variants

This section discusses some avenues to obtain even shorter signatures. Some of these ideas have already been used by other authors [17,13,9]. First we discuss obstructions to very short lattice signatures. The main driver of signature size is that n must be sufficiently large to ensure the lattice problems are hard. Some further issues are:

- The **z** vector has to cover all possible values for **Sc**, so if **Sc** can be made smaller then signatures will be smaller. Unfortunately, we cannot just reject those **c** for which **Sc** is large, since we are unable to simulate such behaviour.
- Lemma 4 requires the simulation to be statistically very close to the real game, and this requires high-grade rejection sampling in the sign algorithm.

If we want to have a constant rejection rate then this leads to a linear factor of n in the bound B for the distribution D_z. In principle, using a Gaussian distribution for D_z reduces this to a $\sqrt{n}$ factor, but large constants are introduced that prevent short signatures for concrete small parameters. Overall, the strong requirement of Lemma 4 is a major contributor to the signature size.

B.1   General Tricks

One can take k very large so that w is smaller. However, the public key grows in size and the improvement is minor (for example, taking $k = 3n$ so that public keys are 3 times larger only reduces w from 18 to 14 when $n = 600$).

One can apply a further rejection sampling to ensure that $\mathbf{z}$ is small. For example, one can save n bits in the signature by replacing B by $B/2$ in the distribution D_z. In other words, we require that $\mathbf{z} \in [-B/2, B/2]^n$. Since $\mathbf{z}$ is sampled uniformly it follows that the acceptance probability goes from $1/e$ to $1/e^2$. Similarly, saving $2n$ bits by reducing D_z to $[-B/4, B/4]$ changes the acceptance probability to $1/e^4 \approx 1/55$.

B.2   Signatures Based on Non-standard LWE

We have seen that signature size depends on both n and $\mathbf{Sc}$. Hence, there is a temptation to choose the entries of $\mathbf{S}$ to be as small as possible.

For instance, we could choose $\mathbf{S}$ to be a binary matrix (entries uniformly chosen from $\{0, 1\}$) and $\mathbf{E}$ from a discrete Gaussian distribution with standard deviation $\sigma_\mathbf{E}$. This is the binary secret LWE problem. Micciancio and Peikert [20] and Brakerski, Langlois, Peikert, Regev and Stenlé [7] have studied the case of LWE with binary secrets. They give some results that imply that such variants of LWE can be hard. However, their results are not useful for our application as they require a large increase in the parameter n for the LWE problem. More precisely, Theorem 4.6 of [20] shows that (m, n, q)-binary-LWE can be hard as long as SIVP_γ is hard in $k = n/\log(n)$ dimensional lattices, where $\gamma = \tilde{O}(\sqrt{k}q)$. The value $n = 512$ corresponds to $k = 82$, and so such parameters give a weak security guarantee.

Alternatively, we could choose $\mathbf{S}$ and $\mathbf{E}$ from Gaussian with some deviation $\sigma \leq 2\sqrt{n}$. As a example we choose $(n, m, \sigma_S, \sigma_E, d, w) = (448, 886, 32, 32, 23, 19)$ and take $q \approx 2^{27.84}$. Here B is about $2^{19.74}$ which gives signatures of size $21n + 128 = 9540$ bits. The Hermite constant γ needed is roughly 1.0060. The acceptance probability is roughly 0.407.

The size of σ_S and σ_E also affects relations in Equation (4). This turns out to be a stricter constraint: it is easier to find suitable parameters when σ_S and σ_E are large. In general, such methods may turn out to provide a relatively minor saving in signature size so we do not pursue this further.

B.3   Bi-Modal

We can also consider the bimodal technique of Ducas, Durmus, Lepoint and Lyubashevsky [9] in our setting. The main idea is to work modulo $2q$ and to choose the matrix $\mathbf{T}$ to be such that $-\mathbf{T} \equiv \mathbf{T} \pmod{2q}$. This can be achieved by ensuring that the entries of the matrix $\mathbf{T}$ are all in $\{0, q\}$. The matrix $\mathbf{T}$ can be represented using mn bits rather than $mn \log_2(2q)$ bits.

One particular choice for $\mathbf{T}$ is q times an $n \times n$ identity matrix (note that this requires $m = n$, which may result in a further increase in q. In this case the public key is further compressed, since there is no need to publish $\mathbf{T}$ at all. Let $k = n$ and suppose the $n \times n$ matrix $\mathbf{S}$ with Gaussian entries is invertible. Construct the public key $(\mathbf{A}, \mathbf{T})$ as follows. Choose $(\mathbf{S}, \mathbf{E})$ first and set $\mathbf{A} \equiv (\mathbf{T} - \mathbf{E})\mathbf{S}^{-1} \pmod{2q}$. The computational assumption is now related to the NTRU assumption: Given $\mathbf{A}$ find matrices $(\mathbf{S}, \mathbf{E})$ with small entries such that $\mathbf{A} \equiv -\mathbf{E}\mathbf{S}^{-1} \pmod{q}$. In particular, it is necessary (but not sufficient as far as we know) for this matrix-NTRU problem to be hard for our scheme to be secure. Note that the security of the short signature scheme of [9] also relies on an NTRU assumption (also in a ring) of a similar form.

The goal of using the bimodal distribution is that is makes the rejection sampling work better, and so one can use smaller distributions for D_y and D_z (indeed, Gaussian distributions). Using a Gaussian distribution for D_y with standard deviation σ and the bi-modal trick we should be able to take (as on page 5 of [9])

$$\sigma = 12\sqrt{n}\sigma_S\sqrt{w}/\sqrt{2}.$$

For instance, from parameters $(n, \sigma_S, w) = (448, 32, 19)$ we can obtain $\sigma = 12\sqrt{wn/2}\sigma_S \approx 25051$. Assuming a perfect encoding of Gaussian data that only requires $\log_2(4\sigma)$ bits to represent elements from this distribution we might hope to have signatures of around $448 \cdot \log_2(4\sigma) + 132 \approx 7575$ bits.

The security analysis of this variant requires a different use of the forking lemma, as well as a non-standard assumption. We do not have space to provide the details here.

B.4   Signatures Based on Ring-LWE/NTRU

Our scheme could be implemented with Ring-LWE. The signature is a single ring element and the hash value. The public key is now a sequence $t_i = a_i s + e_i$ $\pmod q$, for $1 \leq i \leq \ell$, with elements in $\mathbb{Z}_q[x]/(x^{2^k} + 1)$.

To sign we compute $c = H(\lfloor a_1 y \rceil_d \dots \lfloor a_\ell y \rceil_d, \mu)$ and then $z = y + sc$. Verification is that z is short and that $H(\lfloor a_1 z - t_1 c \rceil_d, \dots \lfloor a_\ell z - t_\ell c \rceil_d \mu)$ equals c.

The security proof is identical (one can always consider Ring-LWE as a particular case of the matrix problem), but of course the security now depends on the Ring-LWE assumption. Using Ring-LWE will reduce the public key size and improve speed, but it does not seem to lead to any reduction of the signature size, so we do not consider it further in this paper.

A Generic View on Trace-and-Revoke Broadcast Encryption Schemes

Dennis Hofheinz* and Christoph Striecks**

Karlsruhe Institute of Technology, Karlsruhe, Germany

Abstract. At Eurocrypt 2011, Wee presented a generalization of threshold public key encryption, threshold signatures, and revocation schemes arising from threshold extractable hash proof systems. In particular, he gave instances of his generic revocation scheme from the DDH assumption (which led to the Naor-Pinkas revocation scheme), and from the factoring assumption (which led to a new revocation scheme). We expand on Wee's work in two directions:

(a) We propose threshold extractable hash proof instantiations from the "Extended Decisional Diffie-Hellman" (EDDH) assumption due to Hemenway and Ostrovsky (PKC 2012). This in particular yields EDDH-based variants of threshold public key encryption, threshold signatures, and revocation schemes. In detail, this yields a DCR-based revocation scheme.

(b) We show that our EDDH-based revocation scheme allows for a mild form of traitor tracing (and, thus, yields a new trace-and-revoke scheme). In particular, compared to Wee's factoring-based scheme, our DCR-based scheme has the advantage that it allows to trace traitors.

Keywords: broadcast encryption, revocation scheme, traitor tracing, trace-and-revoke scheme, threshold extractable hash proof system, extended decisional Diffie-Hellman.

1 Introduction

Broadcast Encryption, Revocation Schemes, Traitor Tracing, and Trace-and-Revoke Schemes. In a broadcast encryption (BE) scheme [17], a sender is able to generate ciphertexts that only members of a privileged set $S \subseteq \{1, \ldots, N\}$ of users — each given a long-lived user secret key — can decrypt. There exists a large number of BE schemes under various assumptions and with various efficiency characteristics (e.g., [17, 20, 8, 3, 21, 34, 42, 41]). In this work, we focus on revocation schemes, which are a variant of BE schemes, where a set of revoked users (e.g., non-paying subscribers) $\mathcal{R} = \{1, \ldots, N\} \setminus S$ is given as input to the encryption function. Revocation schemes proposed in the literature are, e.g., [38, 50, 36, 23, 13, 14, 54, 22, 12, 33, 53]. A particularly

* Dennis Hofheinz was supported by a DFG grant (GZ HO 4534/2-1).
** Christoph Striecks was supported by a DFG grant (GZ HO 4534/2-1).

J. Benaloh (Ed.): CT-RSA 2014, LNCS 8366, pp. 48–63, 2014.

interesting property a cryptosystem in the broadcast encryption setting can have is traceability [11], i.e., the ability to trace a "pirate" decryption box back to the corrupted user(s), called traitor(s), who constructed it. Thus, traceability allows to identify a traitor (or a coalition of traitors). Such schemes are called traitor tracing schemes and a variety of them was proposed, e.g., [11, 39, 40, 32, 47, 48, 37, 5, 18, 43, 51, 28, 45, 30, 29, 35, 10, 49, 9, 16, 46, 1, 4, 6]. The combination of revocation and traceability is an aspiring goal. We stress that combining these properties is nontrivial (see [7, Section 4.1]). Nevertheless, there are schemes, e.g., [19, 38, 36, 50, 23, 13, 14, 31, 15, 7, 26][1], which provide a solution for this problem. These schemes are called trace-and-revoke schemes.

Threshold Extractable Hash Proof Systems. In [53], Wee established threshold extractable hash proof systems (TEHPS) as a generalization of extractable hash proof systems (EHPS) [52]. Applying the concept of TEHPSs, Wee explains threshold public key encryption, threshold signatures, and revocation schemes from the Decisional Diffie-Hellman (DDH), from the Computational Diffie-Hellman (CDH), and from the factoring assumptions which — at least in the case of factoring — led to new cryptosystems. We expand the generic view of [53] by providing a TEHPS from the "Extended Decisional Diffie-Hellman" (EDDH) assumption due to Hemenway and Ostrovsky [24]. The EDDH assumption generalizes the DDH and Decisional Composite Residuosity (DCR) assumptions. By our first result, we obtain threshold public key encryption, threshold signatures, and revocation schemes from the EDDH assumption. In particular, our generic system extends the generic view of revocation schemes from [53] (recapped below) and, additionally, via our second result, it yields a new trace-and-revoke scheme from the DCR assumption. (This is not known for the factoring-based instance of [53].)

A Generic Revocation Scheme. Recently, Wee [53] gave a very simple and elegant generic view of revocation schemes. He explains and generalizes previous constructions (e.g., [38, 50]). The public key in these constructions contains the coefficients of a secret polynomial $f(x) = a_0 + a_1 x + \cdots + a_t x^t$ "in the exponent" as $g^{a_0}, g^{a_1}, \ldots, g^{a_t}$. Note that this allows to compute values $g^{f(x)}$ for arbitrary x. A ciphertext is of the form $C = (\mathcal{R}, u, (u^{f(id)})_{id \in \mathcal{R}})$, where $\mathcal{R}$ is a set of t revoked identities. (The $u^{f(id)}$ can be computed from pk, and using knowledge of an exponent r with $u = g^r$.) The corresponding encapsulated key[2] is $s = u^{f(0)}$. Any user with identity id in the system possesses a user secret key $usk_{id} = f(id)$. (Of course, 0 is not an allowed identity for a user.) If $id \notin \mathcal{R}$, then a user can derive a $(t+1)$-st share $u^{usk_{id}} = u^{f(id)}$ and compute $u^{f(0)}$ through Lagrange interpolation of the $t+1$ values $u^{f(id)}$ (for $id \in \mathcal{R} \cup \{id\}$). Depending on the domain over which we are working, and on how a "raw key" $s = u^{f(0)}$

---

[1] Note that the schemes from [36, 23, 13] support a different form of traitor tracing. Particularly, their main goal is to find a setting in which the pirate box is not useful anymore rather than identifying the traitor(s).

[2] Wee's scheme actually is a key encapsulation mechanism, not a full encryption scheme. Hence, a ciphertext does not encrypt a message, but only encapsulates a key that can be used to (symmetrically) encrypt a message.

is post-processed, this yields a revocation scheme from the DDH, the CDH, or the factoring assumption. Note that although similar secret sharing techniques are common in broadcast encryption, Wee's scheme is particularly simple and appealing from a conceptual point of view.

Our First Result: An EDDH-Based TEHPS Instance. By giving a slightly different generic view, we extend the work of Wee to obtain threshold extractable hash proof instantiations from the extended decisional Diffie-Hellman assumption. Concretely, the EDDH assumption works in a group $\mathbb{G}$ with subgroups G, H. It states that, given g, g^x, and g^y, elements g^{xy} are computationally indistinguishable from elements $g^{xy} \cdot h$, where $g \in G$ and $h \in H$ are uniformly chosen, and x, y are uniform exponents. For $G = H$, we have the DDH assumption, and if $\mathbb{G} = \mathbb{Z}_N^*$, $G = \{x^N \mid x \in \mathbb{G}\}$, and $H = \langle 1 + N \rangle$, we have the DCR assumption. In particular, our first result yields EDDH-based threshold encryption, signatures, and revocation schemes. We stress that the EDDH-based instances use a potential stronger assumption (i.e., DCR) as opposed to Wee's factoring-based schemes. Nevertheless, to give a foreshadow, this slightly stronger assumption enables us — via our second result — to obtain a new DCR-based trace-and-revoke scheme which, again, is not known to achieve from Wee's factoring-based scheme. Our revocation scheme is similar to the above generic scheme, but has ciphertexts $C = (\mathcal{R}, u_1, (u_1^{f(id)})_{id \in \mathcal{R}}, u_2)$, for $u_1 \in G$ and $u_2 = u_1^{f(0)} \cdot h$ with $h \in H$. The shared key is extracted from h. Hence, instead of directly using $u_1^{f(0)}$ as shared key, we use it to blind the actual key h. This is consistent with the EDDH assumption: EDDH does not state that g^{xy} looks random — it *does* state however that g^{xy} can be used to blind an H-element. The security analysis of this modified scheme is similar to the analysis of previous schemes. The only difficulties arise out of the fact that the group order of G may not be known (e.g., in the case of DCR). Hence, we must avoid inversion operations in the exponent. (Such inversion operations arise during Lagrange interpolation of the polynomial f in the exponent.) More details about the technique we use to avoid inversions in the exponent are given below.

Our Second Result: Traceability of the EDDH-Based Revocation Scheme. We prove that our EDDH-based revocation scheme also supports a mild form of black-box traitor tracing. That is, we prove that any pirate box produced by a coalition of $T \leq (t+1)/2$ corrupted users can be traced back to a user in that coalition. Tracing requires only completely black-box access to the pirate box and works for imperfect decryption boxes (where the box is allowed to decrypt well-formed ciphertexts invalidly down to some threshold). Further, we allow adversarially chosen revoked sets $\mathcal{R}$. Similar black-box tracing strategies in the revocation setting were considered in previous works, e.g., in [50, 15]. But unlike in, e.g., [50], our tracing algorithm works with imperfect pirate boxes that may even only work for an adversarially chosen set $\mathcal{R}$ of revoked users. The tracing model in [15] also considers imperfect decryption boxes and adversarially chosen revoked users, but for a different scheme. (To achieve black-box traceability in the BE setting we note that similar techniques are common, e.g., in [7].) However, we stress that our focus is on the generic view of constructing trace-and-revoke schemes. Nevertheless, our tracing strategy is explained in more detail below.

More on the Used Techniques. To construct revocation schemes from the EDDH assumption — in which the order of the subgroup G might not be known as opposed to Wee's generic construction above — we use a technique called "clearing the denominator" in the exponent. This tool was used before, but in different scenarios to ours, e.g., in [44, 53, 2]. Hence, we can avoid Lagrangian coefficient inversion in the exponent and are able to construct our EDDH-based revocation scheme. For traceability, consider *random* ciphertexts of the form

$$C_{\mathsf{rnd}}^{\mathcal{R}} = (\mathcal{R}, u_1, (u_1^{f(id)} h^{z_{id}})_{id \in \mathcal{R}}, u_1^{f(0)} h^{z_0}) \quad \text{for uniform } h \in H \text{ and } z_{id}, z_0.$$

Under the EDDH assumption, such random ciphertexts are indistinguishable from real ones, *even when knowing a single user key usk_{id}*. In particular, a pirate box $\mathcal{B}$ decrypts random ciphertexts just as well as real ones. However, the decryption of random ciphertexts depends highly on which user key usk_{id} is used to decrypt. Hence, to trace a pirate box $\mathcal{B}$ back to its creator, we can simply feed $\mathcal{B}$ with random ciphertexts and compare $\mathcal{B}$'s output with decryption results for various user keys. This strategy only works if the pirate box $\mathcal{B}$ knows only one user key. If $\mathcal{B}$ knows, say, two different user keys, it can distinguish real from random ciphertexts. (For instance, $\mathcal{B}$ could decrypt a given ciphertext under the two keys. If the decryptions do not match, the ciphertext cannot be real. See [27] by Kiayias and Yung for a more general case and a formal analysis.) Thus, we adapt our strategy by considering "semi-random ciphertexts" of the form

$$C_{\mathsf{rnd}}^{\mathcal{R},I} = (\mathcal{R}, u_1, (u_1^{f(id)} h^{f'(id)})_{id \in \mathcal{R}}, u_1^{f(0)} h^{f'(0)}) \quad \begin{array}{l} \text{for } f'(x) \in \mathbb{Z}_q[x] \text{ uniform} \\ \text{of degree} \le t, \text{ but subject} \\ \text{to } f'(id) = 0 \text{ for } id \in I. \end{array} \quad (1)$$

Such ciphertexts are indistinguishable from real ones, even when knowing the user keys for I. However, when using user keys for identities outside of I, then we will get a different, random result. Our tracing strategy will hence make a guess for the set I of corrupted users, and confirm the guess by checking if $\mathcal{B}$ decrypts ciphertexts $C_{\mathsf{rnd}}^{\mathcal{R},I}$ correctly. (Note that this is very similar to the "black-box confirmation" argument defined by Boneh and Franklin [5].) The main challenge in our proof consists of handling the case when $\mathcal{B}$ knows *some*, but not all user keys for I. In that case, we have to make sure that we output an identity in I that surely corresponds to a traitor. Similar traceability strategies were already considered, e.g., in [5] (but with a restriction on how the pirate box is built), and in [28, 9, 7] (for very different schemes). In the revocation setting the tracing technique of Tzeng and Tzeng [50] also considers semi-random ciphertexts as those from (1). However, the tracing algorithm of [50] assumes a pirate box with perfect decryption, and, more importantly, has to choose the analog of the revoked set $\mathcal{R}$ from (1) by itself. Dodis, Fazio, Kiayias, and Yung [15] consider imperfect pirate boxes and adversarially chosen revoked users in the revocation setting, but for a different scheme. Again, we stress that the novelty of our work lies in the fact that we extend Wee's generic view of revocation schemes by providing an EDDH-based trace-and-revoke variant which, in particular, generalizes (known) DDH-based and (new) DCR-based trace-and-revoke schemes.

2   Preliminaries

Notation. For $n \in \mathbb{N}$, let $[n] := \{1, \dots, n\}$. Throughout the paper, $k \in \mathbb{N}$ denotes the security parameter. For a finite set $\mathcal{S}$, we denote by $s \leftarrow \mathcal{S}$ the process of sampling s uniformly from $\mathcal{S}$. For a probabilistic algorithm A, we write $y \leftarrow A(x)$ for the process of running A on input x with uniformly chosen random coins, and assigning y the result. If A's running time is polynomial in k, then A is called probabilistic polynomial-time (PPT). A function $f : \mathbb{N} \to \mathbb{R}$ is negligible if it vanishes faster than the inverse of any polynomial (i.e., if $\forall c \exists k_0 \forall k \geq k_0 : |f(k)| \leq 1/k^c$). On the other hand, f is significant if it dominates the inverse of some polynomial (i.e., if $\exists c, k_0 \forall k \geq k_0 : f(k) \geq 1/k^c$).

(Binary) Relations for Hard Search Problems [52, 53]. Following the definition of (binary) relations for hard search problems in [53], let R_{pp} be a family of binary relations, where pp is a public parameter. We assume the existence of two PPT algorithms: given the security parameter k in unary, $\mathsf{SampP}(1^k)$ outputs a public parameter pp together with a secret parameter sp, while $\mathsf{SampR}(1^k, pp)$ outputs a binary relation $(u, s) \in R_{pp}$ such that given only u it is hard to find s. (To make random coins r explicit, we may write $\mathsf{SampR}(1^k, pp; r)$.) Concretely, we define the one-way property of binary relations for hard search problems in the sense that with overwhelming probability over pp, for all u, there exists at most one s such that $(u, s) \in R_{pp}$, and, given an adversary A that gets pp and u with $(u, s) \leftarrow \mathsf{SampR}(1^k, pp)$, there exists an efficiently computable generator G_{pp} such that, for all A, $\mathsf{Adv}_A^{\mathsf{prg}}(k) := \Pr\left[A(pp, u, \mathsf{G}_{pp}(s)) = 1\right] - \Pr\left[A(pp, u, R) = 1\right]$, with uniform R, is negligible in k.

Lagrange Interpolation and Vandermonde Matrices. Fix a field $\mathbb{F}$ and $d + 1$ values $x_0, \dots, x_d \in \mathbb{F}$. The Vandermonde matrix $V_{x_0, \dots, x_d} \in \mathbb{F}^{(d+1) \times (d+1)}$ is defined as

$$
V_{x_0, \dots, x_d} := \begin{pmatrix} 1 & x_0 & \dots & x_0^d \\ \vdots & \vdots & \ddots & \vdots \\ 1 & x_d & \dots & x_d^d \end{pmatrix}.
$$

It is easy to see that $\det(V_{x_0, \dots, x_d}) = \prod_{i<j}(x_j - x_i)$; in particular, $V_{x_0, \dots, x_d}$ is invertible iff all x_i are distinct. We can evaluate a polynomial $f(x) = a_0 + a_1 x + \dots + a_d x^d$ at $x_0, \dots, x_d$ via $(f(x_0), f(x_1), \dots, f(x_d))^\top = V_{x_0, \dots, x_d} \cdot (a_0, a_1, \dots, a_d)^\top$. Conversely, given values $y_0, \dots, y_d \in \mathbb{F}$, we can via $(a_0, a_1, \dots, a_d)^\top = V_{x_0, \dots, x_d}^{-1} \cdot (y_0, y_1, \dots, y_d)^\top$ compute coefficients $a_0, \dots, a_n \in \mathbb{F}$ of a polynomial $f(x) = a_0 + a_1 x + \dots + a_d x^d$ such that $f(x_i) = y_i$. It will be useful to perform such matrix-vector multiplications "in the exponent," where generally a matrix $M = (M_{i,j}) \in \mathbb{F}^{n \times n}$ is known, and a vector $x = (x_i) \in \mathbb{F}^n$ is given in the form $X = (X_i) = (g^{x_i})$ for some g. We will write $M \circ X := (Y_1, \dots, Y_n)$ with $Y_i := \prod_{j=1}^n X_j^{M_{i,j}}$. If we write $y = (y_i)$ for the "exponent vector" with $Y_i = g^{y_i}$, this achieves $M \cdot x = y$.

The Extended Decisional Diffie-Hellman Assumption. In [24], Hemenway and Ostrovsky introduced the Extended Decisional Diffie-Hellman (EDDH) assumption. We say that the EDDH assumption holds for group $\mathbb{G}$ and subgroups $G, H \subseteq \mathbb{G}$ iff $\mathsf{Adv}^{\mathsf{eddh}}_{\mathbb{G},H,D}(k) := \Pr\left[D(1^k, \mathsf{ord}(H), g, g^a, g^b, g^{ab}) = 1\right] - \Pr\left[D(1^k, \mathsf{ord}(H), g, g^a, g^b, g^{ab}h) = 1\right]$ is negligible for any PPT distinguisher D, for uniform group elements g and h from G and H, respectively, for uniform exponents a, b, and group order function ord. Additionally, we require that there exists a randomness extractor $\mathsf{G}^{\mathsf{eddh}}_{\mathbb{G},H}$ such that $\mathsf{G}^{\mathsf{eddh}}_{\mathbb{G},H}(h)$ with uniform $h \in H$ is pseudorandom. We note that the EDDH assumption can be instantiated under the DDH and the DCR assumption. (We refer to [24] for further details.)

3 First Result: An EDDH-Based TEHPS Instance

Threshold Extractable Hash Proof Systems. We first restate the definition of threshold extractable hash proof systems (TEHPS) from [53], in which Wee explains several cryptosystems, i.e., threshold encryption, threshold signatures, and revocation schemes as arising from TEHPSs for a hard search problem with instances u and solution s (defined as above). For public key hk, we define a family of hash functions H_{hk}, which take as input a tag tag and an instance u, and output a hash value $\mathsf{H}_{hk}(tag, u)$. A TEHPS TEHPS = (Gen, Share, Pub, Priv, Ext) with tag space $\mathcal{T}$ consists of the following PPT algorithms:

Setup. Given the security parameter $k \in \mathbb{N}$, the threshold parameter $t \in \mathbb{N}$, and system parameters (pp, sp) (defined as above), $\mathsf{Gen}((pp, sp), 1^k, 1^t)$ generates a public key hk and a master secret key msk.

Key generation. $\mathsf{Share}(msk, tag)$, given the master secret key msk and a tag $tag \in \mathcal{T}$, generates a user secret key usk_{tag} for tag tag.

Public evaluation. $\mathsf{Pub}(hk, tag, r)$, given a public key hk, a tag $tag \in \mathcal{T}$, and random r, outputs a hash value $\mathsf{H}_{hk}(tag, u)$, with $(u, s) = \mathsf{SampR}(1^k, pp; r)$.

Private evaluation. $\mathsf{Priv}(usk_{tag}, u)$, given a user secret key usk_{tag} and an instance u, outputs a hash value $\mathsf{H}_{hk}(tag, u)$.

Extraction. $\mathsf{Ext}(u, (tag_i, \tau_i)_{i \in [t+1]})$, given an instance u, tags $(tag_i)_{i \in [t+1]} \in (\mathcal{T})^{t+1}$, and hash values $(\tau_i)_{i \in [t+1]}$, outputs a value s or $\perp$.

For all $k, t \in \mathbb{N}$ and with overwhelming probability over all values $(pp, sp) \leftarrow \mathsf{SampP}(1^k)$, for all $(hk, msk) \leftarrow \mathsf{Gen}((pp, sp), 1^k, 1^t)$, for all r, for all $(u, s) \leftarrow \mathsf{SampR}(1^k, pp; r)$, we require correctness, $(t+1)$-extraction, and t-simulation:

Correctness. For all $tag \in \mathcal{T}$, all $usk_{tag} \leftarrow \mathsf{Share}(msk, tag)$, we require that $\mathsf{Pub}(hk, tag, r) = \mathsf{H}_{hk}(tag, u) = \mathsf{Priv}(usk_{tag}, u)$.

$(t+1)$-**extraction.** For all distinct tags $(tag_i)_{i \in [t+1]} \in (\mathcal{T})^{t+1}$, and all hash values $(\tau_i := \mathsf{H}_{hk}(tag_i, u))_{i \in [t+1]}$, for $s = \mathsf{Ext}(u, (tag_i, \tau_i)_{i \in [t+1]})$, we require $(u, s) \in R_{pp}$.

t-**simulation.** For all distinct $(tag_i)_{i \in [t]} \in (\mathcal{T})^t$, there exists a PPT algorithm SetupSim such that distributions of $\omega = (hk, usk_{tag_1}, \ldots, usk_{tag_t})$ in the following are statistically close: i.e., we require that

$$\{\omega : (hk, msk) \leftarrow \mathsf{Gen}((pp, sp), 1^k, 1^t), (usk_{tag_i} \leftarrow \mathsf{Share}(msk, tag_i))_{i \in [t]}\}$$

$$\overset{s}{\approx} \{\omega : (hk, usk_{tag_1}, \dots, usk_{tag_t}) \leftarrow \mathsf{SetupSim}(pp, tag_1, \dots, tag_t)\},$$

where $\overset{s}{\approx}$ denotes statistically indistinguishable.

A TEHPS for the EDDH Relation. We now construct a new EDDH-based threshold extractable hash proof system. As opposed to the DDH-based construction in [53], here, the group order of a subgroup $G \subseteq \mathbb{G}$ may not be known (i.e., in the case of DCR). Hence, we must avoid inversion operations in the exponent. We use a technique called "clearing the denominator" that, in a similar way, was used before but in different scenarios; e.g., in [44, 53, 2]. Further, fix a commutative group $\mathbb{G}$ and a subgroup $H \subseteq \mathbb{G}$ of (known) order n. We assume that a (proper) lower bound d on the smallest prime divisor of n is known. Let $G \subseteq \mathbb{G}$ be a cyclic subgroup of (potentially unknown) order q and let $\mathcal{K} := [B]$ such that for $x \leftarrow \mathcal{K}$, the value $x \bmod q$ is statistically close to uniform. In that case we will sample an exponent x uniformly from $[B]$, where $B = B' \cdot 2^k$ for an upper bound B' on q. (Such an upper bound B' will always be known.) Further, we need to specify a (binary) relation for the EDDH problem. Therefor, consider

$$R_{pp}^{\mathsf{eddh}} = \{(u, s) \in ((G \times \mathbb{G}) \times H) \mid u_2 = u_1^{sp} s\},$$

with $u = (u_1, u_2) \in (G \times \mathbb{G})$, for uniform $s \in H$, uniform $sp \in \mathcal{K}$. We set the public parameter pp to be (n, g, g^{sp}) and assume that we can sample g from G efficiently. Thus, sp and pp are efficiently samplable. (This completes the description of the SampP algorithm for the EDDH relation.) For the second EDDH-relation algorithm, we set $\mathsf{SampR}(1^k, pp; r)$ to output

$$(u, s) := ((g^r, (g^{sp})^r \cdot s), s),$$

for randomness $r \in \mathcal{K}$ and uniform $s \in H$. (This completes the description of SampR.) Further, we set $\mathsf{G}_{pp}(s) := \mathsf{G}_{\mathbb{G}, H}^{\mathsf{eddh}}(s)$. Now, we are able to construct:

Construction 3.1 (EDDH-based TEHPS). Let a TEHPS $\mathsf{TEHPS}_{\mathsf{EDDH}} = (\mathsf{Gen}, \mathsf{Share}, \mathsf{Pub}, \mathsf{Ext}, \mathsf{Priv})$ with tag space $\mathcal{T} := [\min\{d, B\}] \subset \mathbb{Z}$, with d and B as above, be as follows:

Setup. $\mathsf{Gen}((pp, sp), 1^k, 1^t)$, with $pp =: (n, g, g^{sp})$, chooses a polynomial $f(x) := sp + a_1 x + \cdots + a_t x^t$ over $\mathcal{K}$, with uniform exponents a_i, for $i \in [t]$. The output is the public key $hk := (n, \tilde{g}, \tilde{g}^{sp}, (\tilde{g}^{a_i})_{i=1}^t)$, with $\tilde{g} := g^v$, for uniform $v \leftarrow \mathcal{K}$, and master secret key $msk := (sp, (a_i)_{i=1}^t)$. We fix a hash function $\mathsf{H}_{hk}(tag, u) := u_1^{f(tag)}$, with $u = (u_1, u_2)$ and some tag $tag \in \mathcal{T}$. For randomness $r \in \mathcal{K}$, we have $(u, s) = ((\tilde{g}^r, \tilde{g}^{sp \cdot r} \cdot s), s) = \mathsf{SampR}(1^k, (n, \tilde{g}, \tilde{g}^{sp}); r)$. (Note that we re-randomize the g-elements of pp here.)

Sharing. $\mathsf{Share}(msk, tag)$, for $tag \in \mathcal{T}$, returns $usk_{tag} := f(tag)$.

Public Evaluation. Given a public key hk, a tag $tag \in \mathcal{T}$, randomness $r \in \mathcal{K}$, $\mathsf{Pub}(hk, tag, r)$ computes

$$\left(\tilde{g}^{sp} \cdot \prod_{i=1}^{t} (\tilde{g}^{a_i})^{tag^i}\right)^r \qquad \left(= (\tilde{g}^{f(tag)})^r = u_1^{f(tag)} = \mathsf{H}_{hk}(tag, u)\right),$$

with $(u, s) = \mathsf{SampR}(1^k, (n, \tilde{g}, \tilde{g}^{sp}); r)$ as above.

Private Evaluation. Given usk_{tag} and $u = (u_1, u_2)$, $\mathsf{Priv}(usk_{tag}, u)$ outputs $u_1^{usk_{tag}} \ (= u_1^{f(tag)})$.

Extraction. $\mathsf{Ext}(u, (tag_i, \tau_{tag_i})_{i \in [t+1]})$, given $u = (u_1, u_2)$, tags $(tag_{t+1})_{i \in [t+1]} \in (\mathcal{T})^{t+1}$, and hash values $(\tau_{tag_i})_{i \in [t+1]}$, efficiently computes fractional Lagrangian coefficients $L_i(0) = \prod_{j=1, i \neq j}^{t+1} \frac{-tag_j}{tag_i - tag_j} \in \mathbb{Q}$ such that $f(0) = \sum_{i=1}^{t+1} L_i(0) \cdot f(tag_i) \bmod q$. (Note that the Lagrangian coefficients can be computed iff all tags $(tag_{t+1})_{i \in [t+1]}$ are distinct. If the tags are not distinct we output $\perp$.) Now, for $\Delta := \mathrm{lcm}\{\prod_{i,j \in [t+1], i \neq j}(tag_i - tag_j) \in \mathbb{Z}\}$ the values $\Delta \cdot L_i(0)$, for all $i \in [t+1]$, are integers. Thus, we are able to extract and output the value

$$\left(\left(\prod_{i=1}^{t+1} \tau_{tag_i}^{\Delta L_i(0)}\right)^{-1} \cdot u_2^{\Delta}\right)^{\Delta^{-1}} \bmod n .$$

(Note that n is always known.)

We now show correctness, $(t+1)$-extraction, and t-simulation of Construction 3.1.

Claim 3.2. *For all $t \in \mathbb{N}$, $\mathsf{TEHPS}_{\mathsf{EDDH}}$ from Construction 3.1 is correct, $(t+1)$-extractable, and t-simulatable.*

Proof sketch. For all $k, t \in \mathbb{N}$, with overwhelming probability over $(pp, sp) \leftarrow \mathsf{SampP}(1^k)$, for all r, for all $(u, s) \leftarrow \mathsf{SampR}(1^k, (n, \tilde{g}, \tilde{g}^{sp}); r)$, with $u = (u_1, u_2)$, for all $(hk, msk) \leftarrow \mathsf{Gen}((pp, sp), 1^k, 1^t)$, for all tags $tag \in \mathcal{T}$, all $usk_{tag} \leftarrow \mathsf{Share}(msk, tag)$, we have:

Correctness. Correctness is easy to verify, i.e., $\mathsf{Pub}(hk, tag, r) = \mathsf{H}_{hk}(tag, u) = \mathsf{Priv}(usk_{tag_i}, u)$.

$(t+1)$-**extraction.** For all distinct tags $(tag_i)_{i \in [t+1]} \in (\mathcal{T})^{t+1}$, all hash values $(\tau_i := \mathsf{H}_{hk}(tag_i, u))_{i \in [t+1]}(= (u_1^{f(tag_i)})_{i \in [t+1]})$, for Δ and fractional Lagrangian coefficients $L_i(0)$ as above, $\mathsf{Ext}(u, (tag_i, \tau_{tag_i})_{i \in [t+1]})$ yields

$$\left(\left(\prod_{i=1}^{t+1} \tau_{tag_i}^{\Delta L_i(0)}\right)^{-1} \cdot u_2^{\Delta}\right)^{\Delta^{-1}} \bmod n \overset{(*)}{=} \left((u_1^{\Delta f(0)})^{-1} \cdot (u_1^{sp} \cdot s)^{\Delta}\right)^{\Delta^{-1}} \bmod n$$

$$= \left(u_1^{-\Delta sp} \cdot u_1^{\Delta sp} \cdot s^{\Delta}\right)^{\Delta^{-1}} \bmod n = s .$$

Recall that all $\Delta \cdot L_i(0)$, for $i \in [t+1]$, are integers and that we used Lagrangian interpolation in the exponent in $(*)$. Thus, we obtain s such that $(u, s) \in R_{pp}^{\mathsf{eddh}}$.

t-**simulation.** For all distinct tags $(tag_i)_{i \in [t+1]} \in (\mathcal{T})^{t+1}$, there exists a PPT algorithm $\mathsf{SetupSim}$ as follows: Choose uniformly $y_1, \ldots, y_t \leftarrow \mathcal{K}$ and set $f(tag_i) := y_i$, for $i \in [t]$. Further, set $\hat{g} := g^v$, for uniform $v \leftarrow \mathcal{K}$, and set $\hat{g}^{f(0)} := (g^{sp})^v = \hat{g}^{sp}$. Note, that this will uniquely define a polynomial f of degree $\leq t$. Let Δ be as above but with $tag_{t+1} = 0$. That (implicitly) determines a vector

$$(\Delta a_0, \Delta a_1, \ldots, \Delta a_t)^{\top} := (\Delta \cdot V_{tag_{t+1}, tag_1, \ldots, tag_t}^{-1}) \cdot (sp, y_1, \ldots, y_t)^{\top} .$$

(That is every Δa_i can be written as linear combination of the y_i, with appropriate integer coefficients. Here, again, we use Δ to "clear the denominator" of V^{-1}'s entries.) Subsequently, output $(n, \tilde{g}, \tilde{g}^{a_0}, \tilde{g}^{a_1}, \ldots, \tilde{g}^{a_t})$, for $\tilde{g} := \hat{g}^{\Delta}$, and $(usk_{tag_1}, \ldots, usk_{tag_t}) := (y_1, \ldots, y_t)$. Thus, the distribution of the output of SetupSim and and the distribution of $(hk, (\mathsf{Share}(msk, tag_i))_{i \in [t]})$ are statistically indistinguishable.   □

Now, by [53, Theorems 1, 2, 3], we derive semantically secure threshold public key encryption, existentially unforgeable threshold signatures in the random oracle model, and semantically secure revocation schemes from the hardness of the EDDH assumption which — at least in the revocation case — yields a new DCR-based revocation scheme. We will now provide details about revocation schemes and recap from [53] how to build them from TEHPSs.

Revocation Schemes. Opposed to a broadcast encryption scheme, where a set of privileged users $\mathcal{S} \subseteq \{1, \ldots, N\}$ (for number of users $N \in \mathbb{N}$) is given as input to the encryption function, a revocation scheme receives a set of revoked users $\mathcal{R} := \{1, \ldots, N\} \setminus \mathcal{S}$ as input instead. The system then guarantees that users in $\{1, \ldots, N\} \setminus \mathcal{R}$ are able to decrypt correctly while users in $\mathcal{R}$ cannot decrypt. We will not directly give a construction of a revocation scheme; rather we will define a revocable key encapsulation mechanism which canonically implies an revocation scheme, but allows for a simpler exposition.

Revocable Key Encapsulation Mechanism. For simplicity, and following [53], we define the notion of a revocable key encapsulation mechanism (RKEM). An RKEM with identity space $\mathcal{ID}$ consists of the following PPT algorithms:

Setup. $\mathsf{Gen}(1^k, 1^t)$, given the security parameter $k \in \mathbb{N}$ and a revocation threshold $t \in \mathbb{N}$, generates a public key pk and a master secret key msk.

Key generation. $\mathsf{Share}(msk, id)$, given the master secret key msk and an identity $id \in \mathcal{ID}$, generates a user secret key usk_{id} for identity id.

Encapsulation. $\mathsf{Enc}(pk, \mathcal{R})$, given the public key pk and a subset $\mathcal{R} \subseteq \mathcal{ID}$ that contains the identities of up to t revoked users, outputs a ciphertext C and a corresponding key K.

Decapsulation. $\mathsf{Dec}(id, usk_{id}, C)$, given an identity id, a corresponding user secret key usk_{id}, and a ciphertext C, outputs a key K.

For correctness, we require that for all $k, t \in \mathbb{N}$, all $(pk, msk) \leftarrow \mathsf{Gen}(1^k, 1^t)$, all set $\mathcal{R} \subseteq \mathcal{ID}$ of up to t identities, all $(C, K) \leftarrow \mathsf{Enc}(pk, \mathcal{R})$, all identities $id \in \mathcal{ID} \setminus \mathcal{R}$, and all $usk_{id} \leftarrow \mathsf{Share}(msk, id)$, we have $\mathsf{Dec}(id, usk_{id}, C) = K$. We will not define security for RKEMs. We note that these notions can be defined in a straightforward way, and the RKEMs based on TEHPSs from [53] can be proven secure in this sense. (In fact, [53] only shows selective-identity security; we expect, however, that adaptive-identity security can be achieved along the lines of Dodis and Fazio [14].) As mentioned before, an RKEM implies a revocation scheme. That is, to build a revocation scheme from an RKEM, use the encapsulated key to symmetrically encrypt the message to be broadcasted; analogously, use the decapsulated key for symmetrically decryption.

RKEMs from TEHPSs. Following [53], we recap the construction of an revocable key encapsulation mechanism $\mathsf{RKEM} = (\mathsf{Gen}, \mathsf{Share}, \mathsf{Enc}, \mathsf{Dec})$ with identity space $\mathcal{ID} := \mathcal{T}$ from a threshold extractable hash proof system $\mathsf{TEHPS} = (\mathsf{Gen'}, \mathsf{Share'}, \mathsf{Pub}, \mathsf{Ext}, \mathsf{Priv})$ with tag space $\mathcal{T}$ as follows:

Setup. $\mathsf{Gen}(1^k, 1^t)$, given security parameter $k \in \mathbb{N}$ and revocation threshold $t \in \mathbb{N}$, samples $(pp, sp) \leftarrow \mathsf{SampP}(1^k)$ and outputs public-key-master-secret-key pair $(pk, msk) := \mathsf{Gen'}((pp, sp), 1^k, 1^t)$.

Key extraction. $\mathsf{Share}(msk, id)$, for $id \in \mathcal{ID}$, returns $usk_{id} \leftarrow \mathsf{Share'}(msk, id)$.

Encapsulation. $\mathsf{Enc}(pk, \mathcal{R})$, for public key pk and $\mathcal{R} \subseteq \mathcal{ID}$ of size exactly t, chooses a random value r, samples $(u, s) \leftarrow \mathsf{SampR}(1^k, pk; r)$, and computes $\tau_{id} := \mathsf{Pub}(hk, id, r)$, for $id \in \mathcal{R}$. The ciphertext is given by $C := (\mathcal{R}, u, (\tau_{id})_{id \in \mathcal{R}})$, the key is $K := \mathsf{G}_{pk}(s)$.

Decapsulation. $\mathsf{Dec}(id, usk_{id}, C)$, with usk_{id} and C as above, retrieves $s := \mathsf{Ext}(u, \mathcal{R} \cup \{id\}, (\tau_{id})_{id \in \mathcal{R}}, \mathsf{Priv}(usk_{id}, u))$ and outputs $K := \mathsf{G}_{pk}(s)$.

Correctness is easy to verify. For semantic security, we point to [53, Theorem 3]. Hence, as a result, we derive an EDDH-based revocation scheme.

4 Second Result: $((t + 1)/2, \varepsilon)$-Traceability of the EDDH-Based RKEM Instance

Trace-and-Revoke Schemes. A trace-and-revoke scheme connects the properties of a revocation scheme and the benefits of a traitor tracing scheme. As mentioned before, combining these is nontrivial (see [7, Section 4.1]). Following [5, 15, 9, 7], we define traceability of an RKEM. (Note, this implicitly defines traceability of a revocation scheme due to the results of Section 3 and, thus, we derive a trace-and-revoke scheme.) Intuitively, we require an efficient algorithm Trace that can, from oracle access to a stateless pirated box $\mathcal{B}$, deduce the identity of at least one party that has been involved in the construction of $\mathcal{B}$. More concretely, suppose an adversary A corrupts a number of devices (i.e., obtains a number of user keys usk_{id}), and constructs a pirate box $\mathcal{B}$. Suppose that $\mathcal{B}$ successfully decrypts ciphertexts for an adversarially specified set $\mathcal{R}$ of revoked users. Then we want that Trace, given oracle access to $\mathcal{B}$, can deduce at least one of the identities id whose device A has corrupted. We will also define a relaxation of traceability, dubbed sid-traceability, in which the adversary has to commit to corrupted identities in advance, before even seeing the public key.

Definition 1 (Traceable/sid-traceable RKEM). *We say that that an adversary A is T-valid if, in experiment $\mathsf{Exp}^{\mathsf{trace}}_{\mathsf{RKEM}, \mathsf{Trace}, A}$ (defined in Figure 1), it always chooses $t \geq T$, it always outputs a set $\mathcal{R}$ of size at most t, and it always makes at most T Share queries. (Note that this definition does not actually depend on Trace, and that t is specified by A itself.) Furthermore, for given $pk, \mathcal{R}$, we define the quality of a pirate box $\mathcal{B}$ output by A as $\mathsf{Q}_{\mathcal{B}, \mathcal{R}} := \Pr[\mathcal{B}(C) = K \mid (C, K) \leftarrow \mathsf{Enc}(pk, \mathcal{R})]$. An RKEM RKEM is (T, ε)-traceable if there exists a PPT algorithm Trace (that may depend on T and ε), so that for every PPT T-valid A, $\mathsf{Adv}^{\mathsf{trace}}_{\mathsf{RKEM}, A}(k) := \Pr[\mathsf{Exp}^{\mathsf{trace}}_{\mathsf{RKEM}, \mathsf{Trace}, A, \varepsilon}(k) = 1]$ is negligible. RKEM is (T, ε)-traceable under selective-identity attacks (short: (T, ε)-sid-traceable) if the analogous statement holds with respect to $\mathsf{Adv}^{\mathsf{sid\text{-}trace}}_{\mathsf{RKEM}, A}(k) :=$*

Experiment $\mathsf{Exp}^{\text{trace}}_{\text{RKEM,Trace},A,\varepsilon}(1^k)$	Experiment $\mathsf{Exp}^{\text{sid-trace}}_{\text{RKEM,Trace},A,\varepsilon}(1^k)$
$1^t \leftarrow A(1^k)$	$(1^t, \mathcal{C}) \leftarrow A(1^k)$
$(pk, msk) \leftarrow \mathsf{Gen}(1^k, 1^t)$	$(pk, msk) \leftarrow \mathsf{Gen}(1^k, 1^t)$
$(\mathcal{B}, \mathcal{R}) \leftarrow A^{\mathsf{Share}(msk,\cdot)}(pk)$	$\forall id \in \mathcal{C}: usk_{id} \leftarrow \mathsf{Share}(msk, id)$
$id \leftarrow \mathsf{Trace}^{\mathcal{B}(\cdot)}(msk, \mathcal{R})$	$(\mathcal{B}, \mathcal{R}) \leftarrow A(pk, (usk_{id})_{id \in \mathcal{C}})$
if A has queried $\mathsf{Share}(msk, id)$	$id \leftarrow \mathsf{Trace}^{\mathcal{B}(\cdot)}(msk, \mathcal{R})$
or $Q_{\mathcal{B},\mathcal{R}} < \varepsilon$ return 0	if $id \in \mathcal{C}$ or $Q_{\mathcal{B},\mathcal{R}} < \varepsilon$ return 0
return 1	return 1

Fig. 1. Security experiments for traceability and sid-traceability of an RKEM

$\Pr\left[\mathsf{Exp}^{\text{sid-trace}}_{\text{RKEM,Trace},A,\varepsilon}(k) = 1\right]$ and $\mathsf{Exp}^{\text{sid-trace}}_{\text{RKEM,Trace},A,\varepsilon}$, defined in Figure 1, in which A has to output an identity set $\mathcal{C}$ of corrupted users of size at most t in advance.

From sid-Traceability to Traceability. There is a trivial (yet expensive) way to convert sid-traceable RKEMs into traceable ones. Namely, we can simply guess the identities for which an adversary (adaptively) requests user keys. Concretely:

Lemma 1 (sid-traceable ⇒ traceable). *Let* RKEM *by a* (T, ε)-*sid-traceable* RKEM *with* N *identities. If* $\binom{N}{T}$ *is polynomial in* k, *then* RKEM *is also* (T, ε)-*traceable (with the same* Trace *algorithm). Concretely, for every adversary* A *on* RKEM*'s traceability, there is an adversary* A' *of roughly the same complexity on* RKEM*'s sid-traceability, such that* $\mathsf{Adv}^{\text{sid-trace}}_{\text{RKEM},A'}(k) \geq \mathsf{Adv}^{\text{trace}}_{\text{RKEM},A}(k)/\binom{N}{T}$.

Proof sketch. See full version [25] for a proof sketch.

Relation to Our Second Result. Our second result (below) shows the $((t + 1)/2, \varepsilon)$-sid-traceability of an EDDH-based RKEM based on threshold extractable hash proofs. Our corresponding tracing algorithm will have a runtime that is linear in $\binom{N}{T}$. Thus, in that case, $\binom{N}{T}$ must be polynomial anyway, and the loss in Lemma 1 seems acceptable.

More about Our Tracing Strategy. We propose a tracing strategy that is similar to the tracing techniques in the revocation setting given by [50, 15]. However, we stress that the tracing algorithm of [50] assumes a pirate box with perfect decryption, i.e., $\varepsilon = 1$, and chooses the revoked set $\mathcal{R}$ by itself. The tracing mode in [15] also considers imperfect decryption boxes, adversarially chosen revoked user sets, and, additionally, allows of querying user secret keys adaptively. (This is possible since their scheme allows to change the public key continuously even after the system setup.) Additionally, both, i.e., [50, 15], only address the DDH setting. Nevertheless, we stress that the novelty of our work lies in the fact that we propose a new generic view of trace-and-revoke schemes.

4.1 Warmup: $(1, 2/3)$-sid-Traceability of the EDDH-Based RKEM

We can now state our second result; i.e., we show the traceability of RKEM$_{\text{EDDH}}$ which is an EDDH-based RKEM as defined and constructed in Section 3. (This immediately translates to an EDDH-based trace-and-revoke scheme.) As a warm-up, we first showcase the $(1, 2/3)$-sid-traceability of $\mathsf{RKEM_{EDDH}}$.

Informal Proof Strategy. To explain the overall idea of our tracing algorithm, observe that the decryption of a ciphertext generated by Enc does not depend on which user key was used to decrypt. (This is necessary for correctness.) Hence, we cannot expect that a pirate box $\mathcal{B}$ can be traced by feeding it valid ciphertexts generated by Enc. Instead, we will feed $\mathcal{B}$ random ciphertexts of the form

$$C_{\mathsf{rnd}}^{\mathcal{R}} = (\mathcal{R}, u_1, (u_1^{f(id)} h^{z_{id}})_{id \in \mathcal{R}}, u_1^{f(0)} h^{z_0}) \quad \text{for uniform } h \in H \text{ and } z_{id}, z_0. \quad (2)$$

We will show that for such random ciphertexts, the result of the (honest) decryption depends on the identity of the used user key usk_{id}. Furthermore, a suitable reduction to the EDDH assumption will show that honestly generated ciphertexts are indistinguishable from random ones. Hence, Trace can go through the set of all possible identities id, and check how often $\mathcal{B}(C_{\mathsf{rnd}}^{\mathcal{R}})$ coincides with $\mathsf{Dec}(id, usk_{id}, C_{\mathsf{rnd}}^{\mathcal{R}})$. In case $\mathcal{B}$ outputs the same as Dec with probability close to $2/3$, chances are that we have found the pirate identity.

Theorem 1 ($(1, 2/3)$-sid-traceability of $\mathsf{RKEM_{EDDH}}$). *Assuming the EDDH assumption, we have that the RKEM $\mathsf{RKEM_{EDDH}} = (\mathsf{Gen}, \mathsf{Share}, \mathsf{Enc}, \mathsf{Dec})$, with identity space $\mathcal{ID}$, polynomial number N of identities, and key derivation function $\mathsf{G}(s) = s$, is $(1, 2/3)$-sid-traceable. The corresponding tracing algorithm Trace runs for $\mathbf{O}(kN \log N)$ steps, and makes $\mathbf{O}(k \log N)$ oracle queries. Concretely, for every T-valid adversary A, there is an EDDH adversary D, such that $\left| \mathsf{Adv}_{\mathsf{RKEM}, A}^{\mathsf{trace}}(k) \right| \leq \mathbf{O}(2^{-k})$, for all k that satisfy $\left| \mathsf{Adv}_{\mathsf{G}, H, D}^{\mathsf{eddh}}(k) \right| \leq 1/9 - \varepsilon_\mathsf{G}$, for negligible ε_G.*

Proof. See the full version [25] for a proof.

4.2 General Case: $((t+1)/2, \varepsilon)$-sid-Traceability of $\mathsf{RKEM_{EDDH}}$

Why Our Tracing Strategy for $T = 1$ Does Not Work. First, observe that our concrete tracing strategy from the proof of Theorem 1 fails if A requests multiple user keys. For instance, A could use multiple user keys to distinguish valid from random ciphertexts. Concretely, A could request two keys usk_{id_1} and usk_{id_2} and let $\mathcal{B}$ first check if a given ciphertext decrypts to the same value under both usk_{id_1} and usk_{id_2}. If the decryptions do not match, then $\mathcal{B}$ immediately fails. (Recall that our proof uses the fact that random ciphertexts decrypt differently under different keys.) Such a box $\mathcal{B}$ would be useless to our tracing algorithm Trace, since Trace feeds $\mathcal{B}$ only random ciphertexts. (See [27] for more details.)

How to Adapt Our Strategy. A natural way to adapt our strategy — this essentially follows the "black-box confirmation" argument from [5] — would seem as follows. Given a set $I \subseteq \mathcal{ID}$ of identities, we can construct "semi-random ciphertexts" of the form $C_{\mathsf{rnd}}^{\mathcal{R}, I} = (\mathcal{R}, u_1, (u_1^{f(id)} h^{f'(id)})_{id \in \mathcal{R}}, u_1^{f(0)} h^{f'(0)})$ for $f'(x) \in \mathbb{Z}_q[x]$ uniform of degree $\leq t$, but subject to $f'(id) = 0$ for $id \in I$. We will also define the *random quality* $\mathrm{RQ}^I_{\mathcal{B},\mathcal{R}}$ of a box $\mathcal{B}$ relative to a given revoked set $\mathcal{R}$, and an identity set $I \subseteq \mathcal{ID}$: $\mathrm{RQ}^I_{\mathcal{B},\mathcal{R}} := \Pr\left[\mathcal{B}(C^{\mathcal{R},I}_{\mathsf{rnd}}) = \mathsf{Dec}(id, usk_{id}, C^{\mathcal{R}}_{\mathsf{rnd}})\right]$, for some $id \in I$. Intuitively, ciphertexts $C^{\mathcal{R},I}_{\mathsf{rnd}}$ look consistent from the point of a pirate box that only knows user keys for identities in I. Hence, our tracing strategy for a larger number T of traitors will be as follows. We iterate over all $\binom{N}{T}$ identity subsets $I \subseteq \mathcal{ID}$ of size T, and approximate $\mathrm{RQ}^I_{\mathcal{B},\mathcal{R}}$. If the approximation indicates that $\mathrm{RQ}^I_{\mathcal{B},\mathcal{R}} \geq \varepsilon$, then we have a candidate for the set $\mathcal{C}$ of traitors. Unfortunately, there may be many candidates, and not all of them contain only traitors. To filter out one identity that surely is a traitor, we remove identities from I, one at a time. If the quality $\mathrm{RQ}^I_{\mathcal{B},\mathcal{R}}$ drops, we must have removed a traitor. (If the removed identity was no traitor, then $\mathcal{B}$ would not have noticed.) Again, this tracing strategy is similar to that of [5, 28, 50, 15, 9, 7]. More formally:

Theorem 2 $(((t+1)/2, \varepsilon)$**-sid-traceability of** $\mathsf{RKEM}_{\mathsf{EDDH}})$. *Assuming EDDH,* $\mathsf{RKEM}_{\mathsf{EDDH}}$ *is* (T, ε)*-sid-traceable for every* $T \leq (t+1)/2$ *for which* $\binom{N}{T}$ *is polynomial, and every significant* ε. *The corresponding tracing algorithm* Trace *runs for* $\mathbf{O}(k\binom{N}{T}/\varepsilon^2)$ *steps, where* N *denotes the number of identities in the system. Concretely, for every* T*-valid adversary* A, *there are adversaries* D, E, F, *such that* $\left|\mathsf{Adv}^{\mathsf{trace}}_{\mathsf{RKEM},A}(k)\right| \leq \mathbf{O}(2^{-k})$, *for all* k *that satisfy* $\left|\mathsf{Adv}^{\mathsf{eddh}}_{\mathsf{G},H,D}(k)\right| + \left(\sum^T_{i=2}\binom{N}{i}\right) \cdot$ $\left|\mathsf{Adv}^{\mathsf{eddh}}_{\mathsf{G},H,E}(k)\right| + (N - T) \cdot \left|\mathsf{Adv}^{\mathsf{eddh}}_{\mathsf{G},F}(k)\right| \leq \frac{\varepsilon}{3T}$.

Proof. See full version [25] for a proof.

Potential Generalizations of Our Tracing Result. There are several dimensions in which one might want to improve our tracing result. We will comment on how our result can be generalized (and when a generalization seems problematic) in the full version [25].

References

[1] Abdalla, M., Dent, A.W., Malone-Lee, J., Neven, G., Phan, D.H., Smart, N.P.: Identity-based traitor tracing. In: Okamoto, T., Wang, X. (eds.) PKC 2007. LNCS, vol. 4450, pp. 361–376. Springer, Heidelberg (2007)

[2] Agrawal, S., Boyen, X., Vaikuntanathan, V., Voulgaris, P., Wee, H.: Functional encryption for threshold functions (or fuzzy ibe) from lattices. In: Fischlin, M., Buchmann, J., Manulis, M. (eds.) PKC 2012. LNCS, vol. 7293, pp. 280–297. Springer, Heidelberg (2012)

[3] Barth, A., Boneh, D., Waters, B.: Privacy in encrypted content distribution using private broadcast encryption. In: Di Crescenzo, G., Rubin, A. (eds.) FC 2006. LNCS, vol. 4107, pp. 52–64. Springer, Heidelberg (2006)

[4] Billet, O., Phan, D.H.: Efficient traitor tracing from collusion secure codes. In: Safavi-Naini, R. (ed.) ICITS 2008. LNCS, vol. 5155, pp. 171–182. Springer, Heidelberg (2008)

[5] Boneh, D., Franklin, M.: An efficient public key traitor tracing scheme. In: Wiener, M. (ed.) CRYPTO 1999. LNCS, vol. 1666, pp. 338–353. Springer, Heidelberg (1999)

[6] Boneh, D., Naor, M.: Traitor tracing with constant size ciphertext. In: Ning, P., Syverson, P.F., Jha, S. (eds.) ACM CCS 2008, pp. 501–510. ACM Press (October 2008)

[7] Boneh, D., Waters, B.: A fully collusion resistant broadcast, trace, and revoke system. In: Juels, A., Wright, R.N., De Capitani di Vimercati, S. (eds.) ACM CCS 2006, pp. 211–220. ACM Press (October/November 2006)

[8] Boneh, D., Gentry, C., Waters, B.: Collusion resistant broadcast encryption with short ciphertexts and private keys. In: Shoup, V. (ed.) CRYPTO 2005. LNCS, vol. 3621, pp. 258–275. Springer, Heidelberg (2005)

[9] Boneh, D., Sahai, A., Waters, B.: Fully collusion resistant traitor tracing with short ciphertexts and private keys. In: Vaudenay, S. (ed.) EUROCRYPT 2006. LNCS, vol. 4004, pp. 573–592. Springer, Heidelberg (2006)

[10] Chabanne, H., Phan, D.H., Pointcheval, D.: Public traceability in traitor tracing schemes. In: Cramer, R. (ed.) EUROCRYPT 2005. LNCS, vol. 3494, pp. 542–558. Springer, Heidelberg (2005)

[11] Chor, B., Fiat, A., Naor, M.: Tracing traitors. In: Desmedt, Y.G. (ed.) CRYPTO 1994. LNCS, vol. 839, pp. 257–270. Springer, Heidelberg (1994)

[12] Delerablée, C., Paillier, P., Pointcheval, D.: Fully collusion secure dynamic broadcast encryption with constant-size ciphertexts or decryption keys. In: Takagi, T., Okamoto, T., Okamoto, E., Okamoto, T. (eds.) Pairing 2007. LNCS, vol. 4575, pp. 39–59. Springer, Heidelberg (2007)

[13] Dodis, Y., Fazio, N.: Public key broadcast encryption for stateless receivers. In: Feigenbaum, J. (ed.) DRM 2002. LNCS, vol. 2696, pp. 61–80. Springer, Heidelberg (2003)

[14] Dodis, Y., Fazio, N.: Public key trace and revoke scheme secure against adaptive chosen ciphertext attack. In: Desmedt, Y.G. (ed.) PKC 2003. LNCS, vol. 2567, pp. 100–115. Springer, Heidelberg (2002)

[15] Dodis, Y., Fazio, N., Kiayias, A., Yung, M.: Scalable public-key tracing and revoking. Distributed Computing 17(4), 323–347 (2005)

[16] Fazio, N., Nicolosi, A., Phan, D.H.: Traitor tracing with optimal transmission rate. In: Garay, J.A., Lenstra, A.K., Mambo, M., Peralta, R. (eds.) ISC 2007. LNCS, vol. 4779, pp. 71–88. Springer, Heidelberg (2007)

[17] Fiat, A., Naor, M.: Broadcast encryption. In: Stinson, D.R. (ed.) CRYPTO 1993. LNCS, vol. 773, pp. 480–491. Springer, Heidelberg (1994)

[18] Fiat, A., Tassa, T.: Dynamic traitor training. In: Wiener, M. (ed.) CRYPTO 1999. LNCS, vol. 1666, pp. 354–371. Springer, Heidelberg (1999)

[19] Gafni, E., Staddon, J., Yin, Y.L.: Efficient methods for integrating traceability and broadcast encryption. In: Wiener, M. (ed.) CRYPTO 1999. LNCS, vol. 1666, pp. 372–387. Springer, Heidelberg (1999)

[20] Garay, J.A., Staddon, J., Wool, A.: Long-lived broadcast encryption. In: Bellare, M. (ed.) CRYPTO 2000. LNCS, vol. 1880, pp. 333–352. Springer, Heidelberg (2000)

[21] Gentry, C., Waters, B.: Adaptive security in broadcast encryption systems (with short ciphertexts). In: Joux, A. (ed.) EUROCRYPT 2009. LNCS, vol. 5479, pp. 171–188. Springer, Heidelberg (2009)

[22] Goodrich, M.T., Sun, J.Z., Tamassia, R.: Efficient tree-based revocation in groups of low-state devices. In: Franklin, M. (ed.) CRYPTO 2004. LNCS, vol. 3152, pp. 511–527. Springer, Heidelberg (2004)

[23] Halevy, D., Shamir, A.: The LSD broadcast encryption scheme. In: Yung, M. (ed.) CRYPTO 2002. LNCS, vol. 2442, pp. 47–60. Springer, Heidelberg (2002)

[24] Hemenway, B., Ostrovsky, R.: Extended-ddh and lossy trapdoor functions. In: Fischlin, M., Buchmann, J., Manulis, M. (eds.) PKC 2012. LNCS, vol. 7293, pp. 627–643. Springer, Heidelberg (2012)

[25] Hofheinz, D., Striecks, C.: A generic view on trace-and-revoke broadcast encryption schemes. Cryptology ePrint Archive (2013)

[26] Jin, H., Lotspiech, J.: Renewable traitor tracing: A trace-revoke-trace system for anonymous attack. In: Biskup, J., López, J. (eds.) ESORICS 2007. LNCS, vol. 4734, pp. 563–577. Springer, Heidelberg (2007)

[27] Kiayias, A., Yung, M.: Self protecting pirates and black-box traitor tracing. In: Kilian, J. (ed.) CRYPTO 2001. LNCS, vol. 2139, pp. 63–79. Springer, Heidelberg (2001)

[28] Kiayias, A., Yung, M.: On crafty pirates and foxy tracers. In: Sander, T. (ed.) DRM 2001. LNCS, vol. 2320, pp. 22–39. Springer, Heidelberg (2002)

[29] Kiayias, A., Yung, M.: Breaking and repairing asymmetric public-key traitor tracing. In: Feigenbaum, J. (ed.) DRM 2002. LNCS, vol. 2696, pp. 32–50. Springer, Heidelberg (2003)

[30] Kiayias, A., Yung, M.: Traitor tracing with constant transmission rate. In: Knudsen, L.R. (ed.) EUROCRYPT 2002. LNCS, vol. 2332, pp. 450–465. Springer, Heidelberg (2002)

[31] Kim, C.H., Hwang, Y.-H., Lee, P.J.: An efficient public key trace and revoke scheme secure against adaptive chosen ciphertext attack. In: Laih, C.-S. (ed.) ASIACRYPT 2003. LNCS, vol. 2894, pp. 359–373. Springer, Heidelberg (2003)

[32] Kurosawa, K., Desmedt, Y.: Optimum traitor tracing and asymmetric schemes. In: Nyberg, K. (ed.) EUROCRYPT 1998. LNCS, vol. 1403, pp. 145–157. Springer, Heidelberg (1998)

[33] Lewko, A.B., Sahai, A., Waters, B.: Revocation systems with very small private keys. In: 2010 IEEE Symposium on Security and Privacy, pp. 273–285. IEEE Computer Society Press (May 2010)

[34] Libert, B., Paterson, K.G., Quaglia, E.A.: Anonymous broadcast encryption: Adaptive security and efficient constructions in the standard model. In: Fischlin, M., Buchmann, J., Manulis, M. (eds.) PKC 2012. LNCS, vol. 7293, pp. 206–224. Springer, Heidelberg (2012)

[35] Matsushita, T., Imai, H.: A public-key black-box traitor tracing scheme with sublinear ciphertext size against self-defensive pirates. In: Lee, P.J. (ed.) ASIACRYPT 2004. LNCS, vol. 3329, pp. 260–275. Springer, Heidelberg (2004)

[36] Naor, D., Naor, M., Lotspiech, J.: Revocation and tracing schemes for stateless receivers. In: Kilian, J. (ed.) CRYPTO 2001. LNCS, vol. 2139, pp. 41–62. Springer, Heidelberg (2001)

[37] Naor, M., Pinkas, B.: Threshold traitor tracing. In: Krawczyk, H. (ed.) CRYPTO 1998. LNCS, vol. 1462, pp. 502–517. Springer, Heidelberg (1998)

[38] Naor, M., Pinkas, B.: Efficient trace and revoke schemes. In: Frankel, Y. (ed.) FC 2000. LNCS, vol. 1962, pp. 1–20. Springer, Heidelberg (2001)

[39] Pfitzmann, B.: Trials of traced traitors. In: Anderson, R. (ed.) IH 1996. LNCS, vol. 1174, pp. 49–64. Springer, Heidelberg (1996)

[40] Pfitzmann, B., Waidner, M.: Asymmetric fingerprinting for larger collusions. In: ACM CCS 1997, pp. 151–160. ACM Press (April 1997)

[41] Phan, D.H., Pointcheval, D., Shahandashti, S.F., Strefler, M.: Adaptive cca broadcast encryption with constant-size secret keys and ciphertexts. Int. J. Inf. Sec. 12(4), 251–265 (2013)

[42] Phan, D.H., Pointcheval, D., Trinh, V.C.: Multi-channel broadcast encryption. In: Chen, K., Xie, Q., Qiu, W., Li, N., Tzeng, W.-G. (eds.) ASIACCS 2013, pp. 277–286. ACM Press (May 2013)

[43] Safavi-Naini, R., Wang, Y.: Sequential traitor tracing. In: Bellare, M. (ed.) CRYPTO 2000. LNCS, vol. 1880, pp. 316–332. Springer, Heidelberg (2000)

[44] Shoup, V.: Practical threshold signatures. In: Preneel, B. (ed.) EUROCRYPT 2000. LNCS, vol. 1807, pp. 207–220. Springer, Heidelberg (2000)

[45] Silverberg, A., Staddon, J., Walker, J.L.: Efficient traitor tracing algorithms using list decoding. In: Boyd, C. (ed.) ASIACRYPT 2001. LNCS, vol. 2248, pp. 175–192. Springer, Heidelberg (2001)

[46] Sirvent, T.: Traitor tracing scheme with constant ciphertext rate against powerful pirates. In: Workshop on Coding and Cryptography (2007)

[47] Stinson, D.R., Wei, R.: Key preassigned traceability schemes for broadcast encryption. In: Tavares, S., Meijer, H. (eds.) SAC 1998. LNCS, vol. 1556, pp. 144–156. Springer, Heidelberg (1999)

[48] Stinson, D.R., Wei, R.: Combinatorial properties and constructions of traceability schemes and frameproof codes. SIAM J. Discrete Math. 11(1), 41–53 (1998)

[49] Tonien, D., Safavi-Naini, R.: An efficient single-key pirates tracing scheme using cover-free families. In: Zhou, J., Yung, M., Bao, F. (eds.) ACNS 2006. LNCS, vol. 3989, pp. 82–97. Springer, Heidelberg (2006)

[50] Tzeng, W.-G., Tzeng, Z.-J.: A public-key traitor tracing scheme with revocation using dynamic shares. In: Kim, K. (ed.) PKC 2001. LNCS, vol. 1992, pp. 207–224. Springer, Heidelberg (2001)

[51] Watanabe, Y., Hanaoka, G., Imai, H.: Efficient asymmetric public-key traitor tracing without trusted agents. In: Naccache, D. (ed.) CT-RSA 2001. LNCS, vol. 2020, pp. 392–407. Springer, Heidelberg (2001)

[52] Wee, H.: Efficient chosen-ciphertext security via extractable hash proofs. In: Rabin, T. (ed.) CRYPTO 2010. LNCS, vol. 6223, pp. 314–332. Springer, Heidelberg (2010)

[53] Wee, H.: Threshold and revocation cryptosystems via extractable hash proofs. In: Paterson, K.G. (ed.) EUROCRYPT 2011. LNCS, vol. 6632, pp. 589–609. Springer, Heidelberg (2011)

[54] Yoo, E.S., Jho, N.-S., Cheon, J.H., Kim, M.-H.: Efficient broadcast encryption using multiple interpolation methods. In: Park, C.-S., Chee, S. (eds.) ICISC 2004. LNCS, vol. 3506, pp. 87–103. Springer, Heidelberg (2005)

Broadcast Steganography

Nelly Fazio[1,3], Antonio R. Nicolosi[2], and Irippuge Milinda Perera[3]

[1] The City College of CUNY
fazio@cs.ccny.cuny.edu
[2] Stevens Institute of Technology
nicolosi@cs.stevens.edu
[3] The Graduate Center of CUNY
{nfazio,iperera}@gc.cuny.edu

Abstract. We initiate the study of broadcast steganography (BS), an extension of steganography to the multi-recipient setting. BS enables a sender to communicate covertly with a dynamically designated set of receivers, so that the recipients recover the original content, while unauthorized users and outsiders remain *unaware* of the covert communication. One of our main technical contributions is the introduction of a new variant of anonymous broadcast encryption that we term *outsider-anonymous broadcast encryption with pseudorandom ciphertexts* (oABE$). Our oABE$ construction achieves sublinear ciphertext size and is secure in the standard model. Besides being of interest in its own right, oABE$ enables an efficient construction of BS secure in the standard model against adaptive adversaries with sublinear communication complexity.

Keywords: Steganography, Broadcast Encryption, Receiver Anonymity.

1 Introduction

Point-to-point encryption schemes are effective at concealing the *meaning* of the communication between two parties. If the parties additionally desire that the very *existence* of their communication over a public channel remains concealed, then the required tool is *steganography*. Conventional steganography allows *two* parties to communicate covertly, even in the presence of an adversary, by *hiding* the intended content within other, seemingly harmless messages. After its initial formalization in the information-theoretic [12] and complexity-theoretic [3,32,34] settings, steganography has received regular attention by the cryptographic community. To a first approximation, existing solutions differ mostly in the degree of adversarial control that they can tolerate, and in the specific trade-off that they achieve among the main efficiency measures of transmission overhead, public/secret key storage, and encryption/decryption complexity.

Steganography. Simmons [44] introduced the cryptographic community to the problem of hidden communication with his famous *prisoners' dilemma*: Alice and Bob are in jail and can only talk in the presence of the jail warden Ward. Ward will not allow any encrypted communication, so Alice and Bob must

J. Benaloh (Ed.): CT-RSA 2014, LNCS 8366, pp. 64–84, 2014.

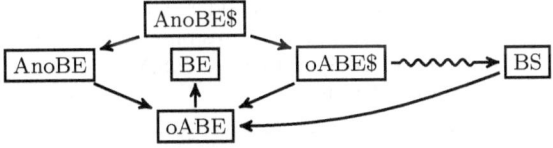

Fig. 1. Relations between broadcast encryption (BE), (outsider) anonymous broadcast encryption (AnoBE and oABE), and broadcast steganography (BS). A straight arrow means that one notion implies the other, while the curly arrow denotes our black-box construction from oABE$ to BS (cf. Sect. 5).

hide their messages about an escape plan (the *hiddentext*) into innocent-looking communication (the *stegotext*) that Ward cannot distinguish from casual chatter (the *covertext*). Modern cryptographic treatment of steganography began with Cachin's formalization in the information-security setting [12] and Hopper *et al.*'s in the complexity-theoretic one [32]. Kiayias *et al.* [35] improve the efficiency of the steganographic protocol of [32] by replacing the use of a pseudorandom function family with the combination of a pseudorandom generator and a *t*-wise independent hash function. This approach was further refined in [36] to obtain a key-efficient steganographic system, where the gain stems from employing a novel *rejection sampling* method based on extractors.

In 2004, von Ahn and Hopper [3] extended the notion of steganography to the public-key setting, but mostly focused on security against passive adversaries. A stronger security model (steganographic secrecy against adaptive chosen-covertext attacks, or SS-CCA) was defined by Backes and Cachin [6], but their constructions attained only an intermediate security notion, termed steganographic secrecy against publicly-detectable, replayable adaptive chosen-covertext attacks (SS-PDR-CCA). Building upon the work of [6], Hopper [31] attained full SS-CCA security under the Decisional Diffie-Hellman (DDH) assumption, in the standard model. Le and Kurosawa [38] suggested a weaker generalization of the model of [6], but with better efficiency than [31].

All steganographic constructions mentioned above assume that the communication channel can be modeled by an efficient covertext sampler that can be queried adaptively, in a black-box manner. Dedic *et al.* [15] looked into communication bounds for stegosystems of this kind, while Lysyanskaya and Meyerovich [40] dealt with the case of imperfect channel oracle samplers.

Work of von Ahn *et al.* [4] and Chandran *et al.* [14] introduced stealthiness to the setting of secure function evaluation, originating the notion of *covert two-party/multi-party computation*. Covert protocols allow parties to carry out distributed computations in a way that hides their very *intent* of taking part in the protocol: that is, unless *all* parties actively participate, nobody can detect that protocol messaging had been initiated (and aborted). This capability supports stealthy coordination between mutually mistrustful parties and enables fascinating applications like covert authentication [4] and co-spy detection [14]. However, it does not imply efficient covert dissemination of information to a chosen subset of (mostly passive) receivers, which is the main focus of this paper.

Table 1. Comparison of the parameters of (outsider) anonymous broadcast encryption schemes. Each scheme is CCA-secure and requires only one decryption attempt. Only our scheme provides pseudorandom ciphertexts ($c \approx \$$:Yes). N is the total number of users and r is the number of revoked users.

Scheme	|MPK|	|sk|	|c|	Security Model	Anonymity	$c \approx \$$
BBW06 [7]	$O(N)$	$O(1)$	$O(N-r)$	Static, RO	Full	No
LPQ12 [39]	$O(N)$	$O(1)$	$O(N-r)$	Adaptive, Standard	Full	No
FP12a [23]	$O(N)$	$O(\log N)$	$O\left(r\log\left(\frac{N}{r}\right)\right)$	Adaptive, Standard	Outsider	No
FP12b [24]	$O(N\log N)$	$O(N)$	$O(r)$	Adaptive, Standard	Outsider	No
oABE\$ [ours]	$O(N)$	$O(\log N)$	$O\left(r\log\left(\frac{N}{r}\right)\right)$	Adaptive, Standard	Outsider	Yes

Broadcast Steganography (BS). In this work, we extend steganography to the broadcast setting. Intuitively, *broadcast steganography* enables a sender to communicate covertly with a dynamically designated set of receivers, so that authorized recipients correctly recover the original content, while unauthorized users and outsiders remain *unaware* of the covert communication. To construct broadcast steganography, we employ the "encrypt-then-embed" paradigm that underpins most steganographic constructions [3,6,31,32] (cf. Sect. 2). Realizing this approach, however, requires solving several technical problems.

The first issue is that, in broadcast encryption, the receiver set is included explicitly in the ciphertext as part of its header (e.g., [8,9,16–19,25,26,28,29,42]). This is a non-starter for steganography, which intrinsically requires that the existence of any data in the channel be concealed. To address this issue, we turn to *private* broadcast encryption, a notion introduced by Barth et al. [7] with the goal of keeping the identities of the authorized receivers anonymous (Sect. 2).

The second hurdle is that the "encrypt-then-embed" paradigm requires the underlying encryption functionality to have *pseudorandom* ciphertexts. This property so far had not been considered in the broadcast encryption literature, and none of the existing constructions support it natively. Interestingly, attaining pseudorandom ciphertexts requires implicitly that the identities of the recipients be unintelligible *in the view of outsiders* (pseudorandomness of the ciphertext clearly cannot hold in the view of the recipients). This condition ties back directly to the previous issue, but in a weaker form, as recipient anonymity is only required to hold against outsiders. As it turns out, Fazio and Perera [23] recently proposed a relaxation of full anonymity of exactly this sort: *outsider-anonymous broadcast encryption* (oABE). This notion trades some degree of anonymity for better efficiency: whereas all known fully-anonymous broadcast encryption schemes [7, 39] have ciphertexts *linear* in the number of receivers, the constructions of [23] obtain *sublinear* ciphertext length, though they do not necessarily guarantee that authorized users will learn no information about other members of the receiver set.

In light of the above observations, we put forth and realize (Sect. 4) a new broadcast encryption variant that we term *outsider-anonymous broadcast encryption with pseudorandom ciphertexts* (oABE\$). oABE\$ enables a black-box construction of BS (cf. Sect. 5). Realizing an efficient oABE\$ scheme requires

Table 2. The parameters of our black-box broadcast steganography schemes. Type-1 channels are the most general, and are modeled as stateful probabilistic oracles whose output distribution *may* depend on past samples. Type-2 channels are slightly more restrictive as they assume history independence, and can then be modeled as efficiently sampleable document distributions, i.e., efficiently computable randomized functions. N is the total number of users and r is the number of revoked users. The notion of BS-CHA (resp. BS-CCA) captures passive (resp. active) security for the BS setting (cf. Sect. 3.2).

Scheme	|MPK|	|sk|	|s|	Security Model	Channel Type
BS-CHA	$O(N)$	$O(\log N)$	$O\left(r\log\left(\frac{N}{r}\right)\right)$	Adaptive, Standard	1
BS-CCA	$O(N)$	$O(\log N)$	$O\left(r\log\left(\frac{N}{r}\right)\right)$	Adaptive, Standard	2

non-trivial enhancements to the oABE construction of [23], for it entails resolving the apparent tension between our ciphertext pseudorandom property and the ciphertext redundancy introduced by common approaches to CCA security [10, 20]. Our solution harmonizes these requirements using a novel Pedersen-like encapsulation mechanism discussed in Sect. 4.2. A comparison of our oABE\$ construction with existing ones is reported in Table 1, whereas Fig. 1 shows how oABE\$ relates to other anonymous broadcast communication tools.

Applications. The combination of stealth and revocation capabilities offered by broadcast steganography enables defenses against insider threats in anti-censorship systems, intelligence scenarios, and other domains that rely on covert communication [41, 45].

For a military example, consider a camp where each soldier has an army smartphone, on which they receive weather forecast, unclassified news and other information in the clear. Suppose that headquarters suspect that a group of officials are conspiring to commit treachery, and decides to carry out an undercover investigation to confirm the identities of the traitors. Conventional broadcast encryption does not suffice to protect the transmission channel to the soldiers involved in the investigation of the traitors, because the selective exclusion of the conspirators from the communication would already put them on notice. Broadcast steganography, instead, would allow delivery of instructions to the investigating parties without risking alerting the traitors to the investigation.

For a civil rights scenario, an activist/blogger may want to hide her commentary into innocent-looking image postings to social media services (e.g., Instagram or Weibo). Because censorship authorities may infiltrate among the activist's followers, the ability of broadcast steganography to authorize/deauthorize recipients at a fine grain would enable the blogger to revoke the infiltrator and prevent him from recovering the hiddentext, *without him noticing that he has been singled out*.

Our Contributions. This work initiates the study of broadcast steganography. After introducing a suitable security framework, we highlight the connections with the issue of recipient-anonymity in broadcast encryption. One of our main technical contributions is the introduction of a new variant of anonymous broadcast encryption that we term outsider-anonymous broadcast encryption with

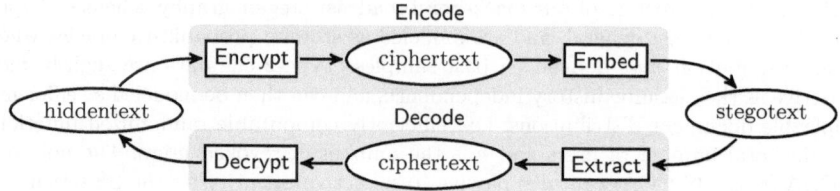

Fig. 2. The "encrypt-then-embed" paradigm underlying (broadcast) steganography

pseudorandom ciphertexts. Our oABE\$ construction achieves sublinear cipher-text size and is secure in the standard model against adaptive adversaries, which required circumventing multiple technical hurdles and is thus of independent interest. Finally, we devise efficient oABE\$-based BS schemes at varying security levels (cf. Table 2), including a construction with sublinear stegotexts secure in the standard model against adaptive adversaries.

2 Background

Documents and Covertexts. Let $\Sigma = \{0,1\}^\sigma$ be a finite set of bit-strings with length σ. Denote by Σ^* the set of sequences of finite length over Σ. We call the strings $u \in \Sigma$ *documents* and the strings $s \in \Sigma^*$ *covertexts*.

Channels. A *channel* $\mathfrak{C}_h$ is a function that takes as input a *channel history* $h \in \Sigma^*$ and produces a probability distribution on Σ. A channel history $h = s_1\|\ldots\|s_l \in \Sigma^*$ is called *legal* if for all $i \in [1,l]$, $\mathrm{Pr}_{\mathfrak{C}_{s_1\|\ldots\|s_{i-1}}}[s_i] > 0$. A sampling of l documents in succession from a channel is denoted by $s = s_1\|\ldots\|s_l \leftarrow \mathfrak{C}_h^l$ (shorthand notation for $s_1 \leftarrow \mathfrak{C}_h, s_2 \leftarrow \mathfrak{C}_{h\|s_1}, \ldots, s_l \leftarrow \mathfrak{C}_{h\|s_1\|\ldots\|s_{l-1}}$). A channel is called *always informative* if for every legal history $h \in \Sigma^*$, $H_\infty(\mathfrak{C}_h^l) = \Omega(l)$, where H_∞ is the min-entropy function. A channel can be modeled either as an oracle or as an efficiently computable randomized function $\mathsf{Channel}(h; r)$ (where r denotes the random coins). While the latter is a stronger assumption on the channel, [31] shows it to be necessary for secure steganography. Efficiently computable channels also enable broadcast steganographic constructions with stronger security guarantees (cf. Sect. 5).

Public-Key Steganography. From an operational standpoint, public-key steganography resembles the setting of asymmetric encryption: a participant with a public/secret key pair is able to receive covert messages (the *hiddentexts*) from another party, who only knows the public key. Unlike the case of public-key cryptography, however, the encoded hiddentexts, termed *stegotexts*, are required to be indistinguishable from the covertexts of the communication channel.

A common approach to realize public-key stegosystems is the "encrypt-then-embed" paradigm [3, 6, 31, 32], depicted in Fig. 2. At a high level, encoding is accomplished by first encrypting the hiddentext using a public-key cryptosystem, and then implanting the resulting ciphertext in the stegotext using an embedding function. The decoding process develops similarly, but in the reverse direction. Based on the security properties of the underlying cryptosystem and embedding function, one obtains stegosystems with a variety of security guarantees (cf. Sect. 1).

Outsider-Anonymous Broadcast Encryption (oABE). The notion of *private* broadcast encryption was initially introduced in [7], with the aim of providing explicit protection for identities of the receivers during each transmission. As a proof-of-concept, therein the authors suggested both generic and number-theoretic public-key constructions that do not leak any information about the list of authorized receivers, and are secure in the standard model and in the random oracle model, respectively. The proposed schemes, however, have communication complexity linear in the number of recipients. In [39], Libert et al. suggested proof techniques to argue the security of (a variant of) the number-theoretic construction of [7] without reliance on random oracles, thus attaining anonymous broadcast encryption with efficient decryption in the standard model. Still, ciphertexts in the resulting construction have length linear in the number of recipients. In [37], Kiayias and Samari put forth lower bounds on the ciphertext size of private broadcast encryption schemes and showed, among other results, that fully anonymous broadcast encryption schemes with a certain "atomicity" property (satisfied, e.g., by the schemes of [7, 39]) must have $\Omega(s \cdot \lambda)$ ciphertext size, where s is the number of authorized receivers and λ is the security parameter.

Fazio and Perera [23] formalized the notion of *outsider-anonymous broadcast encryption* , which lies between the complete lack of protection that characterizes traditional broadcast encryption schemes as introduced in [25], and the full anonymity provided by [7, 39]. In an oABE scheme, an attacker who intercepts a ciphertext of which she is not a legal recipient will be unable to learn anything about the identities of the legal recipients (let alone the contents of the ciphertext). Still, for those ciphertexts for which the adversary is in the authorized set of recipients, she might also garner information about the identities of the other receivers. This seems a natural relaxation, since often the *contents* of the communication already reveals something about the recipient set. Moreover, it enables schemes that achieve *sublinear* ciphertexts size and are secure against adaptive adversaries in the standard model. We observe that, in light of the lower bounds of [37], the trade-off proposed in [23] may be unavoidable.

Entropy Smoothing Hash. A family of hash functions $\mathcal{H}_{es} = \{H : X \to Y\}$ is "entropy smoothing" [33] if it is hard to distinguish $(H, H(x))$ from (H, y), where H is a random element of $\mathcal{H}_{es}$, x is a random element of X, and y is a random element of Y. More formally, $\mathcal{H}_{es}$ is called (t, ϵ)-entropy smoothing if for every t-time adversary $\mathcal{A}$,

$$\left| \Pr\left[\mathcal{A}(H, H(x)) = 1 \mid H \leftarrow_\$ \mathcal{H}_{es}, x \leftarrow_\$ X \right] \right.$$
$$\left. - \Pr\left[\mathcal{A}(H, y) = 1 \mid H \leftarrow_\$ \mathcal{H}_{es}, y \leftarrow_\$ Y \right] \right| \leq \epsilon,$$

where the probability is over the choice of H, x, y and the random coins of $\mathcal{A}$.[1]

3   Broadcast Steganography (BS)

3.1   The Setting

Definition 3.1. *A broadcast steganography scheme, associated with a universe of users $U = [1, N]$, a message space $\mathcal{MSP}$, and a channel $\mathfrak{C}_h$ on a set of documents Σ, is a tuple of probabilistic polynomial-time (PPT) algorithms* (Setup, KeyGen, Encode, Decode) *such that:*

(MPK, MSK) ← **Setup**$(1^\lambda, N)$: Setup *takes the security parameter 1^λ and the number of users in the system N as inputs and outputs the master public key* MPK *and the master secret key* MSK.

sk_i ← **KeyGen**(**MPK, MSK**, i): *Given the master public key* MPK, *the master secret key* MSK, *and a user $i \in U$,* KeyGen *generates a secret key sk_i for user i.*

s ← **Encode**(**MPK**, S, h, m): Encode *takes the master public key* MPK, *a set of receivers $S \subseteq U$, a channel history $h \in \Sigma^*$, and a message $m \in \mathcal{MSP}$ as inputs and outputs a stegotext $s \in \Sigma^*$ from the support of $\mathfrak{C}_h^l$ for some $l = poly(|m|)$.*

$m/\bot$:= **Decode**(**MPK**, sk_i, s): *Given the master public key* MPK, *a secret key sk_i, and a stegotext $s \in \Sigma^*$,* Decode *either outputs a message $m \in \mathcal{MSP}$ or the failure symbol $\bot$. We assume that* Decode *is deterministic.*

Correctness. *For every $S \subseteq U$, $i \in S$, legal channel history $h \in \Sigma^*$, and $m \in \mathcal{MSP}$, if* (MPK, MSK) *is output by* Setup$(1^\lambda, N)$ *and sk_i is generated by* KeyGen(MPK, MSK, i), *then* Decode(MPK, sk_i, Encode(MPK, S, h, m)) = m *except with negligible probability in the security parameter λ.*

Remark 3.2. In contrast to the definition from [31], our definition requires that the Decode algorithm works without receiving the channel history h corresponding to the stegotext s as an input. This is crucial for an efficient broadcast steganography scheme, because requiring that authorized users feed the Decode algorithm with the same h that was used by the sender entails a level of coordination that is unrealistic in a broadcast setting. Our definition also applies to channels whose samples do not depend on h at all, as Encode may simply ignore h.

---

[1] Entropy smoothing is related to strong randomness extraction [46], but it is a much less stringent (and hence easier to realize) notion, as it seeks only computational (rather than information-theoretic) guarantees, and it is specific to *one* entropy source (the uniform distribution over the domain X), whereas strong extractors are applicable to any source of a given min-entropy.

3.2 The Security Models

In broadcast encryption (BE), the adversary's goal is to learn something about the message encrypted within a given ciphertext despite not having a valid decryption key. In broadcast steganography, the adversary's goal is to detect the *presence* of a message in a given covertext without a valid decoding key. In either case, one may consider multiple levels of security, according to the amount of power afforded to the attacker. We discuss below three models of security for broadcast steganography schemes, followed by formal definitions later in this section.

Chosen-Hiddentext Attack (BS-CHA). This is the weakest model of security for a broadcast steganography scheme. Analogous to the chosen-plaintext attack in broadcast encryption, the adversary in this context is only allowed to corrupt users by gaining their secret keys.

Publicly-Detectable Replayable Chosen-Covertext Attack (BS-PDR-CCA). In this model of security, the adversary is additionally given access to a decoding oracle through which they can obtain the hiddentext (if any) in any covertext s of their choice, as recovered by any honest user i of their choice, subject to the following restriction: After receiving the challenge covertext s^* for the set of recipients S^*, the adversary is not allowed to query the decoding oracle with a user index i and a covertext s such that $i \in S^*$ and $s \equiv_{\mathsf{MPK}} s^*$, where $\equiv_{\mathsf{MPK}}$ is an arbitrary *compatible relation*:

Definition 3.3. *Let $\Pi = (\mathsf{Setup}, \mathsf{KeyGen}, \mathsf{Encode}, \mathsf{Decode})$ be a BS scheme. A binary relation on stegotexts of Π induced by a master public key MPK of Π is called a* compatible relation *(denoted by $\equiv_{\mathsf{MPK}}$) if for any two stegotexts s_1, s_2 encoded under sets of receivers S_1, S_2 respectively, we have*

1. *If $s_1 \equiv_{\mathsf{MPK}} s_2$ then for any $i_1 \in S_1$ and $i_2 \in S_2$, $\mathsf{Decode}(\mathsf{MPK}, sk_{i_1}, s_1) = \mathsf{Decode}(\mathsf{MPK}, sk_{i_2}, s_2)$ except with negligible probability in the security parameter λ.*
2. *There exists a PPT algorithm that takes MPK, s_1, s_2 and determines whether $s_1 \equiv_{\mathsf{MPK}} s_2$.*

Chosen-Covertext Attack (BS-CCA). A BS-CCA adversary has the same capabilities from the BS-PDR-CCA model of security, but the restriction for the decoding queries is now lifted. Specifically, the only covertext that the adversary is not allowed to submit to the decoding oracle with a user index $i \in S^*$ is the challenge covertext s^* itself.

We now formally define the BS-CCA security model via the following security game.

Definition 3.4. *For a given BS scheme $\Pi = (\mathsf{Setup}, \mathsf{KeyGen}, \mathsf{Encode}, \mathsf{Decode})$, the BS-IND-CCA game, played between a PPT adversary $\mathcal{A}$ and a challenger $\mathcal{C}$, is defined as follows:*

Setup: *$\mathcal{C}$ runs $(\mathsf{MPK}, \mathsf{MSK}) \leftarrow \mathsf{Setup}(1^\lambda, N)$ and gives $\mathcal{A}$ the resulting master public key MPK, keeping the master secret key MSK to itself. $\mathcal{C}$ also initializes the set of revoked users R to be empty.*

Phase 1: $\mathcal{A}$ *adaptively issues queries* $q_1, \ldots, q_m$ *of one of the following types:*
  • *Secret-key query* i: $\mathcal{A}$ *requests the secret key of a user* $i \in U$. $\mathcal{C}$ *runs* $sk_i \leftarrow \mathsf{KeyGen}(\mathsf{MPK}, \mathsf{MSK}, i)$, *adds* i *to* R, *and sends* sk_i *to* $\mathcal{A}$.
  • *Decoding query* (i, s): $\mathcal{A}$ *issues a decoding query on a user index* $i \in U$ *and a covertext* $s \in \Sigma^*$. $\mathcal{C}$ *computes* $\mathsf{Decode}(\mathsf{MPK}, \mathsf{KeyGen}(\mathsf{MPK}, \mathsf{MSK}, i), s)$ *and gives the result to* $\mathcal{A}$.

Challenge: $\mathcal{A}$ *gives* $\mathcal{C}$ *a message* $m^* \in \mathcal{MSP}$, *a legal history* $h \in \Sigma^*$, *and a set of user identities* $S^* \subseteq U$ *with the restriction that* $S^* \cap R = \emptyset$. $\mathcal{C}$ *picks a random bit* $b^* \in \{0, 1\}$ *and generates the challenge* s^* *depending on it as follows. If* $b^* = 0$, *then* $\mathcal{C}$ *encodes* m^* *into a stegotext* s^* *for the receiver set* S^*, *i.e.,* $s^* \leftarrow \mathsf{Encode}(\mathsf{MPK}, S^*, h, m^*)$. *Otherwise,* $\mathcal{C}$ *sample* s^* *as a covertext of equal length, i.e.,* $s^* \leftarrow\!\!\$\; \mathfrak{C}_h^{l^*}$ *for* $l^* = |\mathsf{Encode}(\mathsf{MPK}, S^*, h, m^*)|/\sigma$. *At the end,* $\mathcal{C}$ *gives* s^* *to* $\mathcal{A}$.

Phase 2: $\mathcal{A}$ *adaptively issues additional queries* $q_{m+1}, \ldots, q_n$ *where each* q_i *is one of the following:*
  • *Secret-key query* i *such that* $i \notin S^*$.
  • *Decoding query* (i, s) *such that, if* $i \in S^*$, *then* $s \neq s^*$.

Guess: $\mathcal{A}$ *outputs a guess* $b \in \{0, 1\}$ *and wins if* $b = b^*$.

The adversary $\mathcal{A}$ *is called a BS-IND-CCA adversary and* $\mathcal{A}$*'s advantage is defined as*

$$\mathsf{Adv}_{\mathcal{A},\Pi}^{BS\text{-}IND\text{-}CCA} := \left| \Pr[b = b^*] - \tfrac{1}{2} \right|,$$

where the probability is over the random coins used by the adversary $\mathcal{A}$ *and the challenger* $\mathcal{C}$.

Definition 3.5. *A BS scheme* Π *is* $(t, Q_{sk}, Q_d, \epsilon)$-*BS-CCA-secure if for any* t-*time BS-IND-CCA adversary making at most* Q_{sk} *adaptive secret-key queries and at most* Q_d *adaptive decoding queries, it is the case that* $\mathsf{Adv}_{\mathcal{A},\Pi}^{BS\text{-}IND\text{-}CCA} \leq \epsilon$.

By restricting the kind of decoding queries allowed in *Phase 2* of the BS-IND-CCA game above, we can obtain the BS-IND-PDR-CCA game. Specifically, the adversary now cannot issue any decoding query (i, s) such that $i \in S^*$ and $s \equiv_{\mathsf{MPK}} s^*$ for some compatible relation $\equiv_{\mathsf{MPK}}$. The adversary $\mathcal{A}$ in this game is called a BS-IND-PDR-CCA adversary and $\mathcal{A}$'s advantage is defined as

$$\mathsf{Adv}_{\mathcal{A},\Pi}^{BS\text{-}IND\text{-}PDR\text{-}CCA} := \left| \Pr[b = b^*] - \tfrac{1}{2} \right|.$$

Definition 3.6. *A BS scheme* Π *is* $(t, Q_{sk}, Q_d, \epsilon)$-*BS-PDR-CCA-secure with respect to some compatible relation* $\equiv_{\mathsf{MPK}}$ *if for any* t-*time BS-IND-PDR-CCA adversary making at most* Q_{sk} *adaptive secret-key queries and at most* Q_d *adaptive decoding queries, it holds that* $\mathsf{Adv}_{\mathcal{A},\Pi}^{BS\text{-}IND\text{-}PDR\text{-}CCA} \leq \epsilon$.

The BS-IND-CHA game is defined similar to the BS-IND-CCA game, with the restriction that the adversary is not allowed to issue any decoding queries during *Phase 1* and *Phase 2*. The adversary is still allowed to issue secret-key queries.

Definition 3.7. *A BS scheme* Π *is* (t, Q_{sk}, ϵ)-*BS-CHA-secure if* Π *is* $(t, Q_{sk}, 0, \epsilon)$-*BS-CCA-secure.*

4 Anonymity and Pseudorandomness in Broadcast Encryption

In Sect. 2, we briefly discussed the notion of outsider-anonymous broadcast encryption [23], a security model for BE whose goal is to hide the identities of the intended receivers of a broadcast ciphertext from unauthorized users. As outlined in Sect. 1, a crucial technical step to realize broadcast steganography is combining receiver anonymity with pseudorandomness of broadcast ciphertexts (cf. Sect. 5). This section develops the notion of *outsider-anonymous broadcast encryption with pseudorandom ciphertexts* (oABE$), and presents an efficient construction secure in the standard model under a stronger security model, *outsider anonymity and ciphertext pseudorandomness against chosen-ciphertext attacks* (oABE$-CCA).

4.1 The Security Models of oABE$

We now present three oABE$ security models: oABE$-CPA, oABE$-PDR-CCA, and oABE$-CCA. In Sect. 4.2, we present an oABE$-CCA-secure construction. At a high level, these security models require that for any message m^* and set of recipients S^*, no PPT adversary $\mathcal{A}$ can distinguish between an actual encryption of m^* intended for the set S^*, and a truly random string of the same length as an encryption of m^* for S^*, so long as $\mathcal{A}$ does not possess the secret key of any user in S^*.

Definition 4.1. *Given an oABE$ scheme Π = (Setup, KeyGen, Encrypt, Decrypt), the oABE$-IND-CCA game, played between a PPT adversary $\mathcal{A}$ and a challenger $\mathcal{C}$, is defined as follows:*

Setup: *$\mathcal{C}$ runs (MPK, MSK) $\leftarrow$ Setup($1^\lambda, N$) and gives $\mathcal{A}$ the resulting master public key MPK, keeping the master secret key MSK to itself. $\mathcal{C}$ also initializes the set of revoked users R to be empty.*

Phase 1: *$\mathcal{A}$ adaptively issues queries $q_1, \ldots, q_m$ where each q_i is one of the following:*
- *Secret-key query i: $\mathcal{A}$ requests the secret key of a user $i \in U$. $\mathcal{C}$ runs $sk_i \leftarrow$ KeyGen(MPK, MSK, i), adds i to R, and sends sk_i to $\mathcal{A}$.*
- *Decryption query (i, c): $\mathcal{A}$ sends a decryption query on a user $i \in U$ and a ciphertext $c \in \mathcal{CSP}$. $\mathcal{C}$ computes Decrypt(MPK, KeyGen(MPK, MSK, i), c) and gives the result to $\mathcal{A}$.*

Challenge: *$\mathcal{A}$ gives $\mathcal{C}$ a message $m^* \in \mathcal{MSP}$ and a set of user identities $S^* \subseteq U$ with the restriction that $S^* \cap R = \emptyset$. $\mathcal{C}$ picks a random bit $b^* \in \{0,1\}$ and generates the challenge ciphertext c^* depending on it: if $b^* = 0$, then $c^* \leftarrow$ Encrypt(MPK, S^*, m^*), else $c^* \leftarrow\!\$ \{0,1\}^{l^*}$ for $l^* = |$Encrypt(MPK, S^*, m^*)$|$. The challenge ciphertext c^* is then given to $\mathcal{A}$.*

Phase 2: *$\mathcal{A}$ adaptively issues additional queries $q_{m+1}, \ldots, q_n$ where each q_i is one of the following:*
- *Secret-key query i such that $i \notin S^*$.*
- *Decryption query (i, c) such that, if $i \in S^*$, then $c \neq c^*$.*

Guess: *$\mathcal{A}$ outputs a guess $b \in \{0,1\}$ and wins if $b = b^*$.*

The adversary $\mathcal{A}$ is called an oABE\$-IND-CCA adversary and $\mathcal{A}$'s advantage is defined as

$$\mathsf{Adv}_{\mathcal{A},\Pi}^{oABE\$-IND-CCA} := \left| \Pr[b = b^*] - \tfrac{1}{2} \right|,$$

where the probability is over the random coins used by the adversary $\mathcal{A}$ and the challenger $\mathcal{C}$.

Observe that the key difference of the above definition from the oABE notion defined in [23] is in the *Challenge* phase, where the challenger either returns the encryption of m^* or a random bit-string with appropriate length.

Definition 4.2. *An oABE\$ scheme Π is $(t, Q_{sk}, Q_d, \epsilon)$-oABE\$-CCA-secure if for any t-time oABE\$-IND-CCA adversary making at most Q_{sk} (resp. Q_d) adaptive secret-key (resp. decryption) queries we have $\mathsf{Adv}_{\mathcal{A},\Pi}^{oABE\$-IND-CCA} \leq \epsilon$.*

The oABE\$-IND-PDR-CCA game is obtained by restricting the adversary during *Phase 2* of the oABE\$-IND-CCA game from submitting any decoding query (i, c) such that $i \in S^*$ and $c \equiv_{\mathsf{MPK}} c^*$, where $\equiv_{\mathsf{MPK}}$ is an arbitrary compatible relation of the oABE\$ scheme.[2] The adversary $\mathcal{A}$ in this game is called an oABE\$-IND-PDR-CCA adversary and $\mathcal{A}$'s advantage is defined as

$$\mathsf{Adv}_{\mathcal{A},\Pi}^{oABE\$-IND-PDR-CCA} := \left| \Pr[b = b^*] - \tfrac{1}{2} \right|.$$

Definition 4.3. *An oABE\$ scheme Π is $(t, Q_{sk}, Q_d, \epsilon)$-oABE\$-PDR-CCA-secure with respect to a compatible relation $\equiv_{\mathsf{MPK}}$ if for any t-time oABE\$-IND-PDR-CCA adversary making at most Q_{sk} adaptive secret-key queries and at most Q_d adaptive decoding queries $\mathsf{Adv}_{\mathcal{A},\Pi}^{oABE\$-IND-PDR-CCA} \leq \epsilon$.*

By restricting the adversary in the oABE\$-IND-CCA game from submitting any decoding queries during *Phase 1* and *Phase 2*, we obtain the oABE\$-IND-CPA game. The adversary is still allowed to issue secret-key queries.

Definition 4.4. *An oABE\$ scheme Π is (t, Q_{sk}, ϵ)-oABE\$-CPA-secure if Π is $(t, Q_{sk}, 0, \epsilon)$-oABE\$-CCA-secure.*

4.2   An oABE\$-CCA-Secure Construction

Our construction builds on the one of [23], so we start with a brief review of the latter. At a high level, the approach of [23] is to: (1) "bundle" multiple ciphertexts of an anonymous identity-based encryption scheme (AIBE, e.g., [1,11,27]) into a single oABE ciphertext; (2) "tag" each AIBE ciphertext to enable the decryptor to efficiently locate the component compatible with her decryption key; and (3) "seal" everything together with a one-time signature to thwart CCA attacks. To attain pseudorandom oABE ciphertexts, we will start with an anonymous identity-based encryption scheme with *pseudorandom ciphertexts* (AIBE\$) like

---

[2] The definition of a compatible relation for an oABE\$ scheme follows analogously to Definition 3.3.

Algorithm: Commit(PK″)
1 $\hat{k} \leftarrow_{\$} \{0,1\}^{\lambda}$
2 **repeat**
3    $\tilde{k} \leftarrow_{\$} \mathbb{Z}_q$, com $:= \mathsf{mp}(g_{\mathsf{com}}^{\hat{k}} h_{\mathsf{com}}^{\tilde{k}})$
4 **until** com $< 2^{\lambda}$
5 decom $:= (\hat{k}, \tilde{k})$
6 **return** $(\hat{k}, \mathsf{com}, \mathsf{decom})$

Algorithm: Open(PK″, com, decom)
1 **parse** decom **as** $(\hat{k}, \tilde{k})$
2 **if** com $= \mathsf{mp}(g_{\mathsf{com}}^{\hat{k}} h_{\mathsf{com}}^{\tilde{k}})$ **then**
3   **return** $\hat{k}$
4 **return** $\perp$

Fig. 3. Our Pedersen-like encapsulation mechanism

the one of [2]. Additionally, we will use an *entropy-smoothing* hash function [33] to hide the structure in the ciphertext tags.

These adjustments do not suffice because the presence of the one-time signature introduces additional structure in the oABE ciphertext of [23]. To get around this, we substitute one-time signatures with MACs (implemented via pseudorandom functions) and employ a variant of an *encapsulation mechanism* [10, 20] with an additional pseudorandom property. In short, an encapsulation mechanism is a "relaxed" commitment scheme consisting of a triplet of algorithms (SetupCom, Commit, Open): SetupCom(1^{λ}) produces a commitment public key PK″; Commit(PK″) samples a random bit string $\hat{k}$ together with associated commitment and decommitment information com and decom; and Open(PK″, com, decom) recovers $\hat{k}$. For *hiding*, triples of the form (PK″, com, $\hat{k}$) ought to be statistically indistinguishable from those of the form (PK″, com, r) for random r. For *relaxed binding*, given a random output ($\hat{k}$, com, decom) of Commit(PK″), it should be hard to produce decom′ such that Open(PK″, com, decom′) $\notin \{\hat{k}, \perp\}$.

Let p, q be primes such that $2^{\lambda} < q < 2^{\lambda+1}$ and $p = 2q + 1$, and g be a square modulo p. Denote by $\mathbb{G} = \langle g \rangle$ the group of quadratic residues modulo p. To "pack" quadratic residues into λ bits, we will use rejection sampling along with the following well-known $\mathbb{G}$–$\mathbb{Z}_q$ bijection (cf. e.g., [31]):

$$\mathsf{mp}(a) = \begin{cases} a & \text{if } a \leq q \\ p - a & \text{otherwise} \end{cases} \qquad \mathsf{mp}^{-1}(b) = \begin{cases} b & \text{if } b^{\frac{p-1}{2}} \equiv 1 \bmod p \\ p - b & \text{otherwise} \end{cases}$$

Figure 3 shows the Commit and Open functionalities of our Pedersen-like [43] encapsulation mechanism over $\mathbb{G}$, whose commitment public keys are random pairs $(g_{\mathsf{com}}, h_{\mathsf{com}})$ of generators of $\mathbb{G}$. The hiding requirement follows from the hiding properties of standard Pedersen commitments, coupled with the observation that $\mathsf{mp}(\cdot)$ is a bijection. Relaxed binding follows from the discrete logarithm assumption in $\mathbb{G}$, again similarly to standard Pedersen commitments. A novel feature of our encapsulation mechanism is that the distribution of commitments com induced by the Commit(PK″) algorithm is *uniform over* $\{0,1\}^{\lambda}$, and hence the relaxed commitment scheme of Fig. 3 has *pseudorandom commitments*.

Let $\Pi' = (\mathsf{Init}, \mathsf{Ext}, \mathsf{Enc}, \mathsf{Dec})$ be an AIBE\$-CCA-secure AIBE\$ scheme with expansion ℓ (i.e., $|\mathsf{Enc}(\mathsf{MPK}', \mathsf{ID}, m)| = \ell(|m|)$). Let $F : \{0,1\}^{\lambda} \times \{0,1\}^* \rightarrow \{0,1\}^{\lambda}$ be a PRF and let $\mathcal{H}_{es} = \{\mathbb{G}^2 \rightarrow \{0,1\}^{\lambda}\}$ be an entropy smoothing hash function family. Below we describe at a high level how we combine these primitives into an oABE$-CCA-secure scheme Π; Fig. 4 reports the details.

Algorithm: Setup($1^\lambda, N$)
1 $(\mathsf{MPK}', \mathsf{MSK}') \leftarrow \mathsf{Init}(1^\lambda)$
2 $\mathsf{PK}'' \leftarrow \mathsf{SetupCom}(1^\lambda), H \leftarrow\!\!\$\ \mathcal{H}_{es}$
3 ▷ Fam – the set of all the subtrees in $\mathcal{T}$
4 **for** $j := 1$ **to** $|\mathsf{Fam}|$ **do**
5   ▷ T_j – the subtree in Fam indexed by j
6   ▷ HID_j – the HID of T_j's root
7     $a_{1,\mathsf{HID}_j}, a_{2,\mathsf{HID}_j}, b_{1,\mathsf{HID}_j}, b_{2,\mathsf{HID}_j} \leftarrow\!\!\$\ \mathbb{Z}_q$
8     $A_{1,\mathsf{HID}_j} := g^{a_{1,\mathsf{HID}_j}}, A_{2,\mathsf{HID}_j} := g^{a_{2,\mathsf{HID}_j}}$
9     $B_{1,\mathsf{HID}_j} := g^{b_{1,\mathsf{HID}_j}}, B_{2,\mathsf{HID}_j} := g^{b_{2,\mathsf{HID}_j}}$
10 $\mathsf{MPK} := (\mathsf{MPK}', \mathsf{PK}'', H, N, \mathbb{G}, g,$
     $\{A_{i,\mathsf{HID}_j}, B_{i,\mathsf{HID}_j}\}_{i \in \{1,2\}, j \in [1,|\mathsf{Fam}|]})$
11 $\mathsf{MSK} := (\mathsf{MSK}',$
     $\{a_{i,\mathsf{HID}_j}, b_{i,\mathsf{HID}_j}\}_{i \in \{1,2\}, j \in [1,|\mathsf{Fam}|]})$
12 **return** $(\mathsf{MPK}, \mathsf{MSK})$

Algorithm: KeyGen($\mathsf{MPK}, \mathsf{MSK}, i$)
1 ▷ HID_i – the HID of leaf i in $\mathcal{T}$
2 **for** $z := 1$ **to** $n+1$ **do**
3     $\overline{sk}_{i,z} := (a_{1,\mathsf{HID}_{i|z}}, a_{2,\mathsf{HID}_{i|z}}, b_{1,\mathsf{HID}_{i|z}}, b_{2,\mathsf{HID}_{i|z}})$
4     $sk_{i,z} \leftarrow \mathsf{Ext}(\mathsf{MPK}', \mathsf{MSK}', \mathsf{HID}_{i|z})$
5 $sk_i := ((\overline{sk}_{i,1}, sk_{i,1}), \ldots, (\overline{sk}_{i,n+1}, sk_{i,n+1}))$
6 **return** sk_i

Algorithm: Encrypt(MPK, S, m)
1 $r := N - |S|, L := \left\lfloor r \log\left(\frac{N}{r}\right) \right\rfloor$
2 $(\hat{k}, \mathsf{com}, \mathsf{decom}) \leftarrow \mathsf{Commit}(\mathsf{PK}'')$
3 **repeat**
4     $s \leftarrow\!\!\$\ \mathbb{Z}_q, \overline{c}_0 := \mathsf{mp}(g^s)$
5 **until** $\overline{c}_0 < 2^\lambda$
6 ▷ Cov – the subtrees covering S in $\mathcal{T}$
7 **for** $j := 1$ **to** $|\mathsf{Cov}|$ **do**
8   ▷ T_j – a subtree in Cov
9   ▷ HID_j – the HID of T_j's root
10    $\overline{c}_j := H((A_{1,\mathsf{HID}_j}^{\mathsf{com}} A_{2,\mathsf{HID}_j})^s,$
       $(B_{1,\mathsf{HID}_j}^{\mathsf{com}} B_{2,\mathsf{HID}_j})^s)$
11    $c_j \leftarrow \mathsf{Enc}(\mathsf{MPK}', \mathsf{HID}_j, \mathsf{com}\|m\|\mathsf{decom})$
12 **for** $j := |\mathsf{Cov}| + 1$ **to** L **do**
13    $\overline{c}_j \leftarrow\!\!\$\ \{0,1\}^\lambda, c_j \leftarrow\!\!\$\ \{0,1\}^{\ell(3\lambda+1+|m|)}$
14 $\hat{c} := \overline{c}_0\|\overline{c}_1\|c_1\| \ldots \|\overline{c}_L\|c_L$
15 $\sigma := F(\hat{k}, \hat{c}), c := \sigma\|\hat{c}\|\mathsf{com}$
16 **return** c

Algorithm: Decrypt(MPK, sk_i, c)
1 **parse** sk_i **as** $((\overline{sk}_{i,1}, sk_{i,1}), \ldots,$
   $(\overline{sk}_{i,n+1}, sk_{i,n+1}))$
2 **parse** c **as** $\sigma\|\hat{c}\|\mathsf{com}$
3 **parse** $\hat{c}$ **as** $\overline{c}_0\|\overline{c}_1\|c_1\| \ldots \|\overline{c}_L\|c_L$
4 $\tilde{c}_0 := \mathsf{mp}^{-1}(\overline{c}_0)$
5 **for** $z := 1$ **to** $n+1$ **do**
6   **parse** $\overline{sk}_{i,z}$ **as** $(\tilde{a}_{1,z}, \tilde{a}_{2,z}, \tilde{b}_{1,z}, \tilde{b}_{2,z})$
7     $tag_z := H(\tilde{c}_0^{\tilde{a}_{1,z}\mathsf{com}+\tilde{a}_{2,z}}, \tilde{c}_0^{\tilde{b}_{1,z}\mathsf{com}+\tilde{b}_{2,z}})$
8   **if** $\exists z \in [1, n+1]\ \exists j \in [1, L] : tag_z = \overline{c}_j$ **then**
9        $m' := \mathsf{Dec}(\mathsf{MPK}', sk_{i,z}, c_j)$
10   **if** $m' \neq \perp$ **then**
11   **parse** m' **as** $\overline{\mathsf{com}}\|m\|\mathsf{decom}$
12   **if** $\overline{\mathsf{com}} = \mathsf{com}$ **then**
13             $\hat{k} := \mathsf{Open}(\mathsf{PK}'', \mathsf{com}, \mathsf{decom})$
14   **if** $\hat{k} \neq \perp \wedge \sigma = F(\hat{k}, \hat{c})$ **then**
15   **return** m
16 **return** $\perp$

Fig. 4. The oABE$-CCA-secure construction. $\mathcal{T}$ is the perfect binary tree with $N = 2^n$ leaves, which represent the users in the system. $\mathsf{HID}_{i|z}$ denotes a prefix of the hierarchical identifier HID_i with length z.

To attain sublinear ciphertexts, we follow the approach of [23], which is based on the Subset Cover Framework [16, 42] (cf. also [21]). We arrange the $N = 2^n$ users in a perfect binary tree with N leaves, and assign to each user (using AIBE$) $n+1$ decryption keys, corresponding to all the nodes in the path to its designated leaf (Line 4 of KeyGen). Each oABE$ ciphertexts consists of multiple AIBE$ components. For efficient decryption, AIBE$ components are tagged using a twin-DH-based [13] technique reminiscent of [24, 39] (Line 10 of Encrypt) so that recipients can single out which AIBE$ component to decrypt, and with which key (Lines 5–8 and 9 of Decrypt). Throughout Encrypt, we make sure that each piece in an oABE\$ ciphertext looks random, with the use of rejection sampling (Lines 3–5), entropy smoothing (Line 10), dummy components (Line 13), and pseudorandom MACs (Line 15) in place of one-time signatures. Forgoing signatures introduce a complication, as the input to the PRF appears to depend on the PRF key $\hat{k}$: the $\bar{c}_j$ values and the oABE\$ components c_j's computed in Lines 10 and 11 are derived from com and decom, which correlate with $\hat{k}$. We solve this circularity by mediating the occurrence of $\hat{k}$ in the ciphertext via the encapsulation scheme of Fig. 3.

Theorem 4.5. *If F is a (t_1, ϵ_1)-hard PRF, Π' is $(t_2, Q_{sk}, Q_d, \epsilon_2)$-AIBE\$-CCA-secure, $\mathcal{H}_{es}$ is a (t_3, ϵ_3)-entropy smoothing hash function, and DDH is (t_4, ϵ_4)-hard in $\mathbb{G}$, then the construction given in Fig. 4 is $\big(t_1 + t_2 + t_3 + t_4, Q_{sk}, Q_d, \big(\epsilon_1 + \epsilon_2 + \epsilon_3 + 2\big(\epsilon_4 + \frac{Q_d}{q}\big)\big) r \log\big(\frac{N}{r}\big)\big)$-oABE\$-CCA-secure, where N is the total number of users and r is the number of revoked users.*

Proof Sketch. We organize our proof as a sequence of games (Game$_0$, $\overline{\text{Game}}_1$, Game$_1$, . . . , $\overline{\text{Game}}_l$, Game$_l$) between an oABE\$-IND-CCA adversary $\mathcal{A}$ and the challenger $\mathcal{C}$, where l denotes the cardinality of the coverset Cov induced by the set of authorized receivers S^* chosen by $\mathcal{A}$ during the *Challenge* phase of the oABE\$-IND-CCA game. In the first game (Game$_0$), $\mathcal{A}$ receives an encryption of m^* for S^* in the *Challenge* phase, and in the last game (Game$_l$), $\mathcal{A}$ receives a uniformly random bit-string of the appropriate length as the challenge ciphertext.

Game$_0$: corresponds to the game given in Definition 4.1 when the challenge bit b^* is fixed to 0. $\mathcal{C}$ computes the challenge ciphertext c^* as follows:

1   $r := N - |S^*|$, $L := \big\lfloor r \log\big(\frac{N}{r}\big)\big\rfloor$

2   $(\hat{k}, \text{com}, \text{decom}) \leftarrow \text{Commit}(\text{PK}'')$

3   **repeat** $s \leftarrow_\$ \mathbb{Z}_q$, $\bar{c}_0 := \text{mp}(g^s)$ **until** $\bar{c}_0 < 2^\lambda$

4   **for** $j := 1$ **to** l **do**

5     $\bar{c}_j := H((A_{1,\text{HID}_j}^{\text{com}} A_{2,\text{HID}_j})^s, (B_{1,\text{HID}_j}^{\text{com}} B_{2,\text{HID}_j})^s)$

6     $c_j \leftarrow \text{Enc}(\text{MPK}', \text{HID}_j, \text{com}\|m^*\|\text{decom})$

7   **for** $j := l+1$ **to** L **do**

8     $\bar{c}_j \leftarrow_\$ \{0,1\}^\lambda$

9     $c_j \leftarrow_\$ \{0,1\}^{\ell(3\lambda+1+|m^*|)}$

10   $\hat{c} := \bar{c}_0 \|\bar{c}_1\| c_1 \| \ldots \|\bar{c}_L\| c_L$

11   $\sigma := F(\hat{k}, \hat{c})$, $c^* := \sigma \|\hat{c}\|\text{com}$

$\overline{\text{Game}}_h (1 \leq h \leq l)$: is similar to Game$_{h-1}$, but, when creating c^*, $\mathcal{C}$ replaces Lines 4–9 with:

1'   **for** $j := 1$ **to** $l - h$ **do**

2' $\bar{c}_j := H((A_{1,\text{HID}_j}^{\text{com}} A_{2,\text{HID}_j})^s, (B_{1,\text{HID}_j}^{\text{com}} B_{2,\text{HID}_j})^s)$

3' $c_j \leftarrow \text{Enc}(\text{MPK}', \text{HID}_j, \text{com}\|m^*\|\text{decom})$

4' $\bar{c}_{l-h+1} := H((A_{1,\text{HID}_{l-h+1}}^{\text{com}} A_{2,\text{HID}_{l-h+1}})^s, (B_{1,\text{HID}_{l-h+1}}^{\text{com}} B_{2,\text{HID}_{l-h+1}})^s)$

5' $c_{l-h+1} \leftarrow_\$ \{0,1\}^{\ell(3\lambda+1+|m^*|)}$

6'   **for** $j := l-h+2$ **to** L **do**

7' $\bar{c}_j \leftarrow_\$ \{0,1\}^\lambda$

8' $c_j \leftarrow_\$ \{0,1\}^{\ell(3\lambda+1+|m^*|)}$

Game$_h$($1 \leq h \leq l$): is similar to $\overline{\text{Game}}_h$, but, when creating c^*, $\mathcal{C}$ replaces
Lines $4'$–$8'$ with:

1″ **for** $j := l - h + 1$ **to** L **do**

2″ $\bar{c}_j \leftarrow\!\!\$ \{0,1\}^\lambda$

3″ $c_j \leftarrow\!\!\$ \{0,1\}^{\ell(3\lambda+1+|m^*|)}$

Note that the only difference between Game$_{h-1}$ and $\overline{\text{Game}}_h$ is that in the former, the ciphertext component c_{l-h+1} is an AIBE\$ ciphertext while in the latter, it is just a random bit string with appropriate length. If $\mathcal{A}$ can distinguish these two games, she can also either break the AIBE\$ security or break the encapsulation mechanism (which eventually leads to breaking the PRF). Therefore, if the underlying PRF F is (t_1, ϵ_1)-hard and the AIBE\$ scheme Π' is $(t_2, Q_{sk}, Q_d, \epsilon_2)$-AIBE\$-CCA-secure, then $\mathcal{A}$'s advantage of distinguishing Game$_{h-1}$ from $\overline{\text{Game}}_h$ must be at most $\epsilon_1 + \epsilon_2$. To formally support this claim, we show in the full version [22] how to reduce an AIBE\$ or a PRF problem instance to an oABE\$ problem instance by building an AIBE\$/PRF adversary $\mathcal{B}$ that uses $\mathcal{A}$ as a subroutine during its execution.

Also note that the only difference between $\overline{\text{Game}}_h$ from Game$_h$ is that in $\overline{\text{Game}}_h$, $\bar{c}_{l-h+1}$ is a well formed tag whereas in Game$_h$, it is a random bit string. We can show that if $\mathcal{H}_{es}$ is an (t_2, ϵ_2)-entropy smoothing family of hash functions and DDH is (t_4, ϵ_4)-hard in $\mathbb{G}$, then $\mathcal{A}$ has at most $\epsilon_3 + 2\left(\epsilon_4 + \frac{Q_d}{q}\right)$ advantage in distinguishing $\overline{\text{Game}}_h$ from Game$_h$ with the help of two intermediate games $\widetilde{\text{Game}}_{1,h}$ and $\widetilde{\text{Game}}_{2,h}$. During the transition from $\overline{\text{Game}}_h$ to $\widetilde{\text{Game}}_{1,h}$, we replace $(B_{1,\text{HID}_{l-h+1}}^{\text{com}} B_{2,\text{HID}_{l-h+1}})^s$ with a random group element $r_2 \in \mathbb{G}$. Next, during the transition from $\widetilde{\text{Game}}_{1,h}$ to $\widetilde{\text{Game}}_{2,h}$, we replace $(A_{1,\text{HID}_{l-h+1}}^{\text{com}} A_{2,\text{HID}_{l-h+1}})^s$ with another random group element $r_1 \in \mathbb{G}$. Finally, during the transition from $\widetilde{\text{Game}}_{2,h}$ to Game$_h$, we replace $H(r_1, r_2)$ with a truly random bit-string of length λ. The idea of the proof of the first two transitions is to reduce from the DDH problem and build a PPT adversary $\mathcal{B}$ that internally executes the oABE\$-IND-CCA game with the adversary $\mathcal{A}$ in order to gain advantage in breaking the DDH assumption. This reduction argument proceeds along the same lines as Lemma 1 of [39]. As for the second transition, we employ the fact that $\mathcal{H}_{es}$ is an entropy smoothing hash function.

Let $\text{Adv}_{\mathcal{A},\Pi}^0$ and $\text{Adv}_{\mathcal{A},\Pi}^l$ denote $\mathcal{A}$'s advantage in winning Game$_0$ and Game$_l$, respectively. Combining the adversary's advantages we explained above in a hybrid argument, we arrive at

$$\left| \text{Adv}_{\mathcal{A},\Pi}^0 - \text{Adv}_{\mathcal{A},\Pi}^l \right| \leq \left(\epsilon_1 + \epsilon_2 + \epsilon_3 + 2\left(\epsilon_4 + \frac{Q_d}{q} \right) \right) r \log\left(\frac{N}{r} \right).$$

5   Constructions of Public-Key Broadcast Steganography

We now present three constructions of broadcast steganography: one for each model of security defined in Sect. 3.2. Our constructions employ the encrypt-then-embed paradigm depicted in Fig. 2, using oABE\$ (Sect. 4) for encryption

Function: Sample(λ, h, H, c)
Input: parameter λ, history h,
    function H, bit-string c
Output: stegotext s
1   $l := |c|$
2   for $i := 1$ to l do
3     $j := 0$
4   repeat
5       $j := j+1, s_i \leftarrow \mathfrak{C}_h$
6   until $H(s_i) = c_i \vee j = \lambda$
7     $h := h \| s_i$
8   $s := s_1 \| \ldots \| s_l$
9   return s

(a) Regular

Function: DSample(λ, H, c, r)
Input: parameter λ, function H,
    bit-string c, randomness r
Output: stegotext s
1   $l := |c|$
2   for $i := 1$ to l do
3     $j := 0$
4   repeat
5       $j := j+1, s_i := \mathsf{Channel}(r^\lambda_{\lambda(i-1)+j})$
6   until $H(s_i) = c_i \vee j = \lambda$
7     $s := s_1 \| \ldots \| s_l$
8   return s

(b) Deterministic

Fig. 5. The rejection-sampler functions

and rejection-sampling [3,5,32] for embedding. In what follows, s_i^σ denotes the ith leftmost non-overlapping substring with length σ of a given bit-string s.

5.1 A BS-CHA-Secure Construction

The rejection-sampler function used in our first construction is given in Fig. 5a. Sample takes as input a security parameter λ, a channel history $h \in \Sigma^*$, a function $H : \Sigma \to \{0,1\}$, and a bit-string $c \in \{0,1\}^*$, and outputs a covertext $s \in \Sigma^*$. Internally, for every bit c_i, Sample attempts to find a covertext $s_i^\sigma \in \Sigma$ such that $H(s_i^\sigma) = c_i$ by repeatedly querying the channel oracle up to λ number of times.[3] This mechanism allows a simple method to extract c from s: compute $c = H(s_1^\sigma) \| \ldots \| H(s_l^\sigma)$ where $l = |s|/\sigma$. As shown in [3,6], if the channel is always informative, H is a strongly universal hash function, and c is uniformly random, then the maximum statistical distance between $s_1 \leftarrow$ Sample(λ, h, H, c) and $s_2 \leftarrow \mathfrak{C}_h^{|c|}$ for any valid $h \in \Sigma^*$ is negligible in the security parameter λ. For simplicity, we denote this statistical distance when $|c| = 1$ by ϵ_1 in the reminder of the paper.

We obtain our BS-CHA-secure scheme by combining the rejection-sampler function from Fig. 5a with our oABE$ scheme (cf. Sect. 4). Formally, given a strongly universal hash function family $\mathcal{H}_{su} = \{H : \Sigma \to \{0,1\}\}$ and an oABE$-CPA-secure oABE$ scheme $\Pi' = $ (Setup', KeyGen', Encrypt', Decrypt') with expansion ℓ (i.e., $|\mathsf{Encrypt}'(\mathsf{MPK}', S, m)| = \ell(|m|)$), we construct a BS-CHA-secure broadcast steganography scheme $\Pi = $ (Setup, KeyGen, Encode, Decode) as shown in Fig. 6.

Theorem 5.1 (Proof in full version [22]). *If the channel is always informative, $\mathcal{H}_{su}$ is a strongly universal hash function family, and Π' is $(t_2, Q_{sk}, \epsilon_2)$-oABE$-CPA-secure, then the construction in Fig. 6 is $(t_2, Q_{sk}, \mu\epsilon_1 + \epsilon_2)$-BS-CHA-secure, where μ is the poly. bound on the total message length.*

---

[3] Sample may fail to find a valid s_i during the λ iterations, but only with negligible probability in the parameter λ.

Algorithm: Setup($1^\lambda, N$)
1 (MPK′, MSK′) ← Setup′($1^\lambda, N$)
2 $H \leftarrow\!\!{\scriptstyle\$}\ \mathcal{H}_{su}$
3 MPK := (MPK′, H)
4 MSK := MSK′
5 **return** (MPK, MSK)

Algorithm: Encode(MPK, S, h, m)
1 $c \leftarrow$ Encrypt′(MPK′, S, m)
2 $s \leftarrow$ Sample(λ, h, H, c)
3 **return** s

Algorithm: KeyGen(MPK, MSK, i)
1 $sk_i \leftarrow$ KeyGen′(MPK′, MSK′, i)
2 **return** sk_i

Algorithm: Decode(MPK, sk_i, s)
1 $l := |s|/\sigma$
2 **for** $j := 1$ to l **do**
3      $c_j := H(s_j^\sigma)$
4 $c := c_1\|\ldots\|c_l$
5 $m := $ Decrypt′(MPK′, sk_i, c)
6 **return** m

Fig. 6. The BS-CHA-secure construction

Remark 5.2. If the oABE\$ scheme employed in Fig. 6 is oABE\$-PDR-CCA-secure, then the resulting BS scheme is BS-PDR-CCA-secure.

5.2 A BS-CCA-Secure Construction

Unfortunately, our first construction fails to provide a BS-CCA-secure broadcast steganography scheme even if the oABE\$ scheme internally used provides oABE\$-CCA security. The problem is that the rejection-sampler function from Fig. 5a allows multiple covertexts corresponding to a given bit-string. However, this limitation can be overcome in the case of channels that are efficiently computable and whose samples are independently distributed. In fact, for channels of this type, Hopper [30] devised a *deterministic* rejection-sampler function DSample that maps a given bit-string to exactly one covertext.

As shown in Fig. 5b, DSample takes in input a security parameter λ, a predicate $H : \Sigma \rightarrow \{0,1\}$ along with a bit-string $c \in \{0,1\}^*$ to embed, and a random bit-string $r \in \{0,1\}^{|c|\cdot\lambda^2}$ that controls the embedding. To sample $s \in \Sigma^*$, for every bit c_i of c, DSample seeks $s_i^\sigma \in \Sigma$ such that $H(s_i^\sigma) = c_i$, by repeatedly drawing from the channel according to the random chunks specified in r. This approach requires that the channel be efficiently computable by a function Channel($\cdot$) whose samples are independent of the history (hence we drop h from its input), but guarantees that an adversary who intercepts a stegotext is unable to tweak it meaningfully. Furthermore, as shown in [3, 6, 31], if H is a strongly universal hash function, and c and r are uniformly random, then the statistical distance between stegotexts produced by DSample and innocent covertexts sampled from Channel($\cdot$) is a negligible function ϵ_1 of λ.

Figure 7 reports the details of our BS-IND-CCA-secure scheme $\Pi = $ (Setup, KeyGen, Encode, Decode), based on a strongly universal hash function family $\mathcal{H}_{su}$, a variable-length pseudorandom generator (vPRG) $G : \{0,1\}^\lambda \times \mathbb{Z} \rightarrow \{0,1\}^*$ (whose second input sets the output length), and an oABE\$-IND-CCA-secure scheme $\Pi' = $ (Setup′, KeyGen′, Encrypt′, Decrypt′) with expansion ℓ.

Theorem 5.3 (Proof in full version [22]). *If the channel is always informative, $\mathcal{H}_{su}$ is a strongly universal hash function family, G is a (t_2, ϵ_2)-hard vPRG, and Π' is $(t_3, Q_{sk}, Q_d, \epsilon_3)$-oABE\$-CCA-secure, then the construction in Fig. 7*

Algorithm: Setup($1^\lambda, N$)
1 $(\mathsf{MPK}', \mathsf{MSK}') \leftarrow \mathsf{Setup}'(1^\lambda, N)$
2 $H \leftarrow\!\!\$ \; \mathcal{H}_{su}$
3 $\mathsf{MPK} := (\mathsf{MPK}', H, G)$
4 $\mathsf{MSK} := \mathsf{MSK}'$
5 **return** $(\mathsf{MPK}, \mathsf{MSK})$

Algorithm: Encode(MPK, S, m)
1 $\hat{r} \leftarrow\!\!\$ \; \{0,1\}^\lambda$
2 $c \leftarrow \mathsf{Encrypt}'(\mathsf{MPK}', S, \hat{r}\|m)$
3 $r := G(\hat{r}, |c| \cdot \lambda^2)$
4 $s := \mathsf{DSample}(\lambda, H, c, r)$
5 **return** s

Algorithm: KeyGen($\mathsf{MPK}, \mathsf{MSK}, i$)
1 $sk_i \leftarrow \mathsf{KeyGen}'(\mathsf{MPK}', \mathsf{MSK}', i)$
2 **return** sk_i

Algorithm: Decode(MPK, sk_i, s)
1 $l := |s|/\sigma$
2 **for** $j := 1$ **to** l **do**
3     $c_j := H(s_j^\sigma)$
4 $c := c_1\| \ldots \|c_l$
5 $m' := \mathsf{Decrypt}'(\mathsf{MPK}', sk_i, c)$
6 **if** $m' \neq \bot$ **then**
7   **parse** m' **as** $\hat{r}\|m$
8     $r := G(\hat{r}, l \cdot \lambda^2)$
9   **if** $\mathsf{DSample}(\lambda, H, c, r) = s$ **then**
10   **return** m
11 **return** $\bot$

Fig. 7. The BS-CCA-secure construction

is $(t_2 + t_3, Q_{sk}, Q_d, \mu\epsilon_1 + \epsilon_2 + \epsilon_3)$-BS-CCA-secure, where μ is the poly. bound on the total message length.

6   Extensions and Future Work

As in the case of broadcast encryption, one may consider extensions of the notion of broadcast steganography that enhance the setting discussed in this paper with additional functionality or security properties. In particular, while broadcast steganography natively protects the recipients' identities from outsiders, it does not aim to prevent recipients from finding out about each other. The natural solution for that is *anonymous* broadcast steganography (AnoBS). By extending the anonymous broadcast encryption schemes of [7, 39] to support ciphertext pseudorandomness, we can use them in place of our oABE$ to achieve fully anonymous broadcast steganography. The resulting AnoBS scheme, however, would have ciphertexts with length *linear* in the number of receivers.

Acknowledgments. Nelly Fazio's research is sponsored in part by NSF CA-REER award #1253927 and NSF award #1117675, and by PSC-CUNY award 64578-00 42 (jointly funded by the Professional Staff Congress and the City University of New York). Nelly Fazio and Irippuge Milinda Perera are supported in part by the U.S. Army Research Laboratory and the U.K. Ministry of Defence under Agreement Number W911NF-06-3-0001. Antonio Nicolosi's research is sponsored in part by NSF awards #1117679 and #1040784. The views and conclusions contained in this document are those of the authors and should not be interpreted as representing the official policies, either expressed or implied, of the U.S. Army Research Laboratory, the U.S. Government, the U.K. Ministry of Defence or the U.K. Government. The U.S. and U.K. Governments are authorized to reproduce and distribute reprints for Government purposes notwithstanding any copyright notation hereon.

References

1. Abdalla, M., Bellare, M., Catalano, D., Kiltz, E., Kohno, T., Lange, T., Malone-Lee, J., Neven, G., Paillier, P., Shi, H.: Searchable encryption revisited: Consistency properties, relation to Anonymous IBE, and extensions. In: Shoup, V. (ed.) CRYPTO 2005. LNCS, vol. 3621, pp. 205–222. Springer, Heidelberg (2005)
2. Agrawal, S., Boyen, X.: Identity-based encryption from lattices in the standard model (2009) (manuscript), http://www.cs.stanford.edu/~xb/ab09/
3. von Ahn, L., Hopper, N.J.: Public-key steganography. In: Cachin, C., Camenisch, J.L. (eds.) EUROCRYPT 2004. LNCS, vol. 3027, pp. 323–341. Springer, Heidelberg (2004)
4. von Ahn, L., Hopper, N.J., Langford, J.: Covert two-party computation. In: ACM Symposium on Theory of Computing, STOC, pp. 513–522 (2005)
5. Anderson, R., Petitcolas, F.: On the limits of steganography. IEEE Journal on Selected Areas in Communications 16(4), 474–481 (1998)
6. Backes, M., Cachin, C.: Public-key steganography with active attacks. In: Kilian, J. (ed.) TCC 2005. LNCS, vol. 3378, pp. 210–226. Springer, Heidelberg (2005)
7. Barth, A., Boneh, D., Waters, B.: Privacy in encrypted content distribution using private broadcast encryption. In: Di Crescenzo, G., Rubin, A. (eds.) FC 2006. LNCS, vol. 4107, pp. 52–64. Springer, Heidelberg (2006)
8. Berkovits, S.: How to broadcast a secret. In: Davies, D.W. (ed.) EUROCRYPT 1991. LNCS, vol. 547, pp. 535–541. Springer, Heidelberg (1991)
9. Boneh, D., Gentry, C., Waters, B.: Collusion resistant broadcast encryption with short ciphertexts and private keys. In: Shoup, V. (ed.) CRYPTO 2005. LNCS, vol. 3621, pp. 258–275. Springer, Heidelberg (2005)
10. Boneh, D., Katz, J.: Improved efficiency for CCA-secure cryptosystems built using identity-based encryption. In: Menezes, A. (ed.) CT-RSA 2005. LNCS, vol. 3376, pp. 87–103. Springer, Heidelberg (2005)
11. Boyen, X., Waters, B.: Anonymous hierarchical identity-based encryption (without random oracles). In: Dwork, C. (ed.) CRYPTO 2006. LNCS, vol. 4117, pp. 290–307. Springer, Heidelberg (2006)
12. Cachin, C.: An information-theoretic model for steganography. Information and Computation 192(1), 41–56 (2004)
13. Cash, D.M., Kiltz, E., Shoup, V.: The twin Diffie-Hellman problem and applications. In: Smart, N.P. (ed.) EUROCRYPT 2008. LNCS, vol. 4965, pp. 127–145. Springer, Heidelberg (2008)
14. Chandran, N., Goyal, V., Ostrovsky, R., Sahai, A.: Covert multi-party computation. In: IEEE Symposium on Foundations of Computer Science, FOCS, pp. 238–248 (2007)
15. Dedic, N., Itkis, G., Reyzin, L., Russell, S.: Upper and Lower Bounds on Black-Box Steganography. Journal of Cryptology 22(3), 365–394 (2009)
16. Dodis, Y., Fazio, N.: Public key broadcast encryption for stateless receivers. In: Feigenbaum, J. (ed.) DRM 2002. LNCS, vol. 2696, pp. 61–80. Springer, Heidelberg (2003)
17. Dodis, Y., Fazio, N.: Public-key trace and revoke scheme secure against adaptive chosen ciphertext attack. In: Desmedt, Y.G. (ed.) PKC 2003. LNCS, vol. 2567, pp. 100–115. Springer, Heidelberg (2002)
18. Dodis, Y., Fazio, N., Kiayias, A., Yung, M.: Scalable public-key tracing and revoking. In: ACM Symposium on Principles of Distributed Computing, pp. 190–199 (2003); invited to the Special Issue of Journal of Distributed Computing, PODC 2003 (2003)

19. Dodis, Y., Fazio, N., Lysyanskaya, A., Yao, D.: ID-based encryption for complex hierarchies with applications to forward security and broadcast encryption. In: ACM Conference on Computer and Communications Security, pp. 354–363 (2004)
20. Dodis, Y., Katz, J.: Chosen-ciphertext security of multiple encryption. In: Kilian, J. (ed.) TCC 2005. LNCS, vol. 3378, pp. 188–209. Springer, Heidelberg (2005)
21. Fazio, N.: On Cryptographic Techniques for Digital Rights Management. Ph.D. thesis, New York University (2006)
22. Fazio, N., Nicolosi, A.R., Perera, I.M.: Broadcast steganography. Cryptology ePrint Archive, Report 2013/078 (2013)
23. Fazio, N., Perera, I.M.: Outsider-anonymous broadcast encryption with sublinear ciphertexts. In: Fischlin, M., Buchmann, J., Manulis, M. (eds.) PKC 2012. LNCS, vol. 7293, pp. 225–242. Springer, Heidelberg (2012)
24. Fazio, N., Perera, I.M.: Outsider-anonymous broadcast encryption with sublinear ciphertexts. Cryptology ePrint Archive, Report 2012/129 (2012), full Version of [23]
25. Fiat, A., Naor, M.: Broadcast encryption. In: Stinson, D.R. (ed.) CRYPTO 1993. LNCS, vol. 773, pp. 480–491. Springer, Heidelberg (1994)
26. Garay, J.A., Staddon, J., Wool, A.: Long-lived broadcast encryption. In: Bellare, M. (ed.) CRYPTO 2000. LNCS, vol. 1880, pp. 333–352. Springer, Heidelberg (2000)
27. Gentry, C.: Practical identity-based encryption without random oracles. In: Vaudenay, S. (ed.) EUROCRYPT 2006. LNCS, vol. 4004, pp. 445–464. Springer, Heidelberg (2006)
28. Gentry, C., Waters, B.: Adaptive security in broadcast encryption systems (with short ciphertexts). In: Joux, A. (ed.) EUROCRYPT 2009. LNCS, vol. 5479, pp. 171–188. Springer, Heidelberg (2009)
29. Halevy, D., Shamir, A.: The LSD broadcast encryption scheme. In: Yung, M. (ed.) CRYPTO 2002. LNCS, vol. 2442, pp. 47–60. Springer, Heidelberg (2002)
30. Hopper, N.J.: Toward a Theory of Steganography. Ph.D. thesis, Carnegie Mellon University (2004)
31. Hopper, N.J.: On steganographic chosen covertext security. In: Caires, L., Italiano, G.F., Monteiro, L., Palamidessi, C., Yung, M. (eds.) ICALP 2005. LNCS, vol. 3580, pp. 311–323. Springer, Heidelberg (2005)
32. Hopper, N.J., Langford, J., von Ahn, L.: Provably Secure Steganography. In: Yung, M. (ed.) CRYPTO 2002. LNCS, vol. 2442, pp. 77–92. Springer, Heidelberg (2002)
33. Impagliazzo, R., Zuckerman, D.: How to recycle random bits. In: IEEE Symposium on Foundations of Computer Science—FOCS, pp. 248–253 (1989)
34. Katzenbeisser, S., Petitcolas, F.A.: Defining security in steganographic systems. In: Security and Watermarking of Multimedia Contents IV, pp. 50–56 (2002)
35. Kiayias, A., Raekow, Y., Russell, A.: Efficient steganography with provable security guarantees. In: Barni, M., Herrera-Joancomartí, J., Katzenbeisser, S., Pérez-González, F. (eds.) IH 2005. LNCS, vol. 3727, pp. 118–130. Springer, Heidelberg (2005)
36. Kiayias, A., Russell, A., Shashidhar, N.: Key-efficient steganography with provable security guarantees. In: Information Hiding—IH, pp. 118–130 (2012)
37. Kiayias, A., Samari, K.: Lower bounds for private broadcast encryption. In: Kirchner, M., Ghosal, D. (eds.) IH 2012. LNCS, vol. 7692, pp. 176–190. Springer, Heidelberg (2013)
38. Le, T., Kurosawa, K.: Efficient Public Key Steganography Secure Against Adaptive Chosen Stegotext Attacks. Cryptology ePrint Archive, Report 2003/244 (2003)
39. Libert, B., Paterson, K.G., Quaglia, E.A.: Anonymous broadcast encryption. In: Fischlin, M., Buchmann, J., Manulis, M. (eds.) PKC 2012. LNCS, vol. 7293, pp. 206–224. Springer, Heidelberg (2012)

40. Lysyanskaya, A., Meyerovich, M.: Provably Secure Steganography with Imperfect Sampling. In: Yung, M., Dodis, Y., Kiayias, A., Malkin, T. (eds.) PKC 2006. LNCS, vol. 3958, pp. 123–139. Springer, Heidelberg (2006)
41. Mazurczyk, W., Karas, M., Szczypiorski, K.: Skyde: A skype-based steganographic method (2013), http://arxiv.org/abs/1301.3632
42. Naor, D., Naor, M., Lotspiech, J.: Revocation and tracing schemes for stateless receivers. In: Kilian, J. (ed.) CRYPTO 2001. LNCS, vol. 2139, pp. 41–62. Springer, Heidelberg (2001)
43. Pedersen, T.P.: Non-interactive and information-theoretic secure verifiable secret sharing. In: Feigenbaum, J. (ed.) CRYPTO 1991. LNCS, vol. 576, pp. 129–140. Springer, Heidelberg (1992)
44. Simmons, G.: The Prisoners' Problem and the Subliminal Channel. In: Advances in Cryptology—CRYPTO, pp. 51–67 (1983)
45. The Economist: Speaking with silence (February 2013)
46. Zuckerman, D.: General weak random sources. In: IEEE Symposium on Foundations of Computer Science—FOCS, pp. 534–543 (1990)

Practical Dual-Receiver Encryption
Soundness, Complete Non-malleability, and Applications

Sherman S.M. Chow[1], Matthew Franklin[2], and Haibin Zhang[2]

[1] Department of Information Engineering, Chinese University of Hong Kong
sherman@ie.cuhk.edu.hk
[2] Department of Computer Science, University of California Davis
{franklin,hbzhang}@cs.ucdavis.edu

Abstract. We reformalize and recast dual-receiver encryption (DRE) proposed in CCS '04, a public-key encryption (PKE) scheme for encrypting to two *independent* recipients in one shot. We start by defining the crucial *soundness* property for DRE, which ensures that two recipients will get the same decryption result. While conceptually simple, DRE with soundness turns out to be a powerful primitive for various goals for PKE, such as complete non-malleability (CNM) and plaintext-awareness (PA). We then construct *practical* DRE schemes without random oracles under the Bilinear Decisional Diffie-Hellman assumption, while prior approaches rely on random oracles or inefficient non-interactive zero-knowledge proofs. Finally, we investigate further applications or extensions of DRE, including DRE with CNM, combined use of DRE and PKE, strengthening two types of PKE schemes with plaintext equality test, off-the-record messaging with a stronger notion of deniability, etc.

Keywords: Dual receiver encryption, soundness, complete non-malleability, plaintext-awareness, combined encryption, off-the-record messaging.

1 Introduction

Dual-receiver encryption (DRE), introduced by Diament, Lee, Keromytis, and Yung [13] (DLKY), is a special kind of public-key encryption (PKE) which allows a ciphertext to be decrypted into the same plaintext by two *independent* users. More concretely, the DRE encryption algorithm produces a ciphertext by taking as input a message and two independently generated public keys pk_1 and pk_2. Both receivers (owners of pk_1 and pk_2) will get the same decryption result.

DRE is a handy tool when sensitive information (may it be political, financial, or medical) should be backed up, and potentially decryptable by some other party (or a threshold number of designated parties which further requires the DRE to support threshold decryption). These scenarios are abundant, e.g., for fulfilling the requirements of law, regulation, policy, or personal needs.

On the other hand, while it appears to be conceptually simple, DRE turns out to be a valuable tool in many cryptographic applications. For example, DLKY show how to construct security puzzles for rate-limiting remote users, e.g., in

J. Benaloh (Ed.): CT-RSA 2014, LNCS 8366, pp. 85–105, 2014.
© Springer International Publishing Switzerland 2014

the TLS protocol [13]. Dodis, Katz, Smith, and Walfish describe the use of DRE to address the deniable authentication problem [14].

Soundness. A crucial requirement for the above applications is that "the ciphertext will be decrypted to the same message by either private key." Unfortunately, the original formulation due to DLKY only ensures the correctness property for honestly generated ciphertexts. As our first contribution, we strengthen the definition by introducing new soundness security notions which formalize the intuition that "two receivers will get the same plaintext and they do *know* this fact."[1] The importance of soundness can be seen when we discuss our second contribution on various applications or extensions of DRE with soundness[2].

Complete Non-Malleability. Complete non-malleability (CNM) [15,32] prohibits adversaries from computing encryptions of related plaintexts even under adversarially generated public keys. This notion is useful both in theory and practice. One can transform our DRE scheme which is secure against chosen-ciphertext attacks (CCA) to a CNM-PKE scheme in the common reference string (CRS) model. Namely, given a DRE scheme, one of the public keys of DRE is added to the CRS, whereas the other serves as the public key of the new scheme; encryption algorithm remains the same as the one for DRE for either public key, while the decryption algorithm is simply the one for DRE decryption scheme with respect to the secret key of the other receiver.

We also study CNM-DRE which remains secure for dynamically generated public keys. It also leads to *dual receiver non-malleable commitment*, a new primitive of independent interests.

Plaintext-Awareness. Roughly, *plaintext-awareness* captures the property that an adversary can decrypt any ciphertext it creates. Assuming *key registration*, Herzog, Liskov, and Micali [19] build a plaintext-aware PKE from general zero-knowledge proof of knowledge and non-malleable non-interactive zero-knowledge (NIZK) proof, which is rather inefficient. We show that one can simply use our DRE schemes which leads to efficient registration-based plaintext-aware PKE.

More Applications. We investigate further applications of our DRE in our full paper [7]. They include two types of PKE schemes with plaintext equality test [34,24,20,8,37], deniable authentication for off-the-record messaging [4,14], practical PKE with non-interactive opening [11], and useful security puzzles without random oracles [13,35].

On Constructing DREs. In this paper, we propose an efficient construction of DRE, a useful primitive that helps achieving various goals as we described. Indeed, the known DRE constructions in the literature are either in the random oracle model (ROM), or rely on CRS to realize the idea of Naor-Yung two-key encryption [25]. The DLKY-DRE scheme [13] uses REACT transformation [26] to achieve CCA-security under the Gap-Bilinear Diffie-Hellman

---

[1] Yet, we can show that the DLKY construction (in the ROM) satisfies our soundness.
[2] When there is no ambiguity from context, we omit "with soundness".

(GBDH) assumption [27].[3] Building DRE using (the most efficient instantiation of) Groth-Sahai proof system [18] will take nearly one hundred group elements [31].[4] From another perspective, given the difficulties, Zhang, Hanaoka, and Imai [35] rely on identity-based encryption [3] to solve the problems that DRE would (in constructing useful security puzzles [13,35]). All these are suggesting that constructing an efficient DRE without random oracles is *non-trivial*.

Broadcast Encryption. While encryption schemes for multiple recipients exist such as broadcast encryption, the group manager needs to prepare the decryption keys for users and can thus decrypt any ciphertexts. The key generation may also be stateful, and the decryption algorithm may also create different intermediate variables for different users. On the other hand, it is natural for DRE to satisfy *independence* of receivers (except, they may share the same security parameter and cryptographic group, and of course, they can be certified by a trusted party). In general, broadcast encryption is more expensive than dual-receiver encryption.

Properties for DRE. In light of these discussion, a *good* DRE should satisfy:

Security under standard assumptions, yet with practical efficiency. As other primitives, a DRE preferably should avoid the use of the less-studied cryptographic assumptions, and its security proof should avoid the use of the ROM. At the same time, it should be efficient so it can be used directly in practice, or as a building block, without introducing much overhead.

Symmetry. Naturally, the role of two receivers should be "symmetric" with respect to all DRE algorithms. This means that the same key generation algorithm will be executed by any user, and the resulting key can be used as the "first" receiver or the "second" receiver, up to the wish of the encryptor. Otherwise, if a DRE user is required to use keys in two different formats for different "positions" in the receivers list, that means each user should generate both kinds of keys, and two implementations (either as software or as circuit) for the same functionality (e.g., decryption) are required. It is also somewhat counter-intuitive to have different decryption algorithms when they can take the CRS as an input.

Symmetry is also useful for applications when the message sender takes the role as one of the receivers of the DRE as well. Section 4 will discuss registration-based plaintext-aware encryption from DRE which benefits from this property.

Public verifiability. Verifying the validity of a ciphertext might be done without decrypting. If a scheme satisfies this requirement we call it publicly verifiable. It is one of the most common cryptographic tasks to prove that two ciphertexts (or commitments) are well-formed and encrypting (or committing to) the same plaintext. In particular, it is useful to achieve threshold decryption [5].

Our Proposed Construction. We provide a practical solution of DRE based on the well-known Bilinear Decisional Diffie-Hellman (BDDH) assumption without random oracles. By analogy with the well-known notions of key encapsulation mechanism (KEM) and hybrid encryption, we also introduce the notions

---

[3] In our full paper [7], we present a more efficient, redundancy-free DRE in the ROM.

[4] The scheme is first described by Smith and Youn in an unpublished manuscript [31] which we will review in our full paper [7].

of dual-receiver KEM (DKEM) and hybrid DRE. It is followed by an efficient construction of DKEM secure under the BDDH assumption. Both of our DRE and DKEM constructions are symmetric, publicly verifiable, and competitive with the most efficient PKE schemes. Also, both can be easily extended to support threshold decryption, which is desirable for the backup application. Both constructions require a trusted setup to acquire a common bilinear group, but all receivers can create their own secret keys, in contrast to the broadcast encryption approach where the users are either assigned with a secret keys or they need to interact with each other before deriving their own secret keys.

Combining DRE and PKE without Key Separation. DRE is of limited use *per se*. For conventional usages, one expects a *combined encryption scheme* which can *securely* provide the functionalities of both DRE and regular PKE simultaneously. This enables users to employ the same key to achieve both functions, and minimizes the risk of misuse and the times of registration with the trusted party. Of course, the combination makes sense only if the schemes retain their efficiency. We first define the security requirements formally, and then give a construction without random oracles from the BDDH assumption which is nearly as efficient as the DRE scheme proposed.

DRE with Complete Non-malleability. It is proven that non-interactive CNM-PKE does not exist with simulation-based black-box simulation in the standard model [15]. A similar impossibility result applies to DRE. We thus instead explore how to design CNM-DRE in the CRS model, just like the study of CNM-PKE in the literature [32,23]. This not only provides a stronger notion for DRE but also for two kinds of plaintext equality testing (as illustrated in our full paper [7]), which apply to settings where on-line authorities are available and adversaries might dynamically and maliciously generate public keys. However, it does not seem to be easy to build CNM-DRE either. Intuitively, this new primitive requires three trapdoors, two of which must be symmetric. We provide two different paradigms in the CRS model. One is to combine Naor-Yung [25] and Rackoff-Simon [29] paradigms, while the other relies on lossy trapdoor functions [28]. Both of these general paradigms can give reasonably efficient instantiations based on a number of assumptions.

2   Refining the Security Model of DRE

All the definitions and security experiments to be described are in the common reference string (CRS) model, where there is a trusted CRS generation algorithm that takes as input the security parameter, and outputs a CRS, which will be part of the inputs of the other algorithms. However, they can be easily adopted for the standard model where the CRS is simply the common security parameter.

Public-Key Dual Receiver Encryption. A public-key *dual receiver encryption* scheme $\mathcal{DRE} = (\mathsf{CGen}_{\mathrm{DRE}}, \mathsf{Gen}_{\mathrm{DRE}}, \mathsf{Enc}_{\mathrm{DRE}}, \mathsf{Dec}_{\mathrm{DRE}})$ consists of algorithms:

-   $\mathsf{CGen}_{\mathrm{DRE}}(1^k)$: The randomized *CRS generation* algorithm takes as input a security parameter k and outputs a CRS crs; we write $\mathsf{crs} \xleftarrow{\$} \mathsf{CGen}_{\mathrm{DRE}}(1^k)$.

- $\mathsf{Gen}_{\mathrm{DRE}}(\mathsf{crs})$: The randomized *key generation* algorithm takes as input crs and outputs a public/secret key pair (pk, sk); we write (pk_1, sk_1) and (pk_2, sk_2) for the key pairs of two independent users. Without loss of generality, for the rest of the paper, we assume $pk_1 <^d pk_2$, where $<^d$ is a "less-than" operator based on lexicographic order.

- $\mathsf{Enc}_{\mathrm{DRE}}(\mathsf{crs}, pk_1, pk_2, M)$: The randomized *encryption algorithm* takes as input crs, two public keys pk_1 and pk_2 (such that $pk_1 <^d pk_2$) and message M, and outputs a ciphertext C; we write $C \xleftarrow{\$} \mathsf{Enc}_{\mathrm{DRE}}(\mathsf{crs}, pk_1, pk_2, M)$.

- $\mathsf{Dec}_{\mathrm{DRE}}(\mathsf{crs}, pk_1, pk_2, sk_i, C)$: The deterministic *decryption algorithm* takes two public keys pk_1 and pk_2 ($pk_1 <^d pk_2$), one of the secret keys sk_i ($i \in \{0, 1\}$), and a ciphertext C as input, and outputs a message M_i (which may be the special symbol $\bot$); we write $M_i \leftarrow \mathsf{Dec}_{\mathrm{DRE}}(\mathsf{crs}, pk_1, pk_2, sk_i, C)$. We may simply write $M_i \leftarrow \mathsf{Dec}_{\mathrm{DRE}}(sk_i, C)$ when there is no ambiguity.

For consistency, we require that, if $\mathsf{crs} \xleftarrow{\$} \mathsf{CGen}_{\mathrm{DRE}}(1^k)$, $(pk_1, sk_1) \xleftarrow{\$} \mathsf{Gen}_{\mathrm{DRE}}(\mathsf{crs})$ and $(pk_2, sk_2) \xleftarrow{\$} \mathsf{Gen}_{\mathrm{DRE}}(\mathsf{crs})$ where $pk_1 <^d pk_2$, and $C \xleftarrow{\$} \mathsf{Enc}_{\mathrm{DRE}}(\mathsf{crs}, pk_1, pk_2, M)$, we have the probability $\Pr[\mathsf{Dec}_{\mathrm{DRE}}(\mathsf{crs}, pk_1, pk_2, sk_1, C) = \mathsf{Dec}_{\mathrm{DRE}}(\mathsf{crs}, pk_1, pk_2, sk_2, C) = M] = 1$ for all integers k and messages M, where the probability is taken over the coins of all the algorithms above. We omit the inclusion of crs when context is clear. Our syntax is slightly different from the initially proposed one [13] for the sake of clarity. We explicitly regard DRE encryption and decryption algorithms as functions of the public keys of two *independent* receivers.

Extending the DLKY Notion—Soundness. In DLKY [13], only the *basic* correctness property is taken into account, which ensures that if the sender honestly follows the protocol then the two receivers will get the same plaintext. However, it is fairly weak or even problematic since there exist solutions satisfying the basic correctness requirement yet failing to provide the functionality of DRE required by its applications. For instance, one can pick a conventional PKE scheme to encrypt the same message using two independent users' public keys as a potential solution of DRE with correctness for a honest sender, but a cheating sender can simply encrypt different messages.

We thus need to formalize the intuition of this rather basic property that any adversary cannot "cheat" by creating a ciphertext which can be decrypted to two different plaintexts. It is also not allowed that one party decrypts it to a message m, while the other decrypts it to $\bot$, i.e., it is a valid ciphertext for one but invalid for another. Besides, there is an additional goal of DRE — both receivers "know" that the ciphertext can be decrypted to the same result. Formally, we consider the following experiment that is associated to an adversary $\mathcal{A}$:

Experiment $\mathbf{Exp}^{\mathrm{sound}}_{\mathcal{DRE}, \mathcal{A}}(k)$

$\mathsf{crs} \xleftarrow{\$} \mathsf{CGen}_{\mathrm{DRE}}(1^k)$

$(pk_1, sk_1) \xleftarrow{\$} \mathsf{Gen}_{\mathrm{DRE}}(\mathsf{crs}); (pk_2, sk_2) \xleftarrow{\$} \mathsf{Gen}_{\mathrm{DRE}}(\mathsf{crs})\ (pk_1 <^d pk_2)$

$C \xleftarrow{\$} \mathcal{A}(\mathsf{crs}, pk_1, sk_1, pk_2, sk_2)$

if $\mathsf{Dec}_{\mathrm{DRE}}(sk_1, C) \neq \mathsf{Dec}_{\mathrm{DRE}}(sk_2, C)$ **then**

return 1 else return 0

We define the advantage of $\mathcal{A}$ in the above experiment as

$$\mathbf{Adv}_{\mathcal{DRE},\mathcal{A}}^{\mathrm{sound}}(k) = \Pr[\mathbf{Exp}_{\mathcal{DRE},\mathcal{A}}^{\mathrm{sound}}(k) = 1].$$

$\mathcal{DRE}$ satisfies *soundness*, if for any adversary $\mathcal{A}$, $\mathbf{Adv}_{\mathcal{DRE},\mathcal{A}}^{\mathrm{sound}}(k)$ is negligible in the security parameter k, where the probability is taken over the choice of $\mathsf{crs} \xleftarrow{\$} \mathsf{CGen}_{\mathrm{DRE}}(1^k)$, $(pk_1, sk_1) \xleftarrow{\$} \mathsf{Gen}_{\mathrm{DRE}}(\mathsf{crs})$, $(pk_2, sk_2) \xleftarrow{\$} \mathsf{Gen}_{\mathrm{DRE}}(\mathsf{crs})$, and coins of $\mathcal{A}$. The adversary can be either computationally bounded or unbounded. If the advantage is always equal to 0, we say that $\mathcal{DRE}$ has *perfect soundness*.

Though DLKY did not formalize any soundness notion, we show in our full paper [7] that the CCA-secure DRE [13] remains a sound and non-trivial DRE which underscores their wisdom in designing DRE.

Weakening/Strengthening Soundness Notions. The above soundness notion allows the adversary to know the secret keys of targeted receivers. One could weaken it by providing the adversary with the full decryption oracles instead of secret keys. Given two honestly generated public keys pk_1 and pk_2, we define the *weak-soundness* advantage $\mathbf{Adv}_{\mathcal{DRE},\mathcal{A}}^{\mathrm{w\text{-}sound}}(k)$ of adversary $\mathcal{A}$ as

$$\Pr[\mathsf{crs} \xleftarrow{\$} \mathsf{CGen}_{\mathrm{DRE}}(1^k); C \xleftarrow{\$} \mathcal{A}^{\mathrm{Dec}_{\mathrm{DRE}}(sk_1, \cdot), \mathrm{Dec}_{\mathrm{DRE}}(sk_2, \cdot)}(\mathsf{crs}, pk_1, pk_2)$$
$$: \mathsf{Dec}_{\mathrm{DRE}}(sk_1, C) \neq \mathsf{Dec}_{\mathrm{DRE}}(sk_2, C)].$$

$\mathcal{DRE}$ satisfies *weak soundness*, if for any $\mathcal{A}$, $\mathbf{Adv}_{\mathcal{DRE},\mathcal{A}}^{\mathrm{w\text{-}sound}}(k)$ is negligible in the security parameter k, where the probability is taken over the random choices of $\mathsf{crs} \xleftarrow{\$} \mathsf{CGen}_{\mathrm{DRE}}(1^k)$, $(pk_1, sk_1) \xleftarrow{\$} \mathsf{Gen}_{\mathrm{DRE}}(\mathsf{crs})$, $(pk_2, sk_2) \xleftarrow{\$} \mathsf{Gen}_{\mathrm{DRE}}(\mathsf{crs})$, and $\mathcal{A}$.

On the other hand, we can give a stronger soundness notion by allowing the adversary to adversarially choose public keys where it does not even know the corresponding secret keys. We have to be a little careful here. Some encryption scheme might support valid-looking keys such that the adversary might produce ciphertexts that can be decrypted in different ways. We call an encryption scheme *admissible* if there is an efficient public verification algorithm such that any valid public key pk that passes the verification algorithm must only correspond to one unique secret key sk. For instance, the basic ElGamal encryption scheme is admissible. In the context of DRE, we *only* consider admissible encryption schemes. If $\mathcal{DRE}$ is an admissible dual receiver encryption scheme and $\mathcal{A}$ is an adversary, we define the *strong-soundness* advantage $\mathbf{Adv}_{\mathcal{DRE},\mathcal{A}}^{\mathrm{s\text{-}sound}}(k)$ of $\mathcal{A}$ as

$$\Pr[\mathsf{crs} \xleftarrow{\$} \mathsf{CGen}_{\mathrm{DRE}}(1^k); (C, pk_1, pk_2) \xleftarrow{\$} \mathcal{A}(\mathsf{crs}): \mathsf{Dec}_{\mathrm{DRE}}(sk_1, C) \neq \mathsf{Dec}_{\mathrm{DRE}}(sk_2, C)],$$

where, above, sk_1 and sk_2 are the unique secret keys of pk_1 and pk_2, respectively, and both the public and secret keys can be chosen by the adversary. $\mathcal{DRE}$ satisfies the *strong soundness* property if for any adversary $\mathcal{A}$, we have that $\mathbf{Adv}_{\mathcal{DRE},\mathcal{A}}^{\mathrm{s\text{-}sound}}(k)$ is negligible in the security parameter k, where the probability is taken over coins of $\mathcal{A}$. Jumping ahead, we stress that the above notion is useful when speaking of completely non-malleable DRE (CNM-DRE).

Security of DRE against Chosen-Ciphertext Attacks. DRE's soundness makes one of the two decryption oracles redundant. To simplify the experiment modelling CCA-security without loss of generality, we assume that the adversary is only given the decryption oracle of the first receiver.

Experiment $\mathbf{Exp}^{\mathrm{cca}}_{\mathcal{DRE},\mathcal{A}}(k)$

    $\mathsf{crs} \xleftarrow{\$} \mathsf{CGen}_{\mathrm{DRE}}(1^k)$

    $(pk_1, sk_1) \xleftarrow{\$} \mathsf{Gen}_{\mathrm{DRE}}(\mathsf{crs}); (pk_2, sk_2) \xleftarrow{\$} \mathsf{Gen}_{\mathrm{DRE}}(\mathsf{crs})\ (pk_1 <^d pk_2)$

    $(M_0, M_1, \mathsf{s}) \xleftarrow{\$} \mathcal{A}^{\mathsf{Dec}_{\mathrm{DRE}}(sk_1, \cdot)}(\mathsf{find}, \mathsf{crs}, pk_1, pk_2)$

    $b \xleftarrow{\$} \{0, 1\}; C^* \xleftarrow{\$} \mathsf{Enc}_{\mathrm{DRE}}(\mathsf{crs}, pk_1, pk_2, M_b)$

    $b' \xleftarrow{\$} \mathcal{A}^{\mathsf{Dec}_{\mathrm{DRE}}(sk_1, \cdot)}(\mathsf{guess}, C^*, \mathsf{s})$

    if $b' = b$ **then return** 1 **else return** 0

In the find stage, it is required that $|M_0| = |M_1|$. In the guess stage, adversary $\mathcal{A}$ is not allowed to query $\mathsf{Dec}_{\mathrm{DRE}}(sk_1, \cdot)$ or $\mathsf{Dec}_{\mathrm{DRE}}(sk_2, \cdot)$ on the challenge ciphertext C^*. We define the advantage of $\mathcal{A}$ in the above experiment as

$$\mathbf{Adv}^{\mathrm{cca}}_{\mathcal{DRE},\mathcal{A}}(k) = \Pr[\mathbf{Exp}^{\mathrm{cca}}_{\mathcal{DRE},\mathcal{A}}(k) = 1] - 1/2.$$

A DRE is said to be *indistinguishable against chosen-ciphertext attacks* (IND-CCA) if for any polynomial-time adversary $\mathcal{A}$, $\mathbf{Adv}^{\mathrm{cca}}_{\mathcal{DRE},\mathcal{A}}(k)$ is negligible in k, where the probability is taken over the choice of $\mathsf{crs} \xleftarrow{\$} \mathsf{CGen}_{\mathrm{DRE}}(1^k)$, $(pk_1, sk_1) \xleftarrow{\$} \mathsf{Gen}_{\mathrm{DRE}}(\mathsf{crs})$, $(pk_2, sk_2) \xleftarrow{\$} \mathsf{Gen}_{\mathrm{DRE}}(\mathsf{crs})$, and coins of $\mathcal{A}$. From a standard hybrid argument, we can show that, similar to PKE [2], single-user, single-query DRE security implies multi-user, multi-query DRE security.

3 Practical DRE and DKEM from BDDH Assumption

We build our efficient CCA-secure dual-receiver schemes in the CRS model. The CRS generation algorithm, which takes an input of security parameter k, will output the description of a symmetric bilinear group $\mathcal{BG} = (q, \mathbb{G}, \mathbb{G}_T, e, g)$ where q is a k-bit integer, $\mathbb{G}$ and $\mathbb{G}_T$ are cyclic groups of prime order q, g generates $\mathbb{G}$, and $e: \mathbb{G} \times \mathbb{G} \to \mathbb{G}_T$ is an efficiently computable bilinear map. This definition of $\mathcal{BG}$ will be used throughout the rest of the paper. Note that the public keys of the two receivers should satisfy the "weak separability" property [6], i.e., they should choose their keys from the same bilinear group. For instance, this can be achieved by going through a standard key-setup procedure.

3.1 DRE from BDDH Assumption

Our scheme, detailed in Fig. 1, is symmetric and publicly verifiable. The starting point is a selective-tag weakly CCA-secure tag-based DRE, which can be transformed to a fully secure one by using a strong one-time signature scheme (OTS) $\mathcal{OT} = (\mathsf{Gen}_{\mathrm{OT}}, \mathsf{Sig}_{\mathrm{OT}}, \mathsf{Vrf}_{\mathrm{OT}})$ [21].

Correctness. A ciphertext $(\mathsf{vk}, c, \pi_1, \pi_2, \phi, \sigma)$ is *consistent*, if $\mathsf{Vrf}_{\mathrm{OT}}(\mathsf{vk}, \sigma, (c, \pi_1, \pi_2, \phi)) = 1$, and $e(g, \pi_1) = e(c, u_1^{\mathsf{vk}} v_1)$, and $e(g, \pi_2) = e(c, u_2^{\mathsf{vk}} v_2)$. It is clear that

$\mathrm{CGen_{DRE}}(1^k)$	$\mathrm{Enc_{DRE}}(\mathcal{BG}, pk_1, pk_2, M)$	$\mathrm{Dec_{DRE}}(\mathcal{BG}, pk_1, pk_2, sk_1, C)$
return $\mathcal{BG}$	$(\mathsf{vk}, \mathsf{sk}) \xleftarrow{\$} \mathrm{Gen_{OT}}(1^k)$	**parse** C **as** $(\mathsf{vk}, c, \pi_1, \pi_2, \phi, \sigma)$
$\mathrm{Gen_{DRE}}(1^k, \mathcal{BG})$	$r \xleftarrow{\$} \mathbb{Z}_q^*;\ c \leftarrow g^r$	**if** $\mathrm{Vrf_{OT}}(\mathsf{vk}, \sigma, (c, \pi_1, \pi_2, \phi)) \neq 1$ **or**
$x_i, y_i \xleftarrow{\$} \mathbb{Z}_q^*$	$\pi_1 \leftarrow (u_1^{\mathsf{vk}} v_1)^r$	$e(g, \pi_1) \neq e(c, u_1^{\mathsf{vk}} v_1)$ **or**
$u_i \leftarrow g^{x_i}; v_i \leftarrow g^{y_i}$	$\pi_2 \leftarrow (u_2^{\mathsf{vk}} v_2)^r$	$e(g, \pi_2) \neq e(c, u_2^{\mathsf{vk}} v_2)$
$pk_i \leftarrow (u_i, v_i)$	$\phi \leftarrow e(u_1, u_2)^r \cdot M$	**return** $\perp$
$sk_i \leftarrow x_i$	$\sigma \xleftarrow{\$} \mathrm{Sig_{OT}}(\mathsf{sk}, (c, \pi_1, \pi_2, \phi))$	$M \leftarrow \phi \cdot e(c, u_2)^{-x_1}$
return (pk_i, sk_i)	**return** $C \leftarrow (\mathsf{vk}, c, \pi_1, \pi_2, \phi, \sigma)$	**return** M

Fig. 1. DRE from the BDDH assumption: The CRS generation algorithm takes as input the security parameter k and outputs $\mathcal{BG} = (q, \mathbb{G}, \mathbb{G}_T, e, g)$. The key generation algorithms are run independently for user $i \in \{1, 2\}$. The decryption algorithm is specified for user 1, and the decryption algorithm is similar for user 2. The schemes in Section 3.2 and Section 5 have similar formulations.

all above can be checked publicly, and in particular, the pairing equations hold if and only if $\pi_1 = c^{x_1 \mathsf{vk} + y_1}$ and $\pi_2 = c^{x_2 \mathsf{vk} + y_2}$. If the ciphertext is consistent then the plaintext can be recovered by either of the two receivers. The receiver obtain the plaintext either via $\phi \cdot e(c, u_2)^{-x_1}$ or $\phi \cdot e(c, u_2)^{-x_2}$. The correctness thus follows from the fact that $e(c, u_2)^{x_1} = e(c, u_1)^{x_2} = e(u_1, u_2)^r$.

Efficiency. The public key for either receiver includes two group elements in $\mathbb{G}$, and the secret key has one element in $\mathbb{Z}_q$. Encryption requires one exponentiation, two multi-exponentiations, one pairing, and a one-time signature computation. Decryption takes five pairings, three exponentiations, and one signature verification. The scheme does not rely on random oracles, having efficiency comparable to the scheme by Kiltz [21] which our scheme relies on.

Security. For soundness, the key point is that the consistency of any ciphertext can be publicly verifiable. If the ciphertext is not consistent then the decryption algorithm for either receiver will reject it (i.e., return $\perp$). Otherwise, any consistent ciphertext $(\mathsf{vk}, c, \pi_1, \pi_2, \phi, \sigma)$ will be decrypted by either of two receivers to the same message, since for any c we have that $e(c, u_2)^{x_1} = e(c, u_1)^{x_2} = e(u_1, u_2)^r$. Therefore, for any ciphertext C (whether consistent or not), we always have that $\mathrm{Dec_{DRE}}(sk_1, C) = \mathrm{Dec_{DRE}}(sk_2, C)$. The soundness security thus follows. For its CCA security, we have the following theorem:

Theorem 1. *If $\mathcal{OT}$ is a strongly-unforgeable OTS scheme and the BDDH assumption holds, then the scheme $\mathcal{DRE}$ described in Fig. 1 is a secure DRE against chosen-ciphertext attacks.* ∎

All the proofs of theorems can be found in our full paper [7].

3.2 DKEM from BDDH Assumption

We extend the concept of dual-receiver encryption to the KEM setting by defining *dual-receiver KEM* $\mathcal{DKEM} = (\mathrm{CGen_{DKEM}}, \mathrm{Gen_{DKEM}}, \mathrm{Enc_{DKEM}}, \mathrm{Dec})$:

- $\mathrm{CGen_{DKEM}}(1^k)$: The randomized *CRS generation* algorithm takes as input a security parameter k and outputs a CRS crs; we write crs $\xleftarrow{\$} \mathrm{CGen_{DKEM}}(1^k)$.

$\mathsf{CGen}_{\mathrm{DKEM}}(1^k)$	$\mathsf{Enc}_{\mathrm{DKEM}}(\mathcal{BG}, pk_1, pk_2)$	$\mathsf{Dec}_{\mathrm{DKEM}}(\mathcal{BG}, pk_1, pk_2, sk_1, C)$
return $\mathcal{BG}$	$r \xleftarrow{\$} \mathbb{Z}_q^*;\ c \leftarrow g^r$	**parse** C **as** (c, π_1, π_2)
$\mathsf{Gen}_{\mathrm{DKEM}}(1^k, \mathcal{BG})\ i \in \{1,2\}$	$t \leftarrow \mathsf{TCR}(c)$	$t \leftarrow \mathsf{TCR}(c)$
$x_i, y_i \xleftarrow{\$} \mathbb{Z}_q^*$	$\pi_1 \leftarrow (u_1^t v_1)^r$	**if** $e(g, \pi_1) \neq e(c, u_1^t v_1)$ **or**
$u_i \leftarrow g^{x_i};\ v_i \leftarrow g^{y_i}$	$\pi_2 \leftarrow (u_2^t v_2)^r$	$e(g, \pi_2) \neq e(c, u_2^t v_2)$
$pk_i \leftarrow (u_i, v_i)$	$K \leftarrow e(u_1, u_2)^r$	**return** $\perp$
$sk_i \leftarrow x_i$	$C \leftarrow (c, \pi_1, \pi_2)$	$K \leftarrow e(c, u_2)^{x_1}$
return (pk_i, sk_i)	**return** (C, K)	**return** K

Fig. 2. DKEM from the BDDH assumption

- $\mathsf{Gen}_{\mathrm{DKEM}}(\mathsf{crs})$: The randomized *key generation* algorithm takes as input crs and outputs a public/secret key pair (pk, sk); we write (pk_1, sk_1) and (pk_2, sk_2) for the key pairs of two independent users.
- $\mathsf{Enc}_{\mathrm{DKEM}}(\mathsf{crs}, pk_1, pk_2)$: The randomized *encapsulation algorithm* takes as input crs and the public keys pk_1 and pk_2 of two users, and outputs a pair (K, C) where $K \in \mathsf{KeySp}$ (i.e, the *encapsulation key space*) is a session key and C is a ciphertext; we write $(K, C) \xleftarrow{\$} \mathsf{Enc}_{\mathrm{DKEM}}(\mathsf{crs}, pk_1, pk_2)$.
- $\mathsf{Dec}_{\mathrm{DKEM}}(\mathsf{crs}, pk_1, pk_2, sk_i, C)$: The deterministic *decapsulation algorithm* takes the CRS crs, the public keys pk_1 and pk_2 of two users, one of the secret keys sk_i $(i \in \{0,1\})$ and a ciphertext C as input, and outputs either a session key K (which may be the special symbol $\perp$); we write $K_i \leftarrow \mathsf{Dec}_{\mathrm{DKEM}}(\mathsf{crs}, pk_1, pk_2, sk_i, C)$ (or simply $K_i \leftarrow \mathsf{Dec}_{\mathrm{DKEM}}(sk_i, C)$).

As before, we require that the public keys for Enc and Dec are ordered by their lexicographic ordering. Conventional consistency is required. Soundness can be defined as that of DRE, i.e., we require that no (polynomial-time) adversary can, with noticeable probability, produce a ciphertext C (whether consistent or not) such that $\mathsf{Dec}_{\mathrm{DKEM}}(sk_1, C) \neq \mathsf{Dec}_{\mathrm{DKEM}}(sk_2, C)$.

DKEM is a useful building block for *dual-receiver hybrid encryption*. One can easily prove that a hybrid usage of DKEM and a symmetric-key encryption gives a secure and efficient DRE scheme.

Our DKEM $\mathcal{DKEM} = (\mathsf{CGen}_{\mathrm{DKEM}}, \mathsf{Gen}_{\mathrm{DKEM}}, \mathsf{Enc}_{\mathrm{DKEM}}, \mathsf{Dec}_{\mathrm{DKEM}})$ is depicted in Fig. 2. It uses a target collision resistant hash function [9] TCR. Such a hash function is usually "keyed," but this raises problems. First, it does not make sense to let either of the receivers choose the key, since this would immediately damage the symmetry property of DRE. Even if we neglect the symmetry property and allow one of them to choose the key, one has to choose multiple keys (each for per pair of receivers) in the multi-recipient setting, which is clearly prohibitive. Last, it does not make sense to let them jointly choose the hash key, as this would violate the key independence requirement of DRE and be less efficient. For our scheme, we can circumvent the problems in using a *non-keyed* TCR by choosing a bijective encoding function from $\mathbb{G}$ to $\mathbb{Z}_q$, as discussed in the literature [5,22]. Correspondingly, the hash function is perfectly collision resistant.

Our DKEM is publicly verifiable, and its correctness easily follows. The perfect soundness is also satisfied similar to the one for the above DRE. The following theorem establishes the chosen-ciphertext security of $\mathcal{DKEM}$:

Theorem 2. *If* TCR *is a target collision resistant hash function and the BDDH assumption holds, then the scheme* $\mathcal{DKEM}$ *described in Fig. 2 is a secure DKEM against chosen-ciphertext attacks.* ∎

Discussion. At the heart of our schemes is an ElGamal-like encryption in bilinear groups, also used in DLKY-DRE [13]. We also borrow ideas from "identity-based technique" due to Boneh and Boyen [3], and our constructions are similar to that of Kiltz's tag-based encryption [21], and KEMs due to Kiltz [21,22], and Boyen, Mei, and Waters [5], respectively. Further optimizations and simplifications are applied on our schemes and symmetry has been taken into account.

4   Plaintext-aware Encryption via Registration from DRE

The notion of *plaintext-awareness via key registration*, due to Herzog, Liskov, and Micali [19], requires the sender to go through a key registration step with the authority. Roughly, it captures that an adversary can decrypt any ciphertext that it creates, as long as the adversary registered its sending key. Their construction [19] relies on general zero-knowledge proof of knowledge and non-malleable NIZK, and thus is rather inefficient. We show that our DRE schemes lead to very efficient registration-based plaintext-aware PKE schemes.

Definitions. A *registration-based plaintext-aware encryption* (RPA) scheme consists of the following algorithms: $\mathcal{RPA} = (\mathsf{CGen}_{\mathrm{RPA}}, \mathsf{Gen}_{\mathrm{RPA}}, \mathsf{Enc}_{\mathrm{RPA}}, \mathsf{Dec}_{\mathrm{RPA}}, \mathsf{RU}, \mathsf{RA})$. $\mathsf{CGen}_{\mathrm{RPA}}$ generates the CRS crs which serves as part of the inputs of the following algorithms. RU and RA are two interactive algorithms (i.e., registration protocol) run by the sender and the key registration authority (KRA), respectively. Each takes as input an incoming message and a state, and outputs an outgoing message, an (updated) state, and a decision (accept, reject, or cont). If the sender accepts, its final state output is a sender key pair (pk_s, sk_s). If the KRA accepts, its final state output is the sender public key pk_s', where $pk_s = pk_s'$ with overwhelming probability. $\mathsf{Gen}_{\mathrm{RPA}}$ generates a key pair (pk_r, sk_r) for the receiver. $\mathsf{Enc}_{\mathrm{RPA}}$ takes as input a message M, the public key of the receiver pk_r, and the public key of the sender pk_s, and outputs a ciphertext C. $\mathsf{Dec}_{\mathrm{RPA}}$ takes as input a ciphertext C, the public key of the receiver pk_r, the public key of the sender pk_s, and the secret key of the receiver sk_r, and outputs a message M.

Apart from the conventional encryption consistency, we expect *honest security*, which ensures that if the receiver and the sender are *both* honest, the scheme should satisfy the (conventional) CCA-security even if the adversary fully controls the KRA. Furthermore, we expect *plaintext-awareness* which guarantees the registered adversary can decrypt any ciphertexts it sends to an receiver, for an honest KRA. We define registration-based plaintext-awareness via the following experiment involving an adversary $\mathcal{A}$ and a simulator $\mathsf{S}_{\mathcal{A}}$:

Experiment $\mathbf{Exp}^{\mathrm{rpa}}_{\mathcal{RPA},S_{\mathcal{A}},\mathcal{A}}(k)$

$\mathsf{crs} \xleftarrow{\$} \mathsf{CGen}_{\mathrm{DKEM}}(1^k)$

$(pk_r, sk_r) \xleftarrow{\$} \mathsf{Gen}_{\mathrm{RPA}}(\mathsf{crs})$

$(pk_{\mathcal{A}}, \mathsf{s}) \xleftarrow{\$} \mathcal{A}^{\mathrm{RA}}(\mathsf{crs}, pk_r)$

$C \xleftarrow{\$} \mathcal{A}^{\mathrm{Dec}_{\mathrm{RPA}}(\mathsf{crs}, \cdot, pk_r, sk_r, \cdot)}(pk_r, pk_{\mathcal{A}}, \mathsf{s})$

if $S_{\mathcal{A}}(\mathsf{s}, C, pk_r, pk_{\mathcal{A}}) = \mathsf{Dec}_{\mathrm{RPA}}(\mathsf{crs}, C, pk_r, sk_r, pk_{\mathcal{A}})$ then

return 1 **else return** 0

We define the advantage of $\mathcal{A}$ in the above experiment as $\mathbf{Adv}^{\mathrm{rpa}}_{\mathcal{RPA},S_{\mathcal{A}},\mathcal{A}}(k) = \Pr[\mathbf{Exp}^{\mathrm{rpa}}_{\mathcal{RPA},S_{\mathcal{A}},\mathcal{A}}(k) = 0]$. An RPA scheme is registration-based plaintext-aware if for any polynomial-time adversary $\mathcal{A}$ there exists $S_{\mathcal{A}}$ such that the advantage $\mathbf{Adv}^{\mathrm{rpa}}_{\mathcal{RPA},S_{\mathcal{A}},\mathcal{A}}(k)$ is negligible in the security parameter k.

The Construction of Herzog, Liskov, and Micali. We briefly recall the Herzog, Liskov, and Micali (crypto/HerzogLM03) scheme [19]: Given a CRS crs, the receiver generates two key pairs (pk_1, sk_1), (pk_2, sk_2) of a PKE scheme ($\mathsf{Gen}_{\mathrm{PKE}}, \mathsf{Enc}_{\mathrm{PKE}}, \mathsf{Dec}_{\mathrm{PKE}}$) which is indistinguishable against chosen-plaintext attack (IND-CPA). The public key is $pk_r = (pk_1, pk_2, \mathsf{crs})$ and the secret key $sk_r = sk_1$. The sender generates another pair of public/secret key pair (pk_3, sk_3) for the same encryption scheme. The sender run a zero-knowledge proof of knowledge protocol with the KRA to prove the knowledge of sk_3. The RPA encryption algorithm computes $C = (c_1 = \mathsf{Enc}_{\mathrm{PKE}}(pk_1, m), c_2 = \mathsf{Enc}_{\mathrm{PKE}}(pk_2, m), c_3 = \mathsf{Enc}_{\mathrm{PKE}}(pk_3, m), \pi)$ where π a non-malleable NIZK proof that c_1, c_2, and c_3 encrypt the same message with respect to pk_1, pk_2, and pk_3, respectively. Authenticated channel is needed to make sure the ciphertext was indeed sent by the entity that registered pk_3. The benefit of the above construction is its generality, but it relies on general non-malleable NIZK proofs, which does not seem to have immediate practical instantiations. Another potential drawback is that it is not symmetric, but in real applications the sender might be also the receiver in another instance.

DRE-Based Plaintext-Awareness. We show that in general our refined DRE naturally leads to a secure RPA overcoming the drawbacks of crypto/HerzogLM03. The transformation is a simple one. Given a DRE scheme, the sender and the receiver correspond to the two receivers of DRE, and the sender further runs a zero-knowledge proof of knowledge of its secret key protocol with the KRA. The RPA encryption is the same as the DRE encryption relative to the public keys of the sender and the receiver, while the decryption algorithm is just the DRE decryption algorithm relative to the receiver. It is easy to see if the receiver and the sender are both honest, the honest security is implied by the DRE CCA-security. Registration-based plaintext-awareness is also simple to see — for any adversary registered its public key, given a ciphertext, we first rewind the adversary to extract its secret key using the proof of knowledge extractor, then decrypt the given ciphertext with this secret key to obtain a plaintext. Via the soundness of DRE, the obtained plaintext is the same as that by decrypting the ciphertext with the secret key of the receiver. It is also easy to see that the conventional formulation of DRE without the soundness requirement is not adequate, since the ciphertext output by the adversary can be maliciously generated.

The general transformation does not rely on NIZK proof (except for the sender registration process). One can instantiate our DRE based PRA schemes with those in Section 3. The key registration protocol simply runs two (well-known and standard) four-round protocol of zero-knowledge proof of knowledge for discrete logarithm or uses more efficient concurrently secure protocol [10] in the auxiliary string model.

5   Combined Encryption Scheme

A combined encryption scheme $\mathcal{CE}$ consists of the following algorithms ($\mathsf{CGen}_{\mathrm{COM}}$, $\mathsf{Gen}_{\mathrm{COM}}$, $\mathsf{Enc}_{\mathrm{DRE}}$, $\mathsf{Dec}_{\mathrm{DRE}}$, $\mathsf{Enc}_{\mathrm{PKE}}$, $\mathsf{Dec}_{\mathrm{PKE}}$):

- $\mathsf{CGen}_{\mathrm{COM}}(1^k)$: The randomized *CRS generation* algorithm takes as input a security parameter k and outputs a CRS crs; we write $\mathsf{crs} \xleftarrow{\$} \mathsf{CGen}_{\mathrm{COM}}(1^k)$.
- $\mathsf{Gen}_{\mathrm{COM}}(\mathsf{crs})$: The randomized *key generation* algorithm takes as input crs and outputs a public/secret key pair (pk, sk); we write (pk_1, sk_1) and (pk_2, sk_2) for the key pairs of two independent users.
- $\mathsf{Enc}_{\mathrm{DRE}}(\mathsf{crs}, pk_1, pk_2, M)$: The randomized *DRE encryption algorithm* takes as input the CRS crs, the public keys pk_1, pk_2, and a message M, and outputs a ciphertext C; we write $C \xleftarrow{\$} \mathsf{Enc}_{\mathrm{DRE}}(\mathsf{crs}, pk_1, pk_2, M)$.
- $\mathsf{Dec}_{\mathrm{DRE}}(\mathsf{crs}, pk_1, pk_2, sk_i, C)$: The deterministic *DRE decryption algorithm* takes as input two public keys pk_1 and pk_2, one of the secret keys sk_i ($i \in \{0, 1\}$), and a ciphertext C, and outputs a message M_i (which may be the special symbol $\bot$); we write $M_i \leftarrow \mathsf{Dec}_{\mathrm{DRE}}(\mathsf{crs}, pk_1, pk_2, sk_i, C)$ or simply $M_i \leftarrow \mathsf{Dec}_{\mathrm{DRE}}(pk_1, pk_2, sk_i, C)$.
- $\mathsf{Enc}_{\mathrm{PKE}}(\mathsf{crs}, pk_1, M')$: The randomized *PKE encryption algorithm* takes as input the CRS crs, the public key pk_1, and a message M', and outputs a ciphertext C'; we write $C' \xleftarrow{\$} \mathsf{Enc}_{\mathrm{PKE}}(\mathsf{crs}, pk_1, M')$.
- $\mathsf{Dec}_{\mathrm{PKE}}(\mathsf{crs}, pk_1, sk_1, C')$: The deterministic *PKE decryption algorithm* takes as input the CRS crs, the public/secret key pair (pk_1, sk_1), and a ciphertext C', and outputs a message M' (which may be the special symbol $\bot$); we write $M' \leftarrow \mathsf{Dec}_{\mathrm{PKE}}(\mathsf{crs}, pk_1, sk_1, C')$ or simply $M' \leftarrow \mathsf{Dec}_{\mathrm{PKE}}(pk_1, sk_1, C')$.

We require that the public keys in the DRE encryption and decryption algorithms respect their lexicographic ordering. Both the PKE consistency and DRE consistency are required.

The formalization of the security of combined encryption schemes is more involved than those of previous combined encryption schemes (e.g. [1,36]), due to the more-than-one receivers nature of DRE. We establish the security of combined encryption scheme by defining *DRE security with PKE decryption oracle* and *PKE security with DRE decryption oracle*. The former captures the security of DRE even with *unrestricted* PKE decryption oracles of the two receivers, while

Experiment $\mathbf{Exp}_{\mathcal{CE},1,\mathcal{A}_1}^{\mathrm{cca}}(k)$	Experiment $\mathbf{Exp}_{\mathcal{CE},2,\mathcal{A}_2}^{\mathrm{cca}}(k)$
$\mathrm{crs} \xleftarrow{\$} \mathrm{CGen}_{\mathrm{COM}}(1^k)$	$\mathrm{crs} \xleftarrow{\$} \mathrm{CGen}_{\mathrm{COM}}(1^k)$
$(pk_i, sk_i) \xleftarrow{\$} \mathrm{Gen}_{\mathrm{COM}}(\mathrm{crs}) \quad i \in \{1,2\}$	$(pk_1, sk_1) \xleftarrow{\$} \mathrm{Gen}_{\mathrm{COM}}(\mathrm{crs})$
$(M_0, M_1, \mathsf{s}) \xleftarrow{\$} \mathcal{A}^{\mathcal{O}_1, \mathcal{O}_2, \mathcal{O}_3}(\mathrm{find}, \mathrm{crs}, pk_1, pk_2)$	$(M_0, M_1, \mathsf{s}) \xleftarrow{\$} \mathcal{A}^{\mathcal{Q}_1, \mathcal{Q}_2, \mathcal{Q}_3}(\mathrm{find}, \mathrm{crs}, pk_1)$
$b \xleftarrow{\$} \{0,1\}; C^* \xleftarrow{\$} \mathrm{Enc}_{\mathrm{DRE}}(\mathrm{crs}, pk_1, pk_2, M_b)$	$b \xleftarrow{\$} \{0,1\}; C^* \xleftarrow{\$} \mathrm{Enc}_{\mathrm{PKE}}(\mathrm{crs}, pk_1, M_b)$
$b' \xleftarrow{\$} \mathcal{A}^{\mathcal{O}_1, \mathcal{O}_2, \mathcal{O}_3}(\mathrm{guess}, C^*, \mathsf{s})$	$b' \xleftarrow{\$} \mathcal{A}^{\mathcal{Q}_1, \mathcal{Q}_2, \mathcal{Q}_3}(\mathrm{guess}, C^*, \mathsf{s})$
if $b' = b$ **then return** 1 **else return** 0	**if** $b' = b$ **then return** 1 **else return** 0

Fig. 3. (**Left:**) DRE security with PKE decryption oracle (**Right:**) PKE security with DRE decryption oracle

the latter formalizes the security of PKE even with *unrestricted* DRE decryption oracles regarding the target public key and some *arbitrary* (valid) public key even if it does *not* know the corresponding secret key.

Fig. 3 (**Left**) depicts DRE security with PKE decryption oracle, where $\mathcal{O}_1 = \mathrm{Dec}_{\mathrm{DRE}}(sk_1, pk_1, pk_2, \cdot)$, $\mathcal{O}_2 = \mathrm{Dec}_{\mathrm{PKE}}(sk_1, \cdot)$, and $\mathcal{O}_3 = \mathrm{Dec}_{\mathrm{PKE}}(sk_2, \cdot)$. In its guess stage, $\mathcal{A}_1$ is not allowed to query the oracles $\mathrm{Dec}_{\mathrm{DRE}}(sk_1, \cdot)$ on the challenge ciphertext C^*. Note that we do not impose any restrictions on $\mathrm{Dec}_{\mathrm{PKE}}(sk_1, \cdot)$ and $\mathrm{Dec}_{\mathrm{PKE}}(sk_2, \cdot)$ oracles. Fig. 3 (**Right**) describes PKE security with DRE decryption, where $\mathcal{Q}_1 = \mathrm{Dec}_{\mathrm{PKE}}(sk_1, \cdot)$, $\mathcal{Q}_2 = \mathrm{Dec}_{\mathrm{DRE}}(sk_1, pk_1, \cdot, \cdot)$, and $\mathcal{Q}_3 = \mathrm{Dec}_{\mathrm{DRE}}(sk_1, \cdot, pk_1, \cdot)$. In the guess stage, $\mathcal{A}_2$ is not allowed to query the oracle $\mathrm{Dec}_{\mathrm{PKE}}(sk_1, \cdot)$ with the challenge ciphertext C^*. The query $\mathrm{Dec}_{\mathrm{DRE}}(sk_1, pk_1, \cdot, \cdot)$ on (pk, C) such that $pk_1 <^d pk$ returns $M \leftarrow \mathrm{Dec}_{\mathrm{DRE}}(sk_1, pk_1, pk, C)$, and the oracle query $\mathrm{Dec}_{\mathrm{DRE}}(sk_1, \cdot, pk_1, \cdot)$ on (pk', C) such that $pk' <^d pk_1$ returns $M \leftarrow \mathrm{Dec}_{\mathrm{DRE}}(sk_1, pk', pk_1, C)$. We levy no restrictions except the validity of keys pk and pk' (i.e., output by $\mathrm{Gen}_{\mathrm{COM}}(\mathrm{crs})$).

In the find stages of both experiments, it is required that $|M_0| = |M_1|$. We define the advantage of $\mathcal{A}_i$ in experiment $\mathbf{Exp}_{\mathcal{CE},i,\mathcal{A}_i}^{\mathrm{cca}}(k)$ $(i \in \{1,2\})$ as

$$\mathbf{Adv}_{\mathcal{CE},i,\mathcal{A}_i}^{\mathrm{cca}}(k) = \Pr[\mathbf{Exp}_{\mathcal{CE},i,\mathcal{A}_i}^{\mathrm{cca}}(k) = 1] - 1/2.$$

The soundness for the DRE functionality is identical to that of a regular DRE.

An Efficient Construction. We describe an efficient combined scheme $\mathcal{CE}$, depicted in Fig. 4, which combines our scheme $\mathcal{DRE}$ in Section 3.1 and a PKE scheme adapted from the one based on the BDDH assumption due to Kiltz [21]. The scheme exploits the "identity-based technique" in a *symmetric* manner, where it can be used to simulate all the unrestricted decryption oracles. It is easy to see that the ciphertext consistency of the combined scheme is also publicly verifiable. Theorem 3 below asserts the security of our combined scheme $\mathcal{CE}$.

Theorem 3. *Our $\mathcal{CE}$ is a combined encryption scheme satisfying DRE security with PKE decryption oracle and PKE security with DRE decryption oracle.* ∎

$\mathsf{CGen}(1^k)$	$\mathsf{Enc}_{\mathrm{DRE}}(\mathcal{BG}, pk_1, pk_2, M)$	$\mathsf{Dec}_{\mathrm{DRE}}(\mathcal{BG}, pk_1, pk_2, sk_1, C)$
return $\mathcal{BG}$	$(\mathsf{vk}, \mathsf{sk}) \xleftarrow{\$} \mathsf{Gen}_{\mathrm{OT}}(1^k)$	**parse** C **as** $(\mathsf{vk}, c, \pi_1, \pi_2, \phi, \sigma)$
$\mathsf{Gen}_{\mathrm{COM}}(1^k, \mathcal{BG})$	$r \xleftarrow{\$} \mathbb{Z}_q^*$	**if** $\mathsf{Vrf}_{\mathrm{OT}}(\mathsf{vk}, \sigma, (c, \pi_1, \pi_2, \phi)) \neq 1$ **or**
$x_i, y_i \xleftarrow{\$} \mathbb{Z}_q^*$	$c \leftarrow g^r$	$e(g, \pi_1) \neq e(c, u_1^{\mathsf{vk}} v_1)$ **or**
$u_i \leftarrow g^{x_i}; v_i \leftarrow g^{y_i}$	$\pi_1 \leftarrow (u_1^{\mathsf{vk}} v_1)^r$	$e(g, \pi_2) \neq e(c, u_2^{\mathsf{vk}} v_2)$
$w_i \leftarrow g^{z_i}$	$\pi_2 \leftarrow (u_2^{\mathsf{vk}} v_2)^r$	**return** $\perp$
$pk_i \leftarrow (u_i, v_i, w_i)$	$\phi \leftarrow e(u_1, u_2)^r \cdot M$	$M \leftarrow \phi \cdot e(c, u_2)^{-x_1}$
$sk_i \leftarrow x_i$	$\sigma \xleftarrow{\$} \mathsf{Sig}_{\mathrm{OT}}(\mathsf{sk}, (c, \pi_1, \pi_2, \phi))$	**return** M
return (pk_i, sk_i)	**return** $C \leftarrow (\mathsf{vk}, c, \pi_1, \pi_2, \phi, \sigma)$	

$\mathsf{Enc}_{\mathrm{PKE}}(\mathcal{BG}, pk_1, M)$	$\mathsf{Dec}_{\mathrm{PKE}}(\mathcal{BG}, pk_1, sk_1, C)$
$(\mathsf{vk}, \mathsf{sk}) \xleftarrow{\$} \mathsf{Gen}_{\mathrm{OT}}(1^k)$	**parse** C **as** $(\mathsf{vk}, c, \pi, \phi, \sigma)$
$r \xleftarrow{\$} \mathbb{Z}_q^*; c \leftarrow g^r$	**if** $\mathsf{Vrf}_{\mathrm{OT}}(\mathsf{vk}, \sigma, (c, \pi, \phi)) \neq 1$ **or**
$\pi \leftarrow (u_1^{\mathsf{vk}} v_1)^r$	$e(g, \pi) \neq e(c, u_1^{\mathsf{vk}} v_1)$ **then**
$\phi \leftarrow e(u_1, w_1)^r \cdot M$	**return** $\perp$
$\sigma \xleftarrow{\$} \mathsf{Sig}_{\mathrm{OT}}(\mathsf{sk}, (c, \pi, \phi))$	$M \leftarrow \phi \cdot e(c, w_1)^{-x_1}$
return $C \leftarrow (\mathsf{vk}, c, \pi, \phi, \sigma)$	**return** M

Fig. 4. A combined encryption scheme from the BDDH assumption

6   Completely Non-malleable DRE

Completely non-malleable DRE provides a stronger notion for DRE, which can apply to settings where on-line authorities are available and adversaries might dynamically and maliciously generate public keys. CNM notion of DRE ensures ciphertext non-malleability even in such settings. This section is also motivated by acquiring stronger notions for plaintext equality test as discussed in our full paper [7]; and by dual-receiver non-malleable commitments to be illustrated.

As argued in the introduction, we need to resort to CRS for constructing CNM-DRE. We will propose two *general* approaches to constructing CNM-DRE followed by *efficient* instantiations. We start with a model of CNM-DRE.

6.1   Modeling Completely Non-Malleable DRE

Fischlin [15] gave a simulation-based definition of CNM extending the original definition of non-malleability, and later Ventre and Visconti [32] introduced the game-based definition. We extend the game-based definition of complete non-malleability [32] to the DRE setting and formalize the definition of CNM for DRE. In this setting, we consider a complete relation R that outputs a boolean variable, and takes as input a plaintext m, two public keys pk_1 and pk_2 for two receivers, two (possibly adversarially generated) public keys pk_1^* and pk_2^*, a vector $\mathbf{m}^*$ of plaintexts, and a vector of DRE ciphertext $\mathbf{c}^*$ encrypting $\mathbf{m}^*$ under pk_1^* and pk_2^*. Consider an experiment with adversary $\mathcal{A}$, as depicted in Fig. 5.

In the experiment, it is mandated that adversary will not query $\mathsf{Dec}_{\mathrm{DRE}}(sk_1, \cdot)$ with c. We also require the chosen distribution M to be valid such that $|m| = |m'|$ for any m and m' having non-zero probability of being sampled. By $\mathbf{m}^* \neq \perp$,

Experiment $\mathbf{Exp}_{\mathcal{DRE},\mathcal{A}}^{\text{cnm-cca-0}}(k)$	Experiment $\mathbf{Exp}_{\mathcal{DRE},\mathcal{A}}^{\text{cnm-cca-1}}(k)$
$\text{crs} \xleftarrow{\$} \text{CGen}_{\text{DRE}}(1^k)$	$\text{crs} \xleftarrow{\$} \text{CGen}_{\text{DRE}}(1^k)$
$(pk_i, sk_i) \xleftarrow{\$} \text{Gen}_{\text{DRE}}(\text{crs}) \quad i \in \{1,2\}$	$(pk_i, sk_i) \xleftarrow{\$} \text{Gen}_{\text{DRE}}(\text{crs}) \quad i \in \{1,2\}$
$(\text{M}, \text{s}) \xleftarrow{\$} \mathcal{A}^{\text{Dec}_{\text{DRE}}(sk_1, \cdot)}(\text{crs}, pk_1, pk_2)$	$(\text{M}, \text{s}) \xleftarrow{\$} \mathcal{A}^{\text{Dec}_{\text{DRE}}(sk_1, \cdot)}(\text{crs}, pk_1, pk_2)$
$m \xleftarrow{\$} \text{M}$	$m, \tilde{m} \xleftarrow{\$} \text{M}$
$c \leftarrow \text{Enc}_{\text{DRE}}(\text{crs}, pk_1, pk_2, m, r)$	$c \leftarrow \text{Enc}_{\text{DRE}}(\text{crs}, pk_1, pk_2, m, r)$
$(\text{R}, pk_1^*, pk_2^*, \mathbf{c}^*) \leftarrow \mathcal{A}^{\text{Dec}_{\text{DRE}}(sk_1, \cdot)}(\text{s}, c)$	$(\text{R}, pk_1^*, pk_2^*, \mathbf{c}^*) \leftarrow \mathcal{A}^{\text{Dec}_{\text{DRE}}(sk_1, \cdot)}(\text{s}, c)$
return 1 iff $\exists (\mathbf{m}^*, \mathbf{r}^*)$ such that	**return** 1 iff $\exists (\mathbf{m}^*, \mathbf{r}^*)$ such that
$(\mathbf{c}^* = \text{Enc}_{\text{DRE}}(\text{crs}, pk_1^*, pk_2^*, \mathbf{m}^*, \mathbf{r}^*))$ and	$(\mathbf{c}^* = \text{Enc}_{\text{DRE}}(\text{crs}, pk_1^*, pk_2^*, \mathbf{m}^*, \mathbf{r}^*))$ and
$(c \notin \mathbf{c}^* \text{ or } (pk_1, pk_2) \neq (pk_1^*, pk_2^*))$ and	$(c \notin \mathbf{c}^* \text{ or } (pk_1, pk_2) \neq (pk_1^*, pk_2^*))$ and
$(\mathbf{m}^* \neq \bot)$ and	$(\mathbf{m}^* \neq \bot)$ and
$(\text{R}(m, \mathbf{m}^*, \text{crs}, pk_1, pk_2, pk_1^*, pk_2^*, \mathbf{c}^*) = 1)$	$(\text{R}(\tilde{m}, \mathbf{m}^*, \text{crs}, pk_1, pk_2, pk_1^*, pk_2^*, \mathbf{c}^*) = 1)$

Fig. 5. Modeling the Security of CNM-DRE

we mean that at least one of the elements of $\mathbf{c}^*$ is a valid ciphertext. We define the advantage of $\mathcal{A}$, $\mathbf{Adv}_{\mathcal{DRE},\mathcal{A}}^{\text{cnm-cca}}(k)$, in the above experiments as

$$\Pr[\mathbf{Exp}_{\mathcal{DRE},\mathcal{A}}^{\text{cnm-cca-0}}(k) = 1] - \Pr[\mathbf{Exp}_{\mathcal{DRE},\mathcal{A}}^{\text{cnm-cca-1}}(k) = 1].$$

To thwart a trivial attack, we require the public keys output from the adversary to be in the lexicographic ordering among bit strings (i.e., $pk_1^* <^d pk_2^*$).

When we restrict the public keys (pk_1^*, pk_2^*) output from $\mathcal{A}$ to be exactly (pk_1, pk_2), our definition is equivalent to NM-CCA (and IND-CCA).

We require for CNM-DRE the *strong soundness* property defined in Section 2 since in the setting of CNM the adversary can choose keys adversarially. (Accordingly, we require the encryption scheme to be admissible.) This also ensures that any final output $\mathbf{c}^*$ will give the same plaintext after decrypting.

6.2 CNM-DRE from Groth-Sahai Proof System

It is known that Naor-Yung "two-key" paradigm [25], where the well-formedness of a ciphertext is ensured by the soundness property of a non-interactive zero-knowledge (NIZK) proof, allows dual encryption and decryption but only achieves IND-CCA1 security. It is later shown by Sahai [30] that one can replace the underlying NIZK proof system with a (one-time) simulation-sound NIZK proof system to get IND-CCA security. To achieve complete non-malleability, we employ an even stronger notion of *simulation-sound and simulation-sound extractable NIZK proof of knowledge* (reviewed in Appendix A) [12,17], which, loosely speaking, requires that the extraction can be achieved even in the simulation setting. The stronger property is needed because it allows the decryption for the forged ciphertext output by the adversary in the simulation setting even if one does not have the corresponding secret key.

Our scheme $\mathcal{CDRE}_1 = (\text{CGen}_{\text{DRE}}, \text{Gen}_{\text{DRE}}, \text{Enc}_{\text{DRE}}, \text{Dec}_{\text{DRE}})$ is detailed in Fig. 6. It employs any *admissible* encryption $\mathcal{PKE} = (\text{Gen}, \text{Enc}, \text{Dec})$ and a simulation-

$\mathsf{CGen}_{DRE}(1^k)$	$\mathsf{Enc}_{DRE}(\text{crs}, pk_1, pk_2, m)$	$\mathsf{Dec}_{DRE}(\text{crs}, pk_1, pk_2, sk_1, C)$
return $\text{crs} \xleftarrow{\$} \mathsf{CGen}(1^k)$	$c_1 \leftarrow \mathsf{Enc}(pk_1, m; r_1)$	**parse** C **as** (c_1, c_2, π)
	$c_2 \leftarrow \mathsf{Enc}(pk_2, m; r_2)$	**if** $\mathsf{V}(\text{crs}, c_1, c_2, pk_1, pk_2, \pi) \neq 1$
$\mathsf{Gen}_{DRE}(1^k)$ $i \in \{1, 2\}$	$\pi \xleftarrow{\$} \mathsf{P}(\text{crs}, (c_1, c_2, pk_1, pk_2), (m, r_1, r_2))$	**return** $\perp$
$(pk_i, sk_i) \xleftarrow{\$} \mathsf{Gen}(1^k)$	$c \leftarrow (c_1, c_2, \pi)$	$m \leftarrow \mathsf{Dec}(c_1, pk_1, sk_1)$
return (pk_i, sk_i)	**return** c	**return** m

Fig. 6. General CNM-DRE from Naor-Yung Paradigm

sound and simulation-sound extractable NIZK argument of knowledge proof system $\mathcal{SSPK} = (\mathsf{CGen}, \mathsf{P}, \mathsf{V}, \mathsf{E}_1, \mathsf{E}_2, \mathsf{S}_1, \mathsf{S}_2)$ for the language $\mathcal{L}_1 := \{(c_1, c_2, pk_1, pk_2) | \exists(m, r_1, r_2) [c_1 = \mathsf{Enc}(pk_1, m; r_1) \wedge c_2 = \mathsf{Enc}(pk_2, m; r_2)]\}$, where r_1 and r_2 denote the randomness used by Enc.

Theorem 4. *If encryption* $\mathcal{PKE}$ *is admissible and indistinguishable under chosen-plaintext attack (IND-CPA), and* $\mathcal{SSPK}$ *is a simulation-sound and simulation-sound extractable NIZK argument of knowledge proof system, then the scheme* $\mathcal{CDRE}_1$ *described in Fig. 6 is a secure CNM-DRE against chosen-ciphertext attacks.*   ∎

Efficient Instantiations. The general construction from simulation-sound and simulation-sound extractable NIZK argument of knowledge can be instantiated with reasonable efficiency. In particular, the simulation-sound NIZK *argument* of knowledge can be achieved by using Groth-Sahai proof system [18] which can be realized based on a number of standard assumptions. More details can be found in our full paper [7].

6.3   CNM-DRE from Lossy Trapdoor Functions

This construction follows the CNM-PKE due to Libert and Yung [23] that modifies the PKE from lossy trapdoor functions by Peikert and Waters [28][5]. In their scheme, the family of all-but-one functions is put in the CRS, rather than being generated by the user key generation. We extend this idea to achieve CNM-DRE. Concretely, in our encryption algorithm, the *same* randomness is used as input to two independent lossy trapdoor functions generated by two receivers, and the rest of the encryption remains as in Peikert and Waters [28]. To achieve soundness, we ask that *both* of the receivers to check the consistency of *both* of the lossy trapdoor functions. Note that it is easy for them to do so, since the decryption algorithm is *witness-recovering*.

Our Construction. We present $\mathcal{CDRE}_2 = (\mathsf{CGen}_{DRE}, \mathsf{Gen}_{DRE}, \mathsf{Enc}_{DRE}, \mathsf{Dec}_{DRE})$ in Fig. 7, from a collection of (n, l) lossy trapdoor functions $\mathcal{LTF} = (\mathcal{S}, \mathcal{F}, \mathcal{F}^{-1})$, a collection of (n, l') all-but-one trapdoor functions $\mathcal{ABO} = (\mathcal{S}_{abo}, \mathcal{G}_{abo}, \mathcal{G}_{abo}^{-1})$, and a collection of pairwise independent hash functions [33] H: $\mathcal{H} \times \{0,1\}^n \to \{0,1\}^d$. We require that $2l + l' \geq n + \lambda$, where $\lambda = \omega(\log n)$ and $\lambda > d + \log(1/\epsilon)$

---

[5] The definitions of lossy and all-but-one trapdoor functions is recalled in Appendix A.

$$\begin{array}{ll}
\mathsf{CGen}_{\mathrm{DRE}}(1^k) & \mathsf{Enc}_{\mathrm{DRE}}(\mathsf{crs}, s_1, s_2, m; r) \\
\quad b_0 \xleftarrow{\$} \{0,1\}^n & \quad (\mathsf{vk}, \mathsf{sk}) \xleftarrow{\$} \mathsf{Gen}_{\mathrm{OT}}(1^k) \\
\quad (s_0, t_0) \xleftarrow{\$} \mathcal{S}_{abo}(1^k, b_0) & \quad r \xleftarrow{\$} \{0,1\}^n \\
\quad h \xleftarrow{\$} \mathcal{H} & \quad C_1 \leftarrow \mathcal{F}(s_1, r) \\
\quad \textbf{return } \mathsf{crs} \leftarrow (s_0, h) & \quad C_2 \leftarrow \mathcal{F}(s_2, r) \\
 & \quad C_3 \leftarrow \mathcal{G}_{abo}(s_0, \mathsf{vk}, r) \\
\mathsf{Gen}_{\mathrm{DRE}}(1^k) \quad i \in \{1,2\} & \quad C_4 \leftarrow M \oplus \mathsf{H}_h(r) \\
\quad (s_i, t_i) \xleftarrow{\$} \mathcal{S}(1^k, 1) & \quad \sigma \xleftarrow{\$} \mathsf{Sig}_{\mathrm{OT}}(\mathsf{sk}, (C_1, C_2, C_3, C_4, pk_1, pk_2)) \\
\quad \textbf{return } (s_i, t_i) & \quad \textbf{return } C \leftarrow (\mathsf{vk}, C_1, C_2, C_3, C_4, \sigma)
\end{array}$$

$$\begin{array}{l}
\mathsf{Dec}_{\mathrm{DRE}}(\mathsf{crs}, s_1, s_2, t_1, C) \\
\quad \textbf{parse } C \textbf{ as } (C_1, C_2, C_3, C_4, pk_1, pk_2, \sigma) \\
\quad \textbf{if } \mathsf{Vrf}_{\mathrm{OT}}(\mathsf{vk}, \sigma, (C_1, C_2, C_3, C_4, pk_1, pk_2)) \neq 1 \textbf{ then} \\
\qquad \textbf{return } \bot \\
\quad r \leftarrow \mathcal{F}^{-1}(t_1, C_1) \\
\quad \textbf{if } C_2 \neq \mathcal{F}(s_2, r) \textbf{ or } C_3 \neq \mathcal{F}(s_0, r) \textbf{ then} \\
\qquad \textbf{return } \bot \\
\quad m \leftarrow C_4 \oplus \mathsf{H}_h(r) \\
\quad \textbf{return } m
\end{array}$$

Fig. 7. General CNM-DRE from Lossy Trapdoor Functions

for some negligible function ϵ. This is the only scheme in our paper that is *not* publicly verifiable, i.e., only the receivers can check if a ciphertext is sound.

Theorem 5. *The scheme $\mathcal{CDRE}_2$ adapted from lossy trapdoor functions as described in Fig. 7 is a secure CNM-DRE against chosen-ciphertext attacks.* ∎

Discussion. The two paradigms (the one based on simulation-sound NIZK argument of knowledge and the one from lossy trapdoor functions) are both general and can be instantiated in a reasonably efficient way. The former can be realized from the SXDH and DLIN assumptions in bilinear groups. It allows short (constant) public keys and constant ciphertext size (more than a hundred group elements though). The latter paradigm has longer ciphertexts, and can be achieved via a number of simpler and more elementary assumptions such as DDH, LWE (learning with errors) [28], and Composite Residuosity [16].

One primary interest in studying CNM encryption schemes springs from non-malleable commitments. Correspondingly, our CNM-DRE's lead to *dual-receiver non-malleable commitments*, generalizing the regular non-malleable commitments, which one can commit to the message in a non-malleable sense for two independent receivers with double trapdoors, where they both know that the de-committed messages will be the same. This is a useful property, and it might find other interesting applications.

Acknowledgement. Many thanks for the valuable comments from the anonymous referees and Jens Groth that largely improved the paper. We would also like to thank Adam Smith for his very helpful discussion and in particular pointing us the OTR protocols, and Rui Zhang for his perceptive comments. Sherman

S.M. Chow is supported by the Early Career Scheme and the Early Career Award of the Research Grants Council, Hong Kong SAR (CUHK 439713), and grants (4055018, 4930034) from Chinese University of Hong Kong. Haibin Zhang is supported by NSF grants CNS 0904380 and CNS 1228828. Haibin Zhang also received support for this project under NSFC 61272035 while visiting Shandong University.

References

1. Baek, J., Safavi-Naini, R., Susilo, W.: On the Integration of Public Key Data Encryption and Public Key Encryption with Keyword Search. In: Katsikas, S.K., López, J., Backes, M., Gritzalis, S., Preneel, B. (eds.) ISC 2006. LNCS, vol. 4176, pp. 217–232. Springer, Heidelberg (2006)
2. Bellare, M., Boldyreva, A., Micali, S.: Public-Key Encryption in a Multi-user Setting: Security Proofs and Improvements. In: Preneel, B. (ed.) EUROCRYPT 2000. LNCS, vol. 1807, pp. 259–274. Springer, Heidelberg (2000)
3. Boneh, D., Boyen, X.: Efficient Selective-ID Secure Identity-Based Encryption Without Random Oracles. In: Cachin, C., Camenisch, J.L. (eds.) EUROCRYPT 2004. LNCS, vol. 3027, pp. 223–238. Springer, Heidelberg (2004)
4. Borisov, N., Goldberg, I., Brewer, E.A.: Off-the-record communication, or, why not to use PGP. In: WPES, pp. 77–84 (2004)
5. Boyen, X., Mei, Q., Waters, B.: Direct Chosen Ciphertext Security from Identity-Based Techniques. In: ACM Conference on Computer and Communications Security, pp. 320–329 (2005)
6. Camenisch, J.L., Michels, M.: Separability and Efficiency for Generic Group Signature Schemes (Extended Abstract). In: Wiener, M. (ed.) CRYPTO 1999. LNCS, vol. 1666, pp. 413–430. Springer, Heidelberg (1999)
7. Chow, S.S.M., Franklin, M., Zhang, H.: Practical Dual-Receiver Encryption: Soundness, Complete Non-Malleability, and Applications. Cryptology ePrint report 2013/858 (2013)
8. Clarkson, M.R., Chong, S., Myers, A.C.: Civitas: Toward a Secure Voting System. In: IEEE Symposium on Security and Privacy, pp. 354–368 (2008)
9. Cramer, R., Shoup, V.: Design and Analysis of Practical Public-Key Encryption Schemes Secure against Adaptive Chosen Ciphertext Attack. SIAM J. Comput. 33(1), 167–226 (2003)
10. Damgård, I.: Efficient Concurrent Zero-Knowledge in the Auxiliary String Model. In: Preneel, B. (ed.) EUROCRYPT 2000. LNCS, vol. 1807, pp. 418–430. Springer, Heidelberg (2000)
11. Damgård, I., Hofheinz, D., Kiltz, E., Thorbek, R.: Public-Key Encryption with Non-interactive Opening. In: Malkin, T. (ed.) CT-RSA 2008. LNCS, vol. 4964, pp. 239–255. Springer, Heidelberg (2008)
12. De Santis, A., Di Crescenzo, G., Ostrovsky, R., Persiano, G., Sahai, A.: Robust Non-interactive Zero Knowledge. In: Kilian, J. (ed.) CRYPTO 2001. LNCS, vol. 2139, pp. 566–598. Springer, Heidelberg (2001)
13. Diament, T., Lee, H.K., Keromytis, A.D., Yung, M.: The Dual Receiver Cryptosystem and its Applications. In: ACM Conference on Computer and Communications Security, pp. 330–343 (2004)
14. Dodis, Y., Katz, J., Smith, A., Walfish, S.: Composability and On-Line Deniability of Authentication. In: Reingold, O. (ed.) TCC 2009. LNCS, vol. 5444, pp. 146–162. Springer, Heidelberg (2009)

15. Fischlin, M.: Completely non-malleable schemes. In: Caires, L., Italiano, G.F., Monteiro, L., Palamidessi, C., Yung, M. (eds.) ICALP 2005. LNCS, vol. 3580, pp. 779–790. Springer, Heidelberg (2005)
16. Freeman, D.M., Goldreich, O., Kiltz, E., Rosen, A., Segev, G.: More Constructions of Lossy and Correlation-Secure Trapdoor Functions. In: Nguyen, P.Q., Pointcheval, D. (eds.) PKC 2010. LNCS, vol. 6056, pp. 279–295. Springer, Heidelberg (2010)
17. Groth, J.: Simulation-Sound NIZK Proofs for a Practical Language and Constant Size Group Signatures. In: Lai, X., Chen, K. (eds.) ASIACRYPT 2006. LNCS, vol. 4284, pp. 444–459. Springer, Heidelberg (2006)
18. Groth, J., Sahai, A.: Efficient Noninteractive Proof Systems for Bilinear Groups. SIAM J. Comput. 41(5), 1193–1232 (2012)
19. Herzog, J.C., Liskov, M., Micali, S.: Plaintext Awareness via Key Registration. In: Boneh, D. (ed.) CRYPTO 2003. LNCS, vol. 2729, pp. 548–564. Springer, Heidelberg (2003)
20. Jakobsson, M., Juels, A.: Mix and Match: Secure Function Evaluation via Ciphertexts. In: Okamoto, T. (ed.) ASIACRYPT 2000. LNCS, vol. 1976, pp. 162–177. Springer, Heidelberg (2000)
21. Kiltz, E.: Chosen-Ciphertext Security from Tag-Based Encryption. In: Halevi, S., Rabin, T. (eds.) TCC 2006. LNCS, vol. 3876, pp. 581–600. Springer, Heidelberg (2006)
22. Kiltz, E.: Chosen-Ciphertext Secure Key-Encapsulation Based on Gap Hashed Diffie-Hellman. In: Okamoto, T., Wang, X. (eds.) PKC 2007. LNCS, vol. 4450, pp. 282–297. Springer, Heidelberg (2007)
23. Libert, B., Yung, M.: Efficient Completely Non-malleable Public Key Encryption. In: Abramsky, S., Gavoille, C., Kirchner, C., Meyer auf der Heide, F., Spirakis, P.G. (eds.) ICALP 2010, Part I. LNCS, vol. 6198, pp. 127–139. Springer, Heidelberg (2010)
24. Lu, Y., Zhang, R., Lin, D.: Stronger Security Model for Public-Key Encryption with Equality Test. In: Abdalla, M., Lange, T. (eds.) Pairing 2012. LNCS, vol. 7708, pp. 65–82. Springer, Heidelberg (2013)
25. Naor, M., Yung, M.: Public-key Cryptosystems Provably Secure against Chosen Ciphertext Attacks. In: STOC, pp. 427–437 (1990)
26. Okamoto, T., Pointcheval, D.: REACT: Rapid Enhanced-Security Asymmetric Cryptosystem Transform. In: Naccache, D. (ed.) CT-RSA 2001. LNCS, vol. 2020, pp. 159–175. Springer, Heidelberg (2001)
27. Okamoto, T., Pointcheval, D.: The Gap-Problems: A New Class of Problems for the Security of Cryptographic Schemes. In: Kim, K.-C. (ed.) PKC 2001. LNCS, vol. 1992, pp. 104–118. Springer, Heidelberg (2001)
28. Peikert, C., Waters, B.: Lossy Trapdoor Functions and Their Applications. In: STOC, pp. 187–196 (2008)
29. Rackoff, C., Simon, D.R.: Non-Interactive Zero-Knowledge Proof of Knowledge and Chosen Ciphertext Attack. In: Feigenbaum, J. (ed.) CRYPTO 1991. LNCS, vol. 576, pp. 433–444. Springer, Heidelberg (1992)
30. Sahai, A.: Non-Malleable Non-Interactive Zero Knowledge and Adaptive Chosen-Ciphertext Security. In: FOCS, pp. 543–553 (1999)
31. Smith, A., Youn, Y.: An Efficient Construction of Dual-Receiver Encryption (2008) (unpublished manuscript)
32. Ventre, C., Visconti, I.: Completely Non-malleable Encryption Revisited. In: Cramer, R. (ed.) PKC 2008. LNCS, vol. 4939, pp. 65–84. Springer, Heidelberg (2008)

33. Wegman, M.N., Carter, L.: New Hash Functions and Their Use in Authentication and Set Equality. J. Comput. Syst. Sci. 22(3), 265–279 (1981)
34. Yang, G., Tan, C.H., Huang, Q., Wong, D.S.: Probabilistic Public Key Encryption with Equality Test. In: Pieprzyk, J. (ed.) CT-RSA 2010. LNCS, vol. 5985, pp. 119–131. Springer, Heidelberg (2010)
35. Zhang, R., Hanaoka, G., Imai, H.: A Generic Construction of Useful Client Puzzles. In: ASIACCS, pp. 70–79 (2009)
36. Zhang, R., Imai, H.: Generic Combination of Public Key Encryption with Keyword Search and Public Key Encryption. In: Bao, F., Ling, S., Okamoto, T., Wang, H., Xing, C. (eds.) CANS 2007. LNCS, vol. 4856, pp. 159–174. Springer, Heidelberg (2007)
37. Zhou, L., Marsh, M.A., Schneider, F.B., Redz, A.: Distributed Blinding for Distributed ElGamal Re-Encryption. In: ICDCS, pp. 815–824 (2005)

A   Building Blocks for CNM-DRE

Simulation-Sound and Simulation-Sound Extractable NIZK Proof of Knowledge. An NIZK proof of knowledge system $\mathcal{SSPK}$ is a *proof system* $(\mathsf{CGen}, \mathsf{P}, \mathsf{V})$ together with *knowledge extraction algorithms* $(\mathsf{E}_1, \mathsf{E}_2)$ and *simulation algorithms* $(\mathsf{S}_1, \mathsf{S}_2)$. The proof system satisfies *completeness, soundness, zero-knowledge, simulation soundness, and simulation sound extractability* properties. We assume some familiarity with NIZK and only recall the latter two.

We say a NIZK proof system *simulation sound* if no adversary can prove any false and new statement even with a simulation oracle. Formally, we define the ss-*advantage* against a polynomial-time adversary $\mathcal{A}$, $\mathbf{Adv}^{\mathrm{ss}}_{\mathcal{SSPK},\mathcal{A}}(k)$, for an efficiently computable relation R and a corresponding language $\mathcal{L}$ as
$\Pr[(\mathsf{crs}, \tau) \xleftarrow{\$} \mathsf{S}_1(1^k); (x, \pi) \xleftarrow{\$} \mathcal{A}^{\mathsf{S}_2(\mathsf{crs},\tau,\cdot)}(\mathsf{crs}) : (x, \pi) \text{ is new} \wedge x \notin \mathcal{L} \wedge \mathsf{V}(\mathsf{crs}, x, \pi) = 1].$

We say a NIZK proof is *simulation sound extractable* if one can always extract a witness, in the simulated setting, whenever the adversary with a simulation oracle makes a new proof. Namely, we define the sse-*advantage* against an adversary $\mathcal{A}$, $\mathbf{Adv}^{\mathrm{sse}}_{\mathcal{SSPK},\mathcal{A}}(k)$, for a relation R and a language $\mathcal{L}$ as the probability
$\Pr[(\mathsf{crs}, \tau, \mathsf{ek}) \xleftarrow{\$} \mathsf{Gen}_{\mathrm{unite}}(1^k); (x, \pi) \xleftarrow{\$} \mathcal{A}^{\mathsf{S}_2(\mathsf{crs},\tau,\cdot)}(\mathsf{crs}, \mathsf{ek}); \omega \xleftarrow{\$} \mathsf{E}_2(\mathsf{crs}, \mathsf{ek}, x, \pi) : (x, \pi) \text{ is new} \wedge (x, \omega) \notin R \wedge \mathsf{V}(\mathsf{crs}, x, \pi) = 1]$, where $\mathsf{Gen}_{\mathrm{unite}}(1^k)$ is a generation algorithm unifying extraction algorithm E_1 and simulation algorithm S_1 such that they share the same simulated common reference string crs.

Lossy Trapdoor Functions. A collection of (n, l)-lossy trapdoor functions $\mathcal{LTF} = (\mathcal{S}, \mathcal{F}, \mathcal{F}^{-1})$: $\mathcal{S}(1^k, 1)$ is the *injective function sampling* algorithm which outputs (s, t) where s is a function index and t is the trapdoor; $\mathcal{F}(s, \cdot)$ computes an *injective function* over the domain $\{0, 1\}^n$, while $\mathcal{F}^{-1}(t, \cdot)$ computes the inverse of the injective function; the *lossy function sampling* algorithm $\mathcal{S}(1^k, 0)$ outputs $(s, \perp)$ where s is a function index; $\mathcal{F}(s, \cdot)$ then computes a deterministic function over $\{0, 1\}^n$ such that its image size is at most 2^{n-l}. The first outputs of $\mathcal{S}(1^k, 1)$ and $\mathcal{S}(1^k, 0)$ are computationally indistinguishable.

All-but-one Trapdoor Functions. Let $\mathcal{B} = \{B_k\}_{k \in \mathbb{N}}$ be a collection of sets whose elements represent the *branches*. A collection of (n, l)-all-but-one trapdoor functions $\mathcal{ABO} = (\mathcal{S}_{abo}, \mathcal{G}_{abo}, \mathcal{G}_{abo}^{-1})$ with branch collection $\mathcal{B}_k$ consists of the following algorithms: With a given lossy branch b^*, the *trapdoor function sampling* algorithm $\mathcal{S}_{abo}(1^k, b^*)$ outputs (s, t) where s is a function index and t is the trapdoor. For any $b \in \mathcal{B}$ such that $b \neq b^*$, $\mathcal{G}_{abo}(s, b, \cdot)$ computes an *injective function* over the domain $\{0, 1\}^n$, while $\mathcal{G}^{-1}(t, b, \cdot)$ computes the inverse of the injective function. $\mathcal{G}^{-1}(t, b^*, \cdot)$ instead computes a deterministic function such that its image size is at most 2^{n-l}. It is required that, for any $b_0^*, b_1^* \in \mathcal{B}$, the first outputs of $\mathcal{S}_{abo}(1^k, b_0^*)$ and $\mathcal{S}_{abo}(1^k, b_1^*)$ are computationally indistinguishable.

Attacking PUF-Based Pattern Matching Key Generators via Helper Data Manipulation

Jeroen Delvaux and Ingrid Verbauwhede

ESAT/COSIC and iMinds, KU Leuven
Kasteelpark Arenberg 10, B-3001 Leuven-Heverlee, Belgium
{firstname.lastname}@esat.kuleuven.be

Abstract. Physically Unclonable Functions (PUFs) provide a unique signature for integrated circuits (ICs), similar to a fingerprint for humans. They are primarily used to generate secret keys, hereby exploiting the unique manufacturing variations of an IC. Unfortunately, PUF output bits are not perfectly reproducible and non-uniformly distributed. To obtain a high-quality key, one needs to implement additional post-processing logic on the same IC. Fuzzy extractors are the well-established standard solution. Pattern Matching Key Generators (PMKGs) have been proposed as an alternative. In this work, we demonstrate the latter construction to be vulnerable against manipulation of its public helper data. Full key recovery is possible, although depending on system design choices. We demonstrate our attacks using a 4-XOR arbiter PUF, manufactured in $65nm$ CMOS technology. We also propose a simple but effective countermeasure.

Keywords: PUF, secret key, helper data, fuzzy extractor, Hamming distance.

1 Introduction

Modern applications for integrated circuits (ICs) increasingly rely on cryptography to protect their sensitive data. Practically all cryptographic implementations require the ability to securely generate, store and retrieve secret keys. Traditionally, the secret keys are stored in non-volatile memory (NVM), using Flash technology for instance. However, providing full system security at a reasonable cost has proven to be very challenging, given that an attacker can easily gain physical access to the IC. NVM tends to be vulnerable against various hardware attacks [13], as the key is stored permanently in electrical form. Additional circuitry to protect the key is usually complemented by practical drawbacks: costly, bulky, battery powered, etc. Furthermore, most NVM technologies are CMOS incompatible, increasing the IC manufacturing cost.

Physically Unclonable Functions (PUFs) have been proposed as a more secure and more efficient alternative. Silicon PUFs leverage the normally undesired manufacturing variations of an IC, enhanced by CMOS technology scaling [6]. The post-manufacturing state of an IC represents an inherently unique secret in

J. Benaloh (Ed.): CT-RSA 2014, LNCS 8366, pp. 106–131, 2014.

non-electrical form. PUFs are electrical circuits that perform a two-step conversion for their own variability: from non-electrical form to analog electrical signals (voltages and currents) and finally to bits. The term 'unclonable' refers to the infeasibility to manufacture a replica of a PUF, as the nanoscale variations are uncontrollable. Input bits might be foreseen, making the PUF a function.

PUFs offer some remarkable advantages for secret key applications, in comparison to on-chip NVM. First, most silicon PUFs are CMOS compatible and hence cost-efficient. Second, PUFs are often assumed to be resistant against invasive attacks. One can argue that invasion damages the physical structure of the PUF, hereby destroying the secret. Third, keys are inherently unique for each manufactured sample of the IC and there is no need to explicitly program them. However, the ability to program an arbitrary key can still be foreseen if desired. Fourth, the key is only generated and stored in volatile memory (VM) whenever key-dependent operations have to be performed. As such, limits are posed on the attacker's time frame.

Unfortunately, PUF output bits are not directly usable as a secret key. One first needs to resolve two issues: (1) the bits are not perfectly reproducible, (2) the bits are non-uniformly distributed. Therefore, digital post-processing logic has to be implemented on the same IC. The use of public helper data is unavoidable hereby, requesting again NVM (preferably off-chip now for cost-efficiency reasons). Fuzzy extractors [2] are the well-established post-processing solution. Typical implementations employ an error-correcting code (ECC) and a cryptographic hash function. Pattern Matching Key Generators (PMKGs) [9] have been proposed as an alternative at the HOST 2011 conference. A patent on the construction has been granted by the World Intellectual Property Organization [10].

PMKGs employ so-called patterns, which are substrings in a long stream of (noisy) PUF output bits. The substring indices are considered to be secret as they directly define the secret key. The patterns are stored as public helper data; other stream bits are not exposed. To reconstruct the key, one does 'slide' the patterns along their regenerated streams, performing a matching procedure (measuring Hamming distance). In this work, we demonstrate the PMKG construction to be vulnerable against malicious modification of its public helper data. Via statistical observation of the PMKG failure rate, one can gradually retrieve the full bitstreams and hence the secret indices, although depending on system design choices. We demonstrate our attacks using a 4-XOR arbiter PUF, manufactured in $65nm$ CMOS technology.

The organization of this paper is as follows. Section 2 and 3 provide an introduction to PUFs and post-processing logic respectively. Section 4 describes the PMKG construction. Its failure characteristics are essential for our attacks: we analyze them in section 5. The attacks are presented in section 6. Countermeasures are discussed in section 7. Section 8 concludes the work.

2   Physically Unclonable Functions

PUFs are functions: their binary input and output vectors are referred to as challenges and responses respectively. In section 2.1, we comment on the number of challenge-response pairs (CRPs) as well as their secrecy. In sections 2.2 and 2.3, we describe two popular PUF architectures: the arbiter PUF and its XOR variant respectively. The latter architecture has been employed for the PMKG implementation of [9]. We do employ the same PUF to illustrate our attacks.

2.1   Challenge-Response Pairs and Their Secrecy

PUFs are often subdivided in two classes, depending on their number of CRPs [11]. Weak PUFs have few CRPs, often linearly increasing with the required IC area. They are primarily used to generate secret keys. Strong PUFs have a huge amount of CRPs, in the ideal case exponentially increasing with the required IC area. The generation of a secret key, assuming a traditional fuzzy extractor as post-processing logic, does not require such a huge amount of response bits. For the PMKG construction however, the use of a strong PUF might be indispensable.

The secrecy of CRPs depends on the use case of the PUF. For traditional secret key generation, it is imperative to keep the responses on-chip. The list of challenges, generating the stream of response bits, is to be considered as publicly known. The secrecy of the responses bits is not affected hereby, given that PUFs are 'random' functions. Hardware attacks (invasive, through side channels and via fault injection) are a threat for the secrecy of the response bits and hence also for the key. One can target the PUF itself as well as the post-processing logic [8]. Remember that PUFs are often assumed to be resistant against invasion. Experimental evidence is generally lacking however, except for the coating PUF [14].

For some PUF use cases, typically employing a strong PUF such as the arbiter PUF or its XOR variant, individual CRPs are exposed on purpose. This is also the case for the PMKG. The security arises from the CRP behavior unpredictability. Given the exposed CRPs, it should be infeasible to construct a mathematical model of the PUF. Machine learning (ML) techniques, like support vector machines and artificial neural networks, form a major threat. Given a limited set of training CRPs, algorithms automatically learn the input-output behavior, trying to generalize the underlying interactions. Both the arbiter PUF and its XOR variant are vulnerable, although the latter construction provides considerably more resistance [12].

2.2   Arbiter PUF

Architecture. Arbiter PUFs [7] quantify manufacturing variability via the propagation delays of logic gates. The high-level functionality is represented by figure 1(a). A rising edge propagates through two paths with identically designed delays. Because of nanoscale manufacturing variations however, there is

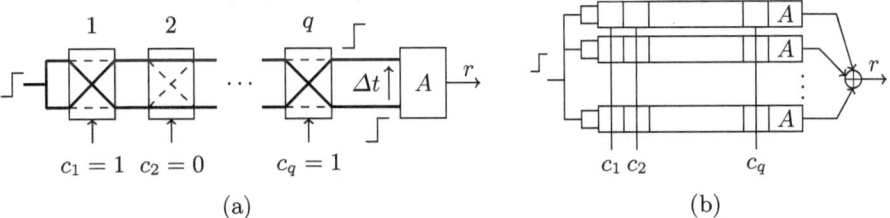

Fig. 1. Arbiter PUF (a) and its XOR variant (b)

a delay difference Δt between both paths. An arbiter decides which path 'wins' the race ($\Delta t \lessgtr 0$) and generates a response bit r.

The two paths are constructed from a series of q switching elements. Challenge bits c_i determine for each stage whether path segments are crossed or uncrossed. Each stage has a unique contribution to Δt, depending on its challenge bit. Challenge vector $\boldsymbol{Chal} = (c_1\ c_2\ \ldots\ c_q)$ determines the time difference Δt and hence the response bit r. The number of CRPs equals 2^q. The reproducibility differs per response bit: the smaller $|\Delta t|$, the easier to flip side because of various perturbations.

Machine Learning. Arbiter PUFs show additive linear behavior, as described in appendix A. This makes them vulnerable to modeling attacks: high accuracies can rapidly be obtained through ML techniques. In the paper proposing arbiter PUFs as a security primitive, ML was already identified as a threat [7]. They reported a modeling accuracy of 97% for their 64-stage $0.18\mu m$ CMOS implementation. The same accuracy was also reported for a more recent $65nm$ implementation, having 64-bit challenges too and using 5000 CRPs as a training set [3].

2.3 XOR Arbiter PUF

Several variants of the arbiter PUF increase the resistance against ML. They introduce various forms of non-linearity for this purpose. We only consider the XOR variant, which has been employed for the PMKG implementation of [9]. The response bits of multiple arbiter chains are XORed to a single response bit, as shown in figure 1(b). All chains have the same challenge as input. The more chains, the more resistance against against ML: the required number of CRPs and the computation time both increase rapidly [12]. However, the reproducibility decreases with the number of chains: the stability of r depends on the stability of all arbiter outputs. As a consequence, the burden of the post-processing logic (PMKG) does increase.

3   Post-Processing Logic: Generating Keys from PUF Responses

Unfortunately, PUF response bits are not directly usable as a secret key. On-chip digital post-processing logic is required to resolve two issues: (1) the response bits are not perfectly reproducible, (2) the response bits are non-uniformly distributed. Section 3.1 clarifies both issues. Section 3.2 introduces the general methodology to resolve them. Section 3.3 describes the well-established solution: the fuzzy extractor. We highlight all interfaces with the user: great care is required to maintain system security.

3.1   PUF Imperfections

A first PUF imperfection concerns the reproducibility of the response bits. The main responsible is noise in CMOS transistors (and interconnect), to be considered as a random time-dependent phenomenon [5]. Its presence is unavoidable. Environmental perturbations, originating from the IC supply voltage or the outside temperature for instance, worsen the problem. Their significance depends on the intended use of the IC. The reproducibility differs per response bit: some bits flip very often, others are very stable. This observation has already been made for arbiter PUFs in specific, although it is true in general.

A second imperfection of PUFs concerns the non-uniform distribution of the responses. The corresponding entropy reduction is clearly disadvantageous for secret key applications. One often considers bias, meaning that a PUF generates on average more 0's than 1's, or vice versa. Correlations between CRPs are another symptom, although harder to quantify. Systematic (spatially dependent) manufacturing variations are a major root cause for both bias and correlations. However, there are various other root causes. Strong PUF responses tend to be very correlated, as an enormous number of bits is extracted from a limited circuit area only. The linear additive delay model of the arbiter PUF (see appendix A) provides some insights in this matter.

3.2   Post-Processing Logic

Fixing the non-uniformity issue is relatively straightforward: one can apply a compression function to restore full entropy. Resolving the reproducibility issue tends to be more complicated. Two procedures are hereby defined. First, a one-time enrollment to mark a response vector $\boldsymbol{Resp}$ as a reference: a string of public helper bits $\boldsymbol{Pub}$, containing information about $\boldsymbol{Resp}$, is stored in (off-chip) NVM. Second, a reconstruction procedure for $\boldsymbol{Resp}$, given a nearby response vector $\boldsymbol{Resp'} = \boldsymbol{Resp} \oplus \boldsymbol{Error}$ and the public helper data. Hamming distance (HD) is the most intuitive proximity criterion, defined as $HD(\boldsymbol{Resp'}, \boldsymbol{Resp}) = HW(\boldsymbol{Error})$, with HW the Hamming weight.

Key reconstruction is performed in a setting where an attacker can easily gain physical access to the IC. The enrollment however, is assumed to take place in a secure environment, as an additional step after IC manufacturing. This assumption facilitates several purposes. First, enrollment procedures might require random uniformly distributed bits as an input. An external source of randomness could then be employed, reducing the IC overhead to a minimum. Furthermore, some constructions hereby enable the user to program an arbitrary key on the IC, despite the immutable PUF randomness. Second, several interfaces need to be disabled permanently after the enrollment. The one-time nature of the enrollment can be imposed with irreversible fuses, for instance.

Helper NVM should be considered as public, meaning that an attacker can read or even modify its data. Remember that PUFs have been proposed as a more secure and more efficient alternative for on-chip NVM: labelling helper data as private would undermine the need for PUFs. Helper string $\boldsymbol{Pub}$ is not supposed to leak any information about the secret key. Malicious modification of $\boldsymbol{Pub}$ is a second security concern.

3.3 Fuzzy Extractor

Fuzzy extractors [2] are the well-established post-processing solution. They form a very generic concept, but we limit ourselves to the most convenient data format for PUFs: binary vectors with HD as a distance metric. Their definition offers two guarantees. First, correctness of reconstruction, given $HD(\boldsymbol{Resp'}, \boldsymbol{Resp}) \leq t$, with t a fixed parameter. Second, a minimum entropy for $\boldsymbol{Resp}$, given an attacker that observes the helper string $\boldsymbol{Pub}$. Typical fuzzy extractor implementations contain two building blocks: an ECC construction and a cryptographic hash function, resolving the reproducibility and non-uniformity issue in a sequential manner.

Figure 2 shows the high-level architecture for secret key generation. A deterministic challenge generator extracts a noisy response vector from the (weak) PUF. A simple counter-based construction might be sufficient. Another option is a pseudorandom number generator (PRNG), starting from a fixed seed value. In either case: the full list of challenges should be considered as publicly known, as mentioned in section 2.1. The fuzzy extractor produces a high-quality secret key $\boldsymbol{Key}$, which is stored in VM for as long as needed. There are two bidirectional interfaces with the user (or attacker). First, an application with key-dependent operations, having input $\boldsymbol{I}$ and output $\boldsymbol{O}$. Second, the public helper string $\boldsymbol{Pub}$ in (off-chip) NVM, providing both read and write access.

Several ECC constructions have been proposed. We limit ourselves to an illustration with the code-offset construction. Its enrollment and reconstruction steps are listed below. Consider a binary $[n,k,2t+1]$ ECC, having block length n, dimension k and error-correcting capability t. Response vector $\boldsymbol{Resp}$, assumed to have length n, is considered as a codeword offset. XORing with a random codeword $\boldsymbol{Cword}$ results in the public helper string $\boldsymbol{Pub}$. During reconstruction, one does compensate the offset using an erroneous response vector $\boldsymbol{Resp'}$: the error vector $\boldsymbol{Error}$ is mapped onto the codeword hereby. Via error-correction, one can retrieve the original codeword $\boldsymbol{Cword}$ and hence also $\boldsymbol{Resp}$, the latter to be hashed to obtain the secret key $\boldsymbol{Key}$.

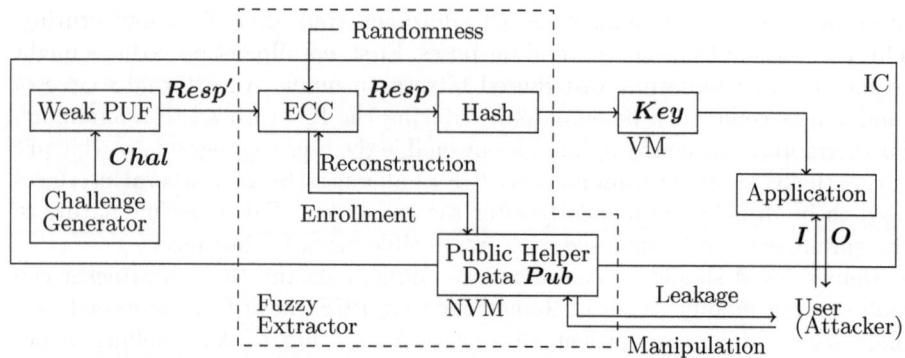

Fig. 2. Key generation via a typical fuzzy extractor

Enrollment	Reconstruction
Choose a random codeword $Cword$	$Cword' \leftarrow Resp' \oplus Pub = Cword \oplus Error$
$Pub \leftarrow Resp \oplus Cword$	Error-correct $Cword'$ to $Cword$
	$Resp \leftarrow Pub \oplus Cword$
	$Key \leftarrow Hash_1(Resp)$

Both helper data leakage and manipulation have been studied extensively. For the code-offset construction, one can prove that Pub does leak $n - k$ bits of information about $Resp$. Hash function $Hash_1$ does compensate for this additional entropy loss, given the initial entropy loss due to non-uniformity. An architectural extension, the so-called robust fuzzy extractor [1], detects modification with very high probability: key reconstruction is aborted in the former case. The enrollment and reconstruction steps are listed below, for the code-offset construction in particular. An additional helper string MAC provides an integrity assurance.

Enrollment	Reconstruction
Choose a random codeword $Cword$	$Cword' \leftarrow Resp' \oplus Pub^\star = Cword \oplus Error$
$Pub^\star \leftarrow Resp \oplus Cword$	Error-correct $Cword'$ to $Cword$
$MAC \leftarrow Hash_2(Resp, Pub^\star)$	Abort reconstruction if $HD(Cword', Cword) > t$
$Pub \leftarrow <Pub^\star, MAC>$	$Resp \leftarrow Pub^\star \oplus Cword$
	Abort reconstruction if $MAC \neq Hash_2(Resp, Pub^\star)$
	$Key \leftarrow Hash_1(Resp)$

4   Pattern Matching Key Generators

PMKGs [9] have been proposed as an alternative post-processing method. We observe that the proposal does not satisfy the fuzzy extractor definition: one can ensure correct reconstruction with a very high probability, but there is never a 100% guarantee, even with $HW(Error) = 0$. No claims about an improved efficiency and/or security are made. The authors present a high-level architecture, hereby suggesting a few alternatives and extensions, without posing a stringent need to implement the latter. We describe the most basic high-level functionality in section 4.1. Extensions and alternatives are considered as countermeasures, as they (unintentionally) increase the resistance against our attacks: we discuss them later in section 7. Section 4.2 further discusses PMKG failures, as we exploit them in our attacks.

4.1 Basic Functionality

Enrollment. Consider a stream of PUF response bits $Resp$. A subset of W consecutive bits is referred to as a pattern. Given a stream of $L + W - 1$ bits, there are L possible patterns one can select. A selection is made at random via an external interface, which is permanently disabled after the enrollment. The index j of the selected pattern is kept secret, but the corresponding response bits $Patt$ are exposed in public helper NVM. The secret index j can provide $log_2(L)$ bits for the construction of a secret key, assuming L to be a power of two. To obtain a secret key of sufficient length, the former mechanism is repeated for multiple streams, with each iteration referred to as a round. There is no reuse of CRPs within this set of streams $\{Resp_h\}$, with $h \in [1, H]$. Indices j_h of all H rounds are concatenated to obtain the full-length secret key $Key = K_0$. Note that the user is able to program an arbitrary key during enrollment.

Reconstruction. To reconstruct K_0, a pattern matching procedure is performed for every round. One does 'slide' each helper pattern $Patt_h$ along its corresponding stream of noisy response bits $Resp'_h$, testing the resemblance with every noisy pattern $Patt'_h$. At each index, one does compute $t = HD(Patt_h, Patt'_h)$. The index with $t \leq T$ is supposed to be the secret index j_h, with T a well-chosen threshold value. As described before, each j_h directly corresponds to a subkey.

High-Level Architecture. The high-level architecture is represented by figure 3. Similarities with figure 2 have been preserved, for ease of comparison. A strong PUF might be required because of the large CRP consumption. A reasonable amount of built-in ML resistance is assumed to be present. An XOR arbiter PUF is therefore suggested in [9]. As a challenge generator, one does suggest a Linear Feedback Shift Register (LFSR), starting from a fixed known seed value. The noisy PUF response bits are fed into a W-bit 'First In, First Out' (FIFO) shift register.

Helper Data. Public helper string Pub consists of H patterns $\{Patt_h\}$. There are two lines of defence against PUF modeling attacks. First, the exposure is small in comparison to the built-in ML resistance of the strong PUF. Note that one does reveal only a subset of the response bits. Second, the link between the exposed response bits and their corresponding challenges is unknown. Retrieving this link is actually equivalent to retrieving the secret key. For each round, there are L possibilities to link the exposed response bits to their challenges. Note that former observations only consider helper data leakage. Our attacks exploit malicious modification of the public helper string Pub.

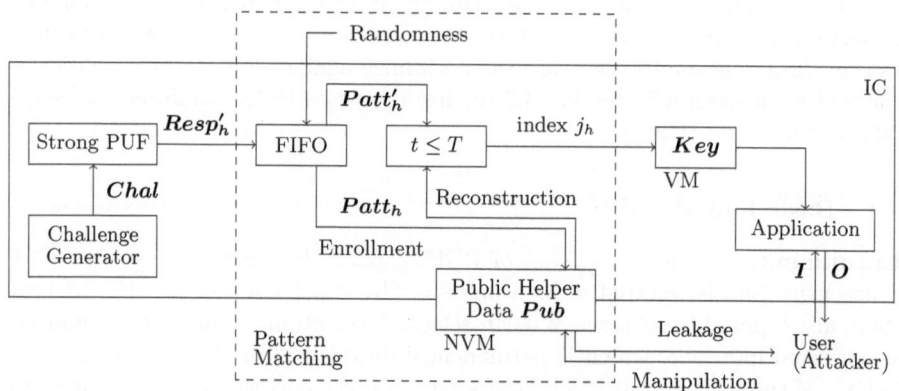

Fig. 3. Pattern matching key generator

Failures. There are two possible failure conditions for key reconstruction: pattern misses and pattern collisions. A pattern miss[1] occurs if $t > T$ at the subkey index of a certain round. A pattern collision occurs if $t \leq T$ for at least one non-subkey index of a certain round.

Parameter Configuration. There are four system parameters: W, L, H and T. Appropriate values need to be chosen for implementation purposes. We summarized the encountered trade-offs hereby in table 1. A better understanding of the failure probabilities is clearly desired. In [9], only intuitive insights are provided, supported by some experimental results. Therefore, we introduce an analytical framework, which also facilitates the understanding of the presented attacks.

Table 1. Choosing parameter values for the PMKG

Design goal	Quantifier/Estimator	Parameter dependencies
Security	Key length	$= H \, log_2(L)$
Speed, energy	PUF bits	$= H(L + W - 1)$
Area, power	FIFO size	$= W$
NVM size	Helper bits	$= HW$
Reliability	Pattern misses: probability of occurrence	Decreases with increasing T. Decreases with increasing W (while preserving the ratio T/W).
	Pattern collisions: probability of occurrence	Decreases with decreasing T. Decreases with increasing W (while preserving the ratio T/W). Decreases with decreasing L.

---

[1] For ease of notation, we do not use the definition given in [9]: a pattern miss occurs if $t > T$ for all indices of a certain round.

4.2 Handling Failures

The precise impact of pattern misses and collisions on the reconstructed key has not been specified in [9]. For each round, one expects a single index to satisfy the condition $t \leq T$. However, it is not clear what happens if either zero or at least two indices provide a match. Note that a single match is no guarantee for correctness: a pattern miss and a single pattern collision might occur simultaneously.

Our attacks do exploit statistical properties of both failure conditions. They are developed in a conservative manner, assuming a minimum level of information propagation. We assume any combination of pattern misses and/or collisions to be detected properly (PMKG extensions in section 7.1 can obtain this goal). This should prevent the application from (unknowingly) processing a data-dependent erroneous key $Key \neq K_0$. In case of a failure, one could force the reconstructed key to have a constant value $Key = K_{FAIL}$, still without notifying the application. Or alternatively, one might raise a flag, commanding the application to abort its execution: $Key = \perp$.

5 PMKG Failure Analysis

There are two failure conditions for the PMKG: pattern misses and pattern collisions. We now study their probability of occurrence extensively: a good understanding will be essential for our attacks. In section 5.1, we construct approximate formulas for the failure probabilities. Except for providing useful insights, they are actually very helpful to determine appropriate system parameters (W, L, H and T), as mentioned before. Section 5.2 provides a graphical illustration.

5.1 Failure Probabilities

The occurrence of both failure conditions indicates an inability to cope with response bit errors. Therefore, we consider the reproducibility of the PUF bits as a starting point. A crucial observation has been stated in section 3.1: the reproducibility differs per response bit. With $R \in [0, 1]$, we denote the probability that a particular response bit evaluates to '1'. To determine the nominal value of the bit, we evaluate $R \lessgtr \frac{1}{2}$. The further from $R = \frac{1}{2}$, the more reproducible the bit.

To obtain workable formulas, providing useful insights, we introduce a few approximations. First, we rely on averaged statistics of R. This approach is accurate for sufficiently wide patterns (large W), which should be the case in practice. Second, we make abstraction of the fact that patterns do overlap. Third, we ignore time-dependencies of R due to low-frequency disturbances (with respect to the sampling rate), regarding either CMOS/interconnect noise or the IC's environment.

We denote the probability of a pattern miss and collision as P_{MISS} and P_{COLL} respectively. The overall failure probability P_{FAIL} is easily expressed as shown below. We now discuss pattern misses and pattern collisions separately. Measurements on our $65nm$ PUF illustrate the theory.

$$P_{FAIL} = 1 - (1 - P_{MISS})^H (1 - P_{COLL})^H$$

Pattern Misses. Before considering a whole pattern, we first study the mismatch behavior of a single response bit. Given its reproducibility R, the probability of a mismatch between its enrolled and regenerated instance is as shown below. As it will be of interest later, we note that a (one-time) majority vote during enrollment could reduce this probability. The more votes, the more likely the enrolled instance to be correct. In the ideal case of negligible enrollment error, the mismatch probability would be as follows: $P_{MISS\_BIT\_IDEAL}(R) = \frac{1}{2} - |R - \frac{1}{2}|$. Figure 4(a) plots both curves as a function of R.

$$P_{MISS\_BIT}(R) = 2R(1 - R).$$

As patterns contain many bits, we have particular interest for an averaged mismatch probability. We define the latter via the probability density function (PDF) of R, as shown below. Figure 4(c) plots $PDF_R(R)$ for our $65nm$ PUF, as measured for 25000 response bits, evaluated 100 times each. We obtain $\overline{P_{MISS\_BIT}} \approx 14\%$. With a perfect majority vote, one could obtain a reduced probability of $\overline{P_{MISS\_BIT\_IDEAL}} \approx 10\%$.

$$\overline{P_{MISS\_BIT}} = \int_0^1 P_{MISS\_BIT}(R) PDF_R(R) \, dR$$

We now consider a full pattern, approximating the mismatch outcome of each bit as a Bernouilli trial, using the averaged probability $\overline{P_{MISS\_BIT}}$. The probability of a pattern miss is then easily described via a cumulative binomial distribution, as expressed below. The formula confirms the intuitive design guidelines

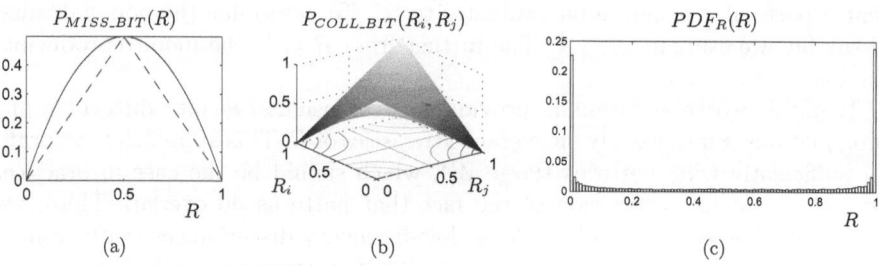

Fig. 4. (a) Probability of a response bit mismatch. The dashed curve corresponds with a majority vote during enrollment, in the ideal case. (b) Probability of a response bit collision. (c) Probability density function of R for our $65nm$ PUF.

of table 1 to reduce pattern misses. The same formula could be employed in case of a perfect majority vote, using $\overline{P_{MISS\_BIT\_IDEAL}}$ instead.

$$P_{MISS} = 1 - \sum_{t=0}^{T} f_{BIN}(t; W, \overline{P_{MISS\_BIT}}) \quad \text{with } f_{BIN}(t; w, p) = \binom{w}{t} p^t (1-p)^{w-t}.$$

Pattern Collisions. For pattern collisions, we again consider the behavior of a single bit first. Now, the enrolled and regenerated instance correspond to different response bits. The probability of a match is as shown below, given their reproducibilities R_i and R_j. Figure 4(b) plots the corresponding surface, together with its contour lines.

$$P_{COLL\_BIT}(R_i, R_j) = R_i R_j + (1 - R_i)(1 - R_j).$$

As patterns contain many bits, we are again interested in an averaged probability. A definition is provided via the PDF of R, as shown below. The probability can be rewritten in terms of the response bit bias. We define R_B as the expected value of R, which should be $\frac{1}{2}$ in the ideal case of zero bias. We estimate $\overline{P_{COLL\_BIT}} \approx 50\%$ for our (very low bias) $65nm$ PUF.

$$\overline{P_{COLL\_BIT}} = \iint_{[0,1] \times [0,1]} P_{COLL\_BIT}(R_i, R_j) PDF_R(R_i) PDF_R(R_j) \, dR_i \, dR_j$$

$$= R_B^2 + (1 - R_B)^2 \quad \text{with } R_B = \int_0^1 R \, PDF_R(R) \, dR.$$

We now consider a full pattern, with the match outcome of each bit again as a Bernouilli trial, using the averaged probability $\overline{P_{COLL\_BIT}}$. The probability of a pattern collision is easily described via a cumulative binomial distribution, as shown below. Parameter Q corresponds with the number of collision candidates. The formula confirms the intuitive design guidelines of table 1 to reduce pattern collisions.

$$P_{COLL} = P_{COLL}(L-1) \quad \text{with } P_{COLL}(Q) = 1 - \left(1 - \sum_{t=0}^{T} f_{BIN}(t; W, 1 - \overline{P_{COLL\_BIT}})\right)^Q$$

5.2 Graphical Interpretation

For a better understanding, we graphically interpret the failure probabilities. We incorporate the averaged characteristics of our PUF: $\overline{P_{MISS\_BIT}} = 0.14$ and $\overline{P_{COLL\_BIT}} = 0.50$. Figure 5 plots the probability of a pattern miss and a pattern collision as a function of T, for $W \in \{64, 128, 256\}$ and fixing $L = 1024$. Pattern misses and collisions are an issue for low and high values of T respectively. The optimal thresholds, minimizing the overall failure probability P_{FAIL}, are indicated by a vertical line.

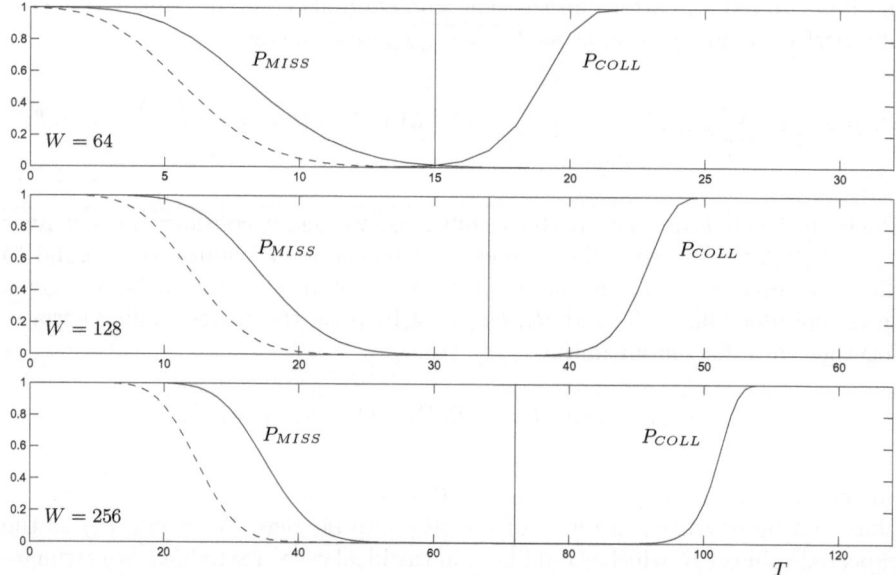

Fig. 5. Failure probabilities, incorporating our PUF statistics $\overline{P_{MISS\_BIT}} = 0.14$ and $\overline{P_{COLL\_BIT}} = 0.50$, using $L = 1024$ and $W \in \{64, 128, 256\}$. Functions are of discrete nature, although drawn continuously. The optimal thresholds are $T = 15$, $T = 34$ and $T = 72$. Dashed curves represent the pattern miss probability in case of a perfect majority vote: $\overline{P_{MISS\_BIT\_IDEAL}} = 0.10$.

The need for sufficiently wide patterns is clearly visible, as one demonstrated experimentally in [9]. For $W = 64$ for instance, it is not possible to make P_{FAIL} negligible. For $W = 128$ however, one is able to fix an appropriate threshold. We employ $W = 256$ to illustrate our attacks, although this setting actually corresponds to a system overdesign. Note that a majority vote during enrollment could alleviate the need for wide patterns.

6   Attacks

We present two key recovery attacks for PMKG devices. They are named Snake I and Snake II, as their graphical representation contains some striking similarities with the well-known video game. We first discuss the attacker model in section 6.1. Section 6.2 describes the setup for our experimental validation. Section 6.3 provides a common framework for the attacks. We discuss Snake I and Snake II separately in sections 6.4 and 6.5 respectively.

6.1   Attacker Model

We consider a PMKG device configured with a secret key $Key = K_0$, assuming the enrollment has been performed in a secure environment. We assume that all parameters $(W, L, H$ and $T)$ are fixed by design and can not be modified. We consider an active attacker with physical access to the device, trying to retrieve K_0 via the IC interfaces: modifying the public helper string Pub, controlling the application input I and observing the application output O. As described in section 4.2, we assume a minimum level of information propagation for the PMKG in case of a failure: $Key = K_{FAIL}$ or $Key = \bot$.

Our attacks rely on a different assumption regarding the application, as formalized below. Application input I is fixed hereby. We consider the requirement for Snake II to be satisfied always: any practical application should behave differently if K_0 is not reconstructed properly. Snake I utilizes key reprogramming: the device is then configured with a key $K_0' \neq K_0$. We require key reconstruction failures of K_0' to be observable via the application output O. We state that many (if not most) practical applications do satisfy. Consider for instance all applications where O contains any form of encrypted data. Furthermore, one might broaden the range of applications via side channel analysis. The occurrence of both $Key = K_{FAIL}$ and $Key = \bot$ might be recognizable via timing information, power consumption, etc.

Failure Handling	Snake I	Snake II
$Key = K_{FAIL}$	$O_{K_0'} \neq O_{K_{FAIL}}$	$O_{K_0} \neq O_{K_{FAIL}}$
$Key = \bot$	$O_{K_0'} \neq O_\bot$	$O_{K_0} \neq O_\bot$

6.2   Experimental Validation

The PMKG implementation of [9] employs a 4-XOR arbiter PUF. We illustrate our attacks using the same PUF architecture, for ease of comparison. More precisely: we use 64-stage arbiter PUFs manufactured in $65nm$ CMOS technology [4]. XORing is not performed on-chip but afterwards in software. However, this fact does not affect the validity of our demonstration.

We implemented the PMKG fully in software. For ease of testing, we emulate the $65nm$ PUF as follows. First, we measured the reproducibility R of many response bits, using 100 evaluations each. These bits are subsequently employed to construct streams of length $L+W-1$. We evaluate bits as $r \leftarrow (rand() < R)$, with $rand() \in [0\ 1]$ the PRNG output of our programming environment, which has a uniform PDF. Like this, there is no limit on the number of evaluations per bit.

The failure probability formulas of section 5.1 rely on approximations. Workability and insights were preferred above analytical complexity. As a consequence, three effects have not been included: (1) an individual R for every pattern/stream bit, (2) pattern overlap and (3) time-dependencies of R due to low-frequency disturbances. Our experimental tests do incorporate (1) and (2) properly. Although (3) has not been addressed explicitly, its impact could be diminished by lowering the sampling rate (the number of key reconstructions per time unit). One could interleave measurements for multiple rounds hereby, to alleviate the execution time penalty.

6.3   Common Framework Snake I and Snake II

Snake I and Snake II recover secret indices j on a per round basis. The initially unexposed bit directly left (or right) of a helper data pattern is retrieved via statistical properties of the overall failure probability P_{FAIL}. Repeating the same mechanism over and over again, we slide (like a snake) along the PUF response string of length $L+W-1$, revealing a bit with every move. Despite the exposure of more response bits, increased ML opportunities are not the main threat here: an abrupt change in failure rate when sliding too far, directly reveals the secret index of the original pattern. Figure 6 provides an illustration.

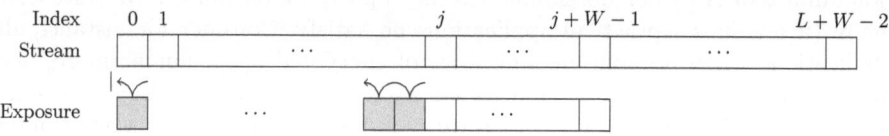

Fig. 6. The common framework for Snake I and Snake II, illustrated for a single round. Newly exposed bits are shaded.

For each move of the snake, there are two hypotheses for the unknown bit: its value is either '0' or '1'. We collect failure rate statistics for patterns $(0\ r_{i+1}\ r_{i+2}\ \ldots\ r_{i+W-1})$ and $(1\ r_{i+1}\ r_{i+2}\ \ldots\ r_{i+W-1})$, with i the index of the unknown bit. The correct guess tends to generate either more or less failures, depending on the snake. Snake I and II use pattern misses and pattern collisions as primary failure condition respectively. Failures are rare events under nominal conditions. To amplify statistical differences between both hypotheses, we intentionally introduce errors in the corrupted patterns.

For ease of notation, we introduce a key reconstruction failure flag: $Failure \in \{0,1\}$, to be raised when any pattern miss or collision did occur. This flag is updated by the attacker after each key reconstruction.

6.4   Snake I

Snake I forces the PMKG device to reconstruct new altered keys, with index i of the unknown bit as a subkey. Therefore, the helper pattern is set to $(0\ r_{i+1}\ r_{i+2}\ \ldots\ r_{i+W-1})$, arbitrarily choosing $r_i = 0$. Given $i \geq 0$, this results with very high probability in a successfully reconstructed key, even if $r_i = 1$. A persistent inability to successfully reconstruct a key, indicates an excess of $i = 0$, hereby revealing the value of j. Figure 7 provides an illustration of the helper data dynamics.

We exploit pattern misses to determine r_i, given $i \geq 0$. A correct guess of r_i results in a lower mismatch rate for this bit: $\frac{1}{2} - \left|R_i - \frac{1}{2}\right| < \frac{1}{2} + \left|R_i - \frac{1}{2}\right|$. As a consequence, less pattern misses are bound to occur for the correct hypothesis: the expected value of Hamming distance t differs $2\left|R_i - \frac{1}{2}\right|$ at pattern index i. The

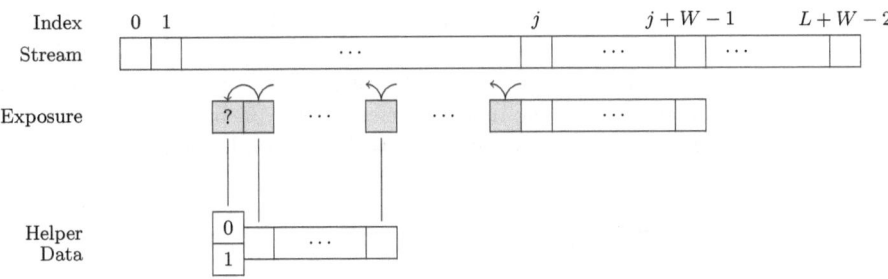

Fig. 7. Snake I helper data, illustrated for a single round. Newly exposed bits are shaded.

Algorithm 1. SNAKE I

Input: Original helper data $\boldsymbol{Patt}_h \in \{0,1\}^{1 \times W}$ of round $h \in [1\ H]$
Key reconstruction failure flag $Failure \in \{0,1\}$
Number of pattern errors $T^\star$
Number of samples N
Output: Modified helper data $\boldsymbol{Patt}_h^\star \in \{0,1\}^{1 \times W}$ of round h
Secret index $j \in [0\ L-1]$ of round h
$j \leftarrow 0$
$stop \leftarrow 0$
while $stop = 0$ **do**
$\quad \boldsymbol{Patt}_h^\star \leftarrow (0\ \boldsymbol{Patt}_h[1:W-1])$
$\quad$ **if** $Failure = 1$ **then**
$\quad\quad |\ stop \leftarrow 1$
$\quad$ **else**
$\quad\quad j \leftarrow j+1$
$\quad\quad FailureRate0 \leftarrow 0$
$\quad\quad FailureRate1 \leftarrow 0$
$\quad\quad$ **for** $n \leftarrow 1$ **to** N **do**
$\quad\quad\quad$ Choose randomly $e \in \{0,1\}^{1 \times W-1}$ with $HW(e) = T^\star$
$\quad\quad\quad \boldsymbol{Patt}_h^\star \leftarrow (0\ \boldsymbol{Patt}_h[1:W-1] \oplus e)$
$\quad\quad\quad FailureRate0 \leftarrow FailureRate0 + Failure/N$
$\quad\quad\quad \boldsymbol{Patt}_h^\star \leftarrow (1\ \boldsymbol{Patt}_h[1:W-1] \oplus e)$
$\quad\quad\quad FailureRate1 \leftarrow FailureRate1 + Failure/N$
$\quad\quad r_i \leftarrow (FailureRate0 > FailureRate1)$
$\quad\quad \boldsymbol{Patt}_h \leftarrow (r_i\ \boldsymbol{Patt}_h[1:W-1])$

---

further from $R_i = \frac{1}{2}$, the easier to observe statistical differences in failure rate. To amplify failure statistics, we randomly flip $T^\star$ bits of the two hypothetical patterns, on corresponding positions for bits r_{i+1} to r_{i+W-1}.

Algorithm 1 provides pseudocode for Snake I, applied on a certain round $h \in [1\ H]$. The larger the number of samples N, the more confidence one should have in the prediction of r_i. Our tests indicate highly feasible values of N, e.g. 10000, to be sufficient. An occasional prediction error, typically occurring if $R_i \approx \frac{1}{2}$, can be tolerated. An appropriate value of $T^\star$ has to be chosen. Algorithm 2 provides pseudocode of a simple method: the (initial) probability of a pattern miss is centered at $\frac{1}{2}$. Note that we observe statistics for all rounds hereby.

Algorithm 2. SNAKE I PROFILING

Input: Original helper data $\langle \boldsymbol{Patt}_1, \boldsymbol{Patt}_2, \ldots, \boldsymbol{Patt}_H \rangle \in \{0,1\}^{H \times W}$
        Key reconstruction failure flag $Failure \in \{0,1\}$
        Number of samples N
Output: Modified helper data $\langle \boldsymbol{Patt}_1^\star, \boldsymbol{Patt}_2^\star, \ldots, \boldsymbol{Patt}_H^\star \rangle \in \{0,1\}^{H \times W}$
        Number of errors $T^\star$
for $t \leftarrow 1$ **to** T **do**
    $FailureRate(t) \leftarrow 0$
    for $n \leftarrow 1$ **to** N **do**
        $\langle \boldsymbol{Patt}_1^\star, \boldsymbol{Patt}_2^\star, \ldots, \boldsymbol{Patt}_H^\star \rangle \leftarrow \langle \boldsymbol{Patt}_1, \boldsymbol{Patt}_2, \ldots, \boldsymbol{Patt}_H \rangle$
        Choose a random $h \in [1\ H]$
        Choose randomly $e \in \{0,1\}^{1 \times W}$ with $HW(e) = t$
        $\boldsymbol{Patt}_h^\star \leftarrow \boldsymbol{Patt}_h \oplus e$
        $FailureRate(t) \leftarrow FailureRate(t) + Failure/N$
$T^\star \leftarrow \arg\min_t |FailureRate(t) - \frac{1}{2}|$

Variants and extensions of former algorithms could serve various purposes. (1) Robustness and/or efficiency could be improved. For algorithm 1 for instance, one could measure samples until a certain level of confidence is obtained regarding the unknown bit r_i. Furthermore, one could adjust the value $T^\star$ at run-time, hereby stabilizing the failure rates. (2) A variant of algorithm 1 could error-correct the initially exposed pattern $\boldsymbol{Patt}_h$, minimizing the pattern miss probability. (3) An extension of algorithm 2 could provide estimates for $\overline{P_{MISS\_BIT}}$, or alternatively $\overline{P_{MISS\_BIT\_IDEAL}}$. (4) One could estimate R, both for initially and newly exposed response bits.

The effect of flipping $T^\star$ bits can be studied with our analytical failure framework. Figure 8 provides an illustration for our 65nm PUF. We rely on two assumptions in order to obtain simple formulas. First, $R_i \in \{0,1\}$, corresponding to the best observable difference between hypotheses. Second, we assume all exposed bits to be correct. For initially exposed bits, this would require a preceding error correction with variant (2) of algorithm 1. For newly exposed bits, this would require a very high N in algorithm 1 to obtain a quasi perfect prediction. Note that one could construct a more generally applicable mathematical model.

6.5 Snake II

Snake II employs pattern collisions as primary failure condition. Figure 9 illustrates the helper data dynamics. The alignment with secret index j is preserved. The pattern at index i is employed as a source of collisions. A correct guess for r_i, provided at index j, does result in more collisions with the former pattern: hypotheses can hence be distinguished. A persistent absence of failures (collisions), indicates an excess of $i = 0$, hereby revealing the value of j.

To stimulate the occurrence of a collision, we again flip $T^\star$ bits, on corresponding positions for bits r_{j+1} to r_{j+W-1}. We only flip bits that represent a mismatch with the intended collision source. As an undesired side effect however, the probability of a pattern miss will increase as well. So both conditions may contribute significantly to the overall failure rate P_{FAIL}, causing difficulties to distinguish hypotheses. Algorithm 3 provides pseudocode for Snake II, applicable in absence

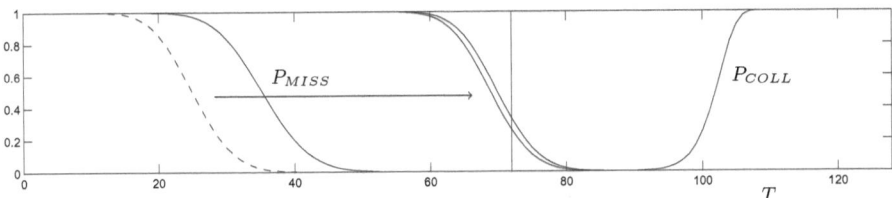

Fig. 8. Snake I failure probabilities using $L = 1024$, $W = 256$ and $T = 72$. We incorporate the reproducibility statistics of our $65nm$ PUF: $\overline{P_{MISS\_BIT}} = 0.14$, $\overline{P_{MISS\_BIT\_IDEAL}} = 0.10$ and $\overline{P_{COLL\_BIT}} = 0.50$. Functions are of discrete nature, although drawn continuously. The pattern miss curve shifts to the right for both hypotheses, as indicated by the arrow. We assume $R_i \in \{0, 1\}$. Furthermore, we assume all exposed bits to be correct. The correct hypothesis then results in $P_{MISS} = \sum_{t_1=0}^{T} f_{BIN}(t_1, W - T^\star - 1, \overline{P_{MISS\_BIT\_IDEAL}}) \sum_{t_2=0}^{T-t_1} f_{BIN}(t_2, T^\star, 1 - \overline{P_{MISS\_BIT\_IDEAL}})$. The incorrect hypothesis then results in $P_{MISS} = \sum_{t_1=0}^{T-1} f_{BIN}(t_1, W - T^\star - 1, \overline{P_{MISS\_BIT\_IDEAL}}) \sum_{t_2=0}^{T-1-t_1} f_{BIN}(t_2, T^\star, 1 - \overline{P_{MISS\_BIT\_IDEAL}})$. We employed $T^\star = 55$.

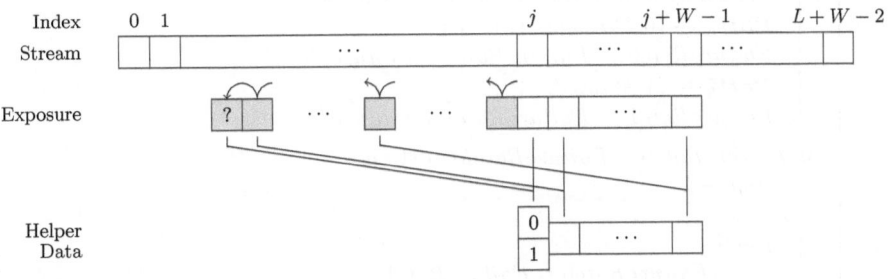

Fig. 9. Snake II helper data, illustrated for a single round. Newly exposed bits are shaded.

of the former issue. Again, very feasible values of N (e.g. 10000) turn out to be successful then.

We study the modified failure probabilities with our analytical framework. Figure 10 provides an illustration for our 65nm PUF. We rely on the same assumptions as before to obtain simple formulas. Threshold value T has a major impact on the feasibility of the attack: it might not be possible to fix $T^\star$ so that hypotheses can be distinguished easily. The smaller T, the larger $T^\star$ in order to obtain collision behavior. For large values of T, as illustrated on the figure, there is typically no problem: only pattern collisions contribute significantly to P_{FAIL}. For small values of T, a pattern miss would occur practically always, completely overshadowing the collision behavior. For medium values of T, both R_i and R_j contribute significantly to the statistical difference in failure rate. Note that [9] does not provide any procedure to determine T or any other system parameters.

Several workarounds could mitigate the former issue. (1) For rounds with $R_j \approx \frac{1}{2}$, pattern misses do not contribute to the statistical difference. A variant of algorithm 1 can determine whether this is the case, as stated before. (2) Or more

---

Algorithm 3. SNAKE II

Input: Original helper data $\boldsymbol{Patt}_h \in \{0,1\}^{1 \times W}$ of round $h \in [1\ H]$
Key reconstruction failure flag $Failure \in \{0,1\}$
Number of pattern errors $T^\star$
Stop condition $FailureRateMin \in [0\ 1]$
Number of samples N
Output: Modified helper data $\boldsymbol{Patt}_h^\star \in \{0,1\}^{1 \times W}$ of round h
Secret index $j \in [0\ L-1]$ of round h
$\boldsymbol{P}_h^\diamond \leftarrow \boldsymbol{Patt}_h$
$j \leftarrow 0$
$stop \leftarrow 0$
while $stop = 0$ **do**
    $FailureRate0 \leftarrow 0$
    $FailureRate1 \leftarrow 0$
    for $n \leftarrow 1$ **to** N **do**
        $\boldsymbol{e} \leftarrow \boldsymbol{Patt}_h[2 : W] \oplus \boldsymbol{Patt}_h^\diamond[1 : W-1]$
        Randomly reduce $HW(\boldsymbol{e})$ so that it equals $T^\star$
        $\boldsymbol{Patt}_h^\star \leftarrow (0\ \boldsymbol{Patt}_h[2 : W] \oplus \boldsymbol{e})$
        $FailureRate0 \leftarrow FailureRate0 + Failure/N$
        $\boldsymbol{Patt}_h^\star \leftarrow (1\ \boldsymbol{Patt}_h[2 : W] \oplus \boldsymbol{e})$
        $FailureRate1 \leftarrow FailureRate1 + Failure/N$
    if $FailureRate0 < FailureRateMin$ **then**
        $stop \leftarrow 1$
    else
        $j \leftarrow j + 1$
        $r_i \leftarrow (FailureRate0 < FailureRate1)$
        $\boldsymbol{Patt}_h^\diamond \leftarrow (r_i\ \boldsymbol{Patt}_h^\diamond[1 : W-1])$

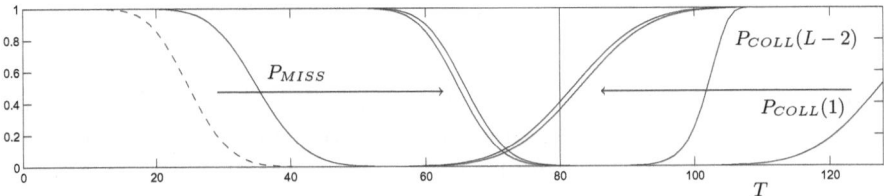

Fig. 10. Snake II failure probabilities using $L = 1024$, $W = 256$ and $T = 80$. We incorporate the reproducibility statistics of our $65nm$ PUF: $\overline{P_{MISS\_BIT}} = 0.14$, $\overline{P_{MISS\_BIT\_IDEAL}} = 0.10$ and $\overline{P_{COLL\_BIT}} = 0.50$. Functions are of discrete nature, although drawn continuously. The pattern miss and collision curve shift to the right and left respectively for both hypotheses, as indicated by the arrows. We assume $R_i, R_j \in \{0,1\}$. Furthermore, we assume all exposed bits to be correct. The correct hypothesis then results in $P_{COLL} = \sum_{t_1=T^\star}^{T^\star+T} f_{BIN}(t_1, W-1, 1-\overline{P_{COLL\_BIT}}) \sum_{t_2=0}^{T^\star+T-t_1} f_{BIN}(t_2, T^\star, \overline{P_{MISS\_BIT\_IDEAL}})$. The incorrect hypothesis then results in $P_{COLL} = \sum_{t_1=T^\star}^{T^\star+T-1} f_{BIN}(t_1, W-1, 1-\overline{P_{COLL\_BIT}}) \sum_{t_2=0}^{T^\star+T-1-t_1} f_{BIN}(t_2, T^\star, \overline{P_{MISS\_BIT\_IDEAL}})$. We employed $T^\star = 50$.

generally applicable: one could estimate R_j and compensate its contribution with respect to the observed statistical difference. (3) In section 4.2, we made the conservative assumption that all pattern misses and collisions are detected properly. However, if this is not the case, one might be able to tell whether a failure is caused by either a miss or a collision. (4) Appendix B discusses a method to generate a large and small shift for the pattern collision and pattern miss curve respectively.

7 Countermeasures

Our attacks have been elaborated for the basic PMKG architecture. We now also consider the various architectural extensions and alternatives: section 7.1 provides a functional description. All of them are treated as countermeasures, as they (unintentionally) increase the resistance against our attacks. Section 7.2 summarizes the corresponding attack capabilities.

7.1 PMKG Extensions and Alternatives

We first describe three extensions of the basic PMKG architecture, all of them to be considered as optional. Subsequently, we describe two alternatives, which are briefly mentioned in the patent application [10] only. We stress that only the first extension has been proposed with increased security as an objective.

Extension: Bi-modal Challenge Generator. Bi-modality of the challenge generator has been proposed as a third ML countermeasure. The secret index of each round is employed to 'fork' the next round of the challenge generator.

Stated otherwise: the PUF challenge/response stream for each round depends on the secret indices of all previous rounds. As a consequence, the CRP link becomes less and less traceable, with a multiplicative rate of L per round.

We make two observations. First, one does not mention that bi-modality could facilitate failure detection. In particular for the combination of a pattern miss and a single pattern collision within a certain round, resulting in a single matching index. Bi-modality would then cause a regular pattern miss for all subsequent rounds, with very high probability. This is straightforward to detect as no matching indices are found. Second, the enormous CRP consumption of bi-modality makes the use of a strong PUF indispensable. However, the use of a weak PUF might even eliminate the ML threat, as their architectures provide considerably lower degrees of correlation (see section 3.1).

Extension: Key Mixing. Secret indices are concatenated to obtain the full secret key. One suggests the optional use of a non further clarified key mixer, post-processing the secret indices. We presume that this could be any deterministic function, not necessarily one-way. Furthermore, one mentions an alternative for the secret indices: state bits of a bi-modal challenge generator could be employed as well.

Extension: Failure Detection Hash. Pattern misses and/or collisions might result in an erroneous reconstructed key. Only with a detection mechanism, an appropriate action can be taken. One suggest the use of a cryptographic hash function, having the bi-modal challenge stream as an input. The digest is stored in public helper NVM during enrollment. Its value is recomputed for every key reconstruction, to check whether there is a match.

We have two remarks. First, there is no adequate detection for the last round. The introduction of an additional dummy round, or simply hashing the set of all secret indices, would resolve this issue. Second, a cryptographic hash function is not readily available as for a traditional fuzzy extractor, leading to a substantial hardware overhead.

Alternative: Best Matching Patterns. During reconstruction, a fixed threshold T is employed to retrieve the secret indices. However, one could also look for the best matching pattern, having the smallest t within a round. The failure characteristics differ considerably with respect to the original proposal, as discussed in appendix C.

Alternative: Non-Overlapping Patterns. Patterns might be chosen in a non-overlapping manner. We consider this as very inefficient however. The number of PUF response bits increases from $H(L + W - 1)$ to HLW, given very comparable failure probabilities.

7.2 Attack Capabilities Overview

Table 2 summarizes the capabilities of our attacks, including all but one countermeasures. The 'best matching patterns' alternative is discussed separately in appendix C. The direct retrieval of (sub)keys is considered to be the main security risk. However, increased ML opportunities due to the exposure of additional response bits, should be taken into account too.

Table 2. Attacks and countermeasures

Counter-measures	Attacks	
	Snake I	Snake II
None	Exposure of all response bits; retrieval of all secret indices; retrieval of the full secret key.	Exposure of all response bits; retrieval of all secret indices; retrieval of the full secret key. Although, small threshold values T might complicate the attack considerably.
Bi-modality[1]	For the last round only: exposure of all response bits and retrieval of the secret index. Retrieval of $log_2(L)$ key bits.	
Bi-modality[1] and key mixing[2,3]	For the last round only: exposure of all response bits and retrieval of the secret index.	
Failure detection hash[2,4]	/	
Non-overlapping patterns[2]	/	/
Circularity (newly proposed)	Exposure of all response bits.	Exposure of all response bits. Although, small threshold values T might complicate the attack considerably.

[1] Assuming the original proposal of [9], without an additional dummy round.
[2] Not initially proposed with a security objective in [9,10].
[3] We assume the worst-case scenario, as there is no precise specification of the key mixing step in [9].
[4] We assume the hash digest to depend on the secret index of the last round too, fixing the issue of [9].

Snake II provides more resistance against the various countermeasures than Snake I. Decreasing T should not be considered as a secure countermeasure against the former, because of the aforementioned workarounds. Furthermore, effectiveness is only offered for very wide patterns, corresponding to a substantial system overdesign (see figure 5). This undermines any efficiency advantage a PMKG might possibly have. For more optimal parameter settings, there is little margin to shift T without affecting the overall failure rate P_{FAIL} significantly.

With non-overlapping patterns, both Snake I and Snake II are fully impeded. However, we consider this countermeasure as very inefficient, as mentioned before. Therefore, we also list a new rather simple countermeasure: circularity of the response bits within a round. Instead of $L + W - 1$ non-circular bits, one could generate L circular bits. As before, there are L pattern indices. Although response bits are still vulnerable to exposure, an attacker will no longer observe an abrupt change in failure statistics at index 0 (or $L - 1$), protecting the secret index as such. One could thwart the increased ML risk by implementing bi-modality as well, or by employing a weak PUF with a negligible amount of correlation (see section 3.1).

8   Conclusion and Further Work

PMKGs offer an alternative for traditional fuzzy extractors, in order to generate reproducible and uniformly distributed keys from PUF responses. However, we presented major vulnerabilities in their architecture. Via manipulation of the public helper data, full key recovery might be possible, although depending on system design choices. Hereby, failure statistics are collected during the key reconstruction phase, observable via the application user interface. We illustrated our attacks using a 4-XOR arbiter PUF, manufactured in $65nm$ CMOS technology.

However, we still see substantial value in the PMKG proposal. One could develop many post-processing variants according to its basic principle: Hamming distance measurements. As all building blocks of such architectures could be rather simple, there might be an efficiency advantage for various use cases. Careful system design should take helper data leakage and manipulation into account. Our (modified) failure framework might be very helpful to determine appropriate system parameters. We consider all of the former as further work.

Acknowledgment. This work was supported in part by the European Commission through the ICT programme under contract FP7-ICT-2011-317930 HINT. In addition this work is supported by the Research Council of KU Leuven: GOA TENSE (GOA/11/007), by the Flemish Government through FWO G.0550.12N and the Hercules Foundation AKUL/11/19. Jeroen Delvaux is funded by IWT-Flanders grant no. 121552.

References

1. Boyen, X., Dodis, Y., Katz, J., Ostrovsky, R., Smith, A.: Secure Remote Authentication Using Biometric Data. In: Cramer, R. (ed.) EUROCRYPT 2005. LNCS, vol. 3494, pp. 147–163. Springer, Heidelberg (2005)
2. Dodis, Y., Ostrovsky, R., Reyzin, L., Smith, A.: Fuzzy Extractors: How to Generate Strong Keys from Biometrics and Other Noisy Data. SIAM J. Comput. 38(1), 97–139 (2008)
3. Hospodar, G., Maes, R., Verbauwhede, I.: Machine Learning Attacks on 65nm Arbiter PUFs: Accurate Modeling poses strict Bounds on Usability. In: Workshop on Information Forensics and Security (WIFS), pp. 37–42. IEEE (December 2012)
4. Koeberl, P., Maes, R., Rožić, V., Van der Leest, V., Van der Sluis, E., Verbauwhede, I.: Experimental Evaluation of Physically Unclonable Functions in 65 nm CMOS. In: 2012 IEEE Conference on European Solid-State Circuits (ESSCIRC), pp. 486–489 (September 2012)
5. Konczakowska, A., Wilamowski, B.M.: Noise in Semiconductor Devices. In: Industrial Electronics Handbook, 2nd edn. Fundamentals of Industrial Electronics, vol. 1, ch. 11. CRC Press (2011)
6. Kuhn, K., Kenyon, C., Kornfeld, A., Liu, M., Maheshwari, A., Shih, W., Sivakumar, S., Taylor, G., Van Der Voorn, P., Zawadzki, K.: Managing Process Variation in Intel's 45nm CMOS Technology. Intel Technology Journal 12(2), 92–110 (2008)
7. Lee, J.W., Lim, D., Gassend, B., Suh, G.E., van Dijk, M., Devadas, S.: A technique to build a secret key in integrated circuits for identification and authentication applications. In: 2004 Symposium on VLSI Circuits, pp. 176–179 (June 2004)
8. Merli, D., Schuster, D., Stumpf, F., Sigl, G.: Side-channel analysis of PUFs and fuzzy extractors. In: McCune, J.M., Balacheff, B., Perrig, A., Sadeghi, A.-R., Sasse, A., Beres, Y. (eds.) TRUST 2011. LNCS, vol. 6740, pp. 33–47. Springer, Heidelberg (2011)

9. Paral, Z., Devadas, S.: Reliable and Efficient PUF-Based Key Generation Using Pattern Matching. In: 2011 IEEE International Symposium on Hardware-Oriented Security and Trust (HOST), pp. 128–133 (June 2011)
10. Paral, Z., Devadas, S., Verayo Inc.: Patent WO/2012/099657, Reliable PUF value generation by pattern matching (July 26, 2012)
11. Rührmair, U., Devadas, S., Koushanfar, F.: Security based on Physical Unclonability and Disorder. Introduction to Hardware Security and Trust. Springer, Book Chapter (2011)
12. Rührmair, U., Sehnke, F., Sölter, J., Dror, G., Devadas, S., Schmidhuber, J.: Modeling attacks on physical unclonable functions. In: 2010 ACM Conference on Computer and Communications Security (CCS), pp. 237–249 (October 2010)
13. Skorobogatov, S.: Semi-invasive attacks - a new approach to hardware security analysis, Technical Report UCAM-CL-TR-630, University of Cambridge, Computer Laboratory (April 2005)
14. Tuyls, P., Schrijen, G.-J., Škorić, B., van Geloven, J., Verhaegh, N., Wolters, R.: Read-Proof Hardware from Protective Coatings. In: Goubin, L., Matsui, M. (eds.) CHES 2006. LNCS, vol. 4249, pp. 369–383. Springer, Heidelberg (2006)

A   Arbiter PUF: Vulnerability to Modeling Attacks

A single stage of the arbiter PUF can be described by two delay parameters: one for each challenge bit state, as illustrated in figure 11. The delay difference at the input of stage i flips in sign for the crossed configuration and is incremented with δt_i^1 or δt_i^0 for crossed and uncrossed configurations respectively.

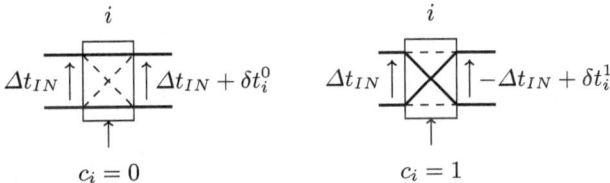

Fig. 11. Modeling a single stage of the arbiter PUF

The impact of a δt on Δt is incremental or decremental for an even and odd number of subsequent crossed stages respectively. By lumping together the δt's of neighboring stages, one can model the whole arbiter PUF with only $q + 1$ independent parameters (and not $2q$). A formal expression for Δt is as follows [12]:

$$\Delta t = \boldsymbol{\gamma \tau} = \left(\gamma_1 \; \gamma_2 \; \ldots \; \gamma_q \; 1\right)\left(\tau_1 \; \tau_2 \; \ldots \; \tau_{q+1}\right)^T$$

$$\text{with } \boldsymbol{\tau} = \frac{1}{2}\begin{pmatrix} \delta t_1^0 + \delta t_1^1 & \delta t_1^0 - \delta t_1^1 \\ & + \delta t_2^0 - \delta t_2^1 \\ & \vdots \\ \delta t_{q-1}^0 + \delta t_{q-1}^1 & + \delta t_q^0 - \delta t_q^1 \\ \delta t_q^0 + \delta t_q^1 & \end{pmatrix} \text{ and } \boldsymbol{\gamma} = \begin{pmatrix} (1-2c_1)(1-2c_2)\ldots(1-2c_{q-1})(1-2c_q) \\ (1-2c_2)\ldots(1-2c_{q-1})(1-2c_q) \\ \vdots \\ (1-2c_{q-1})(1-2c_q) \\ (1-2c_q) \\ 1 \end{pmatrix}^T .$$

Vector $\gamma \in \{\pm1\}^{1\times(q+1)}$ is a transformation of challenge vector **Chal** $\in$ $\{0,1\}^{1\times q}$. Vector $\tau \in \mathbb{R}^{(q+1)\times1}$ contains the lumped stage delays. The more linear a system, the easier to learn its behavior. By using γ instead of **Chal** as ML input, a great deal of non-linearity is avoided. The non-linear threshold operation $\Delta t \lessgtr 0$ remains however.

B   Snake II Extension to Resolve the Threshold Issue

Small and medium values of T complicate the execution of Snake II, as pattern misses then contribute significantly to the overall failure rate. We introduce an extension of Snake II to resolve this issue. Hereby, we generate a large and small shift for the pattern collision and miss curve respectively, referring to the representation of figure 10. The method requires an estimate of R for all exposed bits. Variants of algorithms 1 and 3 can obtain this goal for initially exposed and unexposed bits respectively.

Currently, $T^\star$ patterns errors are introduced fully at random, given the $r_{i+z} \neq r_{j+z}$ constraint, with $z \in [1\ W-1]$. We formulate a simple heuristic to assess the benefit for the remaining positions. Introducing an error at position z shifts the pattern collision and pattern miss curve with $2\left|R_{i+z}-\frac{1}{2}\right|$ and $2\left|R_{j+z}-\frac{1}{2}\right|$ respectively. So the higher $\left|R_{i+z}-\frac{1}{2}\right|-\left|R_{j+z}-\frac{1}{2}\right|$, the more advantageous to flip the bit.

C   PMKG Alternative: Best Matching Patterns

For the 'best matching patterns' alternative, the current notion of pattern misses and collisions gets obsolete. There is only one unified failure condition, which we prefer to denote as a collision. A collision occurs if at least one non-subkey index has a lower or equal value of t with respect to the the subkey index. An approximate formula for the failure probability is given below. The Hamming distance at a subkey and non-subkey index is denoted as t_1 and t_2 respectively.

$$P_{FAIL} = 1 - (1 - P_{COLL})^H \quad \text{with } P_{COLL} = 1 - (1 - P_{COLL}(1))^{L-1} \text{ and}$$

$$P_{COLL}(1) = \sum_{t1=0}^{W} f_{BIN}(t_1; W, \overline{P_{MISS\_BIT}}) \sum_{t2=0}^{t1} f_{BIN}(t_2; W, 1 - \overline{P_{COLL\_BIT}})$$

We briefly introduce two attacks, which are inspired by Snake I and Snake II respectively. They inherit the corresponding assumption regarding the application, as given in section 6.1. A first attack employs the helper data dynamics of figure 7. Again, we randomly introduce $T^\star$ errors for positions r_{i+1} to r_{i+W-1}. The correct hypothesis results in fewer collisions: the expected value of t_1 differs $2\left|R_i-\frac{1}{2}\right|$. The randomized nature of the errors is important: a single collision source would introduce a bias for t_2, causing difficulties to distinguish hypotheses.

A second attack employs the helper data dynamics of figure 9. Again, we randomly introduce $T^\star$ errors for positions r_{j+1} to r_{j+W-1}, but only for bits that represent a mismatch with the intended collision source. The corrects hypothesis should result in more collisions with the intended collision source: the expected value of t_2 differs $2\left|R_i - \frac{1}{2}\right|$. However, the expected value of t_1 differs $2\left|R_j - \frac{1}{2}\right|$, either stimulating or counteracting the collision, with respect to the correct hypothesis. There are a few resolutions, similar to the low threshold issue of Snake II. (1) One could limit the attack to patterns with $R_j \approx \frac{1}{2}$. (2) Or one could perform a compensation for R_j, given a precise estimate of its value.

On Increasing the Throughput
of Stream Ciphers

Frederik Armknecht and Vasily Mikhalev

Universität Mannheim, Germany
{armknecht,mikhalev}@uni-mannheim.de

Abstract. Important practical characteristics of a stream cipher are its throughput and its hardware size. A common hardware implementation technique for improving the throughput is to parallelize computations but this usually requires to insert additional memory cells for storing the intermediate results, hence at the expense of an increased hardware size.

For stream ciphers with feedback shift registers (FSRs), we present an alternative approach for parallelizing operations with almost no grow of the hardware size by cleverly re-using existing structures. It is based on the fact that FSRs are usually specified in Fibonacci configuration, meaning that at each clock-cycle all but one state entries are simply shifted. The idea is to temporarily store values of the stream cipher outside of the FSR, e.g., intermediate results of the output function, directly into the FSRs.

We formally describe the transformation and its preconditions and prove its correctness. Moreover, we demonstrate our technique on Grain-128, one of the eSTREAM finalists with low hardware size. Our technique allows implementations, realized by the Cadence RTL Compiler considering UMC L180 GII technology, where the throughput is increased in the initialization mode by 18% and in the keystream generation mode by 24%, when the compiler was set to optimize the timing, and by 20 % in both modes when the compiler was set to optimize the area. As opposed to other solutions, no additional memory is required. In fact the hardware size even decreased from 1794 GE to 1748 GE in the time-optimized implementation and only slightly increased from 1627 GE to 1656 GE in the area-optimized implementation.

Keywords: Stream Ciphers, Feedback Shift Registers, Efficient Implementation, Throughput, Pipelining, Galois Configuration.

1 Introduction

Motivation. Stream ciphers are designed for efficiently encrypting data streams of arbitrary length. Ideally a stream cipher should not only be secure but also have a low hardware size and high throughput. Consequently huge body of work investigates different techniques for optimizing the hardware implementation of stream ciphers, e.g., [8,10,11,12,14,15,16]. A popular approach for increasing the

J. Benaloh (Ed.): CT-RSA 2014, LNCS 8366, pp. 132–151, 2014.

throughput is pipelining [13] where computations within the cipher are parallelized. However it requires to store intermediate values, making additional memory necessary which is the most expensive part in terms of the area size and power consumption. In general one is interested into techniques which allow for improving one condition without violating the other.

Observe that the majority of stream ciphers are deploying feedback shift registers which are often specified in the so-called Fibonacci configuration. This means that at each clock all but one state entries are simply shifted and only the remaining state entry requires some computation. In particular at each clock significant parts of the FSR state are not involved in any computation and have the only purpose of storing certain data. Hence it is a reasonable strategy to use these almost "free" resources for improving the hardware implementation. One step into this direction has been presented in [5]. The idea was to transform the FSR from Fibonacci-configuration to Galois-configuration [2,6]. In the latter each state entry has a separate update function which are all executed simultaneously. This allowed for accelerating the FSR update process by distributing the computation amongst several update functions with almost no change in the area size. However the improvements are restricted to the FSR itself while the throughput of stream ciphers are often dominated by other components.

Contribution. In this work we introduce a new implementation technique that allows for increasing the throughput but without any (or only small) increase in the hardware size. The technique can be used with stream ciphers that are composed of a (possibly non-linear) feedback shift registers (FSR), an external block (which is treated as a black box), and an output function which combines values from the FSR and the external block. We think that this should cover the majority of stream ciphers proposed so far. The technique can be seen as a combination of the two approaches mentioned above (pipelining and FSR-transformation). The idea is to parallelize the computation of the output function by integrating parts of it into several update functions of the FSR. Of course care needs to be taken that this transformation of the cipher does not alter its functionality. Thus the idea is to correct the changes made in the FSR at a later stage.

A similar idea has been used in [4] for constructing NLFSRs in Galois configuration with a certain period. The author also shortly points out that for analyzing the security, this construction could be re-interpreted as a filter generator. However, the discussion has been restricted to optimizing the area size and the case of filter generators while we aim for a higher throughput and consider a significantly broader class of FSR-based stream ciphers.

We provide a detailed technical description for sufficient conditions and prove that the transformation preserves the functionality of the cipher. As the proof is technically involved, we split it up and prove first an appropriate preserving transformations of FSRs. This transformation might be of independent interest. Moreover, we demonstrate the practicability of our approach by applying it to the stream cipher Grain-128. Grain-128 has been one of the eSTREAM finalists in the second profile portfolio (restricted hardware resources), making it particularly interesting for our transformation. The implementation of Grain-128 was realized by the Cadence RTL Compiler considering UMC L180 GII in two different modes where the compiler was set to optimize the timing and the area size, respectively. In the first case the throughput was increased in the initialization mode by 18% and in the keystream generation mode by 24%, in the second case the improvement of the throughput was 20 % in both modes (compared to a time-optimized and an area-optimized implementations without structural changes). As opposed to other solutions, no additional memory was used. In fact the hardware size even decreased from 1794 GE to 1748 GE for the time-optimized solution and only slightly increased from 1627 GE to 1656 GE for the area-optimized solution.

Outline. In Section 2, we provide the preliminaries for this work. In Section 3 we provide a high level description of the approach. The main results are given in Sections 4 and 5 where we describe and prove the transformations for the FSR and the cipher, respectively. In Section 6, we demonstrate the technique on the cipher Grain-128. Section 7 concludes the paper.

2   Preliminaries

Notation and Boolean Functions. For two integers $n \leq m$, the terms $[n, m]$ and $[n]$ refer to the sets $\{n, \ldots, m\}$ and $\{0, \ldots, n\}$, respectively. Let $\mathbb{F}$ denote the finite field $GF(2)$. For a Boolean function $f(x_0, \ldots, x_{n-1}) \in \mathbb{F}[x_0, \ldots, x_{n-1}]$, we define its *support* to be the smallest set of variables $\{x_{i_1}, \ldots, x_{i_\ell}\} \subseteq \{x_0, \ldots, x_{n-1}\}$ which is required to specify f. That is $f \in \mathbb{F}[x_{i_1}, \ldots, x_{i_\ell}]$ but $f \notin \mathbb{F}[X]$ for any real subset $X \subset \{x_{i_1}, \ldots, x_{i_\ell}\}$.

Feedback Shift Registers. A *Feedback Shift Registers (FSRs)* is an established building block for designing stream ciphers as it allows for generating long bit streams based on a short seed. In a nutshell, a FSR is a regularly clocked finite state machine that is composed of a register and an update mapping F. At each clock, an entry of the state is given out and the state is updated according to the update mapping F. While stream ciphers commonly use a specific type of FSRs, we consider the following, significantly broader class of FSRs:

Definition 1 (FSR with External Input). *A FSR FSR with external input of length n consists of an internal state of length n, an external source which produces a bit sequence $(b_t)_{t\geq 0}$, and update functions $f_i(x_0, \ldots, x_{n-1}, y_0, \ldots, y_\ell)$ for $i = 0, \ldots, n-1$. Given some initial state $S_0 = (S_0[0], \ldots, S_0[n-1]) \in \mathbb{F}^n$, the following steps take place at each clock t:*

1. *The value $S_t[0]$ is given out and forms a part of the* output sequence.
2. *The state $S_t \in \mathbb{F}^n$ is updated to S_{t+1} where $S_{t+1}[i] = f_i(S_t, b_t, \ldots, b_{t+\ell-1})$.*

We denote by seq(FSR, S_0, $(b_t)_{t \geq 0}$) *the output sequence of* FSR *given an initial state* S_0 *and an external bit sequence* $(b_t)_{t \geq 0}$.

Observe that we make no restrictions on the update functions whereas stream ciphers commonly deploy FSRs which are in Fibonacci configuration, i.e, all update functions except of f_{n-1} are *simple*, meaning that $f_i(x_0, \ldots, x_{n-1}) = x_{i+1}$ for $i = 0, \ldots, n - 2$. A further relaxation is that the update of the state depends on the current assignment *and* possibly on bits from an external source. Observe however that the bits $(b_t)_t$ of the external source are not affected by the state bits.

Two FSRs FSR and FSR' of the same length with access to the same external source are called *equivalent*, denoted by FSR $\equiv$ FSR', if for any initial state S_0 for FSR there exists an initial state S_0' for FSR' (and vice versa) such that both produce the same output sequence for any external bit sequence $(b_t)_{t \geq 0}$. A transformation which takes as input some FSR FSR (and possible other inputs) and outputs a FSR FSR' such that FSR $\equiv$ FSR' is called *preserving*.

FSR-Based Stream Ciphers. The majority of stream ciphers can be characterized as follows: They deploy one or several regularly clocked finite state machines, typically including at least one FSR. At each clock several values of these components are fed into an output function h which eventually produces the current keystream bit. We assume that the keystream bit is computed before the FSRs are updated. In principle we investigate if and how certain computations that would take place in h can be shifted to one of the deployed FSRs such that (i) the resulting cipher remains equivalent but (ii) the throughput is increased. Consequently to keep the description as simple and readable as possible and to cover a maximally broad class of stream ciphers, we consider stream ciphers which contain three components only: a FSR FSR of length n, an output function h, and an external block EB. Here we make no restrictions on the processes running inside of EB but consider it as a black box which may contain further FSRs, additional memory, etc. The only assumption we make is that a bitstream $(b_t)_{t \geq 0}$ can be specified which contains all bits produced inside of EB which are relevant for the state updates of FSR and/or for computing the next keystream bit. Observe that this does not exclude the case that EB may contain several components, each producing its own bitstream. For example if we consider ℓ components where the i-th component produces a bitstream $(b_t^{(i)})_{t \geq 0}$, these bitstreams can be joined to one bitstream as follows: $(b_t)_{t \geq 0} = b_0^{(1)}, \ldots, b_0^{(\ell)}, b_1^{(1)}, \ldots$ Adopting the notation from Definition 1, the output function h is defined over some variables $h(x_0, \ldots, x_{n-1}, y_0, \ldots, y_\ell)$ and the t-th keystream bit is

$$z_t = h(S_t, b_t, \ldots, b_{t+\ell-1}). \tag{1}$$

We adopt the notions of *equivalence* and *preserving transformation* from the topic of FSRs for ciphers in a straightforward manner.

Throughput and Hardware Area. Being an essential aspect of our contribution, we shortly recall the notion of the delay of a cipher. In general any hardware implementation can be described by circuits which are composed of one or several logic gates. Upon receiving an input, a circuit C (which may be part of a bigger circuit) processes these values and eventually produces an output. The time period between getting the input and producing the output is called its *delay*: Delay(C). Observe that circuits may run in parallel, e.g., for decreasing the delay of the overall circuit. The operations between circuits are synchronized by clock pulses. Naturally, the time interval between clock pulses must be long enough so that all the logic gates have time to respond to the changes and their outputs "settle" to stable logic values, before the next clock pulse occurs. As long as this condition is met, the circuit is guaranteed to be stable and reliable. Each of the connections between inputs, registers, and outputs of a stream cipher forms a *timing path*. The path which has the biggest delay is called *critical path*. It defines the maximum operating clock frequency of the cipher. The *throughput* is the rate at which a new output is produced with respect to time. It is determined as the number of bits-per-cycle multiplied by the frequency [7]. Therefore, for a given cipher maximum throughput is specified by the delay of its critical path.

The amount of silicon used for the hardware implementation is called *area*, usually expressed in μm^2. To make the area consumption of different circuits comparable, another method is to calculate the Gate Equivalence (GE) which is the total area divided by the lowest power two-input NAND gates area [7].

3 High Level Description

Before we explain the proposed transformation in detail in Sections 4 and 5, we provide first a high level description. A common approach for increasing the throughput of a function is the *pipelining technique* where the circuit is divided into several parts which are computed in parallel. Pipelines can be implemented at a number of layers. During each clock cycle, the output of each block is stored in a memory stage. At the next layer the values from the previous layer are combined to new blocks and so on until the last layer outputs the result of the function. However each layer of the pipelining except the last one requires for storing the intermediate results additional memory, which is the most expensive part in terms of the area size and power consumption and accordingly to [10,11] induces additional latency.

Our technique can be seen as a special case of pipelining but where existing structures are cleverly re-used for avoiding additional memory as much as possible. It is motivated by the observation that FSRs are usually implemented in the Fibonacci configuration. This means that at each clock, all but one state entries are simply shifted while only the remaining entry requires more involved computations.

They idea is now that some of the computations that should take place in the output function are "outsourced" to the FSR update functions and to store the intermediate results in the FSR. To get the idea, assume that the output function h (see Equation 1) can be written as

$$z_t = h(S_t, B_t) = S_t[\beta] + h_1(S_t, B_t) + h_2(S_t, B_t) \tag{2}$$

with $B_t = (b_t, \ldots, b_{t+\ell-1})$. In principle the transformation removes h_1 from h and inserts it into the update function f_β:

$$(f_\beta, h = S_t[\beta] + h_1 + h_2) \stackrel{\text{Transf.}}{\Rightarrow} (f'_\beta := f_\beta + h_1, h' = S_t[\beta] + h_2) \tag{3}$$

Observe that the overall computational effort has not been increased. Moreover, it is not necessary to insert additional memory for storing the intermediate value $h_1(S_t, B_t)$ as it is stored in the FSR register with index β. Finally one sees that h' produces the same output as h but its complexity has been reduced. If possible one may repeat this step several times for different parts of h so that eventually the output function becomes a linear function where simply a selection of FSR state entries is added.

Of course care needs to be taken that the transformation is preserving. To ensure that the FSR output, i.e., the value at index 0, is not affected by the transformation, we apply the following trick: we integrate h_1 into *two* different update functions f_α and f_β for $\alpha < \beta$. The modification of f_β insert the value $h_1(S_t, B_t)$ as explained above such that it can be used directly in the output function. In the subsequent clocks, this value is simply shifted until it reaches position α. Here the modification of f_α has been such that the value is canceled out again. The consequence is that the transformation possibly changes the FSR entries at indexes $\alpha \ldots \beta$ but leaves the state entries outside of this interval unchanged, including the value at index 0 which defines the FSR output. This property is proven for different variants of the transformation (see the proofs of Theorem 1, Lemma 1, and Theorem 2).

While the approach is conceptually simple, several aspects need to be considered:

1. It may not be sufficient to ensure that the FSR output is preserved. If the cipher uses functions where part of the inputs are taken from the interval $\alpha \ldots \beta$, then the output of this function would be altered as well. To avoid such effects, we focus on intervals of state entries such that all other values are independent of this interval in a certain sense. This is made precise by the notion of *isolated intervals* (see Definition 2).

2. For canceling out the change at position α, one cannot simply replace f_α to $f_\alpha + h_1$. The reason is that h_1 would use state entries that are $\beta - \alpha$ clocks later than when the change at index β has been introduced. Thus it is necessary that the value $h_1(S_t, B_t)$ can still be reproduced $\beta - \alpha$ clocks later. We capture this formally by saying that a function has *sustainable outputs* (Definition 3).

In fact, the concrete transformation (including the prerequisites and the proof of correctness) is technically involved. Therefore we split the technical treatment into two parts. In Section 4 we introduce a preserving transformation for *FSRs* where an external bit stream is integrated into some of the update functions (Theorem 1).

As we make no assumptions on this bitstream, the transformation might be of independent interest. Afterwards we explain an extension where this bitstream may depend on the FSR itself (Lemma 1). This requires a careful argumentation why the FSR-transformation is still preserving. For practical reasons, we restrict to bitstreams that depend on values only which are accessible over several clocks without requiring additional memory. These transformations will represent the basic building block for the cipher transformation presented and discussed in Section 5.

4   New Preserving FSR-Transformations

In this section we provide a detailed technical description of a new preserving transformation for FSRs which will be an integral part of the cipher transformation in Section 5. It requires that the FSR state contains an *isolated interval*, meaning a part of the state which has almost no impact on the update of the remaining part and, if existent, is independent of some output function h. The formal definition is as follows:

Definition 2 (Isolated Interval). *Consider a FSR-based stream cipher, being composed of an FSR* FSR *of length n with update mapping $F = (f_0, \ldots, f_{n-1})$, an external block with bit stream $(b_t)_{t \geq 0}$, and a function $h(x_0, \ldots, x_{n-1}, y_0, \ldots, y_\ell)$. We say that an interval $[\alpha \ldots \beta]$ with $0 \leq \alpha \leq \beta \leq n - 1$ of the FSR-state is* isolated *with respect to F and h if the following conditions are met:*

1. *The feedback functions $f_{\alpha-1}, \ldots, f_{\beta-1}$ have all the form*

$$f_i(x_0, \ldots, x_{n-1}, y_0, \ldots, y_{\ell-1}) = x_{(i+1) \bmod n} + g_i(x_0, \ldots, x_{n-1}, y_0, \ldots, y_{\ell-1})$$

   with $\operatorname{supp}(g_i) \cap \{x_\alpha, \ldots, x_\beta\} = \emptyset$. That is these feedback functions depend on the values at indices in $[\alpha, \beta]$ but only in the sense that these values are shifted.

2. *The remaining feedback functions $f_0, \ldots, f_{\alpha-2}, f_\beta, \ldots, f_{n-1}$ and the output function h are completely independent of the values at indices $[\alpha, \beta]$, that is $\operatorname{supp}(f_i) \cap \{x_\alpha, \ldots, x_\beta\} = \emptyset$ for all $i \in [n-1] \setminus [\alpha, \beta]$.*

We describe and prove now a basic preserving transformation where an external bit stream $(b_t)_{t \geq 0}$ is integrated into some update functions:

Theorem 1 (Preserving FSR Transformation). *Consider a FSR* FSR *with update mapping $F = (f_0, \ldots, f_{n-1})$ and an external source producing a bitstream $(b_t)_{t \geq 0}$. Let $[\alpha, \ldots, \beta]$ be an interval which is isolated with respect to F. We define an FSR* FSR' *with update mapping $F' = (f'_0, \ldots, f'_{n-1})$ which is derived from F as follows:*

$$f'_{\alpha-1} := f_{\alpha-1} + y_{\beta-\alpha}, \quad f'_\beta := f_\beta + y_1, \quad f'_i := f_i \text{ for all } i \neq \alpha, \beta \qquad (4)$$

Then both FSRs are equivalent, i.e, FSR $\equiv$ FSR'.

Proof (Theorem 1). We have to show that for any initial state $S_0 \in \mathbb{F}^n$ there exists a corresponding initial state $S'_0 \in \mathbb{F}^n$ such that the output sequences $(S_t[0])_{t \geq 0}$ and $(S'_t[0])_{t \geq 0}$ are equal for any assignment of $(b_t)_{t \geq 0}$. This is an immediate consequence of the following claim:

Claim: We define for each $t \geq 0$ the vector

$$\Delta_t := (0^{\alpha-1}, b_{t+\beta-\alpha}, b_{t+\beta-\alpha-1}, \ldots, b_{t+1}, b_t, 0^{n-\beta}) \tag{5}$$

where 0^r denotes r-times the value zero. Let $S_0 \in \mathbb{F}^n$ be an arbitrary initial state and define $S'_0 := S_0 + \Delta_0$. Then it holds that for each clock t that $S_t + S'_t = \Delta_t$.

It follows from the claim that $S_t[0] + S'_t[0] = \Delta_t[0] = 0$ for each clock if $S_0 + S'_0 = \Delta_0$. That is both produce the same output bitstream which proves the theorem.

It remains to prove the claim which we do by induction. For $t = 0$, the claim holds by definition of S'_0. Next assume that $S_t + S'_t = \Delta_t$ for some clock $t \geq 0$. Recall that by definition of isolated intervals (see Definition 2) that the functions g_i for $i \in [\alpha - 1, \beta - 1]$ and f_i for $i \notin [\alpha - 1, \beta - 1]$ are all independent of the variables $x_\alpha, \ldots, x_\beta$. Moreover, we have $S_t[i] = S'_t[i]$ for all $i \notin [\alpha - 1, \beta - 1]$. Hence, we have $g_i(S_t) = g_i(S'_t)$ for $i \in [\alpha - 1, \beta - 1]$ and $f_i(S_t, b_t, \ldots, b_{t+\ell-1}) = f_i(S'_t, b_t, \ldots, b_{t+\ell-1})$ for $i \notin [\alpha - 1, \beta - 1]$. We investigate now the difference $S_{t+1} + S'_{t+1}$ index by index.

For $i \in [0, \ldots, \alpha - 2, \beta + 1, \ldots, n - 1]$, we have

$$S_{t+1}[i] = f_i(S_t, b_t, \ldots, b_{t+\ell-1}) = f_i(S'_t, b_t, \ldots, b_{t+\ell-1})$$
$$= f'_i(S'_t, b_t, \ldots, b_{t+\ell-1}) = S'_{t+1}[i],$$

showing the zeros at the beginning and the end of $S_{t+1} + S'_{t+1}$.

For $i = \alpha, \ldots, \beta - 1$, it holds

$$S_{t+1}[i] = f_i(S_t, b_t, \ldots, b_{t+\ell-1}) = S_t[i+1] + g_i(S_t, b_t, \ldots, b_{t+\ell-1})$$
$$= S'_t[i+1] + \Delta_t[i+1] + g_i(S'_t, b_t, \ldots, b_{t+\ell-1})$$
$$= S'_t[i+1] + g_i(S'_t, b_t, \ldots, b_{t+\ell-1}) + \Delta_t[i+1] = S'_{t+1}[i] + \Delta_{t+1}[i].$$

In the last equation we made use of the fact that by definition it holds that $\Delta_t[i] = b_{t+\beta-i}$ for all $i = \alpha, \ldots, \beta$ and hence $\Delta_t[i+1] = \Delta_{t+1}[i]$ for $i = \alpha, \ldots, \beta - 1$.

For $i = \alpha - 1$, we have

$$S_{t+1}[\alpha - 1] = f_{\alpha-1}(S_t, b_t, \ldots, b_{t+\ell-1}) = S_t[\alpha] + g_{\alpha-1}(S_t, b_t, \ldots, b_{t+\ell-1})$$
$$= S'_t[\alpha] + \Delta_t[\alpha] + g_{\alpha-1}(S'_t, b_t, \ldots, b_{t+\ell-1})$$
$$= S'_t[\alpha] + g_{\alpha-1}(S'_t, b_t, \ldots, b_{t+\ell-1}) + y_{t+\beta-\alpha}$$
$$= f'_{\alpha-1}(S'_t, b_t, \ldots, b_{t+\ell-1}) = S'_{t+1}[\alpha - 1].$$

Finally, it holds that

$$S_{t+1}[\beta] = f_\beta(S_t) = f_\beta(S'_t, b_t, \ldots, b_{t+\ell-1}) = f_\beta(S'_t, b_t, \ldots, b_{t+\ell-1}) + b_{t+1} + b_{t+1}$$
$$= f'_\beta(S'_t, b_t, \ldots, b_{t+\ell-1}) + b_{t+1} = S'_{t+1}[\beta] + b_{t+1}.$$

Hence $S_{t+1}[\beta] + S'_{t+1}[\beta] = b_{t+1}$ which concludes the claim. $\qquad \square$

Summing up Theorem 1 ensures that XORing an external value to the state entry which marks the beginning of an isolated interval preserves the FSR as long as this value is cancelled out later before it "leaves" this interval. In practice this requires to have access to the same value at two different clocks. For sure a simple solution would be to store this value in some external memory until it is not longer needed but this would increase the hardware area. Hence in practice it is preferable to use values which can be reconstructed several clocks later without the need for additional memory. To this end, we introduce the notion of *sustainability*:

Definition 3 (Function with Sustainable Output). *Consider a FSR-based stream cipher, being composed of an FSR FSR of length n with update mapping $F = (f_0, \ldots, f_{n-1})$, an external block with bit stream $(b_t)_{t \geq 0}$, and a function $h(x_0, \ldots, x_{n-1}, y_0, \ldots, y_\ell)$. We say that h produces values which are r-sustainable if there exists a supplemental function $h^*(x_0, \ldots, x_{n-1}, y_0, \ldots, y_\ell)$ such that*

$$h(S_t, b_t, \ldots, b_{t+\ell-1}) = h^*(S_{t+r}, b_{t+r}, \ldots, b_{t+r+\ell-1}) \quad \forall t \geq 0. \tag{6}$$

Remark 1. Informally the definition means that the output of h at some clock t can likewise be computed r clocks later by h^* without requiring additional storage. Although it may seem like an artificial and strong assumption at the first sight, it is in fact quite often naturally given for FSRs in Fibonacci configuration: as soon as a new state entry is computed, it is only shifted until it forms the output. In particular it remains part of the state for $n - 1$ clocks.

We can now extend the transformation considered in Theorem 1 by replacing the external bits b_t by the outputs of a function that produces $(\beta - \alpha)$-sustainable outputs:

Lemma 1 (Preserving FSR Transformation based on Sustainable Functions). *Consider a FSR-based stream cipher, being composed of an FSR FSR of length n with update mapping $F = (f_0, \ldots, f_{n-1})$, an external block with bit stream $(b_t)_{t \geq 0}$, and a function $h(x_0, \ldots, x_{n-1}, y_0, \ldots, y_\ell)$. Let $[\alpha, \ldots, \beta]$ be an interval which is isolated with respect to F and h. Moreover assume that h produces $(\beta - \alpha)$-sustainable outputs with h^* being the corresponding supplementary function. We define an FSR FSR' with update mapping $F' = (f'_0, \ldots, f'_{n-1})$ which is derived from F as follows:*

$$f'_{\alpha-1} := f_{\alpha-1} + h^*, \quad f'_\beta := f_\beta + h, \quad f'_i := f_i \text{ for all } i \neq \alpha - 1, \beta \tag{7}$$

Then both FSRs are equivalent, i.e, FSR $\equiv$ FSR'.

Proof (Lemma 1). We define $\tilde{b}_t := h(S_t, b_t, \ldots, b_{t+\ell-1})$ for each $t \geq 0$. Assume for a moment that $(\tilde{b}_t)_{t \geq 0}$ is an independent from the FSR and $(b_t)_{t \geq 0}$. We define an FSR FSR'' with update mapping $F'' = (f''_0, \ldots, f''_{n-1})$ which is derived from F as follows:

$$f''_{\alpha-1} := f_{\alpha-1} + \tilde{y}_{\beta-\alpha}, \quad f''_\beta := f_\beta + \tilde{y}_1, \quad f''_i := f_i \text{ for all } i \neq \alpha - 1, \beta \quad (8)$$

Here $\tilde{y}_i$ means a variable which takes the value $\tilde{b}_{t+i}$ at each clock t. It follows directly from Theorem 1 that FSR and FSR″ are equivalent. Moreover the proof shows that at each clock $t \geq 1$, the state S_t and S''_t of FSR and FSR″, respectively, differ by

$$\Delta_t := (0^{\alpha-1}, \tilde{b}_{t+\beta-\alpha}, \tilde{b}_{t+\beta-\alpha-1}, \ldots, \tilde{b}_{t+1}, \tilde{b}_t, 0^{n-\beta}). \quad (9)$$

if the initial states differ by Δ_0 (what we assume in the following). As the interval $[\alpha, \ldots, \beta]$ is isolated with respect to h by assumption, it follows that $h(S_t, b_t, \ldots, b_{t+\ell-1}) = h(S''_t, b_t, \ldots, b_{t+\ell-1})$ and $h^*(S_{t+r}, b_{t+r}, \ldots, b_{t+r+\ell-1}) = h^*(S''_{t+r}, b_{t+r}, \ldots, b_{t+r+\ell-1})$ for $r = \beta - \alpha$. Therefore we can rephrase the definitions of the update functions $f''_{\alpha-1}$ and $f'_\beta := f_\beta + h$ by $f''_{\alpha-1} := f_{\alpha-1}$ and $f''_\beta := f_\beta + h$, respectively. As this results into the exact definition of FSR′, we have FSR′ = FSR″ and in particular FSR ≡ FSR′, showing the claim. □

5   A Preserving Cipher-Transformation

5.1   Technical Description

We are now ready to present the proposed preserving cipher transformation. The idea is to identify appropriate terms of the output function and to integrate them into the update functions of the FSR. This way the delay of the output function can be decreased without any (or very small) increase of the delay of the FSR. More precisely the transformation is as follows:

Theorem 2 (Preserving Cipher Transformation). *Consider a FSR-based stream cipher $\mathcal{C}$, being composed of an FSR FSR of length n with update mapping $F = (f_0, \ldots, f_{n-1})$, an external block with bit stream $(b_t)_{t \geq 0}$, and an output function $h(x_0, \ldots, x_{n-1}, y_0, \ldots, y_\ell)$. Assume that h can be written as*

$$h(x_0, \ldots, x_{n-1}, y_0, \ldots, y_\ell) = x_\beta + h_1(x_0, \ldots, x_{n-1}, y_0, \ldots, y_\ell) + \\ h_2(x_0, \ldots, x_{n-1}, y_0, \ldots, y_\ell) \quad (10)$$

such that the outputs of h_1 could be computed one clock earlier as well. Formally, this means that there exists a function $g((x_0, \ldots, x_{n-1}, y_0, \ldots, y_\ell)$ such that it holds for all clocks $t \geq 1$:

$$h(S_t, b_t, \ldots, b_{t+\ell-1}) = S_t[\beta] + g(S_{t-1}, b_{t-1}, \ldots, b_{t+\ell-2}) + h_2(S_t, b_t, \ldots, b_{t+\ell-1})$$

Moreover the following conditions need to be met:

1. *There exist integers $1 \leq \alpha < \beta < n - 1$ such that the interval $[\alpha, \ldots, \beta]$ is isolated with respect to F and h_2 and the interval $[\alpha+1, \ldots, \beta+1]$ is isolated with respect to g.*
2. *g produces $(\beta - \alpha)$-sustainable outputs with g^* being the corresponding supplementary function.*

A *second cipher is defined as* C' *with an* FSR FSR' *and an output function* h' *which are derived from* FSR *and* h, *respectively. The update mapping* $F' = (f'_0, \ldots, f'_{n-1})$ *of* FSR' *is defined as*

$$f'_{\alpha-1} := f_{\alpha-1} + g^*, \quad f'_\beta := f_\beta + g, \quad f'_i := f_i \text{ for all } i \neq \alpha, \beta \qquad (11)$$

and the output function h' *of* C' *as*

$$h'(x_0, \ldots, x_{n-1}, y_0, \ldots, y_\ell) = x_\beta + h_2(x_0, \ldots, x_{n-1}, y_0, \ldots, y_\ell). \qquad (12)$$

Then both ciphers are equivalent.

Remark 2 (On the Relation between h_1 and g). Before we provide the proof, we shortly explain the relation between h_1 and g. As elaborated before, the goal of the transformation is to remove parts of the output function (here h_1) and to integrate it into the update functions of the FSRs. Here one needs to carefully pay attention to the *order of the computations*. By definition, at each clock t the output function first computes the output and the FSRs are updated afterwards. Hence, when the modified output function is invoked it is necessary that the output of h_1 is already present in the FSR state. The only possibility is that this computation of h_1 has been executed at least one clock before, which is accomplished by the function g.

Proof (Theorem 2). We show that for any initial state of C, there exists a corresponding initial state of C' such that both ciphers produce the same keystream.[1] We assume that in both ciphers, the same external block EB is used, producing the same bitstream $(b_t)_{t\geq0}$. Let S_0 be an arbitrary initial state of FSR. We define for each $t \geq 0$ the vector

$$\Delta_t := (0^{\alpha-1}, g(S_{t+r}, b_{t+r}, \ldots, b_{t+r+\ell-1}), \ldots, g(S_t, b_t, \ldots, b_{t+\ell-1}), 0^{n-\beta}) \quad (13)$$

with $r = \beta - \alpha$. Assume now that FSR' is initialized with $S'_0 := S_0 + \Delta_0$. It follows from Lemma 1 (and the arguments used in its proof) that at each clock $t \geq 1$, the states S_t and S'_t of FSR and FSR', respectively, differ by Δ_t. As the interval $[\alpha, \beta]$ is assumed to be isolated with respect to F, and h_2, and the interval $[\alpha + 1, \ldots, \beta + 1]$ is isolated with respect to g, it follows that for all t it holds that $f_\beta(S'_t, b_t, \ldots, b_{t+\ell-1}) = f_\beta(S_t, b_t, \ldots, b_{t+\ell-1})$ and likewise for g and h_2. We compare now the keystream bits $(z_t)_{t\geq0}$ and $(z'_t)_{t\geq0}$ of C and C', respectively. It is for each $t \geq 0$:

$$\begin{aligned}
z'_t &= h'(S'_t, b_t, \ldots, b_{t+\ell-1}) = S'_t[\beta] + h_2(S'_t, b_t, \ldots, b_{t+\ell-1}) \\
&= f'_\beta(S'_{t-1}, b_{t-1}, \ldots, b_{t+\ell-2}) + h_2(S'_t, b_t, \ldots, b_{t+\ell-1}) \\
&= f_\beta(S'_{t-1}, b_{t-1}, \ldots, b_{t+\ell-2}) + g(S'_{t-1}, b_{t-1}, \ldots, b_{t+\ell-2}) + h_2(S'_t, b_t, \ldots, b_{t+\ell-1}) \\
&= f_\beta(S_{t-1}, b_{t-1}, \ldots, b_{t+\ell-2}) + g(S_{t-1}, b_{t-1}, \ldots, b_{t+\ell-2}) + h_2(S_t, b_t, \ldots, b_{t+\ell-1}) \\
&= S_t[\beta] + h_1(S_t, b_t, \ldots, b_{t+\ell-1}) + h_2(S_t, b_t, \ldots, b_{t+\ell-1}) = z_t.
\end{aligned}$$

This shows that both ciphers produce the same keystream.   □

---

[1] The other direction can be shown analogously.

5.2   Discussion

On the Preconditions. We shortly argue why one might expect in general that the preconditions of Theorem 2 are fulfilled. In a nutshell these conditions are that the output function contains a linear term x_β such that β represents the endpoint of an interval $[\alpha, \beta]$ which is isolated with respect to update functions f_i with $i \notin [\alpha, \beta]$ and the remainder of the output function. First observe that already isolated intervals of length 1, i.e., where $\beta = \alpha$, are sufficient for "outsourcing" h_1 to the FSR. Second ciphers often deploy FSRs in Fibonacci configuration, meaning that all but one update functions are simple (i.e., only shift a value) and in particular depend on one value only. Moreover these FSRs have high length (for security reasons) and the only non-simple update function is sparse (for efficiency reasons). Thus we found several examples where our approach could be applied, Grain-128 being one of them (cf. Section 6). For example in the case of Grain-128 the relation between h_1 and g (see Remark 2) is only a shift in the indices of the variables.

Analysis. In the following we analyze the change of the delay induced by our transformation. As the exact delay strongly depends on the technology used, we discuss from a qualitative point of view how the delay of the cipher depends on the cipher components and under which conditions the transformation increases of the throughput. As our approach considers transformations in the output function and the FSR, no gain can be expected if the critical path goes through the external block EB. Hence we exclude this case in the following and assume that the delay of EB is always smaller than the delay of the output function and of the FSR, i.e, we ignore the delay of EB for simplicity. In fact all expressions can be easily adapted to take $\mathsf{Delay}(\mathsf{EB})$ into account as well. Observe in this context that if the cipher contains more than one FSR, we can apply the transformation with respect to this FSR which is the most appropriate and consider the others as part of the external block.

For the analysis, we distinguish between two different cases. We start with the simpler mode A where the update of FSR is independent of the output of h. This implies both two components can operate in parallel and hence $\mathsf{Delay}(\mathcal{C}) = \max\{\mathsf{Delay}(\mathsf{FSR}), \mathsf{Delay}(h)\}$. As the transformation aims for decreasing $\mathsf{Delay}(h)$, we restrict to the case of $\mathsf{Delay}(h) > \mathsf{Delay}(\mathsf{FSR})$ as otherwise the transformation would not bring any gain. Let h' and FSR' denote the output function and the FSR, respectively, after the transformation.

To apply the transformation explained in Theorem 2, it is necessary that h can be split accordingly, i.e., $h = x_\beta + h_1 + h_2$. Observe that after the transformation the output function becomes smaller, i.e., $h' = x_\beta + h_2$ and therefore likely has smaller delay. In general we have

$$\mathsf{Delay}(h') = \mathsf{Delay}(x_\beta + h_2) \leq \mathsf{Delay}(x_\beta + h_1 + h_2) = \mathsf{Delay}(h). \qquad (14)$$

While the concrete delay of a function depends on the deployed technology, a good approximation is the delay of a depth-optimal tree of 2-input AND and 2-input XOR gates implementing this function. In particular terms with the highest algebraic degree tend to induce the biggest delay. Hence preferable choices of h_1 should contain terms with high algebraic degree.

A FSR of length n is composed of n stages and update functions $f_0, \ldots, f_{n-1}$ which are implemented by flip-flops and logical gates, respectively. The update functions are computed simultaneously but at each clock-cycle, the two steps have to be performed sequentially:

- the values of the update functions have to be computed
- the stages have to be updated with the new values

Therefore the delay of a FSR is the sum of the delay of a flip-flop D_{fl} and of the delay of the slowest of the update functions:

$$\mathsf{Delay}(\mathsf{FSR}) = \max\{\mathsf{Delay}(f_0), \mathsf{Delay}(f_1) \cdots \mathsf{Delay}(f_{n-1})\} + D_{fl}$$
$$= \mathsf{Delay}(f_\mu) + D_{fl} \tag{15}$$

if μ denote the index of the slowest update function. Observe that the update functions within the isolated interval $[\alpha, \beta]$ are simply the shift operators. Hence we can assume that $\mu \notin [\alpha, \beta]$.[2] Recall that the transformation only changes the update functions f_α and f_β. Hence it follows

$$\mathsf{Delay}(\mathsf{FSR}') = \max\{\mathsf{Delay}(f_\mu), \mathsf{Delay}(f_\alpha + g^*), \mathsf{Delay}(f_\beta + g)\} + D_{fl}. \tag{16}$$

Because of $\mathsf{Delay}(\mathcal{C}') = \max\{\mathsf{Delay}(\mathsf{FSR}'), \mathsf{Delay}(h')\}$ and $\mathsf{Delay}(f_\mu) + D_{fl} < \mathsf{Delay}(h)$, the transformation decreases the overall delay if

$$\max \left\{ \begin{array}{l} \mathsf{Delay}(x_\beta + h_2), \\ \mathsf{Delay}(f_\alpha + g^*) + D_{fl}, \\ \mathsf{Delay}(f_\beta + g) + D_{fl} \end{array} \right\} < \mathsf{Delay}(x_\beta + h_1 + h_2). \tag{17}$$

Next we consider mode B where some of the update functions of FSR depend on the output of h. We denote by F^h the part of the circuit that implements FSR which requires the output of h as input and by $F \setminus F^h$ the remaining part of the FSR circuit. In this case it implies that

$$\mathsf{Delay}(\mathcal{C}) = \max\{\mathsf{Delay}(F^h) + \mathsf{Delay}(h), \mathsf{Delay}(F \setminus F^h)\}. \tag{18}$$

Again if $\mathsf{Delay}(F \setminus F^h) \geq \mathsf{Delay}(F^h) + \mathsf{Delay}(h)$, no gain can be expected by shifting computations from h to the FSR. Hence we restrict to the case that $\mathsf{Delay}(F \setminus F^h) < \mathsf{Delay}(F^h) + \mathsf{Delay}(h)$. Recall that by definition, the update functions within the isolated interval simply shifts the preceding state entry. Hence we can assume that $f_\alpha, f_\beta \notin F^h$. In particular $\mathsf{Delay}(F^h)$ will not change

---

[2] Otherwise the whole FSR would consists only of a cyclic shift of its internal state, rendering it useless for cryptographic purposes.

after the transformation. Analogouesly to mode A, we define by μ the index of the slowest update function in $F \setminus F^h$. Thus after the transformation, the delay in the set of update functions which are independent of h is given by $\max\{\mathsf{Delay}(f_\alpha + g^*), \mathsf{Delay}(f_\beta + g)\}, \mathsf{Delay}(f_\mu)\}$. An increase of the delay in this set is tolerable as long as it stays below $\mathsf{Delay}(\mathcal{C}) = \mathsf{Delay}(F^h) + \mathsf{Delay}(\mathsf{FSR})$ which is given for sure for $\mathsf{Delay}(f_\mu)$. A further condition for an improvement is (as in mode A) that the delay of the resulting output function h' is indeed less than the delay of the original output function h. Taking both conditions together yields the following condition for an improvement of the throughput:

$$\max \left\{ \begin{array}{l} \mathsf{Delay}(f_\alpha + g^*) + D_{fl} - \mathsf{Delay}(F^h), \\ \mathsf{Delay}(f_\beta + g) + D_{fl} - \mathsf{Delay}(F^h), \\ \mathsf{Delay}(x_\beta + h_2)\} \end{array} \right\} < \mathsf{Delay}(h). \qquad (19)$$

Observe that if none of the update functions depend on h, it holds that $F^h = \emptyset$. Then, Eq. 19 becomes to Eq. 17 and we are back in mode A.

We want to stress that our approach is applicable in both modes while it is stated in [11] that the pipelining method cannot be used in mode B (at least for Grain-128a). However, the resulting $\mathcal{C}'$ requires the additional computation of g^* (compared to the original cipher $\mathcal{C}$) which may induce a (preferably small) increase in the area size.

6   Application to Grain-128

In this section, we demonstrate our technique by applying it to the Grain-128 stream cipher [9]. Grain-128 consists of an 128-bit LFSR, an 128-bit NLFSR, and an output function h. In the original description of Grain-128 both FSRs are used in Fibonacci configuration, meaning that all bits except the 127th are updated just by shifting the adjacent value. The concrete updates and the output function are given in Appendix A. Grain-128 uses two different modes: initialization and keystream generation. In the keystream generation mode, the result of h forms the output. During the initializing mode the cipher does not produce any output for 256 clock-cycles. Instead the outputs of h are fed back to the LFSR and NLFSR.

Setup. As far as we know the implementation of Grain-128 with the currently highest throughput is given in [10]. Following [10] we used the Cadence RTL Compiler[3] for synthesis and simulation. Two implementations with different compiler settings were examined: optimizing the output for timing and optimizing for area size, respectively. It is well known that changing the compiler setting can lead to unpredictable effects. For example, although our transformation includes additional computations, the area size of the time-optimized solution *reduced* from 1794 GE to 1748 GE. We assume the following reason: when the compiler is set to optimize timing, bigger functions are implemented by gates which consume more area. It seems that such tricks are not necessary

---

[3] See http://www.cadence.com/products/ld/rtl_compiler/pages/default.aspx

anymore (or at least to a lesser extent) after our transformation. In other words, routing of the gates becomes easier for the transformed version of the cipher which outweights the slightly increased logic count. To minimize such effects as far as possible and to get a preferably unbiased view on the results of our transformation, our implementation contains only these blocks that are affected by the transformation. For example, we excluded on purpose the counter that is used in the initialization mode for counting the 256 cycles.

Preparation. Recall that our transformation aims for reducing the delay of the output function. Unfortunately, in the original specification of Grain-128 the critical path goes through the FSRs. Hence, before we applied our transformation, we modified the FSRs to decrease their delays. More precisely, we changed the configurations of the FSRs from Fibonacci to Galois. The idea is to spread the monomials of one update function amongst the others, in order to make them being computed in parallel. The new update functions together with initial state mappings are given in Appendix B. This transformation increased the maximal frequency from 1.03 GHz to 1.11 GHz in the initialization mode (approx. +8%), from 1.29 GHz to 1.45 GHz in the keystream generation mode (approx. +12%) for the timed-optimized solution. For the area-optimized solution the improvement is from 0,42 GHz to 0,60 GHz by 42 % in the initialization mode and from 0,89 GHz to 0,90 GHz in the keystream generation mode. In particular it resulted into the situation that the critical path goes through the output function, making our approach applicable. Of course we used this configuration as the benchmark for estimating the gain of our transformation.

Transformation. For getting the preferably best results from the transformations, we used the following strategy. Originally, the output function h contains several linear and quadratic terms and one cubic term (degree 3). As the terms with the highest degree tend to induce the highest delay (see Sec. 2), we aimed for shifting all monomials with degree bigger than 1 to the FSRs. The exact transformation is explained in App. C. Observe that we took both FSRs into account, i.e., some monomials have been integrated into the LFSR and others into the NLFSR. As both FSRs deploy update functions of degree 2 or less, there was no increase in the delay of the FSRs when the quadratic monomials from h have been integrated. For the single cubic term of h, the situation is different as this may increase the delay of the FSRs. Therefore we implemented both variants, i.e., the cubic term remaining in h or being moved to the FSRs, and it turned out that moving the term yielded the better result.

Results and Discussion. For the time-optimized implementation the maximal frequency within the initialization mode was increased from 1.11 GHz to 1.31 GHz (by 18 %) and for the keystream generation mode from 1.45 GHz to 1.8 GHz (by 24%) while the area size decreased from 1794 GE to 1748 GE. For the area-optimized implementation the maximal frequency within the initialization mode was increased from 0.60 GHz to 0.72 GHz (by 20 %) and for the keystream generation mode from 0.90 GHz to 1.08 GHz (by 20%) while the area slightly increased from 1627 GE to 1656 GE.

Observe that our transformation can be combined with further techniques. For example, we also tested an alternative implementation where the cubic term of the output function was not integrated into the FSR and where the pipelining technique was applied to the resulting output function. It turned out that this variant allowed for even higher frequencies in the keystream generation mode: for 2.1 GHz in the time-optimized solution and for 1,45 GHz in the area-optimized solution.

Unfortunately we had no access to the TSMC 90nm ASIC technology library used in [10] and used instead the Faraday Design Kit for UMC L180 GII technology library. As it turns out, this made the results from [10] incomparable to our results. For example [10] states for their implementation a maximal frequency in the initialization mode of 2 GHz and in the key generation mode of 3.1 GHz, which is roughly 55% faster. In fact this difference is essential for the improvement described there. In order to take advantage of the smaller delay during the keystream generation phase, the dual frequency solution was proposed: the cipher works with the slower frequency during the initialization phase, and when the keystream generation mode begins it switches to the faster clock. To make this possible, a special clock divider block is introduced into the system. Moreover, when the output is not fed back into the inputs of FSRs, the output function can be pipelined. Probably due to the different library, we could not reproduce these results (neither in concrete nor in relative terms), although we tried the same source code. Hence, we leave a meaningful comparison of both approaches for future work.

7   Conclusion

We presented a new approach for parallelizing computations in stream ciphers based on feedback shift registers (FSRs). As opposed to the common pipelining technique, existing structures are re-used for avoiding (or at least reducing) an increase of memory. The transformation has been proven for a broad class of FSRs and FSR-based stream ciphers, Moreover, it and has been applied to Grain-128 where the throughput for a time-optimized implementation is increased in the initialization mode by 18% and in the keystream generation mode by 24%. When the compiler was set to optimize the area size the throughput is increased by 20 % in both modes. As opposed to other solutions, no resp. very few additional memory is required.

We want to remark that we also successfully applied the transformation to Grain-128a [1] which is a recent improvement of Grain-128. The exact results (that are similar as for Grain-128) are not included for space reasons. Nonetheless it remains an open question to apply our technique to other stream ciphers.

Another interesting problem is to automate this approach, i.e., finding an algorithm which automatically finds a (nearly) optimal solution. Our technique is tailored for improving the throughput of FSR-based stream ciphers with a *non-linear* output function by transforming it into a cipher with *linear* output function. Interestingly many recently proposed stream ciphers use a linear output function already in their original configuration. Our transformation may be an indication that when designing FSR-based stream ciphers, it is sufficient to restrict to designs that use a linear output function. In general we expect that the presented technique and theory may be helpful in the design phase already. As the idea is to re-use existing memory, these ideas might be used right from the start for developing new stream ciphers with further decreased hardware size.

References

1. Agren, M., Hell, M., Johansson, T., Meier, W.: Grain-128a: A new version of Grain-128 with optional authentication. Int. J. Wire. Mob. Comput. 5(1), 48–59 (2011)
2. Chabloz, J.-M., Mansouri, S.S., Dubrova, E.: An algorithm for constructing a fastest Galois NLFSR generating a given sequence. In: Carlet, C., Pott, A. (eds.) SETA 2010. LNCS, vol. 6338, pp. 41–54. Springer, Heidelberg (2010)
3. Dubrova, E.: Finding matching initial states for equivalent NLFSRs in the Fibonacci and the Galois configurations. IEEE Transactions on Information Theory 56(6), 2961–2966 (2010)
4. Dubrova, E.: A scalable method for constructing Galois NLFSRs with period $2^n - 1$ using cross-join pairs. IEEE Transactions on Information Theory 59(1), 703–709 (2013)
5. Dubrova, E.: How to speed-up your NLFSR-based stream cipher. In: Proceedings of the Conference on Design, Automation and Test in Europe, DATE 2009, 3001 Leuven, Belgium, Belgium, pp. 878–881. European Design and Automation Association (2009)
6. Dubrova, E.: A transformation from the Fibonacci to the Galois NLFSRs. IEEE Transactions on Information Theory 55(11), 5263–5271 (2009)
7. Good, T., Benaissa, M.: Hardware performance of eSTREAM phase-III stream cipher candidates. In: Proc. of Workshop on the State of the Art of Stream Ciphers (SACS 2008) (2008)
8. Sen Gupta, S., Chattopadhyay, A., Sinha, K., Maitra, S., Sinha, B.P.: High-performance hardware implementation for RC4 stream cipher. IEEE Transactions on Computers 62(4), 730–743 (2013)
9. Hell, M., Johansson, T., Maximov, A., Meier, W.: A stream cipher proposal: Grain-128. In: 2006 IEEE International Symposium on Information Theory, pp. 1614–1618. IEEE (2006)
10. Mansouri, S.S., Dubrova, E.: An improved hardware implementation of the Grain stream cipher. In: 2010 13th Euromicro Conference on Digital System Design: Architectures, Methods and Tools (DSD), pp. 433–440 (September 2010)
11. Mansouri, S.S., Dubrova, E.: An improved hardware implementation of the Grain-128a stream cipher. In: Kwon, T., Lee, M.-K., Kwon, D. (eds.) ICISC 2012. LNCS, vol. 7839, pp. 278–292. Springer, Heidelberg (2013)
12. Nakano, Y., Fukushima, K., Kiyomoto, S., Miyake, Y.: Fast implementation of stream cipher K2 on FPGA. In: International Conference on Computer and Information Engineering (ICCIE), pp. 117–123 (2011)
13. Note, S., Catthoor, F., Goossens, G., De Man, H.J.: Combined hardware selection and pipelining in high-performance data-path design. IEEE Transactions on Computer-Aided Design of Integrated Circuits and Systems 11(4), 413–423 (1992)

14. Stefan, D., Mitchell, C.: On the parallelization of the MICKEY-128 2.0 stream cipher. In: The State of the Art of Stream Ciphers, SASC, pp. 175–185 (2008)
15. Yan, J., Heys, H.M.: Hardware implementation of the Salsa20 and Phelix stream ciphers. In: Canadian Conference on Electrical and Computer Engineering, CCECE 2007, pp. 1125–1128. IEEE (2007)
16. Jing, J., Liu, Z., Zhang, L., Pan, W.: Efficient pipelined stream cipher ZUC algorithm in FPGA. In: The First International Workshop on ZUC Algorithm, Beijing, China, December 2-3 (2010)

A   Specification of Grain-128

Grain-128 consists of an 128-bit LFSR L with update mappings $F = (f_0, \ldots, f_{127})$, an 128-bit NLFSR N with update mappings $Q = (q_0, \ldots, q_{127})$, and an output function h. In the original description of Grain-128 both FSRs are used in Fibonacci configuration, meaning that all bits except the 127th are updated just by shifting the adjacent value. We denote at clock t the state of the LFSR to be $L_t = (L_t[0], \cdots, L_t[127])$ and the state of the NLFSR as $N_t = (N_t[0], \cdots, N_t[127])$. The updates of L and N are as follows:

$$L_{t+1}[i] = L_t[i+1] \text{ and } N_{t+1}[i] = N_t[i+1] \quad \text{for } i = 0, \ldots, 126$$
$$L_{t+1}[127] = L_t[0] + L_t[7] + L_t[38] + L_t[70] + L_t[81] + L_t[96]$$
$$\begin{aligned} N_{t+1}[127] = {}& L_t[0] + N_t[0] + N_t[26] + N_t[56] + N_t[91] + N_t[96] + N_t[3]N_t[67] + \\ & N_t[11]N_t[13] + N_t[17]N_t[18] + N_t[27]N_t[59] + N_t[40]N_t[48] + \\ & N_t[61]N_t[65] + N_t[68]N_t[84] \end{aligned}$$

The output function h of Grain-128 is:

$$\begin{aligned} h = {}& N_t[2] + N_t[15] + N_t[36] + N_t[45] + N_t[64] + N_t[73] + L_t[93] + N_t[89] + \\ & N_t[12]L_t[8] + L_t[13]L_t[20] + N_t[95]L_t[42] + L_t[60]L_t[79] + \\ & N_t[12]N_t[95]L_t[95] \end{aligned}$$

B   Specification of the Change of the FSR Configurations

We specify the update functions of the FSRs after changing the configuration from Fibonacci to Galois. To distinguish the original update functions from the update functions after the change, we use the upper index $(^g)$. That is $(f_0, \ldots, f_{127})$ and $(q_0, \ldots, q_{127})$ denote the original update functions of the LFSR L and the NLFSR N, respectively, while $(f_0^g, \ldots, f_{127}^g)$ and $(q_0^g, \ldots, q_{127}^g)$ refer to the update functions after changing the configuration. Likewise we denote at clock t the state of the LFSR to be $L_t^g = (L_t^g[0], \cdots, L_t^g[127])$ and the state of the NLFSR as $N_t^g = (N_t^g[0], \cdots, N_t^g[127])$. The update functions of the FSRs of Grain-128 in Galois configuration are given in the Table 1. In order to get the same output after this transformation as in original Grain-128, the initial state

Table 1. The Update Functions of the FSRs after Transforming into Galois Configuration

LFSR L^g:

$f_{127}^g = L_t^g[0]$ $\quad\quad\quad\quad\quad\quad\quad\quad$ $f_{111}^g = L_t^g[112] + L_t^g[80]$

$f_{123}^g = L_t^g[124] + L_t^g[3]$ $\quad\quad\quad\quad$ $f_{103}^g = L_t^g[104] + L_t^g[46]$

$f_{119}^g = L_t^g[120] + L_t^g[30]$ $\quad\quad\quad$ $f_{97}^g = L_t^g[98] + L_t^g[51]$

$q_j^g = N_t^g[j+1], 0 \le j \le 127,$ $\quad\quad$ $j \notin \{127, 123, 119, 111, 103, 97\}$

NLFSR N^g:

$q_{127}^g = L_t^g[0] + N_t^g[0]$ $\quad\quad\quad\quad\quad\quad$ $q_{113}^g = N_t^g[114] + N_t^g[77]$

$q_{125}^g = N_t^g[126] + N_t^g[1]N_t^g[65]$ $\quad\quad$ $q_{111}^g = N_t^g[112] + N_t^g[80]$

$q_{123}^g = N_t^g[124] + N_t^g[7]N_t^g[9]$ $\quad\quad$ $q_{100}^g = N_t^g[101] + N_t^g[34]N_t^g[38]$

$q_{121}^g = N_t^g[122] + N_t^g[20]$ $\quad\quad\quad\quad$ $q_{99}^g = N_t^g[100] + N_t^g[40]N_t^g[56]$

$q_{119}^g = N_t^g[120] + N_t^g[9]N_t^g[10]$ $\quad\quad$ $q_{98}^g = N_t^g[99] + N_t^g[11]N_t^g[19]$

$q_{117}^g = N_t^g[118] + N_t^g[17]N_t^g[49]$ $\quad\quad$ $q_{97}^g = N_t^g[98] + N_t^g[26]$

$q_i^g = N_t^g[i+1], 0 \le i \le 127,$ $\quad\quad$ $i \notin \{127, 125, 123, 121, 119, 117, 113, 111, 100, 99, 98, 97\}$

has to be changed. A general treatment of this topic can be found in [3]. For our configuration the initial state needs to be changed as follows.

$$L_0^g[i] = L_0[i], 0 \le i \le 97$$
$$L_0^g[i] = L_0[i] + f_{i-1}^g(L_0) + f_{i-2|+1}^g(L_0) + \cdots + f_{97|+i-98}^g(L_0), 98 \le i \le 127$$
$$N_0^g[j] = N_0[j], 0 \le j \le 97$$
$$N_0^g[j] = N_0[j] + q_{j-1}^g(N_0) + q_{j-2|+1}^g(N_0) + \cdots + q_{97|+j-98}^g(N_0), 98 \le j \le 127$$

were $q_{i|+k}$ and $f_{i|+k}$ denote that every index in the arguments of the functions $q_{i|+k}$ and $f_{i|+k}$ is increased by k.

For example consider the following initial state of Grain-128:

$L_0 = (1010010111100011110011000101000110010111011101111100110100011001$
$1010011001110100110101000111000100101001011100011100011001001100)$

$N_0 = (1100100100010001001011111100110000010111000100101101011011101101$
$1010100010101100101001110111010110011010000011011011010001)$

Then the corresponding initial states after transformation to Galois configuration would be:

$L_0^g = (1010010111100011110011000101000110010111011101111100110100011001$
$1010011001110100110101000111000100110011101100010001100011011010)$

$N_0^g = (1100100100010001001011111100110000010111000100101101011011101101$
$1010100010101100101001110111010110011010000001100011010011111)$

C Specification of Our Transformation

We use the upper index $(^T)$ to indicate that the FSR states and the update function correspond to the configuration after our transformation is done. The exact transformations are provided in the Table 2. All the other update functions are the same as in the configuration explained in App. B. Observe that the modified output function h^T is linear as opposed to the cubic output function h of original Grain-128.

Table 2. The Update and Output Functions after Our Transformation

$$q_{89}^T = N_t^T[90] + N_t^T[3] \qquad q_{87}^T = N_t^T[88] + N_t^T[1]$$
$$q_{73}^T = N_t^T[74] + N_t^T[13]L_t^T[9] \qquad q_{71}^T = N_t^T[72] + N_t^T[11]L_t^T[7]$$
$$q_{64}^T = N_t^T[65] + L_t^T[14]L_t^T[21] \qquad q_{62}^T = N_t^T[63] + L_t^T[12]L_t^T[19]$$
$$q_{36}^T = N_t^T[37] + N_t^T[96]L_t^T[43] \qquad q_{34}^T = N_t^T[35] + N_t^T[94]L_t^T[41]$$
$$q_{15}^T = N_t^T[16] + N_t^T[13]N_t^T[96]L_t^T[96] \quad q_{13}^T = N_t^T[14] + N_t^T[11]N_t^T[94]L_t^T[94]$$
$$f_{93}^T = L_t^T[94] + L_t^T[61]L_t^T[80] \qquad f_{91}^T = L_t^T[92] + L_t^T[59]L_t^T[78]$$
$$h^T = N_t^T[15] + N_t^T[36] + N_t^T[45] + N_t^T[64] + N_t^T[73] + N_t^T[89] + L_t^T[93]$$

In Tab. 3, we provide the concrete mapping between initial states of FSRs before and after the transformation and before it, which is necessary to get the same output. All the other initial state entries are also the same as in the previous configuration.

Table 3. Mapping of the Initial States after Our Transformation

$$N_0^T[89] = N_0^g[89] + N_0^g[2] \qquad N_0^T[88] = N_0^g[88] + N_0^g[1]$$
$$N_0^T[73] = N_0^g[73] + N_0^g[12]L_0^g[8] \qquad N_0^T[72] = N_0^g[72] + N_0^g[11]L_0^g[7]$$
$$N_0^T[64] = N_0^g[64] + L_0^g[13]L_0^g[20] \qquad N_0^T[63] = N_0^g[63] + L_0^g[12]L_0^g[19]$$
$$N_0^T[36] = N_0^g[36] + N_0^g[95]L_0^g[42] \qquad N_0^T[35] = N_0^g[35] + N_0^g[94]L_0^g[41]$$
$$N_0^T[15] = N_0^g[15] + N_0^g[12]N_0^g[95]L_0^g[95] \quad N_0^T[14] = N_0^g[14] + N_0^g[11]N_0^g[94]L_0^g[94]$$
$$L_0^T[93] = N_0^g[93] + L_0^g[60]L_0^g[79] \qquad L_0^T[92] = N_0^g[92] + L_0^g[59]L_0^g[78]$$

On Double Exponentiation for Securing RSA against Fault Analysis

Duc-Phong Le[1], Matthieu Rivain[2], and Chik How Tan[1]

[1] Temasek Laboratories, National University of Singapore
{tslld,tsltch}@nus.edu.sg
[2] CryptoEpxerts, France
matthieu.rivain@cryptoexperts.com

Abstract. At CT-RSA 2009, a new principle to secure RSA (and modular/group exponentiation) against fault-analysis has been introduced by Rivain. The idea is to perform a so-called *double exponentiation* to compute a pair $(m^d, m^{\varphi(N)-d})$ and then check that the output pair satisfies the consistency relation: $m^d \cdot m^{\varphi(N)-d} \equiv 1 \bmod N$. The author then proposed an efficient heuristic to derive an addition chain for the pair $(d, \varphi(N) - d)$. In this paper, we revisit this idea and propose faster methods to perform a double exponentiation. On the one hand, we present new heuristics for generating shorter double addition chains. On the other hand, we present an efficient double exponentiation algorithm based on a right-to-left sliding window approach.

1 Introduction

Fault analysis is a cryptanalytic technique that takes advantage of errors occurring in cryptographic computations. Such errors can be induced in a device by physical means such as the variation of the power supply voltage, the increase in the clock frequency or an intensive lighting of the circuit. The erroneous results of the cryptographic computations can then be exploited in order to retrieve some information about the secret key. Fault attacks have first been introduced by Boneh et al. in [6] against RSA and other public key cryptosystems. In particular, they showed how to break RSA computed in CRT mode from a single faulty signature.

Many countermeasures have been proposed to protect embedded implementations of RSA against fault attacks. They can basically be classified in two different categories: countermeasures based on *a modulus extension* and *self-secure exponentiations*. The former countermeasures add redundancy in the computation by multiplicatively extending the RSA modulus. This approach was first introduced by Shamir in [26], and then further extended in [30,1,5,10,28]. The second approach consists in using an exponentiation algorithm that directly includes redundancy. It was first followed by Giraud in [14], who suggested to use the Montgomery ladder exponentiation algorithm. This approach was also followed by Bosher *et al.* in [8] with the square-and-multiply-always algorithm, and

J. Benaloh (Ed.): CT-RSA 2014, LNCS 8366, pp. 152–168, 2014.
© Springer International Publishing Switzerland 2014

subsequently improved by Baek [2] and by Joye and Karroumi [17]. Eventually, Rivain proposed an alternative method in [22]. His approach is to compute a pair $(m^d, m^{\varphi(N)-d})$ in order to check the computation consistency by the relation $m^d \cdot m^{\varphi(N)-d} \equiv 1 \bmod N$. The author then presents an efficient heuristic to perform such a double exponentiation.

This paper revisits Rivain's idea and presents faster methods for double exponentiation. We first propose efficient improvements of the heuristic for double addition chains proposed in [22]. Namely, we present simple improvements that result in a speed up of 7% compared to the original method, and we investigate the use of sliding-window techniques to further improve its performances. On the other hand, we describe an efficient double exponentiation algorithm based on sliding-window technique and Yao's exponentiation [29]. Finally, we analyze the performances of our proposals and provide a comparison of the various self-secure exponentiation algorithms in the current literature.

2   Preliminaries

2.1   The RSA Cryptosystem

The RSA cryptosystem, introduced by Rivest, Shamir, and Adleman in 1978 [23], is currently the most widely used public key cryptosystem in smart devices. An RSA public key is composed of a public modulus N which is defined as the product of two large secret primes p and q, and of a public exponent e which is co-prime to $\varphi(N) = (p-1) \cdot (q-1)$ (the Euler's totient of N). The underlying RSA private key is composed of the public modulus N and the secret exponent $d = e^{-1} \bmod N$. A signature s (or deciphering) of a message m is computed by raising m to the power d modulo N, that is $s = m^d \bmod N$.

For the sake of efficiency, one often uses the Chinese Remainder Theorem (CRT). This theorem implies that $m^d \bmod N$ can be computed from $m^{d_p} \bmod p$ and $m^{d_q} \bmod q$ where $d_p = d \bmod (p-1)$ and $d_q = d \bmod (q-1)$. The RSA in CRT mode (or RSA-CRT) then consists in computing these two *smaller* modular exponentiations and in combining the two results to recover the signature [13]. As pointed out in [21], this implementation reduces the size of the data stored in memory and is roughly four times faster than the standard implementation.

For both standard RSA and RSA-CRT, the core operation of the signature/deciphering is the modular exponentiation. The efficient implementation of RSA hence relies on an efficient exponentiation algorithm.

2.2   Addition Chains and Exponentiation

An addition chain for a positive integer a is a sequence of integers $\mathcal{C}(a) = \{a_i\}_{0 \leq i \leq n}$ beginning with $a_0 = 1$ and ending with $a_n = a$ such that each element is the sum of two previous elements in the sequence. Namely, for every $i \in \{1, 2, \ldots, n\}$ there exist $j, k \in \{0, 1, \ldots, i-1\}$ such that $a_i = a_j + a_k$. An addition chain for an integer a yields a way to evaluate the exponentiation $m \mapsto m^a$

154   D.-P. Le, M. Rivain, and C.H. Tan

by computing the sequence $m^{a_i} = m^{a_j} \cdot m^{a_k}$ for i from 1 to n. Conversely, any exponentiation process has an underlying addition chain. The problem of designing efficient exponentiation algorithms can hence be considered as the problem of finding short addition chains. A generalization of this problem whose instances are the tuples $(a_1, a_2, \ldots, a_k, n)$ is to find an addition chain of length n containing $a_1, \ldots, a_k$ (see for instance [12]). The later problem arises when one needs to compute simultaneously the monomials $m^{a_1}, m^{a_2}, \ldots, m^{a_k}$ given m and a_1, $a_2, \ldots, a_k$. In this paper, we investigate the case $k = 2$; that is, given a pair of exponent (a, b) we aim at efficiently compute $m \mapsto (m^a, m^b)$. An addition chain for such a pair of exponent was called *double addition chain* in [22].

Given integers a and n, the decision problem of whether there exists an addition chain of length n for a is NP-complete. As a result, finding the shortest addition chain for an exponent a is difficult on average. That is why one relies on heuristics to perform exponentiations in practice. Some heuristics require to perform a preprocessing of the exponent and store the indices (j, k) such that $m^{a_i} = m^{a_j} \cdot m^{a_k}$ for every i. Other heuristics decide on the multiplication to perform at each step by processing the exponent on the fly.

A well-known such heuristic is the binary method also known as *square-and-multiply* method. Let $(a_{\ell-1}, \ldots, a_1, a_0)_2$ denote the binary expansion of a, namely $a = \sum_i 2^i a_i$ where $a_i \in \{0, 1\}$. The equality

$$m^a = \prod_i \left(m^{2^i} \right)^{a_i} = \prod_{i \mid a_i = 1} m^{2^i}$$

gives rise to a simple exponentiation algorithm. At each step one computes m^{2^i} by squaring $m^{2^{i-1}}$ and then multiply it to some accumulator if $a_i = 1$. After ℓ such steps, the accumulator contains the value m^a. This process is summarized in Algorithm 1. This algorithm processes the exponent bits, from the less significant one to the most significant one and is hence often referred to as the *right-to-left* (R2L) binary algorithm. Note that a common *left-to-right* variant also exists that processes the bits in the inverse order (see for instance [19]).

Algorithm 1. R2L binary algorithm	**Algorithm 2.** R2L window algorithm
Input: m, $a = (a_{\ell-1}, \ldots, a_1, a_0)_2 \in \mathbb{N}$	**Input:** m, $a = (u_{n-1}, \ldots, u_1, u_0)_{2^w} \in \mathbb{N}$
Output: m^a	**Output:** m^a
1. $M \leftarrow m$	1. $M \leftarrow m$
2. $A_1 \leftarrow 1$	2. **for** $u \in \{1, 2, \ldots, 2^w - 1\}$ **do** $A_u \leftarrow 1$
3. **for** $i = 0$ **to** $\ell - 1$ **do**	3. **for** $i = 0$ **to** $\ell - 1$ **do**
4. **if** $a_i = 1$ **then** $A_1 \leftarrow A_1 \cdot M$	4. **if** $u_i \neq 0$ **then** $A_{u_i} \leftarrow A_{u_i} \cdot M$
5. $M \leftarrow M^2$	5. $M \leftarrow M^{2^w}$
6. **end for**	6. **end for**
7. **return** A_1	7. **return** $\prod_u A_u^u$

A generalization of the binary method consists in processing the exponent by window of w bits. Let $(u_{n-1}, \ldots, u_1, u_0)_{2^w}$ denote the expansion of some exponent a in radix 2^w where $n = \lceil \log_2(a)/w \rceil$, that is $a = \sum_i u_i 2^{iw}$ with $u_i \in \{0, 1, \ldots 2^w - 1\}$ and $u_{n-1} \neq 0$. The principle of the window method is analogous to that of the binary method and is based on the equality

$$m^a = \prod_i \left(m^{2^{iw}}\right)^{u_i} = \prod_{u=1}^{2^w-1} \left(\prod_{i|u_i=u} 2^{iw} \right)^u.$$

A loop is processed which applies w successive squarings in every iteration to compute $m^{2^{iw}}$ from $m^{2^{(i-1)w}}$, and which multiplies the result to some accumulator A_{u_i}. At the end of the loop each accumulator A_u contains the product $\prod_{i|u_i=u} 2^{iw}$. The different accumulators are finally aggregated as $\prod_u A_u^u = m^a$. The resulting algorithm is summarized in Algorithm 2. This algorithm was first put forward by Yao in [29] and is often referred as Yao's algorithm. It requires more memory than the binary method (specifically 2^w memory registers) but it is faster since the number of multiplications is roughly reduced to $\left(1 + \frac{1-2^{-w}}{w}\right)\ell$.

3   RSA and Fault Analysis

The first fault attacks against RSA were published in the pioneering work of Boneh et al. [6]. In particular, this paper describes a very efficient attack against RSA in CRT mode. The principle of the so-called *Bellcore attack* is to corrupt one of the two CRT exponentiations, and to exploit the difference between the correct and faulty signatures to recover the secret prime factors of the modulus N. For example, suppose an attacker injects a fault during the computation of $s_p = m^{d_p} \bmod p$ so that the RSA computation results in a faulty signature $\tilde{s}$ which is correct modulo q and faulty modulo p (*i.e.* $\tilde{s} \equiv s \bmod q$ and $\tilde{s} \not\equiv s \bmod p$). The difference $\tilde{s} - s$ is hence a multiple of q but is not a multiple of p, and the prime factor q can be recovered by computing $q = \gcd(\tilde{s} - s, N)$.

Implementations of RSA in standard mode (*i.e.* without CRT) are also vulnerable to fault analysis. Some attacks have been described which target the exponent [3], the public modulus [4,9,25] or an intermediate power of the exponentiation [6,7,24]. Although these attacks require several faulty signatures for a full recovery of the secret key, they constitute a practical threat that must be considered by implementors.

3.1   Securing RSA against Fault Analysis

The simplest method to thwart fault analysis is to compute the signature s twice and compare the two results. This method implies a doubling of the computation time and it cannot detect permanent errors. A more efficient way is to verify the signature s with the public exponent e. That is, the cryptographic device checks whether $m \equiv s^e \bmod N$ before returning the signature s. This method provides a perfect security since a faulty signature is systematically detected. On the other hand, this method is efficient as long as e is small (which is widely common), but in the presence of a random e, it is as inefficient as the computation doubling. Besides, in some applications (*e.g.* the Javacard API for RSA signature [27]), the public exponent e is not available to the implementor. That is why, many works have focused on finding alternative solutions.

Shamir [26] first suggested a non-trivial countermeasure that computes exponentiations with some redundancy. The principle is to perform the two CRT exponentiations with extended moduli $p \cdot t$ and $q \cdot t$ where t is a small (random) integer. One can then efficiently check the consistency of the computation modulo t. This method has been extended and improved in many subsequent works [30,1,5,10,28]. In the present paper, we focus on a different approach in which the redundancy is not included in the modular operations but at the exponentiation level. Namely, we focus on *self-secure exponentiations* that provide a direct way to check the consistency of the computation.

3.2 Self-secure Exponentiation Algorithms

The first exponentiation algorithm with built-in security against fault analysis was proposed by Giraud in [14] and is based on the Montgomery ladder [20]. It uses the fact that this exponentiation algorithm works with a pair of registers (R_0, R_1) storing values of the form $(m^\alpha, m^{\alpha+1})$. At the end of the exponentiation loop, the registers contain the pair of values (m^{d-1}, m^d), which enables to verify the computation consistency by checking whether $R_0 \cdot m$ well equals R_1. If a fault is injected during the computation, the coherence between R_0 and R_1 is lost and the fault is detected by the final check.

Another self-secure exponentiation algorithm was proposed by Boscher *et al.* [8] which is based on the right-to-left *square-and-multiply-always* algorithm (originally devoted to thwart *simple power analysis* [11]). Their algorithm works as Algorithm 1 but it involves an additional register A_0 initialized to 1, and when $d_i = 0$ the multiplication $A_0 \leftarrow A_0 \cdot M$ is processed. It is observed in [8] that the triplet (A_0, A_1, M) stores $(m^{2^\ell - d - 1}, m^d, m^{2^\ell})$ at the end of the exponentiation. The computation consistency can be verified by checking whether $A_0 \cdot A_1 \cdot m = M$. In case of fault injection, the relation between the three register values is broken and the fault is detected by the final check. This approach was then generalized by Baek in [2] to the use of the right-to-left window square-and-multiply-always algorithm. It works as Algorithm 2 with a register A_0 so that the multiplication $A_{u_i} \leftarrow A_{u_i} \cdot M$ is also performed whenever $u_i = 0$. At the end of the exponentiation, computing

$$R \leftarrow \prod_{b=1}^{2^w - 1} A_u^u \quad \text{and} \quad L \leftarrow \prod_{b=0}^{2^w - 1} A_u^{2^w - 1 - u} \,,$$

one then gets a triplet (R, L, M) storing $(m^d, m^{2^\ell - d - 1}, m^{2^\ell})$ as in the binary case. If the computation was performed correctly then the equation

$R \cdot L \cdot m = M$ must hold. The obtained self-secure exponentiation achieves better timing performances than the previous ones: it roughly involves $(1 + \frac{1}{w})\ell$ multiplications on average against 2ℓ multiplications for the Giraud and Bosher *et al.* schemes. In [17] Joye and Karroumi further improved this approach with a variant for the aggregation and consistency check achieving a better time-memory trade-off than the original Baek proposal.

Remark 1. The self-secure exponentiations presented above have a drawback: they do not provide detection of errors induced in the exponent. For instance, if the exponent is corrupted before or during the Montgomery ladder (*e.g.* by flipping the current bit in any iteration), it shall output a pair $(m^{d'-1}, m^{d'})$ where d' denotes the corrupted exponent value. One hence clearly see that such a fault is not detected by the consistency check since we still have $m^{d'-1} \cdot m = m^{d'}$. The same applies for the Bosher *et al.* scheme and its variants. The final triplet in presence of a corrupted exponent equals $(m^{d'}, m^{2^\ell - d' - 1}, m^{2^\ell})$ and the fault is undetected by the consistency check. In his paper, Giraud suggests to include integrity checks for the exponent and the loop counter in every iteration of the exponentiation loop. In their paper, Bosher *et al.* suggest to recompute the read exponent on the fly in order to check that it well matches the correct exponent value at the end of the exponentiation (see also [16]). Although such methods may circumvent the problem in theory, their practical implementation is not straightforward and it might leave some unexpected flaws.

3.3   Securing Exponentiation with Double Addition Chains

In [22], Rivain introduced another principle for self-secure exponentiation. It consists in performing a *double exponentiation* to compute m^d and $m^{\varphi(N)-d}$ at the same time and then checking the following consistency relation:

$$m^d \cdot m^{\varphi(N)-d} \equiv 1 \pmod{N}.$$

If there is no fault injected during the computation, then the above equation well holds. Otherwise, if the computation is corrupted, it doesn't hold with high probability (see analysis in [22]).

In order to get an efficient self-secure exponentiation from the above principle, one must then find a way to raise m to both powers d and $\varphi(N)-d$ with the least multiplications possible. In other words, one must find a short addition chain containing both exponents. For such a purpose, Rivain introduces a heuristic to compute a *double addition chain* for any pair of integers (a, b). To construct such a chain, he defines a sequence $\{(\alpha_i, \beta_i)\}_i$ starting from the pair $(\alpha_0, \beta_0) = (a, b)$ down to the pair $(\alpha_n, \beta_n) = (0, 1)$ for some $n \in \mathbb{N}$, such that the inverse sequence is an addition chain for (a, b). Formally, he defines

$$(\alpha_{i+1}, \beta_{i+1}) = \begin{cases} (\alpha_i, \beta_i/2) & \text{if } \alpha_i \le \beta_i/2 \text{ and } \beta_i \text{ is even} \\ (\alpha_i, (\beta_i - 1)/2) & \text{if } \alpha_i \le \beta_i/2 \text{ and } \beta_i \text{ is odd} \\ (\beta_i - \alpha_i, \alpha_i) & \text{if } \alpha_i > \beta_i/2. \end{cases}$$

Without loss of generality, b is assumed to be greater than a and the above sequence keep $\alpha_i \leq \beta_i$ as invariant. Moreover it is shown in [22] that there exists $n \in \mathbb{N}$ such that $(\alpha_n, \beta_n) = (0, 1)$. Then by defining

$$\tau_j = \begin{cases} 0 & \text{if } \beta_i \geq 2\alpha_i, \\ 1 & \text{if } \beta_i < 2\alpha_i, \end{cases} \quad \text{and} \quad \nu_j = \begin{cases} \beta_i \ (\text{mod } 2) & \text{if } \tau_j = 0, \\ \bot & \text{if } \tau_j = 1, \end{cases}$$

where $j = n - i$, the inverse sequence $(a_j, b_j) = (\alpha_i, \beta_i)$ can be computed by initializing (a_0, b_0) to $(0, 1)$ and iterating

$$(a_{j+1}, b_{j+1}) = \begin{cases} (a_j, 2b_j) & \text{if } \tau_{j+1} = 0 \text{ and } \nu_{j+1} = 0 \\ (a_j, 2b_j + 1) & \text{if } \tau_{j+1} = 0 \text{ and } \nu_{j+1} = 1 \\ (b_j, a_j + b_j) & \text{if } \tau_{j+1} = 1 \end{cases} \quad (1)$$

to finally get $(a_n, b_n) = (a, b)$. The sequence (τ_j, ν_j) is hence a sound encoding to process the above double addition chain. The method of [22] consists in computing the (α_i, β_i) sequence in order to derive and store the (τ_j, ν_j) sequence. The double exponentiation $m \mapsto (m^a, m^b)$ is then efficiently computed by evaluating the sequence (m^{a_j}, m^{b_j}) with respect to (1). According to [22], the resulting encoding has a bit-length lower than 2.2ℓ with overwhelming probability and the underlying exponentiation involves 1.65ℓ multiplications on average, where $\ell = \log_2 b$.

4   New Heuristics for Double Addition Chains

As shown above, the problem of finding a double addition chain for a pair (a, b) can be thought as the problem of finding a way to go from the pair (a, b) to the pair $(0, 1)$ using only (and the least possible) subtractions, decrementations and divisions by two. From this starting point, Rivain's method works with two intermediate variables α_i and β_i according to the following principle. If α_i is close to β_i then $\beta_i - \alpha_i$ is small so a *subtraction step* $\beta_{i+1} = \beta_i - \alpha_i$ should be used. Otherwise, if α_i is significantly lower than β_i, then $\beta_i - \alpha_i$ is not significantly lower than β_i, so such a subtraction step should be avoided. One should rather lower β_i so that it get closer to α_i by using a *binary step* $\beta_{i+1} = \beta_i/2$ or $\beta_{i+1} = (\beta_i - 1)/2$ depending on the parity of β_i. In this section, we show that this principle can be improved in several ways.

4.1   First Improvements

Our first improvement starts from the observation that when β_i is odd and lies in $[2\alpha_i; 3\alpha_i]$, it is more efficient to perform a subtraction step $\beta_{i+1} = \beta_i - \alpha_i$ and get $\beta_{i+1} \leq \frac{2}{3}\beta_i$ at the cost of one subtraction (inducing one multiplication at the exponentiation level), rather than performing a binary step $\beta_{i+1} = (\beta_i - 1)/2$ and get $\beta_{i+1} \leq \frac{1}{2}\beta_i$ at the cost of one decrementation and one division by two (inducing two multiplications at the exponentiation level).

Our second improvement focuses on the situation where $\beta_i \geq 2^k \alpha_i$ for some $k \geq 2$. In such a situation, the original method applies k binary steps involving k divisions by two and $H(r)$ decrementations where $r = \beta_i \pmod{2^k}$ and H is the Hamming weight function. We observe that if we have $\alpha_i \pmod{2^k} = \beta_i \pmod{2^k} \neq 0$, then it is more efficient to perform a subtraction step $\beta_{i+1} = \beta_i - \alpha_i$ so that β_{i+1} is a multiple of 2^k. Doing so, the k next steps are divisions by 2 and β_i is lowered by a factor 2^k in $k+1$ operations instead of $k + H(r)$.

From these observations, we suggest to modify the above method by defining the (α_i, β_i) sequence such that $(\alpha_0, \beta_0) = (a, b)$ and for every $i \geq 0$:

$$(\alpha_{i+1}, \beta_{i+1}) = \begin{cases} (\beta_i - \alpha_i, \alpha_i) & \text{if } \beta_i < 2\alpha_i \\ (\alpha_i, \beta_i - \alpha_i) & \text{if } (\beta_i \in [2\alpha_i; 3\alpha_i] \text{ and } \beta_i \text{ is odd}) \text{ or } (\beta_i > 2\alpha_i \\ & \quad \text{and } \exists\, k \text{ s.t. } \alpha_i \ (\mathrm{mod}\, 2^k) = \beta_i \ (\mathrm{mod}\, 2^k) \neq 0) \\ (\alpha_i, (\beta_i - \gamma)/2) & \text{otherwise,} \end{cases}$$

where $\gamma = \beta_i \pmod 2$. Our simulations revealed that the double exponentiation obtained from our heuristic involves an average of 1.55ℓ multiplications, which represents a gain of 7% compared to the original method.

Example 1. We illustrate the effectiveness of the above variant for the pair $(7, 35)$. For this pair, the original method gives:

$$(0,1) \xrightarrow{+} (1,1) \xrightarrow{\times 2\ +1} (1,3) \xrightarrow{\times 2\ +1} (1,7) \xrightarrow{+} (7,8) \xrightarrow{\times 2\ +1} (7,17) \xrightarrow{\times 2\ +1} (7,35)$$

which requires 10 multiplications at the exponentiation level. Using our improvement, we obtain the chain:

$$(0,1) \xrightarrow{\times 2\ +1} (0,3) \xrightarrow{\times 2\ +1} (0,7) \xrightarrow{+} (7,7) \xrightarrow{\times 2} (7,14) \xrightarrow{\times 2} (7,28) \xrightarrow{+} (7,35)$$

which only needs 8 multiplications at the exponentiation level.

Encoding. We have to slightly modify the (τ_j, ν_j) encoding defined in [22] in order to include the proposed improvements. In the original proposal recalled in Section 3.3, a step $(\alpha_{i+1}, \beta_{i+1}) = (\beta_i - \alpha_i, \alpha_i)$ is encoded by a bit $\tau_j = 1$. On the other hand, a step $(\alpha_{i+1}, \beta_{i+1}) = (\alpha_i, (\beta_i - \gamma)/2)$, where $\gamma = \beta_i \pmod 2$, is encoded by a bit $\tau_j = 0$ followed by a bit $\nu_j = \gamma$. In order to include our improvements, we must define an encoding for a step $(\alpha_{i+1}, \beta_{i+1}) = (\alpha_i, \beta_i - \alpha_i)$, namely a subtraction step without swapping of the elements. We suggest to encode every subtraction step by a bit $\tau_j = 1$ followed by a bit ν_j that equals 1 if there is no swap (*i.e.* $\beta_i \geq 2\alpha_i$) and that equals 0 if there is a swap (*i.e.* $\beta_i < 2\alpha_i$). Specifically, we define:

$$\tau_j = \begin{cases} 0 & \text{if } (\alpha_{i+1}, \beta_{i+1}) = (\alpha_i, (\beta_i - \gamma/2)), \\ 1 & \text{otherwise,} \end{cases}$$

and

$$\nu_j = \begin{cases} \beta_i \pmod 2 & \text{if } \tau_j = 0, \\ 0 & \text{if } \tau_j = 1 \text{ and } \beta_i < 2\alpha_i, \\ 1 & \text{if } \tau_j = 1 \text{ and } \beta_i \geq 2\alpha_i, \end{cases}$$

where $j = n - i$. The addition chain $(a_j, b_j) = (\alpha_i, \beta_i)$ can be computed by initializing (a_0, b_0) to $(0, 1)$ and iterating

$$(a_{j+1}, b_{j+1}) = \begin{cases} (a_j, 2b_j + \nu_{j+1}) & \text{if } \tau_{j+1} = 0, \\ (b_j, a_j + b_j) & \text{if } \tau_{j+1} = 1 \text{ and } \nu_{j+1} = 0, \\ (a_j + b_j, b_j) & \text{if } \tau_{j+1} = 1 \text{ and } \nu_{j+1} = 1. \end{cases}$$

Example 2. We construct the encoding $\Gamma(7, 35)$ for the double addition chain given in Example 1. First, we obtain

$$(\tau_0, \tau_1, \tau_2, \tau_3, \tau_4, \tau_5) = (0, 0, 1, 0, 0, 1) \quad \text{and} \quad (\nu_0, \nu_1, \nu_2, \nu_3, \nu_4, \nu_5) = (1, 1, 0, 0, 0, 1)$$

giving the following encoding:

$$\Gamma(7, 35) = 0\ 1\ 0\ 1\ 1\ 0\ 0\ 0\ 0\ 1\ 1$$

Each pattern of two bits correspond to a single step: 00 indicates a $(\times 2)$-step, 01 indicates a $(\times 2 + 1)$-step, 10 and 11 indicate a $(+)$-step (with and without swapping respectively).

4.2 Improved Method Based on Sliding Window

The original and improved methods presented above require only 3 registers to compute a double exponentiation $m \mapsto (m^a, m^b)$ (one for m, one for m^{a_i} and one for m^{b_j}). In this section, we look at the context where more memory is available. For a single exponentiation, window-based methods are natural extensions of the binary method for reducing the number of multiplications. We show hereafter how to improve the performances of double addition chains by using a *sliding window* (see *e.g.* [18]).

In the original method, if we have $\beta_i \geq 2^k \alpha_i$, then the heuristic performs k binary steps to lower β_i by a factor 2^k. At the exponentiation level, this translates by a binary exponentiation involving k squarings and an average of $\frac{k}{2}$ multiplications. It is then natural to replace such binary exponentiation by a more efficient sliding-window exponentiation. The principle is to precompute and store odd values $3, 5, \ldots, 2^w - 1$, for some widow parameter w, so that when $\beta_i \geq 2^k \alpha_i$ for some $k \leq w$, we first subtract $r_i = \beta_i \pmod{2^k} \in \{1, 3, \ldots, 2^w - 1\}$ to β_i and then we perform k successive divisions by two (note that we assume β_i to be odd, otherwise it is simply divided by two). This translates by a multiplication and k squarings at the exponentiation level.

We then modify the original method by defining the sequence (α_i, β_i) such that $(\alpha_0, \beta_0) = (a, b)$, and for every $i \geq 0$:

$$(\alpha_{i+1}, \beta_{i+1}) = \begin{cases} (\alpha_i, \beta_i/2) & \text{if } \alpha_i \leq \beta_i/2 \text{ and } \beta_i \text{ is even}, \\ (\alpha_i, (\beta_i - r_i)/2^{k_i}) & \text{if } \alpha_i \leq \beta_i/2, \beta_i \text{ is odd}, \\ (\beta_i - \alpha_i, \alpha_i) & \text{if } \alpha_i > \beta_i/2, \end{cases}$$

where $r_i = \beta_i \pmod{2^{k_i}}$ and k_i is the greatest integer in $\{1, 2, \ldots, w\}$ such that $\beta_i \geq 2^{k_i} \alpha_i$ and $2^{k_i - 1} \leq r_i < 2^{k_i}$. The latter condition means that the most significant bit of r_i (viewed as a k_i-bit string) is at 1. It is equivalent to the equality $k_i = \lfloor \log_2(r_i) \rfloor + 1$, which is required for our encoding (see below).

Note that the double addition chain is not strictly the inverse of the above sequence. Since it must start with a sequence:

$$1 \xrightarrow{\times 2} 2 \xrightarrow{+1} 3 \xrightarrow{+2} 5 \xrightarrow{+2} 7 \xrightarrow{+2} \cdots \xrightarrow{+2} 2^w - 1$$

in order to precompute the odd values $3, 5, \ldots, 2^w - 1$. This chain translates to one square and $2^{w-1} - 1$ multiplications to compute the powers $m^3, m^5, \ldots, m^{2^w - 1}$ at the exponentiation level. Moreover the resulting implementation has a greater memory consumption since these precomputed powers must be stored during the exponentiation.

Our simulations revealed that the double exponentiation obtained from our sliding-window-based heuristic involves an average of multiplications ranging from 1.59ℓ to 1.53ℓ depending on the window size. This represents a gain between 4% and 8% compared to the original method.

Example 3. We illustrate the effectiveness of our sliding-window-based method for the pair $(6, 27)$. For this pair, the original method gives:

$$(0,1) \xrightarrow{\times 2\ +1} (0,3) \xrightarrow{\times 2} (0,6) \xrightarrow{+} (6,6) \xrightarrow{\times 2\ +1} (6,13) \xrightarrow{\times 2\ +1} (6,27)$$

Using our sliding-window-based method, we obtain the chain:

$$(0,1) \xrightarrow{\times 2\ +1} (0,3) \xrightarrow{\times 2} (0,6) \xrightarrow{+} (6,6) \xrightarrow{\times 2\ \times 2\ +3} (6,27)$$

saving one multiplication at the exponentiation level.

Encoding. In order to define a sound encoding for our window-based double addition chains, we define the three following sequences:

$$\tau_j = \begin{cases} 0 & \text{if } \beta_i \geq 2\alpha_i, \\ 1 & \text{if } \beta_i < 2\alpha_i, \end{cases} \qquad \nu_j = \begin{cases} \beta_i \ (\mathrm{mod}\ 2) & \text{if } \tau_j = 0, \\ \perp & \text{if } \tau_j = 1, \end{cases}$$

and

$$\gamma_j = \begin{cases} (r_i - 1)/2 & \text{if } \tau_j = 0 \text{ and } \nu_j = 1, \\ \perp & \text{if } \tau_j = 1 \text{ or } \nu_j = 0, \end{cases}$$

where $j = n - i$. Note that when r_i is odd (*i.e.* when $\nu_j = 1$), γ_j is the value obtained by shifting $r_i = \beta_i \ (\mathrm{mod}\ 2^{k_i})$ by one bit to the left, and we have $r_i = 2\gamma_j + 1$.

The double addition chain $(a_j, b_j) = (\alpha_i, \beta_i)$ can then be computed from the $(\tau_j, \nu_j, \gamma_j)$ sequence by initializing (a_0, b_0) to $(0, 1)$ and iterating

$$(a_{j+1}, b_{j+1}) = \begin{cases} (a_j, 2b_j) & \text{if } \tau_{j+1} = 0 \text{ and } \nu_{j+1} = 0 \\ (a_j, 2^{k_i} b_j + r_i) & \text{if } \tau_{j+1} = 0 \text{ and } \nu_{j+1} = 1 \\ (b_j, a_j + b_j) & \text{if } \tau_{j+1} = 1, \end{cases}$$

where $r_i = 2\gamma_j + 1$ and $k_i = \lfloor \log_2(r_i) \rfloor + 1$.

Each step is hence encoded by a bit τ_j, followed by a bit ν_j if and only if $\tau_j = 0$, followed by $w - 1$ bits encoding γ_j if and only if $\tau_j = 0$ and $\nu_j = 1$.

Example 4. We construct the encoding $\Gamma(6, 27)$ for the double addition chain given in Example 3 (with window size $w = 2$). First, we obtain

$$(\tau_0, \tau_1, \tau_2, \tau_3) = (0, 0, 1, 0), \quad (\nu_0, \nu_1, \nu_2, \nu_3) = (1, 0, \perp, 1),$$

and

$$(\gamma_0, \gamma_1, \gamma_2, \gamma_3) = (0, \perp, \perp, 1)$$

giving the following encoding:

$$\Gamma(6, 27) = 0\,1\,0\,0\,0\,1\,0\,1\,1$$

The first three bits 010 indicate a $(\times 2 + 1)$-step. The next two bits 00 indicate a $(\times 2)$-step. The next bit 1 indicates a $(+)$-step. And the final three bits 011 indicate a $(\times 2 \times 2 + 3)$-step.

4.3   Combined Improvements

In the previous section we have introduced two different kinds of improvements to Rivain's heuristic for double addition chains. The purpose of our first improvements is to perform subtraction steps (without swapping) instead of binary steps in some cases where it is more advantageous to do so. The purpose of the sliding-window method is to speed up a succession of several binary steps. These two kinds of improvements are hence fully compatible and we can combine them by defining the (α_i, β_i) sequence as:

$$(\alpha_{i+1}, \beta_{i+1}) = \begin{cases} (\beta_i - \alpha_i, \alpha_i) & \text{if } \beta_i < 2\alpha_i \\ (\alpha_i, \beta_i - \alpha_i) & \text{if } (\beta_i \in [2\alpha_i; 3\alpha_i] \text{ and } \beta_i \text{ is odd}) \text{ or } (\beta_i > 2\alpha_i \\ & \quad \text{and } \exists\, k \text{ s.t. } \alpha_i \,(\text{mod } 2^k) = \beta_i \,(\text{mod } 2^k) \neq 0) \\ (\alpha_i, (\beta_i - r_i)/2^{k_i}) & \text{otherwise,} \end{cases}$$

where $r_i = \beta_i \,(\text{mod } 2^{k_i})$ and k_i is the greatest integer in $\{1, 2, \ldots, w\}$ such that $\beta_i \geq 2^{k_i}\alpha_i$ and $2^{k_i-1} \leq r_i < 2^{k_i}$. The encoding of the obtained double addition chain $(a_j, b_j) = (\alpha_i, \beta_i)$ with $j = n - i$ is easily deduced from the encodings of both previous heuristics. Specifically, it is based on the three following sequences:

$$\tau_j = \begin{cases} 0 & \text{if } \beta_i \geq 2\alpha_i, \\ 1 & \text{if } \beta_i < 2\alpha_i, \end{cases} \qquad \nu_j = \begin{cases} \beta_i \,(\text{mod } 2) & \text{if } \tau_j = 0, \\ 0 & \text{if } \tau_j = 1 \text{ and } \beta_i < 2\alpha_i, \\ 1 & \text{if } \tau_j = 1 \text{ and } \beta_i \geq 2\alpha_i, \end{cases}$$

and

$$\gamma_j = \begin{cases} (r_i - 1)/2 & \text{if } \tau_j = 0 \text{ and } \nu_j = 1, \\ \perp & \text{if } \tau_j = 1 \text{ or } \nu_j = 0, \end{cases}$$

where $j = n - i$. The double addition chain $(a_j, b_j) = (\alpha_i, \beta_i)$ can finally be computed from the $(\tau_j, \nu_j, \gamma_j)$ sequence by initializing (a_0, b_0) to $(0, 1)$ and iterating

$$(a_{j+1}, b_{j+1}) = \begin{cases} (a_j, 2b_j) & \text{if } (\tau_{j+1}, \nu_{j+1}) = (0, 0), \\ (a_j, 2^{k_i} b_j + r_i) & \text{if } (\tau_{j+1}, \nu_{j+1}) = (0, 1), \\ (b_j, a_j + b_j) & \text{if } (\tau_{j+1}, \nu_{j+1}) = (1, 0), \\ (a_j + b_j, b_j) & \text{if } (\tau_{j+1}, \nu_{j+1}) = (1, 1), \end{cases}$$

where $r_i = 2\gamma_j + 1$ and $k_i = \lfloor \log_2(r_i) \rfloor + 1$.

5   Sliding-Window Double Exponentiation

In the previous section, we have presented several heuristics for double addition chain improving the original method from [22]. These heuristics give rise to efficient double exponentiation algorithms with different time-memory trade-offs (see Section 6 for a detailed comparison). However, these algorithms have a drawback in practice: they require the precomputation of the chain encoding (involving the evaluation of the (α_i, β_i) sequence). Although this precomputation only involves simple operations compared to the modular multiplications used in the exponentiation, it might not be negligible in practice, especially for implementations using a hardware accelerator for modular arithmetic (which is common in smart cards and other embedded systems).

In this section, we propose an alternative by describing an efficient double exponentiation algorithm that does not rely on any form of precomputation. Our proposed algorithm is a generalization of Yao algorithm for the double exponentiation scenario and it is based on a sliding window approach.

Algorithm 3. Sliding-Window Double Exponentiation

Input: m, a, b
Output: (m^a, m^b)
1. $M \leftarrow m$
2. **for** $d \in \{1, 3, \ldots, 2^w - 1\}$ **do**
3. $A_d \leftarrow 1$; $B_d \leftarrow 1$
4. **end for**
5. **for** $i = 0$ to $\ell - 1$ **do**
6.   **if** $(a_i = 1)$ **then**
7. $d \leftarrow (a_{i+w-1}, \ldots, a_{i+1}, a_i)_2$
8. $A_d \leftarrow A_d \cdot M$
9. $a \leftarrow a - 2^i d$
10.   **endif**
11.   **if** $(b_i = 1)$ **then**
12. $d \leftarrow (b_{i+w-1}, \ldots, b_{i+1}, b_i)_2$
13. $B_d \leftarrow B_d \cdot M$
14. $b \leftarrow b - 2^i d$
15.   **endif**
16. $M \leftarrow M^2$
17. **end for**
18. $A_1 \leftarrow \prod_d A_d^d$
19. $B_1 \leftarrow \prod_d B_d^d$
20. **return** (A_1, B_1)

In a nutshell, the proposed algorithm works as two parallel executions of Yao's algorithm (see Algorithm 2), by using two sets of 2^{w-1} accumulators: A_1, A_3, ..., A_{2^w-1} for exponent a, and B_1, B_3, ..., B_{2^w-1} for exponent b. On the other hand, a single register M is used and the squarings involved to derive the successive powers m, m^2, m^4, ..., m^{2^ℓ} are computed only once, which results in a saving of ℓ squarings compared to two independent applications of Algorithm 2. Moreover, for the sake efficiency, we use a sliding window rather than a fixed window. Namely, instead of cutting the exponent in n fixed windows of w bits, each bit is treated from the less significant one to the most significant one. If the current bit a_i equals 0, the algorithm just squares M and continue with the next bit. Otherwise if a_i equals 1, then the algorithm processes the current w-bit digit $d = \sum_{j=0}^{j=w-1} a_{i+j} 2^j$ by multiplying M to the corresponding accumulator A_d, and by setting the next w bits of a to 0 with $a \leftarrow a - 2^i d$. The same process is performed simultaneously for the exponent b and corresponding accumulators.

The explicit description of the obtained double exponentiation is given in Algorithm 3. This algorithm involves ℓ squarings as a regular sliding window exponentiation. On the other hand, it involves twice more multiplications, that is $2 \times \frac{\ell}{w+1}$ multiplications on average for the exponentiation loop. For the aggregation, we adapt the method proposed in [15] for fixed window algorithms to the case of sliding-window algorithms. Specifically, the aggregation is computed as follows:

1. $M \leftarrow A_{2^w - 1}$
2. **for** $d = 2^w - 3$ **to** 3 **step** $i \leftarrow i - 2$ **do**
3. $\quad A_d \leftarrow A_d \cdot A_{d+2}$
4. $\quad M \leftarrow M \cdot A_d$
5. **end for**
6. $A_1 \leftarrow M^2 \cdot A_3 \cdot A_1$

The above process takes $2^w - 1$ multiplications, and it must be performed twice (in steps 18 and 19 of Algorithm 3). This makes a total of $\left(1 + \frac{2}{w+1}\right)\ell + 2^{w+1} - 2$ multiplications on average.

Example 5. We illustrate hereafter the processing of Algorithm 3 by detailing the successive values of the pair (a, b) and the different registers between each loop iteration for the input pair of exponents $(14, 25)$:

$$
\begin{pmatrix} (a,b) \\ M \\ (A_1, A_3) \\ (B_1, B_3) \end{pmatrix} : \begin{pmatrix} (29,50) \\ m \\ (1,1) \\ (1,1) \end{pmatrix} \rightarrow \begin{pmatrix} (28,50) \\ m^2 \\ (m,1) \\ (1,1) \end{pmatrix} \rightarrow \begin{pmatrix} (28,48) \\ m^4 \\ (m,1) \\ (m^2,1) \end{pmatrix} \rightarrow \begin{pmatrix} (16,48) \\ m^8 \\ (m,m^4) \\ (m^2,1) \end{pmatrix} \rightarrow \begin{pmatrix} (16,48) \\ m^{16} \\ (m,m^4) \\ (m^2,1) \end{pmatrix} \rightarrow \begin{pmatrix} (0,0) \\ m^{32} \\ (m^{17}, m^4) \\ (m^2, m^{16}) \end{pmatrix}
$$

At the end of the exponentiation loop we well have $m^{17} \cdot \left(m^4\right)^3 = m^{29}$ on the one hand and $m^2 \cdot \left(m^{16}\right)^3 = m^{50}$ on the other hand.

6   Performances and Comparison

In this section, we provide performance figures for our proposals and we compare them with other self-secure exponentiations in the literature. Basically, we consider:

- the binary self-secure exponentiations by Giraud [14] (Montgomery ladder) and by Bosher *et al.* [8] (square and multiply always),
- the w-ary square-and-multiply-always (w-ary SMA) method by Baek [2], with the Joye-Karroumi improvement [17],
- the double addition chain method by Rivain [22],
- the improved heuristics for double addition chains described in Section 4 of this paper,
- the sliding-window double exponentiation described in Section 5 of this paper.

The performances of the different methods are summarized in Table 1, for exponent bit-length $\ell \in \{512, 1024, 2048\}$, and for various window sizes. Specifically, we give the average number of multiplications per bit of the exponent as well as the number of ℓ-bit memory registers require by each self-secure exponentiation. We also give the memory overhead required to store the exponent, the chain encoding (for Rivain's method and our improvements) or the pair of exponents (for the double exponentiation described in Section 5). This overhead is given in number of required ℓ-bit registers.

Table 1. Performances of various self-secure exponentiations

	Window size	Multiplications/bit			Reg.	Memory overhead
		$\ell = 512$	$\ell = 1024$	$\ell = 2048$		
Binary exp. [14,8]	-	2	2	2	3	1
w-ary SMA [2,17]	$w = 2$	1.52	1.51	1.50	5	1
	$w = 3$	1.37	1.35	1.34	9	1
	$w = 4$	**1.32**	1.26	1.27	17	1
	$w = 5$	1.34	**1.28**	**1.23**	33	1
	$w = 6$	1.43	1.29	1.23	65	1
Double addition chain [22]	-	1.66	1.66	1.66	3	2.2
First improvements (§4.1)	-	1.55	1.55	1.55	3	3.19
Sliding-window improvement (§4.2)	$w = 2$	1.59	1.59	1.59	4	1.74
	$w = 3$	1.56	1.56	1.56	6	1.89
	$w = 4$	**1.54**	**1.54**	1.54	10	2.09
	$w = 5$	1.54	1.54	**1.53**	18	2.31
	$w = 6$	1.55	1.54	1.53	34	2.55
Combined improvements (§4.3)	$w = 2$	1.55	1.55	1.55	4	2.57
	$w = 3$	1.54	1.54	1.54	6	2.56
	$w = 4$	**1.53**	1.53	1.53	10	2.66
	$w = 5$	1.53	**1.52**	**1.52**	18	2.78
	$w = 6$	1.54	1.53	1.52	34	2.92
Sliding-window double exponentiation (§5)	$w = 2$	1.68	1.67	1.67	5	2
	$w = 3$	1.53	1.51	1.51	9	2
	$w = 4$	**1.46**	1.43	1.42	17	2
	$w = 5$	1.46	**1.39**	1.36	33	2
	$w = 6$	1.53	1.40	**1.35**	65	2

We see that our techniques provide significant improvements of the original heuristic for double addition chain proposed in [22]. The first improved heuristic (Section 4.1) is roughly 7% faster than the original method, whereas the window-based method is 4% to 8% faster depending on the window size. When combined, the two kind of improvements provide a performance gain between 7% and 9%. On the other hand the double exponentiation algorithm described in Section 5 achieves a speed up factor up to 19% depending on the available memory and the exponent length. In comparison, Baek w-ary self-secure exponentiation is roughly 10% faster for a similar memory consumption. However our algorithms (as Rivain's initial proposal) have the advantage of inherently protecting the implementation against corruption of the exponent whereas all other proposals require additional countermeasures for this purpose (see Remark 1).

7   Conclusion

In this paper we have revisited double exponentiation algorithms for fault-analysis resistant RSA. We have introduced new variants of Rivain's heuristic for double addition chains that achieve speed up factors up to 9%. We have also presented a generalization of Yao's right-to-left exponentiation to efficiently perform a double exponentiation. This algorithm achieves a performance gain up to 19% compared to the original double addition chain exponentiation, while requiring no precomputation. These improvements are of interest as self-secure exponentiations based on double exponentiation are currently the only ones that protect the exponent from fault attacks (whereas other self-secure exponentiations need additional countermeasures to this aim).

Interesting open issues include the design of more efficient double exponentiation algorithms (either based on addition chains or not), as well as the investigation of alternative approaches for designing self-secure exponentiation algorithms.

References

1. Aumüller, C., Bier, P., Fischer, W., Hofreiter, P., Seifert, J.-P.: Fault Attacks on RSA with CRT: Concrete Results and Practical Countermeasures. In: Kaliski Jr., B.S., Koç, Ç.K., Paar, C. (eds.) CHES 2002. LNCS, vol. 2523, pp. 260–275. Springer, Heidelberg (2003)
2. Baek, Y.J.: Regular 2^w-ary right-to-left exponentiation algorithm with very efficient dpa and fa countermeasures. International Journal of Information Security 9(5), 363–370 (2010)
3. Bao, F., Deng, R., Han, Y., Jeng, A., Narasimhalu, A.D., Ngair, T.-H.: Breaking Public Key Cryptosystems an Tamper Resistance Devices in the Presence of Transient Fault. In: Christianson, B., Crispo, B., Lomas, M., Roe, M. (eds.) Security Protocols 1997. LNCS, vol. 1361, pp. 115–124. Springer, Heidelberg (1998)
4. Berzati, A., Canovas, C., Goubin, L.: Perturbating RSA Public Keys: An Improved Attack. In: Oswald, E., Rohatgi, P. (eds.) CHES 2008. LNCS, vol. 5154, pp. 380–395. Springer, Heidelberg (2008)

5. Blömer, J., Otto, M., Seifert, J.P.: A New RSA-CRT Algorithm Secure against Bellcore Attacks. In: Jajodia, S., Atluri, V., Jaeger, T. (eds.) ACM Conference on Computer and Communications Security, CCS 2003, pp. 311–320. ACM Press (2003)
6. Boneh, D., DeMillo, R.A., Lipton, R.J.: On the Importance of Checking Cryptographic Protocols for Faults. In: Fumy, W. (ed.) EUROCRYPT 1997. LNCS, vol. 1233, pp. 37–51. Springer, Heidelberg (1997)
7. Boreale, M.: Attacking Right-to-Left Modular Exponentiation with Timely Random Faults. In: Breveglieri, L., Koren, I., Naccache, D., Seifert, J.-P. (eds.) FDTC 2006. LNCS, vol. 4236, pp. 24–35. Springer, Heidelberg (2006)
8. Boscher, A., Naciri, R., Prouff, E.: CRT RSA Algorithm Protected Against Fault Attacks. In: Sauveron, D., Markantonakis, K., Bilas, A., Quisquater, J.-J. (eds.) WISTP 2007. LNCS, vol. 4462, pp. 229–243. Springer, Heidelberg (2007)
9. Brier, E., Chevallier-Mames, B., Ciet, M., Clavier, C.: Why one should also secure rsa public key elements. In: Goubin, L., Matsui, M. (eds.) CHES 2006. LNCS, vol. 4249, pp. 324–338. Springer, Heidelberg (2006)
10. Ciet, M., Joye, M.: Practical Fault Countermeasures for Chinese Remaindering Based RSA. In: Breveglieri, L., Koren, I. (eds.) Workshop on Fault Diagnosis and Tolerance in Cryptography, FDTC 2005, pp. 124–132 (2005)
11. Coron, J.-S.: Resistance against Differential Power Analysis for Elliptic Curve Cryptosystems. In: Koç, Ç.K., Paar, C. (eds.) CHES 1999. LNCS, vol. 1717, pp. 292–302. Springer, Heidelberg (1999)
12. Downey, P., Leong, B., Sethi, R.: Computing Sequences with Addition Chains. SIAM Journal on Computing 10(3), 638–646 (1981)
13. Garner, H.L.: The residue number system. IRE Transactions on Electronic Computers (2), 140–147 (1959)
14. Giraud, C.: An RSA Implementation Resistant to Fault Attacks and to Simple Power Analysis. IEEE Transactions on Computers 55(9), 1116–1120 (2006)
15. Joye, M.: Highly Regular m-Ary Powering Ladders. In: Jacobson Jr., M.J., Rijmen, V., Safavi-Naini, R. (eds.) SAC 2009. LNCS, vol. 5867, pp. 350–363. Springer, Heidelberg (2009)
16. Joye, M.: A Method for Preventing "Skipping" Attacks. In: 2012 IEEE Symposium on Security and Privacy Workshops, pp. 12–15. IEEE Computer Society (2012)
17. Joye, M., Karroumi, M.: Memory-Efficient Fault Countermeasures. In: Prouff, E. (ed.) CARDIS 2011. LNCS, vol. 7079, pp. 84–101. Springer, Heidelberg (2011)
18. Koc, C.K.: Analysis of Sliding Window Techniques for Exponentiation. Computers and Mathematics with Applications 30, 17–24 (1995)
19. Menezes, A.J., Vanstone, S.A., Oorschot, P.C.V.: Handbook of Applied Cryptography, 1st edn. CRC Press, Inc. (1996)
20. Montgomery, P.L.: Speeding the Pollard and Elliptic Curve Methods of Factorization. Mathematics of Computation 48(177), 243–264 (1987)
21. Quisquater, J.J., Couvreur, C.: Fast decipherment algorithm for rsa public-key cryptosystem. Electronics Letters 18(21), 905–907 (1982)
22. Rivain, M.: Securing RSA against Fault Analysis by Double Addition Chain Exponentiation. In: Fischlin, M. (ed.) CT-RSA 2009. LNCS, vol. 5473, pp. 459–480. Springer, Heidelberg (2009)
23. Rivest, R., Shamir, A., Adleman, L.: A Method for Obtaining Digital Signatures and Public-Key Cryptosystems. Communications of the ACM 21(2), 120–126 (1978)

24. Schmidt, J., Herbst, C.: A Practical Fault Attack on Square and Multiply. In: Breveglieri, L., Gueron, S., Koren, I., Naccache, D., Seifert, J.P. (eds.) Fault Diagnosis and Tolerance in Cryptography – FDTC 2008, pp. 53–58 (2008)
25. Seifert, J.-P.: On authenticated computing and rsa-based authentication. In: Atluri, V., Meadows, C., Juels, A. (eds.) Proceedings of the 12th ACM Conference on Computer and Communications Security, CCS 2005, Alexandria, VA, USA, November 7-11, pp. 122–127. ACM (2005)
26. Shamir, A.: Improved Method and Apparatus for Protecting Public Key Schemes from Timing and Fault Attacks. Patent WO9852319 (November 1998); Also presented to EUROCRYPT 1997 rump session
27. Sun Microsystems: Application Programming Interface – Java Card™ Plateform, Version 2.2.2 (March 2006), http://java.sun.com/ products/javacard/specs.html
28. Vigilant, D.: RSA with CRT: A New Cost-Effective Solution to Thwart Fault Attacks. In: Oswald, E., Rohatgi, P. (eds.) CHES 2008. LNCS, vol. 5154, pp. 130–145. Springer, Heidelberg (2008)
29. Yao, A.C.C.: On the evaluation of powers. SIAM Journal on Computing 5(1), 100–103 (1976)
30. Yen, S.M., Joye, M.: Checking Before Output May Not Be Enough Against Fault-Based Cryptanalysis. IEEE Transactions on Computers 49(9), 967–970 (2000)

On the Practical Security of a Leakage Resilient Masking Scheme

Emmanuel Prouff[1], Matthieu Rivain[2], and Thomas Roche[1]

[1] ANSSI, 51, Bd de la Tour-Maubourg, 75700 Paris 07 SP, France
firstname.name@ssi.gouv.fr
[2] CryptoExperts, 41, Bd des Capucines, 75002 Paris, France
matthieu.rivain@cryptoexperts.com

Abstract. Implementations of cryptographic algorithms are vulnerable to Side-Channel Analyses extracting information from the device behaviour. When such an attack targets the manipulation of several, say d, intermediate variables then it is said to be a dth-order one. A privileged way to circumvent this type of attacks is to split any key-dependent variable into n shares, with $n > d$, and to adapt the internal processing in order to securely operate on these shares. The latter step is often very tricky and few schemes have been proposed which address this issue in a sound way.

At Asiacrypt 2012, Balasch *et al.* proposed a new scheme based on the inner-product sharing introduced the same year by Dziembowski and Faust at TCC. This scheme is the first one to aim at provable security in two different security models: the continuous bounded-range leakage model and the dth-order side-channel security model (sometimes called d-probing model).

In this paper, we contradict the dth-order security claim by exhibiting some first-order information leakages. Namely, we show that some intermediate variables of the scheme depend on secret information whatever the number of shares. This result is of importance since this kind of flaw is considered as a dead-end point when evaluating the practical security of an implementation. To illustrate the effectiveness of the flaw, we perform an information theoretic evaluation of the first-order leakage and we provide simulation results for a standard side-channel attack against the scheme.

1 Introduction

In the nineties, Kocher *et al.* showed in [13,14] that cryptosystems implemented in embedded devices are vulnerable to a new kind of attacks called *Side-Channel Analysis* (SCA for short). These attacks exploit the fact that the device behaviour (*e.g.* its power consumption) depends on the logical values being processed, which leaks information about the algorithm secret parameter. Since Kocher *et al.*'s original publications, efficient countermeasures have been developed which essentially consist in implementing the algorithms such that no intermediate variable depends on both a public value and a guessable part of the secret. The efforts made by researchers to design efficient countermeasures and

J. Benaloh (Ed.): CT-RSA 2014, LNCS 8366, pp. 169–182, 2014.
© Springer International Publishing Switzerland 2014

advanced side-channel attacks gave rise to a new research area and to a huge number of publications. In particular, the original attack of [14] was refined to exploit the leakage on several intermediate variables simultaneously [17]. The so-called *higher-order* SCA has been widely studied and improved since then, and its practicality has been demonstrated in several papers [15, 18, 25].

To defeat side-channel attacks, the secret sharing techniques (aka *masking*) are today considered as a good way to design effective countermeasures. They can indeed be applied to get implementations with a scalable security, parametrized by the number of shares and some physical properties of the device [5, 20]. The core principle of a *masking scheme* is to split any sensitive variable occurring in the computation into several (say n) shares, and to process elementary operations on them. The scheme must further ensure that each tuple of intermediate results is independent of any secret-dependent value as long as the tuple size is lower than some threshold d. The latter property is usually called d^{th}-*order security property*. The construction of dth-order secure masking schemes is of great interest for the embedded security community and several works have been published to deal with this issue in the particular context of block cipher implementations.

Related Works. The first scheme achieving d^{th}-order security for an arbitrary chosen d has been designed by Ishai, Sahai and Wagner in [11]. The here-called *ISW scheme* consists in masking the Boolean representation of an algorithm which is composed of logical operations NOT and AND. Most subsequent schemes follow the same strategy and essentially reduces the problem of defining a masking scheme for the entire block cipher algorithm to the problem of defining masking schemes for the internal *elementary operations*, often the addition and multiplication over some finite field. The security of the scheme is then proved locally (*i.e.* for every elementary operations) in a first place, and then globally by composing secure elementary computations with *mask-refreshing* steps.

In [23], Rivain and Prouff extend the ISW scheme to efficiently protect an AES computation. The obtained scheme is based on Boolean masking (*i.e.* intermediate variables are shared using the bitwise addition), and it uses an number of $n = d + 1$ shares to achieve the dth-order security property. Subsequent works have been published to extend and improve this scheme [4, 6, 12]. In a recent paper [20], Prouff and Rivain provide an alternative security proof for these kinds of Bollean masking schemes. They consider an adversary who is not limited in the number of intermediate variables that can be observed, but who get some *noisy leakage* on every elementary computation of the algorithm. Provided that the noise amount can be increased (linearly with the masking order d), and that a leak-free mask-refreshing procedure can be used, the authors show that the overall sensitive information leakage can be made negligible with respect to the masking order.

An alternative to the above Boolean masking schemes has further been proposed by Genelle *et al.* [9] to secure an AES computation by mixing additive and multiplicative sharings, and by involving the ISW scheme to secure the conversion between one sharing to another.

In [22], Prouff and Roche propose masking schemes for the addition and multiplication of variables split thanks to Shamir's secret sharing [24]. The proposed schemes are straightforward applications of those in [2] in the context of secure multi-party computation (MPC for short). The dth-order security property is also directly deduced from the collusion resistance of the secure MPC schemes. It is moreover proved that this security is not impacted by the presence of hardware glitches which are common in CMOS technology [16]. Eventually, the authors of [22] argue that the algebraic complexity of Shamir's sharing compared to the Boolean masking significantly reduces the amount of information leakage. A counterpart of this *masking strength* and of the resistance to glitches is that the complexity of multiplication scheme is $O(n^3)$ which is higher than the $O(n^2)$ complexity for the multiplication in ISW-based masking schemes.

Recently, another approach has been followed by Balasch *et al.*'s [1] to construct a secure higher-order masking scheme. The initial purpose of this scheme is to benefit the complexity advantage of [23] and the security advantages of [22]. Namely, the proposed addition and multiplication schemes have respective complexities $O(n)$ and $O(n^2)$, and enjoy masking strength and resistance to glitches. For such a purpose, the authors use the inner-product secret sharing (IP-sharing for short) introduced by Dziembowski and Faust [7] to construct leakage resilient circuits. The principle of the IP-sharing is to randomly split each intermediate variable V into n shares R_i and n non-zero shares L_i such that

$$V = (L_1 \otimes R_1) \oplus (L_2 \otimes R_2) \oplus \cdots \oplus (L_n \otimes R_n) \, ,$$

where $\oplus$ and $\otimes$ are respectively the addition and multiplication laws over some finite field. In both cases, proofs are given for two different security models: the λ-limited security model (often referred to as the *continuous bounded-range leakage model*) for $n \geqslant 130$ (see Section 4 of [1]), and the dth-order security model, with $d = n - 1$, for any $n \geqslant 2$ (see definitions page 8 of [1]). Those two security proofs together with the masking strength and the resistance to glitches make Balasch *et al.* scheme a valuable alternative to previous higher-order masking schemes.

Our Contribution. In this paper, we contradict the dth-order security claim made by Balasch *et al.* for their IP masking scheme. We indeed exhibit a first-order flaw in the addition and mask-refreshing schemes for any chosen sharing order n. This result is of importance since this kind of flaw is considered as a dead-end point when evaluating the practical security of an implementation. Indeed, a first-order attack is much less influenced by the leakage noise than higher-order attacks are. To confirm this, we quantify the amount of leaking information for different *signal-to-noise ratios* (SNRs) and we present simulations demonstrating the practicality of the exhibited attacks when the SNR is reasonably small.

2   Inner Product Masking Scheme

Let us first recall the basic principle of IP masking. In the following, $\mathbb{F}_q$ will denote some field of characteristic 2 (*i.e.* $q = 2^m$ for some $m \geqslant 1$), and let $\oplus$ and $\otimes$ denote respectively the addition and the multiplication over $\mathbb{F}_q$. The inner product between two vectors $\boldsymbol{X} = (X_1, X_2, \ldots, X_n)$ and $\boldsymbol{Y} = (Y_1, Y_2, \ldots, Y_n)$ from $\mathbb{F}_q^n$ is denoted by:

$$\langle \boldsymbol{X}, \boldsymbol{Y} \rangle = (X_1 \otimes Y_1) \oplus (X_2 \otimes Y_2) \oplus \cdots \oplus (X_n \otimes Y_n).$$

The principle of the IP masking scheme is to manipulate every sensitive variable V as a sharing composed of $2n$ elements, namely the coordinates of two vectors $\boldsymbol{L} = (L_1, L_2, \ldots, L_n)$ and $\boldsymbol{R} = (R_1, R_2, \ldots, R_n)$ such that $V = \langle \boldsymbol{L}, \boldsymbol{R} \rangle$. In order to prevent a direct first-order flaw, the coordinates of $\boldsymbol{L}$ are randomly drawn from $\mathbb{F}_q^* = \mathbb{F}_q \backslash \{0\}$.

To perform computation in the masked domain, the authors of [1] define an addition scheme `IPAdd` and a multiplication scheme `IPMult` to securely process those operations on shared variables. Both schemes are themselves based on two building blocks: the `IPHalfMask` and `IPRefresh` procedures, which are recalled hereafter.[1]

The `IPHalfMask` procedure (Algorithm 1) takes a variable $V \in \mathbb{F}_q$ and a half sharing $\boldsymbol{L} \in (\mathbb{F}_q^*)^n$ and it outputs random half sharing $\boldsymbol{R} \in \mathbb{F}_q^n$ satisfying $V = \langle \boldsymbol{L}, \boldsymbol{R} \rangle$.

Algorithm 1. Half-Masking a variable: $(\boldsymbol{L}, \boldsymbol{R}) \leftarrow \texttt{IPHalfMask}(V, \boldsymbol{L})$

INPUT: a variable $V \in \mathbb{F}_q$ and a vector $\boldsymbol{L}$ of non-zero shares
OUTPUT: a sharing $\boldsymbol{R}$ such that $V = \langle \boldsymbol{L}, \boldsymbol{R} \rangle$

1. **for** $i = 2$ to n **do** $R_i \leftarrow \texttt{rand}()$
2. $R_1 \leftarrow (V \oplus \bigoplus_{i=2}^n L_i \otimes R_i) \otimes L_1^{-1}$
3. **return** $\boldsymbol{R}$

Remark 1. As it can be seen in Algorithm 1, the half-sharing $\boldsymbol{R}$ statistically depends on V. This explains why the security order of the masking is upper bounded by n (the number of shares R_i). In Section 4, the amount of information leaking through the manipulation of the shares R_i will be compared to the flaw exhibited in this paper.

The `IPRefresh` procedure (Algorithm 2), takes a sharing $(\boldsymbol{L}, \boldsymbol{R})$ and computes a new fresh sharing $(\boldsymbol{L}', \boldsymbol{R}')$ such that $\langle \boldsymbol{L}', \boldsymbol{R}' \rangle = \langle \boldsymbol{L}, \boldsymbol{R} \rangle$.

Algorithm 2. Refresh Vector: $(\boldsymbol{L}', \boldsymbol{R}') \leftarrow \texttt{IPRefresh}(\boldsymbol{L}, \boldsymbol{R})$

INPUT: a sharing $(\boldsymbol{L}, \boldsymbol{R})$ of V
OUTPUT: New sharing $(\boldsymbol{L}', \boldsymbol{R}')$ such that $\langle \boldsymbol{L}, \boldsymbol{R} \rangle = \langle \boldsymbol{L}', \boldsymbol{R}' \rangle$

1. $\boldsymbol{L}' \leftarrow (\texttt{randNonZero}())^n$
2. **for** $i = 1$ to n **do** $A_i \leftarrow L_i \oplus L_i'$ $[\boldsymbol{A} \leftarrow \boldsymbol{L} \oplus \boldsymbol{L}']$
3. $X \leftarrow \langle \boldsymbol{A}, \boldsymbol{R} \rangle$
4. $\boldsymbol{B} \leftarrow \texttt{IPHalfMask}(X, \boldsymbol{L}')$
5. $\boldsymbol{R}' \leftarrow \boldsymbol{R} \oplus \boldsymbol{B}$
6. **return** $(\boldsymbol{L}', \boldsymbol{R}')$

---

[1] We do not use the algorithmic presentation from [1] involving two different processors as it is useless for the analysis of the dth-order security model.

Remark 2. In Algorithm 2, the Steps (1-2) for generating A does not correspond to what is described in [1]. We chose this algorithm for simplicity and because it has no incidence whatsoever on the following.

We now recall the masked addition IPAdd and the masked multiplication IPMult in the two following algorithms.

Algorithm 3. Masked Addition: $(X, Y) \leftarrow$ IPAdd$((L, R), (K, Q))$

INPUT: Two sharings (L, R) and (K, Q) of V and V' respectively
OUTPUT: New sharing (X, Y) such that $\langle X, Y \rangle = V \oplus V'$

1. $(A, B) \leftarrow$ IPRefresh$(K, Q \oplus R)$
2. $(C, D) \leftarrow$ IPRefresh$(L \oplus K, R)$
3. $Z \leftarrow \langle C, D \rangle$
4. $Y \leftarrow$ IPHalfMask(Z, A)
5. $X \leftarrow A$
6. $Y \leftarrow Y \oplus B$
7. return (X, Y)

Algorithm 4. Masked Multiplication: $(X, Y) \leftarrow$ IPMult$((L, R), (K, Q))$

INPUT: Two sharings (L, R) and (K, Q) of V and V' respectively
OUTPUT: New sharing (X, Y) such that $\langle X, Y \rangle = V \otimes V'$

1. **for** $i = 0$ **to** $n - 1$ **do**
2.   **for** $j = 1$ **to** n **do**
3. $\tilde{U}_{i*n+j} \leftarrow L_{i+1} \otimes K_j$
4. $\tilde{V}_{i*n+j} \leftarrow R_{i+1} \otimes Q_j$
5.   **end for**
6. **end for**
7. $(U, V) \leftarrow$ IPRefresh$(\tilde{U}, \tilde{V})$
8. $A \leftarrow (U_1, \cdots, U_n)$; $C \leftarrow (U_{n+1}, \cdots, U_{n^2})$
9. $B \leftarrow (V_1, \cdots, V_n)$; $D \leftarrow (V_{n+1}, \cdots, V_{n^2})$
10. $Z \leftarrow \langle C, D \rangle$
11. $Y \leftarrow$ IPHalfMask(Z, A)
12. $X \leftarrow A$
13. $Y \leftarrow Y \oplus B$
14. return (X, Y)

---

3 A First-Order Flaw

Balasch *et al.* claim that their IP masking scheme is secure against any side-channel attack of order $d = n - 1$, or equivalently, that any family of $n - 1$

intermediate variables is independent of any sensitive variable. We contradict this claim hereafter by showing that for any fixed parameter n, there always exists a first-order side-channel attack on the IP masking scheme. To this end, we exhibit an intermediate variable that is statistically dependent on some sensitive variable in both the IPRefresh and IPAdd procedures (Algorithms 2 and 3, Section 2).

3.1   Core Idea of the Attack

For the sake of clarity, we start by developing the core idea of our attack in the IPRefresh setting. Then, we show that a similar flaw occurs in the IPAdd scheme.

Flaw in Mask-Refreshing Procedure. The IPRefresh procedure takes an IP masking (L, R) of V and returns a fresh masking (L', R') of it. The first steps of the procedure generate a random vector $A \in \mathbb{F}_q^n$ whose coordinates are all different from the corresponding ones in L (as $A_i = L_i \oplus L_i'$ and $L_i' \neq 0$ for every i). The next steps compute $X = \langle A, R \rangle$ that is $X = \langle L \oplus L', R \rangle$ where L and L' are mutually independent and both uniformly distributed over $(\mathbb{F}_q^*)^n$. The first-order flaw exhibited in this paper comes from the manipulation of this variable X. Indeed, we will prove in the following sections that this variable statistically depends on V, which implies that its manipulation leaks information on V contrary to what is claimed in [1]. Our dependency proof will consist in showing that the probability mass functions (pmf) $\Pr[X \mid V = v]$ differ according to v. Thanks to the following lemma, the study of the latter functions is reduced to the study of a simpler function f_n.

Lemma 1. *Let L, L' and R be three mutually independent random variables such that L and L' are uniformly distributed over $(\mathbb{F}_q^*)^n$ and R is uniformly distributed over $\mathbb{F}_q^n$. Let X and V respectively denote the result of the inner products $\langle L \oplus L', R \rangle$ and $\langle L, R \rangle$. Then, for any $(x, v) \in \mathbb{F}_q^2$, the probability $\Pr[X = x \mid V = v]$ satisfies:*

$$\Pr[X = x \mid V = v] = \frac{f_n(v, x \oplus v)}{\Pr[V = v]} , \tag{1}$$

where f_n is defined for every $(a, b) \in \mathbb{F}_q^2$ by:

$$f_n(a, b) = \Pr[\langle L, R \rangle = a \wedge \langle L', R \rangle = b] . \tag{2}$$

Proof. By definition of a conditional probability, we have:

$$\Pr[X = x \mid V = v] = \frac{\Pr[V = v \wedge X = x]}{\Pr[V = v]} = \frac{\Pr[V = v \wedge X \oplus V = x \oplus v]}{\Pr[V = v]} .$$

Then, from $\Pr[V = v \wedge X \oplus V = x \oplus v] = \Pr[\langle L, R \rangle = v \wedge \langle L', R \rangle = x \oplus v] = f_n(v, x \oplus v)$ we get (1).   □

Flaw in the Addition Procedure. The IPAdd procedure is subject to a similar flaw that IPRefresh. Indeed at Step 3 of Algorithm 3, a variable $Z = \langle C, D \rangle = \langle L \oplus K, R \rangle$ is computed, where L and K are mutually independent and both uniformly distributed over $(\mathbb{F}_q^*)^n$. Therefore, Lemma 1 applies directly (just by replacing the notation L' by K) and we get:

$$\Pr[Z = z \mid V = v] = \frac{f_n(v, z \oplus v)}{\Pr[V = v]} \ . \tag{3}$$

Hence, for the addition procedure, proving that Z leaks information on V reduces to prove that f_n is not constant with respect to $v \in \mathbb{F}_q$ (as for IPRefresh).

The purpose of the next section is to study the function f_n defined in Lemma 1 and to explicit its expression. In Section 3.3 those expressions will be evaluated to quantify the information flow.

3.2   Study of f_n

The study of f_n developed in this section is recursive. First, in Lemma 2, we give an explicit expression for f_1. Then, in Lemma 3, we exhibit a recursive relationship for f_n. Both lemmas are eventually involved to provide an explicit expression of f_n (Theorem 1).

Lemma 2. *The function f_1 satisfies*

$$f_1(a, b) = \begin{cases} \frac{1}{q} & \text{if } (a, b) = (0, 0) \\ 0 & \text{if } (a, b) \in (\{0\} \times \mathbb{F}_q^*) \cup (\mathbb{F}_q^* \times \{0\}) \\ \frac{1}{q(q-1)} & \text{if } (a, b) \in \mathbb{F}_q^* \times \mathbb{F}_q^* \end{cases}$$

Proof. When n equals 1, vectors A and B are respectively reduced to a single coordinate A_1 and B_1. Since those coordinates are non-zero by definition, f_1 satisfies:

$$f_1(0, 0) \ = \ \Pr[A_1 \otimes R_1 = 0 \wedge B_1 \otimes R_1 = 0] \ = \ \Pr[R_1 = 0] \ = \ \frac{1}{q} \ .$$

Moreover, for any $a \neq 0$, we have

$$f_1(a, 0) \ = \ \Pr[R_1 = a \otimes A_1^{-1} \wedge R_1 = 0] \ = \ 0 \ ,$$

which, by symmetry of f_n, also implies $f_1(0, b) = 0$ for any $b \neq 0$. Eventually, the law of total probability together with the mutual independence between A_1, B_1 and R_1, imply

$$f_1(a, b) \ = \ \sum_{a_1 \in \mathbb{F}_q^*} \Pr[A_1 = a_1] \times \Pr[R_1 = a \otimes a_1^{-1} \wedge B_1 \otimes R_1 = b] \ ,$$

which gives for $a \neq 0$ and $b \neq 0$:

$$f_1(a,b) = \sum_{a_1 \in \mathbb{F}_q^*} \Pr[A_1 = a_1] \times \Pr[R_1 = a \otimes a_1^{-1} \wedge B_1 = b \otimes a^{-1} \otimes a_1]$$

$$= \frac{1}{q(q-1)} \ .$$

$\square$

Lemma 3. *For every $n \geqslant 1$, there exist real values f_n^{00}, f_n^{01} and f_n^{11} such that*

$$f_n(a,b) = \begin{cases} f_n^{00} & \text{if } (a,b) = (0,0) \\ f_n^{01} & \text{if } (a,b) \in (\{0\} \times \mathbb{F}_q^*) \cup (\mathbb{F}_q^* \times \{0\}) \\ f_n^{11} & \text{if } (a,b) \in \mathbb{F}_q^* \times \mathbb{F}_q^* \end{cases} \ .$$

Moreover, we have

$$f_{n+1}^{00} = \frac{1}{q} f_n^{00} + \frac{q-1}{q} f_n^{11} \ ,$$

$$f_{n+1}^{01} = \frac{2}{q} f_n^{01} + \frac{q-2}{q} f_n^{11} \ ,$$

$$f_{n+1}^{11} = \frac{1}{q(q-1)} f_n^{00} + \frac{2(q-2)}{q(q-1)} f_n^{01} + \frac{(q-1)+(q-2)^2}{q(q-1)} f_n^{11} \ .$$

Proof. The first statement is true for $n = 1$ by Lemma 2. It is then implied by recurrence from the second statement. Therefore, we only need to show the latter statement.

For every $n > 1$, the total probability law implies

$$f_{n+1}(a,b) = \sum_{(a_0,b_0) \in \mathbb{F}_q^2} f_n(a \oplus a_0, b \oplus b_0) f_1(a_0, b_0) \ . \qquad (4)$$

1. For $(a,b) = (0,0)$, the terms in the sum in (4) equal $T(a_0, b_0) = f_n(a_0, b_0) f_1(a_0, b_0)$. Moreover, by Lemma 2, the latter product satisfies:

$$T(a_0, b_0) = \begin{cases} \frac{1}{q} f_n(0,0) & \text{if } (a_0,b_0) = (0,0) \\ 0 & \text{if } (a_0,b_0) \in (\{0\} \times \mathbb{F}_q^*) \cup (\mathbb{F}_q^* \times \{0\}) \\ \frac{1}{q(q-1)} f_n(a_0, b_0) & \text{if } (a_0,b_0) \in \mathbb{F}_q^* \times \mathbb{F}_q^* \end{cases} \ .$$

We deduce

$$f_{n+1}(a,b) = \frac{1}{q} f_n^{00} + (q-1)^2 \frac{1}{q(q-1)} f_n^{11} \ . \qquad (5)$$

2. For $(a,b) \in \{0\} \times \mathbb{F}_q^*$, the terms in the sum in (4) equal $T(a_0, b_0) = f_n(a_0, b \oplus b_0) f_1(a_0, b_0)$. Moreover, by Lemma 2, the latter product satisfies:

$$T(a_0, b_0) = \begin{cases} \frac{1}{q} f_n(0,b) & \text{if } (a_0,b_0) = (0,0) \\ 0 & \text{if } (a_0,b_0) \in (\{0\} \times \mathbb{F}_q^*) \cup (\mathbb{F}_q^* \times \{0\}) \\ \frac{1}{q(q-1)} f_n(a_0, 0) & \text{if } (a_0,b_0) \in \mathbb{F}_q^* \times \{b\} \\ \frac{1}{q(q-1)} f_n(a_0, b_0) & \text{if } (a_0,b_0) \in \mathbb{F}_q^* \times (\mathbb{F}_q^* \backslash \{b\}) \end{cases} \ .$$

We deduce

$$f_{n+1}(a,b) = \frac{1}{q}f_n^{01} + (q-1)\frac{1}{q(q-1)}f_n^{01} + (q-1)(q-2)\frac{1}{q(q-1)}f_n^{11} . \quad (6)$$

For $(a,b) \in \mathbb{F}_q^* \times \{0\}$, we have the same equality by symmetry of the function $f_{n+1}S$.

3. For $(a,b) \in \mathbb{F}_q^* \times \mathbb{F}_q^*$, the terms in the sum in (4) equal $T(a_0,b_0) = f_n(a \oplus a_0, b \oplus b_0)f_1(a_0,b_0)$. Moreover, by Lemma 2, the latter product satisfies:

$$T(a_0,b_0) = \begin{cases} \frac{1}{q}f_n(a,b) & \text{if } (a_0,b_0) = (0,0) \\ \frac{1}{q(q-1)}f_n(0,0) & \text{if } (a_0,b_0) = (a,b) \\ 0 & \text{if } (a_0,b_0) \in (\{0\} \times \mathbb{F}_q^*) \cup (\mathbb{F}_q^* \times \{0\}) \\ \frac{1}{q(q-1)}f_n(a \oplus a_0, 0) & \text{if } (a_0,b_0) \in (\mathbb{F}_q^* \backslash \{a\}) \times \{b\} \\ \frac{1}{q(q-1)}f_n(0, b \oplus b_0) & \text{if } (a_0,b_0) \in \{a\} \times (\mathbb{F}_q^* \backslash \{b\}) \\ \frac{1}{q(q-1)}f_n(a \oplus a_0, b \oplus b_0) & \text{if } (a_0,b_0) \in (\mathbb{F}_q^* \backslash \{a\}) \times (\mathbb{F}_q^* \backslash \{b\}) \end{cases} .$$

We deduce

$$f_{n+1}(a,b) = \frac{1}{q}f_n^{11} + \frac{1}{q(q-1)}f_n^{00} + 2\left((q-2)\frac{1}{q(q-1)}f_n^{01}\right)$$
$$+ (q-2)^2 \frac{1}{q(q-1)}f_n^{11} . \quad (7)$$

Equations (5), (6) and (7) directly yield to the second statement. □

Theorem 1. *For every $n \geqslant 1$ we have*

$$f_n(a,b) = \begin{cases} \frac{1}{q^2} + \frac{1}{q^2(q-1)^{n-2}} & \text{if } (a,b) = (0,0) \\ \frac{1}{q^2} - \frac{1}{q^2(q-1)^{n-1}} & \text{if } (a,b) \in (\{0\} \times \mathbb{F}_q^*) \cup (\mathbb{F}_q^* \times \{0\}) \\ \frac{1}{q^2} + \frac{1}{q^2(q-1)^{n}} & \text{if } (a,b) \in \mathbb{F}_q^* \times \mathbb{F}_q^* \end{cases}$$

Proof. From Lemma 3, we have

$$\begin{pmatrix} f_{n+1}^{00} \\ f_{n+1}^{01} \\ f_{n+1}^{11} \end{pmatrix} = \begin{pmatrix} \frac{1}{q} & 0 & \frac{q-1}{q} \\ 0 & \frac{2}{q} & \frac{q-2}{q} \\ \frac{1}{q(q-1)} & \frac{2(q-2)}{q(q-1)} & \frac{(q-1)+(q-2)^2}{q(q-1)} \end{pmatrix} \cdot \begin{pmatrix} f_n^{00} \\ f_n^{01} \\ f_n^{11} \end{pmatrix} ,$$

that is

$$\begin{pmatrix} f_{n+1}^{00} \\ f_{n+1}^{01} \\ f_{n+1}^{11} \end{pmatrix} = P \cdot \begin{pmatrix} 1 & 0 & 0 \\ 0 & 0 & 0 \\ 0 & 0 & \frac{1}{q-1} \end{pmatrix} \cdot P^{-1} \cdot \begin{pmatrix} f_n^{00} \\ f_n^{01} \\ f_n^{11} \end{pmatrix} , \quad (8)$$

where P is the eigenvectors matrix defined by:

$$P = \begin{pmatrix} 1 & 1-q & q^2 - 2q + 1 \\ 1 & \frac{1}{2}(2-q) & 1-q \\ 1 & 1 & 1 \end{pmatrix} .$$

After recursively applying (8), we can express $(f_n^{00}, f_n^{01}, f_n^{11})$ with respect to $(f_1^{00}, f_1^{01}, f_1^{11})$ as

$$
\begin{pmatrix} f_n^{00} \\ f_n^{01} \\ f_n^{11} \end{pmatrix} = P \cdot \begin{pmatrix} 1 & 0 & 0 \\ 0 & 0 & 0 \\ 0 & 0 & \frac{1}{(q-1)^{n-1}} \end{pmatrix} \cdot P^{-1} \cdot \begin{pmatrix} f_1^{00} \\ f_1^{01} \\ f_1^{11} \end{pmatrix}
$$

Finally, Lemma 2 implies $(f_1^{00}, f_1^{01}, f_1^{11}) = (\frac{1}{q}, 0, \frac{1}{q(q-1)})$, which together with the above equation yields to the theorem statement. $\square$

3.3   Exhibiting the Flaws in `IPRefresh` and `IPAdd` Procedures

Due to Lemma 1 and Theorem 1, and given that $\Pr[V = v]$ equals $\frac{1}{q}$, we get:

$$
\Pr[X = x \mid V = v] = \begin{cases} \frac{1}{q} + \frac{1}{q(q-1)^{n-2}} & \text{if } x = 0 \\ \frac{1}{q} - \frac{1}{q(q-1)^{n-1}} & \text{if } x \neq 0 \end{cases} \tag{9}
$$

for $v = 0$, and

$$
\Pr[X = x \mid V = v] = \begin{cases} \frac{1}{q} - \frac{1}{q(q-1)^{n-1}} & \text{if } x = v \\ \frac{1}{q} + \frac{1}{q(q-1)^{n}} & \text{if } x \neq v \end{cases}, \tag{10}
$$

otherwise. Hence, when the sensitive variable V equals 0, then the intermediate variable X manipulated in `IPRefresh` is more likely to equal 0 than another value in $\mathbb{F}_q$. On the other hand, when V equals a non-zero value $v \neq 0$, then X is more likely to be any value of $\mathbb{F}_q$ but v. Although the bias is exponentially small in n, for small values of n it may induce a significant information leakage (see Section 4).

For the reasons given in Section 3.1, Equations (9) and (10) also stand for the dependency of Z and V in `IPAdd`. The manipulation of Z hence leaks information on V and $\Pr[Z = z \mid V = v]$ satisfies (9) and (10).

Remark 3. The flaw in `IPMult` seems less informative than in `IPRefresh` and `IPAdd`. Indeed except for the `IPRefresh` call, we did not find any flaw in the actual algorithm. Moreover the `IPRefresh` procedure is called on a sharing of dimension n^2. Hence, even for small values of n, the observed bias quickly becomes very small.

4   Information Theoretic Evaluation of the Flaw

We have seen in Section 3.3 that Balasch *et al.*'s proposal possesses a first-order flaw whatever the masking dimension n of their scheme. To complete our study, we conduct hereafter an information theoretic evaluation of the flaw exhibited in (9) and (10), following the same outlines as the security analyses in [8, 10, 22, 25]. Moreover, the quantity of sensitive information leakage due to the flaw is compared with the amount of intrinsic information leakage from the manipulation of the right-half sharing $\boldsymbol{R}$.

To quantify the amount of leaking information, we model the relationship between the physical leakage and the manipulated variables as follows. Each tuple of variables $(I_1, I_2, \cdots, I_t)$ is associated with a tuple of leakages $\mathcal{L} = (\mathcal{L}_1, \mathcal{L}_2, \cdots, \mathcal{L}_t)$ s.t. $\mathcal{L}_j = \mathrm{HW}(I_j) + \mathcal{N}_j$, where HW denotes the Hamming weight function and $\mathcal{N}_j$ denotes an independent Gaussian variable with mean 0 and standard deviation σ. We use the notation $\mathcal{L} \leftrightarrow (I_1, I_2, \cdots, I_t)$ to refer to this association. To compare the information revealed by the flaw and that inherently revealed by the leakage on the right-half sharing (see Remark 1 in Section 2), we computed the mutual information[2] $\mathrm{I}(V; \mathcal{L})$ between the sensitive variable $V = \langle \boldsymbol{L}, \boldsymbol{R} \rangle$ and the leakage $\mathcal{L}$ in the following situations where we recall that X equals $\langle \boldsymbol{L} \oplus \boldsymbol{L}', \boldsymbol{R} \rangle$ (see Section 3.1):

right-half leakage for $n = 2$: $\mathcal{L} \leftrightarrow \boldsymbol{R} = (R_1, R_2)$,   (11)

right-half leakage for $n = 3$: $\mathcal{L} \leftrightarrow \boldsymbol{R} = (R_1, R_2, R_3)$,   (12)

first-order flaw for $n = 2$: $\mathcal{L} \leftrightarrow X$,   (13)

first-order flaw for $n = 3$: $\mathcal{L} \leftrightarrow X$.   (14)

Figure 1 summarizes the information theoretic evaluation for each leakage (11) to (14). It can be observed that for each sharing dimension $n \in \{2, 3\}$, there exists a threshold for σ up to which the first-order flaw becomes more informative than the overall right-half leakage. For instance, for $n = 2$, this gap value is $\sigma \approx 2$. This observation is in accordance with the soundness of the dth-order security notion: a security at a greater order implies a smaller asymptotic leakage (with respect to an increasing noise).

5   Attack Simulations

To study the difficulty of exploiting the sensitive information leakage exhibited in Figure 1, we compared the effectiveness of a classical Correlation Power Analysis (CPA for short) against the flaw with that of a second-order CPA targeting the half IP-Masking $\boldsymbol{R}$ (which, according to Remark 1, leaks sensitive information).

The target variable V in our attack was defined as the output of the s-box of the light-weight block cipher PRESENT [3], and hence V, R_1, R_2 and X were defined as elements of $\mathbb{F}_{16}$. The leakages on these values were simulated in the Hamming weight model with Gaussian Noise, as in (11) and (13), for different noise standard deviations $\sigma \in [0, 4.5]$. For each key hypothesis, the predictions were computed with the *optimal prediction function* defined in [21] (with the Hamming weight as model function). The results of our attack simulations are reported in Figure 2.

---

[2] As shown in [25], the number of measurements required to achieve a given success-rate in a maximum likelihood attack is related to the mutual information evaluation and it roughly equals $c \times \mathrm{I}(V; \mathcal{L})^{-1}$, where c is a constant related to the chosen success-rate and the leakage model.

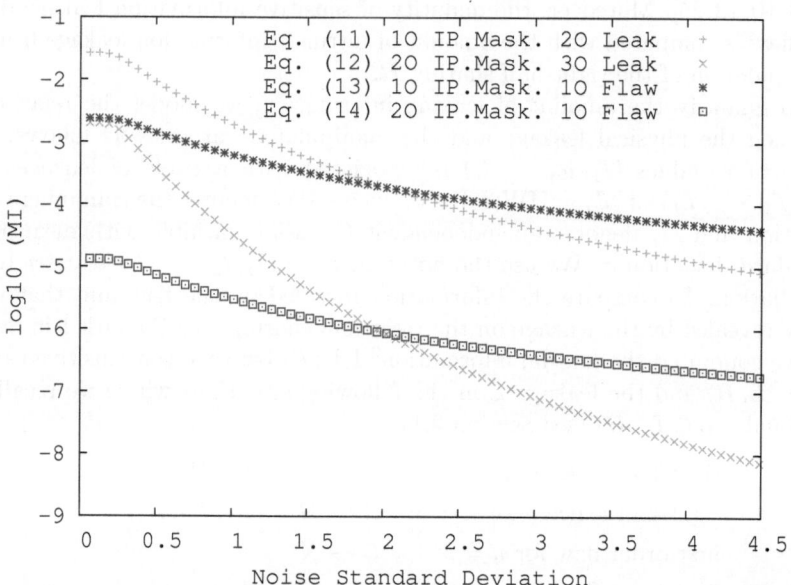

Fig. 1. Mutual information ($\log_{10}$) between the leakage and the sensitive variable over an increasing noise standard deviation (x-axis)

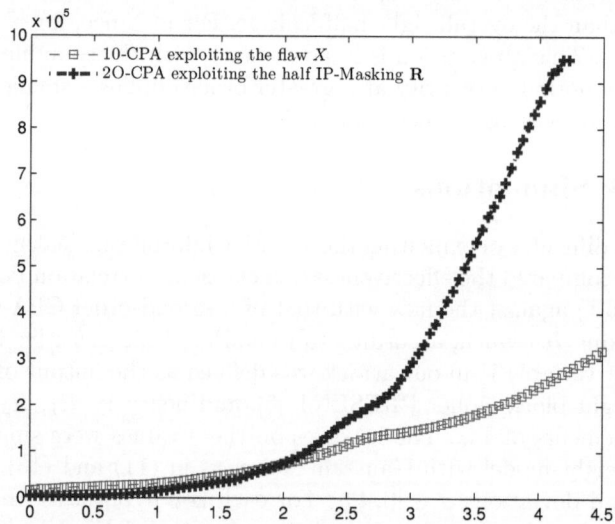

Fig. 2. Number of measurements (y-axis) required to achieve a 90% attack success rate against IP-Masking ($n = 2$) *versus* the noise standard deviation (x-axis)

It may be observed that the attack efficiencies are close when the standard deviation of the noise is lower than 2 (less than 75000 measurements), which corresponds to the crossing point of the mutual information traces in Figure 1. After this threshold, the difference between the slops of the two efficiency traces quickly increases. Eventually, for $\sigma = 4.5$, the second-order CPA against the right-half IP masking fails, even with 1 million measurements, whereas the first-order CPA against the flaw succeeds with around 300 000 measurements. This clearly illustrates the importance of the exhibited flaw. We also emphasize that the resynchronization of leakage traces and the detection of points of interest usually make higher-order attacks much more difficult to mount in practice than first-order ones. This further increases the practical insecurity resulting from a first-order leakage compared to a higher-order leakage.

References

1. Balasch, J., Faust, S., Gierlichs, B., Verbauwhede, I.: Theory and practice of a leakage resilient masking scheme. In: Wang, X., Sako, K. (eds.) ASIACRYPT 2012. LNCS, vol. 7658, pp. 758–775. Springer, Heidelberg (2012)
2. Bellare, M., Goldwasser, S., Micciancio, D.: "Pseudo-random" number generation within cryptographic algorithms: The DSS case. In: Kaliski Jr., B.S. (ed.) CRYPTO 1997. LNCS, vol. 1294, pp. 277–291. Springer, Heidelberg (1997)
3. Bogdanov, A.A., Knudsen, L.R., Leander, G., Paar, C., Poschmann, A., Robshaw, M., Seurin, Y., Vikkelsoe, C.: PRESENT: An Ultra-Lightweight Block Cipher. In: Paillier, P., Verbauwhede, I. (eds.) CHES 2007. LNCS, vol. 4727, pp. 450–466. Springer, Heidelberg (2007)
4. Carlet, C., Goubin, L., Prouff, E., Quisquater, M., Rivain, M.: Higher-order masking schemes for s-boxes. In: Canteaut, A. (ed.) FSE 2012. LNCS, vol. 7549, pp. 366–384. Springer, Heidelberg (2012)
5. Chari, S., Jutla, C., Rao, J., Rohatgi, P.: A Cautionary Note Regarding Evaluation of AES Candidates on Smart-Cards. In: Second AES Candidate Conference – AES 2 (March 1999)
6. Coron, J.-S., Prouff, E., Rivain, M., Roche, T.: Higher-order side channel security and mask refreshing. In: Moriai, S. (ed.) FSE. LNCS, Springer (2013) (to appear)
7. Dziembowski, S., Faust, S.: Leakage-resilient circuits without computational assumptions. In: Cramer, R. (ed.) TCC 2012. LNCS, vol. 7194, pp. 230–247. Springer, Heidelberg (2012)
8. Fumaroli, G., Martinelli, A., Prouff, E., Rivain, M.: Affine Masking against Higher-Order Side Channel Analysis. In: Biryukov, A., Gong, G., Stinson, D.R. (eds.) SAC 2010. LNCS, vol. 6544, pp. 262–280. Springer, Heidelberg (2011)
9. Genelle, L., Prouff, E., Quisquater, M.: Thwarting higher-order side channel analysis with additive and multiplicative maskings. In: Preneel, Takagi [19], pp. 240–255
10. Grosso, V., Standaert, F.-X., Faust, S.: Masking vs. multiparty computation: How large is the gap for aes? In: Bertoni, G., Coron, J.-S. (eds.) CHES 2013. LNCS, vol. 8086, pp. 400–416. Springer, Heidelberg (2013)
11. Ishai, Y., Sahai, A., Wagner, D.: Private Circuits: Securing Hardware against Probing Attacks. In: Boneh, D. (ed.) CRYPTO 2003. LNCS, vol. 2729, pp. 463–481. Springer, Heidelberg (2003)
12. Kim, H., Hong, S., Lim, J.: A fast and provably secure higher-order masking of aes s-box. In: Preneel, Takagi [19], pp. 95–107

13. Kocher, P.: Timing Attacks on Implementations of Diffie-Hellman, RSA, DSS, and Other Systems. In: Koblitz, N. (ed.) CRYPTO 1996. LNCS, vol. 1109, pp. 104–113. Springer, Heidelberg (1996)
14. Kocher, P., Jaffe, J., Jun, B.: Differential Power Analysis. In: Wiener, M. (ed.) CRYPTO 1999. LNCS, vol. 1666, pp. 388–397. Springer, Heidelberg (1999)
15. Lomné, V., Prouff, E., Roche, T.: Behind the Scene of Side Channel Attacks. In: Sako, K., Sarkar, P. (eds.) ASIACRYPT 2013, Part I. LNCS, vol. 8269, pp. 506–525. Springer, Heidelberg (2013)
16. Mangard, S., Popp, T., Gammel, B.M.: Side-Channel Leakage of Masked CMOS Gates. In: Menezes, A. (ed.) CT-RSA 2005. LNCS, vol. 3376, pp. 351–365. Springer, Heidelberg (2005)
17. Messerges, T.: Using Second-order Power Analysis to Attack DPA Resistant software. In: Paar, C., Kocc, cC.K. (eds.) CHES 2000. LNCS, vol. 1965, pp. 238–251. Springer, Heidelberg (2000)
18. Oswald, E., Mangard, S., Herbst, C., Tillich, S.: Practical Second-order DPA Attacks for Masked Smart Card Implementations of Block Ciphers. In: Pointcheval, D. (ed.) CT-RSA 2006. LNCS, vol. 3860, pp. 192–207. Springer, Heidelberg (2006)
19. Preneel, B., Takagi, T. (eds.): CHES 2011. LNCS, vol. 6917. Springer, Heidelberg (2011)
20. Prouff, E., Rivain, M.: Masking against Side-Channel Attacks: A Formal Security Proof. In: Johansson, T., Nguyen, P.Q. (eds.) EUROCRYPT 2013. LNCS, vol. 7881, pp. 142–159. Springer, Heidelberg (2013)
21. Prouff, E., Rivain, M., Bévan, R.: Statistical Analysis of Second Order Differential Power Analysis. IEEE Transactions on Computers 58(6), 799–811 (2009)
22. Prouff, E., Roche, T.: Higher-order glitches free implementation of the aes using secure multi-party computation protocols. In: Preneel, Takagi [19], pp. 63–78
23. Rivain, M., Prouff, E.: Provably secure higher-order masking of aes. In: Mangard, S., Standaert, F.-X. (eds.) CHES 2010. LNCS, vol. 6225, pp. 413–427. Springer, Heidelberg (2010)
24. Shamir, A.: How to Share a Secret. Commun. ACM 22(11), 612–613 (1979)
25. Standaert, F.-X., Veyrat-Charvillon, N., Oswald, E., Gierlichs, B., Medwed, M., Kasper, M., Mangard, S.: The World is not Enough: Another Look on Second-Order DPA. In: Abe, M. (ed.) ASIACRYPT 2010. LNCS, vol. 6477, pp. 112–129. Springer, Heidelberg (2010)

The Myth of Generic DPA... and the Magic of Learning

Carolyn Whitnall[1], Elisabeth Oswald[1], and François-Xavier Standaert[2]

[1] University of Bristol, Department of Computer Science,
Merchant Venturers Building, Woodland Road, BS8 1UB, Bristol, UK
{carolyn.whitnall,elisabeth.oswald}@bris.ac.uk
[2] Université catholique de Louvain, UCL Crypto Group
Place du Levant 3, B-1348 Louvain-la-Neuve, Belgium
fstandae@uclouvain.be

Abstract. A *generic* DPA strategy is one which is able to recover secret information from physically observable device leakage without any *a priori* knowledge about the device's leakage characteristics. Here we provide much-needed clarification on results emerging from the existing literature, demonstrating precisely that such methods (strictly defined) are *inherently* restricted to a very limited selection of target functions. Continuing to search related techniques for a 'silver bullet' generic attack appears a bootless errand. However, we find that a minor relaxation of the strict definition—the incorporation of some minimal non-device-specific intuition—produces scope for *generic-emulating* strategies, able to succeed against a far wider range of targets. We present stepwise regression as an example of such, and demonstrate its effectiveness in a variety of scenarios. We also give some evidence that its practical performance matches that of 'best bit' DoM attacks which we take as further indication for the necessity of performing profiled attacks in the context of device evaluations.

Keywords: side-channel analysis, differential power analysis.

1 Introduction

Ever since Kocher et al. showed that differential power analysis (DPA) could be successful even with very little information about the target implementation [16], the research community has pursued 'generic' methods—informally, techniques able to recover secret information even in the total absence of knowledge about the attacked device's data-dependent power consumption. Recent suggestions include mutual information analysis (MIA) using an identity power model [12], distinguishers based on the Kolmogorov–Smirnov (KS) two-sample test statistic [30,35] and the Cramér–von Mises test [30], linear regression (LR)-based methods which can be seen as a sort of on-the-fly profiling [9,24], and an innovative approach using copulas [31].

However, all existing proposals share a common shortfall when applied to injective target functions: in order to distinguish between hypotheses the attacker

J. Benaloh (Ed.): CT-RSA 2014, LNCS 8366, pp. 183–205, 2014.

must, after all, have some meaningful piece of knowledge by which to partition the measurements (in the case of MIA and KS-based DPA) or select the appropriate set of covariates (in the case of LR-based DPA) [31]. Unfortunately, this dependence on prior knowledge has been under-appreciated because of the apparent success of 'arbitrary' work-arounds such as the practice of partitioning intermediate variables according to their 7 least significant bits (sometimes called the 7LSB model). However, it is shown in [34] that this strategy is far from universally-applicable and only works to the extent that the seemingly indifferent partition captures something meaningful about the leakage after all. For example, noise on top of a typical CMOS Hamming weight consumption distorts the trace measurements *towards* the 7LSB model sufficiently for MIA to succeed, but this is not the case in general (i.e in arbitrary leakage scenarios). Such attacks can no longer be considered 'generic', a description which is earned primarily by virtue of the non-reliance on *a priori knowledge* rather than the chosen statistical methodology. The focus on defining universally-applicable *distinguishers* indicates a confusion about the role of the distinguisher and that of the power model in what has so far been only informally defined as 'generic' DPA. It also raises the fundamental question of whether *truly* 'generic' tools exist at all.

Establishing whether or not generic DPA attacks exist has fundamental consequences for the process of cryptographic device evaluation. The presence of generic attacks would imply that any device could potentially be attacked without any information about its internal functioning or leakage characteristics. Consequently, attacks based on profiling would only be 'better' in terms of efficiency (number of power traces needed)—not in terms of applicability. The absence of generic attacks would imply that there exist devices (leakage characteristics) which can only be evaluated soundly by performing profiled attacks—a practice which is not commonly undertaken at present (see, e.g., [19] Appendix F). In the following, we tackle this important question in the practically relevant context of standard DPA as investigated, e.g., in [9,12,16,24,30,35]. That is, we assume that the mean of the side-channel leakage distributions is key-dependent.

1.1 Our Contribution

We first develop a theory of power models according to Stevens' 'levels of measurement' [28], enabling us to formally define what constitutes a *generic power model*. We show that different distinguishers require different types of power model and derive the notion of a *generic-compatible distinguisher* accordingly. The pairing of a *generic-compatible distinguisher* with the *generic power model* we call a *generic strategy*. These definitions provide a basis for making conclusive general statements about generic DPA. We show that the noninjectivity of the target function is a prerequisite for *any* first-order generic strategy to succeed, proving the absence of a universally-applicable generic distinguisher in the context of first-order DPA! (Generic higher-order DPA can only be *more* difficult, so this conclusive statement naturally extends upwards). As a further finding we observe that noninjectivity alone is not sufficient for generic success, and investigate additional requirements on the target function. It is already known that there is an inverse relationship between performance against certain S-box criteria and susceptibility to DPA [21]; we demonstrate a sufficient condition for first-order generic success which is promoted (though not inevitably produced) by the desirable S-box property of *differential uniformity* [20].

Having ruled out the possibility of a universally-applicable generic distinguisher, we investigate *minimal* relaxations on the generic criteria producing theoretically plausible attack strategies. As a starting point we take the LR-based distinguisher [9,24], which (we show) qualifies as generic-compatible but returns more auxiliary information than other such methods when applied against an injective target. Hence, even though the keys remain indistinguishable in the ranking (as is consistent with the first half of this paper and with earlier studies [31]), the hypothesis-dependent model estimates—i.e. the estimated coefficients in the polynomial expression for the leakage—contain additional clues about the correct key. At this stage we introduce some 'non-device-specific intuition' regarding the simplicity of the leakage function relative to the cryptographic target function (typically an S-box). This extremely minimal assumption (which we will explain more formally in due course) allows us to exploit the model estimates, which we propose to do using the techniques of *stepwise regression*. Such a strategy is no longer strictly generic, but the general device-independent nature of the extra assumption prompts us to coin the description *generic emulating*. We verify that this proposed strategy truly is effective—even against injective target functions such as the AES and PRESENT S-boxes, and even as the true leakage becomes increasingly unusual or complex (high-degree polynomials, for example). We also show that the proposed strategy is efficient, albeit seemingly no better in performance than difference-of-means (DoM) based attacks.

2 Preliminaries

2.1 Differential Power Analysis

We consider a 'standard DPA attack' scenario as defined in [18], and briefly explain the underlying idea as well as introduce the necessary terminology here. We assume that the power consumption T of a cryptographic device depends on some internal value (or state) $F_{k^*}(X)$ which we call the *target*: a function $F_{k^*} : \mathcal{X} \to \mathcal{Z}$ of some part of the known plaintext—a random variable $X \overset{R}{\in} \mathcal{X}$—which is dependent on some part of the secret key $k^* \in \mathcal{K}$. Consequently, we have that $T = L \circ F_{k^*}(X) + \varepsilon$, where $L : \mathcal{Z} \to \mathbb{R}$ describes the data-dependent component and ε comprises the remaining power consumption which can be modeled as independent random noise (this simplifying assumption is common in the literature—see, again, [18]). The attacker has N power measurements corresponding to encryptions of N known plaintexts $x_i \in \mathcal{X}$, $i = 1, \ldots, N$ and wishes to recover the secret key k^*. The attacker can accurately compute the internal values as they would be under each key hypothesis $\{F_k(x_i)\}_{i=1}^N$, $k \in \mathcal{K}$ and uses whatever information he possesses about the true leakage function L to construct a prediction model $M : \mathcal{Z} \to \mathcal{M}$.

DPA is motivated by the intuition that the model predictions under the correct key hypothesis should give more information about the true trace measurements than the model predictions under an incorrect key hypothesis. A distinguisher D is some function which can be applied to the measurements and the hypothesis-dependent predictions in order to quantify the correspondence between them. For a given such comparison statistic, D, the *theoretic* attack vector is $\mathbf{D} = \{D(L \circ F_{k*}(X) + \varepsilon, M \circ F_k(X))\}_{k \in \mathcal{K}}$, and the *estimated* vector from a practical instantiation of the attack is $\hat{\mathbf{D}}_N = \{\hat{D}_N(L \circ F_{k*}(\mathbf{x}) + \mathbf{e}, M \circ F_k(\mathbf{x}))\}_{k \in \mathcal{K}}$ (where $\mathbf{x} = \{x_i\}_{i=1}^N$ are the known inputs and $\mathbf{e} = \{e_i\}_{i=1}^N$ is the observed noise). Then the attack is *o-th order theoretically successful* if $\#\{k \in \mathcal{K} : \mathbf{D}[k^*] \leq \mathbf{D}[k]\} \leq o$ and *o-th order successful* if $\#\{k \in \mathcal{K} : \hat{\mathbf{D}}_N[k^*] \leq \hat{\mathbf{D}}_N[k]\} \leq o$.[1]

Definition 1. *A practical instantiation of a standard univariate DPA attack computes, given a set of power traces $\mathbf{T}$, a prediction model M, a set of inputs $\mathbf{X}$, and a comparison statistic D, the distinguishing vector $\hat{\mathbf{D}}_N = \{\hat{D}_N(L \circ F_{k*}(\mathbf{x}) + \mathbf{e}, M \circ F_k(\mathbf{x}))\}_{k \in \mathcal{K}}$. A practical instantiation is said to be o-th order successful if $\#\{k \in \mathcal{K} : \hat{\mathbf{D}}_N[k^*] \leq \hat{\mathbf{D}}_N[k]\} \leq o$.*

2.2 Measuring DPA Outcomes

Metrics to compare the *efficiency* of DPA attacks include the *(o-th order) success rate* and the *guessing entropy* of [27]—defined respectively as the probability of o-th order success and the expected number of key hypotheses remaining to test after a practical attack on a given number of traces. However, in the evaluation of generic strategies, the question of asymptotic feasibility takes precedence over that of efficiency. By the law of large numbers $\frac{1}{N}\sum_{i=1}^N L \circ F_{k*}(x) + e_i \rightarrow L \circ F_{k*}(x)$ as $N \rightarrow \infty$ (as long as the samples are independent and identically distributed). We can therefore discuss feasibility from the perspective of the *ideal* distinguishing vector $\mathbf{D}_{IDEAL} = \{D(L \circ F_{k*}(X), M \circ F_k(X))\}_{k \in \mathcal{K}}$, noting that this no longer depends on the noise but only on the hypothesis-dependent power models relative to the true leakage. Indeed, averaging the trace measurements conditioned on the inputs is a popular pre-processing step in practice as it strips out irrelevant variance and reduces the dimensionality of the computations (see, for example, [1]); it is a sound approach as long as the side-channel information to be exploited originates in differences between the mean values of the leakage distributions, which *is* the case in our standard DPA scenario.

For the purposes of evaluating the theoretic capabilities of generic emulating and related strategies, we will focus on first-order asymptotic success, as captured by the (ideal) nearest-rival distinguishing margin (see [33,34]):
$NRMarg(\mathbf{D}_{IDEAL}) = \mathbf{D}_{IDEAL}[k^*] - \max\{\mathbf{D}_{IDEAL}[k] | k \neq k^*\}$. In Sect. 4.6, where we investigate the practical performance of our proposed generic emulating distinguisher, we report success rates for attacks against simulated leakages.

---

[1] Note that standard DPA attacks do not include collision-based attacks [25], which exploit information from several leakage points per observation, and do not require a power model at all.

2.3 Boolean Vectorial Functions

We are often interested in the special case that the key-indexed functions F_k can be expressed as $F_k(X) = F(k * X)$ where $F : \mathbb{F}_2^n \to \mathbb{F}_2^m$ is an $(n\text{-}m)$ Boolean vectorial function and $*$ denotes the *key combining* operator (e.g., XOR). It particularly pertains to the study of block ciphers, and their associated S-boxes.

Certain algebraic properties of such functions are known to be particularly important to the *cryptanalytic* robustness of a cipher system. We (very) briefly recall those concepts that will play a role in our later analysis; for a good basic introduction see [14] or, for a more comprehensive explanation, [6,7].

F is *affine* if it can be expressed as a linear map followed by a translation—that is, if there exists a matrix $M \in \mathbb{F}_2^{m \times n}$ and a vector $v \in \mathbb{F}_2^m$ such that $F(x) = Mx \oplus v$. *Nonlinearity* is defined as: $N_F = \min_{u \in \mathbb{F}_2^n, v \in \mathbb{F}_2^m \setminus \{0\}} \sum_{x \in \mathbb{F}_2^n} u \cdot x \oplus v \cdot F(x)$.

F is *balanced* if the preimages in F of all singleton subsets of $\mathbb{F}_2^m$ are uniformly sized: that is, $\forall y \in \mathbb{F}_2^m$, $\#\{x \in \mathbb{F}_2^n | F(x) = y\} = 2^{n-m}$. This property applies to many functions used in block ciphers, particularly S-boxes [36] where any bias on the unobserved inputs is extremely undesirable.

Another desirable S-box property is *differential uniformity* [20]—that the derivatives of F with respect to $a \in \mathbb{F}_2^n$ (defined as $D_a F(x) = F(x) \oplus F(x \oplus a)$) be *as uniform as possible*. If there exists a vector $a \in \mathbb{F}_2^n$ such that $D_a F(x)$ is constant over $\mathbb{F}_2^n$ then a is called a *linear structure* of F and (as per [10]) can be exploited by a cryptanalyst. $\{a \in \mathbb{F}_2^n | D_a F = cst\}$ is the *linear space* of F.

3 Clarifying Generic DPA

What does it mean for an attack to be 'generic'? The discussion in the literature has focused on appropriating, as distinguishers, statistics which 'require few distributional assumptions'—trawling the statistical literature for nonparametric, distribution-comparing procedures such as the Kullback-Leibler divergence (a.k.a. Mutual Information Analysis) [12], the Kolmogorov–Smirnov [30,35] and Cramér–von Mises [30] tests, and copulas [31]. However, the emphasis on finding 'distribution-free' statistics for use as distinguishers somewhat distracts from the essential defining feature of generic DPA which is that *no assumptions have been made about the device leakage*. Clearly, the (fairly common) practice of combining such distinguishers with an informed prior model does not produce a generic attack: we need to begin by establishing what constitutes a *generic power model*.

We first delineate the different types of model used in DPA attacks, and discuss which distinguishers are suitable in each instance. We can then define a generic power model, a generic-compatible distinguisher, and a generic DPA strategy. These definitions form the basis for a number of propositions that clarify the cases in which any generic strategy is bound to fail (we spell out necessary conditions for success and discuss further the feasibility of generic DPA).

3.1 Delineating Leakage Assumptions

Firstly we must distinguish between assumptions about the *data-dependent* leakage, as captured by the power model, and assumptions about the *distribution of the noise*—which in most cases play a less visible role, but can affect how accurately or efficiently certain statistics may be estimated. Fig. 1 visualises this two-dimensional continuum, and indicates the suitability of popular distinguishers as assumptions vary.

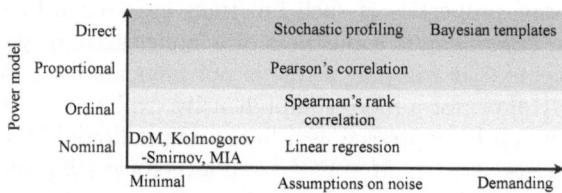

Fig. 1. Types of leakage model and the assumptions required by common distinguishers

Assumptions about the noise range from *fully characterised distributions* as exploited (e.g.) by Bayesian template attacks, down to *no knowledge whatsoever*, when the robustness of nonparametric statistics such as mutual information and the Kolmogorov–Smirnov test may come in handy. Fortunately, the often reasonable assumption of approximate normality opens up a broad range of (semi-)parametric options, which are to be preferred as they are inherently less costly to estimate.

We now consider the *nature* of the power model, with which this paper is primarily concerned. Previous studies have talked about 'good' power models, in an arbitrary sense, and most have missed the very material distinction between different *levels* of model. As hinted towards in [2,11], the widely-accepted 'levels of measurement'—ratio, interval, ordinal, nominal—laid out by Stevens [28] present a natural framework for delineation. It is important to understand the appropriate (type-specific) notion of accuracy for a given model, and to select a compatible distinguisher; that is, one which (implicitly) interprets the model according to the correct type.

The type of power model exploited by profiled attacks (e.g. Bayesian templates [8] and stochastic profiling [24]) amounts to a *direct approximation* of the actual power consumed by processing the data, in contribution to the overall consumption. This requirement is the most demanding possible, expressed as $M \approx L$ (c.f. the 'ratio scale' of [28]). The outcome of an attack will depend on how accurately the templates approximate the actual data-dependent consumption (as well as the noise distribution). The error sum-of-squares is a natural way of quantifying the appropriate notion of accuracy.

Less demanding is the requirement that the attacker has a power model which is a good approximation for L *up to proportionality*: $M \approx \alpha L$ (c.f. the 'interval scale' of [28]). Pearson's correlation coefficient provides a natural way to quantify accuracy and can be directly adapted for use as a distinguisher [4] (a popular strategy since, as a simple, moment-based statistic, it can usually be estimated very efficiently with respect to the number of trace measurements required).

Less demanding again is the requirement that M approximates L up to ordinality: $\{z|M(z) < M(z')\} \approx \{z|L(z) < L(z')\}$ $\forall z' \in \mathcal{Z}$ (c.f. the 'ordinal scale' of [28]). Such a model could be exploited via a variant of correlation DPA using Spearman's rank correlation coefficient, as proposed in [2]. And, again, the accuracy of the model can be quantified via the rank correlation itself.

The least demanding requirement to place on a model is that it approximates the leakage function *up to nominality* only: $\{z|M(z) = M(z')\} \approx \{z|L(z) = L(z')\}$ $\forall z' \in \mathcal{Z}$ (c.f. the 'nominal scale' of [28]). As ever, such a model must be paired with a statistic which interprets the values appropriately: that is to say, as arbitrary labels only. In fact, these correspond to the 'partition-based' distinguishers of [26]. Typical examples include statistics which are used to compare arbitrary distributions, such as MI [12] and the KS test statistic [30,35]. Kocher et al.'s original Difference-of-Means (DoM) test [16] also falls into this category, but is limited in how much information it is able to exploit as it is only able to operate with a two-way partition model. To produce this partition, either the value of a single bit is used (in which case the other bits act as algorithmic noise, increasing the data complexity of the attack), or combinations of multiple bits are used, which results in discarded traces (instances not fitting into either category).

Appropriate notions of accuracy for a nominal model are drawn from classification theory. *Precision* is the probability that items grouped according to the model really do belong together, whilst *recall* is the probability that items which belong together are identified as such (see, e.g. [17]).[2]

$$Precision(M) = \mathbb{P}(L(z) = L(z')|M(z) = M(z')),$$
$$Recall(M) = \mathbb{P}(M(z) = M(z')|L(z) = L(z')).$$

3.2 Defining 'Genericity'

We are now in a position to discuss the generic power model: what, in practice, does it mean to make *no* assumptions about the data-dependent leakage? Essentially, that we do no more than to assign a distinct label to each value in the range of the target function. These labels can be seen to correspond to the key-dependent equivalence classes produced by the preimages of F_k: $[x]_k = F_k^{-1}[F_k(x)]$ $\forall x \in \mathcal{X}$.

Definition 2. *The* generic power model *associated with key hypothesis $k \in \mathcal{K}$ is the nominal mapping to the equivalence classes induced by the key-hypothesised target function F_k.*

---

[2] The classification theory literature more frequently states these definitions in terms of ratios of counts—practically convenient but less directly translatable across contexts. See [13] for a more explicit probabilistic interpretation; though in our case we are, of course, averaging over multiple classes.

The 'identity' power model emphasised in previous literature is fine for this purpose as long as it is understood that the mapping is simply a convenient labelling system and should be interpreted *nominally* only. It is clear, then, that the *generic-compatible distinguishers* are precisely those (described in Sect. 3.1 above) which interpret hypothesis-dependent predictions as an approximation up to nominality of the data-dependent leakage.

Definition 3. *A distinguisher is* generic-compatible *if it is built from a statistic which operates on nominal scale measurements.*

This provides valuable clarification on previous work such as [3], which demonstrated successful attacks against Hamming weight leakage using correlation DPA with an 'identity' power model. The authors rightly remarked that this was possible precisely because, over $\mathbb{F}_2^4$, the identity is sufficiently accurate as a *proportional* approximation of the Hamming weight to produce a successful correlation attack. Far from operating generically, the identity mapping in such a strategy is interpreted as an interval scale model—not a perfect approximation but adequate in the specific case that L can be well-approximated by the Hamming weight. And even in this restricted case it is not, of course, invariant to permutation of the 'identity' labels.

Definitions 2 and 3 combine towards a natural notion of a 'generic strategy':

Definition 4. *A* generic strategy *performs a standard univariate DPA attack using the generic power model paired with a generic-compatible distinguisher.*

However, as previous work on 'partition-based' distinguishers (separately, e.g. [12,31,35], and collectively [26]) has consistently noted, not all (indeed, not many) scenarios are suited to a generic strategy.

3.3   Conditions for a Generic Strategy to Succeed

All distinguishers operate by identifying the key hypotheses producing the most accurate model predictions for the actual measurements, according to the appropriate notion of accuracy for the model type (some are able to perform this comparison more effectively or from fewer trace measurements). In the generic setting each key hypothesis $k \in \mathcal{K}$ gives rise to a model M_k s.t. $M_k^{-1}[z] = F_k^{-1}[z]$ $\forall z \in F_k(\mathcal{X})$, and it is the comparative *nominal* accuracy which will determine key-recovery success. We can therefore explore the conditions necessary for a successful attack—independently of any particular distinguisher—by reasoning directly about the accuracy of F_{k^*} and F_k, $\forall k \in \mathcal{K} \setminus \{k^*\}$ as nominal approximations for $L \circ F_{k^*}$. Recall the precision and recall measures introduced in Sect. 3.1 (with $\mathbb{E}$ to denote expectation):

$$Precision(M_k) = \mathbb{P}(L \circ F_{k^*}(x) = L \circ F_{k^*}(x') | F_k(x) = F_k(x'))$$

$$= \mathbb{E}_{x \in \mathcal{X}} \left[\frac{\#F_{k^*}^{-1}[L^{-1}[L \circ F_{k^*}(x)]] \cap F_k^{-1}[F_k(x)]}{\#F_k^{-1}[F_k(x)]} \right]$$

$$Recall(M_k) = \mathbb{P}(F_k(x) = F_k(x')|L \circ F_{k^*}(x) = L \circ F_{k^*}(x'))$$

$$= \mathbb{E}_{x \in \mathcal{X}} \left[\frac{\#F_{k^*}^{-1}[L^{-1}[L \circ F_{k^*}(x)]] \cap F_k^{-1}[F_k(x)]}{\#F_{k^*}^{-1}[L^{-1}[L \circ F_{k^*}(x)]]} \right]$$

Trivially, the precision of the generic model under the correct hypothesis is always maximal (the leakage preimage must contain the function preimage). By contrast, the recall depends additionally on the true leakage function, so that even under the correct hypothesis we do not get perfect recall unless it happens that L is also injective. The ability of a strategy to reject an *incorrect* alternative requires the corresponding model to be of inferior quality; whether this is so depends on features of F_k and L. An immediate and quite restrictive pre-requisite arises from the inherent nature of the generic power model:

Proposition 1. *No generic strategy is able to distinguish the correct key k^* from an alternative hypothesis k if F_{k^*} and F_k are injective.*

Proof. If F_{k^*}, F_k are injective then $\forall x \in \mathcal{X}$, $F_k^{-1}[F_k(x)] = F_{k^*}^{-1}[F_{k^*}(x)] = \{x\}$. Each hypothesis produces models of equivalent nominal accuracy—no generic-compatible distinguisher can separate the candidates.

Indeed, all of the known generic-compatible distinguishers, from the seminal CHES '08 paper on MIA [12] to the recent copula-based method presented at Crypto '11 [31], have individually been shown to fail whenever the *composition* of the target function and the power model is injective; the same observation was made for the entire class of 'partition-based' distinguishers described in [26]. The authors duly noted that some restriction was required on the power model in order for these distinguishers to operate against an injective target, but left as an open question the existence (or demonstrable non-existence) of an as-yet undiscovered method which would somehow circumvent this requirement. Demonstrating that the limitation is attributable directly to the generic power model rules out this possibility.

Noninjectivity is therefore a necessary condition, but not, as we next establish, a sufficient one. In the general case it is rather difficult to formulate useful, concrete observations so we will henceforth narrow down to the restricted but highly relevant case that F is a *balanced* $(n\text{-}m)$ function and k is introduced by key addition (as described in Sect. 2.3). It then becomes fairly straightforward to draw out such function characteristics as will obstruct a generic strategy.

Proposition 2. *Suppose F is a balanced, non-injective $(n\text{-}m)$ function, with k introduced by (XOR) key addition, i.e. $F_k(x) = F(x \oplus k)$. Then:*

(a) *If F is affine then no generic strategy is able to distinguish the correct key k^* from any $k \in \mathcal{K} \setminus \{k^*\}$.*

(b) *If $a \in \mathbb{F}_2^n$ is a linear structure of F then no generic strategy is able to distinguish between k^* and $k^* \oplus a$.*

(c) *If, for some $a \in \mathbb{F}_2^n$ we have that $D_a F(x)$ depends on x only via $F(x)$, then no generic strategy is able to distinguish between k^* and $k^* \oplus a$.*

The proof of Proposition 2 can be found in Appendix A. Part (a) arises from the fact that all key hypotheses produce indistinguishably 'good' models for the leakage; the distinguishing vector produced by such an attack would be flat and maximal across all hypotheses.

The implication of 2(b) is that $k^* \oplus a$ cannot be rejected if the derivative of F with respect to a is *constant* over the *domain* of F, i.e $\#D_a F(\mathbb{F}_2^n) = 1$. In such a case we would expect a practical attack to exhibit a *ghost peak* at $k^* \oplus a$ [4]; [21], notes a corresponding phenomenon for correlation DPA.

Part (c) can be otherwise expressed as the fact that $k^* \oplus a$ cannot be rejected if the derivative of F with respect to a is *constant* over *each singleton preimage* of F, i.e. $\#D_a F(F^{-1}[F(x)]) = 1 \ \forall x \in \mathbb{F}_2^n$. We have actually observed this property in the fourth DES S-box, for the key-offset $a = 47_{(10)} = 101111_{(2)}$: consequently, $k^* \oplus 47$ produces a 'ghost peak' in the distinguishing vector, with a nonetheless substantial margin between these *two* and the remaining hypotheses—a good example of an attack scenario with a low first-order, but high second-order, success rate [27]. Our observation is consistent with (and illuminates) past works such as [5] which recognised the unusual operation of DPA distinguishers confronted with this particular S-box/offset combination.

Thus emerges a minimal requirement for k^* to be distinguished from k:

Proposition 3. *Suppose F is a balanced, noninjective (n-m) function, with k introduced by (XOR) key-addition. A necessary condition for a generic strategy to distinguish k^* from k is: $\exists x \in \mathbb{F}_2^n$ such that $\#D_{k^* \oplus k} F(F^{-1}[F(x)]) \neq 1$. If L is injective then this becomes a sufficient condition.*

This is informally expressed as the requirement that there is at least one (singleton) preimage over which the derivative with respect to $k^* \oplus k$ is *not* constant. The proof follows from our reasoning in support of Proposition 2 and can be found in Appendix A along with a toy example to demonstrate that we can no longer claim sufficiency if L is noninjective.

Recall from Sect. 2.3 the idea that the derivatives of an S-box should ideally be close to uniform—thus maximising entropy; affine functions or functions with non-null linear spaces represent the extreme in terms of cryptanalytic vulnerability. The pursuit of such a design goal would not guarantee the minimal condition above, as even a perfectly balanced derivative could be so arranged as to be constant over the singleton preimages (which are of cardinality 2^{n-m} since F is also balanced). However, it would certainly seem to increase the chance that the condition be met for a given key-offset, as the more finely $D_a F$ partitions $\mathbb{F}_2^n$, the fewer the possible *refinements* into 2^m (balanced) parts. Therefore, among the (already restricted) class of noninjective S-boxes we would expect ghost peaks and indistinguishable keys to be a rarity—even more so as the size of the S-box increases.

4   Introducing Generic-Emulating DPA

Most existing generic-compatible distinguishers return only some sort of 'classification accuracy', leading them to fail against injective targets. But, on examination of the literature, LR-based attacks emerge as an interesting candidate for generic DPA: they can be used with a full basis of polynomial terms (equivalent, we shall show, to a generic power model), but possess additional features that may possibly be exploited. In particular, further to the distinguishing vector of goodness-of-fit values, LR-based DPA also returns the estimated model coefficients, which differ by key hypothesis. In this section we explore how the coefficients may be interpreted in the light of some simple, non-device-specific intuition to reveal the correct key, and show that the process can be automated straightforwardly using LR in a stepwise mode.

We begin by introducing (standard) LR-based DPA, explaining the mechanism by which it distinguishes the correct key, and demonstrating that it is among the class of generic-compatible distinguishers. We then present the 'generic-emulating' stepwise linear regression- (SLR-) inspired variant which exploits the non-device-specific intuition to successfully attack injective targets even with 'no' (other) prior knowledge. We finally demonstrate the effectiveness of these distinguishers against well-known (injective and noninjective) S-boxes, as the level of prior knowledge available varies from 'complete' to 'none'.

4.1 Introduction to Linear Regression-Based DPA

The motivation for an LR-based approach begins with the observation that $L : \mathbb{F}_2^m \to \mathbb{R}$ can be viewed as a pseudo-Boolean vectorial function with a unique expression in numerical normal form [6]. That is to say, there exists coefficients $\alpha_u \in \mathbb{R}$ such that $L(z) = \sum_{u \in \mathbb{F}_2^m} \alpha_u z^u$, $\forall z \in \mathbb{F}_2^m$ (z^u denotes the monomial $\prod_{i=1}^m z_i^{u_i}$ where z_i is the ith bit of z). Finding those coefficients amounts to finding a power model for L in polynomial function of the coordinate functions of F. As first observed in [24], and demonstrated in [9], linear regression can be adapted to non-profiled key-recovery: the true leakage function is estimated 'on-the-fly' and recovered synchronously with the true key.

Appendix B provides background on linear regression; in short, the LR-based attack uses ordinary least squares to estimate, for each $k \in \mathcal{K}$, the parameters of the model $L_{k^*}(X) + \varepsilon = \alpha_0 + \sum_{u \in \mathcal{U}} F_k(X)^u \alpha_u$ where $\mathcal{U} \subseteq \mathbb{F}_2^m \setminus \{0\}$. The distinguishing vector comprises the R^2 measure of fit from each of these models: $D_{\text{LR}}(k) = \rho(L_{k^*}(X) + \varepsilon, \hat{\alpha}_{k,0} + \sum_{u \in \mathcal{U}} F_k(X)^u \hat{\alpha}_{k,u})^2$ (where ρ denotes Pearson's correlation coefficient). It can be viewed as a generalisation of correlation DPA, where the power model M is known a priori: $D_\rho(k) = \rho(L_{k^*}(X) + \varepsilon, M \circ F_k(X))$. In each case, the value of k which produces the largest distinguisher value is selected as the key guess.

4.2 Linear Regression Is Generic-Compatible

In the way the distinguisher is naturally presented, the attacker's prior knowledge is contained within $\mathcal{U}$; it is not immediately obvious exactly what is the power model, or where it fits alongside the various types presented in Sect. 3.1. In fact, each $u \in \mathcal{U}$ could be seen to represent a *separate* power model which divides the traces into two nominal classes: $\{x \in \mathbb{F}_2^n | F_k(x)^u = 1\}$ and $\{x \in \mathbb{F}_2^n | F_k(x)^u = 0\}$.[3] Intuitively, as long as the power consumption really *does* differ systematically according to the bit-interaction term represented by u, then this 'approximation' has low precision but high recall under the correct key hypothesis, and loses accuracy under an incorrect hypothesis as long as the function F is such that changes to the input produce nonuniform changes to the output. In fact, this is the mechanism by which the original difference-of-means DPA [16] operates!

So the linear regression distinguisher could be viewed as an extension of difference-of-means DPA—a means of exploiting *multiple* (overlapping) nominal approximations, each of low precision (and therefore weak as standalone models) but in conjunction providing a refined description of the leakage.

Intuitively, the generic instantiation should correspond to $\mathcal{U} = \mathbb{F}_2^m \setminus \{0\}$ (i.e., imposing no restrictions on the leakage form). But our previous reasoning about the operation of generic strategies supposed a *single* power model (F_k, interpreted nominally) and it is hard to see how we might begin to reason about the impact of multiple power models. Fortunately, in the $\mathcal{U} = \mathbb{F}_2^m \setminus \{0\}$ case *only*, the operation of the distinguisher *can* be re-framed in terms of the generic power model as defined above, so that all of our prior reasoning applies.

Proposition 4. *The linear regression-based DPA attack with a full set of covariates $\mathcal{U} = \mathbb{F}_2^m \setminus \{0\}$ constitutes a generic strategy.*

We sketch a proof as follows: If M_k is an arbitrary labelling on F_k, we can always map bijectively to $\mathbb{F}_2^m$ to acquire an arbitrary *permutation* of the function outputs $M'_k(x) = p \circ F_k(x)$. For each $u \in \mathbb{F}_2^m$, the associated monomial $M'_k(x)^u$ has a unique expression in numerical normal form $M'_k(x)^u = \sum_{v \in \mathbb{F}_2^m} b_v F_k(x)^v$, $b_v \in \mathbb{R}$ [6]. So the system of equations relating to an incorrect hypothesis k can be rewritten in function of $F_k(x)$ by substituting in these expressions, expanding out and collecting up the terms. We end up with different values of α_u, $u \in \mathbb{F}_2^m$ whenever we reparametrise in this way, but, crucially, the terms in the equation *collectively* explain the measured traces equally well—and it is in this sense that linear regression DPA is *invariant to re-labelling* and therefore can be discussed alongside other generic-compatible strategies (though it is not usually used in this way—particularly as meaningful restrictions on $\mathcal{U}$ contribute to efficiency gains in the estimation stage).

As we would expect from Sect. 3, LR-based DPA fails against injective targets when used generically (i.e. with $\mathcal{U} = \mathbb{F}_2^m \setminus \{0\}$). This failure can be better understood when we consider that the data-dependent part of the power consumption can be expressed as a system of 2^n equations (in function of $F_k(x)$) with 2^n unknowns. Because this system is fully-determined and consistent under any key

---

[3] Note that the labeling is irrelevant since they are represented in the regression equation by dummy variables: the 1/0 assignment is arbitrary and will impact only the estimated coefficients, not the R^2.

hypothesis it *always* has a perfect solution, so as to produce a flat distinguishing vector of maximal R^2s.[4]

4.3   Exploiting Non-Device-Specific Intuition

The unique opportunity presented by generic LR arises from the fact that it produces, not just the distinguishing vector of R^2 values (which are unable to discriminate between hypotheses when the target is injective), but also the hypothesis-dependent sets of estimated coefficients. When $k = k^*$ these give the correct expression for L in function of the output bits; the rest of the time, they give an expression for $L \circ F_k \circ F_{k^*}^{-1}$. If, then, the attacker was able to recognise the correct expression, he would be able to identify the secret key.

Thus motivated, we examine the correct and incorrect expressions for L in the case that the target function is an injective S-box (of size 8 bits in the case of AES, or 4 bits in the case of PRESENT) and that the true form of the leakage is the Hamming weight: $L(z) = \sum_{i=0}^{m} z^{2^i}$. Fig. 2 shows the coefficients, in the polynomial expression for L, on the covariates as produced by the true key k^* (in black) and on those as produced under an incorrect hypothesis k' (in grey). The high nonlinearity of the S-box functions ensure that, when viewed as a polynomial in $F_k(X)$ rather than $F_{k^*}(X)$, the leakage function L is also highly nonlinear in form.

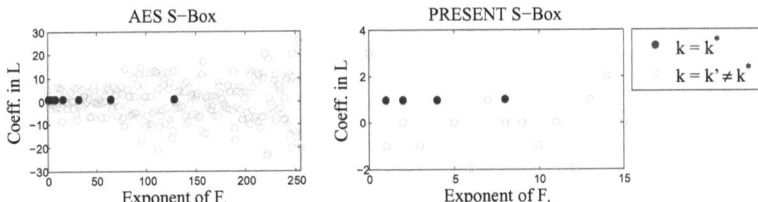

Fig. 2. Coefficients, in the fitted expression for L, on the covariates as predicted under the correct and an alternative hypothesis

In the face of such evidence an attacker would be justified in favouring hypothesis k^* over k: intuitively, it seems more likely (especially given the known high nonlinearity of F) that the 'simpler' expression (i.e. the one corresponding to the black circles in Fig. 2) is the correct one. To exploit the extra information represented by the coefficients, we therefore need to trust this intuition (which implicitly also assumes that $M_k = F_k$). This takes us a step away from the generic strategy—but since the intuition is not specific to any particular device it appears to be a very small step. That is, we just need to assume that the leakage function is 'sufficiently simple' compared to the target function. This is

---

[4] In the case of noninjective targets, the system is *overdetermined* (2^n equations, 2^m unknowns). Provided the target satisfies the criteria in Sect. 3.3 then this system is *only* consistent under the correct key hypothesis (thus only then does it have a perfect solution—there are only 2^m *linearly independent* equations).

justified for a wide range of devices manufactured in CMOS technologies, including advanced 65-nanometer processes [23]. In fact, even for protected logic styles such as introduced by Tiri and Verbauwhede [29], it turns out that ensuring a complex (e.g. highly nonlinear) leakage function is a challenging task [22]. Besides, the results in Sect. 4.5 will also demonstrate that this 'simplicity constraint' on the leakage function can be quite relaxed.

Of course, comparing graphs is not ideal from a practical perspective, besides which the true leakage function may not always have so simple a form as to be visibly discernible: we would like to encapsulate the underlying reasoning into an automated and systematic procedure for testing hypotheses. In the next section we introduce a learning technique from data mining which uses our non-device-specific intuition about 'what the leakage should look like' to produce, in a wide range of leakage scenarios, asymptotically successful key recovery against injective targets *even when provided with the full set of covariates* $\mathcal{U} = \mathbb{F}_2^m \setminus \{\mathbf{0}\}$. Such a strategy, whilst not *generic*, may reasonably be described as *generic-emulating*.

4.4   A Stepwise Regression-Based Distinguisher

Stepwise regression [15] is a model-building tool whereby potential explanatory variables are iteratively added and removed depending on whether they contribute sufficient explanatory power to meet certain threshold criteria (see Appendix C for full details). The resulting regression model should therefore exclude 'unimportant' terms whilst retaining all of the 'significant' terms. In the context of LR-based DPA this equates to testing each of the multiple binary models represented by $u \in \mathcal{U}$ separately (conditioned on the current model) and then privileging those which appear most meaningful.

Under a correct key hypothesis, and *beginning with a full basis* $\mathcal{U} = \mathbb{F}_2^n \setminus \{\mathbf{0}\}$ we would expect to obtain a 'good' regression model which explains most of the variance in L, although with some minor terms absent if they do not meet our threshold criteria for statistical significance. The example depicted in Fig. 2 above justifies the hope that the model produced under an incorrect hypothesis might be 'less good': with the explanatory power being so much more dispersed, the contribution of any individual term decreases. These small contributions are prejudiced against in the model building process (depending on the threshold criteria) but their *actual* contributions are real and so, therefore, is the loss in excluding them. If the aggregate loss is sufficient then the resulting R^2 will be enough reduced relative to the true key R^2 to distinguish between the two.

We therefore explore next whether stepwise linear regression (SLR) can indeed be used as a 'generic-emulating' distinguisher, i.e. as generic compatible distinguisher that only uses the additional non-device-specific intuition as introduced in this paper.

4.5   Theoretic Distinguishing Margins for SLR-Based DPA

Fig. 3 shows the distinguishing margins achieved (asymptotically) against AES, PRESENT and DES S-boxes by our proposed generic-emulating SLR-based distinguisher (labelled 'GenEm SLR'). The strategy is effective against all three targets and remains so even as the degree of the leakage polynomial increases.

For comparison, we also show the margins for several related strategies. The optimal strategy is a correlation DPA with a known power model; as expected, this has the largest margins in all scenarios (the margins we report are for the *squared* correlation coefficients, so as to be directly comparable to the R^2-based margins reported for the LR variants). Generic LR-based DPA only succeeds against the (noninjective) DES S-box, where it can be seen to underperform relative to generic-emulating SLR. LR with an appropriately restricted basis (i.e. comprising terms up to and including the true order of the leakage function, labelled 'MaxDeg LR') succeeds (and outperforms generic-emulating SLR) against low-degree leakage but decreases in effectiveness as the degree increases, eventually coinciding with generic LR. Restricting the initial basis for SLR (again, up to the degree of the true leakage, labelled 'MaxDeg SLR') likewise produces increased distinguishing margins in low-degree settings, but of course can no longer be considered generic-emulating.[5]

The DoM distinguisher is considered sub-optimal as it only exploits the leakage of a single bit, but is generally seen as the 'best' an attacker can do without prior knowledge on the power model—a sort of 'last resort'. Therefore, it is an important baseline comparison for our proposed strategy. Since the DoM distinguisher is SCA-equivalent to correlation DPA with a single-bit power model (see [9])[6], what we actually report (labelled 'Best DoM') are the margins produced by the squared correlation coefficients for the best out of every possible single-bit partition (again, so as to place it on a like-for-like scale with our other distinguishers).

As can be seen from Fig. 3, the bit-by-bit DoM strategy does (on average) distinguish the key once an appropriate bit has been identified. However, it achieves this by smaller margins than the generic emulating SLR-based distinguisher, at least in the case of the AES and DES S-boxes. This is in line with our expectation that it is more informative to exploit the entire intermediate value than it is to exploit a single bit only. In the case of PRESENT, DoM and SLR appear close, with a slight advantage to DoM. We conjecture that this is due to the smallness of the S-box, which limits the attainable degree of cryptographic nonlinearity—the particular feature which SLR exploits.

It is perhaps surprising to note that the example attacks above succeed even when the leakage degree is maximal. The success of generic-emulating SLR rests on the comparative 'complexity' (in some sense) of $L \circ F_k \circ F_{k*}^{-1}$ relative to L. Evidently, high *polynomial degree* is not a relevant criteria on L for predicting attack failure. We have constructed example failure cases (e.g. random

---

[5] The asymptotic outcomes appear to be reliably consistent over the 500 repeated experiments—see Appendix D for more information.

[6] That is, the distinguishing vectors are exactly proportional so that the relative margins are identical. The result also matches that resulting from LR-based DPA with a single bit term in the regression equation, as should be obvious from Sect. 4.2.

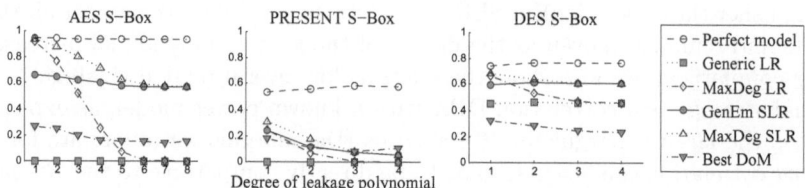

Fig. 3. Median distinguishing margins of attacks against AES, PRESENT and DES S-boxes as the leakage degree increases (500 experiments with uniformly random coefficients between -10 and 10)

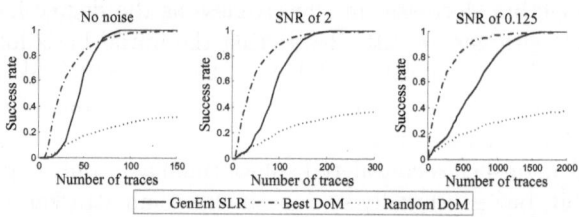

Fig. 4. Success rates as the number of traces increases, for DoM and SLR attacks against the AES S-box with high degree leakage (500 experiments with uniformly random coefficients between -10 and 10)

permutations over $\{0, \ldots, 2^m - 1\}$, indicating that SLR fails if L has a high *cryptographic* nonlinearity when interpreted as a function over $\mathbb{F}_2^m$), but we leave as an open question the precise properties of L which will cause failures in general.

4.6 Practical Success Rate Evaluation

The above analysis shows the AES S-box to be the most interesting scenario (of the three) for generic-emulating SLR : its large size ensures sufficiently high cryptographic nonlinearity (by contrast with PRESENT), and its injectivity means that it is not vulnerable to generic attacks (by contrast with DES). Therefore, in order to establish its effectiveness in practice, we performed experimental attacks against AES with (arbitrarily generated) degree-8 polynomial leakages—the most challenging of the leakage forms considered above. Fig. 4 shows the success rate as the number of traces increases, as compared with the success rates of DoM in the best case (the strongest of all 8 possible one-bit attacks) and the average case (the outcome of a single, randomly-chosen one-bit attack). In practice, an attacker does *not* know the best bit to attack, and so is in this latter scenario, where success is by no means guaranteed and the SLR strategy is far more likely to recover the key from a given number of traces. However, by trying each bit in turn (or all in parallel) an attacker can greatly improve their chances, and indeed the *best* DoM is consistently more data efficient than generic-emulating SLR despite the fact that the latter exploits the leaked information far more comprehensively. This is because of the increased estimation costs incurred by stepwise regression, which requires fitting a model with up to 2^8 unknown coefficients, whilst DoM amounts to the estimation of two means.[7]

5   Conclusion

Implementers and evaluators routinely perform DPA attacks against devices to identify vulnerabilities. Yet the current state of the art, e.g. [19] Appendix F, is often based on incomplete understanding of the myriad attack methods and how they relate. Practitioners are rightly concerned about the increasingly unmanageable amount of work required for a thorough evaluation, e.g. [32]—but testing only a subset of methods risks overestimating security if the best possible strategy is omitted.

The non-existence of universally-applicable generic attacks—as shown in the first part of this paper—implies that profiled attacks are necessary in security evaluations. It also leads to questions about the existence of 'almost generic' methods that would connect worst-case security evaluations with (more realistic) non-profiled adversaries, as addressed in the second part of the paper. In the absence of a viable power model a usual strategy is to 'revert' back to single-bit models, e.g. using Kocher et al.'s DoM-based methods. However, using our non-device-specific intuition, we were able to define a novel tweak on the LR-based method that works in a generic-emulating manner and, for large enough (i.e. nonlinear enough) S-boxes, produces outcomes comparable to those attainable by single-bit strategies (based on the 'most leaky' bit). The practical advantage of generic-emulating SLR is unclear because of the substantial estimation costs involved; however, it greatly improves over the success rates of a randomly-selected DoM and is not too far behind the 'best' DoM, which looks to remain the most practically-effective known non-profiled distinguisher for use against unknown leakage distributions, by virtue of the minimal data complexity associated with estimating sample means.

Acknowledgements. This work has been funded in part by the ERC project 280141 (acronym CRASH), and in part by the EPSRC via grant EP/I005226/1. François-Xavier Standaert is an associate researcher of the Belgian Fund for Scientific Research (FNRS-F.R.S.).

References

1. The DPA Contest, http://www.dpacontest.org/
2. Batina, L., Gierlichs, B., Lemke-Rust, K.: Comparative Evaluation of Rank Correlation Based DPA on an AES Prototype Chip. In: Wu, T.-C., Lei, C.-L., Rijmen, V., Lee, D.-T. (eds.) ISC 2008. LNCS, vol. 5222, pp. 341–354. Springer, Heidelberg (2008)

---

[7] It is well-recognised that the data complexity of different statistical estimators varies widely; the subsequent gap between the theoretic and practical capabilities of DPA distinguishers is discussed in more detail in [33].

3. Batina, L., Gierlichs, B., Prouff, E., Rivain, M., Standaert, F.-X., Veyrat-Charvillon, N.: Mutual Information Analysis: A Comprehensive Study. Journal of Cryptology 24, 269–291 (2011)
4. Brier, E., Clavier, C., Olivier, F.: Correlation Power Analysis with a Leakage Model. In: Joye, M., Quisquater, J.-J. (eds.) CHES 2004. LNCS, vol. 3156, pp. 16–29. Springer, Heidelberg (2004)
5. Canovas, C., Clediere, J.: What Do S-boxes Say in Differential Side Channel Attacks? Cryptology ePrint Archive, Report 2005/311 (2005)
6. Carlet, C.: Boolean Functions for Cryptography and Error Correcting Codes. In: Boolean Models and Methods in Mathematics, Computer Science, and Engineering, 1st edn., pp. 257–397. Cambridge University Press, New York (2010)
7. Carlet, C.: Vectorial Boolean Functions for Cryptography. In: Boolean Models and Methods in Mathematics, Computer Science, and Engineering, 1st edn., pp. 398–469. Cambridge University Press, New York (2010)
8. Chari, S., Rao, J., Rohatgi, P.: Template attacks. In: Kaliski Jr., B.S., Koç, Ç.K., Paar, C. (eds.) CHES 2002. LNCS, vol. 2523, pp. 13–28. Springer, Heidelberg (2003)
9. Doget, J., Prouff, E., Rivain, M., Standaert, F.-X.: Univariate Side Channel Attacks and Leakage Modeling. J. Cryptographic Engineering 1(2), 123–144 (2011)
10. Evertse, J.-H.: Linear Structures in Block Ciphers. In: Price, W.L., Chaum, D. (eds.) EUROCRYPT 1987. LNCS, vol. 304, pp. 249–266. Springer, Heidelberg (1988)
11. Gierlichs, B.: Statistical and Information-Theoretic Methods for Power Analysis on Embedded Cryptography. PhD thesis, Katholieke Universiteit Leuven, Faculty of Engineering (2011)
12. Gierlichs, B., Batina, L., Tuyls, P., Preneel, B.: Mutual Information Analysis: A Generic Side-Channel Distinguisher. In: Oswald, E., Rohatgi, P. (eds.) CHES 2008. LNCS, vol. 5154, pp. 426–442. Springer, Heidelberg (2008)
13. Goutte, C., Gaussier, É.: A Probabilistic Interpretation of Precision, Recall and F-Score, with Implication for Evaluation. In: Losada, D.E., Fernández-Luna, J.M. (eds.) ECIR 2005. LNCS, vol. 3408, pp. 345–359. Springer, Heidelberg (2005)
14. Heys, H.M.: A tutorial on linear and differential cryptanalysis. Cryptologia 26, 189–221 (2002)
15. Hocking, R.R.: The Analysis and Selection of Variables in Linear Regression. Biometrics 32(1), 1–49 (1976)
16. Kocher, P.C., Jaffe, J., Jun, B.: Differential Power Analysis. In: Wiener, M. (ed.) CRYPTO 1999. LNCS, vol. 1666, pp. 388–397. Springer, Heidelberg (1999)
17. Kowalski, G.: Information retrieval architecture and algorithms. Springer, New York (2011)
18. Mangard, S., Oswald, E., Standaert, F.-X.: One for All – All for One: Unifying Standard DPA Attacks. IET Information Security 5(2), 100–110 (2011)
19. NIST. Security Requirements for Cryptographic Modules (Revised Draft). Technical Report FIPS PUB 140-3, US Department of Commerce (December 2009)
20. Nyberg, K.: Differentially Uniform Mappings for Cryptography. In: Helleseth, T. (ed.) EUROCRYPT 1993. LNCS, vol. 765, pp. 55–64. Springer, Heidelberg (1994)
21. Prouff, E.: DPA Attacks and S-Boxes. In: Gilbert, H., Handschuh, H. (eds.) FSE 2005. LNCS, vol. 3557, pp. 424–441. Springer, Heidelberg (2005)

22. Renauld, M., Kamel, D., Standaert, F.-X., Flandre, D.: Information Theoretic and Security Analysis of a 65-Nanometer DDSLL AES S-Box. In: Preneel, B., Takagi, T. (eds.) CHES 2011. LNCS, vol. 6917, pp. 223–239. Springer, Heidelberg (2011)
23. Renauld, M., Standaert, F.-X., Veyrat-Charvillon, N., Kamel, D., Flandre, D.: A formal study of power variability issues and side-channel attacks for nanoscale devices. In: Paterson, K.G. (ed.) EUROCRYPT 2011. LNCS, vol. 6632, pp. 109–128. Springer, Heidelberg (2011)
24. Schindler, W., Lemke, K., Paar, C.: A Stochastic Model for Differential Side Channel Cryptanalysis. In: Rao, J.R., Sunar, B. (eds.) CHES 2005. LNCS, vol. 3659, pp. 30–46. Springer, Heidelberg (2005)
25. Schramm, K., Wollinger, T.J., Paar, C.: A new class of collision attacks and its application to des. In: Johansson, T. (ed.) FSE 2003. LNCS, vol. 2887, pp. 206–222. Springer, Heidelberg (2003)
26. Standaert, F.-X., Gierlichs, B., Verbauwhede, I.: Partition *vs*. Comparison Side-Channel Distinguishers: An Empirical Evaluation of Statistical Tests for Univariate Side-Channel Attacks against Two Unprotected CMOS Devices. In: Lee, P.J., Cheon, J.H. (eds.) ICISC 2008. LNCS, vol. 5461, pp. 253–267. Springer, Heidelberg (2009)
27. Standaert, F.-X., Malkin, T.G., Yung, M.: A Unified Framework for the Analysis of Side-Channel Key Recovery Attacks. In: Joux, A. (ed.) EUROCRYPT 2009. LNCS, vol. 5479, pp. 443–461. Springer, Heidelberg (2009)
28. Stevens, S.S.: On the theory of scales of measurement. Science 103, 677–680 (1946)
29. Tiri, K., Verbauwhede, I.: Securing Encryption Algorithms against DPA at the Logic Level: Next Generation Smart Card Technology. In: Walter, C.D., Koç, Ç.K., Paar, C. (eds.) CHES 2003. LNCS, vol. 2779, pp. 125–136. Springer, Heidelberg (2003)
30. Veyrat-Charvillon, N., Standaert, F.-X.: Mutual Information Analysis: How, When and Why? In: Clavier, C., Gaj, K. (eds.) CHES 2009. LNCS, vol. 5747, pp. 429–443. Springer, Heidelberg (2009)
31. Veyrat-Charvillon, N., Standaert, F.-X.: Generic side-channel distinguishers: Improvements and limitations. In: Rogaway, P. (ed.) CRYPTO 2011. LNCS, vol. 6841, pp. 354–372. Springer, Heidelberg (2011)
32. Wagner, M.: 700+ attacks published on smart cards: The need for a systematic counter strategy. In: Schindler, W., Huss, S.A. (eds.) COSADE 2012. LNCS, vol. 7275, pp. 33–38. Springer, Heidelberg (2012)
33. Whitnall, C., Oswald, E.: A Comprehensive Evaluation of Mutual Information Analysis Using a Fair Evaluation Framework. In: Rogaway, P. (ed.) CRYPTO 2011. LNCS, vol. 6841, pp. 316–334. Springer, Heidelberg (2011)
34. Whitnall, C., Oswald, E.: A Fair Evaluation Framework for Comparing Side-Channel Distinguishers. Journal of Cryptographic Engineering 1(2), 145–160 (2011)
35. Whitnall, C., Oswald, E., Mather, L.: An Exploration of the Kolmogorov-Smirnov Test as Competitor to Mutual Information Analysis. Cryptology ePrint Archive, Report 2011/380 (2011), http://eprint.iacr.org/
36. Youssef, A.M., Tavares, S.E.: Resistance of Balanced S-Boxes to Linear and Differential Cryptanalysis. Inf. Process. Lett. 56, 249–252 (1995)

A   Conditions for a Generic Strategy to Succeed

Here we provide simple proofs for the claims stated in Sect. 3.3. For conciseness we first prove Proposition 2 part (c) and then show that parts (a) and (b) are covered as special cases.

Proof. (Of 2(c)). Ultimately, k^* is indistinguishable from k if $F_k^{-1}[F_k(x)] \subseteq F_{k^*}^{-1}[L^{-1}[L \circ F_{k^*}(x)]]$ $\forall x \in \mathbb{F}_2^n$ as this implies that F_k is just as accurate a model for $L \circ F_{k^*}$ as F_{k^*} (that is $Precision(F_k) = Precision(F_{k^*}) = 1$ and $Recall(F_k) = Recall(F_{k^*})$ as follows directly from the formulae).

It is sufficient to show that $\forall x \in \mathbb{F}_2^n$, $x' \in F_k^{-1}[F_k(x)] \Rightarrow x' \in F_{k^*}^{-1}[F_{k^*}(x)]$, since, trivially, $F_{k^*}^{-1}[F_{k^*}(x)] \subseteq F_{k^*}^{-1}[L^{-1}[L \circ F_{k^*}(x)]]$.

If $D_a F(x)$ depends on x only via $F(x)$ we can write $D_a F(x) = c(F(x))$ for some function $c : \mathbb{F}_2^m \to \mathbb{F}_2^m$.

It thus follows that $F_{k^*}(x) = F(x \oplus k^* \oplus a \oplus a) = D_a F(x \oplus k^* \oplus a) \oplus F(x \oplus k^* \oplus a) = c(F(x \oplus k^* \oplus a)) \oplus F(x \oplus k^* \oplus a) = c(F_{k^* \oplus a}(x)) \oplus F_{k^* \oplus a}(x)$.

So if $x' \in F_{k^* \oplus a}^{-1}[F_{k^* \oplus a}(x)]$ then:

$$F_{k^*}(x') = c(F_{k^* \oplus a}(x')) \oplus F_{k^* \oplus a}(x')$$
$$= c(F_{k^* \oplus a}(x)) \oplus F_{k^* \oplus a}(x)$$
$$= F_{k^*}(x).$$

I.e. $x' \in F_{k^*}^{-1}[F_{k^*}(x)]$ and thus $F_{k^* \oplus a}^{-1}[F_{k^* \oplus a}(x)] \subseteq F_{k^*}^{-1}[F_{k^*}(x)] \subseteq F_{k^*}^{-1}[L^{-1}[L \circ F_{k^*}(x)]]$.

Part (b) follows trivially once we notice that, if $a \in \mathbb{F}_2^n$ is a linear structure of F, we can replace $c(F(x))$ in the above argument with c for some $c \in \mathbb{F}_2^m$ constant over all x.

Part (a) follows from the observation that if F is affine, the linear space of F is the whole of $\mathbb{F}_2^n$ so that k^* is indistinguishable from $k = k' \oplus a$ for *all* $a \in \mathbb{F}_2^n \setminus \{0\}$ (and thus for all $k \in \mathcal{K} \setminus \{k^*\} \subseteq \mathbb{F}_2^n$) by the same argument.

Proof. (Of Proposition 3). That the condition is necessary follows directly from Proposition 2(c). Now suppose that, additionally, L is injective.

Choose $x' \in \mathbb{F}_2^n$ such that $\#D_{k^* \oplus k}F(F^{-1}[F(x' \oplus k)]) \neq 1$—which can be re-written as $\#D_{k^* \oplus k}F(F_k^{-1}[F_k(x')]) \neq 1$.

Thus $\exists x'' \in F_k^{-1}[F_k(x')]$ such that:

$$D_{k^* \oplus k}F(x' \oplus k) \neq D_{k^* \oplus k}F(x'' \oplus k)$$
$$\Rightarrow \quad F(x' \oplus k \oplus k^* \oplus k) \oplus F(x' \oplus k) \neq F(x'' \oplus k \oplus k^* \oplus k) \oplus F(x'' \oplus k)$$
$$\Rightarrow \qquad F(x' \oplus k^*) \oplus F(x' \oplus k) \neq F(x'' \oplus k^*) \oplus F(x'' \oplus k)$$
$$\Rightarrow \qquad\quad F_{k^*}(x') \oplus F_k(x') \neq F_{k^*}(x'') \oplus F_k(x'')$$
$$\Rightarrow \qquad\qquad F_{k^*}(x') \neq F_{k^*}(x'') \qquad (\text{since } x'' \in F_k^{-1}[F_k(x')])$$
$$\Rightarrow \qquad\qquad\qquad x'' \notin F_{k^*}^{-1}[F_{k^*}(x')]$$
$$\Rightarrow \qquad\qquad F_{k^*}^{-1}[F_{k^*}(x')] \neq F_k^{-1}[F_k(x')]$$

Now we look at what this does to the precision and recall of F_k as a nominal model for F_{k^*}, beginning with the summands in the numerator of both expressions:

$$\#F_{k^*}^{-1}[L^{-1}[L \circ F_{k^*}(x)]] \cap F_k^{-1}[F_k(x)] = \#F_{k^*}^{-1}[F_{k^*}(x)] \cap F_k^{-1}[F_k(x)]$$

$$\begin{cases} < 2^{n-m}, & \text{if } x = x' \\ \leq 2^{n-m}, & \text{if } x \neq x'. \end{cases}$$

By the balancedness of F and the injectivity of L the denominator summands in the precision and recall expressions always take the value 2^{n-m}. In this case, then, we get that $Precision(F_{k^*}) = Recall(F_{k^*}) = 1$ whilst $Precision(F_k) = Recall(F_k) < 1$, so that a sufficiently sensitive generic-compatible distinguisher will be able to reject the hypothesis k.

It only remains to show that sufficiency cannot be claimed when L is noninjective, which we do with a simple illustrative example:

Define $F : \mathbb{F}_2^3 \to \mathbb{F}_2^2$ and $L : \mathbb{F}_2^2 \to \{1, 2\}$ such that:

$$F(x) = \begin{cases} 0, & x \in \{0, 3\} \\ 1, & x \in \{1, 2\} \\ 2, & x \in \{4, 5\} \\ 3, & x \in \{6, 7\}, \end{cases} \qquad L(z) = \begin{cases} 1, & z \in \{0, 1\} \\ 2, & z \in \{2, 3\}. \end{cases}$$

$$\text{So } F_0(x) = F(x \oplus 0) = F(x)$$

$$\text{and } F_4(x) = F(x \oplus 4) = \begin{cases} 0, & x \in \{4, 7\} \\ 1, & x \in \{5, 6\} \\ 2, & x \in \{0, 1\} \\ 3, & x \in \{2, 3\}. \end{cases}$$

Then (for example) $F_0^{-1}[F_0(0)] = \{0, 3\} \neq \{0, 1\} = F_4^{-1}[F_4(0)]$, but nonetheless $F_0^{-1}[L^{-1}[L \circ F_0(0)]] = \{0, 1, 2, 3\} = F_4^{-1}[L^{-1}[L \circ F_4(0)]] \supset F_4^{-1}[F_4(0)]$ and in fact it can be checked that $F_4^{-1}[F_4(x)] \subset F_0^{-1}[L^{-1}[L \circ F_0(x)]] \; \forall x \in \mathbb{F}_2^3$ so that $Precision(M_4) = Precision(M_0) = 1$ and $Recall(M_4) = Recall(M_0)$, implying that key candidates 0 and 4 cannot be distinguished from one another.

B   Linear Regression

Linear regression is a statistical method for modelling the relationship between a single dependent variable Y and one or more explanatory variables Z. It operates by finding a least-squares solution $\hat{\beta}$ to the system of linear equations $Y = Z\beta + \varepsilon$, where Y is an N-dimensional vector of measured outcomes, Z is an N-by-p matrix of p measured 'covariates', β is the p-dimensional vector of unknown parameters, and ε is the noise or error term, that is, all remaining variation in Y

which is *not* caused by Z. Once the model has been estimated, the goodness-of-fit can be measured (for example) by the 'coefficient of determination', R^2, which quantifies the proportion of variance explained by the model: $R^2 = 1 - \frac{SS_{error}}{SS_{total}}$, where $SS_{total} = \sum_{i=1}^{N}(Y_i - \frac{1}{N}\sum_{i=1}^{N} Y_i)^2$ is the total sum of squares and $SS_{error} = \sum_{i=1}^{N}(Y_i - Z_i\hat{\beta})^2$ is the error sum of squares.

In the case that Z includes a constant term (the associated parameter estimate is called the intercept), the coefficient of determination is the square of the correlation coefficient between the outcomes and their predicted values: $R^2 = \rho(Z\hat{\beta}, Y)^2$. It is appealing as an attack distinguisher by virtue of this close relationship with correlation, coupled with the fact that it requires far less knowledge about the true form of the leakage to succeed. In correlation DPA the attacker has *prior knowledge* of a power model M and the distinguishing vector takes the form $D_\rho(k) = \rho(L_{k^*}(X) + \varepsilon, M \circ F_k(X))$. In linear regression DPA the challenge is to *simultaneously recover the true power model* along with the correct key as follows:

- Model the measured traces in function of the predicted coordinate function outputs and such higher-order interactions as you believe to be influential.
- Estimate the parameters and compute the resulting R^2 under each possible key hypothesis.
- If the largest R^2 is produced by the predictions relating to the correct key hypothesis then the attack has succeeded.

The LR-based distinguishing vector is thus: $D_{LR}(k) = \rho(L_{k^*}(X) + \varepsilon, \hat{\alpha}_{k,0} + \sum_{u \in \mathcal{U}} F_k(X)^u \hat{\alpha}_{k,u})^2$, where ρ is Pearson's correlation coefficient, defined for two random variables A, B as $\rho(A, B) = \frac{\text{Cov}(A,B)}{\sqrt{\text{Var}(A)\text{Var}(B)}}$.

C   Stepwise Regression

The inputs to the procedure are an $N \times 1$ vector Y containing observations of the dependent variable, p $N \times 1$ vectors $\{Z_i\}_{i=1}^{p}$ for each of the candidate explanatory variables, a set of indices indicating terms to be included regardless of explanatory power $I_{fix} \subset \{1, \ldots, p\}$ and a set of indices indicating *additional* terms to include in the initial model $I_{initial} \subseteq \{1, \ldots, p\}$ (s.t. $I_{fix} \cap I_{initial} = \emptyset$).

1. Set $I_{in} = I_{initial}$. Set $I_{test} = \{1, \ldots, p\} \setminus \{I_{in} \cup I_{fix}\}$.
2. For all $j \in I_{test}$ fit the model $Y = \beta_0 + \sum_{i \in I_{fix} \cup I_{in}} \beta_i Z_i + \beta_j Z_j + \varepsilon$ using least-squares regression and obtain the p-value on Z_j (call it $pval_j$).
3. If $\min_{j \in I_{test}} pval_j \leq pval_{add}$ then set $I_{in} = I_{in} \cup \text{argmin}_{j \in I_{test}} pval_j$, $I_{test} = I_{test} \setminus \text{argmin}_{j \in I_{test}} pval_j$ and repeat from step 2.
4. Else fit the model $Y = \beta_0 + \sum_{i \in I_{fix} \cup I_{in}} \beta_i Z_i + \varepsilon$ using least-squares regression and obtain $\{pval_i\}_{i \in I_{in}}$.
5. If $\max_{i \in I_{in}} pval_i \geq pval_{rem}$ then set $I_{in} = I_{in} \setminus \text{argmax}_{i \in I_{test}} pval_i$, $I_{test} = I_{test} \cup \text{argmax}_{i \in I_{test}} pval_i$ and return to step 2.
6. Else return I_{in}.

Note that the p-values on included terms change when other terms are added or removed—hence the need for an iterative procedure that re-tests the significance of included terms to identify candidates for removal. The threshold p-values for model entry and removal, $pval_{add}$ and $pval_{rem}$, are user-determined and will influence the resulting model. The terms included in the initial model will also influence the result. The MatLab defaults are $pval_{add} = 0.05$, $pval_{rem} = 0.1$ and $I_{initial} = I_{fix} = \emptyset$.

D   Variability of Measured Outcomes

The asymptotic outcomes reported in Sect. 4.5 are based on 500 different leakage functions constructed to have uniformly random coefficients between -10 and 10. Fig. 3 displays the medians but provide a reliable indication of the behaviour over the whole sample as the variance is moderate, at least in the case of AES and DES S-boxes. By way of illustration, Fig. 5 below shows the 1st percentiles of the measured outcomes observed. Successful outcomes against AES and DES are preserved (although diminished); there are more failure cases against the PRESENT S-box, which we conjecture is due to its smaller size, which restricts the degree of cryptographic nonlinearity attainable. It should, of course, be noted that these attacks use *fixed* stepwise inclusion/exclusion thresholds, and that the failure cases may respond to more sensitive tuning.

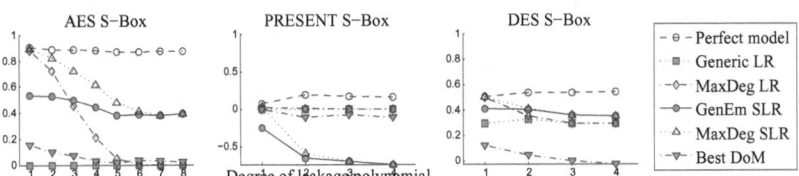

Fig. 5. First percentile of the distinguishing margins of attacks against AES, PRESENT and DES S-boxes as the actual degree of the leakage polynomial increases (500 experiments with uniformly random coefficients between -10 and 10)

Hardware Implementation and Side-Channel Analysis of Lapin

Lubos Gaspar[1,*], Gaëtan Leurent[1,2], and François-Xavier Standaert[1]

[1] ICTEAM/ELEN/Crypto Group, Université catholique de Louvain, Belgium
[2] Inria, EPI SECRET, Rocquencourt, France
{lubos.gaspar,fstandae}@uclouvain.be, gaetan.leurent@inria.fr

Abstract. Lapin is a new authentication protocol that has been designed for low-cost implementations. In a work from RFIDsec 2012, Berstein and Lange argued that at similar (mathematical) security levels, Lapin's performances are below the ones of block cipher based authentication. In this paper, we suggest that as soon as physical security (*e.g.* against side-channel attacks) is taken into account, this criticism can be mitigated. For this purpose, we start by investigating masked hardware implementations of Lapin, and discuss the gains obtained over software ones. Next, we observe that the structure of our implementations significantly differs from block cipher ones (for which most results in side-channel analysis apply), hence raising questions regarding how to evaluate physical security in this case. We then provide first results of side-channel analyzes against unprotected and masked Lapin. Despite interesting properties of the masked implementations, our conclusions are still contrasted because of the on-chip randomness requirements of Lapin protocol. These results give strong incentive to design similar but deterministic protocols, *e.g.* based on the recently introduced Learning With Rounding assumption.

Keywords: LPN, Ring-LPN, masking, side-channel analysis.

1 Introduction

In [9], Heyse at al. proposed the Lapin authentication protocol based on the hardness of the Ring-LPN problem. Authors described two different Lapin variants based on a carefully chosen ring $R = \mathbb{F}_2[X]/f(X)$. In the first variant, the ring is constructed with respect to an irreducible polynomial $f(X)$ in $\mathbb{F}_2$. This way the ring becomes a Galois field. In the second variant the polynomial $f(X)$ is reducible and it factors into distinct irreducible factors over $\mathbb{F}_2$, leading to improved performances (only this second variant will be considered next).

* This work has been funded in part by the ERC project 280141 (acronym CRASH), by the European Commissions 7th framework program's project TAMPRES, and by the Belgian Cybercrime Center of Excellence for Training Research and Education (B-CCENTRE). F.-X. Standaert is an associate researcher of the Belgiam Fund for Scientific Research (FNRS-F.R.S).

J. Benaloh (Ed.): CT-RSA 2014, LNCS 8366, pp. 206–226, 2014.
© Springer International Publishing Switzerland 2014

The claim that such a protocol could provide better performances than standard solutions using block ciphers gave rise to some debate, as witnessed by the work of Bernstein and Lange [3]. In this paper, the authors strongly argued against Lapin, because of its unclear security level, and performances that are anyway below the ones of lightweight ciphers. In this paper, we aim to mitigate these criticisms in light of the interesting properties of Lapin regarding side-channel resistance. Namely, we would like to argue that[1] as the (physical) security level against side-channel attacks required by some application increases, Lapin gradually becomes an interesting alternative over the AES. The main reason of this interesting feature is the linearity found in its core operations.

For this purpose, we first propose a generic hardware architecture for Lapin, and detail the performance gains that can be obtained from its implementation in an FPGA (compared to previous software implementations of unprotected Lapin and masked AES). Next, we provide a preliminary evaluation of its side-channel properties. Interestingly, the situation of Lapin can be compared to recent investigations of randomness extractors against side-channel attacks [15]. Namely, they can both be masked quite efficiently, while raising questions regarding how to best exploit/evaluate side-channel leakage. As a first step in this direction, we suggest two ways to mount attacks against Lapin: one non-divide-and-conquer DPA-like attack, and one divide-and-conquer collision-like attack, exploiting the correlation between the leakage corresponding to multiple messages.

Overall, these results suggest that Lapin could be a promising candidate for (reasonably) lightweight and physically secure implementations. Yet, and admittedly, a significant drawback remains that it requires the generation of randomness on-chip, which may be an issue both from the performance and the physical security point of view. As the previous work in [9], we ignored this part of the problem so far, leading to two important questions for further research. First, how to generate this noise efficiently and in a leakage-resilient manner. Second, can we build an authentication protocol similar to Lapin, but deterministic, e.g. using the recently introduced Learning With Rounding assumption [1,2].

2   Background

In this section we recall the Lapin authentication protocol and the masking countermeasure.

2.1   The Lapin Protocol

Lapin is a two-round authentication protocol, illustrated in Figure 1. It is defined over the ring $R = \mathbb{F}_2[X]/f(X)$, where f is a polynomial over $\mathbf{F}_2$ of degree n. The initial public parameters are: λ – security level parameter (in bits); π – mapping $\{0,1\}^\lambda \to R$; $\tau \in (0, 1/2)$ – Bernoulli distribution parameter; $\tau' \in (\tau, 1/2)$ – reader acceptance threshold. Besides, the secret key of the tag and reader is defined as $K = (s, s')$, with $(s, s') \xleftarrow{\$} R$. The protocol is executed as follows.

---

[1] Up to some limitations related to the randomness requirements of Lapin - see next.

Public parameters: R, $\pi:\{0,1\}^\lambda \to R, \tau, \tau', \lambda$.
Secret key: $K = (s, s') \in R^2$.

	Tag		**Reader**
①		$\xleftarrow{\quad c \quad}$	$c \xleftarrow{\$} \{0,1\}^\lambda$
②	$r \xleftarrow{\$} R^*; e \xleftarrow{\$} Ber_\tau^R \in R$		
③	$z := r \cdot (s \cdot \pi(c) \oplus s') \oplus e$	$\xrightarrow{\quad (r,z) \quad}$	
④			if $r \notin R^*$ reject
⑤			$e' := z - r \cdot (s \cdot \pi(c) \oplus s')$
⑥			if $HW(e') > n \cdot \tau'$ reject
			else accept

Fig. 1. Two-round Lapin authentication protocol

After the tag is detected in the reader's vicinity, the reader randomly generates a challenge $c \in \{0,1\}^\lambda$ and sends it to the tag (step ① in Fig. 1). The λ
parameter determines the security level of the protocol (*e.g.* $\lambda = 80$ bits). In the
meantime, the tag generates parameters r and e (step ②). The parameter r is an
uniformly chosen element of the ring R^* and e is a low-weight ring element chosen
with Bernoulli distribution over $\mathbb{F}_2$ (Ber$_\tau$) with parameter (bias) $\tau \in]0, 1/2[$ (*i.e.*,
$\Pr[X = 1] = \tau$ if $X \leftarrow$ Ber$_\tau$). After receiving the challenge c, the tag maps the
challenge to the ring through π, where π satisfies $\pi(c) \oplus \pi(c') \in R \setminus R^* \Leftrightarrow c = c'$.
We denote R^* the set of elements in R that have a multiplicative inverse. Subse-
quently, the tag responds with $(r, z = r \cdot K(c) \oplus e) \in R \times R$ (step ③), where
$K(c) = s \cdot c \oplus s'$ is the session key that depends on the shared secret key
$K = (s, s') \in R^2$ and the challenge c. The reader accepts if $e' = z \oplus r \cdot K(c)$
(computed in the step ⑤) is a polynomial of low weight (step ⑥). More details
on the Lapin protocol and all necessary security proofs can be find in [9].

Chinese Reminder Theorem Representation (CRT): In this work, we
focus on versions of Lapin over a ring $R = \mathbb{F}_2[X]/f(X)$ where $f(X)$ factors into
distinct irreducible factors over $\mathbb{F}_2$. For an element h in the ring $\mathbb{F}_2[X]/f(X)$,
we will denote $\hat{h}$ its CRT representation with respect to the factors of $f(X)$
(for simplicity $f(X)$ will be further denoted only as f). In other words, if $f = f_1 \cdot f_2 \cdots f_m$ where all f_j are irreducible, then:

$$\hat{h} \doteq (h \bmod f_1, \ldots, h \bmod f_m), \qquad \hat{h}_i \doteq h \bmod f_i.$$

For the protocol to be implemented efficiently, all public and private values must
be transformed to the CRT domain. However, in order to obtain the resulting
tag response (r, z), it must be reconstructed from the response $(\hat{r}, \hat{z})$ as follows:

$$(r, z) = \left(\bigoplus_{i=1}^m \hat{r}_i \cdot \overbrace{\frac{f}{f_i} \cdot \left[\left(\frac{f}{f_i} \right)^{-1} \right]_{f_i}}^{\text{constant}}, \bigoplus_{i=1}^m \hat{z}_i \cdot \overbrace{\frac{f}{f_i} \cdot \left[\left(\frac{f}{f_i} \right)^{-1} \right]_{f_i}}^{\text{constant}} \right). \tag{1}$$

Although constants in the equation can be precomputed, this transformation still involves m multiplications and additions of size n. Since the transformation from and to the CRT representation only uses public values, the tag response (r, z) can be sent to the reader in its CRT representation $(\widehat{r}, \widehat{z})$ without decreasing Lapin's security. This way, the computationally extensive transformation can be performed at the reader side.

The challenge mapping π is defined as $\widehat{\pi(c)} = (c, c, c, c, c)$, *i.e.* each CRT component is just the challenge padded with zeroes.

2.2   The Masking Countermeasure

Masking is a countermeasure against power analysis attacks based on secret sharing, first proposed by Chari et al. [5] and Goubin et al. [7]. Its main objective is to decrease the correlation between the power consumed by a device and the data being processed, by applying one (or several) random mask(s) to intermediate values. More formally, prior to the execution of the algorithm, all sensitive values (*i.e.* all key-dependent intermediate results used during the cryptographic computations) must be split into shares. Next, the algorithm is implemented in such a way that the processing is only performed on these shares, which are recombined at the end of the computation to produce the correct output result. Given that the shares are refreshed for each new authentication[2], masking provides an increase of the side-channel attacks data complexity that is exponential in their number, under the assumption that the leakage of each share is independent of the others. However, for this exponential security increase to materialize into strong concrete security, it is required that sufficient noise is present in the leakage measurements [18].

Different types of masking schemes have been proposed in the literature. Boolean masking (where the sharing is performed using a bitwise XOR operation) appears as the most natural candidate in our context, since it can take advantage of the linearity of the computations in Lapin. In this context, the split of a sensitive value h into d shares requires the generation of $d-1$ random mask values q_i, and is defined as follows:

$$h_1 = q_1, \qquad \dots, \qquad h_{d-1} = q_{d-1}, \qquad h_d = h \oplus \bigoplus_{i=1}^{d-1} q_i.$$

Based on this sharing, a masked version of Lapin becomes straightforward to implement. The secret keys s, s' and low-weight element e are first divided to shares $s_1, s_2, \dots, s_d$; $s'_1, s'_2, \dots, s'_d$ and $e_1, e_2, \dots, e_d$, respectively. The final result z is then obtained by recombining shares $z_1, z_2, \dots, z_d$ that are computed as follows:

---

[2] This implies storing all the shares of the secret key, for which the initial split is assumed to be performed once without leakage (otherwise this initialization can always be the target of simple attacks).

$$z = (\pi(c) \cdot s \oplus s') \cdot r \oplus e,$$
$$= [\pi(c) \cdot (s_1 \oplus \cdots \oplus s_d) \oplus (s'_1 \oplus \cdots \oplus s'_d)] \cdot r \oplus (e_1 \oplus \cdots \oplus e_d),$$
$$= [(\pi(c) \cdot s_1 \oplus s'_1) \cdot r \oplus e_1] \oplus \cdots \oplus [(\pi(c) \cdot s_d \oplus s'_d) \cdot r \oplus e_d],$$
$$= z_1 \oplus \cdots \oplus z_d,$$

with

$$z_i \doteq (\pi(c) \cdot s_i \oplus s'_i) \cdot r \oplus e_i.$$

Since Lapin is linear, we can compute the shares z_i independently, and there is no need of interaction between them nor refreshing during the computations, as opposed to masking non-linear gates within the AES [16], for instance. This leads to very efficient implementations.

On the Independent Leakage Assumption: In addition, the linearity of Lapin also allows to compute the shares sequentially. This time separation typically reduces the risk of glitches and other hardware effects that are well known to contradict the independence assumption [13]. This is especially interesting in the context of hardware implementations as considered in the next section; this is the typical context in which glitches can appear [14].

3   Hardware Implementation

In this section we discuss our design choices for (unprotected and masked) Lapin. We present several implementations of a Lapin co-processor and report their area and timing performance. A hardware implementation takes advantage of parallel computing in order to generate sufficient algorithmic noise, which allows significant security gains in practice (and improved performances).

3.1   Generic Architecture

In order to implement the Lapin protocol, we use the same parameter values as defined in Heyse at al. [9]. The degree of the polynomial f is chosen as $n = 621$, the security level parameter $\lambda = 80$ bits, Bernoulli distribution bias parameters $\tau = 1/6$, $\tau' = 0.29$ and the number of factors of f as $m = 5$. The five f_j polynomials are defined as follows:

$$f_1(X) = X^{127} \oplus X^8 \oplus X^7 \oplus X^3 \oplus 1,$$
$$f_2(X) = X^{126} \oplus X^9 \oplus X^6 \oplus X^5 \oplus 1,$$
$$f_3(X) = X^{125} \oplus X^9 \oplus X^7 \oplus X^4 \oplus 1,$$
$$f_4(X) = X^{122} \oplus X^7 \oplus X^4 \oplus X^3 \oplus 1,$$
$$f_5(X) = X^{121} \oplus X^8 \oplus X^5 \oplus X \quad \oplus 1.$$

Assuming that the Lapin protocol is performed on d shares (each of them computed for all m CRT parts), we will denote the $i-th$ share of the $j-th$ CRT part for a sensitive variable h as $\widehat{h_{i,j}}$. Next, we propose a flexible architecture that allows splitting the sensitive variables into arbitrary number of shares. Taking advantage of generic VHDL coding enables the generation of such implementations by re-synthetizing the same code with different parameters. For this purpose, we present the masked Lapin algorithm, the combined polynomial multiplication-reduction algorithm, and the hardware implementation of the complete Lapin core.

Masked Lapin: The generic masked Lapin algorithm is illustrated in Algorithm 1. First, a padded public challenge $\pi(c)$ is multiplied by a secret key s divided into shares $\widehat{s_{i,j}}$ for $1 \leq i \leq d$, $1 \leq j \leq m$. Following, the result is added to the secret key s' divided into shares $\widehat{s'_{i,j}}$. The sum is then multiplied by a public random tag response $\widehat{r_j}$. Subsequently, the product is added to a low-weight element $\widehat{e_{i,j}}$. The last step is to sum all resulting shares to form an unmasked tag response $\widehat{z_j}$. Finally, $\widehat{r_j}$ and $\widehat{z_j}$ are sent back to the reader to finish the authentication process. Note that all computations are performed on all m CRT parts.

Algorithm 1. Masked Lapin algorithm

Input:
1: Padded public challenge $\pi(c)$
2: Public random element $\widehat{r}$
3: Secret keys s and s' divided to shares $\widehat{s}$ and $\widehat{s'}$ respectively
4: Secret low-weigh error element e divided into shares $\widehat{e}$

Output: Response $(\widehat{z}, \widehat{r})$
5: **for** j from 1 to m **do**
6:    $\widehat{z_j} \leftarrow 0$
7:    **for** i from 1 to d **do**
8:       $\widehat{t_{i,j}} \leftarrow (\pi(c) \cdot \widehat{s_{i,j}} \oplus \widehat{s'_{i,j}}) \cdot \widehat{r_j} \oplus \widehat{e_{i,j}}$
9:    **end for**
10:   **for** i from 1 to d **do**
11:      $\widehat{z_j} \leftarrow \widehat{z_j} \oplus \widehat{t_{i,j}}$
12:   **end for**
13: **end for**
14: Return $\widehat{z}$

Reduction of a Low-Weight Error Element e: Unlike the other parameters in Lapin, the low-weight error element e cannot be generated or pre-stored in CRT representation directly: its m CRT parts must be calculated prior to other computations. The reduction of such a large element is not straightforward and requires additional hardware resources. In order to simplify this problem, we first write each share of e (a polynomial of degree 621) in Horner form using five polynomials $[e^{(4)}, e^{(3)}, e^{(2)}, e^{(1)}, e^{(0)}]$ of degree 127 (except for $e^{(4)}$ of degree 109):

$$\widehat{e_{i,j}} = \left(\left(\left(\left(e_i^{(4)} \cdot X^{128} \oplus e_i^{(3)}\right) \cdot X^{128} \oplus e_i^{(2)}\right) \cdot X^{128} \oplus e_i^{(1)}\right) \cdot X^{128} \oplus e_i^{(0)}\right) \bmod f_j. \quad (2)$$

Next, the polynomial X^{128} can be reduced by each characteristic polynomial f_j resulting in constant polynomials g_j of degree less than $\deg(f_j)$. After substitution Equation 2 becomes:

$$\widehat{e_{i,j}} = \left(\left(\left(e_i^{(4)} g_j \bmod f_j \oplus e_i^{(3)}\right) \cdot g_j \bmod f_j \oplus e_i^{(2)}\right) \cdot g_j \bmod f_j \oplus e_i^{(1)}\right) \cdot g_j \bmod f_j \oplus e_i^{(0)}. \quad (3)$$

This way, only four multiplications, four reductions and four additions have to be computed to obtain each $\widehat{e_{i,j}}$. Moreover, the same hardware as used for performing the computations in Algorithm 1 can be re-used to calculate the $\widehat{e_{i,j}}$'s. Note that since $e^{(3)}$, $e^{(2)}$, $e^{(1)}$ and $e^{(0)}$ are of degree 127, some extra hardware is still necessary for their reduction.

Polynomial Multiplication and Reduction: Examining the previous algorithms reveals that $6 \times d \times m$ polynomial multiplications, reductions and polynomial additions have to be performed to generate a response $\widehat{z}$. Among those, the most time-consuming operations are the polynomial multiplications and subsequent reductions of the products. Although the performances of the "schoolbook" multiplication algorithm is theoretically lower ($\mathcal{O}(2^n)$) than the Karatsuba algorithm ($\mathcal{O}(n^{log_2 3})$), it has a very simple structure, and so the resulting implementation is area-efficient and can operate at high clock frequencies. Moreover, polynomial reduction and multiplication operations can be executed simultaneously in this case, so that no computational time is lost for the reduction step. For this reason, we have implemented a combined polynomial multiplication-reduction based on the schoolbook multiplication, as explained in Algorithm 2. Two input polynomials $\widehat{a_{i,j}}$ and $\widehat{b_{i,j}}$ of degree at most $n_j - 1$ (represented with bit arrays $A[n_j - 1 : 0]$ and $B[n_j - 1 : 0]$) are multiplied together while partial products are reduced by the characteristic polynomial f_j of degree n_j (represented with the bit array $F[n_j : 0]$) simultaneously. A closer examination of the algorithm shows that B is multiplied by one bit of A at a time. Therefore, if A contains a secret value, Lapin will be vulnerable to a Simple Power Analysis (SPA) attack, where each partial multiplication leaks one bit of a key. For this reason, A must contain only public data. On the contrary, B is processed in larger blocks (according to the datapath size), so we used it to manipulate sensitive data (that will additionally be protected against DPA thanks to masking).

Lapin Architecture: We implemented Lapin as a hardware co-processor core, synthesized using Xilinx ISE 12.4 for Xilinx Virtex-5 XC5VLX50T FPGAs. Our implementation is illustrated in Figure 2. All variables are stored in the data register that is implemented in a dual-port embedded RAM. Random ring elements $\widehat{r}$ and low-weight error elements e have to be generated by a TRNG. Three distinctive parts can be identified in the datapath of this Lapin core: the polynomial multiplication logic (shown in blue in Figure 2), the reduction logic (in red)

Algorithm 2. Combined polynomial multiplication-reduction

Input:

1: polynomial $\widehat{a_{i,j}}$, $\deg\left(\widehat{a_{i,j}}\right) \leq n_j - 1$ represented as bit array $A[n_j - 1 : 0]$

2: polynomial $\widehat{b_{i,j}}$, $\deg\left(\widehat{b_{i,j}}\right) \leq n_j - 1$ represented as bit array $B[n_j - 1 : 0]$

3: characteristic polynomial $f_j(X)$ of degree n_j represented as bit array $F_j[n_j : 0]$

Output: $c(X) = \left(\widehat{a_{i,j}}.\widehat{b_{i,j}}\right) \bmod f_j)$

4: $C \leftarrow 0$

5: **for** i from 1 to n_j **do**

6:     **if** $A[n_j - i] = 1$ **then**

7:         $C \leftarrow C \oplus B$

8:     **end if**

9:     **if** $C[n_j - 1] = 1$ **then**

10:         $C \leftarrow (C \ll 1) \oplus F_j[n_j - 1 : 0]$

11:     **else**

12:         $C \leftarrow (C \ll 1)$

13:     **end if**

14: **end for**

15: Return $C[n_j - 1 : 0]$

---

and the addition logic (in green). During multiplication, a public parameter is stored in the shift register (implemented in logic). By shifting this register, one bit is selected at a time and multiplied with the secret parameter. The resulting partial product is stored in the accumulator (also implemented in a dual-port RAM). Subsequently, this partial product is shifted and added to the next partial product. Whenever the size of this sum exceeds n_j bits ($n_j = \deg(f_j)$), reduction circuitry is activated in the next clock cycle to reduce the exceeding bit. Once the multiplication is finished, the result can be summed with a next secret parameter stored in the data register. Prior to this addition, all exceeding bits of this parameter are reduced by an auxiliary reduction circuitry. As can be observed from the figure, multiplication involves shifting of partial products stored in the accumulator. However, if a partial product of size n_j is shifted in more than one clock cycle (which is the case when $k < 128$), the most significant bit of each shifted word must be stored in a carry bit register Cr. This way a stored carry bit becomes a least significant bit of the next word in the next clock cycle.

3.2   Performance Evaluation

Implementation Results: In order to investigate the performance trends resulting from different datapath sizes, we implemented our design for different values of the k parameter in Figure 2, namely we considered $k =$8-, 16-, 32-, 64- or 128-bit wide architectures, as summarized in Table 1. These results correspond to an unprotected implementation (*i.e.* $d = 1$) – but thanks to the linear structure of Lapin, the masked versions have essentially the same cost: only the memory requirements will increase proportionally to the number of

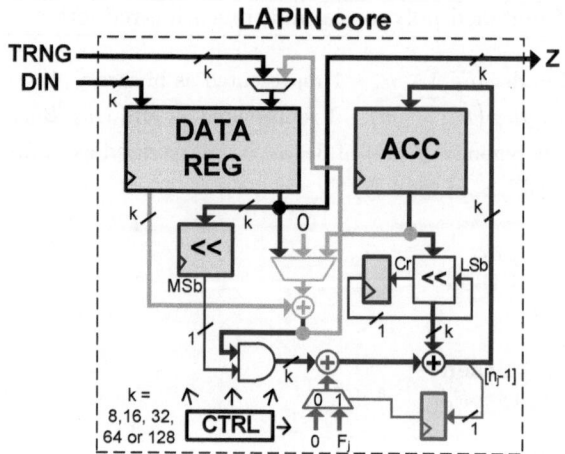

Fig. 2. Datapath with multiplication (blue), reduction (red) and addition (green) circuitry

shares, in order to store intermediate results. We observe that if the datapath size is decreased by half, the number of allocated fine-grained FPGA resources does not always decrease accordingly. This can be explained by the fact that narrower datapaths usually require more multiplexers and more complex control logic. Moreover, this extra logic increases the overall datapath delays, resulting in lower maximal clock frequency (see the fifth column in Table 1).

Table 1. Implementation results: resource usage and timing information

Datapath (k)	Slices	BRAM 18kb	36kb	f_{max} (MHz)	Clock cycles $d=1$	$d=2$	$d=3$
8	213	2	0	125.3	20,977	41,969	62,961
16	232	2	0	127.5	10,489	20,985	31,481
32	311	1	1	127.2	5,245	10,493	15,741
64	330	0	3	130.2	2,623	5,247	7,871
128	451	0	6	140.3	1,332	2,664	3,996

Timing Results: The detailed timing characteristics of our implementations are given in Table 2 (see Appendix B), in which each line corresponds to the number of clock cycles required for the computations in one characteristic polynomial domain (f_j), and the last line represents the total number of clock cycles for the full Lapin execution, *i.e.* one tag response for one authentication request. The left part of the table shows results if no masking is used (secret variables are not divided into shares, *i.e.* $d = 1$); its right part summarizes results for three-share computations (*i.e.* $d = 3$). For completeness, timing characteristics

are again provided for all the aforementioned datapath sizes. The datapath and
the control logic were designed in order to eliminate cycles with no activity (*i.e.*
pipeline bubbles). As a result, decreasing the datapath size by half results in
doubling the number of clock cycles in most cases. The only exception is the
128-bit datapath where some extra dummy cycles were necessary to avoid RAM
read/write collisions.

Comparison: The timing comparison of software AES [16], software Lapin [9]
and our hardware Lapin are given in Figure 3. In the case of software Lapin,
the cycle counts for the masked versions are extrapolated from the unprotected
implementation. These results lead to two main observations.

First, we see that masked Lapin implementations indeed become interesting
alternatives over AES ones, as the number of shares increases. This is caused
by the fact the the implementation cost of non-linear operations (which become
dominant in masked AES implementations) increases quadratically with d, while
this increase is only linear in the case of Lapin. Interestingly, the number of
shares for which this gain concretely appears is reasonably small, hence close to
practical interest. The software figures we have for protected implementations of
AES and Lapin on ATMega suggest that Lapin could become more efficient than
AES even with $d = 2$, but the crossing point can move significantly depending
on the masking scheme used, and the optimization level of the implementation.

Second, we see that (as usual) specialized hardware implementations allow
a significant optimization of the performances of Lapin. Gains already appear
in the comparison of 8-bit architectures: computing a tag response in software
requires 112,500 clock cycles (that can be decreased to 30,000 clock cycles if
precomputation is allowed); our 1-share 8-bit hardware implementation requires
only 20,977 clock cycles in this case (without precomputations). These advantages naturally amplify as we consider larger datapath sizes.

# of shares d	AES —●— softw. [16, 8]	Lapin —■— softw. [9]	Lapin —▲— 8b hardw.
1	5100	112500	20977
2	286844	225016	41969
3	572069	337532	62961
4	1003154	450048	83953
5	1489539	562564	104945
6	2095756	675080	125937
7	2779561	787596	146929

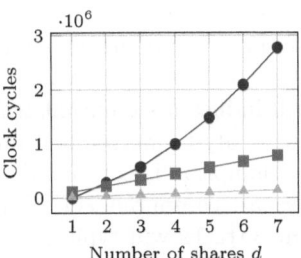

Fig. 3. Number of clock cycles vs. number of shares (d) for software AES [16,8], software
Lapin [9] and hardware Lapin. With increase of used shares, the computation time
increases quadratically for the AES and only linearly for both Lapin implementations.

4   Side-Channel Analysis of Lapin

The previous section suggests that Lapin is an interesting candidate for masking. First, its linearity allows increasing the number of shares for only a linear implementation cost penalty. Second, it also allows manipulating the shares independently, which implies a better chance to fulfill the independent leakage requirements that is crucial for masking to provide its expected security improvements. Third, it is efficiently implemented in hardware with large datapaths, providing algorithmic noise that is needed for the exponential data complexity increase of masking to materialize into strong security levels. On the other hand, a limitation of this analysis remains that it "only" considers the security orders of the masking schemes (*i.e.* the minimum number of shares of which the leakage must be exploited to recover key-dependent information). While this is a traditional approach in side-channel analysis, it remains to understand how these security orders translate into actual attack complexities. In particular, since Lapin has a significantly different structure than block ciphers (to which most published higher-order side-channel attacks apply), it is interesting to study attacks that exploit the design of its multiplier. In this section, we consequently suggest several scenarios to analyze/evaluate a Lapin implementation using side-channel information, and we study the efficiency of those attacks depending on the masking order of this implementation. As will be seen, these attacks differ from classical DPA in some interesting respects.

We first point out that we can attack the CRT components independently: each component is computed separately, and we can test a key candidate $\widehat{s_i}$ from the an authentication transcript without knowing the other CRT components. In the following we describe attacks on a single CRT component.

As a starting point, we consider a non-protected implementation of Lapin, and we study how to apply a standard DPA attack. In order to evaluate power analysis on our implementation of Lapin, we first have to study what parts of the computations are key-dependent, and how it might affect the power consumption. In our analysis we target the first multiplication $s \cdot \pi(c)$ in the Lapin protocol, where s is a secret value, and c is a challenge that can be set by the attacker. Our architecture for Lapin includes a large accumulator that is updated at each clock cycle, as shown in Figure 2, and we assume that this accumulator will induce a significant leakage dependent on its value a. In order to simplify our analysis, we use a Hamming weight model, *i.e.* we assume that the power consumption is correlated with $\mathrm{HW}(a)$, and we run simulations where the samples are computed as $\mathrm{HW}(a) + N$, with N a Gaussian-distributed random noise. Our attacks will typically exploit the fact that, when computing $a \cdot c$, the multiplication algorithm updates the accumulator a as (we consider the optimized multiplication with an 80-bit c):

$$a_0 = 0 \qquad\qquad a_{i+1} \leftarrow \begin{cases} 2 \cdot a_i \oplus s & \text{if } c[80 - i] = 1 \\ 2 \cdot a_i & \text{otherwise.} \end{cases}$$

Hence, the value of the a after a few cycles of computation is a small multiple of the secret:

$$a_{80} = s \cdot c \qquad\qquad a_i = s \cdot \sum_{j=1}^{i} c[80 - j] X^{i-j}.$$

Cautionary Note: Assuming Hamming weight leakages is admittedly a simplification of the real measurements used in side-channel attacks. However, it is a reasonable abstraction for preliminary analyses, that has been used in numerous contexts [12]. While the actual complexities provided by these simulated attacks are only meaningful up to the extent that true leakages behave similarly, they are usually informative to confirm whether some attack techniques can be successful. This is typically what the following results aim to exhibit, *i.e.* how side-channel attacks against Lapin differ from standard DPA against block ciphers.

4.1   A First DPA-Like Attack against Unprotected Lapin

In an unprotected design, the leakage reveals the Hamming weight of multiples of the secret, with a chosen multiplier $m_i(c) = \sum_{j=1}^{i} c[80 - j] X^{i-j}$, depending on the challenge c and the cycle i we target. If we exploit several different cycles in a given trace, we can get information about $\mathrm{HW}(a_i) = \mathrm{HW}(s \cdot m_i(c))$ for the same c and different values of i. However, the same information can also be obtained by targeting a fixed cycle ι of the computation if we capture several traces and send the appropriate challenges c_j so that $m_\iota(c_j) = m_j(c)$.

In a DPA attack, we guess a small part of the key, then predict the value of the leakage for a key guess according to a model, and compare the prediction to the actual measurements in order to rank the key candidates. For a block cipher, the key is usually divided according to the structure of the cipher; for instance, an attack on the AES will target the key bytes independently because each SBox in the first round depends on a single key byte. In the case of Lapin there is no such natural division of the key, but we can study the key bits required to compute some bits of the accumulator.

Recovering a Few Key Bits. For a given t, if $m_i(c)$ is of degree at most t (*e.g.* if $i \le t$), we can compute the p *least* significant bits of $s \cdot m_i(c)$ from the p *least* significant and the $t - 1$ *most* significant bits of s. This allows to build a simple DPA attack: after guessing the key bits, we compute the least significant bits of a_i and we consider the remaining bits as algorithmic noise. We can then compute the correlation between the leaked weight of a and the weight of the predicted bits, and use it to rank the key candidates.

Note that if there is no measurement noise, we can only use 2^t different measures in this attack, because there are only 2^t different polynomials of degree t or lower. Extra measures are only useful to reduce the measurement noise.

We implemented this attack using Pearson's correlation coefficient as a comparison tool [4], and we show an example of results in Figure 8 in Appendix A. We can see from this example that the information from the measures is not sufficient to recover exactly the secret key bits; there is a cluster of key candidates with the same correlation coefficient. This is due to the algebraic structure of the multiplier; for instance, if we consider two key candidate s and $s' = s \cdot X$, our prediction for the least significant bit of the accumulator using the key s will match the second-least significant bit of the accumulator for candidate s'. Therefore, both candidates will be in the same cluster.

Recovering the Full Key. As opposed to a typical side channel attack on a block cipher, we don't have independent parts of the key affecting different parts of the computation. Therefore, we don't attack key parts independently using a divide-and-conquer approach, but we recover key information gradually: if we have a good candidate for n bits of the key, we generate key candidates for $n+1$ bits by considering both values for the next key bit. This defines a tree of key candidates, and we explore the tree following the best candidates.

More precisely, we compute a score for the candidates as the ratio of Pearson's correlation coefficient over the expected correlation coefficient for the right key (the square root of the number of predicted bits divided by the total number of bits on the bus, over which the Hamming weight is computed). This allows to compare the quality of key guesses of different lengths: if more key bits are guessed, we can predict more bits, and we expect a better correlation coefficient. The score of a node is computed when its parent is explored, and we select the node with the higher score among all nodes whose score has been computed. In practice, we use a priority queue to store the nodes and to extract the best one efficiently.

If we have 2^t traces, we begin by guessing the $t - 1$ most significant bits, and one least significant bit of the key; this allows to predict one bit of the accumulator a_t after t cycles. Next, we guess the second-least significant bit of the key, so that we can predict two bits of a_t.

Figure 5 in Appendix A shows the success rate of this DPA-like attack, with various parameters. The attack becomes less efficient with a large datapath, because the Hamming weight over a larger bus size introduces more algorithmic noise to the predicted value.

Those experiments clearly show the effect of the algorithmic noise from the unknown bits in the Hamming weight (with variance $k/4$ for a k-bit datapath), and of the physical noise (with variance σ^2). When the physical noise is dominant, i.e. $\sigma^2 > k/4$, we see the data complexity increasing linearly with the variance of the noise, as expected [11]. For instance, our experiment show a data complexity of about $2^7.\sigma^2$ to reach a high success rate with $k = 8$. When k increases, this increases the algorithmic noise, and we have a similar increase of the data complexity if the algorithmic noise is dominant, i.e. when $\sigma^2 < k/4$. We note that this increase is somewhat faster than $k/4$ because there are more nodes to explore to locate the correct key when k is larger, but we stop after a fixed number of nodes are explored.

4.2   Collision-Like Attack

We now describe an attack based on the structure of the operations in Lapin. The main advantage of this attack is that we can eliminate the algorithmic noise due to the Hamming weight with a large datapath by comparing the leakage with two different inputs. This is similar to side-channel collision attacks [17] where two traces are compared to detect specific events.

More precisely, we use the fact that the operation $\alpha \mapsto \alpha \cdot X$ has a predictable effect on the Hamming weight of α. We have:

$$\alpha \cdot X \bmod f = \begin{cases} (\alpha \ll 1) & \text{if MSB}(\alpha) = 0 \\ (\alpha \ll 1) \oplus f & \text{if MSB}(\alpha) = 1, \end{cases}$$

where $\ll$ to denotes a left shift. Alternatively, we can write it using a rotation $\lll$ over $\deg(f)$ bits:

$$\alpha \cdot X \bmod f = \begin{cases} (\alpha \lll 1) & \text{if MSB}(\alpha) = 0 \\ (\alpha \lll 1) \oplus \bar{f} & \text{if MSB}(\alpha) = 1, \end{cases}$$

where $\bar{f} = f \oplus X^{\deg(f)} \oplus 1$ is f without the highest and lowest coefficients. Since the polynomials f used in Lapin are pentanomials, we have $\text{HW}(\bar{f}) = 3$, and we can relate the Hamming weight of α and the Hamming weight of $\alpha \cdot X \bmod f$:

$$\text{HW}(\alpha \cdot X \bmod f) = \begin{cases} \text{HW}(\alpha) & \text{if MSB}(\alpha) = 0 \\ \text{HW}(\alpha) + 3 & \text{if MSB}(\alpha) = 1 \text{ and } \text{HW}(\alpha \lll 1 \wedge \bar{f}) = 0 \\ \text{HW}(\alpha) + 1 & \text{if MSB}(\alpha) = 1 \text{ and } \text{HW}(\alpha \lll 1 \wedge \bar{f}) = 1 \\ \text{HW}(\alpha) - 1 & \text{if MSB}(\alpha) = 1 \text{ and } \text{HW}(\alpha \lll 1 \wedge \bar{f}) = 2 \\ \text{HW}(\alpha) - 3 & \text{if MSB}(\alpha) = 1 \text{ and } \text{HW}(\alpha \lll 1 \wedge \bar{f}) = 3. \end{cases}$$

Therefore, the distribution of $\text{HW}(\alpha \cdot X) - \text{HW}(\alpha)$ for a random α is the following:

if MSB(α) = 0: $\text{HW}(\alpha \cdot X) - \text{HW}(\alpha) = 0$,

if MSB(α) = 1: $\text{HW}(\alpha \cdot X) - \text{HW}(\alpha) = \begin{cases} +3 & \text{with probability } 1/8 \\ +1 & \text{with probability } 3/8 \\ -1 & \text{with probability } 3/8 \\ -3 & \text{with probability } 1/8. \end{cases}$

To exploit this property, we will use two measures such that $m_i(c) = m$ and $m_{i'}(c') = m \cdot X$. Then, we can recover the value $\text{MSB}(m \cdot s)$ (*i.e.* a linear equation in s) by comparing $\text{HW}(m \cdot s)$ and $\text{HW}(m \cdot X \cdot s)$ (we use the analysis above with $\alpha = m \cdot s$). If there is no noise, we will recover a key bit with only two measures, with probability one.

As opposed to the attack of Section 4.1, this analysis uses the full state of the multiplier, and avoids algorithmic noise due to the Hamming weight. This makes the attack quite efficient. However, there is also an important limitation:

because the challenge used in Lapin is only 80-bit long, the multiplication $m \cdot c$ only takes 80 cycles, and we can only recover 80 bits from each CRT component of the key with this technique.

If there is some measurement noise, we can remove it either by repeating the measures of $\mathrm{HW}(m \cdot s)$ and $\mathrm{HW}(m \cdot X \cdot s)$ and averaging them, or by using all the measures in a template attack [6]. We performed simulations with various levels of noise using a template attack, and the rank estimation code from [19] to compute the rank of the full key from the estimated key bits probability. We report our results in Appendix A, Figure 6. Those experiments show that with a 128-bit datapath we can recover 80 key bits with very few candidates using only 2^6 traces with a noise variance of 1. Again, the data complexity grows linearly with the noise variance σ^2, and we need about $2^6 \cdot \sigma^2$ traces to reduce the key space to a few candidates.

If the datawidth k is smaller than 128, we have to combine $128/k$ measures to build the full Hamming weight $\mathrm{HW}(a)$ in order to perform the attack. If the noise variance is σ^2 this becomes equivalent to a noise variance of $128/k \cdot \sigma^2$ for an attack with a 128-bit datapath, and the number of traces required is about $2^6 \cdot \sigma^2 \cdot 128/k$. As expected, this behavior is opposite to what happens in the attack of Section 4.1 where a larger datapath implies a higher attack complexity because of the extra algorithmic noise.

For the acquisition of the data, one can either extract the two leakages from a single trace at two different points of interest, or use two traces with chosen challenges and extract the leakage from each trace at the same point in time. In order to minimize the number of traces required for the attack, we use all the clock cycles of the multiplier. More precisely, we send the challenge $c = 2^{79}$, so that $m_i(c) = X^{i-1}$ and $m_{i+1}(c) = X^i = m_i(c) \cdot X$.

Order of the Attack. This attack exploits information from two different measures, and combines them using the difference operation. Since we use a single pair of challenges for each key bit, we can average the measures and the information can be extracted from the average leakage values by testing whether it is zero or in $\{-3, -1, +1, +3\}$. Therefore, this attack can be seen as a first-order bivariate attack.

4.3   Attack on Masked Lapin

We now study how this attack can be applied against a masked implementation of Lapin such as the implementation described in Algorithm 1. In a masked implementation the multiplication $\pi(c) \cdot s$ is split in d computations $\pi(c) \cdot s_j$, with $s = \bigoplus_{j=1}^d s_j$. Therefore we have to combine leakages from each of the d computations to recover information about the secret s.

First, we can see that if there is no noise, it is still easy to recover the key using the attack of Section 4.2. If we send the challenge $c = 2^{79}$, we have $m_i(c) = X^{i-1}$ and $m_{i+1}(c) = X^i = m_i(c) \cdot X$. By comparing $\mathrm{HW}(X^{i-1} \cdot s_j)$ and $\mathrm{HW}(X^i \cdot s_j)$, we can recover $\mathrm{MSB}(X^{i-1} \cdot s_j)$, and we can rebuild a bit of s using $\mathrm{MSB}(X^{i-1} \cdot s) = \bigoplus_j \mathrm{MSB}(X^{i-1} \cdot s_j)$.

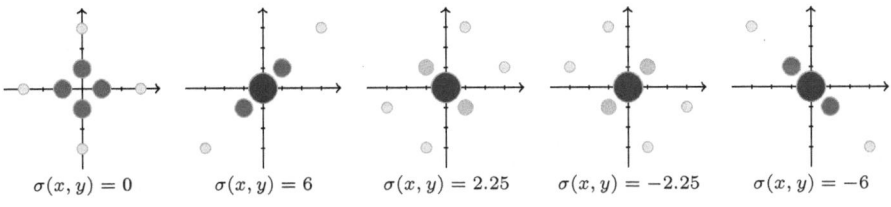

$\sigma(x,y)=0$ $\sigma(x,y)=6$ $\sigma(x,y)=2.25$ $\sigma(x,y)=-2.25$ $\sigma(x,y)=-6$

4.1. MSB(α)=1   **4.2.** MSB(α)=0   **4.3.** MSB(α)=0   **4.4.** MSB(α)=0   **4.5.** MSB(α)=0

HW($\alpha \lll 1 \wedge \bar{f}$)=0   HW($\alpha \lll 1 \wedge \bar{f}$)=1   HW($\alpha \lll 1 \wedge \bar{f}$)=2   HW($\alpha \lll 1 \wedge \bar{f}$)=3

Fig. 4. Possible distributions for $\big(\mathrm{HW}(\alpha_1 \cdot X) - \mathrm{HW}(\alpha_1), \mathrm{HW}(\alpha_2 \cdot X) - \mathrm{HW}(\alpha_2)\big)$. The probabilities are represented as: ☐: 1/16, ▨: 2/16, ■: 3/16, ■: 8/16

More generally, we study the $2d$-dimensional distribution of:

$$\big(\mathrm{HW}(\alpha_j), \mathrm{HW}(\alpha_j \cdot X)\big)_{j=1}^{d}, \quad \text{with } \alpha = \bigoplus_{j=1}^{d} \alpha_j.$$

Following the analysis of Section 4.2, we combine the measures using a difference operation, and reduce them to d dimensions:

$$\big(\mathrm{HW}(\alpha_j \cdot X) - \mathrm{HW}(\alpha_j)\big)_{j=1}^{d}, \quad \text{with } \alpha = \bigoplus_{j=1}^{d} \alpha_j.$$

We will later use this analysis with $\alpha = m \cdot s$ and $\alpha_j = m \cdot s_j$.

We now study the case $d = 2$ in more details. Following the analysis of Section 4.2, we expect different distributions depending on the most significant bit of α.

MSB(α) = 1: If MSB(α) = 1, then we have either MSB(α_1) = 0 and MSB(α_2) = 1, or MSB(α_1) = 1 and MSB(α_2) = 0. This results in the distribution of Figure 4.1: either $\mathrm{HW}(\alpha_1 \cdot X) - \mathrm{HW}(\alpha_1) = 0$ and $\mathrm{HW}(\alpha_2 \cdot X) - \mathrm{HW}(\alpha_2) \in \{-3, -1, +1, +3\}$, or $\mathrm{HW}(\alpha_1 \cdot X) - \mathrm{HW}(\alpha_1) \in \{-3, -1, +1, +3\}$ and $\mathrm{HW}(\alpha_2 \cdot X) - \mathrm{HW}(\alpha_2) = 0$.

MSB(α) = 0: If MSB(α) = 0, then we have either MSB(α_1) = 0 and MSB(α_2) = 0, or MSB(α_1) = 1 and MSB(α_2) = 1. The first case gives $\mathrm{HW}(\alpha_1 \cdot X) - \mathrm{HW}(\alpha_1) = 0$ and $\mathrm{HW}(\alpha_2 \cdot X) - \mathrm{HW}(\alpha_2) = 0$. In the second case, we have $\mathrm{HW}(\alpha_1 \cdot X) - \mathrm{HW}(\alpha_1) \in \{-3, -1, +1, +3\}$ and $\mathrm{HW}(\alpha_2 \cdot X) - \mathrm{HW}(\alpha_2) \in \{-3, -1, +1, +3\}$, but we need to look at $\mathrm{HW}(\alpha \lll 1 \wedge \bar{f})$ in order to predict all the possibilities. The results are shown in Figure 4.

We can use those distributions to mount a template attack against a masked implementation of Lapin. We use $c = 2^{79}$, in order to collect traces with $\mathrm{HW}(X^{i-1} \cdot s_j)$ and $\mathrm{HW}(X^i \cdot s_j)$, and we recover $\mathrm{MSB}(X^{i-1} \cdot s)$ by distinguishing the distributions (i.e. we have $\alpha = X^{i-1} \cdot s$). We report our simulations results in Figure 7 in Appendix A. We can see that the data complexity increases roughly like the squared variance σ^4, which is typical of a second-order attack [5]. In our simulations, the rank of the correct key becomes smaller than 2^{10} when the data complexity is about $2^{10} \cdot \sigma^4$.

Order of the Attack. This attack exploits information from four different measures, and combines pairs of measures using the difference operation. Then we have to distinguish the distributions of Figure 4, which can be done by computing the covariance and testing whether it is zero or in $\{-6, -2.25, 2.25, 6\}$. Therefore, this attack can be seen as a second-order 4-variate attack.

5   Conclusion

The previous results suggest that Lapin has interesting properties for secure and efficient masking, because it can be implemented by manipulating shares independently. They also exhibit that the exploitation of its leakage does not directly derive from standard DPA such as applied in the context of block ciphers. Yet, it is possible to mount attacks against both unprotected and masked Lapin, with similar intuition regarding the security order as for block ciphers. Admittedly, our side-channel experiments are only a first step, and several problems remain open. Technically, it would certainly be worth investigating other leakage models (*e.g.* distance-based) and actual measurements. Besides, it could be interesting to further study the possible presence of more data-dependent algorithmic noise in an implementation (*i.e.* capturing more than the main register activity), and how to get rid of it taking advantage of multiple plaintexts in a collision-like attack. Eventually, and as pointed out in introduction, the problem of on-chip randomness generation remains an important drawback of Lapin. Analyzing its leakage, or designing deterministic protocols based on the Learning With Rounding assumption are interesting scopes for further research.

References

1. Alwen, J., Krenn, S., Pietrzak, K., Wichs, D.: Learning with Rounding, Revisited - New Reduction, Properties and Applications. In: Canetti, R., Garay, J.A. (eds.) CRYPTO 2013, Part I. LNCS, vol. 8042, pp. 57–74. Springer, Heidelberg (2013)
2. Banerjee, A., Peikert, C., Rosen, A.: Pseudorandom Functions and Lattices. In: Pointcheval, D., Johansson, T. (eds.) EUROCRYPT 2012. LNCS, vol. 7237, pp. 719–737. Springer, Heidelberg (2012)
3. Bernstein, D.J., Lange, T.: Never Trust a Bunny. In: Hoepman, J.-H., Verbauwhede, I. (eds.) RFIDSec 2012. LNCS, vol. 7739, pp. 137–148. Springer, Heidelberg (2013)
4. Brier, E., Clavier, C., Olivier, F.: Correlation Power Analysis with a Leakage Model. In: Joye, Quisquater [10], pp. 16–29
5. Chari, S., Jutla, C.S., Rao, J.R., Rohatgi, P.: Towards Sound Approaches to Counteract Power-Analysis Attacks. In: Wiener, M. (ed.) CRYPTO 1999. LNCS, vol. 1666, pp. 398–412. Springer, Heidelberg (1999)

6. Chari, S., Rao, J.R., Rohatgi, P.: Template Attacks. In: Kaliski Jr., B.S., Koç, Ç.K., Paar, C. (eds.) CHES 2002. LNCS, vol. 2523, pp. 13–28. Springer, Heidelberg (2003)
7. Goubin, L., Patarin, J.: DES and Differential Power Analysis (The "Duplication" Method). In: Koç, Ç.K., Paar, C. (eds.) CHES 1999. LNCS, vol. 1717, pp. 158–172. Springer, Heidelberg (1999)
8. Grosso, V., Standaert, F.-X., Faust, S.: Masking vs. Multiparty Computation: How Large Is the Gap for AES? In: Bertoni, G., Coron, J.-S. (eds.) CHES 2013. LNCS, vol. 8086, pp. 400–416. Springer, Heidelberg (2013)
9. Heyse, S., Kiltz, E., Lyubashevsky, V., Paar, C., Pietrzak, K.: Lapin: An Efficient Authentication Protocol Based on Ring-LPN. In: Canteaut, A. (ed.) FSE 2012. LNCS, vol. 7549, pp. 346–365. Springer, Heidelberg (2012)
10. Joye, M., Quisquater, J.-J. (eds.): CHES 2004. LNCS, vol. 3156. Springer, Heidelberg (2004)
11. Mangard, S.: Hardware Countermeasures against DPA – A Statistical Analysis of Their Effectiveness. In: Okamoto, T. (ed.) CT-RSA 2004. LNCS, vol. 2964, pp. 222–235. Springer, Heidelberg (2004)
12. Mangard, S., Oswald, E., Popp, T.: Power analysis attacks - revealing the secrets of smart cards. Springer (2007)
13. Mangard, S., Popp, T., Gammel, B.M.: Side-Channel Leakage of Masked CMOS Gates. In: Menezes, A. (ed.) CT-RSA 2005. LNCS, vol. 3376, pp. 351–365. Springer, Heidelberg (2005)
14. Mangard, S., Pramstaller, N., Oswald, E.: Successfully Attacking Masked AES Hardware Implementations. In: Rao, J.R., Sunar, B. (eds.) CHES 2005. LNCS, vol. 3659, pp. 157–171. Springer, Heidelberg (2005)
15. Medwed, M., Standaert, F.-X.: Extractors against side-channel attacks: weak or strong? J. Cryptographic Engineering 1(3), 231–241 (2011)
16. Rivain, M., Prouff, E.: Provably Secure Higher-Order Masking of AES. In: Mangard, S., Standaert, F.-X. (eds.) CHES 2010. LNCS, vol. 6225, pp. 413–427. Springer, Heidelberg (2010)
17. Schramm, K., Leander, G., Felke, P., Paar, C.: A Collision-Attack on AES: Combining Side Channel- and Differential-Attack. In: Joye, Quisquater [10], pp. 163–175
18. Standaert, F.-X., Veyrat-Charvillon, N., Oswald, E., Gierlichs, B., Medwed, M., Kasper, M., Mangard, S.: The World Is Not Enough: Another Look on Second-Order DPA. In: Abe, M. (ed.) ASIACRYPT 2010. LNCS, vol. 6477, pp. 112–129. Springer, Heidelberg (2010)
19. Veyrat-Charvillon, N., Gérard, B., Standaert, F.-X.: Security Evaluations beyond Computing Power. In: Johansson, T., Nguyen, P.Q. (eds.) EUROCRYPT 2013. LNCS, vol. 7881, pp. 126–141. Springer, Heidelberg (2013)

A   Simulation Results of the Side-Channel Attacks

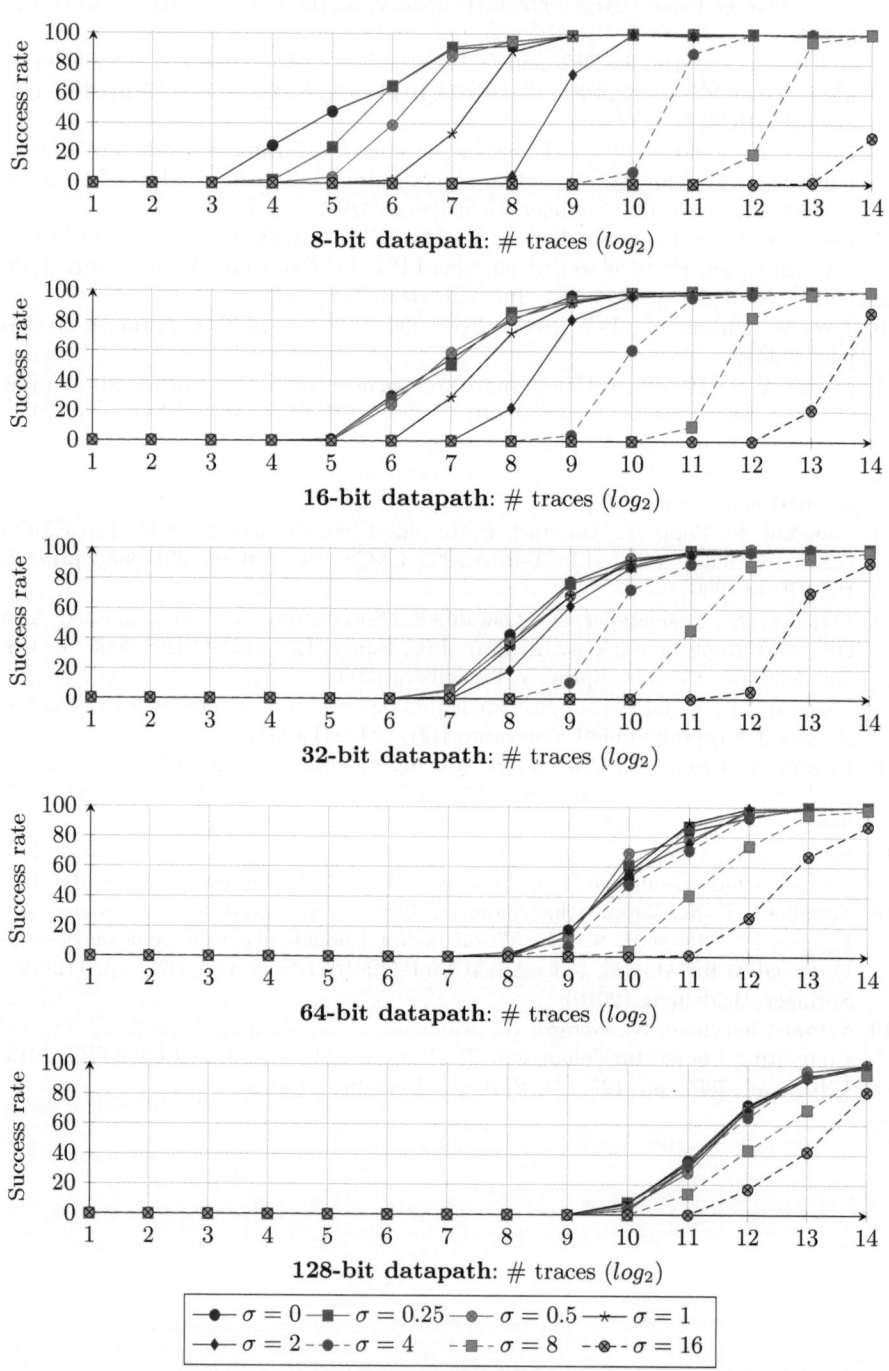

Fig. 5. DPA attack success rate for full-key recovery, after exploring 2^{16} tree nodes

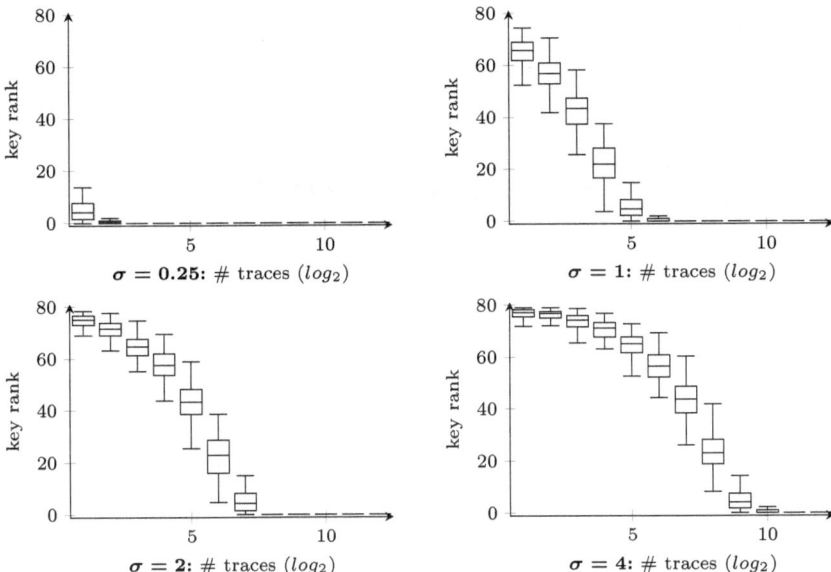

Fig. 6. Security graphs for the collision-like attack, with $k = 128$. We assume that all the clock cycles are used for each trace. Alternatively, the attack can be mounted targeting a single point of interest if the data complexity is multiplied by 80.

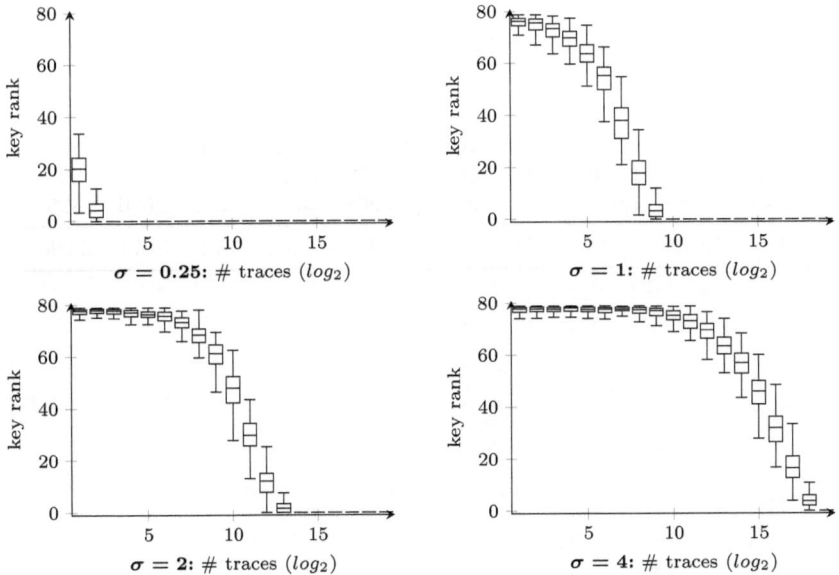

Fig. 7. Security graphs for the collision-like attack on a masked Lapin, with $k = 128$

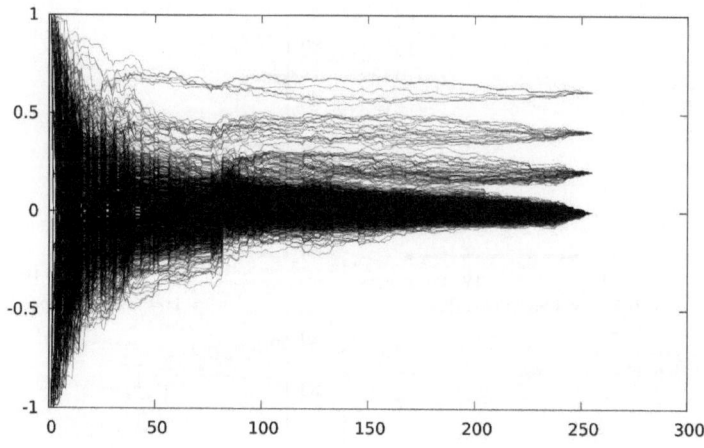

Fig. 8. Correlation coefficient for the key candidates, depending on the number of traces. We use $t = 7$ and $p = 3$, and don't add any noise to the Hamming weights.

B Additional Implementation Results

Table 2. Number of clock cycles required for Lapin calculation

	One share ($d = 1$)					Three shares ($d = 3$)				
	8-bit	16-bit	32-bit	64-bit	128-bit	8-bit	16-bit	32-bit	64-bit	128-bit
f_1	4,048	2,024	1,012	506	257	12,144	6,072	3,036	1,518	771
f_2	4,160	2,080	1,040	520	264	12,480	6,240	3,120	1,560	792
f_3	4,208	2,104	1,052	526	267	12,624	6,312	3,156	1,578	801
f_4	4,224	2,112	1,056	528	268	12,672	6,336	3,168	1,584	804
f_5	4,336	2,168	1,084	542	275	13,008	6,504	3,252	1,626	825
Total	20,977	10,489	5,245	2,623	1,332	62,961	31,481	15,741	7,871	3,996

Automatic Search for Differential Trails in ARX Ciphers

Alex Biryukov and Vesselin Velichkov

Laboratory of Algorithmics, Cryptology and Security (LACS)
University of Luxembourg
{Alex.Biryukov,Vesselin.Velichkov}@uni.lu

Abstract. We propose a tool[1] for automatic search for differential trails in ARX ciphers. By introducing the concept of a *partial difference distribution table* (pDDT) we extend Matsui's algorithm, originally proposed for DES-like ciphers, to the class of ARX ciphers. To the best of our knowledge this is the first application of Matsui's algorithm to ciphers that do not have S-boxes. The tool is applied to the block ciphers TEA, XTEA, SPECK and RAIDEN. For RAIDEN we find an iterative characteristic on all 32 rounds that can be used to break the full cipher using standard differential cryptanalysis. This is the first cryptanalysis of the cipher in a non-related key setting. Differential trails on 9, 10 and 13 rounds are found for SPECK32, SPECK48 and SPECK64 respectively. The 13 round trail covers half of the total number of rounds. These are the first public results on the security analysis of SPECK. For TEA multiple full (i.e. not truncated) differential trails are reported for the first time, while for XTEA we confirm the previous best known trail reported by Hong et al. . We also show closed formulas for computing the exact additive differential probabilities of the left and right shift operations.

Keywords: symmetric-key, differential trail, tools for cryptanalysis, automatic search, ARX, TEA, XTEA, SPECK, RAIDEN.

1 Introduction

A broad class of symmetric-key cryptographic algorithms are designed by combining a small set of simple operations such as modular addition, bit rotation, bit shift and XOR. Although such designs have been proposed as early as the 1980s, only recently the term *ARX* (from *Addition, Rotation, XOR*) was adopted in reference to them.

Some of the more notable examples of ARX algorithms, ordered chronologically by the year of proposal are: the block cipher FEAL [37] (1987), the hash functions MD4 [34] (1990) and MD5 [35] (1992), the block ciphers TEA [40] (1994), RC5 [36] (1994), XTEA [30] (1997), XXTEA [31] (1998) and HIGHT [15] (2006), the stream cipher Salsa20 [4] (2008), the SHA-3 [28] finalists Skein [13]

---

[1] The source code of the tool is made publicly available as part of a larger toolkit for the analysis of ARX at the following address: https://github.com/vesselinux/yaarx .

J. Benaloh (Ed.): CT-RSA 2014, LNCS 8366, pp. 227–250, 2014.
© Springer International Publishing Switzerland 2014

and BLAKE [2] (2011) and the recently proposed hash function for short messages SipHash [1] (2012).

By combining linear (XOR, bit shift, bit rotation) and non-linear (modular addition) operations, and iterating them over multiple rounds, ARX algorithms achieve strong resistance against standard cryptanalysis techniques such as linear [24] and differential [5] cryptanalysis. Additionally, due to the simplicity of the underlying operations, they are typically very fast in software.

Although ARX designs have many advantages and have been widely used for many years now, the methods for their rigorous security analysis are lagging behind. This is especially true when compared to algorithms such as AES [9] and DES [29]. The latter were designed using fundamentally different principles, based on the combination of linear transformations and non-linear substitution tables or S-boxes.

Since a typical S-box operates on 8 or 4-bit words, it is easy to efficiently evaluate its differential (resp. linear) properties by computing its difference distribution table (DDT) (resp. linear approximation table (LAT)). In contrast, ARX algorithms use modular addition as a source of non-linearity, rather than S-boxes. Constructing a DDT or a LAT for this operation for n-bit words would require $2^{3n} \times 4$ bytes of memory and would clearly be infeasible for a typical word size of 32 bits.

In this paper we demonstrate that although the computation of a full DDT for ARX is infeasible, it is still possible to efficiently compute a *partial DDT* containing (a fraction of) all differentials that have probability above a fixed threshold. This is possible due to the fact that the probabilities of XOR (resp. ADD) differentials through the modular addition (resp. XOR) operation are monotonously decreasing with the bit size of the word.

Based on the concept of partial DDT-s we develop a method for automatic search for differential trails in ARX ciphers. It is based on Matsui's branch-and-bound algorithm [23], originally proposed for S-box based ciphers. While other methods for automatic search for differential trails in ARX designs exist in literature [12,25,20] they have been exclusively applied to the analysis of hash functions where the key (the message) is known and can be freely chosen. With the proposed algorithm we address the more general setting of searching for trails in block ciphers, where the key is fixed and unknown to the attacker.

Beside the idea of using partial DDT-s another fundamental concept at the heart of the proposed algorithm is what we refer to as *the highways and country roads analogy*. If we liken the problem of finding high probability differential trails in a cipher to the problem of finding fast routes between two cities on a road map, then differentials that have high probability (w.r.t. a fixed threshold) can be thought of as *highways* and conversely differentials with low probability can be viewed as slow roads or *country roads*. To further extend the analogy, a differential trail for n rounds represents a route between points 1 and n composed of some number of highways and country roads. A search for high probability trails is analogous to searching for a route in which the number of highways is maximized while the number of country roads is minimized.

The differentials from the pDDT are the highways on the road map from the above analogy. Beside those highways, the proposed search algorithm explores also a certain number of country roads (low probability differentials). While the list of highways is computed offline prior to the start of the search, the list of country roads is computed on-demand for each input difference to an intermediate round that is encountered during the search. Of all possible country roads that can be taken at a given point (note that there may be a huge number of them), the algorithm considers only the ones that lead back on a highway. If such are not found, then the shortest country road is taken (resp. the maximum probability transition). This strategy prevents the number of explored routes from exploding and at the same time keeps the total probability of the resulting trail high.

Due to the fact that it uses a partial, rather than the full DDT, our algorithm is not guaranteed to find the best differential trail. However experiments[2] on small word sizes of 11, 14 and 16 bits show that the probabilities of the found trails are within a factor of at most 2^{-3} from the probability of the best one.

We demonstrate the proposed tool on block ciphers TEA [40], XTEA [30], SPECK [3] and RAIDEN [32]. Beside being good representatives of the ARX class of algorithms, these ciphers are of interest also due to the fact that results on full (i.e. not truncated) differential trails on them either do not exist (as is the case for TEA, RAIDEN and SPECK) or are scarce (in the case of XTEA). For TEA specifically, in [16, Sect. 1] the authors admit that *it is difficult to find a good differential characteristic.*

By applying our tool, we are able to find multiple differential characteristics for TEA. They cover between 15 and 18 rounds, depending on the value of the key and have probabilities $\approx 2^{-60}$. The 18 round trail, in particular, has probability $\approx 2^{-63}$ for approx. 2^{116} ($\approx 0.1\%$) of all keys. To put those results in perspective, we note that the best differential attack on TEA covers 17 rounds and is based on an impossible differential [8] while the best attack overall applies zero-correlation cryptanalysis and is on 23 rounds but requires the full codebook [6]. For XTEA, we confirm the best previously known full differential trail based on XOR differences [16], but this time it was found in a fully automatic way.

For RAIDEN an iterative characteristic on 3 rounds with probability 2^{-4} is reported. When iterated over all 32 rounds a characteristic with probability 2^{-42} on the full cipher is constructed that can be used to fully break RAIDEN using standard differential cryptanalysis. This is the first analysis of the cipher in a non-related key setting.

We also present results on versions of the recently proposed block cipher SPECK [3] with word sizes 16, 24 and 32 bits resp. SPECK32, SPECK48 and SPECK64. For SPECK64 the best trail found by the tool covers half of the total number of rounds (13 out of 26) and has probability 2^{-58}. The best found trails for 16 and 24 bits cover resp. 9 and 10 rounds out of 22/23 with probabilities resp. 2^{-31} and 2^{-45}.

---

[2] For 11 and 14 bits 50 experiments were performed, while for 16 bits 20 experiments were performed. In each experiment a new fixed key was chosen uniformly at random. More details are provided in Appendix C.1.

Table 1. Maximum number of rounds covered by single (truncated) differential trails used in existing differential attacks on TEA, XTEA, SPECK and RAIDEN compared to the best found trails reported in this paper

Cipher	Type of Trail	#Rounds Covered	#Rounds Total	Ref.
TEA	Trunc.	5	64	[26]
	Trunc.	7		[8]
	Trunc.	8		[16,6]
	Full	**18**		**Sect. 6**
XTEA	Trunc.	6	64	[26]
	Trunc.	7		[8]
	Trunc.	8		[16,6]
	Full	14		[16]
	Full	**14**		**Sect. 6**
SPECK32	**Full**	**9**	22	**Sect. 6**
SPECK48	**Full**	**10**	22/23	**Sect. 6**
SPECK64	**Full**	**13**	26/27	**Sect. 6**
RAIDEN	**Full**	**32**	32	**Sect. 6**

In Table 1 we provide a comparison between the number of rounds covered by single (truncated) differential trails used in existing attacks (where applicable) on TEA, XTEA, SPECK and RAIDEN to the number of rounds covered by the trails found with the tool.

An additional contribution is that the paper is the first to report closed formulas for computing the exact additive differential probabilities of the left and right shift operations. These formulas are derived in a similar way as the ones for computing the DP of left and right rotation reported by Daum [11, Sect. 4.1.3]. Note that Fouque et al. [14] have previously analyzed the propagation of additive differences through the shift operations, but not the corresponding differential probabilities.

The outline is as follows. In Sect. 2 we define partial difference distribution tables (pDDT) and present an efficient method for their computation. Our extension of Matsui's algorithm using pDDT, referred to as *threshold search*, is presented in Sect. 3. It is followed by the description of a general methodology for automatic search for differential trails in ARX ciphers with Feistel structure in Sect. 4. A brief description of block ciphers TEA, XTEA, SPECK and RAIDEN is given in Sect. 5. In Sect. 6 we apply our methods to search for differential trails in the studied ciphers and we show the most relevant experimental results. Finally, in Sect. 7 are discussed general problems and limitations arising when studying differential trails in ARX ciphers. Sect. 8 concludes the paper. Proofs of all theorems and propositions and more experimental results are provided in Appendix.

A few words on notation: with $x[i]$ is denoted the i-th bit of x; $x[i:j]$ represents the sequence of bits $x[j], x[j+1], \ldots, x[i] : j \le i$ where $x[0]$ is the least-significant bit (LSB); x_n denotes the n-bit word x (equivalent to $x[n-1:0]$, but more concise); $\#A$ denotes the number of elements in the set A and $x|y$ is the concatenation of the bit strings x and y.

2   Partial Difference Distribution Tables

In this section as well as in the rest of the paper with xdp^+ and $\mathrm{adp}^\oplus$ are denoted respectively the XOR differential probability (DP) of addition modulo 2^n and the additive DP of XOR. Similarly, the additive differential probability of the operations right bit shift (RSH) and left bit shift (LSH) are denoted resp. with $\mathrm{adp}^{\gg r}$ and $\mathrm{adp}^{\ll r}$. Due to space constrains the formal definition and details on the efficient computation of those probabilities are given in Appendix A and Appendix B.

Definition 1. *A **partial difference distribution table (pDDT)** D for the ADD (resp. XOR) operation is a DDT that contains all XOR (resp. ADD) differentials $(\alpha, \beta \to \gamma)$ whose probabilities are larger than or equal to a pre-defined threshold* p_{thres}:

$$(\alpha, \beta, \gamma) \in D \iff \mathrm{DP}(\alpha, \beta \to \gamma) \geq \mathrm{p}_{thres} \ . \tag{1}$$

*If a DDT contains only a fraction of all differentials that have probability above a pre-defined threshold, it is an **incomplete pDDT**.*

The following proposition is crucial for the efficient computation of a pDDT:

Proposition 1. *The DP of ADD and XOR (resp. xdp^+ and $\mathrm{adp}^\oplus$) are monotonously decreasing with the word size n of the differences α, β, γ:*

$$p_n \leq \cdots \leq p_k \leq p_{k-1} \leq \cdots \leq p_1 \leq p_0 \ , \tag{2}$$

where $p_k = \mathrm{DP}(\alpha_k, \beta_k \to \gamma_k)$, $n \geq k \geq 1$, $p_0 = 1$, and x_k denotes the k LSB-s of the difference x i.e. $x_k = x[k-1:0]$.

Proof. Appendix D.1.

For xdp^+, the proposition follows from the following result by Lipmaa et al. [21]: $\mathrm{xdp}^+(\alpha, \beta \to \gamma) = 2^{-\sum_{i=0}^{n-2} \neg \mathrm{eq}(\alpha[i], \beta[i], \gamma[i])}$, where $\mathrm{eq}(\alpha[i], \beta[i], \gamma[i]) = 1 \iff \alpha[i] = \beta[i] = \gamma[i]$. Proposition 1 is also true for $\mathrm{adp}^\oplus$.

Due to Proposition 1 a recursive procedure for computing a pDDT for a given probability threshold p_{thres} can be defined as follows. Starting at the least-significant (LS) bit position $k = 0$ recursively assign values to bits $\alpha[k]$, $\beta[k]$ and $\gamma[k]$. At every bit position $k : n > k \geq 0$ check if the probability of the partially constructed $(k+1)$-bit differential is still bigger than the threshold i.e. check if $p_k = \mathrm{DP}(\alpha_k, \beta_k \to \gamma_k) \geq p_{thres}$ holds. If yes, then proceed to the next bit position, otherwise backtrack and assign other values to $(\alpha[k], \beta[k], \gamma[k])$. This process is repeated recursively until $k = n$, at which point the differential $(\alpha_n, \beta_n \to \gamma_n)$ is added to the pDDT together with its probability p_n. A pseudo-code of the described procedure is listed in Algorithm 1. The initial values are: $k = 0$, $p_0 = 1$ and $\alpha_0 = \beta_0 = \gamma_0 = \emptyset$.

Algorithm 1. Computation of a pDDT for ADD and XOR.

Input: n, p_{thres}, k, p_k, α_k, β_k, γ_k.
Output: pDDT D: $(\alpha, \beta, \gamma) \in D : \mathrm{DP}(\alpha, \beta \to \gamma) \geq p_{\text{thres}}$.
1: **procedure compute_pddt**$(n, p_{\text{thres}}, k, p_k, \alpha_k, \beta_k, \gamma_k)$ **do**
2:     **if** $n = k$ **then**
3:         Add $(\alpha, \beta, \gamma) \leftarrow (\alpha_k, \beta_k, \gamma_k)$ to D
4:         **return**
5:     **for** $x, y, z \in \{0, 1\}$ **do**
6:         $\alpha_{k+1} \leftarrow x|\alpha_k, \quad \beta_{k+1} \leftarrow y|\beta_k, \quad \gamma_{k+1} \leftarrow z|\gamma_k$.
7:         $p_{k+1} = \mathrm{DP}(\alpha_{k+1}, \beta_{k+1} \to \gamma_{k+1})$
8:         **if** $p_{k+1} \geq p_{\text{thres}}$ **then**
9:             **compute_pddt**$(n, p_{\text{thres}}, k + 1, p_{k+1}, \alpha_{k+1}, \beta_{k+1}, \gamma_{k+1})$

The correctness of Algorithm 1 follows directly from Proposition 1. After successful termination the computed pDDT contains all differentials with probability equal to or larger than the threshold. The complexity of Algorithm 1 depends on the value of the threshold p_{thres}. Some timings for both ADD and XOR differences for different thresholds are provided in Table 2. As can be seen from the data in the table it is infeasible to compute pDDT-s for XOR differences for values of the threshold $p_{\text{thres}} \leq 0.01 = 2^{-6.64}$, while for ADD differences this is still possible, but requires significant time (more than 17 hours).

Table 2. Timings on the computation of pDDT for ADD and XOR on 32-bit words using Algorithm 1. Target machine: Intel® Core™ i7-2600, 3.40GHz CPU, 8GB RAM.

	ADD		XOR	
p_{thres}	#elements in pDDT	Time	#elements in pDDT	Time
0.1	252 940	36 *sec.*	3 951 388	1.23 *min.*
0.07	361 420	37 *sec.*	3 951 388	2.29 *min.*
0.05	3 038 668	5.35 *min.*	167 065 948	44.36 *min.*
0.01	2 715 532 204	17.46 *hours*	$\geq$ 72 589 325 174	$\geq$ 29 *days*

3 Threshold Search

In his paper from 1994 [23] Matsui proposed a practical algorithm for searching for the best differential trail (and linear approximation) for the DES block cipher. The algorithm performs a recursive search for differential trails over a given number of rounds $n \geq 1$. From knowledge of the best probabilities $B_1, B_2, \ldots, B_{n-1}$ for the first $(n - 1)$ rounds and an initial estimate $\overline{B}_n$ for the probability for n rounds it derives the best probability B_n for n rounds. For the estimate the following must hold: $\overline{B}_n \leq B_n$. As already noted, Matsui's algorithm is applicable to block ciphers that have S-boxes. In this section we extend it to the case of ciphers without S-boxes such as ARX by applying the concept of pDDT.

We describe the extended algorithm next. Its description in pseudo-code is listed in Algorithm 2.

In addition to Matsui's notation for the probability of the best n-round trail B_n and of its estimate $\overline{B}_n$ we introduce $\widehat{B}_n$ to denote the probability of *the best found* trail for n rounds: $\overline{B}_n \leq \widehat{B}_n \leq B_n$. Given a pDDT H of size m, an estimation for the best n-round probability $\overline{B}_n$ with its corresponding n-round differential trail $\overline{T}$ and the probabilities $\widehat{B}_1, \widehat{B}_2, \ldots, \widehat{B}_{n-1}$ of the best found trails for the first $n - 1$ rounds, Algorithm 2 outputs an n-round trail $\widehat{T}$ that has probability $\widehat{B}_n \geq \overline{B}_n$.

Similarly to Matsui's algorithm, Algorithm 2 operates by recursively extending a trail for i rounds to $(i + 1)$ rounds, beginning with $i = 1$ and terminating at $i = n$. The recursion at level i continues to level $(i + 1)$ only if the probability of the constructed i-round trail multiplied by the probability of the best found trail for $(n - i)$ rounds is at least $\overline{B}_n$ i.e. if $p_1 p_2 \ldots p_i \widehat{B}_{n-i} \geq \overline{B}_n$. For $i = n$ the last equation is equivalent to: $p_1 p_2 \ldots p_n = \widehat{B}_n \geq \overline{B}_n$. If the latter holds, the initial estimate is updated with the new: $\overline{B}_n \leftarrow \widehat{B}_n$ and the corresponding trail is also updated accordingly: $\overline{T}_n \leftarrow \widehat{T}_n$.

During the search process Algorithm 2 explores multiple differential trails. It is important to stress that the differentials that compose those trails are not restricted to the entries from the initial pDDT H. The latter represent only the starting point of the first two rounds of the search, as in those rounds both the input and the output differences of the round transformation can be freely chosen (due to the specifics of the Feistel structure). From the third round onwards, excluding the last round, beside the entries in H the algorithm explores also an additional set of low-probability differentials stored in a temporary pDDT C and sharing the same input difference.

The table C is computed on demand for each input difference to an intermediate round (any round other than the first two and the last) encountered during the search. All entries in C additionally satisfy the following two conditions: (1) Their probabilities are such that they can still improve the probability of the best found trail for the given number of rounds i.e. if (α_r, β_r, p_r) is an entry in C for round r, then $p_r \geq \overline{B}_n / (p_1 p_2 \cdots p_{r-1} \widehat{B}_{n-r})$; (2) Their structure is such that they guarantee that the input difference for the next round $\alpha_{r+1} = \alpha_{r-1} + \beta_r$ will have a matching entry in H. While the need for condition (1) is self-evident, condition (2) is necessary in order to prevent the exploding of the size of C while at the same time keeping the probability of the resulting trail high. The meaning of the tables H and C is further clarified with the following analogy.

Example 1 (The Highways and Country Roads Analogy). The two tables H and C employed in the search performed by Algorithm 2 can be thought of as lists of highways and country roads on a map. The differentials contained in H have high probabilities w.r.t. to the fixed probability threshold and correspond therefore to fast roads such as *highways*. Analogously, the differentials in C have low probabilities and can be seen as slow roads or *country roads*. To continue this analogy, the problem of finding a high probability differential trail for n rounds can be seen as a problem of finding a fast route between points 1 and n on the

---

Algorithm 2. Matsui Search for Differential Trails Using pDDT (Threshold Search).

Input: n: number of rounds; **r**: current round; **H**: pDDT; $\widehat{\mathbf{B}} = (\widehat{\mathbf{B}}_1, \widehat{\mathbf{B}}_2, \ldots, \widehat{\mathbf{B}}_{n-1})$: probs. of best found trails for the first $(n-1)$ rounds; $\overline{\mathbf{B}}_n \leq \mathbf{B}_n$: initial estimate; $\overline{\mathbf{T}} = (\overline{\mathbf{T}}_1, \ldots, \overline{\mathbf{T}}_n)$: trail for n rounds with prob. $\overline{B}_n$; $\mathbf{p}_{thres}$: probability threshold.
Output: $\widehat{\mathbf{B}}_n, \widehat{\mathbf{T}} = (\widehat{\mathbf{T}}_1, \ldots, \widehat{\mathbf{T}}_n)$: trail for n rounds with prob. $\widehat{B}_n : \overline{B}_n \leq \widehat{B}_n \leq B_n$.

1: **procedure** threshold_search($n, r, H, \widehat{B}, \overline{B}_n, \overline{T}$) **do**
2:     // Process rounds 1 and 2
3:     **if** $((r = 1) \lor (r = 2)) \land (r \neq n)$ **then**
4:         **for** all (α, β, p) in H **do**
5:             $p_r \leftarrow p, \quad \widehat{B}_n \leftarrow p_1 \cdots p_r \widehat{B}_{n-r}$
6:             **if** $\widehat{B}_n \geq \overline{B}_n$ **then**
7:                 $\alpha_r \leftarrow \alpha, \quad \beta_r \leftarrow \beta, \quad$ **add** $\widehat{T}_r \leftarrow (\alpha_r, \beta_r, p_r)$ to $\widehat{T}$
8:                 call **threshold_search**($n, r + 1, H, \widehat{B}, \overline{B}_n, \widehat{T}$)
9:     // Process intermediate rounds
10:    **if** $(r > 2) \land (r \neq n)$ **then**
11:        $\alpha_r \leftarrow (\alpha_{r-2} + \beta_{r-1}); \quad p_{r,\min} \leftarrow \overline{B}_n/(p_1 p_2 \cdots p_{r-1} \widehat{B}_{n-r})$
12:        $C \leftarrow \emptyset$ // Initialize the country roads table
13:        **for** all $\beta_r : (p_r(\alpha_r \rightarrow \beta_r) \geq p_{r,\min}) \land ((\alpha_{r-1} + \beta_r) = \gamma \in H)$ **do**
14:            **add** (α_r, β_r, p_r) to C // Update country roads table
15:        **if** $C = \emptyset$ **then**
16:            $(\beta_r, p_r) \leftarrow p_r = \max_\beta p(\alpha_r \rightarrow \beta);$ **add** (α_r, β_r, p_r) to C
17:        **for** all $(\alpha, \beta, p) : \alpha = \alpha_r$ in H and all $(\alpha, \beta, p) \in C$ **do**
18:            $p_r \leftarrow p, \quad \widehat{B}_n \leftarrow p_1 p_2 \ldots p_r \widehat{B}_{n-r}$
19:            **if** $\widehat{B}_n \geq \overline{B}_n$ **then**
20:                $\beta_r \leftarrow \beta, \quad$ **add** $\widehat{T}_r \leftarrow (\alpha_r, \beta_r, p_r)$ to $\widehat{T}$
21:                call **threshold_search**($n, r + 1, H, \widehat{B}, \overline{B}_n, \widehat{T}$)
22:    // Process last round
23:    **if** $(r = n)$ **then**
24:        $\alpha_r \leftarrow (\alpha_{r-2} + \beta_{r-1})$
25:        **if** $(\alpha_r$ in $H)$ **then**
26:            $(\beta_r, p_r) \leftarrow p_r = \max_{\beta \in H} p(\alpha_r \rightarrow \beta)$ // Select the max. from the highway table
27:        **else**
28:            $(\beta_r, p_r) \leftarrow p_r = \max_\beta p(\alpha_r \rightarrow \beta)$ // Compute the max.
29:            **if** $p_r \geq p_{thres}$ **then**
30:                **add** (α_r, β_r, p_r) to H
31:        $p_n \leftarrow p_r, \quad \widehat{B}_n \leftarrow p_1 p_2 \ldots p_n$
32:        **if** $\widehat{B}_n \geq \overline{B}_n$ **then**
33:            $\alpha_n \leftarrow \alpha_r, \quad \beta_n \leftarrow \beta, \quad$ **add** $\widehat{T}_n \leftarrow (\alpha_n, \beta_n, p_n)$ to $\widehat{T}$
34:            $\overline{B}_n \leftarrow \widehat{B}_n, \quad \overline{T} \leftarrow \widehat{T}$
35:    $\widehat{B}_n \leftarrow \overline{B}_n, \quad \widehat{T} \leftarrow \overline{T}$ // Update the target bound and the best found trail
36:    **return** $\widehat{B}_n, \widehat{T}$

---

map. Clearly such a route must be composed of as many highways as possible. Condition (2), mentioned above, essentially guarantees that any country road that we may take in our search for a fast route will bring us back on a highway. Note that it is possible that the fastest route contains two or more country roads in sequence. While such a case will be missed by Algorithm 2, it may be accounted for by lowering the initial probability threshold.

Algorithm 2 terminates when the initial estimate $\overline{B}_n$ can not be further improved. The complexity of Algorithm 2 depends on the following factors: (1) the closeness of the best found probabilities $\widehat{B}_1, \widehat{B}_2, \ldots, \widehat{B}_{n-1}$ for the first $(n-1)$ rounds to the actual best probabilities, (2) the tightness of the initial estimate $\overline{B}_n$ and (3) the number of elements m in H. The latter is determined by the probability threshold used to compute H.

4   General Methodology for Automatic Search for Differential Trails in ARX

We describe a general methodology for the automatic search for differential trails in ARX algorithms. In our analysis we restrict ourselves to Feistel ciphers, although the proposed method is applicable to other ARX designs as well.

Let F be the round function (the F-function) of a Feistel cipher E, designed by combining a number of ARX operations, such as XOR, ADD, bit shift and bit rotation. To search for differential trails for multiple rounds of E perform the following steps:

1. Derive an expression for computing the differential probability (DP) of F for given input and output difference. The computation may be an approximation obtained as the multiplication of the DP of the components of F.
2. Compute a pDDT for F. It can be an incomplete pDDT obtained e.g. by merging the separate pDDT-s of the different components of F.
3. Execute the threshold search algorithm described in Sect.3 with the (incomplete) pDDT computed in Step. 2 as input.

In the following sections we apply the proposed methodology to automatically search for differential trails in several ARX-based block ciphers.

5   Description of TEA, XTEA, SPECK and RAIDEN

The Tiny Encryption Algorithm (TEA) is a block cipher designed by Wheeler and Needham and presented at FSE 1994 [40]. It has a Feistel structure composed of 64 rounds. Each round operates on 64-bit blocks divided into two 32-bit words $L_i, R_i : 0 \leq i \leq 64$, so that $P = L_0 | R_0$ is the plaintext and $C = L_{64} | R_{64}$ is the ciphertext. TEA has 128-bit key K composed of four 32-bit words: $K = K_3 | K_2 | K_1 | K_0$. The key schedule is such that the same two key words are used at every second round i.e. K_0, K_1 are used in all odd rounds and K_2, K_3 are used in all even rounds. Additionally, thirty-two 32-bit constants $\delta_r : 1 \leq r < 32$ (the

δ constants) are defined. A different δ constant is used at every second round. The round function F of TEA takes as input a 32-bit value x, two 32-bit key words k_0, k_1 and a round constant δ and produces a 32-bit output $F(x)$. For fixed δ, k_0 and k_1, F is defined as:

$$(\delta, k_0, k_1) : F(x) = ((x \ll 4) + k_0) \oplus (x + \delta) \oplus ((x \gg 5) + k_1) . \qquad (3)$$

For fixed round keys $K_j, K_{j+1} : j \in \{0,2\}$ and round constant δ_r, round i of TEA $(1 \leq i < 64)$ is described as: $L_{i+1} = R_i$, $R_{i+1} = L_i + F(R_i)$.

XTEA is an extended version of TEA proposed in [30] by the same designers. It was designed in order to address two weaknesses of TEA pointed by Kelsey et al. [18]: (1) a related-key attack on the full TEA and (2) the fact that the effective key size of TEA is 126, rather than 128 bits. The structure of XTEA is very similar to the one of TEA: 64-round Feistel network operating on 64-bit blocks using a 128-bit key. The main difference is in the key schedule: at every round XTEA uses one rather than two 32-bit key words from the original key according to a new non-periodic key schedule. Additionally, the number of δ constants is increased from 32 to 64 and thus a different constant is used at every round. The F-function of XTEA is also slightly modified and for a fixed round key k and round constant δ is defined as:

$$(\delta, k) : F(x) = (\delta + k) \oplus (x + ((x \ll 4) \oplus (x \gg 5))) . \qquad (4)$$

The F-functions of TEA and XTEA are depicted in Fig. 1.

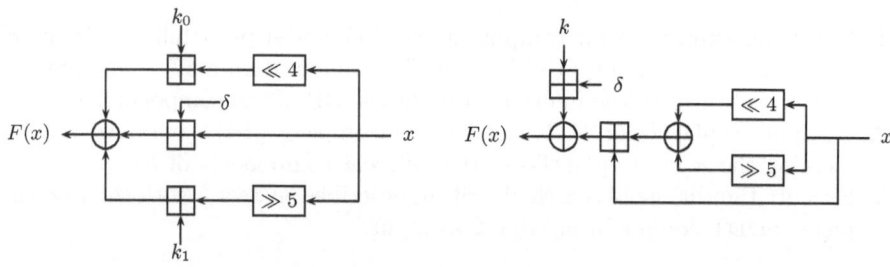

Fig. 1. The F-functions of TEA (left) and XTEA (right)

In [32] Polimón et al. have proposed a variant of TEA called RAIDEN. It has been designed by applying genetic programming algorithms to automatically evolve a highly non-linear round function. The latter is composed of the same operations as TEA (arranged in different order) but is more efficient and has better mixing properties as measured by its avalanche effect. As a result RAIDEN is claimed to be competitive to TEA in terms of security. It has 32 rounds and its round function is:

$$F_k(x) = ((k + x) \ll 9) \oplus (k - x) \oplus ((k + x) \gg 14) . \qquad (5)$$

The key k in (5) is updated every second round according to a new key schedule and therefore every two consecutive rounds use the same key. The main differences with TEA are that in (5) the round constant δ is discarded, the shift constants are changed and the shift operations are moved *after* the key addition (see Fig. 2, left). For more details on the RAIDEN cipher we refer the reader to [32]. The only previous security result for RAIDEN is a related-key attack reported in [17].

Most recently, in June 2013, a new family of ARX-based lightweight block ciphers SPECK [3] was proposed by researchers from the National Security Agency (NSA) of the USA. Its design bears strong similarity to Threefish – the block cipher used in the hash function Skein [13]. The round function of SPECK under a fixed round key k is defined on inputs x and y as

$$F_k(x, y) = (f_k(x, y), \; f_k(x, y) \oplus (y \lll t_2)) \; , \qquad (6)$$

where the function $f_k(\cdot, \cdot)$ is defined as $f_k(x, y) = ((x \ggg t_1) + y) \oplus k$. The rotation constants t_1 and t_2 are equal to 7 and 2 resp. for word size $n = 16$ bits and to 8 and 3 for all other word sizes: $24, 32, 48$ and 64. Note that although SPECK is not a Feistel cipher itself, it can be represented as a composition of two Feistel maps as described in [3]. At the time of this writing we are not aware of any published results on the security analysis of SPECK. The round functions of RAIDEN and SPECK are shown in Fig. 2.

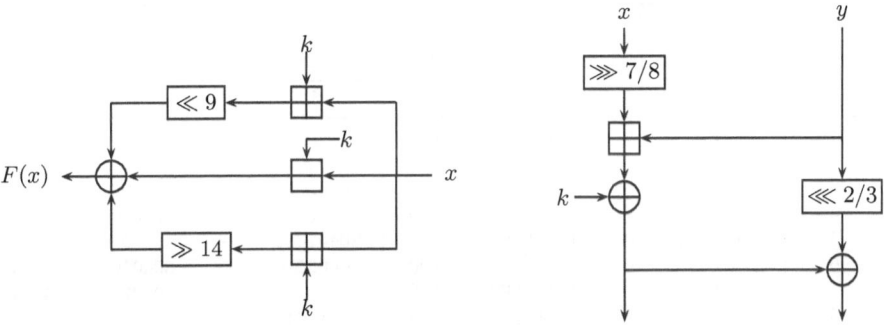

Fig. 2. The F-functions of RAIDEN (left) and SPECK (right)

In Table 1 are listed the maximum number of rounds covered by differential trail/s used in published differential attacks on TEA, XTEA, RAIDEN and SPECK. These results are compared with the best trails found using our method.

6 Automatic Search for Differential Trails

We apply the steps from Sect. 4 to search for differential trails for multiple rounds of the block ciphers described in Sect. 5. We analyze TEA, RAIDEN and SPECK w.r.t. ADD differences and XTEA w.r.t. XOR differences. Additive differences are more appropriate for the differential analysis of the former (as opposed to XOR differences) due to two reasons. First, the round keys and round constants are ADD-ed. Second, the number of ADD vs. XOR operations in one round is larger and therefore more components are linear w.r.t. ADD than to XOR. Similarly, XTEA is more suitably analyzed with XOR differences since the round keys are XOR-ed.

In Table 3 (left) is shown the best found ADD differential trail for 18 rounds of TEA with probability $2^{-62.6}$ and on the right side is shown the best found XOR trail for 14 rounds of XTEA with probability $2^{-60.76}$ confirming a previous result by Hong et al. [16]. Note that while the rule that a country road must be followed by a highway is strictly respected in the trail for TEA, this is not the case for XTEA. For example transitions 6 and 7 in the trail for XTEA have prob. resp. $2^{-5.35}$ and $2^{-5.36}$ both of which are below the threshold $p_{\text{thres}} = 2^{-4.32}$. In those cases no country road that leads back on a highway was found and so the shortest country road was taken (resp. the maximum probability transition for the given input difference was computed: lines 15–16 of Algorithm 2).

The top line of Table 3 shows the fixed values of the keys for which the two trails were found and for which their probabilities were experimentally verified.

Table 3. Differential trails for TEA and XTEA. The leftmost key word is K_0, the next is K_1, etc. #hways lists the number of elements in the pDDT (the highways).

	TEA				XTEA			
key	11CAD84E 96168E6B 704A8B1C 57BBE5D3				E15C838 DC8DBE76 B3BB0110 FFBB0440			
r	β		α	$\log_2 p$	β		α	$\log_2 p$
1	F	←	FFFFFFFF	−3.62	0	←	80402010	−4.61
2	0	←	0	−0.00	80402010	←	0	−3.01
3	F	←	FFFFFFFF	−2.87	80402010	←	80402010	−5.48
4	0	←	F	−7.90	0	←	80402010	−3.30
5	FFFFFFF1	←	FFFFFFFF	−3.60	80402010	←	0	−3.01
6	0	←	0	−0.00	80402010	←	80402010	−5.35
7	FFFFFFF1	←	FFFFFFFF	−2.78	0	←	80402010	−5.36
8	2	←	FFFFFFF1	−8.66	80402010	←	0	−2.99
9	F	←	1	−3.57	80402010	←	80402010	−5.45
10	0	←	0	−0.00	0	←	80402010	−5.42
11	FFFFFFF1	←	1	−2.87	80402010	←	0	−2.99
12	FFFFFFFE	←	FFFFFFF1	−7.90	80402010	←	80402010	−5.38
13	F	←	FFFFFFFF	−3.59	0	←	80402010	−5.40
14	0	←	0	−0.00	80402010	←	0	−2.99
15	11	←	FFFFFFFF	−2.79				
16	0	←	11	−8.83				
17	FFFFFFEF	←	FFFFFFFF	−3.61				
18	0	←	0	−0.00				
$\sum_r \log_2 p_r$				−62.6				−60.76
$\log_2 p_{\text{thres}}$				−4.32				−4.32
#hways				68				474
Time:				21.36 min.				315 min.

The reason to perform the search for a fixed key rather than averaged over all keys is the fact that for TEA the assumption of independent round keys, commonly made in differential cryptanalysis, does not hold. This is a consequence of the simple key schedule of the cipher according to which the same round keys are re-used every second round. Thus a trail that has very good probability computed as an average over all keys, may in fact have zero probability for many or even all keys. This problem is further discussed in Sect. 7.

The mentioned effect is not so strong for XTEA due to the slightly more complex key schedule of the latter. In XTEA, the round keys are re-used according to a non-periodic schedule and, more importantly, a round constant that is different for every round, is added to the key before it is applied to the state (see Fig. 1). In this way the round keys are randomized in every round and thus the traditional differential analysis with probabilities computed as an average over all keys is more appropriate for XTEA.

A major consequence of the key dependency effect discussed above is that while the 14 round trail for XTEA from Table 3 can directly be used in a key-recovery attack, as has indeed been already done in [16], it is not straightforward to do so for the 18 round trail for TEA. The reason is that this trail is valid only for a fraction of all keys. We have estimated the size of this fraction to be approx. $0.098\% \approx 0.1\%$, which is equal to 2^{116} weak keys (note that the effective key size of TEA is 126 bits [18]). The size of the weak key class was computed by observing that only the 9 LS bits of K_2 and the 3 LS bits of K_3 influence the probability of the trail. By fixing those 12 bits to the corresponding bits of the key values in Table 3 (resp. 0x11C and 0x3), we have experimentally verified that for any assignment of the remaning 116 bits of the key the 18 round trail has probability $\approx 2^{-63}$. Note that other assignments of the relevant 12 bits may also be possible and therefore the size of the weak key class may be actually bigger.

While the fixed-key trails for TEA found by the threshold search algorithm may have limited use for an attacker due to the reasons discussed above, they already provide very useful information for a designer. By running Algorithm 2 for many fixed keys we saw that the best found trails typically cover between 15 and 17 rounds and in more rare cases 18 rounds. If this information has been available to the designers of TEA at the time of the design, they may have considered reducing the total number of rounds from 64 to 32 or less. Similarly, the threshold search algorithm can be used in order to estimate the security of new ARX designs and to help to select the appropriate number of rounds accordingly.

Comparisons of the trails found with the tool to the actual best trails on TEA with reduced word size of 11 and 16 bits are shown in Appendix C.1.

After applying the threshold search to RAIDEN the best characteristic that was found is iterative with period 3 with probability 2^{-4} (shown in Table 4). By iterating it for 32 rounds we construct a charactersistic with probability 2^{-42}. The latter can be used in a standard differential attack on the full cipher under a non related-key setting. Note that in contrast to TEA, the probabilities of the

Table 4. Three round iterative characteristic for RAIDEN beginning at round i

r	β		α	$\log_2 p$
i	0	$\leftarrow$	0	-0
$i+1$	7FFFFF00	$\leftarrow$	7FFFFF00	-2
$i+2$	80000100	$\leftarrow$	7FFFFF00	-2
...	...	$\leftarrow$	0	-0
$\sum_r \log_2 p_r$				-4

reported differentials for RAIDEN are independent of the round key due to the fact that the shift operations are moved *after* the key addition.

We applied the threshold search algorithm using XOR differences to three instances of block cipher SPECK with 16, 24 and 32 bit word sizes respectively. The best trail found for the 32-bit version covers half of the rounds (13 out of 26) and has probability 2^{-58} while the best found trails for 16 and 24 bits cover resp. 9 and 10 rounds out of 22/23 and have probabilities resp. 2^{-31} and 2^{-45}. All trails are shown in Table 5.

Table 5. Differential trails for SPECK32, SPECK48 and SPECK64. #hways lists the number of elements in the pDDT (the highways).

	SPECK32			SPECK48			SPECK64		
r	Δ_L	Δ_R	$\log_2 p$	Δ_L	Δ_R	$\log_2 p$	Δ_L	Δ_R	$\log_2 p$
0	A60	4205	-0	88A	484008	-0	802490	10800004	-0
1	211	A04	-5	424000	4042	-5	80808020	4808000	-5
2	2800	10	-4	202	20012	-4	24000080	40080	-5
3	40	0	-2	10	100080	-3	80200080	80000480	-3
4	8000	8000	-0	80	800480	-2	802480	800084	-4
5	8100	8102	-1	480	2084	-2	808080A0	84808480	-5
6	8000	840A	-2	802080	8124A0	-3	24000400	42004	-6
7	850A	9520	-4	A480	98184	-6	202000	12020	-4
8	802A	D4A8	-6	888020	C48C00	-7	10000	80100	-3
9	A8	520B	-7	240480	6486	-7	80000	480800	-2
10				800082	8324B2	-6	480000	2084000	-3
11							2080800	124A0800	-4
12							12480008	80184008	-7
13							880A0808	88C8084C	-7
$\sum_r \log_2 p_r$		-31			-45			-58	
$\log_2 p_{thres}$		-5.00			-5.00			-5.00	
#hways		2^{30}			2^{30}			2^{30}	
Time:		≈ 240 min.			≈ 400 min.			≈ 500 min.	

7   Difficulties, Limitations and Common Problems

In this section we discuss the common problems and difficulties encountered when studying differential trails in ARX ciphers. This discussion is also naturally related to the limitations of the methodology proposed in Sect. 4. Although below we often use the TEA block cipher as an example, our observations are general and are therefore applicable to a broader class of ARX algorithms.

Accuracy of the Approximation of the DP of F. The first step in the methodology presented in Sect. 4 is to derive an expression for computing the DP of the F-function of the target cipher. Since it is often difficult to efficiently compute the exact probability, this expression would usually be an approximation obtained as the multiplication of the DP of the separate components of F. The probability computed in this way will often deviate from the actual value due to the dependency between the inputs of the different components. Indeed, this phenomenon is well-known and has been studied before e.g. in [38]. The mentioned problem can be addressed with experimental *re-adjustment* of the probability by evaluating the F-function over a number of random chosen input pairs satisfying the input difference.

Dependency of the DP of F on the Round Keys. Another difficulty arises from the fact that in some cases the DP of the F-function is dependent on the value of the round key(s). Ciphers for which this is the case are *not* key-alternating ciphers (cf. [10, Definition 2]) and are typically harder to analyze. The block cipher TEA is an example of a non-key-alternating cipher. The DP of its F-function is key-dependent w.r.t. both XOR and ADD differences. A solution to the problem of key-dependency of the DP of the F-function is to search for differential trails with probabilities computed for (multiple) fixed keys rather than for trails with probabilities averaged over all keys. As discussed in Sect. 6, this is the approach that we took in the analysis of TEA.

Dependency Between the Round Keys. In differential cryptanalysis of keyed primitives it is common practice to assume that the round keys are independent [19]. This is known as *making the hypothesis of independent round keys* [10]. In ciphers with weak key schedule such as TEA the hypothesis of independent round keys does not hold. As a consequence, obtaining an accurate estimation of the expected probabilities of differential trails in such ciphers is difficult. A possible solution to the dependent round keys problem is to analyze the cipher with respect to a set of randomly chosen fixed keys and consider the minimum probability, among all keys within the set (rather than the expected probabilities averaged over all keys). The reason to select the minimum probability is to guarantee that the resulting differential trail is possible (i.e. has non-zero probability) for every key in the set.

Influence of the Round Constants. Fixed constants are commonly used in the design of symmetric-key primitives in order to destroy similarities between the rounds. Since they are typically added to the state by applying the same operation as for the round keys, it is generally assumed that constants influence neither the probabilities nor the structure of differential trails and hence can be safely ignored. Surprisingly, this assumption does not hold for TEA and possibly for other ARX constructions as well. After modifying TEA to use the same δ constant at every round, for many keys the best found trail after several rounds eventually becomes iterative with period 2 and of the form $(\alpha \to 0), (0 \to 0), (\alpha \to 0), \dots$. The difference that maximizes the probability of the differential $(\alpha \to 0)$ is $\alpha = \texttt{0xF}$ and has probability 2^{-8} for exactly $6 \cdot 2^{59} \approx 2^{61.6}$ keys (approx. 10% of all keys). We use the two-round iterative trail $(\texttt{0xF} \to 0), (0 \to 0)$ to construct a trail over 15 rounds with probability 2^{-56}. We also found a 4-round iterative pattern with probability $< 2^{-15}$ which holds for a smaller number of key and is used to construct a trail with probability $2^{-61.36}$ on 18 rounds of the modified TEA.

8   Conclusions and Future Work

In this paper we proposed the first extension of Matsui's algorithm for automatic search for differential trails, originally proposed for S-box based ciphers, to the class of ARX ciphers. We used the block ciphers TEA, XTEA, RAIDEN and SPECK as a testbed for demonstrating the practical application of this method.

Using the proposed algorithm, the first full (i.e. not truncated) differential trails for block cipher TEA were found. The best one covers 18 rounds which is one round more than the best differential attack on TEA (17 rounds) and significantly improves the best previously known truncated trail which is on 8 rounds. Trails on 9, 10 and 13 rounds of SPECK32, SPECK48 and SPECK64 resp. were also reported. They represent the first public security analysis of the cipher. For RAIDEN, a trail on all 32 rounds was shown that can be used to break the full cipher. The best trail for XTEA found by the tool confirms the previous known best trail, but this time it was found in a fully automatic way.

For future work, an important problem on the theoretical side would be to compute a bound on how far the probabilities of the best found trails can be from the actual best trail in terms of the fixed probability threshold. On the practical side it would be interesting to extend the algorithm to search for differentials rather than characteristics. Applying the tool to other ARX constructions is another natural direction for future work.

Acknowledgments. We thank our colleagues from the laboratory of algorithmics, cryptology and security (LACS) at the university of Luxembourg for the useful discussions, and especially Yann Le Corre for his help with visualizing the experimental data. We further thank the anonymous reviewers for their time and helpful comments. Some of the experiments presented in this paper were carried out using the HPC facility of the University of Luxembourg.

References

1. Aumasson, J.-P., Bernstein, D.J.: SipHash: a fast short-input PRF. IACR Cryptology ePrint Archive, 2012:351 (2012)
2. Aumasson, J.-P., Henzen, L., Meier, W., Phan, R.C.-W.: SHA-3 proposal BLAKE. Submission to the NIST SHA-3 Competition, Round 2 (2008)
3. Beaulieu, R., Shors, D., Smith, J., Treatman-Clark, S., Weeks, B., Wingers, L.: The SIMON and SPECK Families of Lightweight Block Ciphers. Cryptology ePrint Archive, Report 2013/404 (2013), http://eprint.iacr.org/
4. Bernstein, D.J.: The Salsa20 Family of Stream Ciphers. In: Robshaw, M., Billet, O. (eds.) New Stream Cipher Designs. LNCS, vol. 4986, pp. 84–97. Springer, Heidelberg (2008)
5. Biham, E., Shamir, A.: Differential Cryptanalysis of DES-like Cryptosystems. J. Cryptology 4(1), 3–72 (1991)
6. Bogdanov, A., Wang, M.: Zero Correlation Linear Cryptanalysis with Reduced Data Complexity. In: Canteaut [7], pp. 29–48
7. Canteaut, A. (ed.): FSE 2012. LNCS, vol. 7549. Springer, Heidelberg (2012)
8. Chen, J., Wang, M., Preneel, B.: Impossible Differential Cryptanalysis of the Lightweight Block Ciphers TEA, XTEA and HIGHT. In: Mitrokotsa, A., Vaudenay, S. (eds.) AFRICACRYPT 2012. LNCS, vol. 7374, pp. 117–137. Springer, Heidelberg (2012)
9. Daemen, J., Rijmen, V.: The Design of Rijndael: AES - The Advanced Encryption Standard. Springer (2002)
10. Daemen, J., Rijmen, V.: Probability distributions of Correlation and Differentials in Block Ciphers. IACR Cryptology ePrint Archive, 2005:212 (2005)
11. Daum, M.: Cryptanalysis of Hash Functions of the MD4-Family. PhD thesis, Ruhr-Universität Bochum (2005)
12. De Cannière, C., Rechberger, C.: Finding SHA-1 Characteristics: General Results and Applications. In: Lai, X., Chen, K. (eds.) ASIACRYPT 2006. LNCS, vol. 4284, pp. 1–20. Springer, Heidelberg (2006)
13. Ferguson, N., Lucks, S., Schneier, B., Whiting, D., Bellare, M., Kohno, T., Callas, J., Walker, J.: The Skein Hash Function Family. Submission to the NIST SHA-3 Competition, Round 2 (2009)
14. Fouque, P.-A., Leurent, G., Nguyen, P.Q.: Automatic Search of Differential Path in MD4. IACR Cryptology ePrint Archive, 2007:206 (2007)
15. Hong, D., Sung, J., Hong, S., Lim, J., Lee, S., Koo, B., Lee, C., Chang, D., Lee, J., Jeong, K., Kim, H., Kim, J., Chee, S.: Hight: A new block cipher suitable for low-resource device. In: Goubin, L., Matsui, M. (eds.) CHES 2006. LNCS, vol. 4249, pp. 46–59. Springer, Heidelberg (2006)
16. Hong, S., Hong, D., Ko, Y., Chang, D., Lee, W., Lee, S.: Differential Cryptanalysis of TEA and XTEA. In: Lim, J.-I., Lee, D.-H. (eds.) ICISC 2003. LNCS, vol. 2971, pp. 402–417. Springer, Heidelberg (2004)
17. Karroumi, M., Malherbe, C.: Related-key cryptanalysis of raiden. In: International Conference on Network and Service Security, N2S 2009, pp. 1–5 (2009)
18. Kelsey, J., Schneier, B., Wagner, D.: Related-key cryptanalysis of 3-WAY, Biham-DES, CAST, DES-X, NewDES, RC2, and TEA. In: Han, Y., Quing, S. (eds.) ICICS 1997. LNCS, vol. 1334, pp. 233–246. Springer, Heidelberg (1997)

19. Lai, X., Massey, J.L.: Markov ciphers and differential cryptanalysis. In: Davies, D.W. (ed.) EUROCRYPT 1991. LNCS, vol. 547, pp. 17–38. Springer, Heidelberg (1991)

20. Leurent, G.: Construction of Differential Characteristics in ARX Designs - Application to Skein. IACR Cryptology ePrint Archive, 2012:668 (2012)

21. Lipmaa, H., Moriai, S.: Efficient Algorithms for Computing Differential Properties of Addition. In: Matsui, M. (ed.) FSE 2001. LNCS, vol. 2355, pp. 336–350. Springer, Heidelberg (2002)

22. Lipmaa, H., Wallén, J., Dumas, P.: On the Additive Differential Probability of Exclusive-Or. In: Roy, B., Meier, W. (eds.) FSE 2004. LNCS, vol. 3017, pp. 317–331. Springer, Heidelberg (2004)

23. Matsui, M.: On Correlation between the Order of S-Boxes and the Strength of DES. In: De Santis, A. (ed.) EUROCRYPT 1994. LNCS, vol. 950, pp. 366–375. Springer, Heidelberg (1995)

24. Matsui, M., Yamagishi, A.: A New Method for Known Plaintext Attack of FEAL Cipher. In: Rueppel, R.A. (ed.) EUROCRYPT 1992. LNCS, vol. 658, pp. 81–91. Springer, Heidelberg (1993)

25. Mendel, F., Nad, T., Schläffer, M.: Finding SHA-2 Characteristics: Searching through a Minefield of Contradictions. In: Lee, D.H., Wang, X. (eds.) ASIACRYPT 2011. LNCS, vol. 7073, pp. 288–307. Springer, Heidelberg (2011)

26. Moon, D., Hwang, K., Lee, W.I., Lee, S.-J., Lim, J.-I.: Impossible Differential Cryptanalysis of Reduced Round XTEA and TEA. In: Daemen, J., Rijmen, V. (eds.) FSE 2002. LNCS, vol. 2365, pp. 49–60. Springer, Heidelberg (2002)

27. Mouha, N., Velichkov, V., De Cannière, C., Preneel, B.: The Differential Analysis of S-Functions. In: Biryukov, A., Gong, G., Stinson, D.R. (eds.) SAC 2010. LNCS, vol. 6544, pp. 36–56. Springer, Heidelberg (2011)

28. National Institute of Standards and Technology. Announcing Request for Candidate Algorithm Nominations for a New Cryptographic Hash Algorithm (SHA-3) Family. Federal Register 27(212), 62212–62220 (November 2007), http://csrc.nist.gov/groups/ST/hash/documents/FR_Notice_Nov07.pdf (October 17, 2008)

29. National Institute of Standards, U.S. Department of Commerce. FIPS 47: Data Encryption Standard (1977)

30. Needham, R.M., Wheeler, D.J.: TEA extensions. Computer Laboratory, Cambridge University, England (1997), http://www.movable-type.co.uk/scripts/xtea.pdf

31. Needham, R.M., Wheeler, D.J.: Correction to XTEA. Technical report, University of Cambridge (October 1998)

32. Polimón, J., Castro, J.C.H., Estévez-Tapiador, J.M., Ribagorda, A.: Automated design of a lightweight block cipher with Genetic Programming. KES Journal 12(1), 3–14 (2008)

33. Preneel, B. (ed.): FSE 1994. LNCS, vol. 1008. Springer, Heidelberg (1995)

34. Rivest, R.L.: The MD4 Message Digest Algorithm. In: Menezes, A., Vanstone, S.A. (eds.) CRYPTO 1990. LNCS, vol. 537, pp. 303–311. Springer, Heidelberg (1991)

35. Rivest, R.L.: The MD5 Message-Digest Algorithm. RFC 1321 (April 1992)

36. Rivest, R.L.: The RC5 Encryption Algorithm. In: Preneel [33], pp. 86–96

37. Shimizu, A., Miyaguchi, S.: Fast Data Encipherment Algorithm FEAL. In: Price, W.L., Chaum, D. (eds.) EUROCRYPT 1987. LNCS, vol. 304, pp. 267–278. Springer, Heidelberg (1988)
38. Velichkov, V., Mouha, N., De Cannière, C., Preneel, B.: The Additive Differential Probability of ARX. In: Joux, A. (ed.) FSE 2011. LNCS, vol. 6733, pp. 342–358. Springer, Heidelberg (2011)
39. Velichkov, V., Mouha, N., Preneel, C.D.B.: UNAF: A Special Set of Additive Differences with Application to the Differential Analysis of ARX. In: Canteaut, [7] pp. 287–305
40. Wheeler, D.J., Needham, R.M.: TEA, a Tiny Encryption Algorithm. In: Preneel [33], pp. 363–366

A   The Differential Probabilities of ADD and XOR

In this section we recall the definitions of the differential probabilities of the operations XOR and modular addition. Before we begin – a brief remark on notation: in the same way as XOR is used to denote both the XOR operation and an XOR difference, we use ADD to denote both the modular addition operation and an additive difference.

Definition 2. *Let α, β and γ be fixed n-bit XOR differences. The XOR differential probability (DP) of addition modulo 2^n (xdp$^+$) is the probability with which α and β propagate to γ through the ADD operation, computed over all pairs of n-bit inputs (x, y):*

$$\mathrm{xdp}^+(\alpha, \beta \to \gamma) = 2^{-2n} \cdot \#\{(x,y) : ((x \oplus \alpha) + (y \oplus \beta)) \oplus (x + y) = \gamma\} . \quad (7)$$

The dual of xdp$^+$ is the probability adp$^\oplus$ and is defined analogously:

Definition 3. *Let α, β and γ be fixed n-bit ADD differences. The additive DP of XOR (adp$^\oplus$) is the probability with which α and β propagate to γ through the XOR operation, computed over all pairs of n-bit inputs (x, y):*

$$\mathrm{adp}^\oplus(\alpha, \beta \to \gamma) = 2^{-2n} \cdot \#\{(x,y) : ((x + \alpha) \oplus (y + \beta)) - (x + y) = \gamma\} . \quad (8)$$

The probabilities xdp$^+$ and adp$^\oplus$ have been studied in [21] and [22] respectively, where methods for their efficient computation have been proposed. In [21] is also described an efficient algorithm for the computation of xdp$^+$ maximized over all output differences: $\max_\gamma \mathrm{xdp}^+(\alpha, \beta \to \gamma)$. In [27] the methods for the computation of xdp$^+$ and adp$^\oplus$ are further generalized using the concept of S-functions. Finally, in [39, Appendix C, Algorithm 1] a general algorithm for computing the maximum probability output difference for certain types of differences and operations is described. It is applicable to both $\max_\gamma \mathrm{xdp}^+(\alpha, \beta \to \gamma)$ and $\max_\gamma \mathrm{adp}^\oplus(\alpha, \beta \to \gamma)$.

B   The Additive DP of Left and Right Shift

Definition 4. *For fixed input and output ADD differences resp. α and β, the additive differential probability of the operation* **right bit shift** *(RSH) by r positions is defined over all n-bit $(n \geq r)$ inputs x as:*

$$\text{adp}^{\gg r}(\alpha \to \beta) = 2^{-n} \cdot \#\{x : ((x + \alpha) \gg r) - (x \gg r) = \beta\} \ . \tag{9}$$

Analogously, the additive differential probability of the operation **left bit shift** *(LSH) by r positions is defined as in (9) after replacing $\gg r$ with $\ll r$.*

Theorem 1. *The LSH operation is linear with respect to ADD differences i.e. $((x + \alpha) \ll r) - (x \ll r) = (\alpha \ll r)$, where x, α and r are as in Definition 4. It follows that*

$$\text{adp}^{\ll r}(\alpha \to \beta) = \begin{cases} 1 \ , & \text{if } (\beta = \alpha \ll r) \ , \\ 0 \ , & \text{otherwise} \ . \end{cases} \tag{10}$$

Proof. Appendix D.2.

In contrast to LSH, the RSH operation is not linear w.r.t. ADD differences. The following theorem provides expressions for the computation of $\text{adp}^{\gg r}$.

Theorem 2. *Let α be a fixed n-bit input ADD difference to an RSH operation with shift constant $r \leq n$. Then there are exactly four possibilities for the output difference β. The four differences together with their corresponding probabilities computed over all n-bit inputs are:*

$$\text{adp}^{\gg r}(\alpha \to \beta) = \begin{cases} 2^{-n}(2^{n-r} - \alpha_{\text{L}})(2^r - \alpha_{\text{R}}) \ , & \beta = (\alpha \gg r) \ , \\ 2^{-n}\alpha_{\text{L}}(2^r - \alpha_{\text{R}}) \ , & \beta = (\alpha \gg r) - 2^{n-r} \ , \\ 2^{-n}\alpha_{\text{R}}(2^{n-r} - \alpha_{\text{L}} - 1) \ , & \beta = (\alpha \gg r) + 1 \ , \\ 2^{-n}(\alpha_{\text{L}} + 1)\alpha_{\text{R}} \ , & \beta = (\alpha \gg r) - 2^{n-r} + 1 \ . \end{cases}$$
$$\tag{11}$$

where α_{L} and α_{R} denote respectively the $(n - r)$ most-significant (MS) bits and the r least-significant (LS) bits of α so that: $\alpha = \alpha_{\text{L}} 2^r + \alpha_{\text{R}}$ and additions and subtractions are performed modulo 2^n. If $\alpha : \beta = \beta_i = \beta_j$ for some $0 \leq i \neq j < 4$ then $\text{adp}^{\gg r}(\alpha \to \beta) = \text{adp}^{\gg r}(\alpha \to \beta_i) + \text{adp}^{\gg r}(\alpha \to \beta_j)$.

Proof. Appendix D.3.

C   More Experimental results

C.1   Threshold Search on TEA with Reduced Word Size

In Fig. 3 and Fig. 4 are compared the probabilities of the best trails found by the threshold search algorithm using pDDT to the actual best trails found by applying Matsui's search using full DDT on TEA with word size reduced to 11 and 16 bits respectively. For 11 bits 50 experiments are performed and in

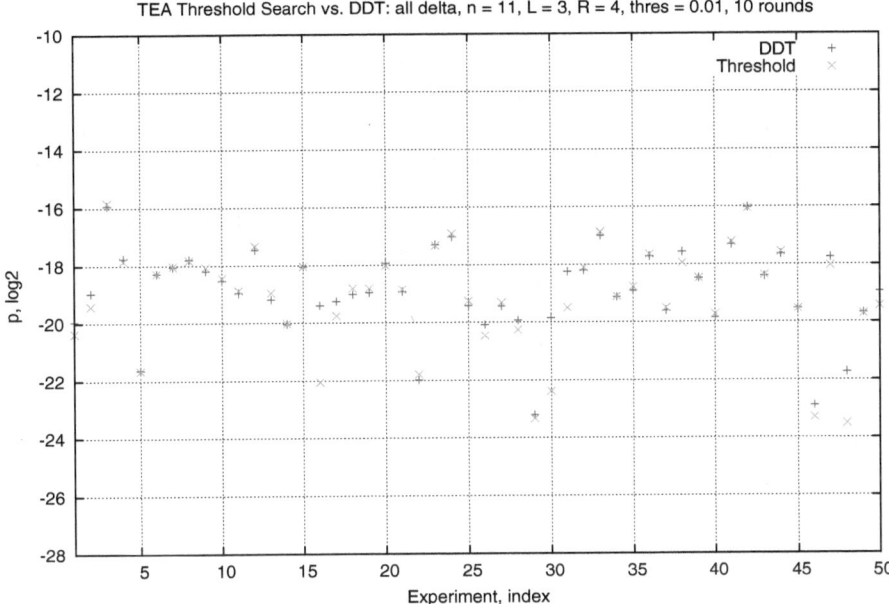

Fig. 3. Threshold Search vs. DDT Search: word size $n = 11$ bits

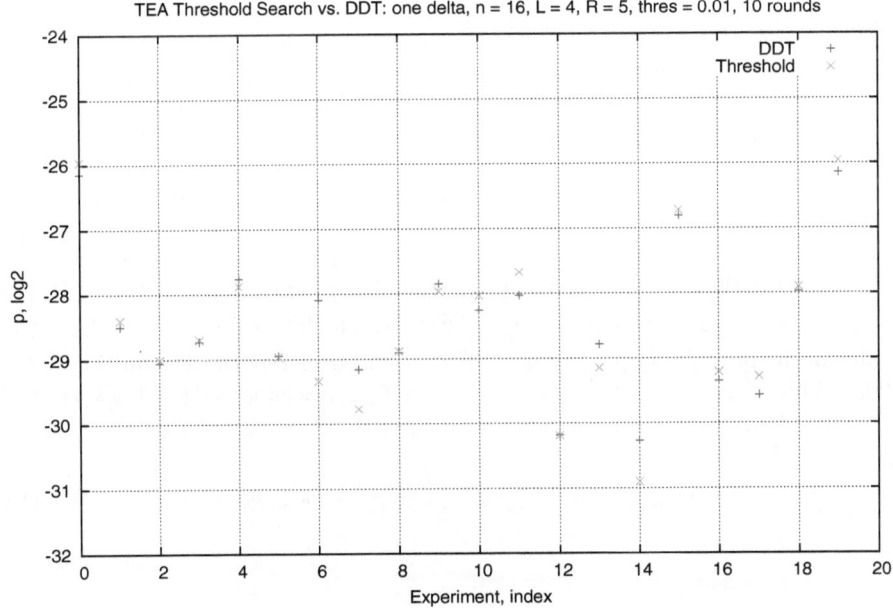

Fig. 4. Threshold Search vs. DDT Search: word size $n = 16$ bits; same δ is used in every round

A. Biryukov and V. Velichkov

each experiment a new fixed key is chosen uniformly at random. For 16 bits, the number of experiments is 20. In the experiments on 16 bits the same δ constant (equal to the initial value) was used in every round. The reason is that if different constants are used, then a separate DDT has to be computed for every round, which for more than a couple of rounds quickly becomes infeasible. Also note that for 16 bits it takes longer to compute the full DDT-s due to their larger size (compared to the 11 bit case). The memory consumption is also much bigger – 320 GB of RAM are required to store all DDT-s. Due to the mentioned limitations, less number of experiments on 16 bits were performed.

D Proofs

D.1 Proof of Proposition 1

Proof. We shall prove the proposition for $\mathrm{adp}^{\oplus}$. In this case α, β and γ are ADD differences propagating through the XOR operation. The proof for xdp^{+} is analogous.

We induct over the word size n. The proposition is trivially true for the base case $n = 1$: $p_1 \leq p_0 = 1$. Let $n = k > 1$. We have to prove that $p_k \leq p_{k-1}$.

Let x and y be n-bit integers. Define L_i to be the set of i-bit pairs (x_i, y_i) that satisfy the differential $(\alpha_i, \beta_i \rightarrow \gamma_i)$ for the operation addition modulo 2^i:

$$L_i = \{(x_i, y_i) : ((x_i + \alpha_i) \oplus (y_i + \beta_i)) - (x_i + y_i) = \gamma_i\}, \quad n \geq i \geq 1 . \quad (12)$$

Let $l_i = \#L_i$. By definition $p_k = l_k/2^{2k}$ and $p_{k-1} = l_{k-1}/2^{2(k-1)}$ (cf. (8)). Note that every element of L_k can be obtained from an element (x_{k-1}, y_{k-1}) of L_{k-1} by appending bits $x[k-1]$ and $y[k-1]$ to x_{k-1} and y_{k-1} respectively. Assume that this is not true i.e. assume:

$$\exists x_k, y_k : \quad (x_k = x[k-1]|x_{k-1}, \ y_k = y[k-1]|y_{k-1}, \ (x_k, y_k) \in L_k) \wedge$$
$$((x_{k-1}, \ y_{k-1}) \notin L_{k-1}) . \quad (13)$$

If (13) is true then we can construct a new set $L^*_{k-1} = (x_{k-1}, y_{k-1}) \cup L_{k-1}$. Its size is $l^*_{k-1} = l_{k-1} + 1$ and so $p_{k-1} = l^*_{k-1}/2^{2(k-1)}$. The latter differs from the actual value of the probability $p_{k-1} = l_{k-1}/2^{2(k-1)}$ and therefore the assumption (13) is false. Thus $\forall(x_k, y_k) \in L_k : (x_{k-1}, y_{k-1}) \in L_{k-1}$. Because $\#\{(x[k], y[k])\} = 2^2$, the size of L_k can be at most 2^2 times bigger than the size of L_{k-1}:

$$l_k \leq 2^2 l_{k-1} \Rightarrow \frac{l_k}{2^{2k}} \leq \frac{l_{k-1}}{2^{2(k-1)}} \Rightarrow p_k \leq p_{k-1} . \quad (14)$$

$\square$

D.2 Proof of Theorem 1

Proof. Let x be an n-bit input to LSH with shift constant $r \leq n$. Let $x_L, x_R :$ $x = x_L 2^{n-r} + x_R$. Then $(x \ll r) = x_R 2^r$. Similarly, for the input ADD difference

α let $\alpha_L, \alpha_R : \alpha = \alpha_L 2^{n-r} + \alpha_R$ and thus $(\alpha \ll r) = \alpha_R 2^r$. The sum $(x + \alpha)$ can then be represented as:

$$(x + \alpha) = (x_L + \alpha_L) 2^{n-r} + (x_R + \alpha_R)$$
$$= ((x_L + \alpha_L + c_R) \mod 2^r) 2^{n-r} + ((x_R + \alpha_R) \mod 2^{n-r}) , \quad (15)$$

where c_R is the carry generated from the addition $(x_R + \alpha_R) \mod 2^{n-r}$. From (15) follows that $(x + \alpha) \ll r = (x_R + \alpha_R) 2^r$. Thus for the output difference β we get:

$$\beta = ((x + \alpha) \ll r) - (x \ll r) = (x_R + \alpha_R) 2^r - x_R 2^r = \alpha_R 2^r = (\alpha \ll r) . \quad (16)$$

Note that (16) is independent of the input x and therefore holds with probability 1 over all values of x. From this the expression (10) for the probability $\text{adp}^{\ll r}$ immediately follows. $\qquad\square$

D.3   Proof of Theorem 2

Proof. Let x be an n-bit input to RSH with shift constant $r \leq n$. Let x_L, x_R : $x = x_L 2^r + x_R$. Then $(x \gg r) = x_L$. Similarly, for the input ADD difference α let $\alpha_L, \alpha_R : \alpha = \alpha_L 2^r + \alpha_R$ and thus $(\alpha \gg r) = \alpha_L$. Denote by c_R the carry generated from the addition $(a_R + \alpha_R) \mod 2^r$:

$$c_R = \begin{cases} 0 , & \text{if } (x_R + \alpha_R) < 2^r , \\ 1 , & \text{otherwise} . \end{cases} \quad (17)$$

The sum $(x + \alpha)$ can then be represented as:

$$(x + \alpha) = (x_L + \alpha_L) 2^r + (x_R + \alpha_R)$$
$$= ((x_L + \alpha_L + c_R) \mod 2^{n-r}) 2^r + ((x_R + \alpha_R) \mod 2^r) . \quad (18)$$

Therefore $(x + \alpha) \gg r = (x_L + \alpha_L + c_R) \mod 2^{n-r}$ and for the output difference β we derive:

$$\beta = ((x + \alpha) \gg r) - (x \gg r) = ((x_L + \alpha_L + c_R) \mod 2^{n-r}) - x_L$$
$$= \alpha_L - c_L 2^{n-r} + c_R , \quad (19)$$

where

$$c_L = \begin{cases} 0 , & \text{if } (x_L + \alpha_L + c_R) < 2^{n-r} , \\ 1 , & \text{otherwise} . \end{cases} \quad (20)$$

The term $-c_L 2^{n-r}$ in (19) is introduced in order to cancel the carry 2^{n-r} that is generated in the cases in which the sum $(x_L + \alpha_L + c_R)$ is bigger than $(2^{n-r} - 1)$. In such a case $c_L = 1$ and $-c_L 2^{n-r} + (x_L + \alpha_L + c_R) = -2^{n-r} + 2^{n-r} + (x_L + \alpha_L + c_R) \mod 2^{n-r} = (x_L + \alpha_L + c_R) \mod 2^{n-r}$.

In the expression for β (19), for each distinct value of the tuple (c_L, c_R) we get one of the four possibilities for β:

$$\beta = \begin{cases} (\alpha \gg r) \,, & c_L = 0, c_R = 0 \,, \\ (\alpha \gg r) - 2^{n-r} \,, & c_L = 1, c_R = 0 \,, \\ (\alpha \gg r) + 1 \,, & c_L = 0, c_R = 1 \,, \\ (\alpha \gg r) - 2^{n-r} + 1 \,, & c_L = 1, c_R = 1 \,. \end{cases} \tag{21}$$

In order to compute the corresponding probabilities, we have to count the number of inputs x, that result in a given value for (c_L, c_R). Note that c_L and c_R depend on x and α, of which α is fixed and x can take on all values from 0 to $2^n - 1$. From (17) it is easy to compute that $c_R = 0$ for exactly $(2^r - \alpha_R)$ values of x_R and therefore $c_R = 1$ for the remaining $2^r - (2^r - \alpha_R) = \alpha_R$ values. Note that x_R is an r-bit word. Similarly, if $c_R = 0$ then $c_L = 0$ for $(2^{n-r} - \alpha_L)$ values of x_L and $c_L = 1$ for the remaining α_L values. If $c_R = 1$ then $c_L = 0$ for $(2^{n-r} - \alpha_L - 1)$ values and $c_L = 1$ for the remaining $\alpha_L + 1$ values. Therefore $(c_L, c_R) = (0, 0)$ for $(2^{n-r} - \alpha_L)(2^r - \alpha_R)$ values of x. Since the total number of values is 2^n we obtain the probability:

$$\mathrm{adp}^{\gg r}(\alpha \to \beta = (\alpha \gg r)) = 2^{-n}(2^{n-r} - \alpha_L)(2^r - \alpha_R) \,. \tag{22}$$

The expressions for the remaining three probabilities are derived analogously.

□

CBEAM: Efficient Authenticated Encryption from Feebly One-Way ϕ Functions

Markku-Juhani O. Saarinen

Kudelski Security, Switzerland
mjos@cblnk.com

Abstract. We show how efficient and secure cryptographic mixing functions can be constructed from low-degree rotation-invariant ϕ functions rather than conventional S-Boxes. These novel functions have surprising properties; many exhibit inherent feeble (Boolean circuit) one-wayness and offer speed/area tradeoffs unobtainable with traditional constructs. Recent theoretical results indicate that even if the inverse is not explicitly computed in an implementation, its degree plays a fundamental role to the security of the iterated composition. To illustrate these properties, we present CBEAM, a Cryptographic Sponge Permutation based on a single 5×1-bit Boolean function. This simple nonlinear function is used to construct a 16-bit rotation-invariant ϕ function of Degree 4 (but with a very complex Degree 11 inverse), which in turn is expanded into an efficient 256-bit mixing function. In addition to flexible tradeoffs in hardware we show that efficient implementation strategies exist for software platforms ranging from low-end microcontrollers to the very latest x86-64 AVX2 instruction set. A rotational bit-sliced software implementation offers not only comparable speeds to AES but also increased security against cache side channel attacks. Our construction supports Sponge-based Authenticated Encryption, Hashing, and PRF/PRNG modes and is highly useful as a compact "all-in-one" primitive for pervasive security.

Keywords: CBEAM, Authenticated Encryption, Cryptographic Sponge Functions, Trapdoor ϕ functions, Lightweight Cryptography.

1 Introduction

The only nonlinear component of the SHA-3 algorithm KECCAK [1,2] is not a traditional S-Box but a rotation-invariant ϕ function [3]. It has been widely observed [4] that this 5×5 - bit function, χ, has a lower algebraic degree and circuit complexity than its inverse χ^{-1} (See Figure 1). This is a desirable quality in a Sponge-based cryptoprimitive as computation of inverse is not required in normal operation. Boura and Canteaut have showed that complex inverse makes the resulting iteration strong even if it is not explicitly computed [5]. We have discovered new functions of ϕ type which exhibit much more radical asymmetry than the χ function of KECCAK.

Sponge-based constructions offer perhaps the best route to shared-resource (combined encryption and MAC state) authenticated encryption via the Duplex construction [6,7,8,9,10]. This motivates our investigation of higher-degree ϕ functions as we believe that they are better suited for Sponge constructions than traditional block cipher design methodologies that require efficient computation in both directions.

J. Benaloh (Ed.): CT-RSA 2014, LNCS 8366, pp. 251–269, 2014.

Our contributions and structure of this paper. We first give some basic observations on ϕ functions and their cryptanalysis in Section 2. Inspired by our discovery of a unique, particularly strong 5-input ϕ function, we propose a cryptographic permutation named CBEAM which can be used for hashing, authenticated encryption, and other purposes. Section 3 gives a formal definition of the CBEAM Sponge Permutation π, followed by analysis in Section 4.

This "Cryptographic Swiss Army Knife" Sponge primitive uses a fast 16×16 -bit ϕ function of Degree 4, with 13 terms in its ANF polynomial for each output bit. Its asymmetry is evident as its inverse has degree 11 and 13465 terms for output each bit – see Section 4.3 and Appendix D.

Based on extensive experimentation we conjecture that these functions exhibit inherent feeble one-wayness as defined by Hiltgen for circuit complexity. This indicates high algebraic resistance for our construct [5] and shows that ϕ functions are in some ways superior to conventional designs based on S-Box lookups.

In Section 5 we describe implementations of CBEAM for x86-64 AVX2 instruction set and for the 16-bit MSP 430 ultra-low power microcontroller. CBEAM is as fast as fastest AES implementations (without dedicated AES hardware) on both of these platforms, but has significantly smaller implementation footprint on both. Significant area-speed trade-offs are possible in hardware, as demonstrated by our two reference VHDL implementations.

Our conclusions in Section 6 are followed by test vectors and cryptanalytic tables in Appendices.

2   Rotation-Invariant ϕ Functions

Introduced in Daemen's 1995 PhD Thesis [3], ϕ functions are rotation-invariant n-bit invertible (bijective) functions. We use a slightly different notation from Daemen who used ϕ to denote non-invertible as well as invertible rotation-invariant functions.

Definition 1. *Let $f : \{0,1\}^n \mapsto \{0,1\}^n$ be a function from n-bit vectors to n-bit vectors. f is a ϕ function if it is bijective (uniquely invertible) and rotation-invariant: $f(x) = y \Rightarrow f(x \lll r) = y \lll r$ for all r.*

Lemma 1. *Any $n \times n$-bit ϕ function f is unambiguously characterized by an $n \times 1$ - bit function $f_{(1)}$ that satisfies $f_{(1)}(x) = f(x) \wedge 1$.*

Proof. Directly from rotation invariance. Constant 1 has Hamming weight 1.   □

Each output bit of the function may be dependent only on some subset of n input bits. This subset is not arbitrary; we found that neighboring input bits are more likely to yield invertible functions. In the present work ϕ_5 is a specific 5×1 - bit function and ϕ_{16} is a 16×16 - bit function defined by it as per Lemma 1. We note that each output bit of the inverse function f^{-1} may be dependent on all input bits even though this is not the case for f (See Figure 1.)

2.1 Invertibility

It is easy to see that there are invertible $n \times n$ - bit ϕ functions for any $n > 1$ by considering $f(x) = cx \pmod{2^n - 1}$, where $\gcd(c, 2^n - 1) = 1$. Rotation invariance: $2^n \equiv 1 \pmod{2^n - 1}$ and $f(2^k x) = 2^k cx \pmod{2^n - 1}$. For invertibility $f^{-1}(x) = c^{-1} x \pmod{2^n - 1}$.

The inverse function f^{-1} can also be characterized by an $n \times 1$ - bit function $f_{(1)}^{-1}$ (Lemma 1) since the inverse of any ϕ function is clearly also a ϕ function. It may also be the case that $f = f^{-1}$. Hummingbird-2ν is an example of a cipher that utilizes two 16-bit ϕ functions which are in fact involutions [11]. The SIMON family of block ciphers from NSA is an example of a cipher that utilizes a *non-surjective* rotation-invariant function f as part of a Feistel construction [12].

It is nontrivial to characterize which one-bit $f_{(1)}$ functions generate invertible f functions apart from simple properties such as bit balance: $\sum_{x=0}^{2^n-1} f_{(1)}(x) = 2^{n-1}$. Good ϕ functions appear to be rather hard to find – we resorted to optimized exhaustive tabulation methods to find our implementation-friendy and "feebly asymmetric" ϕ_5.

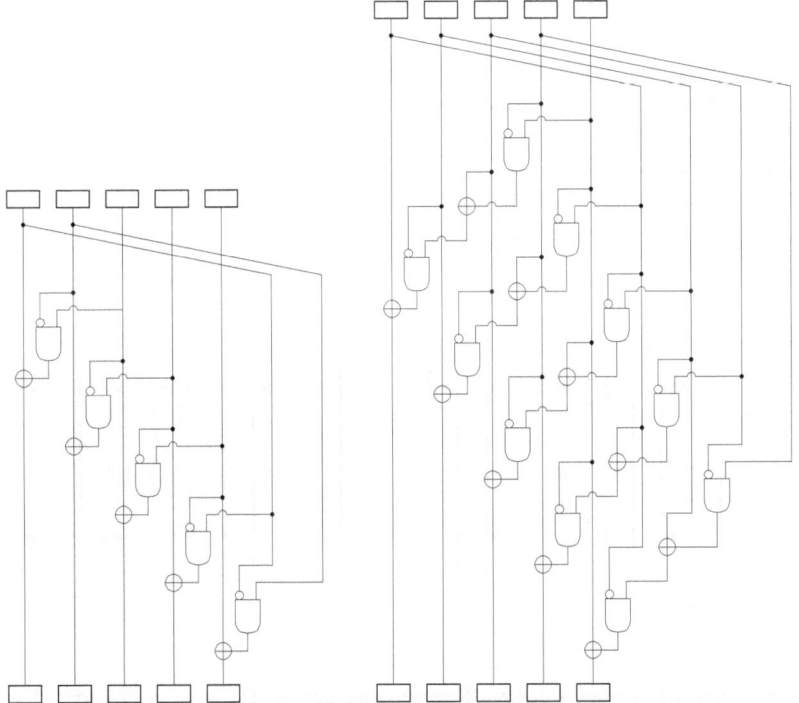

Fig. 1. On left, a circuit implementing KECCAK's 5×5 - bit χ component, which happens to be a rotation-invariant ϕ function of degree 2. On right, a circuit implementing its inverse permutation, χ^{-1}, which has Degree 3 with each output bit dependent on all input bits. Such asymmetric Boolean and circuit complexity is characteristic of ϕ functions.

2.2   On Cryptanalysis of ϕ Functions

Algorithms for finding differential [13] and linear [14,15] cryptanalytic properties of a ϕ function are relatively fast and straightforward to implement. Thanks to Lemma 1, when determining linear bounds we may assume that the input mask is a subset of the input bits to its $f_{(1)}$.

For differential cryptanalysis we must consider the convolution of the input differential w.r.t. a single output bit. Due to rotation we may always by convention set the bit at index 0 in the input differential.

Countermeasures must be taken against rotational cryptanalysis [16] due to inherent rotational invariance of ϕ functions. Algebraically these functions have surprising properties. See Section 4.3 and Appendix D for tables and conjectures related to ϕ_5.

2.3   General Implementation Features

One the most useful features of ϕ functions is the extreme amount of implementation trade-offs allowed. Computation of a $n \times n$ - bit ϕ function can take anywhere from 1 (fully unrolled) to $c \times n$ cycles (serial implementation – here c is some constant), depending on target hardware platform. This is illustrated in Figure 3.

On software platform, ϕ functions allow efficient implementation of large "S-boxes" via a Boolean sequence programming technique resembling bit-slicing [17]. Finding a good bit-slicing Boolean description for an $n \times 1$ - bit function is much easier than for a generic $n \times n$ - bit S-Box.

Such straight-line code is resistant to cache-based side-channel timing attacks such as those reported against AES implementations [18,19,20].

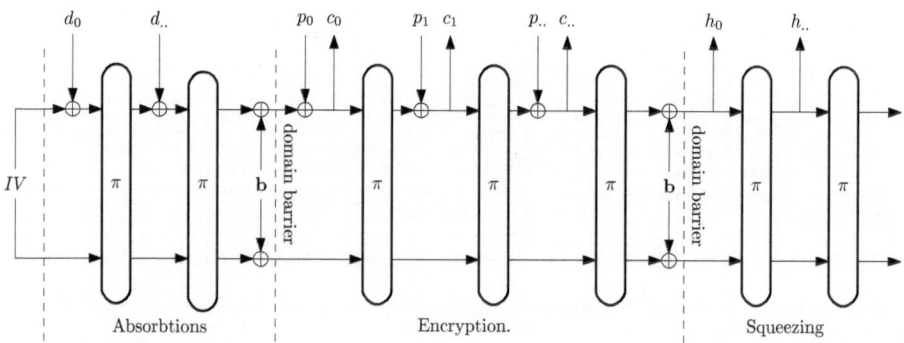

Fig. 2. A simplified view of a generic Sponge construction. The state is first loaded with an Initialization Vector or the final state of previous message. In CBEAM, the mixing function is $\pi = \text{mx}^6$. Then Secret Key, Nonce, and Associated Authenticated Data (AAD) are absorbed and mixed - all represented by d words. $\mathbf{b}$ represents some domain separating padding mechanism. The same π function is then be used to encrypt and decrypt data and finally to extract ("squeeze") out a MAC or a hash h.

3   CBEAM and Its π Permutation

The design of CBEAM was driven by the following goals:

1. KISS: A simple design based on a single feebly one-way unkeyed permutation.
2. Fulfills all symmetric cryptographic needs of a communications security suite with a single core primitive. Usable as a Pseudorandom Function, Authenticated Encryption Algorithm, and a Collision-resistant Hash.
3. Have high performance on high-end CPUs, yet be efficiently implementable on low-end MCUs and lightweight hardware platforms such as RFID.
4. Have a high security level against attacks (2^{128}).

CBEAM is based on the Sponge construction (Section 3.2) with a 256-bit state size and 64-bit data rate; data transfer generally occurs in 64-bit increments.

3.1   Mixing Function mx

The basic building block of CBEAM is mx, which is a bijective transform on a 256-bit state variable. Six rounds of mx make up π, the fundamental permutation of CBEAM.

The mixing function mx is composed of addition of a round constant rc^r, bit matrix transpose, linear mixing λ, and nonlinear mixing ϕ:

$$\mathsf{mx}_r(\mathbf{s}) = (\phi \circ \lambda)(\mathbf{s} \oplus rc^r)^T. \tag{1}$$

Practical software implementation notes are presented in Section 5.2 and a test trace of six rounds in Appendix A.

Formal Definition. We index the state $\mathbf{s}$ interchangeably as a 16×16 - bit matrix $s[\,0..15\,][\,0..15\,]$, a vector of 16-bit words $s_w[\,0..15\,]$ with $s_w[\,i\,] = \sum_{j=0}^{15} 2^j s[\,i\,][\,j\,]$ or as four quadwords $s_q[\,0..3\,]$ with $s_q[\,i\,] = \sum_{j=0}^{3} 2^{16j} s_w[\,4i + j\,]$. All data is stored in little-endian format.

In the following description modulo 16 arithmetic in indexing is equivalent to logical masking with 0xF; $a \bmod 16$ is always in the range $0, 1, \cdots, 15$. To evaluate $\pi = \mathsf{mx}^6$ we compute six rounds $r = 0 \ldots 5$ of the following three steps:

1. Round Constant rc^r. Let the individual round bits be $r = 4r_2 + 2r_1 + r_0$. We have $s'[\,i\,][\,j\,] = s[\,i\,][\,j\,]$ for all $0 \leq i, j \leq 15$ except the following:

$$s'[\,0\,][\,0\,] = s[\,0\,][\,0\,] \oplus (r_0 \wedge \neg r_1) \qquad s'[\,8\,][\,2\,] = s[\,8\,][\,2\,] \oplus (r_0 \wedge r_1)$$
$$s'[\,1\,][\,0\,] = s[\,1\,][\,0\,] \oplus (r_0 \wedge r_2) \qquad s'[\,10\,][\,2\,] = s[\,10\,][\,2\,] \oplus r_0$$
$$s'[\,3\,][\,0\,] = s[\,3\,][\,0\,] \oplus r_0 \qquad s'[\,11\,][\,2\,] = s[\,11\,][\,2\,] \oplus (r_0 \wedge r_2)$$
$$s'[\,4\,][\,1\,] = s[\,4\,][\,1\,] \oplus r_0 \qquad s'[\,13\,][\,3\,] = s[\,13\,][\,3\,] \oplus r_0$$
$$s'[\,5\,][\,1\,] = s[\,5\,][\,1\,] \oplus (r_0 \wedge \neg r_1) \qquad s'[\,14\,][\,3\,] = s[\,14\,][\,3\,] \oplus (r_0 \wedge r_1)$$
$$s'[\,6\,][\,1\,] = s[\,6\,][\,1\,] \oplus (r_0 \wedge r_2) \qquad s'[\,15\,][\,3\,] = s[\,15\,][\,3\,] \oplus (r_0 \wedge r_2).$$

Observe that the round constants are active only on odd rounds ($r_0 = 1$).

Table 1. Truth table for ϕ_5 (Equation 4.)

x_4 x_3 x_2 x_1 x_0	ϕ_5	x_4 x_3 x_2 x_1 x_0	ϕ_5	x_4 x_3 x_2 x_1 x_0	ϕ_5	x_4 x_3 x_2 x_1 x_0	ϕ_5
0 0 0 0 0	0	0 1 0 0 0	1	1 0 0 0 0	1	1 1 0 0 0	1
0 0 0 0 1	0	0 1 0 0 1	0	1 0 0 0 1	1	1 1 0 0 1	0
0 0 0 1 0	1	0 1 0 1 0	1	1 0 0 1 0	0	1 1 0 1 0	1
0 0 0 1 1	1	0 1 0 1 1	0	1 0 0 1 1	1	1 1 0 1 1	0
0 0 1 0 0	0	0 1 1 0 0	0	1 0 1 0 0	0	1 1 1 0 0	0
0 0 1 0 1	0	0 1 1 0 1	0	1 0 1 0 1	0	1 1 1 0 1	0
0 0 1 1 0	1	0 1 1 1 0	1	1 0 1 1 0	1	1 1 1 1 0	1
0 0 1 1 1	1	0 1 1 1 1	1	1 0 1 1 1	0	1 1 1 1 1	1

2. Linear transform λ^T. Let $\mathbf{s}' = \lambda(\mathbf{s}^T)$ for $0 \le i, j \le 15$:

$$
\begin{aligned}
s'[\,i\,][\,j\,] =\ & s[\,(j+4) \bmod 16\,][\,i\,] \oplus \\
& s[\,(j+8) \bmod 16\,][\,i\,] \oplus \\
& s[\,(j+12) \bmod 16\,][\,i\,].
\end{aligned}
\tag{2}
$$

We note that the λ^T transform consists of a transpose of the matrix and a bit parity operation. The transpose and bit parity operations are individually involutions but applying their compound operation λ^T four times results in the original matrix.

3. Nonlinear transform ϕ. We define $\mathbf{s}' = \phi(\mathbf{s})$ for $0 \le i, j \le 15$ as:

$$
\begin{aligned}
s'[\,i\,][\,j\,] = \phi_5\big(& s[\,i\,][\,j\,], \\
& s[\,i\,][\,(j-1) \bmod 16\,], \\
& s[\,i\,][\,(j-2) \bmod 16\,], \\
& s[\,i\,][\,(j-3) \bmod 16\,], \\
& s[\,i\,][\,(j-4) \bmod 16\,]\big),
\end{aligned}
\tag{3}
$$

where ϕ_5 is defined the following Algebraic Normal Form (ANF) polynomial in $\mathbb{Z}_2$:

$$
\begin{aligned}
\phi_5(x_0, x_1, x_2, x_3, x_4) =\ & x_0 x_1 x_3 x_4 + x_0 x_2 x_3 + x_0 x_1 x_4 + x_1 x_2 x_3 + x_2 x_3 x_4 + \\
& x_0 x_3 + x_1 x_3 + x_2 x_3 + x_2 x_4 + x_3 x_4 + x_1 + x_3 + x_4.
\end{aligned}
\tag{4}
$$

Selection of ϕ_5 is discussed in Section 4.1 and Table 1 gives its truth table.

3.2 Hashing and Authenticated Encryption

We claim that π can be used in all of the following proposed Sponge modes of operation. However, we suggest that unique message nonces or randomizers are always used for AE and MAC modes.

- Authenticated Encryption (AE) with SPONGEWRAP[9].
- Keyed Message Authentication Codes (MACs) [21].

- Collision resistant hashing [6].
- Tree hashing with SAKURA [22].
- Pseudorandom extractors (PRFs and PRNGs) [8].
- BLINKER two-party protocols [23].

For CBEAM described in this paper $b = 256$ and a natural choice for rate is $r = 64$, leaving a capacity of $c = 192$. This is more suitable for low-resource platforms and short messages than KECCAK with its 1600-bit state [1].

For SPONGEWRAP and other modes with frame bits it may be appropriate to have $r = 65$ or 66 in order to not break input byte boundaries. For 2^{38} bits of data per key we claim 2^{128} security based on Theorems of [10], equivalent to AES-128 and suitable for SECRET data. For 2^{46} data we claim 2^{112} security, superior to 3DES / TDEA [24].

If even faster speeds are required and unique nonces are available, one may reduce the number of rounds to mx^4 or even mx^2 and use the MONKEYDUPLEX construction of [25]. However, many of the security assurances will break down in this case.

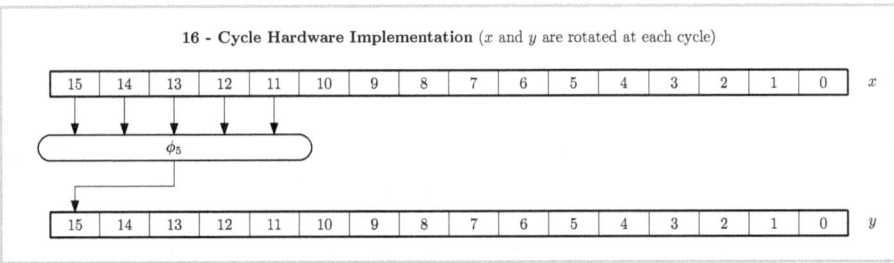

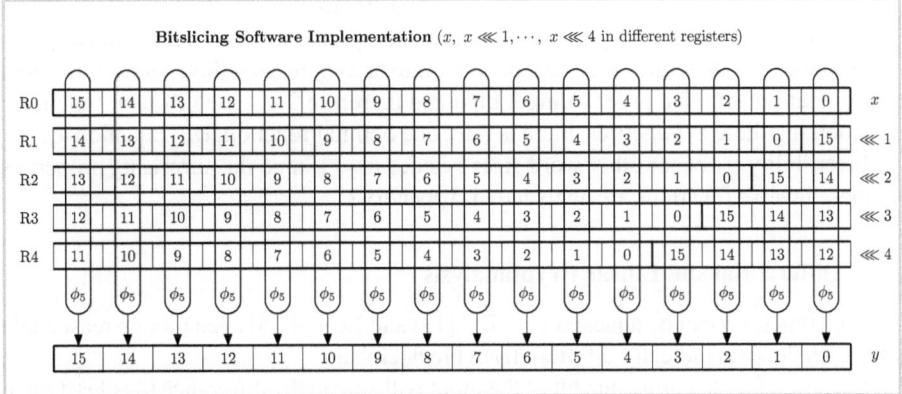

Fig. 3. Example of a 16×16 - bit ϕ function based on a 5×1 - bit Boolean function ϕ_5. We observe 16 and 1 cycle implementations of the same function. Note that the latter example is equivalent to "bit slicing" software implementation using rotated words.

4 Design and Analysis

Ignoring the round constant, the mx transform may be viewed as a transpose of a matrix followed by 16 parallel, independent invocations of a 16 - bit permutation, $(\phi \circ \lambda)_{16}$. We start with the most fundamental observation:

Theorem 1. *The mx transform is bijective (reversible).*

Proof. The mx transform is bijective as all of its component functions are individually reversible. It is trivial to see that the linear transform λ is bijective. Since convolution by a nonlinear Boolean function is generally not reversible, one may compute the 2^{16} - entry table of ϕ_{16} to verify that it is indeed bijective. □

The choice of round constants was specially crafted to deter rotational [16] and slide [26,27] attacks.

Theorem 2. *Without the round constants the mx transform is shift-invariant both horizontally and vertically. Let $s' = mx(s)$ and $t' = mx(t)$. If each element $s[i][j] = t[(i+4\Delta_i) \bmod 16][(j+\Delta_j) \bmod 16]$ for some offsets Δ_i and Δ_j, then $s'[i][j] = t'[(i+\Delta_j) \bmod 16][(j+4\Delta_i) \bmod 16]$.*

Proof. The theorem follows form shift-invariant properties of all component functions. Note the exchange of indices $4\Delta_i$ and Δ_j due to transpose. □

4.1 Selection of ϕ_5

We analyzed all $2^{2^5} = 2^{32}$ five-input Boolean functions, searching for ones that result in invertible 16-bit ϕ functions with particularly good properties. Five neighboring bits are used since rotation amounts that would yield better branching (such as the set $\{0,1,2,4,8\}$) didn't result in any appropriate functions. Single left rotations are used as it is universally available (addition of number to self with carry flow-over to LSB).

There were 260 invertible functions, of which 56 were dependent on all five input bits in nonlinear fashion. Eight of these exhibited optimal differential and linear properties. However there are three independent mirror symmetries (inversion of all input and output bits and the order of input bits) and therefore $2^3 = 8$ equivalent functions. Discounting these symmetries, there is only one optimal function, ϕ_5 (Equation 4).

Invertibility ϕ_5 of for other word sizes besides $n = 16$ and the surprising properties of these inverse functions are analyzed in Appendix D.

4.2 Differential and Linear Cryptanalysis

Sponge functions can be attacked with DC [13] and LC [14,15] even though reasonable attack models are radically different from block ciphers.

Because of λ, changing one bit of the input will spread the difference to at least three bit positions outside the first quadword which can be modified by the attacker. After four of six mx iterations, there is no easily detectable bias regardless of input difference, which we feel is an appropriate security margin. See Table 4 for an illustration of progress of differentials in the state during forward and reverse iterations.

For this analysis we view $(\phi \circ \lambda)_{16}$ row operation as a 16×16 - bit "S-Box". The highest-probability differential is 0CCC $\rightarrow$ 8001 and its rotational equivalents. The probability of this differential is $\frac{12032}{2^{16}} \approx 0.1836$. From Table 2 in Appendix C we observe that a 1-bit input difference never yields a 1-bit output difference (branch number is greater than 2).

The best linear approximation for $(\phi \circ \lambda)_{16}$ is 0888 $\rightarrow$ 0001 and its rotational equivalents, which have a bias of $\frac{16384}{2^{16}} = \frac{1}{4}$. The other best approximations are given in Table 3. Significantly, all single bit approximations have 0 linear bias, as do 2-to-1 and 1-to-2 - bit approximations.

4.3 Algebraic Properties

The truth table for ϕ_5 Boolean function is given in Table 1. From its definition in Equation 4 one easily see that the degree of ϕ_5 is 4 (and ANF weight 13), and that is also the algebraic degree of ϕ state transform mx (see Equation 3).

The mx function has been designed to have a significant amount of algebraic "one-wayness" in the sense discussed by Hiltgen [28]. The following somewhat surprising observation can be verified by examining the inverse of ϕ_{16}:

Observation 1 *The algebraic degree of the ϕ_{16}^{-1} inverse function is 11. The weight (number of nonzero terms) of the ANF polynomial for each output bit of ϕ_{16}^{-1} is 13465.*

For a characterization of the Algebraic properties of the inverse of ϕ_n^{-1} for $n \neq 16$, we refer to Appendix D, where tables and conjectures are presented.

The algebraic degree of mx^n is bound by 4^n. We have verified that the output after six invocations actually has a degree up to 256. If state bits are observed as a function of $s_q[\,0\,]$, the number of terms of each degree are distributed in a way that indicates that CBEAM is not vulnerable to d-monomial distinguishers [29] or other traditional algebraic attacks.

Higher-degree inverse indicates high-degree iteration. Research by Boura and Canteaut on the algebraic degree of iterated permutations seen as multivariate polynomials shows that the degree depends on the algebraic degree of the *inverse* of the permutation which is iterated [5]. This indicates exceptional algebraic security for our proposal.

5 Padding and Implementation Notes

A special padding mode of operation, BLINKER [23], is proposed together with CBEAM. This multi-use padding mode allows full encryption protocols to be built from CBEAM. We note that an early version of CBEAM and BLINKER was used in the HA-GRAT academic Remote Access Trojan [30], minimizing the size of the encryption component.

CBEAM is highly flexible when it comes to implementation platforms. A standard C implementation may compute four rows in parallel using 64-bit data types whereas specific implementation strategies exist that fully utilize architectures from 16-bit to

256-bit word size. Figure 4 shows how the state fits into the register sets of various CPU architectures.

In hardware implementations, an invocation of the mx^n transform can take anywhere between 1 and several thousand clock cycles, depending on the number of gates, peak energy and amount of surface area available. Figure 3 shows sixteen- and single clock versions of a ϕ_{16} - type convolution.

5.1 Hardware Implementations

We have designed and written VHDL for two implementations, dubbed Serial-CBEAM and Block-CBEAM. These have been found to function correctly on a Xilinx Virtex 3E FPGA board with the ISE 14.4 design flow.

Serial Implementation. The Serial implementation assumes external 256-bit memory for the state and operates on that state one bit at a time. The implementation sacrifices a lot of clock cycles for reduction of gates and area. The implementation requires only 16 internal register bits in addition to address/clock counters. The implementation with a 1-bit data bus requires 256 read cycles and 256 write cycles for each MX iteration, 3072 clocks in total for full $\pi = mx^6$. We estimate that the implementation footprint is only about 300 GE without the 256-bit external state memory.

Block Implementation. This is a 1 - cycle implementation of the mx function (with e.g. 256 parallel ϕ_5 circuits). Depending on target platform and area, timing constraints, it is possible to implement more than one round of mx^2 in a single cycle. Pipelined operation using SAKURA-like [22] hopping hash trees can also be considered with this mx core.

5.2 Implementing CBEAM in Software without Matrix Transpose

Since transposing a binary matrix is generally slow in software, one would typically want to combine two mx operations into a double-round with separate "vertical" and "horizontal" parts. We give some generic guidance on how to implement mx^2 in software this way. However, one should examine the reference 16-bit, 64-bit, and 256-bit implementations for architecture-specific optimizations.

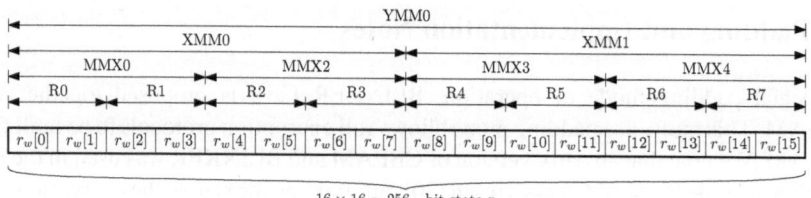

$$16 \times 16 = 256 \text{ - bit state } \mathbf{r}$$

Fig. 4. Illustration on how to fit the 256-bit state into a single Haswell+ AVX2 YMM register, two Pentium 3+ SSE XMM registers, four Pentium+ MMX or ARM NEON registers or eight ARM general purpose registers for bit-slicing computation

Step 1: Vertical linear transform λ. This step is easiest to implement by viewing the state as 64-bit words ("quadwords") $s_q[0..3]$ with $\mathbf{s} = (\,s_q[\,0\,],\,s_q[\,1\,],\,s_q[\,2\,],\,s_q[\,3\,]\,)$.

$$t = s_q[\,0\,] \oplus s_q[\,1\,] \oplus s_q[\,2\,] \oplus s_q[\,3\,]$$
$$\mathbf{s}' = (s_q[\,0\,] \oplus t,\, s_q[\,1\,] \oplus t,\, s_q[\,2\,] \oplus t,\, s_q[\,3\,] \oplus t\,). \tag{5}$$

Step 2: Vertical nonlinear transform. An optimized bit-slicing method for ϕ_5 is used (See Appendix B). Note that the input words may be stored in registers and contents of registers values in shifted for each new input word. For $0 \le i \le 15$:

$$s'_w[\,i\,] = \phi_5\big(s_w[\,i\,], s_w[\,(i-1) \bmod 16\,], s_w[\,(i-2) \bmod 16\,],$$
$$s_w[\,(i-3) \bmod 16\,], s_w[\,(i-4) \bmod 16\,]\big). \tag{6}$$

Step 3: Round Constant. As the round constants are only active at odd rounds, they are in fact always applied between vertical and horizontal rounds in this type of implementation. Written as transposed quadwords, the three nonzero round constants are:

$$rc_q^1 = \text{0x2000040000300009}$$
$$rc_q^3 = \text{0x6000050000100008} \tag{7}$$
$$rc_q^3 = \text{0xA0000C000070000B}$$

Constants from Equation 7 are XORed over the first quadword of state at round i:

$$s'_q[\,0\,] = s_q[\,0\,] \oplus rc_q^i. \tag{8}$$

Step 4: Horizontal linear transform λ. This step is relatively slow in this type of implementation. There are many ways to do this; we note that each nibble of t is equivalent to each other. This step is also parallelizable. For $0 \le i \le 15$:

$$t = s_w[\,i\,] \oplus (s_w[\,i\,] \lll 4) \oplus (s_w[\,i\,] \lll 8) \oplus (s_w[\,i\,] \lll 12)$$
$$s'_w[\,i\,] = s_w[\,i\,] \oplus t. \tag{9}$$

Step 5: Horizontal nonlinear transform. Again a bit-slicing implementation of ϕ_5 (Appendix B) is used, but on rotated values of each word. For $0 \le i \le 15$:

$$s'_w[\,i\,] = \phi_5\big(s_w[\,i\,], s_w[\,i\,] \lll 1, s_w[\,i\,] \lll 2, s_w[\,i\,] \lll 3, s_w[\,i\,] \lll 4\big). \tag{10}$$

5.3 Latest Server/Desktop/Laptop Systems: x86-64 with AVX2

The Intel Haswell (Generation 4 Core) and later x86-64 CPUs support 256-bit AVX2 (Advanced Vector Extensions 2) SIMD instructions. The AVX2 platform provides shuffle and vector shift instructions for 16-bit vector sub-units in addition to 256-bit Boolean logic for the nonlinear function ϕ_5 (Equation 4). We can implement full 256-bit ϕ_5 with only eight instructions (Appendix B.1). This roughly doubles the overall execution speed when compared to optimized 64-bit gcc versions.

The following speeds were measured on a MacBook Air (Q3/2013) with Intel Core i5 - 4250U CPU @ 1.30 GHz running Ubuntu Linux 13.04. The internal clock frequency was 1.90 GHz for all tests.

We compare to OpenSSL 1.0.1e AES implementation, which is the de facto standard AES implementation. Generic assembler optimizations were enabled but we disabled the full hardware AES for fairness.

Implementation	Troughput	Cycles/Byte
CBEAM-GCC	58.5 MB/s	32.5
CBEAM-AVX2	117.5 MB/s	16.1
OpenSSL AES-128	106.5 MB/s	17.8
OpenSSL AES-192	86.0 MB/s	22.1
OpenSSL AES-256	71.9 MB/s	26.4

5.4 Sensors and Pervasive Devices: MSP430

Texas Instruments MSP430 is a well known family of low-cost and ultra-low power 16-bit SoC microcontrollers, widely used in sensor networks. CBEAM beats the more than dozen MSP430 encryption algorithm implementations reported in [31], often by an order of magnitude.

Our implementation of π is able to execute entirely on 12 general-purpose registers without having to resort to stack (except the top value) and therefore the running RAM requirement is equivalent to the state size, 32 bytes. The ϕ_5 function was realized with nine logic instructions (Appendix B.2). Unfortunately the target only has 1-bit shifts and no multi-bit rotation instructions, which results in a bottleneck for "horizontal" λ.

The cipher is as fast as the very fastest AES implementations on this platform but has significantly smaller implementation footprint. The following numbers are only for cores, modes of operation not included. The IAIK [32] implementation is commercial and written in hand-optimized assembly. The Texas Instruments [33] implementation is recommended by the SoC vendor.

Code	Flash	Ram	Encryption	Decryption	Cycles/Byte
CBEAM	386	32	4369	4404	550.5
AES-128 [32]	2536	?	5432	8802	550.1
AES-128 [33]	2423	80	6600	8400	525.0
AES-256 [32]	2830	?	7552	12258	766.1

6   Conclusions

We propose the use of novel rotation-invariant ϕ functions in cryptographic primitives such as hashes and authenticated encryption. These functions have fascinating and attractive properties such as "feeble one-wayness"; the Boolean complexity of inversion appears to be much higher than the Boolean complexity of computing the permutation in forward direction. We have experimentally verified that the polynomial degree for the inverse of a ϕ_5 function grows linearly as the number of input bits grows, while it remains constant in forward direction. Hence the function and its inverse are in different complexity classes (linear vs. polynomial or super-polynomial).

In a Sponge construction a large and efficient cryptographic permutation is required. The permutation needs to be computed only in one direction during normal operation. It has been shown that complexity of inversion makes collision search and other attacks more difficult. Here an asymmetric ϕ function is an ideal choice. This motivates us to propose a new 256-bit Sponge function, CBEAM, which can be used for cryptographic hashing, authenticated encryption, and other purposes.

In addition to the theoretical side, the main attractive feature of CBEAM is its extreme implementation flexibility; a single word encryption operation may require anywhere between 1 to thousands of cycles, depending on the area and energy requirements of the implementation. We also demonstrate that it is approximately as fast as AES on both high-end CPUs and low-end MCUs, while having a significantly smaller implementation footprint.

Acknowledgements. The author wishes to thank Kudelski Security, University of Haifa, and Nanyang Technological University for supporting his work. Program Committee members of CT-RSA 2014 provided invaluable suggestions for improving the quality of this paper.

References

1. Bertoni, G., Daemen, J., Peeters, M., Assche, G.V.: The Keccak reference, version 3.0. NIST SHA3 Submission Document (January 2011)
2. NIST: NIST selects winner of secure hash algorithm (SHA-3) competition. NIST Tech Beat Newsletter (October 2, 2012)
3. Daemen, J.: Cipher and Hash Function Design Strategies based on linear and differential cryptanalysis. PhD thesis, K.U. Leuven (March 1995)
4. Dinur, I., Dunkelman, O., Shamir, A.: New attacks on keccak-224 and keccak-256. In: Canteaut, A. (ed.) FSE 2012. LNCS, vol. 7549, pp. 442–461. Springer, Heidelberg (2012)
5. Boura, C., Canteaut, A.: On the influence of the algebraic degree of F^{-1} on the algebraic degree of G o F. IEEE Transactions on Information Theory 59(1) (January 2013)
6. Bertoni, G., Daemen, J., Peeters, M., Assche, G.V.: Sponge functions. In: Ecrypt Hash Workshop (May 2007)
7. Bertoni, G., Daemen, J., Peeters, M., Van Assche, G.: On the indifferentiability of the sponge construction. In: Smart, N.P. (ed.) EUROCRYPT 2008. LNCS, vol. 4965, pp. 181–197. Springer, Heidelberg (2008)
8. Bertoni, G., Daemen, J., Peeters, M., Van Assche, G.: Sponge-based pseudo-random number generators. In: Mangard, S., Standaert, F.-X. (eds.) CHES 2010. LNCS, vol. 6225, pp. 33–47. Springer, Heidelberg (2010)
9. Bertoni, G., Daemen, J., Peeters, M., Van Assche, G.: Duplexing the sponge: Single-pass authenticated encryption and other applications. In: Miri, A., Vaudenay, S. (eds.) SAC 2011. LNCS, vol. 7118, pp. 320–337. Springer, Heidelberg (2012)
10. Bertoni, G., Daemen, J., Peeters, M., Assche, G.V.: Cryptographic sponge functions, version 0.1. STMicroelectronics and NXP Semiconductors (January 2011), http://sponge.noekeon.org/

11. Saarinen, M.J.O.: Related-key attacks against full Hummingbird-2. In: FSE 2013: 20th International Workshop on Fast Software Encryption, Singapore, March 11-13 (to appear, 2013)
12. Beaulieu, R., Shors, D., Smith, J., Treatman-Clark, S., Weeks, B., Wingers, L.: The SIMON and SPECK families of lightweight block ciphers. IACR ePrint 2013/404 (June 2013), http://eprint.iacr.org/2013/404
13. Biham, E., Shamir, A.: Differential Cryptanalysis of the Data Encryption Standard. Springer (1993)
14. Matsui, M.: Linear cryptanalysis method for DES cipher. In: Helleseth, T. (ed.) EUROCRYPT 1993. LNCS, vol. 765, pp. 386–397. Springer, Heidelberg (1994)
15. Matsui, M.: The first experimental cryptanalysis of the data encryption standard. In: Desmedt, Y.G. (ed.) CRYPTO 1994. LNCS, vol. 839, pp. 1–11. Springer, Heidelberg (1994)
16. Khovratovich, D., Nikolić, I.: Rotational cryptanalysis of ARX. In: Hong, S., Iwata, T. (eds.) FSE 2010. LNCS, vol. 6147, pp. 333–346. Springer, Heidelberg (2010)
17. Biham, E.: A fast new DES implementation in software. In: Biham, E. (ed.) FSE 1997. LNCS, vol. 1267, pp. 260–272. Springer, Heidelberg (1997)
18. Bernstein, D.J.: Cache-timing attacks on AES. Technical report, University of Chigaco (2005)
19. Acıiçmez, O., Schindler, W., Koç, Ç.K.: Cache based remote timing attack on the AES. In: Abe, M. (ed.) CT-RSA 2007. LNCS, vol. 4377, pp. 271–286. Springer, Heidelberg (2006)
20. Weiß, M., Heinz, B., Stumpf, F.: A cache timing attack on AES in virtualization environments. In: Keromytis, A.D. (ed.) FC 2012. LNCS, vol. 7397, pp. 314–328. Springer, Heidelberg (2012)
21. Bertoni, G., Daemen, J., Peeters, M., Assche, G.V.: On the security of the keyed sponge construction. In: SKEW 2011 Symmetric Key Encryption Workshop (February 2011)
22. Bertoni, G., Daemen, J., Peeters, M., Assche, G.V.: Sakura: a flexible coding for tree hashing. IACR ePrint 2013/213 (April 2013), http://eprint.iacr.org/2013/213
23. Saarinen, M.-J.O.: Beyond modes: Building a secure record protocol from a cryptographic sponge permutation. In: Benaloh, J. (ed.) CT-RSA 2014. LNCS, vol. 8366, Springer, Heidelberg (2014)
24. NIST: Recommendation for the Triple Data Encryption Algorithm (TDEA) block cipher, revision 1. NIST Special Publication 800-67 (January 2012)
25. Bertoni, G., Daemen, J., Peeters, M., Assche, G.V.: Permutation-based encryption, authentication and authenticated encryption. In: DIAC 2012 (2012), http://keccak.noekeon.org/KeccakDIAC2012.pdf
26. Biryukov, A., Wagner, D.: Slide attacks. In: Knudsen, L.R. (ed.) FSE 1999. LNCS, vol. 1636, pp. 245–259. Springer, Heidelberg (1999)
27. Biryukov, A., Wagner, D.: Advanced slide attacks. In: Preneel, B. (ed.) EUROCRYPT 2000. LNCS, vol. 1807, pp. 589–606. Springer, Heidelberg (2000)
28. Hiltgen, A.P.: Towards a better understanding of one-wayness: Facing linear permutations. In: Nyberg, K. (ed.) EUROCRYPT 1998. LNCS, vol. 1403, pp. 319–333. Springer, Heidelberg (1998)
29. Saarinen, M.-J.O.: Chosen-IV statistical attacks against eSTREAM ciphers. In: Proc. SECRYPT 2006, International Conference on Security and Cryptography, Setubal, Portugal, August 7-10 (2006)
30. Saarinen, M.J.O.: Developing a grey hat C2 and RAT for APT security training and assessment. In: GreHack 2013 Hacking Conference, Grenoble, France, November 15 (to appear, 2013)
31. Cazorla, M., Marquet, K., Minier, M.: Survey and benchmark of lightweight block ciphers for wireless sensor networks. In: SECRYPT 2013 (May 2013), http://eprint.iacr.org/2013/295

32. IAIK: AES for Texas Instruments MSP430 microcontrollers. Technical report, IAIK SIC T. U. Graz, `http://jce.iaik.tugraz.at/sic/Products/Crypto_Software_for_Microcontrollers`
33. TI: AES128 - A C implementation for encryption and decryption. Technical Report SLAA397A, Texas Instruments (July 2009), `http://www.ti.com/lit/an/slaa397a/slaa397a.pdf`

A   Trace of Execution for CBEAM

A trace (test vector) of six rounds of computation for the $\pi = mx^6$ function:

$$\mathbf{b} = (\ 0123,\ 1234,\ 2345,\ 3456,\ 4567,\ 5789,\ 6789,\ 789A,$$
$$89AB,\ 9ABC,\ ABCD,\ BCDE,\ CDEF,\ DEF0,\ EF01,\ F012\ )$$

$$mx(\mathbf{b}) = (\ 88A8,\ 3333,\ BDBD,\ BFC1,\ DD5D,\ B87B,\ BF7D,\ A3B5,$$
$$88A8,\ CCCC,\ F6F6,\ FF06,\ 5555,\ 9999,\ EDED,\ FE0D\ )$$

$$mx^2(\mathbf{b}) = (\ 6F0D,\ E713,\ 4B47,\ B151,\ 25BD,\ 929F,\ 2540,\ 7780,$$
$$4985,\ 511D,\ 818C,\ A135,\ 8426,\ 9911,\ FB65,\ 3991\ )$$

$$mx^3(\mathbf{b}) = (\ E50C,\ EAE4,\ 07F3,\ B08A,\ 6476,\ 2138,\ D90D,\ F629,$$
$$3919,\ 3071,\ 1E59,\ 1458,\ DEEC,\ 15F3,\ 96DF,\ 1FB2\ )$$

$$mx^4(\mathbf{b}) = (\ 8922,\ B751,\ 6648,\ 0EED,\ C285,\ 89E5,\ 2DFC,\ DBBF,$$
$$4310,\ 77FA,\ 3494,\ 7F13,\ 47D9,\ 6DD3,\ 1E59,\ E502\ )$$

$$mx^5(\mathbf{b}) = (\ 2CA0,\ 67B3,\ 4F96,\ 0A46,\ B209,\ AC7E,\ 5C64,\ A125,$$
$$CF7C,\ B46F,\ EB8A,\ FAED,\ 1130,\ 934D,\ CC02,\ 0D67\ )$$

$$mx^6(\mathbf{b}) = \pi(\mathbf{b}) = (\ 5432,\ 281E,\ B184,\ 9481,\ AAF0,\ C9BE,\ A028,\ 4C79,$$
$$4B69,\ 53BF,\ 53C0,\ CFE8,\ 8839,\ 9D2A,\ 89E3,\ 1300\ )$$

B   Bit-Slicing for ϕ_5

The ANSI C reference implementation `cbref/mx6-gcc.c` implements ϕ_5 as a macro as follows:

```
#define CBEAM_PHI5(x0, x1, x2, x3, x4) \
    (~(x0 & ((~x3 & x4) ^ (~x2 & x3))) & \
    (x1 | (~x2 & x3))) ^ (~x2 & (~x3 & x4))
```

Here we put our trust to compiler for common subexpression elimination of $(\sim\!x3\ \&\ x4)$ and $(\sim\!x2\ \&\ x3)$. One can assign these to temporary variables if necessary. We have exhaustively verified that ϕ_5 cannot be implemented with less than eight logical instructions (ANDN $(\sim\!x\ \&\ y)$ is a single op).

B.1   AVX 2

Here is a code snippet written in AVX2 C intrinsics for implementing the ϕ_5 function with 8 logical instructions on 256-bit registers:

```
// t0 = Phi5(x0,x1,x2,x3,x4)
t0 = _mm256_andnot_si256(x3, x4);
t1 = _mm256_andnot_si256(x2, x3);
t2 = _mm256_andnot_si256(x2, t0);
t3 = _mm256_or_si256(x1, t1);
t0 = _mm256_xor_si256(t0, t1);
t1 = _mm256_and_si256(x0, t0);
t0 = _mm256_andnot_si256(t1, t3);
t0 = _mm256_xor_si256(t0, t2);
```

Please see the reference implementation file cbref/mx6-avx2.c for tricks on how to implement λ and various shifts efficiently on this platform.

B.2   MSP430

TI MSP430 has only two-operand machine instructions and hence the code is slightly longer with 9 instructions on 16-bit registers:

```
/* r14 = Phi5(r15,r14,r13,r12,r11) */
bic      r12, r11
inv      r13
and      r13, r12
and      r11, r13
xor      r12, r11
and      r11, r15
bis      r12, r14
bic      r15, r14
xor      r13, r14
```

The MSP430 reference implementation cbeam430/mx430.s can compute $\pi = mx^6$ without utilizing stack (except the top value, which is basically free).

C   Auxiliary Tables

Table 2. Probabilities (%) of best differentials for $(\lambda \circ \phi)_{16}$ with specific input weight (rows) and output weight (columns). The best overall differential and the best differential with output weight 1 are emphasized.

Wt	1	2	3	4	5	6	7	8	9	10	11	12	13	14	15	16
1	0	0	1.07	.513	.635	.562	.385	.330	.140	.137	.064	.021	.003	0	0	0
2	0	4.30	2.15	2.54	2.15	1.37	.592	.443	.284	.256	.116	.098	.037	.027	.006	.006
3	**17.2**	5.47	5.47	3.91	1.78	.922	.787	.476	.330	.195	.177	.119	.079	.052	.027	.003
4	.009	1.46	3.37	5.15	1.95	1.32	.903	.439	.305	.375	.232	.159	.101	.064	.049	.021
5	.684	2.93	6.74	2.49	2.20	1.76	.885	.635	.446	.363	.266	.192	.140	.085	.064	.021
6	7.03	**18.4**	5.47	3.91	2.34	1.37	.894	.702	.412	.354	.214	.168	.131	.128	.052	.018
7	.928	2.00	4.17	2.12	3.09	1.64	1.14	.671	.470	.299	.247	.223	.165	.101	.040	.024
8	2.93	3.22	3.22	4.15	3.12	1.95	1.20	.732	.522	.360	.220	.256	.140	.070	.049	.034
9	8.20	4.00	11.1	4.59	3.52	1.95	1.28	.885	.525	.366	.253	.171	.134	.101	.067	.024
10	.598	1.39	1.66	2.73	1.46	2.27	1.44	.781	.586	.323	.220	.208	.131	.153	.043	.021
11	.964	2.44	3.27	2.05	3.96	2.22	1.27	.879	.403	.232	.266	.192	.165	.092	.037	.027
12	.781	5.57	2.83	6.74	2.34	1.86	.696	.439	.290	.296	.198	.171	.128	.058	.040	.031
13	0	.122	.159	.323	.247	.269	.327	.317	.272	.214	.223	.119	.082	.058	.031	.009
14	0	.018	.073	.150	.177	.250	.269	.424	.235	.275	.140	.104	.061	.052	.024	.015
15	0	0	.003	.006	.079	.064	.122	.058	.076	.064	.055	.037	.043	.034	.021	0
16	0	0	0	0	0	.006	.006	.049	.024	.055	.031	.058	.015	.021	0	.012

Table 3. Absolute biases (%) of best linear approximations for $(\lambda \circ \phi)_{16}$ with specific input mask weight (rows) and output weight (columns)

Wt	1	2	3	4	5	6	7	8	9	10	11	12	13	14	15	16
1	0	0	6.25	3.71	4.69	3.12	2.73	1.56	1.17	.586	.439	0	0	0	0	0
2	0	12.5	7.03	9.38	6.25	4.88	3.71	2.93	3.32	1.86	1.27	1.27	.684	.391	0	0
3	**25.0**	12.5	9.38	6.25	5.08	4.49	4.59	3.71	2.73	1.95	1.66	1.42	1.37	.830	.684	0
4	0	7.03	9.38	7.81	7.81	7.03	3.91	3.81	3.03	2.88	4.39	6.15	3.37	2.73	1.27	2.15
5	6.25	12.5	9.38	8.59	9.38	5.86	5.08	3.91	5.27	6.05	6.84	3.47	2.64	2.49	1.95	1.07
6	18.8	18.8	15.6	10.9	7.03	5.47	5.27	6.45	6.25	8.01	4.83	3.32	2.15	1.95	1.46	1.17
7	0	7.81	10.9	12.5	7.81	6.64	7.42	8.40	8.40	4.59	3.91	4.15	4.74	2.78	3.42	1.27
8	6.25	15.6	14.1	9.38	10.2	8.59	8.59	9.77	6.45	4.79	4.83	3.96	3.76	3.76	2.25	.977
9	18.8	18.8	15.6	10.9	8.59	10.5	10.9	6.25	4.69	3.96	4.39	3.56	2.88	2.15	1.95	.879
10	0	7.03	7.81	9.38	9.38	14.1	8.59	5.08	4.49	4.54	3.61	3.96	3.76	4.98	2.83	2.25
11	6.25	7.81	7.81	10.9	15.6	7.81	6.25	4.59	3.61	3.32	4.20	4.88	3.08	2.98	1.86	1.17
12	6.25	9.38	14.1	17.2	9.38	6.25	3.91	3.32	3.37	3.32	3.66	4.20	2.98	2.59	1.46	1.56
13	0	0	1.95	2.93	2.93	2.93	3.71	2.88	3.27	4.20	3.52	2.78	3.27	3.52	5.08	.586
14	0	0	.391	.684	1.90	2.05	2.44	2.29	2.93	2.98	2.59	2.98	2.69	2.78	1.46	.977
15	0	0	0	.684	.635	1.22	1.66	1.76	1.81	1.76	2.05	1.86	2.29	1.17	.684	0
16	0	0	0	0	0	0	0	.488	.537	.684	.977	1.37	1.32	2.78	1.17	9.38

Table 4. Progression of differentials in consecutive invocations of mx. Here the zeroth bit has been flipped; $\Delta = 0^{255} \parallel 1$. We observe that the full state is affected and there is no detectable bias after mx^4. The π transform has six rounds by default.

$mx(x) \oplus mx(x \oplus \Delta)$

#	15 14 13 12	11 10 09 08	07 06 05 04	03 02 01 00
00	38 50 63 50	37 50 62 50	37 50 63 38	00 00 00 **25**
01	00 00 00 00	00 00 00 00	00 00 00 00	00 00 00 00
02	00 00 00 00	00 00 00 00	00 00 00 00	00 00 00 00
03	00 00 00 00	00 00 00 00	00 00 00 00	00 00 00 00
04	00 00 00 00	00 00 00 00	00 00 00 00	00 00 00 00
05	00 00 00 00	00 00 00 00	00 00 00 00	00 00 00 00
06	00 00 00 00	00 00 00 00	00 00 00 00	00 00 00 00
07	00 00 00 00	00 00 00 00	00 00 00 00	00 00 00 00
08	00 00 00 00	00 00 00 00	00 00 00 00	00 00 00 00
09	00 00 00 00	00 00 00 00	00 00 00 00	00 00 00 00
10	00 00 00 00	00 00 00 00	00 00 00 00	00 00 00 00
11	00 00 00 00	00 00 00 00	00 00 00 00	00 00 00 00
12	00 00 00 00	00 00 00 00	00 00 00 00	00 00 00 00
13	00 00 00 00	00 00 00 00	00 00 00 00	00 00 00 00
14	00 00 00 00	00 00 00 00	00 00 00 00	00 00 00 00
15	00 00 00 00	00 00 00 00	00 00 00 00	00 00 00 00

$mx^2(x) \oplus mx^2(x \oplus \Delta)$

#	15 14 13 12	11 10 09 08	07 06 05 04	03 02 01 00
00	09 12 16 12	09 12 16 12	09 12 16 09	00 00 00 06
01	00 00 00 00	00 00 00 00	00 00 00 00	00 00 00 00
02	00 00 00 00	00 00 00 00	00 00 00 00	00 00 00 00
03	00 00 00 00	00 00 00 00	00 00 00 00	00 00 00 00
04	14 19 23 19	14 19 23 19	14 19 23 14	00 00 00 09
05	23 31 39 31	23 31 39 31	23 31 39 23	00 00 00 16
06	19 25 31 25	19 25 31 25	19 25 31 19	00 00 00 12
07	14 19 23 19	14 19 23 19	14 19 23 14	00 00 00 09
08	19 25 31 25	19 25 31 25	19 25 31 19	00 00 00 13
09	23 31 39 31	23 31 39 31	23 31 39 23	00 00 00 16
10	19 25 31 25	19 25 31 25	19 25 31 19	00 00 00 13
11	14 19 23 19	14 19 23 19	14 19 23 14	00 00 00 09
12	19 25 31 25	19 25 31 25	19 25 31 19	00 00 00 12
13	23 31 39 31	23 31 39 31	23 31 39 23	00 00 00 16
14	19 25 31 25	19 25 31 25	19 25 31 19	00 00 00 12
15	14 19 24 19	14 19 23 19	14 19 23 14	00 00 00 09

$mx^3(x) \oplus mx^3(x \oplus \Delta)$

#	15 14 13 12	11 10 09 08	07 06 05 04	03 02 01 00
00	33 34 33 32	33 34 33 32	33 36 36 37	38 39 36 32
01	00 00 00 00	00 00 00 00	00 00 00 00	00 00 00 00
02	00 00 00 00	00 00 00 00	00 00 00 00	00 00 00 00
03	00 00 00 00	00 00 00 00	00 00 00 00	00 00 00 00
04	40 42 41 39	40 42 41 39	40 43 43 42	44 45 43 39
05	47 48 47 45	47 49 47 45	46 48 48 47	49 49 48 45
06	44 46 45 43	44 46 46 43	44 46 46 46	47 48 46 43
07	40 42 41 39	40 42 41 39	40 43 43 42	44 45 43 39
08	44 46 45 43	44 46 45 43	44 46 46 46	47 48 46 43
09	46 48 47 45	47 49 47 45	46 48 48 47	48 49 48 45
10	44 46 45 43	44 46 45 42	44 46 46 46	47 48 46 43
11	40 42 41 39	40 42 41 39	40 42 43 42	44 45 43 39
12	44 46 45 43	44 46 45 43	44 46 46 46	47 48 46 43
13	46 48 47 45	47 49 47 45	46 48 48 47	48 49 48 45
14	44 46 45 43	44 46 45 43	44 46 46 46	47 48 46 43
15	40 42 41 39	40 42 41 39	40 43 43 42	44 45 43 39

$mx^4(x) \oplus mx^4(x \oplus \Delta)$

#	15 14 13 12	11 10 09 08	07 06 05 04	03 02 01 00
00	49 49 49 49	49 49 49 49	49 49 49 50	50 50 49 49
01	49 49 50 49	49 50 50 49	49 50 50 50	50 50 50 49
02	50 50 50 50	50 50 50 50	50 50 50 50	50 50 50 50
03	50 50 50 50	50 50 50 49	50 50 50 50	50 50 50 50
04	49 50 50 49	49 50 50 49	49 50 50 50	50 50 50 49
05	49 49 50 49	49 49 50 49	49 49 50 50	50 50 50 49
06	49 50 50 49	49 50 50 49	49 50 50 50	50 50 50 49
07	49 49 49 49	49 49 49 49	49 49 50 50	50 50 50 49
08	49 49 49 49	49 49 49 49	49 49 49 49	49 49 49 49
09	49 49 49 49	49 49 49 49	49 49 50 50	50 50 50 49
10	50 50 50 49	49 49 50 49	49 50 50 50	50 50 50 49
11	49 49 49 49	49 49 49 49	49 49 49 50	50 50 50 49
12	49 49 49 49	49 49 49 49	49 49 49 49	49 49 49 49
13	49 49 49 49	49 49 49 49	49 49 49 49	49 49 49 49
14	50 50 50 49	50 50 50 49	49 50 50 50	50 50 50 49
15	49 49 49 49	49 49 49 49	49 49 50 50	50 50 50 49

Progression of differentials in consecutive invocations of inverse function mx^{-1}. Here again the zeroth bit is flipped. After third round there is no longer any detectable bias.

$mx^{-1}(x) \oplus mx^{-1}(x \oplus \Delta)$

#	15 14 13 12	11 10 09 08	07 06 05 04	03 02 01 00
00	00 00 00 00	00 00 00 00	00 00 00 00	50 50 50 **50**
01	00 00 00 00	00 00 00 00	00 00 00 00	50 50 50 50
02	00 00 00 00	00 00 00 00	00 00 00 00	50 50 50 50
03	00 00 00 00	00 00 00 00	00 00 00 00	50 50 50 50
04	00 00 00 00	00 00 00 00	00 00 00 00	50 50 50 50
05	00 00 00 00	00 00 00 00	00 00 00 00	50 50 50 50
06	00 00 00 00	00 00 00 00	00 00 00 00	50 50 50 50
07	00 00 00 00	00 00 00 00	00 00 00 00	50 50 50 50
08	00 00 00 00	00 00 00 00	00 00 00 00	50 50 50 50
09	00 00 00 00	00 00 00 00	00 00 00 00	50 50 50 50
10	00 00 00 00	00 00 00 00	00 00 00 00	50 50 50 50
11	00 00 00 00	00 00 00 00	00 00 00 00	50 50 50 50
12	00 00 00 00	00 00 00 00	00 00 00 00	50 50 50 50
13	00 00 00 00	00 00 00 00	00 00 00 00	50 50 50 50
14	00 00 00 00	00 00 00 00	00 00 00 00	50 50 50 50
15	00 00 00 00	00 00 00 00	00 00 00 00	50 50 50 50

$mx^{-2}(x) \oplus mx^{-2}(x \oplus \Delta)$

#	15 14 13 12	11 10 09 08	07 06 05 04	03 02 01 00
00	20 25 19 25	34 34 24 25	24 25 25 25	25 25 25 25
01	24 21 22 20	20 20 20 21	20 21 21 20	21 21 21 21
02	23 21 21 21	21 21 20 21	20 21 21 21	21 21 21 22
03	39 39 39 39	40 40 39 39	39 39 39 39	39 39 39 39
04	50 50 50 50	50 50 50 50	50 50 50 50	50 50 50 50
05	49 50 50 50	49 50 50 50	50 50 50 50	50 50 50 50
06	46 47 47 48	49 49 48 47	48 47 47 48	47 47 47 47
07	49 48 47 47	47 47 46 47	46 48 48 47	48 48 48 49
08	50 50 50 50	50 50 50 50	50 50 50 50	50 50 50 50
09	49 50 50 50	47 47 49 50	49 50 50 50	50 50 50 50
10	44 46 44 47	51 51 47 46	47 46 46 47	46 46 46 46
11	50 47 48 47	47 47 46 47	46 47 47 47	47 47 48 48
12	50 50 50 50	50 50 50 50	50 50 50 50	50 50 50 50
13	49 49 49 49	47 47 49 49	49 49 49 49	49 49 49 50
14	41 45 42 45	50 50 46 45	46 45 45 45	45 45 45 45
15	47 38 40 36	38 38 35 37	34 38 37 36	39 38 39 40

D   Tables and Conjectures on Algebraic Properties of ϕ_n^{-1}

The ϕ_5 (Equations 4 and 10) Boolean mapping also defines reversible $n \times n$ - bit shift-invariant functions for other n apart from $n = 16$. Each forward function has degree 4. The characteristics of the Algebraic Normal Form of inverse functions up to $n = 32$ are given below. Each column contains the number of monomials of given degree; the last column has the number of nonzero terms for all degrees.

Conjecture 1. The inverse of ϕ_n is defined for each $n \geq 5$ with $n \neq 0 \pmod 3$ and $\deg \phi_n^{-1} = \lceil \frac{2}{3} n \rceil$.

Conjecture 2. Computation of ϕ_n^{-1} has at least polynomial complexity (with degree ≥ 2).

The computation of ϕ_n has linear complexity $O(n)$ but the complexity of ϕ_n^{-1} is at least $O(n^2)$ since the number of input bits grows with n as per observation in Conjecture 1. Super-polynomial complexity has not been ruled out as we do not know a polynomial time algorithm for ϕ_n^{-1}. Based on current evidence we are reluctant to believe in exponential complexity, however.

n	1	2	3	4	5	6	7	8	9	10	11	12	13	14	15	16	17	18	19	20	21	22	Poly n.z.t.
6																							*Nonsurjective.*
7	4	11	17	15	6																		53
8	3	9	13	13	9	2																	49
9																							*Nonsurjective.*
10	5	21	55	91	95	56	14																337
11	4	18	45	75	88	69	28	4															331
12																							*Nonsurjective.*
13	6	34	125	303	502	565	408	168	30														2141
14	5	30	106	253	433	543	471	252	72	8													2173
15																							*Nonsurjective.*
16	7	50	236	753	1705	2797	3293	2686	1430	446	62												13465
17	6	45	205	640	1456	2504	3236	3017	1912	766	172	16											13975
18																							*Nonsurjective.*
19	8	69	397	1570	4506	9678	15684	19001	16832	10532	4402	1104	126										83909
20	7	63	351	1356	3866	8472	14450	18965	18645	13266	6554	2114	396	32									88537
21																							*Nonsurjective.*
22	9	91	617	2910	10112	26816	55170	88281	109077	102570	71834	36250	12464	2618	254								519073
23	8	84	553	2548	8750	23352	49428	83181	110136	112723	87302	49868	20260	5510	892	64							554659
24																							*Nonsurjective.*
25	10	116	905	4956	20216	63770	158824	315095	498190	624397	614364	467824	269904	114084	33356	6036	510						3192557
26	9	108	820	4390	17654	55622	140638	288151	477827	636095	671875	555352	353222	168890	58546	13834	1980	128					3445141
27																							*Nonsurjective.*
28	11	144	1270	7918	37078	135562	396082	936082	1801051	2816653	3568633	3636674	2955688	1887016	925480	336844	85766	13646	1022				19545961
29	10	135	1161	7083	32664	118764	349392	843177	1676448	2740338	3661044	3966297	3452310	2386518	1289610	532002	161404	33822	4348	256			21256783
30																							*Nonsurjective.*
31	12	175	1721	12033	63606	264432	886320	2431089	5500476	10297548	15947808	20378433	21385950	18304116	12646968	6947652	2965474	948556	214062	30408	2046		119228885
32	11	165	1585	10855	56487	232938	781992	2171889	5029839	9731040	15696456	21023385	23257191	21114276	15602790	9279726	5389364	1589364	429714	81042	9468	512	130470385

Beyond Modes: Building a Secure Record Protocol from a Cryptographic Sponge Permutation

Markku-Juhani O. Saarinen

Kudelski Security, Switzerland
mjos@cblnk.com

Abstract. BLINKER is a light-weight cryptographic suite and record protocol built from a single permutation. Its design is based on the Sponge construction used by the SHA-3 algorithm KECCAK. We examine the SpongeWrap authenticated encryption mode and expand its padding mechanism to offer explicit domain separation and enhanced security for our specific requirements: shared secret half-duplex keying, encryption, and a MAC-and-continue mode. We motivate these enhancements by showing that unlike legacy protocols, the resulting record protocol is secure against a two-channel synchronization attack while also having a significantly smaller implementation footprint. The design facilitates security proofs directly from a single cryptographic primitive (a single security assumption) rather than via idealization of multitude of algorithms, paddings and modes of operation. The protocol is also uniquely suitable for an autonomous or semi-autonomous hardware implementation of protocols where the secrets never leave the module, making it attractive for smart card and HSM designs.

Keywords: Lightweight Security, Sponge-based Protocols, Sponge Construction, Autonomous Hardware Encryption, Half-duplex security, BLINKER.

1 Introduction

The last decade has seen significant advances in encryption algorithm design for pervasive and low-resource platforms; PRESENT [1] (2007),Grain-128a [2, 3] (2006-2011), Hummingbird-2 [4, 5] (2009-2011), and FIDES [6] (2013) are some notable examples, each representing a different cipher design methodology; block ciphers, stream ciphers, and authenticated encryption algorithms have been proposed [7]. However, there have been few general-purpose security suite proposals that have been designed from ground up for lightweight platforms.

In this work we forgo traditional ciphers and hashes and take a fresh look at designing light-weight security protocols. We see that a single cryptographic sponge permutation can fulfill all security requirements of such a protocol, leading to a reduction of implementation footprint and facilitating straight-forward security proofs.

Our aim is to create a generic short-distance link layer security provider that can function independently from upper layer application functions. Ideally this would be realizable with autonomous hardware, without much CPU or MCU involvement.

J. Benaloh (Ed.): CT-RSA 2014, LNCS 8366, pp. 270–285, 2014.

Contributions and Structure of This Paper. After a brief introduction to resource-hungry legacy record protocols (Section 2), we describe the two-channel synchronization problem which affects most of them – the interwoven order of messages from two communicating parties is left unauthenticated (Section 3).

Our design avoids much of the complexity of traditional security protocols by adopting a sequential state authentication mode (Section 4) which can better meet our security and efficiency requirements while facilitating straight-forward security proofs.

In order to counter the synchronization problem and to reduce implementation footprint we adopt a half-duplex mode that utilizes a fully shared state between the two parties (Section 5).

With the term *half-duplex* we are referring to a mode of communication where two parties take turns on a single channel – the corresponding ITU-T term is "simplex circuit". This is unrelated to the "Duplexing" primitive of SPONGEWRAP.

The "rolling" shared state will not only authenticate the current message but also all previous messages and secrets sent and received during the session by both parties together with their relative order.

We then recall basic facts about Sponge-based cryptography (Section 6), popularized by the NIST SHA-3 algorithm KECCAK [8, 9] and expand its functionality to two-party encryption and authentication with domain-separating multiplex padding (Section 6.1). This also addresses MAC truncation issues of the proposed authenticated encryption mode, SPONGEWRAP and the considerations expressed by NIST [10, 11].

After a brief technical description of authentication and (re)keying flow (Section 7), we give implementation notes (Section 8), followed by Conclusions (Section 9).

2 Legacy Record and Transport Protocols

All of the standard networking security protocols - SSL3 [12], SSH2 [13, 14], TLS [15], IPSEC [16–18], PPTP [19], and wireless WPA2 [20] together with its predecessors - can be divided into two largely independent protocols: the handshake / authentication protocol and the transport / record protocol. In this work we concentrate on the latter protocol which performs encryption and authentication of bulk data. We call these collectively as "legacy record protocols".

The record transport mechanisms of these protocols require that a diverse set of binary strings are fed to various padding, wrapping, encryption and message authentication algorithms. We denote this compound operation by f_{cs} for some "ciphersuite" determined during the handshake phase of the protocol.

In addition to the plaintext P, data items required to perform authenticated encryption usually include at least the following:

S Incremental message sequence number for MACs.
IV Initialization vector for block ciphers.
K_e Secret key for the symmetric encryption algorithm.
K_a Secret key for the message authentication algorithm.

All of this state data is required to create a protected record C which contains plaintext headers, encrypted headers, encrypted payload, padding, and the MAC.

$$C = f_{cs}(P, S, IV, K_e, K_a). \tag{1}$$

The inverse typically yields either the plaintext or failure and closure of the channel:

$$f_{cs}^{-1}(C, S, IV, K_e, K_a) = P \ or \ \mathsf{FAIL}. \tag{2}$$

We note that this was not the original specified behavior of these legacy protocols; various error messages were specified and implemented but these have been found to act as oracles and leak secret information in cryptanalytic attacks [21–23].

Details of f_{cs} process vary depending on the particular protocol and version, but generally a header is appended to the message, followed by passes with a MAC algorithm such as HMAC [24] and an encryption algorithm (typically AES [25] in CBC [26] mode or the RC4 stream cipher [27]). In recent years the AES-GCM [28] authenticated encryption mode has also been integrated with many of these protocols, but it is not very popular in implementations. The Wireless Protected Access 802.11i (WPA / WPA2) protocol [20] requires AES in two-pass CCM [29] mode to implement its CCMP protocol and SHA-1 [30] for key derivation. Furthermore TLS-based EAP-TLS [31] authentication is recommended.

State and Algorithmic Complexity. At least two sets of data items (state) are required since these protocols view the server-to-client and client-to-server channels as entirely independent from each other. In IPSEC the two separate Security Associations (SAs) may even theoretically utilize different algorithms.

Even if we ignore various error conditions, the security of legacy record protocols depends upon the security of a large number of unrelated component designs, including: Key derivation (PRF), HMAC and its Hash, padding, the cipher and its mode of operation, and header encoding. Furthermore all data is processed at least twice – by the encryption algorithm and the MAC algorithm, independently of each other. This is why these protocols cannot be considered fully suitable for embedded and lightweight applications or fully autonomous hardware implementations.

3 Two-Party Synchronization

As previously mentioned in Section 2, two independent channels are established by legacy protocols, one from client to server ($A \rightarrow B$) and another from server to client ($B \rightarrow A$). As these security protocols are often implemented as *communication layers* (e.g. HTTPS is just HTTP over a TLS layer), typically no API interface is even available to synchronize communications between the two channels.

Example: Consider the following three transcripts

$$T1: \quad B \rightarrow A : M_2, \quad A \rightarrow B : M_1, \quad A \rightarrow B : M_3$$
$$T2: \quad A \rightarrow B : M_1, \quad B \rightarrow A : M_2, \quad A \rightarrow B : M_3$$
$$T3: \quad A \rightarrow B : M_1, \quad A \rightarrow B : M_3, \quad B \rightarrow A : M_2$$

These three transcripts have precisely the same, valid, representation on the two channels when sent over IPSEC, TLS, SSL, or SSH protocols. The same authentication codes will match.

Therefore the upper protocol layers cannot determine whether M_2 was sent spontaneously by B ($T1$) or as a response to M_1 ($T2$) or to both M_1 and M_3 ($T3$). Such ambiguity can significantly affect the interpretation of M_2 in an upper layer application such as a transaction protocol and lead to security failures.

The Synchronization Problem of Two-Channel Protocols. This illustrates a fundamental security issue; despite individual message authentication, the interwoven order of the sequence of back-and-forth messages cannot be unambiguously determined and authenticated with the legacy protocols, a fundamental requirement for reliable transactions. This is why transaction records are often authenticated on the application level as well, adding another layer of complexity.

This issue also affects basic end-user interactive security as portions of server messaging can be maliciously delayed, encouraging the user to react to partial information.

We note this issue is already partially addressed by some national or regional payment terminal standards such as [32].

4 Rethinking Privacy and Authentication

Legacy record protocols apply authentication to each message individually; authentication of an individual message does not affect others any more than the $A \to B$ channel affects $B \to A$ channel. We note that such approach is not necessary as these protocols are not generally fault tolerant and therefore require reliable rather than datagram transport.

We simplify the abstraction of Equations 1 and 2 by defining an encoding transform enc() that takes in a state variable S_i, plaintext P_i, and padding, outputting a new state S_{i+1} and ciphertext message C_i. The ciphertext message C_i may be longer than plaintext P_i if it contains a t-bit authentication tag, which must be checked by the recipient.

$$(S_{i+1}, C_i) = \mathsf{enc}(\ S_i, P_i, pad\ ). \tag{3}$$

The decoding function dec() produces the same S_{i+1} and P_i from the ciphertext and equivalent S_i and padding, synchronizing the state between sender and receiver – or resulting in a failure in case of an authentication error:

$$(S_{i+1}, P_i) = \mathsf{dec}(\ S_i, C_i, pad\ )\ or\ \mathsf{FAIL}. \tag{4}$$

Here the intended utility of legacy protocols' MAC and Encryption secret keys and algorithms (for encryption and message authentication), sequence numbers, and initialization vectors boils down to a singular synchronized state variable whose contents depend on absorbed keying and initialization data together with all encrypted messaging transmitted thus far. The new state S_{i+1} can be then used for transmitting an another message; this is a "MAC-and-Continue" mode.

Our main security goals are largely compatible with those laid out for Authenticated Encryption [33, 34] and Duplex Sponges in particular – proofs in [35, 36] are applicable if appropriate domain-separating padding is used. See Section 6.1 for claimed security bounds for the following security goals:

priv The ciphertext result C of $enc(S, P, pad)$ must be indistinguishable from random when S is random and P may be chosen by the attacker.

auth The probability of an adversary of choosing a message C that does not result in a FAIL in $dec(S, C, pad)$ without knowledge of S is bound by a function of the authentication tag size t and number of trials.

We define an additional nonstandard, informal goal which relates to solving the synchronization problem of actual two-party protocols described in Section 3. It can be viewed as a direct extension of auth from an unidirectional communications channel to bidirectional channels and multi-party protocols:

sync Each party can verify that all previous messages of the session have been correctly received and the absolute order in which messages were sent.

Our security argument for this goal is derived from the fact that an encoding exists that effectively expresses each two-party session as a single, unique hash. However, it may be possible to achieve such verifiability in a protocol which is not strictly synchronous or has more than two parties, so we leave the formal definition of sync to latter work.

Comparison with Legacy Protocols. Our requirements are stronger than those commonly expected from security protocols; for example all protocols of Section 2 are easily identifiable, a concern in the operation of Firewalls and Intrusion Detection Systems (IDS) which try to profile and filter various protocols being used in a network.

Our design tries to avoid visible unencrypted sequence numbers and paddings that would allow trivial protocol and protocol version identification as it is very difficult to block something you cannot create an IDS signature for. [1]

The third, informal requirement sync appears to be new and is not met by current protocols as shown in Section 3. Here we are trying to address a real-world security concern rather than adding a vehicle for theoretical research.

We find that with Sponge approach we do not have to over-simplify our protocol when modeling it for security proofs. In analysis of a typical real world protocol, one is faced with a combinatorial explosion of interplay between details such as: crypto algorithms, message formatting and padding, modes of operation, hash constructions, MAC constructions, error codes, and key derivation. Such complexity is the main reason why "provably secure" protocols often fail in practice; the protocols have been be severely simplified and idealized for analysis.

During the 10-15 years since the protocols of Section 2 largely took their present form, a large number number of security proofs, counter-proofs and attacks have been presented, starting with [38–40] and [23, 41–44] representing some of the more recent work.

---

[1] Our BLINKER implementation has its origins in the stealthy communications mechanisms of an Academic RAT tool [37]. Here a HTTP port 80 channel was used and hence our traffic could not be "picked up" amongst other random things that are transmitted during web surfing.

5   Half-Duplex Security Protocols with a Shared State

In BLINKER, we implement communications security for the shared channel using a single, synchronized state S_i for both directions, saving resources and 50% of state memory in the implementation. A domain separation padding mechanism distinguishes between the two communicating parties as well as data input types. Figure 1 shows an interchange of three messages with a synchronized state.

From security viewpoint, this setup has the advantage that the entire interchange or "conversation" is continually authenticated as the evolving state includes full contents of messages from both parties and the order they were sent. The security proofs interpret the state S_i as equivalent to a cryptographic hash of a full transcript of the session up to message or input i; this is achieved with specific padding.

Asymmetrically Signed Sessions and Transactions. The entire session up to point i can be cryptographically validated by signing a hash "squeezed" from the state S_i. Even if the initial session authentication is based on digital signatures, as is often the case with legacy protocols, this does not mean that the session is signed. Without Alice's signature of the protocol transcript, Bob (who also knows all symmetric authentication and encryption secrets) can easily forge a session transcript. It is rather difficult to sign a session with a protocol such as TLS, SSH2, or IPSEC since application-level hashing and processing is required. With a BLINKER-type protocol such final authentication is relatively easy to implement, an excellent feature for transaction protocols.

Real-Life Prevalence of Half-Duplex Links. Half-duplex links may seem rare to a software developer due to the widespread use of the socket programming paradigm. This illusion is often achieved by time-division duplexing (TDD). However, half-duplex is physically prevalent on sensor networks, IoT and last-hop radio links – Bluetooth and IEEE 802.15.4 ZigBee being two notable examples.

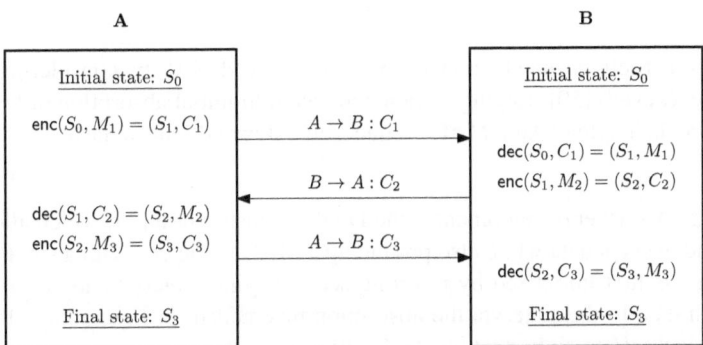

Fig. 1. Simplified interchange of three messages whose plaintext equivalents are $A \rightarrow B : M_1$, $B \rightarrow A : M_2$, $A \rightarrow B : M_3$, utilizing a synchronized secret state variables S_i. The order of messages cannot be modified and hence this exchange is sync - secure.

Half-duplex links can be established wirelessly with unpaired frequencies (same frequency in both directions), a typical scenario in light-weight time-divide communications, our specific targets. An another example are embedded twisted-wire serial links.

We note that in addition to wireless last-hop transports, most RFID, Smart Card, and industrial control (MODBUS) communications are implemented under a query-response model and are therefore effectively half-duplex [45–47].

6 Extending the Sponge Construction

Sponge constructions generally consist of a state $S = (S^r \mathbin{\|} S^c)$ which has $b = r + c$ bits and a b-bit keyless cryptographic permutation π. The S^r component of the state has r "rate" bits which interact with the input and the internal S^c component has c private "capacity" bits.

These components, together with suitable padding and operating rules can be used to build provable Sponge-based hashes [48], Tree Hashes [49], Message Authentication Codes (MACs) [50], Authenticated Encryption (AE) algorithms [35], and pseudorandom extractors (PRFs and PRNGs) [51].

Absorbing and Squeezing. We recall the basic Sponge hash [48] concepts of "absorbing" and "squeezing" which intuitively correspond to insertion and extraction of data to or from the sponge. Let S_i and S_{i+1} be b-bit input and output states. For absorption of padded data blocks M_i (of r bits each) we iterate:

$$S_{i+1} = \pi(S_i^r \oplus M_i \mathbin{\|} S_i^c). \tag{5}$$

This stage is followed by squeezing out the hash $H = H(M)$ by consecutive iterations of:

$$H = H \mathbin{\|} S_i^r$$
$$S_{i+1} = \pi(S_i). \tag{6}$$

These constructions may be transformed into a keyed MAC by considering the state S_i as secret (keyed) [50]. Keying is then equivalent to initial absorption of keying material before the payload data. MAC is squeezed out exactly like a hash.

Duplexing. A further development is the Duplex construction [35] which allows us to encrypt and decrypt data while also producing a MAC in the end with a single pass.

The state is first initialized by inserting secret keying material and non-secret randomization data to the state via the absorption mechanism of Equation 5. To encrypt plaintext blocks P_i to ciphertext blocks C_i we iterate:

$$C_i = S_i^r \oplus P_i$$
$$S_{i+1} = \pi(C_i \mathbin{\|} S_i^c). \tag{7}$$

The effect on the state is the same as that of Equation 5. The inverse – decryption operation – is almost equivalent to encryption, which in itself has significant implementation advantages:

$$P_i = S_i^r \oplus C_i$$
$$S_{i+1} = \pi(C_i \parallel S_i^c). \tag{8}$$

After encryption or decryption, a message authentication code for the message may be squeezed out as in Equation 6 and verified. To simplify exposition, we have left some key details regarding padding. We will come back to these in Section 6.1.

MAC-and-Continue. There is really no need to constrain the iteration to a single message. With appropriate domain-separating padding the security proofs allow the sponge states to be used for any number of consecutive authenticated messages ("MAC-and-Continue") without the need for sequence numbers, and re-keying. This is one of the main observations which led to the present work and greatly reduces the latency of implementation as "initialization rounds" are not required for each message. This was also proposed as part of the original SPONGEWRAP construction.

6.1 Multiplex Padding

The SPONGEWRAP [35] and MONKEYDUPLEX [36] padding rules offer concrete Sponge-based methods for performing authenticated encryption. Recent work on implementation of SPONGEWRAP and its variants on low-resource platforms is reported in [7].

The requirements laid out in [35] for the padding rule are that they are reversible, non-empty and that the last block is non-zero. The padding rule in KECCAK is that a single 1 bit is added after the last bit of the message and also at the end of the input block.

In the Duplex construction of SPONGEWRAP additional padding is included for each input block; a secondary information bit called *frame bit* is used for domain separation. SAKURA [49] uses additional frame bits to facilitate tree hashing. It is essential that the various bits of information such as the key, authenticated data, and authenticated ciphertext can be exactly "decoded" from the Sponge input to avoid trivial padding collisions. We use a more explicit padding mechanism but the following priv and auth bounds proven in [35] (Section 5.2 on Page 332) and [50] also hold for enc():

Theorem 1 (Theorem 1 from [35]). *The* SPONGEWRAP *and BLINKER authenticated encryption modes satisfy the following privacy and authentication security bounds:*

$$\mathrm{Adv}_{\mathsf{enc}}^{\mathsf{priv}}(\mathcal{A}) < q2^{-k} + \frac{N(N+1)}{2^{c+1}} \tag{9}$$

$$\mathrm{Adv}_{\mathsf{enc}}^{\mathsf{auth}}(\mathcal{A}) < q2^{-k} + 2^{-t} + \frac{N(N+1)}{2^{c+1}} \tag{10}$$

against any single adversary $\mathcal{A}$ *if* $K \xleftarrow{\$} \{0,1\}^k$, *tags of* $l \geq t$ *bits are used,* π *is a randomly chosen permutation,* q *is the number of queries and* N *is the number of times* π *is called.*

Note that even the Squeezing phase can utilize padding to mark the size of desired output (as we do in Section 6.2). In KECCAK and SPONGEWRAP a convention has been adopted to have a null S_r input to π during squeezing in order to separate it from other phases (hence the requirement that padding rule does not produce null blocks). However this may lead to problems in some applications where the MAC length is not clear.

Context collision in KECCAK and SPONGEWRAP. There is no indicator for MAC length in SPONGEWRAP construction – output is simply truncated. If the sender and recipient have a different idea about the length, there is no way to detect truncation of the MAC. Different length-variants of KECCAK give different outputs for the same data simply because different data rates r are used and this affects the placing of the final padding bit. Earlier members of the SHA standard avoid this issue by having different IV values depending on the desired output length [30].

6.2   Multiplexing the Sponge

Our new padding rule is called Multiplex. Input and output blocks, encrypted and authenticated data, keys, and nonces are all different input domains and must be encoded unambiguously as Sponge inputs. Rather than using frame bits per block for domain separation as in SPONGEWRAP, the data domains are explicitly encoded. This allows many more data types to be entered into the sponge as well and clearer domain separation between them. It is essential in a shared-state two-party protocol that the originating party of the block (Alice or Bob) is also used to mark domain separation between the two.

We retain one d-bit word D in S^c for domain separation; $S^c = (S^d \parallel S^{c'})$ with $c' = c - d$. The iteration for arbitrary absorption, squeezing, and encryption is now:

$$S_{i+1} = \pi(S_i^r \oplus M_i \parallel S_i^d \oplus D_i \parallel S_i^{c'}). \qquad (11)$$

For decryption we have the following update function:

$$S_{i+1} = \pi(C_i \parallel S_i^d \oplus D_i \parallel S_i^{c'}). \qquad (12)$$

In our implementation $d = 16$ bits. Table 1 gives a description of padding mask word bits (which may be OR'ed together). Message blocks are always padded with a single "1" bit and by zeros to fill r bits, followed by the multiplex padding word. If full r bits are used in a block, the padding bit is the bit 0 in the multiplex word.

The effective information theoretic capacity is reduced by the Multiplex construction to no more than $c - 3$ rather than $c' = c - d$ if tree functions are not used.

Unlike message data, the domain separation word is always XORed with the S state bits on all operations (Equations 11 and 12). Apart from few options, the domains follow each other in application-specific predetermined order and hence two bits of entropy is sufficient to mark that separation between block types in our protocol. In addition there is a padding bit that may be located in the domain separation word if the input block is full (bit 0).

Therefore the effective c for values bounds of Theorem 1 need to be modified only by 3 bits when multiplex padding is used. We do this in order to remove the requirement for additional message padding buffers and also to follow Horton's Principle [40, 52], *"Authenticate what is being meant, not what is being said."*

The separation of the domain mask word from main input allows later expansions of functionality without breaking interface designs; for example we may adopt tree-based hashing - and by extension, tree MACs and encryption - by utilizing bits 14 and 15 of D_i for this purpose rather than adding more frame bits as in SAKURA [49]. If tree structure is used, the capacity should be reduced to $c - 4$ for security analysis. Furthermore, increasing $d > 16$ will not break existing implementations.

Since the protocol exchange can be unambiguously decoded from the sponge input $(M_1 \parallel D_1) \parallel (M_2 \parallel D_2) \parallel ..$, and we do not reset the state between messages, the proofs of Theorem 1 [35, 50] seem to apply to the protocol as a whole as well as individual messages. If one can forge an individual message authentication code or (by induction) a multi-message exchange, one can also break the Sponge in a SHA-3 - type hash construction. However, we leave the formalization and proof machinery of our informal sync goal for latter work.

Padding while Squeezing. In the squeezing phases of our construction the (inputless) output blocks are virtually padded as if $M_i = 0^r$ in Equation 11. If $s < r$ bits of the block is begin squeezed out, a single "1" bit is XORed at state S after the location of last output bit; $M_i = 0^s \parallel 1 \parallel 0^{r-s-1}$. This resolves the SPONGEWRAP context collision described in Section 6.1 since at least the last output block will differ for different output sizes.

We acknowledge that the solution is perhaps not ideal if the extracted hash is longer than the block size; two hashes of different size from the same message are equivalent except for the final blocks.

6.3   Sourcing π

BLINKER was originally designed together with the CBEAM algorithm [53] for integrated use in low-resource and small-footprint applications.

However, the choice of π is arbitrary if it satisfies the required security properties. KECCAK is a strong candidate as it has been selected as the NIST SHA-3 algorithm [8, 9, 54], albeit its 1600-bit state is often seen as too large for low-resource platforms and short messages. However, there are nonstandard reduced-state variants KECCAK-$f[b]$ where $b = 25 \times 2^l$ for $1 \le l \le 6$.

Other candidates as π donors include PHOTON [55]. QUARK [56, 57], and SPONGENT [58]. Each of these can be used to construct extremely lightweight protocols based on our Multiplex / BLINKER construction.

Note that some clearly "non-hermetic" Sponge permutations such as FIDES [6] are probably not secure enough. It may be possible to be somewhat flexible in this requirement as we assume a randomized session S, as is done in the MONKEYDUPLEX [36] construct.

Table 1. Proposed bits used in the Multiplex Padding Word which is XORed with the state. Depending on protocol state and the intended usage of message block, multiple bits are set simultaneously.

Bit	Mask	When set
0	0x0001	This is a full input or output block (r bits).
1	0x0002	This is the final block of this data element.
4	0x0004	Block is an input to sponge ("absorption").
3	0x0008	Block is output from sponge ("squeezing").
4	0x0010	Associated Authenticated Data input.
5	0x0020	Secret key block.
6	0x0040	Nonce input block.
7	0x0080	Encryption / Decryption block.
8	0x0100	Hash block.
9	0x0200	Keyed Message Authentication Code (MAC) output block.
10	0x0400	Block for state storage or reloading.
11	0x0800	Pseudo Random Number Generator (PRNG) block.
12	0x1000	Originating from Alice (client / slave).
13	0x2000	Originating from Bob (server / master).
14	0x4000	Tree chaining Node.
15	0x8000	Tree final Node.

Comparison with AES-based Protocols. For most of these π permutations the working memory required to implement the entire two-way BLINKER protocol is only slightly more than b bits for the state. It is difficult if not impossible to implement AES in any reasonable authenticated mode of operation with such a small amount of memory in a two-party protocol as additional storage is required for two round / nonce counters, authenticators, and round keys.

7   Basic Shared Secret Authentication and Record Protocol Flow

We assume that the shared secret K is simply stored by both parties; however it may be derived with a lightweight asymmetric key exchange method such as Curve25519 [59]. K may also be combined from passwords or composed in other ways.

We use the shorthand $enc(state, input, pad)$ in the following for encoding operations. Corresponding synchronized decoding may result in FAIL and immediate closure of channel. We do not explicitly describe these operations; see Sections 4 and 5. However, in order to clarify exposition, we are "writing out" the authentication tag generation phases.

We first absorb the identities I_a and I_b of Alice and Bob into the state. Note that it may not be necessary to transmit the messages M_1 and M_2 if the identities are self-evident. The key is never transmitted but simply mixed with the state. Let S_0 be some initialization value.

$$(S_1, M_1) = \text{enc}(S_0, I_a, \texttt{0x108C}) \mid A \to B : M_1$$
$$(S_2, M_2) = \text{enc}(S_1, I_b, \texttt{0x208C}) \mid B \to A : M_2$$
$$S_3 = \text{enc}(S_2, K, \texttt{0x3024}) \mid$$

Two random nonces R_a and R_b are required for challenge-response authentication and to make the session unique.

$$(S_4, M_3) = \text{enc}(S_3, R_a, \texttt{0x10CC}) \mid A \to B : M_3$$
$$(S_5, M_4) = \text{enc}(S_4, R_b, \texttt{0x20CC}) \mid B \to A : M_4$$

We may now perform mutual authentication with tags of t bits:

$$(S_6, M_5) = \text{enc}(S_5, 0^t, \texttt{0x1208}) \mid A \to B : M_5$$
$$(S_7, M_6) = \text{enc}(S_6, 0^t, \texttt{0x2208}) \mid B \to A : M_6$$

Checking M_5 and M_6 completes mutual authentication. By an inductive process we see that the session secret S_7 is now dependent upon randomizers from both parties and the original shared secret is not leaked if the Sponge satisfies our security axioms.

After this, plaintexts P_a (for $A \to B$) and P_b (for $B \to A$) can be encrypted, transmitted and authenticated by repeating the following exchange:

$$(S_{i+1}, M_a) = \text{enc}(S_i, P_a, \texttt{0x108C}) \mid A \to B : M_a$$
$$(S_{i+2}, T_a) = \text{enc}(S_{i+1}, 0^t, \texttt{0x1208}) \mid A \to B : T_a$$
$$(S_{i+3}, M_b) = \text{enc}(S_{i+2}, P_b, \texttt{0x208C}) \mid B \to A : M_b$$
$$(S_{i+4}, T_b) = \text{enc}(S_{i+3}, 0^t, \texttt{0x2208}) \mid B \to A : T_b$$

Due to explicit padding it is easy to show that the entire message flow is authenticated if appropriate checks are made.

8   Implementation Notes

We have already fielded BLINKER in a tiny security application that communicates with a server over a HTTP 1.1 stay-alive link [37]. Such a link is essentially half-duplex as messages are sent and received over HTTP POST method within a single stay-alive TCP session. On the target platform this proved to be an ideal method for communicating with a server over the Internet; SSL is essentially unimplementable on the target platform. The same is true for many low-end embedded devices that have only rudimentary TCP stacks or use some non-TCP protocol for the initial hop.

Figure 2 shows a simplified interface for a module that implements BLINKER in hardware. The mode of operation is determined by the domain separation padding word PADDING IN (as specified in Table 1) together with the SEND / RECEIVE signal that distinguishes between encryption and decryption, MAC generation and verification. It is noteworthy that the S^c secret state bits never have to leave the module and can be isolated from CPU with the interface provided.

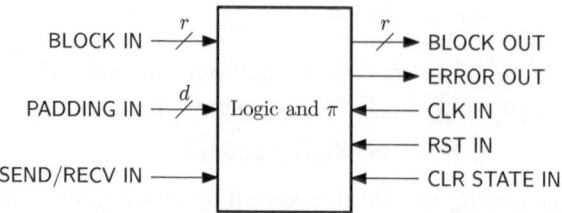

Fig. 2. A simplified interface architecture for a semi-autonomous hardware component implementing BLINKER

9   Conclusions

We have described the use of Sponge permutations to build complete lightweight two-way communications links (record protocols). In terms of embedded RAM and ROM our design has much smaller implementation footprint when compared to traditional approaches. Furthermore the "half-duplex" design is naturally suited for these platforms and is resistant to synchronization flaws; each authentication tag essentially authenticates the entire session up to that point.

In a hardware implementation the session secrets never have to leave (and cannot leave) a specific hardware component, making the design attractive in HSM and smart card applications. Such separation is very difficult (and costly) to achieve with SSL and other legacy protocols which generally require CPU/MCU interaction to create encryption and authentication keys from session secrets.

Our design is especially suitable for last-lap and autonomous hardware communications, such as those with sensors, Radio Frequency Identification (RFID) and Near Field Communication (NFC) systems, smart cards, and Internet-of-Things applications.

Acknowledgements. The author wishes to thank Kudelski Security, University of Haifa, and Nanyang Technological University for supporting his work. Program Committee members of CT-RSA 2014 provided invaluable suggestions for improving the quality of this paper.

References

1. Bogdanov, A., Knudsen, L.R., Leander, G., Paar, C., Poschmann, A., Robshaw, M.J.B., Seurin, Y., Vikkelsoe, C.: PRESENT: An ultra-lightweight block cipher. In: Paillier, P., Verbauwhede, I. (eds.) CHES 2007. LNCS, vol. 4727, pp. 450–466. Springer, Heidelberg (2007)
2. Hell, M., Johansson, T., Meier, W.: Grain - a stream cipher for constrained environments. International Journal of Wireless and Mobile Computing, Special Issue on Security of Computer Network and Mobile Systems 2(1), 86–93 (2006)
3. Gren, M.A., Hell, M., Johansson, T., Meier, W.: Grain-128a: a new version of Grain-128 with optional authentication. International Journal of Wireless and Mobile Computing 5(1), 48–59 (2011)
4. Engels, D., Fan, X., Gong, G., Hu, H., Smith, E.M.: Ultra-lightweight cryptography for low-cost RFID tags: Hummingbird algorithm and protocol. Technical Report CACR-2009-29, University of Waterloo (2009)

5. Engels, D., Saarinen, M.-J.O., Schweitzer, P., Smith, E.M.: The hummingbird-2 lightweight authenticated encryption algorithm. In: Juels, A., Paar, C. (eds.) RFIDSec 2011. LNCS, vol. 7055, pp. 19–31. Springer, Heidelberg (2012)
6. Bilgin, B., Bogdanov, A., Knežević, M., Mendel, F., Wang, Q.: FIDES: Lightweight authenticated cipher with side-channel resistance for constrained hardware. In: Bertoni, G., Coron, J.-S. (eds.) CHES 2013. LNCS, vol. 8086, pp. 142–158. Springer, Heidelberg (2013)
7. Yalçın, T., Kavun, E.B.: On the implementation aspects of sponge-based authenticated encryption for pervasive devices. In: Mangard, S. (ed.) CARDIS 2012. LNCS, vol. 7771, pp. 141–157. Springer, Heidelberg (2013)
8. NIST: NIST selects winner of secure hash algorithm (SHA-3) competition. NIST Tech Beat Newsletter (October 2, 2012)
9. Bertoni, G., Daemen, J., Peeters, M., Assche, G.V.: The Keccak reference, version 3.0. NIST SHA3 Submission Document (January 2011)
10. Kelsey, J.: SHA3: Where we've been, where we're going. Talk Given at RSA Security Conference USA 2013 (February 2013)
11. Kelsey, J.: SHA3: Past, present, and future. Invited Talk Given at CHES 2013 (August 2013)
12. Freier, A., Karlton, P., Kocher, P.: The secure sockets layer (SSL) protocol version 3.0. IETF RFC 6101 (Historic) (August 2011)
13. Ylönen, T., Lonvick, C.: The secure shell (SSH) protocol architecture. IETF RFC 4251 (Standards Track) (January 2006)
14. Ylönen, T., Lonvick, C.: The secure shell (SSH) transport layer protocol. IETF RFC 4253 (Standards Track) (January 2006)
15. Dierks, T., Rescorla, E.: The transport layer security (TLS) protocol version 1.2. IETF RFC 5246 (Standards Track) (August 2008)
16. Kent, S., Seo, K.: Security architecture for the internet protocol. IETF RFC 4301 (Standards Track) (December 2005)
17. Kent, S.: IP authentication header. IETF RFC 4302 (Standards Track) (December 2005)
18. Kent, S.: IP encapsulating security payload (ESP). IETF RFC 4303 (Standards Track) (December 2005)
19. Hamzeh, K., Pall, G., Verthein, W., Taarud, J., Little, W., Zorn, G.: Point-to-point tunneling protocol (PPTP). IETF RFC 2637 (July 1999)
20. IEEE: IEEE standard for information technology - telecommunications and information exchange between systems - local and metropolitan area networks - specific requirements. part 11: Wireless LAN medium access control (MAC) and physical layer (PHY) specifications. amendment 6: Medium access control (MAC) security enhancements (July 2004)
21. Bleichenbacher, D.: Chosen ciphertext attacks against protocols based on the RSA encryption standard PKCS #1. In: Krawczyk, H. (ed.) CRYPTO 1998. LNCS, vol. 1462, pp. 1–12. Springer, Heidelberg (1998)
22. Vaudenay, S.: Security flaws induced by CBC padding - applications to SSL, IPSEC, WTLS.. In: Knudsen, L.R. (ed.) EUROCRYPT 2002. LNCS, vol. 2332, pp. 534–546. Springer, Heidelberg (2002)
23. AlFardan, N.J., Paterson, K.G.: Lucky thirteen: Breaking the TLS and DTLS record protocols. In: IEEE Symposium on Security and Privacy 2013 (to appear, 2013)
24. Bellare, M., Canetti, R., Krawczyk, H.: Message authentication using hash functions - the HMAC construction. CryptoBytes 2(1) (1996)
25. NIST: Advanced Encryption Standard (AES). Federal Information Processing Standards 197 (2001)
26. Dworkin, M.: Recommendation for block cipher modes of operation. Special Publication 800-38A (December 2001)
27. Rivest, R.: The RC4 encryption algorithm (March 1992)

28. NIST: Recommendation for block cipher modes of operation: Galois/counter mode (GCM) and GMAC. NIST Special Publication 800-38D (2007)
29. Whiting, D., Housley, R., Ferguson, N.: Counter with CBC-MAC (CCM). IETF RFC 3610 (September 2003)
30. NIST: Secure Hash Standard (SHS). Federal Information Processing Standards Publication 180-4 (March 2012)
31. Simon, D., Aboba, B., Hurst, R.: The EAP-TLS authentication protocol. IETF RFC 5216 (March 2008)
32. UKPA: Acquirers' interface requirements for electronic data capture terminals. UKPA / APACS Standard 40, incorporated into Standard 70 Book 2, 4 & 5 (2007)
33. Rogaway, P., Bellare, M., Black, J., Krovetz, T.: OCB: A block-cipher mode of operation for efficient authenticated encryption. In: Reiter, M.K., Samarati, P. (eds.) CCS 2001: Proceedings of the 8th ACM Conference on Computer and Communications Security, pp. 196–205. ACM (2001)
34. Rogaway, P., Bellare, M., Black, J.: OCB: A block-cipher mode of operation for efficient authenticated encryption. ACM Transactions on Information and System Security (TISSEC) 6(3), 365–403 (2003)
35. Bertoni, G., Daemen, J., Peeters, M., Van Assche, G.: Duplexing the sponge: Single-pass authenticated encryption and other applications. In: Miri, A., Vaudenay, S. (eds.) SAC 2011. LNCS, vol. 7118, pp. 320–337. Springer, Heidelberg (2012)
36. Bertoni, G., Daemen, J., Peeters, M., Assche, G.V.: Permutation-based encryption, authentication and authenticated encryption. In: DIAC 2012 (2012), http://keccak.noekeon.org/KeccakDIAC2012.pdf
37. Saarinen, M.J.O.: Developing a grey hat C2 and RAT for APT security training and assessment. In: GreHack 2013 Hacking Conference, Grenoble, France, November 15, 2013 (to appear)
38. Bellovin, S.M.: Problem areas for the IP security protocols. In: Proc. Sixth USENIX Security Symposium, pp. 205–214 (1996)
39. Mitchell, J., Shmatikov, V., Stern, U.: Finite-state analysis of SSL 3.0. In: USENIX Security Symposium 1998, 201–216. USENIX (1998)
40. Wagner, D., Schneier, B.: Analysis of the SSL 3.0 protocol. In: The Second USENIX Workshop on Electronic Commerce Proceedings, pp. 29–40. USENIX Press (November 1996)
41. Degabriele, J.P., Paterson, K.G.: Attacking the IPsec standards in encryption-only configurations. In: IEEE Symposium on Security and Privacy, pp. 335–349. IEEE Computer Society (2007)
42. Degabriele, J.P., Paterson, K.G.: On the (in)security of IPsec in MAC-then-encrypt configurations. In: Al-Shaer, E., Keromytis, A.D., Shmatikov, V. (eds.) ACM Conference on Computer and Communications Security, pp. 493–504. ACM (2010)
43. Paterson, K.G., Ristenpart, T., Shrimpton, T.: Tag size *does* matter: Attacks and proofs for the TLS record protocol. In: Lee, D.H., Wang, X. (eds.) ASIACRYPT 2011. LNCS, vol. 7073, pp. 372–389. Springer, Heidelberg (2011)
44. Krawczyk, H., Paterson, K.G., Wee, H.: On the security of the TLS protocol: A systematic analysis. In: Canetti, R., Garay, J.A. (eds.) CRYPTO 2013, Part I. LNCS, vol. 8042, pp. 429–448. Springer, Heidelberg (2013)
45. International Standardization Organization: ISO/IEC 7816-4:2013 Identification cards – Integrated circuit cards – Part 4: Organization, security and commands for interchange (2013)
46. International Standardization Organization: ISO/IEC 18000-63. Information technology – Radio frequency identification for item management – Part 6: Parameters for air interface communications at 860 MHz to 960 MHz Type C (2012)

47. MODBUS: MODBUS Application Protocol Specification V1.1B (April 2012),
    `http://www.modbus.org/docs/`
    `Modbus_Application_Protocol_V1_1b3.pdf`
48. Bertoni, G., Daemen, J., Peeters, M., Assche, G.V.: Sponge functions. In: Ecrypt Hash Workshop 2007 (May 2007)
49. Bertoni, G., Daemen, J., Peeters, M., Assche, G.V.: Sakura: a flexible coding for tree hashing. IACR ePrint 2013/213 (April 2013), `http://eprint.iacr.org/2013/213`
50. Bertoni, G., Daemen, J., Peeters, M., Assche, G.V.: On the security of the keyed sponge construction. In: SKEW 2011 Symmetric Key Encryption Workshop (February 2011)
51. Bertoni, G., Daemen, J., Peeters, M., Van Assche, G.: Sponge-based pseudo-random number generators. In: Mangard, S., Standaert, F.-X. (eds.) CHES 2010. LNCS, vol. 6225, pp. 33–47. Springer, Heidelberg (2010)
52. Ferguson, N., Schneier, B.: Practical Cryptography. John Wiley & Sons (2003)
53. Saarinen, M.-J.O.: CBEAM: Efficient authenticated encryption from feebly one-way *phi* functions. In: Benaloh, J. (ed.) CT-RSA 2014. LNCS, vol. 8366, Springer, Heidelberg (2014)
54. Chang, S., Perlner, R., Burr, W.E., Turan, M.S., Kelsey, J.M., Paul, S., Bassham, L.E.: Third-round report of the SHA-3 cryptographic hash algorithm competition. Technical Report NISTIR 7896, National Institute of Standards and Technology (November 2012)
55. Guo, J., Peyrin, T., Poschmann, A.: The PHOTON family of lightweight hash functions. In: Rogaway, P. (ed.) CRYPTO 2011. LNCS, vol. 6841, pp. 222–239. Springer, Heidelberg (2011)
56. Aumasson, J.-P., Henzen, L., Meier, W., Naya-Plasencia, M.: QUARK: A lightweight hash. In: Mangard, S., Standaert, F.-X. (eds.) CHES 2010. LNCS, vol. 6225, pp. 1–15. Springer, Heidelberg (2010)
57. Aumasson, J.P., Henzen, L., Meier, W., Naya-Plasencia, M.: Quark: A lightweight hash. Journal of Cryptology (2012), doi: 10.1007/s00145-012-9125-6
58. Bogdanov, A., Knežević, M., Leander, G., Toz, D., Varıcı, K., Verbauwhede, I.: SPONGENT: A lightweight hash function. In: Preneel, B., Takagi, T. (eds.) CHES 2011. LNCS, vol. 6917, pp. 312–325. Springer, Heidelberg (2011)
59. Bernstein, D.J.: Curve25519: New diffie-hellman speed records. In: Yung, M., Dodis, Y., Kiayias, A., Malkin, T. (eds.) PKC 2006. LNCS, vol. 3958, pp. 207–228. Springer, Heidelberg (2006)

Group Signatures with Message-Dependent Opening in the Standard Model

Benoît Libert and Marc Joye

Technicolor
975 Avenue des Champs Blancs
35576 Cesson-Sévigné Cedex, France

Abstract. Group signatures allow members of a group to anonymously sign messages in the name of this group. They typically involve an opening authority that can identify the origin of any signature if the need arises. In some applications, such a tracing capability can be excessively strong and it seems desirable to restrict the power of the authority. Sakai *et al.* recently suggested the notion of group signatures with message-dependent opening (GS-MDO), where the opening operation is made contingent on the knowledge of a trapdoor information – generated by a second authority – associated with the message. Sakai *et al.* showed that their primitive implies identity-based encryption (IBE). In the standard model, efficiently constructing such a system thus requires a structure-preserving IBE scheme, where the plaintext space is the source group $\mathbb{G}$ (rather than the target group $\mathbb{G}_T$) of a bilinear map $e : \mathbb{G} \times \mathbb{G} \to \mathbb{G}_T$. Sakai *et al.* used a structure-preserving IBE which only provides bounded collusion-resistance. As a result, their GS-MDO construction only provides a weak form of anonymity where the maximal number of trapdoor queries is determined by the length of the group public key. In this paper, we construct the first fully collusion-resistant IBE scheme that encrypts messages in $\mathbb{G}$. Using this construction, we obtain a GS-MDO system with logarithmic signature size (in the number N of group members) and prove its security in the standard model under simple assumptions.

Keywords: Group signatures, message-dependent opening, efficiency, collusion-resistance, structure-preserving cryptography.

1 Introduction

Group signatures are central anonymity-related primitives, suggested by Chaum and van Heyst [20], which allow users to sign messages while hiding their identity within a population they belong to. They notably find applications in trusted computing platforms, auction protocols, anonymous subscription systems or in mechanisms for protecting the privacy of commuters in public transportation. To prevent users from abusing the system, group signatures usually involve an opening authority (OA) which is capable of identifying the signer using some trapdoor information. Although the opening authority can remain most frequently offline, group members have no privacy at all against this all powerful

J. Benaloh (Ed.): CT-RSA 2014, LNCS 8366, pp. 286–306, 2014.
© Springer International Publishing Switzerland 2014

entity that can spy on all signature generations and identify the signer every time. To address this problem, Sakai *et al.* [35] advocated the design of a special kind of group signatures, called *group signatures with message-dependent opening* (GS-MDO), where restrictions are placed on the power of the OA. In the GS-MDO primitive, opening authorities cannot open any signature on their own. In order to open a signature on a message M, they need both their private key *and* a message-specific trapdoor t_M generated by a separate authority called *admitter*.

While the notion of group signatures dates back to Chaum and van Heyst [20], truly scalable and secure solutions remained elusive until the construction put forth by Ateniese *et al.* [6]. For lack of well-understood definitions, the security of their scheme was analyzed w.r.t. a list of sometimes redundant properties. A suitable security model was studied later on by Bellare, Micciancio and Warinschi [7] in the setting of static groups, where previous properties were subsumed by two security notions named *full anonymity* and *full traceability*. The case of dynamically growing groups was independently considered by Bellare, Shi and Zhang [9] and Kiayias and Yung [29].

During the last decade, a number of practical schemes were analyzed (e.g., [6, 12, 21, 29, 32]) in the random oracle model [8], which is known [18] to only provide heuristic arguments in terms of security. While theoretical standard model constructions were given under general assumptions [7, 9], they were "only" proofs of concept. Viable constructions were suggested for the first time by Boyen and Waters [14, 15] and Groth [23, 24] who took advantage of breakthrough results [22, 25] in the construction of non-interactive zero-knowledge (NIZK) and witness indistinguishable (NIWI) proofs. The most efficient standard model realizations to date rely on the Groth-Sahai methodology [25], which is tailored to specific languages involving elements in bilinear groups.

GROUP SIGNATURES WITH MESSAGE-DEPENDENT OPENING. Traditional group signature models allow opening authorities to identify the originator of every single signature. As discussed by Sakai *et al.* [35], it may be desirable to restrict this extremely high power in many real-life applications.

One way to address this problem is to use techniques from threshold cryptography and share the opening key among several distributed opening authorities (as considered in, e.g., [10]) in such a way that none of these can individually open signatures and hurt the privacy of group members. While this approach may be sufficient in some applications, it requires the distributed openers to run a joint opening protocol whenever they want to trace a signature back to its source. In applications where many signatures on the same message have to be opened, this may become impractical. For example, suppose that group signatures are used to verify anonymous access rights to a parking or to enhance the privacy of users in public transportation systems: by issuing a group signature on a message consisting of the current date and time, users can demonstrate that they hold a valid credential and paid the subscription without being linkable to their previous rides. If a crime is committed, the police may want to find out who used a given metro line during a specific time interval. This requires a mechanism allowing for the opening of all signatures generated for a given date-time message and only those. Running a distributed opening protocol for each individual signature may be a bottleneck in this scenario. The same is true when group signatures are used in auction protocols: if group members are bidders who anonymously sign their bids, the threshold opening approach entails a communication cost proportional to the number of winners who offered the highest amount.

The above use cases motivated Sakai *et al* [35] to formalize the notion of *group signatures with message-dependent opening* (GS-MDO), which splits the role of the opening authority between two entities called *opener* and *admitter*. In order to identify the author of a signature on a message M, the opener needs both its opening key ok *and* a trapdoor t_M generated by the admitter for the message M: the opening operation must be approved by the admitter, depending on the content of the message. Importantly, neither entity is powerful enough to open a signature by itself. A crucial difference with the aforementioned threshold opening approach is that, once a trapdoor t_M has been released for a sensitive message M, the opener can trace all signatures on M without any further interaction with the admitter.

We believe this message-dependent opening property to be of interest even in the setting of a centralized opening authority. Indeed, it features a complementary property to that of traceable signatures [28]. These involve opening authorities which can release a user-specific trapdoor allowing anyone to trace all signatures issued by a misbehaving group member. The GS-MDO primitive is important when the tracing criterion is the signed message (which could contain keywords associated with an illegal transaction) instead of the group member's identity. Both techniques could actually be used in conjunction: one could first use a message-specific trapdoor to identify all group members who signed a suspicious message before tracing all other signatures created by these members.

RELATED WORK. Sakai *et al.* [35] gave a general construction of GS-MDO and notably showed that it implies Identity-Based Encryption [13, 36] (IBE): in their specific construction, the trusted authority naturally serves as an admitter and message-specific trapdoors are nothing but IBE private keys associated with the message. They also pointed out that, in order to build an efficient GS-MDO system in the standard model with the current state of knowledge in the area, they need a form of structure-preserving IBE scheme. Recall that a cryptographic primitive is called *structure-preserving* (see [1–4, 17, 19, 23] for examples) if it handles objects – like ciphertexts or signatures – that only consist of elements from a group $\mathbb{G}$ over which a bilinear map is efficiently computable and if the validity of these objects can be checked using pairing-product equations. The latter properties make the primitive compatible with the Groth-Sahai techniques [25], which is crucial when one seeks to prove security in the standard model.

The main difficulty is that no structure-preserving IBE scheme is available to date: all pairing-based schemes proceed either by XORing the message with a hashed Bilinear Diffie-Hellman key [13] or encrypting messages that live in the target group $\mathbb{G}_T$ of the bilinear map $e : \mathbb{G} \times \mathbb{G} \to \mathbb{G}_T$ (see, e.g., [11, 37]). In order to construct an efficient GS-MDO in the standard model, what we need is an IBE scheme that encrypts messages in the domain group $\mathbb{G}$. We call such a system *partially* structure-preserving since identities do not have to be group elements and private keys can be ordinary (non-structure-preserving) signatures. For lack of a fully collusion-resistant such IBE, Sakai *et al.* [35] used a variant of the k-resilient construction of Heng and Kurosawa [27]: in the latter, semantic security is only guaranteed against adversaries that obtain private keys for no more than an *a priori* bounded number of identities. Moreover, the master public key has linear size in the pre-determined upper bound k. As a consequence, the standard model GS-MDO realization of [35] only achieves a relaxed flavor of security: namely, anonymity against the opener is only guaranteed as long as the adversary obtains trapdoors for at most k distinct messages. Moreover, the group public key inherits the $\mathcal{O}(k)$ size of the underlying IBE system.

In the random oracle model, Ohara *et al.* [33] recently proposed a construction allowing for an unbounded number of trapdoor queries. However, for the time being, building a fully secure GS-MDO system in the standard model remains an open problem.

OUR CONTRIBUTION. In this paper, we describe a GS-MDO system with $\mathcal{O}(\log N)$ size signatures, where N is the number of group members, and prove its security in the standard model under simple, constant-size assumptions (*i.e.*, we do not use q-type assumptions where the number of input elements depends on the number of adversarial queries or other system-related parameters).

As a result of independent interest, we describe the first fully collusion-resistant pairing-based IBE scheme that allows encrypting messages in the source group $\mathbb{G}$. This property is useful when it comes to proving properties about IBE-encrypted data: for example, the techniques of Camenisch *et al.* [16] can be used in combination with Groth-Sahai proofs to provide evidence that an IBE-encrypted plaintext belongs to a public set. Our system proceeds by blinding the plaintext $M \in \mathbb{G}$ using a random mask obtained by multiplying a random subset $\prod_{i \in S} Z_i$ of public elements $(Z_1, \ldots, Z_\ell) \in \mathbb{G}^\ell$, where ℓ is proportional to the security parameter. The ℓ-bit string K identifying the subset S (so that $K[i] = 1$ if and only if $Z_i \in S$) is in turn encoded in a bit-wise manner using a variant of the Waters IBE scheme, each bit $K[i]$ of K being encoded as an independent IBE ciphertext entirely comprised of elements in $\mathbb{G}$. A consequence of this bit-by-bit encoding is that we need $O(\ell)$ group elements to encrypt one element $M \in \mathbb{G}$. Despite its relatively large ciphertext size, our construction suffices to provide $\mathcal{O}(\log N)$ size signatures.

If we naively plug our IBE scheme into the general GS-MDO construction of Sakai *et al.* [35], we obtain signatures consisting of $\mathcal{O}(\lambda)$ group elements (or $\mathcal{O}(\lambda^2)$ bits), where λ is the security parameter, as each signature includes an IBE ciphertext. Fortunately, we can obtain signatures of only $\mathcal{O}(\log N)$ group elements – which is substantially shorter since $\log N \ll \lambda$ for any group of polynomial cardinality N – by combining the bit-wise encoding of our IBE scheme with the technique used in the Boyen-Waters group signature [14]. In the latter, membership certificates consist of Waters signatures $\left(g^\omega \cdot (v_0 \cdot \prod_{j=1}^\ell v_j^{\mathrm{id}[j]})^r, g^r \right)$

on the group members' identifiers $\mathrm{id} \in \{0,1\}^{\ell}$, where $\ell = \log N$, and each group signature contains commitments to the individual bits $\mathrm{id}[j]$ of id as well as NIWI proofs showing that committed values are actually bits. Our idea is thus to encode each bit $\mathrm{id}[j]$ of id using a structure-preserving identity-based bit encryption scheme where the receiver's identity is the message to be signed. In order to guarantee anonymity against the admitter, we follow [35] and super-encrypt each IBE ciphertext under the opener's public key using a CCA2-secure public-key cryptosystem. For groups of $N = 10^6$ users, we eventually obtain signatures of 68 kB at the 128-bit security level, which is approximately twice the signature length of the k-resilient scheme of [35].

ORGANIZATION. In the forthcoming sections, we first recall the syntax and the security definitions of group signatures with message-dependent opening in Section 2. Section 3 describes our structure-preserving IBE system and our GS-MDO scheme is detailed in Section 4.

2 Background

2.1 Bilinear Maps and Complexity Assumptions

We use bilinear maps $e : \mathbb{G} \times \mathbb{G} \to \mathbb{G}_T$ over groups of prime order p where $e(g, h) \neq 1_{\mathbb{G}_T}$ if and only if $g, h \neq 1_{\mathbb{G}}$. In these groups, we rely on two hardness assumptions that are both non-interactive and stated using a constant number of elements.

Definition 1 ([12]). *The* **Decision Linear** *(DLIN) Problem in* $\mathbb{G}$*, is to distinguish between the distributions* $(g^a, g^b, g^{ac}, g^{bd}, g^{c+d})$ *and* $(g^a, g^b, g^{ac}, g^{bd}, g^z)$*, with* $a, b, c, d \stackrel{R}{\leftarrow} \mathbb{Z}_p$, $z \stackrel{R}{\leftarrow} \mathbb{Z}_p$*. The Decision Linear assumption is the intractability of DLIN for any PPT distinguisher.*

Definition 2 ([13]). *The* **Decision 3-party Diffie-Hellman** *(D3DH) Problem in* $\mathbb{G}$*, is to distinguish the distributions* $(g, g^a, g^b, g^c, g^{abc})$ *and* (g, g^a, g^b, g^c, g^z)*, where* $a, b, c, z \stackrel{R}{\leftarrow} \mathbb{Z}_p$*.*

2.2 Groth-Sahai Proof Systems

Groth-Sahai (GS) proofs [25] can be based on the DLIN assumption, where they use prime order groups and a common reference string containing three vectors $\vec{f_1}, \vec{f_2}, \vec{f_3} \in \mathbb{G}^3$, where $\vec{f_1} = (f_1, 1, g)$, $\vec{f_2} = (1, f_2, g)$ for some $f_1, f_2 \in \mathbb{G}$. To commit to $X \in \mathbb{G}$, one chooses $r, s, t \stackrel{R}{\leftarrow} \mathbb{Z}_p$ and computes $\vec{C} = (1, 1, X) \cdot \vec{f_1}^r \cdot \vec{f_2}^s \cdot \vec{f_3}^t$. In the soundness setting, we have $\vec{f_3} = \vec{f_1}^{\xi_1} \cdot \vec{f_2}^{\xi_2}$ where $\xi_1, \xi_2 \in \mathbb{Z}_p$. Commitments $\vec{C} = (f_1^{r+\xi_1 t}, f_2^{s+\xi_2 t}, X \cdot g^{r+s+t(\xi_1+\xi_2)})$ are then extractable using $\beta_1 = \log_g(f_1)$, $\beta_2 = \log_g(f_2)$. In the witness indistinguishability (WI) setting, $\vec{f_1}, \vec{f_2}, \vec{f_3}$ are linearly independent and $\vec{C}$ is a perfectly hiding commitment. Under the DLIN assumption, the two kinds of CRS are indistinguishable.

To commit to an exponent $x \in \mathbb{Z}_p$, the prover computes $\vec{C} = \vec{\varphi}^x \cdot \vec{f_1}^r \cdot \vec{f_2}^s$, where $r, s \xleftarrow{R} \mathbb{Z}_p$, using a CRS consisting of vectors $\vec{\varphi}, \vec{f_1}, \vec{f_2}$. In the perfect soundness setting, $\vec{\varphi}, \vec{f_1}, \vec{f_2}$ are linearly independent while, in the perfect WI setting, choosing $\vec{\varphi} = \vec{f_1}^{\xi_1} \cdot \vec{f_2}^{\xi_2}$ gives a perfectly hiding commitment.

To prove that committed variables satisfy a set of relations, the prover computes one commitment per variable and one proof element per relation. Such non-interactive witness indistinguishable (NIWI) proofs are available for pairing-product equations, which are equations of the form

$$\prod_{i=1}^{n} e(\mathcal{A}_i, \mathcal{X}_i) \cdot \prod_{i=1}^{n} \cdot \prod_{j=1}^{n} e(\mathcal{X}_i, \mathcal{X}_j)^{a_{ij}} = t_T, \qquad (1)$$

for variables $\mathcal{X}_1, \ldots, \mathcal{X}_n \in \mathbb{G}$ and constants $t_T \in \mathbb{G}_T$, $\mathcal{A}_1, \ldots, \mathcal{A}_n \in \mathbb{G}$, $a_{ij} \in \mathbb{Z}_p$, for $i, j \in \{1, \ldots, n\}$. Efficient NIWI proofs also exist for multi-exponentiation equations, which are of the form $\prod_{i=1}^{m} \mathcal{A}_i^{y_i} \cdot \prod_{j=1}^{n} \mathcal{X}_j^{b_j} \cdot \prod_{i=1}^{m} \cdot \prod_{j=1}^{n} \mathcal{X}_j^{y_i \gamma_{ij}} = T$, for variables $\mathcal{X}_1, \ldots, \mathcal{X}_n \in \mathbb{G}$, $y_1, \ldots, y_m \in \mathbb{Z}_p$ and constants $T, \mathcal{A}_1, \ldots, \mathcal{A}_m \in \mathbb{G}$, $b_1, \ldots, b_n \in \mathbb{Z}_p$ and $\gamma_{ij} \in \mathbb{G}$, for $i \in \{1, \ldots, m\}, j \in \{1, \ldots, n\}$.

In pairing-product equations, proofs for quadratic equations require 9 group elements whereas linear equations (*i.e.*, where $a_{ij} = 0$ for all i, j in equation (1)) only cost 3 group elements each. Linear multi-exponentiation equations of the type $\prod_{i=1}^{m} \mathcal{A}_i^{y_i} = T$ require 2 group elements.

2.3   Group Signatures with Message-Dependent Opening

We use the syntax of [35], which extends the static model of Bellare, Micciancio and Warinschi [7].

Keygen(λ, N): given a security parameter $\lambda \in \mathbb{N}$ and a maximal number of group members $N \in \mathbb{N}$, this algorithm outputs a group public key gpk, a vector **gsk** = (gsk[0], ..., gsk[$N-1$]) of group members' private keys as well as private keys msk$_{\mathsf{ADM}}$ and ok for the admitter and the opener.

Sign: takes as input a message M, a private key gsk[i] and gpk, it outputs a signature σ.

Verify: is a deterministic algorithm taking as input a signature σ, a message M and a group public key gpk. It returns either 0 or 1.

TrapGen: is a possibly randomized algorithm that takes as input the admitter's private key msk$_{\mathsf{ADM}}$ and a message M. It outputs a trapdoor t_M allowing the OA to open all signatures on M.

Open: takes as input a message M, a valid signature σ w.r.t. gpk, the opening authority's private key ok and a trapdoor t_M for the message M. It outputs $i \in \{0, \ldots, N-1\} \cup \{\bot\}$, which is either the index of a group member or a symbol indicating an opening failure.

Definition 3. *A GS-MDO scheme provides full traceability if, for any $\lambda \in \mathbb{N}$, any $N \in \mathsf{poly}(\lambda)$ and any PPT adversary $\mathcal{A}$ involved in the experiment hereafter, it holds that*

$$\mathbf{Adv}_{\mathcal{A}}^{\mathrm{trace}}(\lambda) = \Pr[\mathbf{Exp}_{\mathcal{A}}^{\mathrm{trace}}(\lambda, N) = 1] \in \mathsf{negl}(\lambda).$$

$Exp_{\mathcal{A}}^{trace}(n, N)$

$(\mathsf{gpk}, \mathsf{ok}, \mathsf{msk}_{\mathsf{ADM}}, \mathbf{gsk}) \leftarrow \mathsf{Keygen}(\lambda, N)$

$\mathsf{st} \leftarrow (\mathsf{ok}, \mathsf{msk}_{\mathsf{ADM}}, \mathsf{gpk})$; $\mathcal{C} \leftarrow \emptyset$; $K \leftarrow \varepsilon$; $Cont \leftarrow \mathbf{true}$

while $(Cont = \mathbf{true})$ do

   $(Cont, \mathsf{st}, j) \leftarrow \mathcal{A}^{\mathsf{Sign}(\mathbf{gsk}[\cdot], \cdot)}(choose, \mathsf{st}, K)$

   if $Cont = \mathbf{true}$ then $\mathcal{C} \leftarrow \mathcal{C} \cup \{j\}$; $K \leftarrow K \cup \{\mathbf{gsk}[j]\}$ end if

end while

$(M^{\star}, \sigma^{\star}) \leftarrow \mathcal{A}^{\mathsf{Sign}(\mathbf{gsk}[\cdot], \cdot)}(guess, \mathsf{st})$

if $\mathsf{Verify}(\mathsf{gpk}, M^{\star}, \sigma^{\star}) = 0$ then *Return* 0

if $\mathsf{Open}(\mathsf{gpk}, \mathsf{ok}, \mathsf{TrapGen}(\mathsf{gpk}, \mathsf{msk}_{\mathsf{ADM}}, M^{\star}), M^{\star}, \sigma^{\star}) = \bot$ then *Return* 1

if $\exists j^{\star} \in \{0, \ldots, N-1\}$ *such that*

   $(\mathsf{Open}(\mathsf{gpk}, \mathsf{ok}, t_{M^{\star}}, M^{\star}, \sigma^{\star}) = j^{\star}) \wedge (j^{\star} \notin \mathcal{C}) \wedge ((j^{\star}, M^{\star})$ *not queried by* $\mathcal{A})$

   with $t_{M^{\star}} \leftarrow \mathsf{TrapGen}(\mathsf{gpk}, \mathsf{msk}_{\mathsf{ADM}}, M^{\star})$

then *Return* 1

else *Return* 0

Definition 4. *A GS-MDO scheme provides full anonymity against the admitter if, for any $\lambda \in \mathbb{N}$, any $N \in \mathsf{poly}(\lambda)$ and any PPT adversary $\mathcal{A}$, the function*

$$\mathbf{Adv}_{\mathcal{A}}^{\mathrm{anon\text{-}adm}}(\lambda) = |\Pr[\mathbf{Exp}_{\mathcal{A}}^{\mathrm{anon\text{-}adm}}(\lambda, N) = 1] - 1/2| \in \mathsf{negl}(\lambda)$$

is a negligible function in the security parameter if the experiment proceeds as follows

$Exp_{\mathcal{A}}^{anon-adm}(\lambda, N)$

$(\mathsf{gpk}, \mathsf{ok}, \mathsf{msk}_{\mathsf{ADM}}, \mathbf{gsk}) \leftarrow \mathsf{Keygen}(\lambda, N)$

$(\mathsf{st}, j_0, j_1, M^{\star}) \leftarrow \mathcal{A}^{\mathcal{O}_{\mathsf{ok}}}(choose, \mathsf{gpk}, \mathbf{gsk}, \mathsf{msk}_{\mathsf{ADM}})$

$b \xleftarrow{R} \{0, 1\};\quad \sigma^{\star} \leftarrow \mathsf{Sign}(\mathsf{gpk}, \mathbf{gsk}[j_b], M^{\star})$

$b' \leftarrow \mathcal{A}^{\mathcal{O}_{\mathsf{ok}}}(guess, \mathsf{st}, \sigma^{\star})$

Return 1 *if* $b' = b$ *and* 0 *otherwise*

In the above notation, $\mathcal{O}_{\mathsf{ok}}$ denotes an oracle that takes as input any adversarially chosen signature $\sigma \neq \sigma^{\star}$ and uses ok and $\mathsf{msk}_{\mathsf{ADM}}$ to determine and return the identity of the signer.

Definition 5. *A GS-MDO scheme provides full anonymity against the opener if, for any $\lambda \in \mathbb{N}$, any $N \in \mathsf{poly}(\lambda)$ and any PPT adversary $\mathcal{A}$, the function*

$$\mathbf{Adv}_{\mathcal{A}}^{\mathrm{anon\text{-}oa}}(\lambda) = |\Pr[\mathbf{Exp}_{\mathcal{A}}^{\mathrm{anon\text{-}oa}}(\lambda, N) = 1] - 1/2| \in \mathsf{negl}(\lambda)$$

is a negligible function in the security parameter if the experiment goes as follows

$Exp_{\mathcal{A}}^{anon-oa}(\lambda, N)$

$(\mathsf{gpk}, \mathsf{ok}, \mathsf{msk}_{\mathsf{ADM}}, \mathbf{gsk}) \leftarrow \mathsf{Keygen}(\lambda, N)$

$(\mathsf{st}, j_0, j_1, M^{\star}) \leftarrow \mathcal{A}^{\mathcal{O}_{\mathsf{msk}_{\mathsf{ADM}}}}(choose, \mathsf{gpk}, \mathbf{gsk}, \mathsf{ok})$

$b \xleftarrow{R} \{0, 1\};\quad \sigma^{\star} \leftarrow \mathsf{Sign}(\mathsf{gpk}, \mathbf{gsk}[j_b], M^{\star})$

$b' \leftarrow \mathcal{A}^{\mathcal{O}_{\mathsf{msk}_{\mathsf{ADM}}}}(guess, \mathsf{st}, \sigma^{\star})$

Return 1 *if* $b' = b$ *and* 0 *otherwise*

In the above notation, $\mathcal{O}_{\mathsf{msk}_{\mathsf{ADM}}}(.)$ is an oracle that returns trapdoors for arbitrary messages $M \neq M^{\star}$ chosen by the adversary.

3 A Fully Collusion-Resistant Partially Structure-Preserving IBE

3.1 Intuition

The scheme is only partially structure-preserving in that identities are still encoded as binary strings and private keys are ordinary signatures (recall that, in any IBE, private keys are signatures on the corresponding identity, as mentioned in [13]) instead of structure-preserving ones. It can be seen as a variant of Waters' IBE [37] (see Appendix A for syntactic definitions) and builds on a consequence of the Leftover Hash Lemma [26]: namely, if $\ell > 2\log_2(p)$ and $a_1, \ldots, a_\ell \in_R \mathbb{Z}_p$ are uniformly distributed in $\mathbb{Z}_p$, then random subset sums $\sum_{i=1}^{\ell} \beta_i a_i$ with $(\beta_1, \ldots, \beta_\ell) \in_R \{0,1\}^\ell$ are statistically indistinguishable from uniformly random values in $\mathbb{Z}_p$.

The idea is to include a vector $(Z_1, \ldots, Z_\ell) \in \mathbb{G}^\ell$ in the master public key. The message $M \in \mathbb{G}$ will be encrypted by choosing a random ℓ-bit string $K \in \{0,1\}^\ell$ and multiplying M with a product of elements in the set $S = \{Z_i \mid K[i] = 1\}$. Then, each bit $K[i]$ of K will be individually encrypted using a variant of the Waters IBE. In the latter variant, an encryption of 1 will consist of a tuple $(C_{i,1}, C_{i,2}, C_{i,3}, C_{i,4}) = (g^{s_i}, H_\mathbb{G}(\mathsf{ID})^{s_i}, g_1^{s_i/\omega_i}, g_2^{\omega_i})$, where $s_i, \omega_i \in_R \mathbb{Z}_p$. In an encryption of 0, the pair $(C_{i,3}, C_{i,4})$ is chosen uniformly in $\mathbb{G}^2$. Upon decryption, the receiver can use his private key (d_1, d_2) to test whether the equality $e(C_{i,3}, C_{i,4}) = e(C_{i,1}, d_1)/e(C_{i,2}, d_2)$ holds. If it does, the receiver decodes the i-th bit of K as $K[i] = 1$. Otherwise, it sets $K[i] = 0$. The security of the resulting scheme can be proved under the D3DH assumption (instead of the DBDH assumption).

Although the latter scheme allows encrypting messages in the group $\mathbb{G}$, it still does not provide all the properties we need for the problem at hand. When it comes to proving that a ciphertext encrypts a message that coincides with the content of Groth-Sahai commitment, the difficulty is to prove that the equality $e(C_{i,3}, C_{i,4}) = e(C_{i,1}, d_1)/e(C_{i,2}, d_2)$ is *not* satisfied when $K[i] = 0$. For this reason, we need to modify the scheme as suggested in Section 3.2.

3.2 Construction

In order to be able to efficiently prove that a ciphertext and a Groth-Sahai commitment hide the same group element, we modify the scheme of Section 3.1 as follows. In the master public key, the element g_1 is replaced by a pair $(g_0, g_1) = (g^{\alpha_0}, g^{\alpha_1})$. The master secret key is twinned in the same way and now consists of $(g_2^{\alpha_0}, g_2^{\alpha_1})$. Likewise, each identity is assigned a private key of the form $(d_{0,1}, d_{0,2}, d_{1,1}, d_{1,2}) = (g_2^{\alpha_0} \cdot H_\mathbb{G}(\mathsf{ID})^{r_0}, g^{r_0}, g_2^{\alpha_1} \cdot H_\mathbb{G}(\mathsf{ID})^{r_1}, g^{r_1})$.

In the encryption algorithm, when the sender wants to "encrypt" a bit $K[i]$ of $K \in \{0,1\}^\ell$, it generates $(C_{i,3}, C_{i,4})$ as $(C_{i,3}, C_{i,4}) = (g_{K[i]}^{s_i/\omega_i}, g_2^{\omega_i})$, so that the receiver can easily determine the value of $K[i]$ using his private key.

The modification will make it easier to prove equalities between the plaintext and a committed value. The reason is that the prover does not have to prove an inequality when $K[i] = 0$: he essentially has to prove statements of the form "$(C_{i,3}, C_{i,4}) = \left(g_0^{s_i/\omega_i}, g_2^{\omega_i}\right)$ OR $(C_{i,3}, C_{i,4}) = \left(g_1^{s_i/\omega_i}, g_2^{\omega_i}\right)$". Our construction of Groth-Sahai-compatible IBE thus goes follows.

Setup(λ) : Choose bilinear groups $(\mathbb{G}, \mathbb{G}_T)$ of prime order $p > 2^\lambda$. Then, do the following.

1. Choose $\alpha_0, \alpha_1 \xleftarrow{R} \mathbb{Z}_p$, $g \xleftarrow{R} \mathbb{G}$, $g_2 \xleftarrow{R} \mathbb{G}$ and set $g_0 = g^{\alpha_0}$, $g_1 = g^{\alpha_1}$.
2. Choose $u_0, u_1, \ldots, u_L \xleftarrow{R} \mathbb{G}$, for a suitably large $L \in \text{poly}(\lambda)$. These will be used to implement a number-theoretic hash function $H_{\mathbb{G}} : \{0,1\}^L \to \mathbb{G}$ such that any L-bit string $\tau = \tau[1] \ldots \tau[L] \in \{0,1\}^L$ is mapped to the value $H_{\mathbb{G}}(\tau) = u_0 \cdot \prod_{i=1}^{L} u_i^{\tau[i]}$.
3. Choose group elements $(Z_1, \ldots, Z_\ell) \xleftarrow{R} \mathbb{G}^\ell$, where $\ell = 2\lceil \log_2(p) \rceil > 2\lambda$.

The master secret key is $\mathsf{msk} := (g_2^{\alpha_0}, g_2^{\alpha_1})$ and the master public key is defined as

$$\mathsf{mpk} = \left((\mathbb{G}, \mathbb{G}_T),\ p,\ g,\ g_0 = g^{\alpha_0},\ g_1 = g^{\alpha_1},\ g_2,\ \{u_i\}_{i=0}^{L},\ \{Z_i\}_{i=1}^{\ell}\right)$$

Keygen($\mathsf{msk}, \mathsf{ID}$) : given the master secret key $\mathsf{msk} = (g_2^{\alpha_0}, g_2^{\alpha_1})$ and an identity $\mathsf{ID} \in \{0,1\}^L$, choose $r_0, r_1 \xleftarrow{R} \mathbb{Z}_p$ to compute and return

$$d_{\mathsf{ID}} = (d_{0,1}, d_{0,2}, d_{1,1}, d_{1,2}) = \left(g_2^{\alpha_0} \cdot H_{\mathbb{G}}(\mathsf{ID})^{r_0}, g^{r_0}, g_2^{\alpha_1} \cdot H_{\mathbb{G}}(\mathsf{ID})^{r_1}, g^{r_1}\right).$$

Encrypt($\mathsf{mpk}, \mathsf{ID}, M$) : to encrypt a message $M \in \mathbb{G}$, conduct the following steps.

1. Choose a random ℓ-bit string $K \xleftarrow{R} \{0,1\}^\ell$, where $\ell = 2\log_2(p)$.
2. Choose $s_1, \ldots, s_\ell \xleftarrow{R} \mathbb{Z}_p$ and $\omega_1, \ldots, \omega_\ell \xleftarrow{R} \mathbb{Z}_p$.
3. Parse K as $K[1] \ldots K[\ell] \in \{0,1\}^\ell$. For $i = 1$ to ℓ, compute

$$C_{i,1} = g^{s_i} \qquad C_{i,2} = H_{\mathbb{G}}(\mathsf{ID})^{s_i} \qquad C_{i,3} = g_{K[i]}^{s_i/\omega_i} \qquad C_{i,4} = g_2^{\omega_i} \qquad (2)$$

4. Then, compute $C_0 = M \cdot \prod_{i=1}^{\ell} Z_i^{K[i]}$.

Return the ciphertext $C = \left(C_0, \{(C_{i,1}, C_{i,2}, C_{i,3}, C_{i,4})\}_{i=1}^{\ell}\right) \in \mathbb{G}^{4\ell+1}$.

Decrypt($\mathsf{mpk}, d_{\mathsf{ID}}, C$) : parse C as $C = \left(C_0, \{(C_{i,1}, C_{i,2}, C_{i,3}, C_{i,4})\}_{i=1}^{\ell}\right)$.

1. For $i = 1$ to ℓ compute $\mu_b = e(C_{i,1}, d_{b,1})/e(C_{i,2}, d_{b,2})$ for each $b \in \{0,1\}$. If there exists $b \in \{0,1\}$ such that $\mu_b = e(C_{i,3}, C_{i,4})$, set $K[i] = b$. Otherwise, return $\bot$.
2. Compute and return $M = C_0/(\prod_{i=1}^{\ell} Z_i^{K[i]})$.

Unlike the IBE system of Sakai *et al.* [35], the above scheme provides full collusion-resistance and the size of the master public key only depends on the security parameter and not on a pre-determined bound on the number of corrupted users.

Theorem 1. *The above IBE scheme provides IND-ID-CPA security under the D3DH assumption.*

Proof. We consider a sequence of games which begins with the real game and ends with a game where the adversary's view is independent of the challenger's bit $\beta \in \{0,1\}$. For each i, we denote by S_i the event that the adversary wins in Game i and we define the adversary's advantage as $Adv_i := |\Pr[S_i] - 1/2|$.

Game 0: This is the real attack game where the challenger generates a proper encryption of M_β, with $\beta \xleftarrow{R} \{0,1\}$, in the challenge phase. The game ends with the adversary $\mathcal{A}$ outputting $\beta' \in \{0,1\}$ and we denote by S_0 the event that $\beta' = \beta$.

Game i ($1 \leq i \leq \ell$): In this game, the challenger generates the challenge ciphertext in a hybrid manner. Namely, for each $j \in \{1, \ldots, \ell\}$, the challenger generates the ciphertext components $\{(C_{j,1}, C_{j,2}, C_{j,3}, C_{j,4})\}$ as follows.

- If $j \leq i$, its picks $s_j \xleftarrow{R} \mathbb{Z}_p$, computes $(C_{j,1}, C_{j,2}) = (g^{s_j}, H_{\mathbb{G}}(\mathsf{ID})^{s_j})$ but chooses $(C_{j,3}, C_{j,4}) \xleftarrow{R} \mathbb{G}^2$ at random.
- If $j > i$, it runs the normal encryption algorithm and sets

$$(C_{j,1}, C_{j,2}, C_{j,3}, C_{j,4}) = (g^{s_j}, H_{\mathbb{G}}(\mathsf{ID})^{s_j}, g_{K[j]}^{s_j/\omega_j}, g_2^{\omega_j})$$

for randomly chosen $s_j, \omega_j \xleftarrow{R} \mathbb{Z}_p$.

Game $\ell + 1$: This game is identical to Game ℓ with the difference that, in the challenge ciphertext, C_0 is chosen as a uniformly random $C_0 \xleftarrow{R} \mathbb{G}$ instead of being computed as $C_0 = M_\beta \cdot \prod_{j=1}^{\ell} Z_j^{K[j]}$.

For each $j \in \{1, \ldots, \ell\}$, Lemma 1 shows that Game j is computationally indistinguishable from Game $j - 1$ if the D3DH assumption holds.

In Game ℓ, the ciphertext components $\{(C_{j,1}, C_{j,2}, C_{j,3}, C_{j,4})\}_{j=1}^{\ell}$ are completely uncorrelated to the string $K = K[1] \ldots K[\ell] \in \{0,1\}^\ell$ that is used to compute $C_0 = M_\beta \cdot \prod_{j=1}^{\ell} Z_j^{K[j]}$. For this reason, we argue that the adversary's view is statistically independent of M_β. This is easily seen by observing that the Leftover Hash Lemma implies that the two distributions

$$D_0 = \{(a, \langle a, z \rangle) \mid a \xleftarrow{R} \mathbb{Z}_p^\ell, \ z \xleftarrow{R} \{0,1\}^\ell\} \qquad D_1 = \{(a, w) \mid a \xleftarrow{R} \mathbb{Z}_p^\ell, \ w \xleftarrow{R} \mathbb{Z}_p\},$$

are statistically close when $\ell > 2 \log_2(p)$. Consequently, Game ℓ is statistically close to Game $\ell + 1$, where C_0 is replaced by a uniformly random group element in the challenge ciphertext. In the latter game, we have $\Pr[S_{\ell+1}] = 1/2$ (and thus $Adv_{\ell+1} = 0$) since the challenge ciphertext is independent of M_β. $\qquad\square$

Lemma 1. *If the D3DH assumption holds, Game i is computationally indistinguishable from Game $i - 1$ for each $i \in \{1, \ldots, \ell\}$. More precisely, if $\mathcal{A}$ runs in time t and has significantly different advantages in Game i and Game $i-1$, then there exists a PPT algorithm $\mathcal{B}$ with running time $t + O(\varepsilon^{-2} \ln(\varepsilon^{-1})\eta^{-1} \ln(\eta^{-1}))$ such that*

$$|Adv_i(\mathcal{A}) - Adv_{i-1}(\mathcal{A})| \leq 16 \cdot (L+1) \cdot q \cdot \mathbf{Adv}^{\mathrm{D3DH}}(\mathcal{B}),$$

where $\eta = 1/(4(L+1)q)$ and q is the maximal number of private key queries. (The proof is given in Appendix B.)

We note that the same idea can be applied to construct other partially structure-preserving primitives. For example, it can be applied to selectively-secure attribute-based encryption schemes based on the Decision Bilinear Diffie-Hellman assumption [34].

3.3 Proving Properties about Encrypted Messages

Our solution retains the useful property of the scheme in [35] as it allows efficiently proving relations about the plaintext using the Groth-Sahai techniques. If $\vec{C}_M = (1,1,M) \cdot \vec{f_1}^{r_M} \cdot \vec{f_2}^{s_M} \cdot \vec{f_3}^{t_M}$ denotes a Groth-Sahai commitment to $M \in \mathbb{G}$ which is also encrypted with the above IBE, the sender can proceed as follows to prove the equality between the committed message and the plaintext.

For each i, the sender computes $\vec{C}_{K_i} = (1, 1, g^{K[i]}) \cdot \vec{f_1}^{r_{K[i]}} \cdot \vec{f_2}^{s_{K[i]}} \cdot \vec{f_3}^{t_{K[i]}}$ as a commitment to the group element $K_i = g^{K[i]}$ and generates a non-interactive proof $\vec{\pi}_{K[i]}$ that $K[i] \in \{0, 1\}$. This is typically achieved by proving the equality $K[i]^2 = K[i] \bmod p$ with a proof $\vec{\pi}_{K[i]}$ consisting of 9 group elements. Next, the sender generates a commitment $\vec{C}_{G_i}$ to the group element $G_i = g_{K[i]}$ and generates a non-interactive proof $\vec{\pi}_{G_i}$ that committed elements G_i and $K[i]$ satisfy $G_i = g_1^{K[i]} \cdot g_0^{1-K[i]}$ or, equivalently, $e(G_i, g) = e(g_1, K_i) \cdot e(g_0, K_i^{-1} \cdot g)$. The latter is a linear equation for which the proof $\vec{\pi}_{G_i}$ requires three group elements. Then, the sender generates a commitment $\vec{C}_{\Theta_i}$ to the auxiliary variable $\Theta_i = g^{s_i/\omega_i}$ and generate non-interactive proofs $\vec{\pi}_{\Theta_i,1}$, $\vec{\pi}_{\Theta_i,2}$ for the relations

$$e(\Theta_i, C_{i,4}) = e(C_{i,1}, g_2) \qquad e(\Theta_i, G_i) = e(g, C_{i,3}). \qquad (3)$$

Since the first equation of (3) is linear equation, $\vec{\pi}_{\Theta_i,1}$ only requires 3 group elements. On the other hand, the second equation is quadratic, so that $\vec{\pi}_{\Theta_i,2}$ costs 9 group elements to prove.

Finally, the sender is left with proving that $e(C_0/M, g) = \prod_{i=1}^{\ell} e(Z_i, K_i)$, which is a linear equation whose proof $\vec{\pi}_{C_0}$ requires 3 group elements.

The whole NIWI proof $\left(\{\vec{C}_{K_i}, \vec{C}_{G_i}, \vec{C}_{\Theta_i}, \vec{\pi}_{K[i]}, \vec{\pi}_{G_i}, \vec{\pi}_{\Theta_i,1}, \vec{\pi}_{\Theta_i,2}\}_{i=1}^{\ell}, \vec{\pi}_{C_0}\right)$ thus takes $35\ell + 3$ group elements overall.

In some cases, the above proof might have to be a NIZK (and not just NIWI) proof. In pairing-product equations, NIZK proofs are not known to always exist. Fortunately, we can solve this issue by introducing a constant number of extra variables, as we will see in Section 4.

4 A Fully Anonymous GS-MDO Scheme with Logarithmic-Size Signatures

Our construction departs from the general approach suggested in [35] in order to obtain shorter signatures. The signing algorithm of [35] proceeds by choosing two random session keys K^{PKE} and K^{IBE} which are separately encrypted using a CCA2-secure public-key encryption scheme and an IBE scheme, respectively. These two keys K^{PKE} and K^{IBE} are then used to hide the group member's credential in the fashion of nested multiple encryptions while adding a proof that the hidden value is a valid and properly encrypted credential. If we naively apply this approach using our IBE scheme, we will eventually obtain signatures consisting of $O(\lambda^2)$ bits, where λ is the security parameter.

To reduce the signature size to $O(\lambda \log N)$ bits (recall that $\log N \ll \lambda$ since the cardinality N of the group is assumed to be polynomial), we use a different approach. Instead of encrypting random session keys which conceal the group member's credential under two randomly generated session keys, we directly encrypt the bits of the group member's identity as if it were the session key K in the IBE scheme of Section 3.2. This allows reducing the number of bit-carrying IBE ciphertext components from $O(\lambda)$ to $O(\log N)$. In order to make sure that neither the admitter or the opening authority will be able to individually open any signature, we add a second encryption layer and additionally encrypt – under the admitter's public key using Kiltz's DLIN-based CCA2-secure encryption scheme [31] – the IBE ciphertext components which depend on the bits of the group member's identity.

The rest of the signing algorithm proceeds as in the Boyen-Waters group signature [14], by having the signer verifiably encrypt a two-level hierarchical signature [30], where the first-level (resp. second-level) message is the signer's identity (resp. the actual message). Like [14], we use a two-level hierarchical extension of Waters' signature [37].

4.1   Construction

Keygen(λ, N): given a security parameter $\lambda \in \mathbb{N}$ and $N = 2^\ell$,

1. Choose bilinear groups $(\mathbb{G}, \mathbb{G}_T)$ of prime order $p > 2^\lambda$, with $g \overset{R}{\leftarrow} \mathbb{G}$.
2. As a CRS for the Groth-Sahai proof system, select vectors $\mathbf{f} = (\vec{f_1}, \vec{f_2}, \vec{f_3})$ such that $\vec{f_1} = (f_1, 1, g) \in \mathbb{G}^3$, $\vec{f_2} = (1, f_2, g) \in \mathbb{G}^3$, and $\vec{f_3} = \vec{f_1}^{\,\xi_1} \cdot \vec{f_2}^{\,\xi_2}$, where $f_1 = g^{\beta_1}, f_2 = g^{\beta_2} \overset{R}{\leftarrow} \mathbb{G}$ and $\beta_1, \beta_2, \xi_1, \xi_2 \overset{R}{\leftarrow} \mathbb{Z}_p$. We also define the vector $\vec{\varphi} = \vec{f_3} \cdot (1, 1, g)$.
3. Generate a master key pair $(\mathsf{msk}_{\mathrm{IBE}}, \mathsf{mpk}_{\mathrm{IBE}})$ for the identity-based key encapsulation scheme of Section 3.2[1]. These consist of $\mathsf{msk}_{\mathrm{IBE}} = (g_2^{\alpha_0}, g_2^{\alpha_1})$ and

$$\mathsf{mpk}_{\mathrm{IBE}} = \Big(g_0 = g^{\alpha_0}, \ g_1 = g^{\alpha_1}, \ g_2, \ \{u_i\}_{i=0}^L, \Big),$$

where $L \in \mathsf{poly}(\lambda)$ denotes the length of (hashed) messages to be signed. For a message $M \in \{0,1\}^L$, we define the function $H_U(M) \in \mathbb{G}$ as $H_U(M) = u_0 \cdot \prod_{i=1}^L u_i^{M[i]}$, where $M[i] \in \{0,1\}$ denotes the i-th bit of M.
4. Generate a key pair (sk_W, pk_W) for a two-level hierarchical Waters signature. At level 1 (resp. level 2), messages will be of length ℓ (resp. L).

---

[1] Note that the $\{Z_i\}_{i=1}^\ell$ components are not needed here and can be discarded.

This key pair consists of $sk_W = g^\omega$ and

$$pk_W = \left(e(g,g)^\omega, \ \{v_i\}_{i=0}^\ell, \ \{w_i\}_{i=0}^L \right),$$

where $\omega \in_R \mathbb{Z}_p$. Analogously to step 3, we denote by $H_W(M)$ the function that maps the message $M \in \{0,1\}^L$ to $H_W(M) = w_0 \cdot \prod_{i=1}^L w_i^{M[i]}$, where $M[i] \in \{0,1\}$ is the i-th bit of M.

5. For each $i \in \{0, \ldots, N-1\}$ generate the private key $\mathsf{gsk}[i]$ of member i as a Waters signature $\mathsf{gsk}[i] = \left(g^\omega \cdot (v_0 \cdot \prod_{j=1}^\ell v_j^{\mathrm{id}_i[j]})^r, \ g^r \right)$, with $r \xleftarrow{R} \mathbb{Z}_p$, on the message $\mathrm{id}_i = \mathrm{id}_i[1] \ldots \mathrm{id}_i[\ell] \in \{0,1\}^\ell$ which is obtained as the binary expansion of $i \in \{0, \ldots, N-1\}$. The private key $sk_W = g^\omega$ is not needed beyond this point and can be erased after the generation of the vector of private keys $\mathsf{gsk} = (\mathsf{gsk}[0], \ldots, \mathsf{gsk}[N-1])$.

6. Generate a public key $(X, Y, U, V) = (g^{\beta_x}, g^{\beta_y}, g^{\beta_u}, g^{\beta_v})$, with random $\beta_x, \beta_y, \beta_u, \beta_v \xleftarrow{R} \mathbb{Z}_p$, for Kiltz's CCA2-secure encryption scheme.

7. Select a strongly unforgeable one-time signature scheme $\Sigma = (\mathcal{G}, \mathcal{S}, \mathcal{V})$.

The admitter's message specification key consists of $\mathsf{msk}_{\mathrm{ADM}} := \mathsf{msk}_{\mathrm{IBE}}$. The private key ok of the opening authority is defined as $\mathsf{ok} := (\beta_x, \beta_y, \beta_u, \beta_v)$. The private key of member i is $\mathsf{gsk}[i]$ while the group public key is be

$$\mathsf{gpk} := \left((\mathbb{G}, \mathbb{G}_T), \ p, \ g, \ \mathbf{f} = (\vec{f_1}, \vec{f_2}, \vec{f_3}), \ \mathsf{mpk}_{\mathrm{IBE}}, \ pk_W, \ (X, Y, U, V), \ \Sigma \right)$$

Sign$(\mathsf{gpk}, \mathsf{gsk}[i], M)$: to sign a message $M \in \{0,1\}^L$ using the i-th group member's private key $\mathsf{gsk}[i] = (S_{i,1}, S_{i,2}) = (g^\omega \cdot (v_0 \cdot \prod_{j=1}^\ell v_j^{\mathrm{id}_i[j]})^r, \ g^r)$, generate a one-time signature key pair $(\mathsf{SK}, \mathsf{VK}) \leftarrow \Sigma.\mathcal{G}(\lambda)$ and do the following.

1. Generate a two-level Waters signature where the message is $\mathrm{id}_i \in \{0,1\}^\ell$ at the first level and $M \in \{0,1\}^L$ at level 2. The signature consists of

$$(\Omega_1, \Omega_2, \Omega_3) = \left(S_{i,1} \cdot (v_0 \cdot \prod_{j=1}^\ell v_i^{\mathrm{id}_i[j]})^{r'} \cdot H_W(M)^s, \ S_{i,2} \cdot g^{r'}, \ g^s \right)$$

$$= \left(g^\omega \cdot (v_0 \cdot \prod_{j=1}^\ell v_i^{\mathrm{id}_i[j]})^{r''} \cdot H_W(M)^s, \ g^{r''}, \ g^s \right),$$

where $r'' = r + r'$.

2. Generate a commitment $\vec{C}_{H_V}$ to $H_V = v_0 \cdot \prod_{j=1}^\ell v_j^{\mathrm{id}_i[j]}$. Then, for each $j \in \{1, \ldots, \ell\}$, generate a commitment $\vec{C}_{F_j}$ to $F_j = g^{\mathrm{id}_i[j]}$ and generate a NIWI proof $\vec{\pi}_{H_V} \in \mathbb{G}^3$ that

$$e(H_V, g) \cdot \prod_{j=1}^\ell e(v_j, F_j)^{-1} = e(v_0, g) \tag{4}$$

Since (4) is a linear equation, $\vec{\pi}_{H_V}$ only requires 3 group elements.

3. Choose $s_1, \ldots, s_\ell \xleftarrow{R} \mathbb{Z}_p$ and $\omega_1, \ldots, \omega_\ell \xleftarrow{R} \mathbb{Z}_p$. For $j = 1$ to ℓ, compute

$$C_{j,1} = g^{s_j} \qquad\qquad C_{j,2} = H_U(M)^{s_j} \qquad\qquad (5)$$
$$C_{j,3} = g_{\mathrm{id}_i[j]}^{s_j/\omega_j} \qquad\qquad C_{j,4} = g_2^{\omega_j}.$$

Then, encrypt $C_{j,3}$ using Kiltz's encryption scheme, by randomly choosing $z_{j,1}, z_{j,2} \xleftarrow{R} \mathbb{Z}_p$ and computing

$$\begin{aligned}\Psi_j &= (\Psi_{j,1}, \Psi_{j,2}, \Psi_{j,3}, \Psi_{j,4}, \Psi_{j,5}) \\ &= \left(X^{z_{j,1}}, Y^{z_{j,2}}, C_{j,3} \cdot g^{z_{j,1}+z_{j,2}}, (g^{\mathrm{VK}} \cdot U)^{z_{j,1}}, (g^{\mathrm{VK}} \cdot V)^{z_{j,2}} \right)\end{aligned}$$

The next step will be to prove that the ciphertexts $\{\Psi_j\}_{j=1}^\ell$ encrypt $\{C_{j,3}\}_{j=1}^\ell$ such that $\{(C_{j,1}, C_{j,2}, C_{j,3}, C_{j,4})\}_{j=1}^\ell$ are of the form (5) with $\mathrm{id}_i[j] \in \{0,1\}$.

4. To generate NIZK proofs for the next statements, generate commitments $\vec{C}_\theta = \vec{\varphi}^\theta \cdot \vec{f_1}^{r_\theta} \cdot \vec{f_2}^{s_\theta}$, as well as $\vec{C}_{\Gamma_1}$ and $\vec{C}_{\Gamma_2}$ to the variables

$$\theta = 1, \qquad\qquad \Gamma_1 = g^\theta, \qquad\qquad \Gamma_2 = g_2^\theta, \qquad\qquad (6)$$

and a non-interactive proof $\vec{\pi}_\Gamma$ for the three equalities (6), which requires 9 group elements (3 for each equation). Then, for each $j \in \{1, \ldots, \ell\}$, generate Groth-Sahai commitments $\vec{C}_{G_j}, \vec{C}_{\Theta_j}, \vec{C}_{z_{j,1}}, \vec{C}_{z_{j,2}}$ to the variables $G_j = g_1^{\mathrm{id}_i[j]} \cdot g_0^{1-\mathrm{id}_i[j]}$, $\Theta_j = g^{s_j/\omega_j}$, $Z_{j,1} = g^{z_{j,1}}$ and $Z_{j,2} = g^{z_{j,2}}$. Then, generate NIZK proofs $\vec{\pi}_j, \vec{\pi}_{G_j}, \vec{\pi}_{\Theta_j}, \{\vec{\pi}_{\Psi_{j,k}}\}_{k=1}^3$ for the relations

$$e(F_j, F_j) = e(g, F_j) \qquad\qquad (7)$$
$$e(G_j, g) = e(g_1, F_j) \cdot e(g_0, F_j^{-1} \cdot g) \qquad\qquad (8)$$
$$e(\Theta_j, C_{j,4}) = e(C_{j,1}, g_2) \qquad\qquad (9)$$
$$e(\Psi_{j,1}, g) = e(X, Z_{j,1}) \qquad\qquad (10)$$
$$e(\Psi_{j,2}, g) = e(Y, Z_{j,2}) \qquad\qquad (11)$$
$$e(\Psi_{j,3}, g) = e(\Theta_j, G_j) \cdot e(g, Z_{j,1} \cdot Z_{j,2}) \qquad\qquad (12)$$

This is done by proving that

$$e(F_j, F_j) = e(g, F_j) \qquad\qquad (13)$$
$$e(G_j, g) = e(g_1, F_j) \cdot e(g_0, F_j^{-1} \cdot g) \qquad\qquad (14)$$
$$e(\Theta_j, C_{j,4}) = e(C_{j,1}, \Gamma_2) \qquad\qquad (15)$$
$$e(\Psi_{j,1}, \Gamma_1) = e(X, Z_{j,1}) \qquad\qquad (16)$$
$$e(\Psi_{j,2}, \Gamma_1) = e(Y, Z_{j,2}) \qquad\qquad (17)$$
$$e(\Psi_{j,3}, \Gamma_1) = e(\Theta_j, G_j) \cdot e(\Gamma_1, Z_{j,1} \cdot Z_{j,2}) \qquad\qquad (18)$$

Note that relation (7) guarantees that each $\mathrm{id}_i[j]$ is indeed a bit. Relations (13) and (18) are quadratic equation and thus require 9 elements each whereas 12 elements suffice for relations (14)-(17). Note that the same variable $\theta \in \mathbb{Z}_p$ can be re-used for each $j \in \{1, \ldots, \ell\}$, so that (6) only needs to be proved once.

5. Generate a commitment $\vec{C}_{\Omega_1}$ to Ω_1 with a NIWI proof $\vec{\pi}_W \in \mathbb{G}^3$ that variables (Ω_1, H_V) satisfy the verification equation

$$e(g, g)^\omega \cdot e(H_W(M), \Omega_3) = e(\Omega_1, g) \cdot e(H_V, \Omega_2^{-1}) \qquad (19)$$

of the two-level Waters signature.
6. Finally, use SK to generate a one-time signature σ_{ots} on the entire set of commitments and NIWI/NIZK proofs in order to achieve anonymity in the CCA2 sense.

The whole signature σ consists of

$$
\sigma = \Big(\mathsf{VK}, \vec{C}_{H_V}, \ \vec{C}_\theta, \ \vec{C}_{\Gamma_1}, \ \vec{C}_{\Gamma_2}, \ \vec{\pi}_\Gamma, \ \vec{\pi}_{H_V}, \ \vec{\pi}_W, \ \{\vec{C}_{F_j}, \ (C_{j,1}, C_{j,2}, C_{j,4}, \Psi_j),
$$
$$
\vec{C}_{G_j}, \ \vec{\pi}_{G_j}, \ \vec{\pi}_{\Theta_j}, \ \vec{C}_{\Theta_j}, \ \vec{C}_{Z_{j,1}}, \ \vec{C}_{Z_{j,2}}, \ \vec{\pi}_j, \ \{\vec{\pi}_{\Psi_{j,k}}\}_{k=1}^3 \}_{j=1}^\ell, \ \vec{C}_{\Omega_1}, \ \Omega_2, \ \Omega_3, \ \sigma_{ots} \Big)
$$

Verify(gpk, M, σ): parse σ as above. Return 1 if and only if: (i) σ_{ots} is a valid one-time signature on the entire bundle; (ii) $\{\Psi_j\}_{j=1}^\ell$ are all valid ciphertexts for Kiltz's cryptosystem (*i.e.*, by testing if $e(\Psi_{j,4}, X) = e(\Psi_{j,1}, g^{\mathsf{VK}} \cdot U)$ and $e(\Psi_{j,5}, Y) = e(\Psi_{j,2}, g^{\mathsf{VK}} \cdot V)$); (iii) It holds that $e(C_{j,1}, H_U(M)) = e(g, C_{j,2})$ for each $j \in \{1, \ldots, \ell\}$; (iv) All proofs properly verify.

TrapGen(gpk, msk$_{\mathsf{ADM}}$, M): given the admitter's key msk$_{\mathsf{ADM}} = (g_2^{\alpha_0}, g_2^{\alpha_1})$ and a message $M \in \{0,1\}^L$, choose $r_0, r_1 \xleftarrow{R} \mathbb{Z}_p$ to compute and return

$$t_M = (t_{0,1}, t_{0,2}, t_{1,1}, t_{1,2}) = \big(g_2^{\alpha_0} \cdot H_U(M)^{r_0}, g^{r_0}, g_2^{\alpha_1} \cdot H_U(M)^{r_1}, g^{r_1} \big). \qquad (20)$$

Open(gpk, ok, t_M, M, σ): return $\bot$ if σ is not a valid group signature w.r.t. gpk and M. Otherwise, parse t_M as in (20). For $i = 1$ to ℓ, do the following.

1. Decrypt $\Psi_j = (\Psi_{j,1}, \Psi_{j,2}, \Psi_{j,3}, \Psi_{j,4}, \Psi_{j,5})$ using ok $= (\beta_x, \beta_y, \beta_u, \beta_v)$ to obtain $C_{j,3} \in \mathbb{G}$.
2. Use t_M to determine the bit id$[i] \in \{0,1\}$ for which the equalities (5) are satisfied.

Return the identifier id $=$ id$[1] \ldots$ id$[\ell] \in \{0,1\}^\ell$.

Overall, each signature consists of $53\ell + 35$ group elements if the scheme is instantiated with Groth's discrete-logarithm-based one-time signature [23]. For groups of $N \approx 10^6$ members (which can accommodate the population of a city), we can set $\ell = 20$ and obtain signatures of 68 kB at the 128-bit security level assuming that each group element has a 512-bit representation. In comparison, the k-resilient system of Sakai *et al.* [35] already requires signatures of 32 kB for the same security level. While less efficient than the random-oracle-based realization of [33], our scheme is not unrealistically expensive for practical applications.

4.2 Security

The traceability of the scheme relies on the standard CDH assumption whereas the anonymity properties rely on the D3DH and DLIN assumptions. In the proof of anonymity against the admitter, we also need to assume that the one-time signature is strongly unforgeable [5], which is implied by the DLIN assumption in Groth's scheme [23]. Since the CDH assumption is implied by both D3DH and DLIN, we only need two assumptions to prove the following result (as detailed in the full version of the paper).

Theorem 2. *The scheme provides full traceability as well as full anonymity against the opener and the admitter assuming that: (i) Σ is a strongly unforgeable one-time signature; (ii) The DLIN and D3DH assumption both hold in $\mathbb{G}$.*

References

1. Abe, M., Fuchsbauer, G., Groth, J., Haralambiev, K., Ohkubo, M.: Structure-Preserving Signatures and Commitments to Group Elements. In: Rabin, T. (ed.) CRYPTO 2010. LNCS, vol. 6223, pp. 209–236. Springer, Heidelberg (2010)
2. Abe, M., Groth, J., Haralambiev, K., Ohkubo, M.: Optimal Structure-Preserving Signatures in Asymmetric Bilinear Groups. In: Rogaway, P. (ed.) CRYPTO 2011. LNCS, vol. 6841, pp. 649–666. Springer, Heidelberg (2011)
3. Abe, M., Haralambiev, K., Ohkubo, M.: Signing on Elements in Bilinear Groups for Modular Protocol Design. Cryptology ePrint Archive: Report 2010/133 (2010)
4. Abe, M., Haralambiev, K., Ohkubo, M.: Group to Group Commitments Do Not Shrink. In: Pointcheval, D., Johansson, T. (eds.) EUROCRYPT 2012. LNCS, vol. 7237, pp. 301–317. Springer, Heidelberg (2012)
5. An, J.-H., Dodis, Y., Rabin, T.: On the Security of Joint Signature and Encryption. In: Knudsen, L.R. (ed.) EUROCRYPT 2002. LNCS, vol. 2332, pp. 83–107. Springer, Heidelberg (2002)
6. Ateniese, G., Camenisch, J., Joye, M., Tsudik, G.: A practical and provably secure coalition-resistant group signature scheme. In: Bellare, M. (ed.) CRYPTO 2000. LNCS, vol. 1880, pp. 255–270. Springer, Heidelberg (2000)
7. Bellare, M., Micciancio, D., Warinschi, B.: Foundations of group signatures: Formal definitions, simplified requirements, and a construction based on general assumptions. In: Biham, E. (ed.) EUROCRYPT 2003. LNCS, vol. 2656, pp. 614–629. Springer, Heidelberg (2003)
8. Bellare, M., Rogaway, P.: Random Oracles are Practical: A Paradigm for Designing Efficient Protocols. In: 1st ACM Conference on Computer and Communications Security, pp. 62–73. ACM Press (1993)
9. Bellare, M., Shi, H., Zhang, C.: Foundations of group signatures: The case of dynamic groups. In: Menezes, A. (ed.) CT-RSA 2005. LNCS, vol. 3376, pp. 136–153. Springer, Heidelberg (2005)
10. Benjumea, V., Choi, S.G., Lopez, J., Yung, M.: Fair traceable multi-group signatures. In: Tsudik, G. (ed.) FC 2008. LNCS, vol. 5143, pp. 231–246. Springer, Heidelberg (2008)
11. Boneh, D., Boyen, X.: Efficient Selective-ID Secure Identity-Based Encryption Without Random Oracles. In: Cachin, C., Camenisch, J.L. (eds.) EUROCRYPT 2004. LNCS, vol. 3027, pp. 223–238. Springer, Heidelberg (2004)

12. Boneh, D., Boyen, X., Shacham, H.: Short Group Signatures. In: Franklin, M. (ed.) CRYPTO 2004. LNCS, vol. 3152, pp. 41–55. Springer, Heidelberg (2004)

13. Boneh, D., Franklin, M.: Identity-Based Encryption from the Weil Pairing. SIAM Journal of Computing 32(3), 586–615 (2003); earlier version in Kilian, J. (ed.) CRYPTO 2001. LNCS, vol. 2139, pp. 213–229. Springer, Heidelberg (2001)

14. Boyen, X., Waters, B.: Compact Group Signatures Without Random Oracles. In: Vaudenay, S. (ed.) EUROCRYPT 2006. LNCS, vol. 4004, pp. 427–444. Springer, Heidelberg (2006)

15. Boyen, X., Waters, B.: Full-Domain Subgroup Hiding and Constant-Size Group Signatures. In: Okamoto, T., Wang, X. (eds.) PKC 2007. LNCS, vol. 4450, pp. 1–15. Springer, Heidelberg (2007)

16. Camenisch, J.L., Chaabouni, R., Shelat, A.: Efficient Protocols for Set Membership and Range Proofs. In: Pieprzyk, J. (ed.) ASIACRYPT 2008. LNCS, vol. 5350, pp. 234–252. Springer, Heidelberg (2008)

17. Camenisch, J., Haralambiev, K., Kohlweiss, M., Lapon, J., Naessens, V.: Structure Preserving CCA Secure Encryption and Applications. In: Lee, D.H., Wang, X. (eds.) ASIACRYPT 2011. LNCS, vol. 7073, pp. 89–106. Springer, Heidelberg (2011)

18. Canetti, R., Goldreich, O., Halevi, S.: The random oracle methodology, revisited. Journal of the ACM 51(4), 557–594 (2004)

19. Cathalo, J., Libert, B., Yung, M.: Group Encryption: Non-Interactive Realization in the Standard Model. In: Matsui, M. (ed.) ASIACRYPT 2009. LNCS, vol. 5912, pp. 179–196. Springer, Heidelberg (2009)

20. Chaum, D., van Heyst, E.: Group Signatures. In: Davies, D.W. (ed.) EUROCRYPT 1991. LNCS, vol. 547, pp. 257–265. Springer, Heidelberg (1991)

21. Delerablée, C., Pointcheval, D.: Dynamic Fully Anonymous Short Group Signatures. In: Nguyên, P.Q. (ed.) VIETCRYPT 2006. LNCS, vol. 4341, pp. 193–210. Springer, Heidelberg (2006)

22. Groth, J., Ostrovsky, R., Sahai, A.: Perfect non-interactive zero knowledge for NP. In: Vaudenay, S. (ed.) EUROCRYPT 2006. LNCS, vol. 4004, pp. 339–358. Springer, Heidelberg (2006)

23. Groth, J.: Simulation-Sound NIZK Proofs for a Practical Language and Constant Size Group Signatures. In: Lai, X., Chen, K. (eds.) ASIACRYPT 2006. LNCS, vol. 4284, pp. 444–459. Springer, Heidelberg (2006)

24. Groth, J.: Fully anonymous group signatures without random oracles. In: Kurosawa, K. (ed.) ASIACRYPT 2007. LNCS, vol. 4833, pp. 164–180. Springer, Heidelberg (2007)

25. Groth, J., Sahai, A.: Efficient non-interactive proof systems for bilinear groups. In: Smart, N.P. (ed.) EUROCRYPT 2008. LNCS, vol. 4965, pp. 415–432. Springer, Heidelberg (2008)

26. Håstad, J., Impagliazzo, R., Levin, L., Luby, M.: A pseudorandom generator from any one-way function. SIAM Journal on Computing 28(4), 1364–1396 (1999)

27. Heng, S.-H., Kurosawa, K.: k-Resilient Identity-Based Encryption in the Standard Model. In: Okamoto, T. (ed.) CT-RSA 2004. LNCS, vol. 2964, pp. 67–80. Springer, Heidelberg (2004)

28. Kiayias, A., Tsiounis, Y., Yung, M.: Traceable signatures. In: Cachin, C., Camenisch, J.L. (eds.) EUROCRYPT 2004. LNCS, vol. 3027, pp. 571–589. Springer, Heidelberg (2004)

29. Kiayias, A., Yung, M.: Secure scalable group signature with dynamic joins and separable authorities. International Journal of Security and Networks (IJSN) 1(1/2), 24–45 (2006)

30. Kiltz, E., Mityagin, A., Panjwani, S., Raghavan, B.: Append-Only Signatures. In: Caires, L., Italiano, G.F., Monteiro, L., Palamidessi, C., Yung, M. (eds.) ICALP 2005. LNCS, vol. 3580, pp. 434–445. Springer, Heidelberg (2005)
31. Kiltz, E.: Chosen-ciphertext security from tag-based encryption. In: Halevi, S., Rabin, T. (eds.) TCC 2006. LNCS, vol. 3876, pp. 581–600. Springer, Heidelberg (2006)
32. Nguyen, L., Safavi-Naini, R.: Efficient and Provably Secure Trapdoor-Free Group Signature Schemes from Bilinear Pairings. In: Lee, P.J. (ed.) ASIACRYPT 2004. LNCS, vol. 3329, pp. 372–386. Springer, Heidelberg (2004)
33. Ohara, K., Sakai, Y., Emura, K., Hanaoka, G.: A Group Signature Scheme with Unbounded Message-Dependent Opening. In: AsiaCCS 2013. ACM Press (2013)
34. Sahai, A., Waters, B.: Fuzzy Identity-Based Encryption. In: Cramer, R. (ed.) EUROCRYPT 2005. LNCS, vol. 3494, pp. 457–473. Springer, Heidelberg (2005)
35. Sakai, Y., Emura, K., Hanaoka, G., Kawai, Y., Matsuda, T., Omote, K.: Group Signatures with Message-Dependent Opening. In: Abdalla, M., Lange, T. (eds.) Pairing 2012. LNCS, vol. 7708, pp. 270–294. Springer, Heidelberg (2013)
36. Shamir, A.: Identity-Based Cryptosystems and Signature Schemes. In: Blakely, G.R., Chaum, D. (eds.) CRYPTO 1984. LNCS, vol. 196, pp. 47–53. Springer, Heidelberg (1985)
37. Waters, B.: Efficient identity-based encryption without random oracles. In: Cramer, R. (ed.) EUROCRYPT 2005. LNCS, vol. 3494, pp. 114–127. Springer, Heidelberg (2005)

A   Definitions for Identity-Based Encryption

Definition 6 ([13]). *An IBE scheme consists of a tuple of efficient algorithms* (**Setup, Keygen, Encrypt, Decrypt**) *such that:*

- **Setup** *takes as input a security parameter* $\lambda \in \mathbb{N}$ *and outputs a master public key* mpk *and a matching* master secret key msk.
- **Keygen** *takes as input an identity* ID *and a master secret key* msk. *It outputs a private key* d_{ID} *for the identity* ID.
- **Encrypt** *takes as input the master public key* mpk, *an identity* ID *and a message* m *and outputs a* ciphertext C.
- **Decrypt** *takes as input the master public key* mpk, *a decryption key* d_{ID} *and a ciphertext* C *and outputs a message* M.

Correctness requires that, for any $\lambda \in \mathbb{N}$, *any outputs* (mpk, msk) *of* **Setup**(λ), *any plaintext* M *and any identity* ID, *if* $d_{ID} \leftarrow$ **Keygen**(msk, ID), *it holds that* **Decrypt**(mpk, d_{ID}, **Encrypt**(mpk, ID, M)) = M.

The standard security notion captures the semantic security of messages encrypted under some identity, even when the adversary has corrupted polynomially-many other identities.

Definition 7. *[13] An IBE system is semantically secure (or* IND-ID-CPA *secure) if no PPT adversary* $\mathcal{A}$ *has non-negligible advantage in this game:*

1. *The challenger generates a master key pair* (mpk, msk) ← **Setup**(λ) *and gives* mpk *to* $\mathcal{A}$.
2. $\mathcal{A}$ *issues a number of key extraction queries for identities* ID *of its choice. The challenger responds with* d_{ID} ← **Keygen**(msk, ID).
3. *When the adversary* $\mathcal{A}$ *decides that phase 2 is over, it chooses distinct equal-length messages* M_0, M_1 *and an identity* ID* *that has never been queried to the key extraction oracle at step 2. The challenger flips a coin* $d \xleftarrow{R} \{0,1\}$ *and returns a challenge ciphertext* $C^\star = $ **Encrypt**(mpk, ID, $M_d^\star$).
4. $\mathcal{A}$ *issues new queries but cannot ask for the private key of* ID*.
5. $\mathcal{A}$ *finally outputs a bit* $d' \in \{0,1\}$ *and wins if* $d' = d$. $\mathcal{A}$*'s advantage is defined as the distance* $\mathbf{Adv}^{\text{ind-id-cpa}}(A) := |\Pr[d' = d] - 1/2|$.

In k-resilient IBE schemes [27], the adversary is restricted to make private key extraction queries on at most k distinct identities. In this paper, we consider the standard definition where the maximal number of private key queries is not fixed in advance.

B   Proof of Lemma 1

Proof. Let us assume that there exists $i \in \{1, \ldots, \ell\}$ for which a PPT adversary $\mathcal{A}$ can tell Game i apart from Game $i - 1$. We show how to build an algorithm $\mathcal{B}$ that takes in an instance (g, g^a, g^b, g^c, T) of the D3DH problem and uses its interaction with $\mathcal{A}$ to decide if $T = g^{abc}$ or $T \in_R \mathbb{G}$.

To this end, algorithm $\mathcal{B}$ prepares the master public key mpk by randomly choosing $\gamma_0, \gamma_1 \xleftarrow{R} \mathbb{Z}_p$ and setting $g_0 = (g^a)^{\gamma_0}$, $g_1 = (g^a)^{\gamma_1}$ as well as $g_2 = g^b$. Note that this implicitly defines $\alpha_0 = a \cdot \gamma_0$ and $\alpha_1 = a \cdot \gamma_1$. Next, $\mathcal{B}$ chooses random values $\nu \xleftarrow{R} \{0, \ldots, L\}$, $\rho_0, \rho_1, \ldots, \rho_L \xleftarrow{R} \{0, \ldots, \zeta - 1\}$ and $\delta_0, \delta_1, \ldots, \delta_L \xleftarrow{R} \mathbb{Z}_p$, with $\zeta = 2q$ and where q is the maximal number of private key queries throughout the game. These are used to define

$$
\begin{aligned}
u_0 &= g^{\delta_0} \cdot (g^b)^{\nu \cdot \zeta - \rho_0} \\
u_i &= g^{\delta_i} \cdot (g^b)^{-\rho_i}, \qquad\qquad i \in \{1, \ldots, L\},
\end{aligned}
\tag{21}
$$

so that any L-bit identity ID $=$ ID[1]...ID[L] $\in \{0,1\}^L$ has a hash value $H_{\mathbb{G}}(\text{ID}) = u_0 \cdot \prod_{i=1}^{L} u_i^{\text{ID}[i]}$ that can be written $H_{\mathbb{G}}(\text{ID}) = g^{J_2(\text{ID})} \cdot (g^b)^{J_1(\text{ID})}$ if we define the functions

$$
J_1(\text{ID}) = \nu \cdot \zeta - \rho_0 - \sum_{i=1}^{L} \rho_i \cdot \text{ID}[i], \qquad\qquad J_2(\text{ID}) = \delta_0 - \sum_{i=1}^{L} \delta_i \cdot \text{ID}[i].
$$

The generation of mpk is completed by having $\mathcal{B}$ choose $Z_1, \ldots, Z_\ell \xleftarrow{R} \mathbb{G}$ at random.

Whenever $\mathcal{A}$ queries an identity ID for private key extraction, $\mathcal{B}$ uses the same strategy as in the security proofs of [11, 37]. Namely, it first evaluates the function $J_1(\mathsf{ID})$. If $J_1(\mathsf{ID}) = 0$, it aborts and outputs a random bit. Otherwise, it chooses $r_0, r_1 \xleftarrow{R} \mathbb{Z}_p$ and computes $(d_{0,1}, d_{0,2}, d_{1,1}, d_{1,2})$ as

$$\left(H_\mathbb{G}(\mathsf{ID})^{r_0} \cdot (g^a)^{-\gamma_0 \cdot J_2(\mathsf{ID})}, g^{r_0} \cdot (g^a)^{-\gamma_0/J_1(\mathsf{ID})}, \right.$$

$$\left. H_\mathbb{G}(\mathsf{ID})^{r_1} \cdot (g^a)^{-\gamma_1 \cdot J_2(\mathsf{ID})}, g^{r_1} \cdot (g^a)^{-\gamma_1/J_1(\mathsf{ID})} \right)$$

which equals $(g_2^{\gamma_0 \cdot a} \cdot H_\mathbb{G}(\mathsf{ID})^{\tilde{r}_0}, g^{\tilde{r}_0}, g_2^{\gamma_1 \cdot a} \cdot H_\mathbb{G}(\mathsf{ID})^{\tilde{r}_1}, g^{\tilde{r}_1})$ if $\tilde{r}_0 = r_0 - \gamma_0 \cdot a/J_1(\mathsf{ID})$ and $\tilde{r}_1 = r_1 - \gamma_1 \cdot a/J_1(\mathsf{ID})$. The 4-uple $d_{\mathsf{ID}} = (d_{0,1}, d_{0,2}, d_{1,1}, d_{1,2})$ thus forms a valid private key and is returned to $\mathcal{A}$.

When $\mathcal{A}$ decides to enter the challenge phase, it chooses messages $M_0, M_1 \in \mathbb{G}$ and a target identity $\mathsf{ID}^\star$. At this point, $\mathcal{B}$ aborts and outputs a random bit in the event that $J_1(\mathsf{ID}^\star) \neq 0$. Otherwise (i.e., if $J_1(\mathsf{ID}^\star) = 0$), $\mathcal{B}$ chooses a bit $\beta \xleftarrow{R} \{0,1\}$ as well as a random ℓ-bit string $K \xleftarrow{R} \{0,1\}^\ell$ and generates the challenge ciphertext as follows.

- For each $j \in \{1, \ldots, i-1\}$, $\mathcal{B}$ chooses $s_j, \omega_j \xleftarrow{R} \mathbb{Z}_p$, $\tilde{C}_{j,3}, \tilde{C}_{j,4} \xleftarrow{R} \mathbb{G}$ at random and sets $(C_{j,1}, C_{j,2}, C_{j,3}, C_{j,4}) = (g^{s_j}, H_\mathbb{G}(\mathsf{ID})^{s_j}, \tilde{C}_{j,3}, \tilde{C}_{j,4})$.
- For each $j \in \{i+1, \ldots, \ell\}$, $\mathcal{B}$ faithfully chooses $s_j, \omega_j \xleftarrow{R} \mathbb{Z}_p$ and sets $(C_{j,1}, C_{j,2}, C_{j,3}, C_{j,4}) = \left(g^{s_j}, H_\mathbb{G}(\mathsf{ID})^{s_j}, g_{K[j]}^{s_j/\omega_j}, g_2^{\omega_j} \right)$.
- For $j = i$, $\mathcal{B}$ $(C_{i,1}, C_{i,2}, C_{i,3}, C_{i,4}) = \left(g^c, (g^c)^{J_2(\mathsf{ID}^\star)}, T^{\gamma_{K[i]}/\omega_i}, g^{\omega_i} \right)$ for a randomly drawn $\omega_i \xleftarrow{R} \mathbb{Z}_p$.

Finally, $\mathcal{B}$ computes $C_0 = M_\beta \cdot \prod_{j=1}^\ell Z_j^{K[j]}$ and provides the adversary with the challenge ciphertext $C = (C_0, \{(C_{j,1}, C_{j,2}, C_{j,3}, C_{j,4})\}_{j=1}^\ell)$.

We remark that, if $T = g^{abc}$, the challenge ciphertext C is distributed as in Game $i-1$ as $(C_{i,1}, C_{i,2}, C_{i,3}, C_{i,4})$ can be written

$$(C_{i,1}, C_{i,2}, C_{i,3}, C_{i,4}) = \left(g^c, H_\mathbb{G}(\mathsf{ID}^\star)^c, g^{ac \cdot \gamma_{K[i]}/\bar{\omega}_i}, (g^b)^{\bar{\omega}_i} \right)$$

$$= \left(g^c, H_\mathbb{G}(\mathsf{ID}^\star)^c, g_{K[i]}^{c/\bar{\omega}_i}, g_2^{\bar{\omega}_i} \right).$$

where $\bar{\omega}_i = \omega_i/b$. In contrast, if $T \in_R \mathbb{G}$, then the pair $(C_{i,3}, C_{i,4})$ is uniformly distributed in $\mathbb{G}^2$, which means that $(C_{i,1}, C_{i,2}, C_{i,3}, C_{i,4})$ has the same distribution as in Game i.

At this stage, the adversary's probability may be correlated with the probability that the simulator $\mathcal{B}$ has to abort (i.e., because $\mathcal{A}$ queries the private key of an identity ID for which $J_1(\mathsf{ID}) = 0$ or because $J_1(\mathsf{ID}^\star) \neq 0$ in the challenge phase). As in [37], one way to address this problem is to introduce an artificial abort step in order to guarantee that $\mathcal{B}$ always aborts with the maximal probability, no matter which particular set of queries is made by $\mathcal{A}$.

Namely, with $\zeta = 2q$, the same analysis as [37] shows that $\mathcal{B}$'s probability not to abort for any set of queries is at least $\eta = 1/(4(L+1)q)$.

When the game ends, $\mathcal{B}$ considers the sequence of identities $(\mathsf{ID}_1, \ldots, \mathsf{ID}_q, \mathsf{ID}^\star)$

chosen by $\mathcal{A}$ during the game and estimates the probability that this choice causes the simulation to abort. This process does not require to run $\mathcal{A}$ again but rather involves repeatedly sampling vectors $(\rho_0, \rho_1, \ldots, \rho_L) \xleftarrow{R} \mathbb{Z}_\zeta^{L+1}$ and evaluate $J_1(\mathsf{ID}_1), \ldots, J_1(\mathsf{ID}_q)$ and $J_1(\mathsf{ID}^\star)$ accordingly. When the estimated probability η' is obtained after $O(\varepsilon^{-2} \ln(\varepsilon^{-1}) \eta^{-1} \ln(\eta^{-1}))$ samples, if $\eta' > \eta$, $\mathcal{B}$ artificially aborts and outputs a random bit with probability $1 - \eta/\eta'$. With probability η/η', it continues.

After the artificial abort step, if the simulator $\mathcal{B}$ did not naturally or artificially abort, it outputs 1 if $\mathcal{A}$ successfully guesses $\beta' = \beta$ and 0 otherwise. We now argue that $\mathcal{B}$ has non-negligible advantage as a D3DH distinguisher if $\mathcal{A}$ can distinguish Game i from Game $i - 1$. Indeed, depending on the distribution of T, $\mathcal{B}$ is playing either Game $i - 1$ or Game i with $\mathcal{A}$. Using the same analysis as in [37], we find that, if the difference $|Adv_{i-1} - Adv_i|$ between $\mathcal{A}$'s advantage functions in Game $i-1$ and Game i is ε, then $\mathcal{B}$ can break the D3DH assumption with probability $\varepsilon/(16(L+1)q)$. ☐

Practical Distributed Signatures in the Standard Model*

Yujue Wang[1,2], Duncan S. Wong[2], Qianhong Wu[3],
Sherman S.M. Chow[4], Bo Qin[5], and Jianwei Liu[3]

[1] Key Laboratory of Aerospace Information Security and Trusted Computing
Ministry of Education, School of Computer, Wuhan University, China
[2] Department of Computer Science
City University of Hong Kong, Hong Kong, China
[3] School of Electronics and Information Engineering, Beihang University, China
[4] Department of Information Engineering
Chinese University of Hong Kong, Hong Kong, China
[5] School of Information, Renmin University of China, Beijing, China
yjwang@whu.edu.cn, duncan@cityu.edu.hk,
{qianhong.wu,liujianwei}@buaa.edu.cn,
sherman@ie.cuhk.edu.hk, bo.qin@ruc.eud.cn

Abstract. A distributed signature scheme allows participants in a qualified set to jointly generate a signature which cannot be forged even when all the unqualified participants collude together. In this paper, we propose an efficient scheme for any monotone access structure and show its unforgeability and robustness under the computational Diffie-Hellman (CDH) assumption in the standard model. For 112-bit security, its secret key shares and signature fragments are as short as 255 bits and 510 bits, which are shorter than existing schemes assuming random oracle. We then propose two extensions. The first one allows new participants to dynamically join the system without any help from the dealer. The second one supports a type of multipartite access structures, where the participant set is divided into multiple disjoint groups, and each group is bounded so that a distributed signature cannot be generated unless a pre-defined number of participants from multiple groups work together.

Keywords: Distributed signature, threshold signature, secret sharing, monotone span program, multipartite access structure, standard model.

* This work is supported by the National Key Basic Research Program (973 program) through project 2012CB315905, by the National Nature Science Foundation of China through projects 61003214, 61173154, 61272501, 61202465 and 61370190, by the Beijing Natural Science Foundation through project 4132056, by the Fundamental Research Funds for the Central Universities, and the Research Funds of Renmin University of China and by Open Research Fund of Beijing Key Laboratory of Trusted Computing. Sherman Chow is supported by the Early Career Scheme and the Early Career Award of the Research Grants Council, Hong Kong SAR (CUHK 439713), and grants (4055018, 4930034) from Chinese University of Hong Kong.

J. Benaloh (Ed.): CT-RSA 2014, LNCS 8366, pp. 307–326, 2014.
© Springer International Publishing Switzerland 2014

1   Introduction

A distributed signature scheme [12, 24, 25] enables a qualified set of participants to jointly generate a signature on a message. The participants have their shares of a (secret) signing key so that each of them can generate a signature fragment for a given message. A full signature can then be reconstructed by collecting the signature fragments from a qualified set of participants. This full signature would be computationally indistinguishable from the one generated directly using the signing key, and it should be unforgeable even if all the participants in the unqualified sets collude together. How the qualified set is represented may differ from construction to construction. The qualified set can be simply a threshold structure (which reduces distributed signature to its special case of threshold signature), or a more general notion of monotone access structure. For instance, a signing key may be shared among three participants $\{p_1, p_2, p_3\}$ such that the minimal qualified sets are $\{p_1, p_2\}$ and $\{p_2, p_3\}$. As $\{p_1, p_3\}$ is unqualified, existing threshold signature schemes does not apply to this distributed setting.

When multiple signers are involved, there are at least two properties we may expect from a distributed signature scheme. First, we want *robustness* such that the full signature can be reconstructed even if there were some invalid signature fragments. Second, it is also desirable if the scheme is *non-interactive* in both signature fragment generation and final signature reconstruction, i.e., every participant can locally compute a signature fragment for any given message, and after all these fragments are collected, reconstruction can take place without further help from any participants.

Non-interactive robust distributed cryptosystem is a useful cryptographic primitive for distributed systems [38]. A canonical example involves issuing signature from a number of parties for security and availability, such as issuing digital certificates and certifying transactions between companies. Daza, Herranz, and Sáez [13] discussed its application in metering, which provides a publicly-verifiable cryptographic proof counting the number of interactions between servers and clients, such as counting the number of visits to a web server (say, for advertisement accounting) by collecting signature fragments from the clients. On the other hand, one may use this scheme in another way. A company can launch a promotion campaign such that users can get reward when they see the ad-banner from this company from a sufficient number of different web sites.

1.1   Our Contributions

There are several known distributed signature schemes [12, 24, 25]. Our work improves the state-of-the-art in a few different dimensions. In detail, our scheme achieves these appealing properties:

1. *Provable Security under Standard Assumption.* Our scheme is proven secure under Computational Diffie-Hellman (CDH) assumption *without* relying on random oracles. Prior to our work, only the RSA-based scheme by Damgård-Dupont [12] is proved secure without random oracles.

2. *Expressive Access Structure.* Our construction is generic and applicable to any linear secret sharing schemes. As a result, our scheme supports expressive access structure since monotone span programs are equivalent to linear secret sharing schemes [4] and every monotone access structure can be realized by a linear secret sharing scheme [24, 43]. Sharing secret key can be tricky. In existing distributed RSA-based signature schemes [12, 24], the Euler's totient function of RSA modulus should remain secret even for share-holder. Any non-trivial linear dependence of the rows allows reconstruction of the Euler's totient function. This requires the sub-matrices regarding all unqualified sets in the monotone span program to be full rank.

3. *Practical Efficiency.* Compared to the existing schemes (see Table 1), our scheme is more efficient as its secret key shares and signature fragments are 4 times and 2 times shorter than others, e.g., for 112-bit security, secret key shares and signature fragments of our scheme are as short as 255 bits and 510 bits, respectively. Moreover, our construction is *non-interactive*. All the existing distributed signature schemes [12, 24, 25] are interactive.

1.2   Extensions

We consider two extensions of our proposed schemes.

Dynamic Joining. In some scenarios, e.g., ad-hoc networks, new participants are expected to join the group dynamically. A trivial solution needs the help from a trusted dealer. Our first extension is a threshold signature scheme, which supports dynamic join without the presence of a dealer. A new participant just needs to talk to at least t existing users for a threshold t. To the best of our knowledge, the only known such scheme is proposed by Gennaro et al. under the RSA assumption [21] in random oracle model, yet our scheme is in standard model and more efficient (see Table 2).

Multipartite Access Structures. All participants have the same power in a regular threshold signature scheme. However, in real world applications, participants may be classified by their attributes such as titles, positions, etc., which in turn determine their power in signature generation. In a multipartite access structure [2,3,6,10,17–19,33,41,44], the participant set is divided into multiple disjoint groups and the participants in the same group have the equal power when reconstructing the signature. Obviously, this generalizes the threshold case. In recent years, multipartite access structures have been received considerable attentions, such as compartmented access structures [10, 17, 19, 44, 46, 47], weighted access structures [2,3,33,41], multi-level (hierarchical) access structures [6,10,17–19,44], partially hierarchical access structures [17], etc. For some of these, linear and efficient secret sharing schemes have been found [10, 41, 44, 46, 47].

Our second extension is designed specifically for *compartmented access structure with upper bounds* [17, 46]. There exists a threshold for all the participants, and an upper bound for each separate group, i.e., there is a quorum for signature issuing, but any group can not contribute more than the given upper bound even when all the participants in this group participate.

1.3 Related Work

There are a few different notions of signature related to distributed signatures.

Threshold Signatures. Threshold signatures have been received considerable attentions (e.g., see [11, 14, 15, 21–23, 31, 42, 45]). A signature can be created from the participation of any t or more signers among n potential signers. When $2t - 1 \leq n$, the scheme can be made robust. To realize robustness, Gennaro et al. [22] proposed two approaches to verify RSA signature fragments, which are based on the non-interactive information checking protocol, and undeniable signature requiring interactions between the verifier and the signers. The robust threshold RSA signature schemes also have been discussed in random oracle model [21, 42] and without random oracles [11, 31]. There is also a threshold version for digital signature standard (DSS) signatures [23].

Distributed Signatures. An RSA-based distributed signature scheme for general access structures was proposed by Herranz, Padró and Sáez [24]. An RSA-based scheme in the standard model was given by Damgård and Thorbek [12], which introduced *linear integer secret sharing* to distribute RSA secret keys. Stinson and Strobl [45] generalized discrete-logarithm-based Schnorr's signature [37, 40] into a threshold version. Distributed Schnorr's signature was studied by Herranz and Sáez [25], which also served as a building block for constructing distributed proxy signature [25, 26]. However, these schemes are analyzed in the random oracle model.

Mesh Signatures. As a generalization of ring signatures, mesh signatures [9] can be generated by a qualified set of valid atomic signatures with anonymity. The only construction known [9] has complexities linear in the number of signers. In fact, the corresponding arborescent monotone access structure is a linear combination of *threshold gates*, as both *AND* and *OR gates* are special cases of threshold access structures. However, this scheme [9] cannot support monotone access structures without arborescent representations. Both distributed signature and mesh signature can be used to express that the signers are from a qualified group. A mesh signature can be generated by a single signer, while a distributed signature is usually generated by multiple signers.

Attribute-Based Signatures. In attribute-based signature [32], each signer is assigned with a set of attributes. A signer can generate a signature if the claim-predicate is satisfied by her attributes. Both monotone [29, 32] and non-monotone access structures [34, 35] can be realized by span programs. Like distributed signatures, the scheme has collusion resistance such that signers cannot create a signature that none of them are qualified to even if they pool their attributes together. Unlike distribute signatures, an attribute-based signature is generated by a single signer (with a qualified set of attributes). The claim-predicate can be different for each signature, which inherently makes the signature more complex, either in terms of signature size or underlying assumption. For example, the schemes of Okamoto-Takashima [34, 35], which are based on decisional linear assumption, produce signatures of lengths increase linearly with the complexity of the access structure. The attribute-based signature scheme with threshold access structure due to Herranz et al. [29] is constant-size, yet based on a non-static assumption. Bellare and

Fuchsbauer [8] considered a more general primitive known as *policy-based signature*, which allows a signer to generate signature on some message that fits in some policy, while the privacy of the policy is preserved.

2   Definitions and Security Requirements

2.1   Secret Sharing and Monotone Span Program

In a secret sharing scheme [7,28,41], a *dealer* distributes the *shares* of some secret information to *participants* in such a way that the secret can be recovered when participants in a *qualified set* pool their shares together. An *access structure* is the collection of all qualified sets. An access structure is said to satisfy the *monotone increasing property* if any set that contains a qualified set is also qualified. In this paper, we will require all the secret sharing schemes are *perfect*, that is, unqualified sets cannot get any information about the secret.

Notations. Consider a group of participants $\mathcal{P} = \{p_1, \cdots, p_n\}$. We use Γ to denote the monotone access structure defined on $\mathcal{P}$. Due to its monotone increasing property of Γ, there exists a collection of minimal qualified sets which denoted by $min\Gamma$, such that their proper subsets are not qualified, that is, $\forall A \in min\Gamma$ and $\forall B \subsetneq A$, we have $B \notin \Gamma$. We also use $\overline{\Gamma} = 2^{\mathcal{P}} \setminus \Gamma$ to represent the collection of all unqualified sets of participants where $2^{\mathcal{P}}$ is the power set of $\mathcal{P}$. Clearly, $\overline{\Gamma}$ satisfies monotone decreasing property, i.e., $\forall A \in \overline{\Gamma}$ and $\forall B \subseteq A$, $B \in \overline{\Gamma}$. Similarly, let $max\overline{\Gamma}$ be the collection of all the maximal unqualified sets of participants which are not contained in any other unqualified ones.

Definition 1 (Perfect Secret Sharing [4]). *Let Γ be an access structure defined on a group of participants $\mathcal{P}$. For a secret sharing scheme $\mathcal{S}$ realizing Γ, $\mathcal{S}$ is said to be perfect if the following two properties are satisfied:*

- *for any qualified set $A \in \Gamma$, $\Pr[Re(s_A(k)) = k] = 1$ for every $k \in \mathbb{F}$;*
- *for any unqualified set $B \notin \Gamma$, $\Pr[s_B(k_1) = (s_i)_{p_i \in B}] = \Pr[s_B(k_2) = (s_i)_{p_i \in B}]$ for any two distinct secrets $k_1, k_2 \in \mathbb{F}$, and a list of any possible shares $(s_i)_{p_i \in B}$;*

where $Re(\cdot)$ is the reconstruction function of $\mathcal{S}$ and $s_A(k)$ denotes the shares of the secret k which are assigned to the participants in set A.

In this paper, we are interested in the *linear secret sharing schemes* (LSSS), that is, the shares are calculated by using a linear mapping, and also the secret information can be linearly represented by the shares in any qualified set. In the upcoming sections, we will use *monotone span programs* (MSP) to model linear secret sharing schemes, which was introduced in [30] by Karchmer and Wigderson. In fact, MSP was implicitly proposed before [10] by Brickell which was called *vector space secret sharing scheme.*

Definition 2 (Monotone Span Program [4,30]). *Let $\mathcal{P}$ be a group of participants, a and b be two positive integers. A monotone span program is a quadruple $\mathcal{M} = (\mathbb{F}, \tau, M, \rho)$, where $\mathbb{F}$ is a field, τ is a target vector in $\mathbb{F}^b$, M is an $a \times b$*

matrix over $\mathbb{F}$ *and* $\rho : \{1, 2, \cdots, a\} \to \mathcal{P}$ *labels each row of* M *by a participant in* $\mathcal{P}$. *The size of* $\mathcal{M}$ *is defined as the row number of* M. *For any set* $P \subseteq \mathcal{P}$, *there is a sub-matrix* M_P *of* M, *which consists of all the rows labeled by the participants in* P. *A set* $P \subseteq \mathcal{P}$ *is accepted by* $\mathcal{M}$ *if the target vector* $\boldsymbol{\tau}$ *can be spanned by the vectors in* M_P. *An access structure* Γ *defined on* $\mathcal{P}$ *is accepted by* $\mathcal{M}$ *if and only if* $\mathcal{M}$ *accepts all the sets* $P \in \Gamma$.

It is easy to see that, $\mathcal{M}$ not only defines a linear mapping from the matrix M to the participants in $\mathcal{P}$, but also defines a linear relationship between $\boldsymbol{\tau}$ and each sub-matrix M_P ($P \in \Gamma$) because $\boldsymbol{\tau}$ can be spanned by the rows of M_P. It is well known that, each monotone access structure can be realized by an LSSS [24,43] and MSP is equivalent to LSSS [4,30]. Thus, every monotone access structure can be realized by an MSP, and in such a way that, there may be several rows of M labeled to one participant $p_i \in \mathcal{P}$. However, for convenience to express our results in next sections, we assume there is a one to one correspondence between the rows of M and the participants in $\mathcal{P}$, and will use the vector $\boldsymbol{\omega_i}$ to denote the row of M which labeled by the participant $p_i \in \mathcal{P}$, i.e., $\boldsymbol{\omega_i} = \rho^{-1}(p_i)$.

For other details on secret sharing, the readers can refer to [4].

2.2   Distributed Signature Scheme

We proceed to review the definitions and security model of distributed signature schemes [12,24,25], which are in fact generalizations of threshold signature schemes [22,23]. Besides a group of participants $\mathcal{P} = \{p_1, p_2, \cdots, p_n\}$, we assume there exists a special trusted dealer D and a collector C. Anyone (including that in $\mathcal{P}$) can act as the collector C to run the public-known signature reconstruction algorithm without requiring or producing any secret. We also assume that there exists a secure channel between D and each participant p_i ($1 \leq i \leq n$), but we do not assume that between any pair of participants (including C). The access structure Γ will be represented by an MSP $\mathcal{M} = (\mathbb{F}, \boldsymbol{\tau}, M, \rho)$, and in which the target vector $\boldsymbol{\tau}$ is implicitly assigned to the dealer D.

Definition 3 (Γ-Distributed Signature Scheme). *Let* $SS = \langle \mathsf{KGen}, \mathsf{Sig}, \mathsf{Ver} \rangle$ *be a signature scheme and* Γ *be a general monotone access structure realized by MSP on the participant set* $\mathcal{P}$ *and a trusted dealer* D. *A* Γ-*distributed signature scheme* DS *for* SS *is a quadruple* $DS = \langle \mathsf{DKGen}, \mathsf{SFGen}, \mathsf{SReCon}, \mathsf{Ver} \rangle$ *where all algorithms are polynomial-time computable.*

- *DKGen: On input* 1^κ *where* $\kappa \in \mathbb{N}$ *is a security parameter, and access structure* Γ, *the (randomized) distributed signature key generation algorithm, which is carried out by the dealer* D, *computes* $(PK, SK) \leftarrow \mathsf{KGen}(1^\kappa)$, *then generates* n *secret key shares* $(SK_1, \cdots, SK_n)$ *based on* Γ. *This algorithm also publishes some additional verification parameters* VP. *We denote* $(PK, SK_1, \cdots, SK_n, VP) \leftarrow \mathsf{DKGen}(1^\kappa, \Gamma)$.
- *SFGen: On input* 1^κ, *a message* m, *secret key share* SK_i, *public key* PK, *and public verification parameters* VP, *the signature fragment generation algorithm, which is carried by each participant* $p_i \in \mathcal{P}$, *generates a signature fragment* σ_i. *We denote* $\sigma_i \leftarrow \mathsf{SFGen}(1^\kappa, m, SK_i, PK, VP)$ *for any* $p_i \in \mathcal{P}$.

- SReCon: *On input 1^κ, a message m, signature fragments $\{\sigma_i : p_i \in \mathbb{P}\}$ where $\mathbb{P} \subseteq \mathcal{P}$, public key PK, public verification parameters VP, and access structure Γ, the signature reconstruction algorithm is carried out by the collector, reconstructs the signature σ from the signature fragments σ_i's based on Γ. If the set of signature fragments is unqualified with respect to Γ, then outputs $\bot$. We denote $\{\sigma, \bot\} \leftarrow$ SReCon$(1^\kappa, m, \{\sigma_i : p_i \in \mathbb{P}$ such that $\mathbb{P} \subseteq \mathcal{P}\}, PK, VP, \Gamma)$.*
- Ver: *On input 1^κ, a message-signature pair (m, σ) and a public key PK, the deterministic verification algorithm, which can be carried out by anyone (including who are not in $\mathcal{P}$), outputs "1" if σ is a valid signature for m under the public key PK, or "0" otherwise. We denote $\{1, 0\} \leftarrow$ Ver$(1^\kappa, m, \sigma, PK)$.*

When the verification algorithm Ver in $\mathcal{DS}$ is just the same as that in $\mathcal{SS}$, no one can tell whether a signature is generated in a distributed or the typical centralized manner.

A distributed signature scheme is *correct*, if for all messages and all key tuples consisting of public key, secret key shares and public verification parameters, the signatures produced by signature reconstruction algorithm can be verified as valid under the corresponding public key. Formally, the correctness of a Γ-distributed signature scheme $\mathcal{DS} = \langle$DKGen, SFGen, SReCon, Ver$\rangle$ can be defined as follows.

Definition 4 (Correctness). *Γ-distributed signature scheme $\mathcal{DS}$ is **correct** if Ver$(1^\kappa, m, \sigma, PK) = 1$ for any $(PK, SK_1, \cdots, SK_n, VP) \leftarrow$ DKGen$(1^\kappa, \Gamma)$, any $P \in \Gamma$, any $m \in \{0, 1\}^\star$, and any $\sigma \leftarrow$ SReCon$(1^\kappa, m, \{\sigma_i \leftarrow$ SFGen$(1^\kappa, m, SK_i, PK, VP) : p_i \in P\}, PK, VP, \Gamma)$.*

Definition 5 (Unforgeability). *Given a Γ-distributed signature scheme $\mathcal{DS}$. Suppose $\mathcal{A}$ be a probabilistic polynomial time adversary who controls an unqualified set $P' \in \overline{\Gamma}$ of participants. Consider the following experiment for $\mathcal{A}$:*

- *On input 1^κ and Γ, DKGen is executed to get (PK, SK) and $(SK_1, \cdots, SK_n)$;*
- *$\mathcal{A}$ is given 1^κ, PK, and a list of secret key shares which belong to P'.*
- *$\mathcal{A}$ adaptively chooses q_s ($q_s \in \mathbb{N}$) messages $m_1, \cdots, m_{q_s}$ and interacts with SFGen and SReCon to obtain their signatures $\sigma_1, \cdots, \sigma_{q_s}$.*
- *$\mathcal{A}$ outputs a pair (m, σ). $\mathcal{A}$ succeeds the game if Ver$(1^\kappa, m, \sigma, PK) = 1$ and $m \notin \{m_1, \cdots, m_{q_s}\}$.*

*If there is no such adversary $\mathcal{A}$ who could succeed with non-negligible probability in κ, then $\mathcal{DS}$ is said to be **existentially unforgeable against adaptively chosen message attacks**.*

If an adversary $\mathcal{A}$ controls an unqualified set $P' \in \overline{\Gamma}$ of participants, then $\mathcal{A}$'s view contains not only all the signatures $\sigma_1, \cdots, \sigma_{q_s}$ for the adaptively chosen messages, but also all the intermediate states of the participants in P' and the public outputs on the execution of $\mathcal{DS}$. Furthermore, suppose $\mathcal{A}$ is a *malicious* adversary, then $\mathcal{A}$ can also make participants in P' deviate from the algorithms running, e.g., the corrupted participants can provide invalid signature fragments for SReCon. If a distributed signature scheme resists such an adversary $\mathcal{A}$, then it is *robust*.

Definition 6 (Robustness). *Given a Γ-distributed signature scheme $\mathcal{DS}$. Suppose $\mathcal{A}$ be a malicious adversary who controls an unqualified set $P' \in \overline{\Gamma}$ of participants. $\mathcal{DS}$ is said to be $\overline{\Gamma}$-**robust** if for any $(PK, SK_1, \cdots, SK_n, VP) \leftarrow$ $\mathsf{DKGen}(1^\kappa, \Gamma)$ and any message $m \in \{0,1\}^\star$, there exists $P \subseteq \mathcal{P} \setminus P'$ such that $\mathsf{Ver}(1^\kappa, m, \sigma, PK) = 1$ for any $\sigma \leftarrow \mathsf{SReCon}(1^\kappa, m, \{\sigma_i' : p_i \in P'\} \cup \{\sigma_i \leftarrow \mathsf{SFGen}(1^\kappa, m, SK_i, PK, VP) : p_i \in P\}, PK, VP, \Gamma)$.*

In fact, all the existing distributed signature schemes [12, 24, 25] are robust. Similar to the threshold cases, there is a requirement on the access structures to implement robust distributed signature schemes. In our case, the union of any two unqualified sets cannot cover the universal set of the participants. Otherwise, after discarding an unqualified set of signature fragments provided by malicious participants, the remaining ones will also be unqualified to recover the signature.

3   Our Basic Scheme

We first briefly review bilinear groups which will be used in our construction.

Definition 7 (Bilinear Groups [20]). *Let q be a prime. Suppose $\mathbb{G}_1$ and $\mathbb{G}_2$ are cyclic groups of order q, and generated by g_1 and g_2, respectively. A group pair $(\mathbb{G}_1, \mathbb{G}_2)$ are said to be bilinear if there exists a cyclic group $\mathbb{G}_T$ and a bilinear map $e : \mathbb{G}_1 \times \mathbb{G}_2 \to \mathbb{G}_T$ such that:*

1. *Bilinearity: $\forall \mu \in \mathbb{G}_1$, $\forall \nu \in \mathbb{G}_2$, and $\forall a, b \in \mathbb{Z}$, $e(\mu^a, \nu^b) = e(\mu, \nu)^{ab}$;*
2. *Non-degeneracy: $e(g_1, g_2) \neq 1$ and thus is a generator of $\mathbb{G}_T$;*
3. *Efficiency: the map e and the group operations in $\mathbb{G}_1, \mathbb{G}_2$ and $\mathbb{G}_T$ could be calculated efficiently.*

Our Construction. Our construction is based on the Waters signature scheme [27, 48]. Let $\mathbb{G}$ be a group of order q, where q is a prime. For simplicity of presentation we set $\mathbb{G}_1 = \mathbb{G}_2 = \mathbb{G}$ such that $e : \mathbb{G} \times \mathbb{G} \to \mathbb{G}_T$ is an efficient bilinear map. Suppose $H : \{0,1\}^\star \to \{0,1\}^\ell$ is a public collision-resistant hash function, where ℓ is derived from the system security parameter. The access structure Γ is represented by an MSP $\mathcal{M} = (\mathbb{Z}_q, \boldsymbol{\tau}, M, \rho)$.

- DKGen: The dealer randomly chooses a secret key k from $\mathbb{Z}_q$, and also a series of elements $g, g_0, \cdots, g_\ell \in \mathbb{G}$. The public key is a tuple

$$PK = (g, g_0, \cdots, g_\ell, e(g, g)^k).$$

To share the secret key k among the participants in $\mathcal{P}$, the dealer randomly chooses a vector $\boldsymbol{v} \in (\mathbb{Z}_q)^b$ that satisfies $\boldsymbol{v} \cdot \boldsymbol{\tau} = k \mod q$ and calculates the secret key shares as $k_i = \boldsymbol{v} \cdot \boldsymbol{\omega_i} \mod q$ for every $p_i \in \mathcal{P}$. The algorithm also publishes the verification parameters

$$VP = (e(g, g)^{k_1}, \cdots, e(g, g)^{k_n}).$$

- SFGen: All messages are taken as ℓ-bit strings. For any longer messages, hash function H should be applied first on them in order to shorten their length to ℓ. Given a message m denoted by $(m_1, \cdots, m_\ell)$, the algorithm randomly chooses a value $r_i \in \mathbb{Z}_q$ and generates signature fragment $\sigma_i = (\alpha_i, \beta_i)$ for the participant p_i ($p_i \in \mathcal{P}$) using the secret key share k_i as

$$\alpha_i = g^{k_i} \left(g_0 \prod_{j=1}^{\ell} g_j^{m_j} \right)^{r_i} \quad , \quad \beta_i = g^{r_i}.$$

- SReCon: Given a message m, signature fragments $\{\sigma_i : p_i \in \mathbb{P} \text{ such that } \mathbb{P} \subseteq \mathcal{P}\}$, public key $PK = (g, g_0, \cdots, g_\ell, e(g,g)^k)$ and verification parameters $VP = (e(g,g)^{k_1}, \cdots, e(g,g)^{k_n})$, the collector discards all the invalid signature fragments by checking if

$$e(\alpha_i, g) \stackrel{?}{=} e(g,g)^{k_i} e(g_0 \prod_{j=1}^{\ell} g_j^{m_j}, \beta_i)$$

holds. If the remaining signature fragments constitute a qualified set P with regard to the access structure Γ, then there exist a series of values $\{d_i \in \mathbb{Z}_q : p_i \in P\}$ which can be efficiently found by solving the system of equations, such that

$$\boldsymbol{\tau} = \sum_{p_i \in P} d_i \boldsymbol{\omega_i} \mod q.$$

Thus, the signature $\sigma = (\alpha, \beta)$ can be reconstructed as follows

$$\alpha = \prod_{p_i \in P} \alpha_i^{d_i}, \quad \beta = \prod_{p_i \in P} \beta_i^{d_i}.$$

Otherwise, outputs $\bot$.
- Ver: Given a message-signature pair $(m, \sigma = (\alpha, \beta))$ and public key $PK = (g, g_0, \cdots, g_\ell, e(g,g)^k)$, checks whether the following equality holds

$$e(\alpha, g) \stackrel{?}{=} e(g,g)^k e(g_0 \prod_{j=1}^{\ell} g_j^{m_j}, \beta).$$

If it is true, then the purported signature σ on message m is valid and accepted; otherwise it is invalid.

Theorem 1. *The proposed distributed signature scheme is correct.*

Proof. According to the definition of MSP, $\boldsymbol{\tau}$ can be linearly represented by using all $\boldsymbol{\omega_i}$'s of M_P where P is a qualified set $P \in \Gamma$. Thus, there exists a group of numbers $\{d_i \in \mathbb{Z}_q : p_i \in P\}$ such that $\sum_{p_i \in P} d_i \boldsymbol{\omega_i} = \boldsymbol{\tau} \mod q$ and they can be found by solving linear equations. Furthermore, we know

$$k = \boldsymbol{v} \cdot \boldsymbol{\tau} = \boldsymbol{v} \cdot \left(\sum_{p_i \in P} d_i \boldsymbol{\omega_i} \right) = \sum_{p_i \in P} d_i (\boldsymbol{v} \cdot \boldsymbol{\omega_i}) = \sum_{p_i \in P} d_i k_i \mod q.$$

Then, the signature $\sigma = (\alpha, \beta)$ can be computed as

$$\alpha = \prod_{p_i \in P} \alpha_i{}^{d_i} = g^{\sum_{p_i \in P} d_i k_i} \left(g_0 \prod_{j=1}^{\ell} g_j^{\mathsf{m}_j} \right)^{\sum_{p_i \in P} d_i r_i} = g^k \left(g_0 \prod_{j=1}^{\ell} g_j^{\mathsf{m}_j} \right)^r,$$

and

$$\beta = \prod_{p_i \in P} \beta_i{}^{d_i} = g^{\sum_{p_i \in P} d_i r_i} = g^r,$$

where $r = \sum_{p_i \in P} d_i r_i \mod q$ is also random because all the r_i's are randomly chosen.

Given a message-signature pair $(m, \sigma = (\alpha, \beta))$ and public key $PK = (g, g_0, \cdots, g_\ell, e(g, g)^k)$, the signature σ can be validated due to the following equalities

$$e(\alpha, g) = e\left(g^k \left(g_0 \prod_{j=1}^{\ell} g_j^{\mathsf{m}_j} \right)^r, g \right) = e(g^k, g) e\left(\left(g_0 \prod_{j=1}^{\ell} g_j^{\mathsf{m}_j} \right)^r, g \right)$$

$$= e(g, g)^k e(g_0 \prod_{j=1}^{\ell} g_j^{\mathsf{m}_j}, g^r) = e(g, g)^k e(g_0 \prod_{j=1}^{\ell} g_j^{\mathsf{m}_j}, \beta).$$

$\square$

3.1   Security Analysis

We first review a modular approach to prove unforgeability of distributed (threshold) signature schemes, which has been used in previous works (e.g., [22–24,42]). In detail, the unforgeability of a Γ-distributed signature scheme can be proved by first showing that the underlying standard signature scheme is unforgeable and then showing that the Γ-distributed signature scheme itself is *simulatable*. A simulatable Γ-distributed signature scheme $\mathcal{DS}$ requires that DKGen, SFGen and SReCon are simulatable for any probabilistic polynomial time adversary $\mathcal{A}$, that is, $\mathcal{A}$'s view on the execution of DKGen, SFGen and SReCon can be efficiently simulated only based on the public key PK and access structure Γ (represented by MSP) of $\mathcal{DS}$.

Definition 8 (Simulatability [22–24,42]). *A Γ-distributed signature scheme $\mathcal{DS} = \langle \mathsf{DKGen}, \mathsf{SFGen}, \mathsf{SReCon}, \mathsf{Ver} \rangle$ is said to be **simulatable**, if for any probabilistic polynomial time adversary $\mathcal{A}$ who controls an unqualified set $P' \in \overline{\Gamma}$, there exist efficient (polynomial time) algorithms $\mathcal{S}_1$ to simulate $\mathcal{A}$'s view on the execution of DKGen, and $\mathcal{S}_2$ to simulate $\mathcal{A}$'s view on the execution of SFGen and SReCon:*

- *$\mathcal{S}_1$: on input public key PK, corrupted set P', and MSP which represents Γ in $\mathcal{DS}$, can simulate the adversary $\mathcal{A}$'s view on the execution of DKGen.*

- $\mathcal{S}_2$: on input the outputs of $\mathcal{S}_1$ (including all the secret information with regard to the corrupted participants in P', e.g., secret key shares), a message-signature pair (m, σ), the public key PK, the corrupted set P' and MSP which represents Γ in $\mathcal{DS}$, can simulate the adversary $\mathcal{A}$'s view on the execution of SFGen and SReCon for generating σ.

The next lemma states the requirements for the unforgeability of $\mathcal{DS}$, and will show that holding the view on the executions of DKGen and SFGen is useless for $\mathcal{A}$ to generate a signature forgery. The counterpart of the lemma for threshold signatures is given in [22,23,42]. It was used in distributed signature schemes [24].

Lemma 1. *The $\mathcal{DS}$ scheme is also unforgeable if the underlying signature scheme $\mathcal{SS} = \langle \mathsf{KGen}, \mathsf{Sig}, \mathsf{Ver}\rangle$ is unforgeable and the corresponding Γ-distribute signature scheme $\mathcal{DS} = \langle \mathsf{DKGen}, \mathsf{SFGen}, \mathsf{SReCon}, \mathsf{Ver}\rangle$ is simulatable.*

Regarding the security of our scheme, we have the following claim.

Theorem 2. *Let $\Gamma \subset 2^{\mathcal{P}}$ be an access structure and $\mathcal{M} = (\mathbb{Z}_q, \boldsymbol{\tau}, M, \rho)$ be a monotone span program realizing Γ. Then our Γ-distributed signature scheme is secure (robust and unforgeable under chosen message attacks) in the standard model, assuming that the underlying Waters signature scheme is unforgeable.*

Proof. It is easy to verify that the robustness can be achieved if $\mathcal{P} \setminus P' \in \Gamma$ for any $P' \in \overline{\Gamma}$. In detail, suppose the adversary $\mathcal{A}$ controls an unqualified set $P' \in \overline{\Gamma}$, then all the invalid signature fragments provided by P' can be detected during the execution of SReCon, and the signature can be reconstructed by $\mathcal{P} \setminus P'$.

For unforgeability, we will give two algorithms $\mathcal{S}_1$ and $\mathcal{S}_2$ to simulate the adversary $\mathcal{A}$'s view when $\mathcal{A}$ controls an unqualified set $P' \in \overline{\Gamma}$, then Lemma 1 can be used accordingly.

$\mathcal{S}_1$ takes the public key $PK = (g, g_0, \cdots, g_\ell, e(g, g)^k)$, the controlled set P' and access structure Γ with an MSP realization $\mathcal{M} = (\mathbb{Z}_q, \boldsymbol{\tau}, M, \rho)$ as input. In the proposed scheme, every participant $p_i \in P'$ holds a secret key share $k_i = \boldsymbol{v} \cdot \boldsymbol{\omega}_i \bmod q$, where the vector $\boldsymbol{v}$ is randomly chosen from $(\mathbb{Z}_q)^b$ such that $k = \boldsymbol{v} \cdot \boldsymbol{\tau} \bmod q$. As $\overline{\Gamma}$ is monotone decreasing, there exists a maximal unqualified set $\hat{P}' \in max\overline{\Gamma}$ such that $P' \subseteq \hat{P}'$. In order to simulate the adversary $\mathcal{A}$'s view, $\mathcal{S}_1$ randomly chooses a vector $\tilde{\boldsymbol{v}} \in (\mathbb{Z}_q)^b$ and gives every participant $p_i \in \hat{P}'$ a value $\tilde{k}_i = \tilde{\boldsymbol{v}} \cdot \boldsymbol{\omega}_i \bmod q$. In fact, the outputs $\{\tilde{k}_i : p_i \in P'\}$ of $\mathcal{S}_1$ are computationally indistinguishable from the real secret key shares $\{k_i : p_i \in P'\}$, because both $\tilde{k}_i$'s and k_i's are uniformly distributed in $\mathbb{Z}_q$. Furthermore, it has been proved [4] that MSP is equivalent to the perfect linear secret sharing scheme, which means that the distribution of $\{k_i : p_i \in \hat{P}'\}$ are perfectly secure with regard to Γ. Thus, $\{\tilde{k}_i : p_i \in \hat{P}'\}$ are also perfectly secure towards the same Γ.

$\mathcal{S}_1$ also calculates the simulated verification parameters $\widetilde{VP}$ which are computationally indistinguishable from the real verification parameters VP. In detail, a part of $\widetilde{VP}$ which related to the participants in $\hat{P}'$ can be calculated as $\{e(g, g)^{\tilde{k}_i} : p_i \in \hat{P}'\}$, while the other ones can be computed as follows. Since $\hat{P}' \in max\overline{\Gamma}$, we know $\hat{P}' \cup \{p_s\} \in \Gamma$ for any participant $p_s \in \mathcal{P} \setminus \hat{P}'$. According to the definition of monotone span program, $\boldsymbol{\omega_s}$ can be linearly represented by $\boldsymbol{\tau}$ and $\{\boldsymbol{\omega_i} : p_i \in \hat{P}'\}$:

$$\boldsymbol{\omega_s} = d_D \boldsymbol{\tau} + \sum_{p_i \in \hat{P}'} d_i \boldsymbol{\omega_i} \mod q,$$

where d_D and $\{d_i : p_i \in \hat{P}'\}$ are elements in $\mathbb{Z}_q$. Thus, for any participant $p_s \in \mathcal{P} \setminus \hat{P}'$, $\mathcal{S}_1$ computes

$$e(g,g)^{\tilde{k}_s} = e(g,g)^{d_D k + \sum_{p_i \in \hat{P}'} d_i \tilde{k}_i} = \left(e(g,g)^k\right)^{d_D} \cdot \prod_{p_i \in \hat{P}'} \left(e(g,g)^{\tilde{k}_i}\right)^{d_i}.$$

$\mathcal{S}_2$ takes the public key $PK = (g, g_0, \cdots, g_\ell, e(g,g)^k)$, the outputs $\{\tilde{k}_i : p_i \in \hat{P}'\}$ of $\mathcal{S}_1$, the controlled set P', a public known hash function H, and a message-signature pair (m, σ) as input. For each participant $p_i \in \hat{P}'$, $\mathcal{S}_2$ calculates the simulated signature fragment $\tilde{\sigma}_i = (\tilde{\alpha}_i, \tilde{\beta}_i)$ as

$$\tilde{\alpha}_i = g^{\tilde{k}_i} \left(g_0 \prod_{j=1}^{\ell} g_j^{\mathsf{m}_j}\right)^{\tilde{r}_i} \quad, \quad \tilde{\beta}_i = g^{\tilde{r}_i},$$

where $\tilde{r}_i \in \mathbb{Z}_q$ is randomly chosen by $\mathcal{S}_2$. Under the above $\widetilde{VP}$, for any participant $p_s \in \mathcal{P} \setminus \hat{P}'$, $\mathcal{S}_2$ can generate a simulated signature fragment $\tilde{\sigma}_s = (\tilde{\alpha}_s, \tilde{\beta}_s)$ as

$$\tilde{\alpha}_s = \alpha^{d_D} g^{\sum_{p_i \in \hat{P}'} d_i \tilde{k}_i} \left(g_0 \prod_{j=1}^{\ell} g_j^{\mathsf{m}_j}\right)^{\tilde{r}_s} \quad, \quad \tilde{\beta}_s = \beta^{d_D} g^{\tilde{r}_s},$$

where $\tilde{r}_s \in \mathbb{Z}_q$ is randomly chosen by $\mathcal{S}_2$. As it is easy to check the validity of these simulated signature fragments $\{\tilde{\sigma}_i : p_i \in \mathcal{P}\}$ under the public key PK and the simulated verification parameters $\widetilde{VP}$, $\{\tilde{\sigma}_i : p_i \in \mathcal{P}\}$ are computationally distinguishable from the real signature fragments $\{\sigma_i : p_i \in \mathcal{P}\}$ with regard to the given (m, σ).

Thus, the proposed Γ-distributed signature scheme is simulatable. Since Waters signature scheme is unforgeable under chosen message attacks [27,48], then by Lemma 1, so does our scheme.   □

3.2   Comparison

We compare the proposed scheme with existing distributed Schnorr signature scheme [25] and distributed RSA signature schemes [12,24] in terms of key (share) sizes and signature (fragment) sizes at the same security level. It is well known that the bilinear map can be realized by utilizing pairings on some elliptic curves. We give a comparison according to the key sizes recommended by NIST [1,20] in Table 1. Consider 112-bit security level, distributed Schnorr signature scheme requires the longest signature fragments (2272 bits), while distributed RSA signature scheme requires the longest secret key shares (2048 bits). Thus, our scheme is more practical with secret key shares and signature fragments as short as 255 bits and 510 bits, respectively.

Table 1. Comparison of distributed signature schemes for $\kappa = 112$ (bits)

Schemes	Key size	Key share size	Signature (fragment) size	Standard model
DL-based [25]	224	448	2272	×
RSA-based [24]	2048	2048	2052	×
RSA-based [12]	2048	2048	2048	✓
Our CDH-based	224-255	224-255	448-510	✓

4 Extensions

In this section, we will give two special extensions of our distributed signature scheme, which can capture some specific requirements in real-world applications.

4.1 Threshold Signatures with Dynamic Addition of Participants

We first give an extension of our distributed signature scheme by using a symmetric bivariate polynomial to share the signing key. Any two secret key shares generated by our scheme are correlated according to the symmetric property. We will give one more algorithm (i.e., PtAdd), which is executed by the new participants to generate his/her secret key share, on inputting the information that generated by other t or more participants. The same technique is used in the scheme of Gennaro et al. [21], which was originally used for admitting node in a short-lived mobile ad hoc network [39].

- DKGen: The dealer randomly chooses a secret key k from $\mathbb{Z}_q$, and also a series of elements $g, g_0, \cdots, g_\ell \in \mathbb{G}$. The public key is a tuple

$$PK = (g, g_0, \cdots, g_\ell, e(g,g)^k).$$

To share the secret key k among the participants in $\mathcal{P}$, the dealer constructs a symmetric bivariate polynomial

$$f(x,y) = \sum_{u=0}^{t-1} \sum_{v=0}^{t-1} c_{u,v} x^u y^v,$$

where the coefficients $c_{u,v}$'s are randomly chosen from $\mathbb{Z}_q$ such that $c_{u,v} = c_{v,u}$, $c_{0,0} = k$ and $c_{t-1,t-1}$ is nonzero. Thus, the secret key shares are computed as $k_i(x) = f(x,i) \mod q$ for all participants $p_i \in \mathcal{P}$. The algorithm also publishes the verification parameters $VP = \{e(g,g)^{k_i(0)} : p_i \in \mathcal{P}\}$.
- PtAdd: When a new participant p_s joining the group, he/she should be given a share of the secret key. In fact, his/her share can be computed with the help of other t participants and do not need the dealer. We assume the new participant p_s received t shares $k_i(s) = f(s,i) \mod q$ from the other parties. Without loss of generality, we assume these values are calculated by the participants in $P = \{p_1, \cdots, p_t\}$, that is, the new participant p_s holds

$$\{k_1(s) = f(s,1), \cdots, k_t(s) = f(s,t)\}.$$

Due to the symmetric property of the bivariate polynomial $f(x, y)$, i.e. $k_i(j) = f(j, i) = f(i, j) = k_j(i) \mod q$, the new participant p_s indeed holds $\{k_s(1) = f(1, s), \cdots, k_s(t) = f(t, s)\}$ and his/her share of the secret key can be calculated by using polynomial interpolation

$$k_s(x) = \sum_{i=1}^{t} \lambda_i(x) k_s(i) \mod q,$$

where $\lambda_i(x) = \prod_{j=1, j \neq i}^{t} \frac{x-j}{i-j} \mod q$. Then, he/she also publishes $e(g, g)^{k_s(0)}$. Thus, the participant set $\mathcal{P}$ and verification parameters VP are dynamically updated.

In fact, the new participant p_s can validate $k_s(0)$ by checking if the following equalities holds

$$e(g, g)^{k_s(0)} = e(g, g)^{\sum_{i=1}^{t} \lambda_i k_i(0)} = \prod_{i=1}^{t} \left(e(g, g)^{k_i(0)} \right)^{\lambda_i},$$

which is due to

$$k_s(0) = f(0, s) = \sum_{i=1}^{t} \lambda_i f(0, i) = \sum_{i=1}^{t} \lambda_i k_i(0) \mod q,$$

where λ_i's are the Lagrange coefficients $\lambda_i = \prod_{j=1, j \neq i}^{t} \frac{s-j}{i-j} \mod q$.

- SFGen: Given a message m denoted by $(\mathfrak{m}_1, \cdots, \mathfrak{m}_\ell)$, the algorithm randomly chooses a value $r_i \in \mathbb{Z}_q$ and generates signature fragment $\sigma_i = (\alpha_i, \beta_i)$ for the participant p_i $(p_i \in \mathcal{P})$ as

$$\alpha_i = g^{k_i(0)} \left(g_0 \prod_{j=1}^{\ell} g_j^{\mathfrak{m}_j} \right)^{r_i}, \quad \beta_i = g^{r_i}.$$

- SReCon: Given a message m, signature fragments $\{\sigma_i : p_i \in \mathbb{P} \text{ such that } \mathbb{P} \subseteq \mathcal{P}\}$, public key PK, and verification parameters VP, the collector discards all the invalid signature fragments by checking if

$$e(\alpha_i, g) \stackrel{?}{=} e(g, g)^{k_i(0)} e(g_0 \prod_{j=1}^{\ell} g_j^{\mathfrak{m}_j}, \beta_i)$$

holds. If there are remaining t or more valid signature fragments (e.g., $\{\sigma_1, \cdots, \sigma_t\}$), the signature $\sigma = (\alpha, \beta)$ of m can be reconstructed as follows

$$\alpha = \prod_{i=1}^{t} \alpha_i^{\lambda_i}, \quad \beta = \prod_{i=1}^{t} \beta_i^{\lambda_i},$$

where λ_i's are the Lagrange coefficients $\lambda_i = \prod_{j=1, j \neq i}^{t} \frac{j}{j-i} \mod q$. Otherwise, outputs $\perp$.

- Ver: Given a message m, a signature $\sigma = (\alpha, \beta)$, and a public key $PK = (g, g_0, \cdots, g_\ell, e(g,g)^k)$, check if the following equality holds

$$e(\alpha, g) \stackrel{?}{=} e(g,g)^k e(g_0 \prod_{j=1}^{\ell} g_j^{\mathsf{m}_j}, \beta).$$

If it is true, the signature σ is valid; otherwise it is invalid.

As the secret sharing scheme being used in the distributed secret key generation algorithm DKGen is a special linear threshold scheme, thus, according to Theorem 1, we have the following corollary.

Corollary 1. *The above threshold signature scheme is correct.*

Also, according to Theorem 2, we have the following claim.

Corollary 2. *The above threshold signature scheme is secure under CDH assumption in the standard model.*

Table 2 illustrates a performance comparison between our scheme with Gennaro et al.'s scheme [21]. Our scheme has shorter secret key shares and signature fragments, and introduces no additional parameters. As we have noted, due to the Euler's totient function of RSA modulus should keep unknown to all the participants, some additional parameters $(\Delta, \{\delta_i\}, \delta)$ should be introduced for realizing the same functionality in RSA setting.

Table 2. Comparison of threshold signature schemes for $\kappa = 112$ (bits)

	Key share size	Signature fragment size	Additional parameters	Standard model
[21]	$2048t$	2048	$\Delta, \{\delta_i\}, \delta$	×
Ours	$224t$ to $255t$	448-510	×	✓

4.2 Distributed Signature Scheme for Multipartite Access Structures

In a multipartite access structure, the participant set $\mathcal{P}$ can be divided into u disjoint groups $\mathcal{G}_i$ ($i \in [1, u]$), i.e., $\mathcal{P} = \cup_{i=1}^{u}\mathcal{G}_i$ and $\mathcal{G}_i \cap \mathcal{G}_j = \varnothing$ if $i \neq j$. Furthermore, all participants in the same group $\mathcal{G}_i$ are equally powerful, that is, if a participant $p \in \mathcal{G}_i$ is in a qualified set $P \in \Gamma$, then p can be replaced by any participant $p' \in \mathcal{G}_i \setminus P$.

Our second extension is a distributed signature scheme for *compartmented access structures with upper bounds* [17, 46]. Our construction is based on the linear secret sharing scheme proposed by Tassa and Dyn [46]. Compartmented access structures with upper bounds can be defined as

$$\Gamma = \{\mathcal{I} \subseteq \mathcal{P} : \exists \mathcal{J} \subseteq \mathcal{I} \text{ such that } |\mathcal{J} \cap \mathcal{G}_i| \leq t_i, 1 \leq i \leq u, \text{ and } |\mathcal{J}| = t\},$$

where $1 \leq t \leq \min\{\sum_{i=1}^{u} t_i, n\}$. That is, t_i determines the power of group $\mathcal{G}_i$ ($i \in [1, u]$). As we will see in the following, for the scheme presented by Tassa and Dyn [46], more than t_i participants of $\mathcal{G}_i$ cannot contribute more to recovering the secret.

- DKGen: The dealer randomly chooses a secret key $k \in \mathbb{Z}_q$, and also a series of elements $g, g_0, \cdots, g_\ell \in \mathbb{G}$. The public key is a tuple

$$PK = (g, g_0, \cdots, g_\ell, e(g, g)^k).$$

To share the secret key k among the participants in $\mathcal{P}$, for each group $\mathcal{G}_i$ ($i \in [1, u]$), the dealer first constructs a random univariate polynomial

$$f_i(y) = \sum_{j=0}^{t_i-1} c_{i,j} y^j$$

over $\mathbb{Z}_q$, where c_{i,t_i-1} is nonzero, and specifies a distinct identity $x_i \in \mathbb{Z}_q$. Furthermore, it is required that

$$\sum_{i=1}^{u} \sum_{j=0}^{t_i-1} c_{i,j} = k \mod q.$$

Then using Lagrange interpolation to construct

$$f(x, y) = \sum_{i=1}^{u} \lambda_i(x) f_i(y) = \sum_{i=1}^{u} \sum_{j=0}^{t_i-1} c_{i,j} \lambda_i(x) y^j \mod q,$$

where $\lambda_i(x) = \prod_{h=1, h \neq i}^{u} \frac{x - x_h}{x_i - x_h} \mod q$. The secret key share for participant $p_{i,j} \in \mathcal{G}_i$ ($i \in [1, u]$) can be calculated as $k_{i,j} = f(x_i, y_{i,j}) \mod q$, in which $y_{i,j}$ is the identity of $p_{i,j}$ such that $y_{i,j} \neq 1$. The verification parameters are published as

$$VP = \{e(g, g)^{k_{i,j}} : p_{i,j} \in \mathcal{P}\}.$$

In addition, as $t \leq \sum_{i=1}^{u} t_i$, the dealer should also publish $s = \sum_{i=1}^{u} t_i - t$ secret key shares, that is, the dealer random chooses s different points (x_i', z_i') where $x_i' \notin \{x_1, \cdots, x_u\}$ and calculates $k_i' = f(x_i', z_i') \mod q$.
- SFGen: Given a message m denoted by $(\mathfrak{m}_1, \cdots, \mathfrak{m}_\ell)$, the algorithm generates a signature fragment $\sigma_{i,j} = (\alpha_{i,j}, \beta_{i,j})$ for the participant $p_{i,j} \in \mathcal{P}$ as

$$\alpha_{i,j} = g^{k_{i,j}} \left(g_0 \prod_{h=1}^{\ell} g_h^{\mathfrak{m}_h} \right)^{r_{i,j}}, \quad \beta_{i,j} = g^{r_{i,j}},$$

where $r_{i,j}$ is randomly chosen from $\mathbb{Z}_q$.

- SReCon: Given a message m, signature fragments $\{\sigma_{i,j} : p_{i,j} \in \mathbb{P}$ such that $\mathbb{P} \subseteq \mathcal{P}\}$, public key $PK = (g, g_0, \cdots, g_\ell, e(g,g)^k)$, and verification parameters $VP = \{e(g,g)^{k_{i,j}} : p_{i,j} \in \mathcal{P}\}$, the collector discards all the invalid signature fragments by checking if

$$e(\alpha_{i,j}, g) \stackrel{?}{=} e(g,g)^{k_{i,j}} e(g_0 \prod_{h=1}^{\ell} g_h^{m_h}, \beta_{i,j})$$

holds. If there are remaining t or more valid signature fragments $\sigma_{i,j}$'s (suppose they belong to the participants in $P \subseteq \mathbb{P}$), the signature $\sigma = (\alpha, \beta)$ of m can be reconstructed as follows: because there exist $\sum_{i=1}^{u} t_i$ values of $d_{i,j}$'s and d_i's over $\mathbb{Z}_q$ (which can be efficiently found by solving the system of equations) such that

$$k = \sum_{p_{i,j} \in P} d_{i,j} k_{i,j} + \sum_{i=1}^{s} d_i k_i' \mod q,$$

the signature σ is calculated as

$$\alpha = \prod_{p_{i,j} \in P} \alpha_{i,j}^{d_{i,j}} \cdot \prod_{i=1}^{s} (g^{k_i'})^{d_i}, \quad \beta = \prod_{p_{i,j} \in P} \beta_{i,j}^{d_{i,j}}.$$

Otherwise, outputs $\perp$.
- Ver: Given a message m, a signature $\sigma = (\alpha, \beta)$, and a public key $PK = (g, g_0, \cdots, g_\ell, e(g,g)^k)$, check whether the following equality holds

$$e(\alpha, g) \stackrel{?}{=} e(g,g)^k e(g_0 \prod_{h=1}^{\ell} g_h^{m_h}, \beta).$$

If it holds, then the signature σ is valid; otherwise it is invalid.

Tassa and Dyn [46] proved their linear secret sharing scheme for the compartmented access structures with upper bounds is perfect with probability $1 - O(1/q)$. It is easy to rewrite their scheme in a MSP representation, thus, according to Theorem 1 and Theorem 2, we have following corollaries.

Corollary 3. *The above distributed signature scheme for compartmented access structures with upper bounds is correct.*

Corollary 4. *The above distributed signature scheme for compartmented access structures with upper bounds is secure with probability $1 - O(1/q)$ under CDH assumption in the standard model.*

5   Conclusion

We proposed a distributed signatures scheme in the standard model based on the CDH assumption. Our scheme offers higher efficiency when compared with existing schemes in the random oracle model. We also presented two special extensions of our construction. The first one can be used in the situation in which new participants can join the system without the help from a centralized dealer. The second one can be used for a type of multipartite access structures where all the disjoint groups are bounded to jointly generate a signature.

References

1. Barker, E., Barker, W., Burr, W., Polk, W., Smid, M.: Recommendation for Key Management-Part 1: General (Revision 3). NIST Special Publication 800-57, 1-147 (2012), http://csrc.nist.gov/publications/nistpubs/800-57/sp800-57_part1_rev3_general.pdf
2. Beimel, A., Weinreb, E.: Monotone Circuits for Monotone Weighted Threshold Functions. Information Processing Letters 97, 12–18 (2006)
3. Beimel, A., Tassa, T., Weinreb, E.: Characterizing Ideal Weighted Threshold Secret Sharing. SIAM J. Discrete Math. 22, 360–397 (2008)
4. Beimel, A.: Secret-Sharing Schemes: A Survey. In: Chee, Y.M., Guo, Z., Ling, S., Shao, F., Tang, Y., Wang, H., Xing, C. (eds.) IWCC 2011. LNCS, vol. 6639, pp. 11–46. Springer, Heidelberg (2011)
5. Benaloh, J., Leichter, J.: Generalized Secret Sharing and Monotone Functions. In: Goldwasser, S. (ed.) CRYPTO 1988. LNCS, vol. 403, pp. 27–35. Springer, Heidelberg (1990)
6. Beutelspacher, A., Wettl, F.: On 2-level Secret Sharing. Designs, Codes and Cryptography 3, 127–134 (1993)
7. Blakley, G.R.: Safeguarding Cryptographic Keys. In: National Computer Conference, vol. 48, pp. 313–317. AFIPS Press (1979)
8. Bellare, M., Fuchsbauer, G.: Policy-based Signatures. Cryptology ePrint Archive, Report 2013/413 (2013)
9. Boyen, X.: Mesh Signatures. In: Naor, M. (ed.) EUROCRYPT 2007. LNCS, vol. 4515, pp. 210–227. Springer, Heidelberg (2007)
10. Brickell, E.F.: Some Ideal Secret Sharing Schemes. In: Quisquater, J.-J., Vandewalle, J. (eds.) EUROCRYPT 1989. LNCS, vol. 434, pp. 468–475. Springer, Heidelberg (1990)
11. Damgård, I., Dupont, K.: Efficient Threshold RSA Signatures with General Moduli and No Extra Assumptions. In: Vaudenay, S. (ed.) PKC 2005. LNCS, vol. 3386, pp. 346–361. Springer, Heidelberg (2005)
12. Damgård, I., Thorbek, R.: Linear Integer Secret Sharing and Distributed Exponentiation. In: Yung, M., Dodis, Y., Kiayias, A., Malkin, T. (eds.) PKC 2006. LNCS, vol. 3958, pp. 75–90. Springer, Heidelberg (2006)
13. Daza, V., Herranz, J., Sáez, G.: Protocols Useful on the Internet from Distributed Signature Schemes. Int. J. Inf. Secur. 3, 61–69 (2004)
14. Desmedt, Y.: Society and Group Oriented Cryptography: A New Concept. In: Pomerance, C. (ed.) CRYPTO 1987. LNCS, vol. 293, pp. 120–127. Springer, Heidelberg (1988)
15. Desmedt, Y., Frankel, Y.: Threshold Cryptosystems. In: Brassard, G. (ed.) CRYPTO 1989. LNCS, vol. 435, pp. 307–315. Springer, Heidelberg (1990)
16. El Gamal, T.: A Public Key Cryptosystem and a Signature Scheme Based on Discrete Logarithms. IEEE Transactions on Information Theory IT-31(4), 469–472 (1985)

17. Farràs, O., Padró, C., Xing, C., Yang, A.: Natural Generalizations of Threshold Secret Sharing. In: Lee, D.H., Wang, X. (eds.) ASIACRYPT 2011. LNCS, vol. 7073, pp. 610–627. Springer, Heidelberg (2011)
18. Farràs, O., Padró, C.: Ideal Hierarchical Secret Sharing Schemes. In: Micciancio, D. (ed.) TCC 2010. LNCS, vol. 5978, pp. 219–236. Springer, Heidelberg (2010)
19. Farràs, O., Martí-Farré, J., Padró, C.: Ideal Multipartite Secret Sharing Schemes. Journal of Cryptology 25(3), 434–463 (2012)
20. Galbraith, S.D., Paterson, K.G., Smart, N.P.: Pairings for Cryptographers. Discrete Applied Mathematics 156(16), 3113–3121 (2008)
21. Gennaro, R., Halevi, S., Krawczyk, H., Rabin, T.: Threshold RSA for Dynamic and Ad-Hoc Groups. In: Smart, N.P. (ed.) EUROCRYPT 2008. LNCS, vol. 4965, pp. 88–107. Springer, Heidelberg (2008)
22. Gennaro, R., Jarecki, S., Krawczyk, H., Rabin, T.: Robust and Efficient Sharing of RSA Functions. J. Cryptol. 13, 273–300 (2000)
23. Gennaro, R., Jarecki, S., Krawczyk, H., Rabin, T.: Robust Threshold DSS Signatures. Information and Computation 164, 54–84 (2001)
24. Herranz, J., Padró, C., Sáez, G.: Distributed RSA Signature Schemes for General Access Structures. In: Boyd, C., Mao, W. (eds.) ISC 2003. LNCS, vol. 2851, pp. 122–136. Springer, Heidelberg (2003)
25. Herranz, J., Sáez, G.: Verifiable Secret Sharing for General Access Structures, with Application to Fully Distributed Proxy Signatures. In: Wright, R.N. (ed.) FC 2003. LNCS, vol. 2742, pp. 286–302. Springer, Heidelberg (2003)
26. Herranz, J., Sáez, G.: Revisiting Fully Distributed Proxy Signature Schemes. In: Canteaut, A., Viswanathan, K. (eds.) INDOCRYPT 2004. LNCS, vol. 3348, pp. 356–370. Springer, Heidelberg (2004)
27. Hohenberger, S., Waters, B.: Short and Stateless Signatures from the RSA Assumption. In: Halevi, S. (ed.) CRYPTO 2009. LNCS, vol. 5677, pp. 654–670. Springer, Heidelberg (2009)
28. Ito, M., Saito, A., Nishizeki, T.: Secret Sharing Scheme Realizing General Access Structure. In: IEEE Global Telecommunications Conference, pp. 99–102 (1987)
29. Herranz, J., Laguillaumie, F., Libert, B., Ràfols, C.: Short Attribute-Based Signatures for Threshold Predicates. In: Dunkelman, O. (ed.) CT-RSA 2012. LNCS, vol. 7178, pp. 51–67. Springer, Heidelberg (2012)
30. Karchmer, M., Wigderson, A.: On Span Programs. In: Proc. of the 8th IEEE Structure in Complexity Theory, pp. 102–111 (1993)
31. Li, J., Yuen, T.H., Kim, K.: Practical Threshold Signatures without Random Oracles. In: Susilo, W., Liu, J.K., Mu, Y. (eds.) ProvSec 2007. LNCS, vol. 4784, pp. 198–207. Springer, Heidelberg (2007)
32. Maji, H.K., Prabhakaran, M., Rosulek, M.: Attribute-Based Signatures. In: Kiayias, A. (ed.) CT-RSA 2011. LNCS, vol. 6558, pp. 376–392. Springer, Heidelberg (2011)
33. Morillo, P., Padró, C., Sáez, G., Villar, J.L.: Weighted Threshold Secret Sharing Schemes. Information Processing Letters 70, 211–216 (1999)
34. Okamoto, T., Takashima, K.: Efficient Attribute-Based Signatures for Non-monotone Predicates in the Standard Model. In: Catalano, D., Fazio, N., Gennaro, R., Nicolosi, A. (eds.) PKC 2011. LNCS, vol. 6571, pp. 35–52. Springer, Heidelberg (2011)
35. Okamoto, T., Takashima, K.: Decentralized Attribute-Based Signatures. In: Kurosawa, K., Hanaoka, G. (eds.) PKC 2013. LNCS, vol. 7778, pp. 125–142. Springer, Heidelberg (2013)

36. Padró, C., Sáez, G., Villar, J.L.: Detection of Cheaters in Vector Space Secret Sharing Schemes. Designs, Codes and Cryptography 16(1), 75–85 (1999)
37. Pointcheval, D., Stern, J.: Security Arguments for Digital Signatures and Blind Signatures. Journal of Cryptology 13(3), 361–396 (2000)
38. Qin, B., Wu, Q., Zhang, L., Farràs, O., Domingo-Ferrer, J.: Provably Secure Threshold Public-Key Encryption with Adaptive Security and Short Ciphertexts. Information Sciences 210, 67–80 (2012)
39. Saxena, N., Tsudik, G., Yi, J.H.: Efficient Node Admission for Short-lived Mobile Ad Hoc Networks. In: 13th IEEE International Conference on Network Protocols, ICNP, pp. 269–278 (2005)
40. Schnorr, C.P.: Efficient Signature Generation by Smart Cards. J. Cryptol. 4, 161–174 (1991)
41. Shamir, A.: How to Share a Secret. Commun. of the ACM 22, 612–613 (1979)
42. Shoup, V.: Practical Threshold Signatures. In: Preneel, B. (ed.) EUROCRYPT 2000. LNCS, vol. 1807, pp. 207–220. Springer, Heidelberg (2000)
43. Simmons, G.J., Jackson, W.-A., Martin, K.M.: The Geometry of Shared Secret Schemes. Bulletin of the Institute of Combinatorics and Its Applications 1, 71–88 (1991)
44. Simmons, G.J.: How to (Really) Share a Secret. In: Goldwasser, S. (ed.) CRYPTO 1988. LNCS, vol. 403, pp. 390–448. Springer, Heidelberg (1990)
45. Stinson, D.R., Strobl, R.: Provably Secure Distributed Schnorr Signatures and a (t, n) Threshold Scheme for Implicit Certificates. In: Varadharajan, V., Mu, Y. (eds.) ACISP 2001. LNCS, vol. 2119, pp. 417–434. Springer, Heidelberg (2001)
46. Tassa, T., Dyn, N.: Multipartite Secret Sharing by Bivariate Interpolation. J. Cryptol. 22, 227–258 (2009)
47. Tassa T.: Hierarchical Threshold Secret Sharing. Journal of Cryptology 20, 237–264 (2007)
48. Waters, B.: Efficient Identity-based Encryption without Random Oracles. In: Cramer, R. (ed.) EUROCRYPT 2005. LNCS, vol. 3494, pp. 114–127. Springer, Heidelberg (2005)

Decentralized Traceable Attribute-Based Signatures

Ali El Kaafarani[1], Essam Ghadafi[2], and Dalia Khader[3]

[1] University of Bath, UK
[2] University of Bristol, UK
[3] Interdisciplinary Centre for Security, Reliability and Trust (SnT), Luxembourg

Abstract. We provide a formal security model for traceable attribute-based signatures. Our focus is on the more practical case where attribute management is distributed among different authorities rather than relying on a single central authority. By specializing our model to the single attribute authority setting, we overcome some of the shortcomings of the existing model for the same setting.

Our second contribution is a generic construction for the primitive which achieves a strong notion of security. Namely, it achieves CCA anonymity and its security is w.r.t. adaptive adversaries. Moreover, our framework permits expressive signing polices. Finally, we provide some instantiations of the primitive whose security reduces to falsifiable intractability assumptions without relying on idealized assumptions.

Keywords: Attribute-based signatures, security definitions, standard model.

1 Introduction

Attribute-based cryptography has emerged as an important research topic in recent years. It offers a versatile solution for designing role-based cryptosystems. In such systems, users are assigned attributes, and private operations (e.g. decryption/signing) are associated with security policies. Only users possessing attributes satisfying the policy in question can perform such operations. The first proposals of attribute-based cryptosystems were: an encryption scheme by Goyal et al. [20] (inspired by Sahai and Waters [39]) and a signature scheme by Maji et al. [33].

In Attribute-Based Signatures (ABS) [33,34], messages are signed w.r.t. a signing policy expressed as a predicate. Thus, the recipient is convinced that someone with a set of attributes satisfying the signing predicate has indeed authenticated the message without learning the identity of the signer or learning which set of attributes was used in the signing.

There are many applications of attribute-based signatures such as attribute-based messaging, e.g. [7], trust negotiation, e.g. [13], and leaking secrets. Refer to [34] for more details and comparison with related notions.

J. Benaloh (Ed.): CT-RSA 2014, LNCS 8366, pp. 327–348, 2014.

Besides correctness, the security of attribute-based signatures requires signer privacy and unforgeability. Informally, signer privacy (sometimes is also referred to as anonymity), requires that a signature reveals neither the identity of the signer nor which set of attributes was used to satisfy the associated predicate. On the other hand, unforgeability requires that a signer cannot forge a signature w.r.t. a signing predicate that her individual attributes do not satisfy, even if she colludes with other signers.

Traceable Attribute-Based Signatures (TABS) [11] extend standard attribute-based signatures by adding an anonymity revocation mechanism which allows a tracing authority to recover the identity of the signer if needed. This added feature is very important in scenarios where accountability and abuse prevention are required.

Related Work. Variants of attribute-based signatures exist in the literature each supporting policies that differ in their expressiveness. Those can be categorized into three main types of policies: non-monotonic policies, e.g. [36], monotonic policies, e.g. [34], and threshold-based policies, e.g. [31,40,30,24,16]. Schemes with more expressive policies are more interesting since they cover a larger scale of potential applications. Nevertheless, their current state–of–the–art instantiations are less efficient. The size of the signatures in existing instantiations of those supporting "monotonic" and "non-monotonic" policies, in the best case, are linearly dependent on the number of attributes in the policy [34,36]. While the works of [24,16] yield constant-size signatures, they only support threshold policies.

Early proposals of attribute-based signatures considered the case of multiple attribute authorities where each authority is responsible for a sub–universe of attributes [33,36]. However, the multi–authority case still had the problem of relying on the existence of a central trusted authority. Moreover, in some cases, the security (unforgeability) of the whole system is compromised if the central authority is corrupted. Okamoto and Takashima [37] recently proposed the first decentralized construction.

Traceability in attribute-based signatures was first addressed by Khader [27] who proposed the notion of attribute-based group signatures. In this notion, only the anonymity of the identity of the signer is preserved, whereas the attributes used are not hidden. This is an undesirable property for many applications. Later, Khader et al. [28] proposed a traceable attribute-based signature scheme that relies on the verifier to decide the policy and thus requiring interaction in the signing protocol. Even though this can be useful in certain applications (see [28] for details), such interaction is prohibitive for many applications. A more recent construction by Escala et al. [11] adds the traceability feature (it was called revocation by the authors) to standard ABS schemes. The proposed scheme in [11] is in the inefficient composite-order groups setting and was originally proven in the Random Oracle Model (ROM) [3]. The authors informally described how the reliance on random oracles may be removed. The model and the construction proposed by [11] rely on a central attribute authority which could be a bottleneck when the number of members of the system increases.

Our Contribution. Our first contribution is a formal security model for traceable attribute-based signatures. Our focus is on the more interesting setting where there are multiple attribute authorities. We refer to this setting as Decentralized Traceable Attribute-Based Signatures (DTABS). By restricting the number of attribute authorities to one, we get a new model which addresses some of the shortcomings of the previous model for the same setting [11].

Our second contribution is generic construction for DTABS. Our construction meets strong security requirements and permits expressive signing policies. Namely, it is CCA-anonymous under full-key exposure attacks, and its unforgeability is w.r.t. adaptively chosen messages and signing policies.

Finally, we present example instantiations of the generic construction and provide the first provably secure construction not relying on idealized assumptions. The security of all our instantiations rely on intractability assumptions which are falsifiable [35].

Paper Organization. In Section 2, we give preliminary definitions. We formally define DTABS and provide their security model in Sections 3 and 4, respectively. We list the building blocks we use in Section 5. In Section 6, we present our generic construction and prove its security. In Section 7, we present constructions in the standard model.

Notation. A function $\nu(.) : \mathbb{N} \to \mathbb{R}^+$ is negligible in c if for every polynomial $p(.)$ and all sufficiently large values of c, it holds that $\nu(c) < \frac{1}{p(c)}$. Given a probability distribution S, we denote by $y \leftarrow S$ the operation of selecting an element according to S. If A is a probabilistic machine, we denote by $A(x_1, \ldots, x_n)$ the output distribution of A on inputs $(x_1, \ldots, x_n)$. By PPT we mean running in probabilistic polynomial time in the relevant security parameter.

2   Preliminaries

Bilinear Groups. A bilinear group is a tuple $\mathcal{P} := (\mathbb{G}_1, \mathbb{G}_2, \mathbb{G}_T, p, G, \tilde{G}, e)$ where $\mathbb{G}_1, \mathbb{G}_2$ and $\mathbb{G}_T$ are groups of a prime order p and G and $\tilde{G}$ generate $\mathbb{G}_1$ and $\mathbb{G}_2$, respectively. The function e is a non-degenerate bilinear map $\mathbb{G}_1 \times \mathbb{G}_2 \longrightarrow \mathbb{G}_T$. We will use multiplicative notation for all the groups although usually $\mathbb{G}_1$ and $\mathbb{G}_2$ are chosen to be additive groups. We let $\mathbb{G}_1^\times := \mathbb{G}_1 \setminus \{1_{\mathbb{G}_1}\}$ and $\mathbb{G}_2^\times := \mathbb{G}_2 \setminus \{1_{\mathbb{G}_2}\}$. For clarity, elements from $\mathbb{G}_2$ will be accented with $\tilde{}$.

In this paper, we will be working with Type-1 groups [17] where $\mathbb{G}_1 = \mathbb{G}_2 = \mathbb{G}$ and Type-3 groups [17] where $\mathbb{G}_1 \neq \mathbb{G}_2$ and there is no efficient isomorphism between the groups in either direction.

Complexity Assumptions. We use the following assumptions from the literature:

SXDH. The DDH assumption holds in both groups $\mathbb{G}_1$ and $\mathbb{G}_2$.
DLIN [8]. For a group $\mathbb{G} := \langle G \rangle$ of a prime order p, given $(G^a, G^b, G^{ra}, G^{sb}, G^t)$ where $a, b, r, s, t \in \mathbb{Z}_p$ are unknown, it is hard to tell whether $t = r + s$ or t is random.

q-**SDH** [6]. For a group $\mathbb{G} := \langle G \rangle$ of a prime order p, given $(G, G^x, \ldots, G^{x^q})$ for $x \leftarrow \mathbb{Z}_p$, it is hard to output a pair $(c, G^{\frac{1}{x+c}}) \in \mathbb{Z}_p \times \mathbb{G}$ for an arbitrary $c \in \mathbb{Z}_p \backslash \{-x\}$.

WFCDH [14]. In symmetric bilinear groups, given $(G, G^a, G^b) \in \mathbb{G}^3$ for $a, b \leftarrow \mathbb{Z}_p$, it is hard to output a tuple $(G^r, G^{ra}, G^{rb}, G^{rab}) \in \mathbb{G}^{\times 4}$ for an arbitrary $r \in \mathbb{Z}_p$.

AWFCDH [14]. In asymmetric bilinear groups, given $(G, G^a, \tilde{G}) \in \mathbb{G}_1{}^2 \times \mathbb{G}_2$ for $a \leftarrow \mathbb{Z}_p$, it is hard to output a tuple $(G^b, G^{ab}, \tilde{G}^b, \tilde{G}^{ab}) \in \mathbb{G}_1^{\times 2} \times \mathbb{G}_2^{\times 2}$ for an arbitrary $b \in \mathbb{Z}_p$.

q-**ADHSDH** [14]. In asymmetric bilinear groups [1], given $(G, F, K, G^x, \tilde{G}, \tilde{G}^x) \in \mathbb{G}_1^4 \times \mathbb{G}_2^2$ for $x \leftarrow \mathbb{Z}_p$, and $q-1$ tuples $(W_i := (K \cdot G^{u_i})^{\frac{1}{x+v_i}}, U_i := G^{u_i},$ $\tilde{U}_i := \tilde{G}^{u_i}, V_i := F^{v_i}, \tilde{V}_i := \tilde{G}^{v_i})_{i=1}^{q-1}$ for $u_i, v_i \leftarrow \mathbb{Z}_p$, it is hard to output a new tuple $(W^*, U^*, \tilde{U}^*, V^*, \tilde{V}^*)$ of this form.

Span Programs. For a field $\mathbb{F}$ and a variable set $A = \{a_1, \ldots, a_n\}$, a monotone span program [25] is define by a $\alpha \times \beta$ matrix $\mathbf{Z}$ (over $\mathbb{F}$) along with a labeling map ρ which associates each row in $\mathbf{Z}$ with an element $a_i \in A$.

The span program accepts a set γ iff $\mathbf{1} \in \text{Span}(\mathbf{Z}_\gamma)$, where $\mathbf{Z}_\gamma$ is the submatrix of $\mathbf{Z}$ containing only rows with labels $a_i \in \gamma$. In other words, the span program only accepts the set γ if there exists a vector $\boldsymbol{s}$ s.t. $\boldsymbol{s}\mathbf{Z}_\gamma = [1, 0, \ldots, 0]$.

3   Syntax of Decentralized Traceable Attribute-Based Signatures

The parties involved in a DTABS scheme are: κ attribute authorities each with a unique identity aid and a pair of secret/verification keys ($\mathsf{aask}_{\mathsf{aid}}, \mathsf{aavk}_{\mathsf{aid}}$); a tracing authority T which possesses a secret tracing key tk that can be used to trace the identity of the signer of a given signature; a set of signers each with a unique identity sid and a set of attributes $\mathcal{A} \subseteq \mathbb{A}$, where $\mathbb{A}$ is the universe of attributes. An attribute can be uniquely identified by concatenating the identity of the managing attribute authority with the name of the attribute itself. A DTABS scheme is a tuple of polynomial-time algorithms

$$\mathsf{DTABS} := (\mathsf{Setup}, \mathsf{AuthSetup}, \mathsf{KeyGen}, \mathsf{Sign}, \mathsf{Verify}, \mathsf{Trace}, \mathsf{Judge}),$$

whose definitions are below; where all algorithms bar Setup and AuthSetup take as implicit input the public parameters pp output by algorithm Setup.

Setup(1^λ) is run by some trusted third party. It takes as input a security parameter 1^λ and outputs public parameters pp and the tracing key tk. We assume that pp contains the attribute universe $\mathbb{A}$.

AuthSetup(pp, aid) used by attribute authority $\mathsf{Auth}_{\mathsf{aid}}$ to generate its key pair ($\mathsf{aask}_{\mathsf{aid}}, \mathsf{aavk}_{\mathsf{aid}}$). The attribute authority publishes its public verification key $\mathsf{aavk}_{\mathsf{aid}}$.

---

[1] This can also be instantiated in symmetric groups. See [14].

KeyGen($\mathsf{aask_{aid}}$, sid, a) takes as input an attribute authority's secret key $\mathsf{aask_{aid}}$, a signer's identity sid and an attribute $a \in \mathbb{A}$ that signer sid owns and generates a secret key $\mathsf{sk_{sid,}}_a$ for attribute a for the signer. The key $\mathsf{sk_{sid,}}_a$ is given to sid. The attribute authority may locally maintain a list of signers for which it ran the KeyGen algorithm.

Sign($\{\mathsf{aavk_{aid}}_{(a)}\}_{a \in \mathcal{A}}, \{\mathsf{sk_{sid,}}_a\}_{a \in \mathcal{A}}, m, \Psi$) signer sid who possesses a set of attributes $\mathcal{A} \subseteq \mathbb{A}$ uses this algorithm to produce a signature on m w.r.t. the signing policy Ψ where $\Psi(\mathcal{A}) = 1$. The algorithm takes as input an ordered list of attribute authorities' verification keys $\{\mathsf{aavk_{aid}}_{(a)}\}_{a \in \mathcal{A}}$, an ordered list of attributes' secret keys $\{\mathsf{sk_{sid,}}_a\}_{a \in \mathcal{A}}$, a message m and a signing predicate Ψ, and outputs a signature σ. Here $\mathsf{aid}(a)$ denotes the identity of the attribute authority managing attribute $a \in \mathbb{A}$.

Verify($\{\mathsf{aavk_{aid}}_{(a)}\}_{a \in \Psi}, m, \sigma, \Psi$) is a deterministic algorithm which takes as input an ordered list of attribute authorities' verification keys $\{\mathsf{aavk_{aid}}_{(a)}\}_{a \in \Psi}$, a message m, a signature σ and a signing predicate Ψ, and outputs 1 if σ is valid on m w.r.t. the signing predicate Ψ or 0 otherwise.

Trace(tk, m, σ, Ψ) is a deterministic algorithm which takes as input T's key tk, a message m, a signature σ and a signing predicate Ψ, and outputs the identity sid of the signer plus a proof π attesting to this claim. If the algorithm is unable to trace the signature to a signer, it returns the special symbol $\bot$. Note that if the tracing authority additionally gets a read-only access to the local registration tables maintained by the attribute authorities (whose identities can be inferred from the signing policy Ψ), then the tracing authority could additionally check whether or not sid has run the KeyGen algorithm.

Judge($\{\mathsf{aavk_{aid}}_{(a)}\}_{a \in \Psi}, m, \sigma, \Psi, \mathsf{sid}, \pi$) is a deterministic algorithm which takes as input an ordered list of attribute authorities' verification keys $\{\mathsf{aavk_{aid}}_{(a)}\}_{a \in \Psi}$, a message m, a signature σ, a signing predicate Ψ, a signer identity sid, and a tracing proof π, and outputs 1 if π is a valid proof that sid has produced σ or 0 otherwise.

4 Security of Decentralized Traceble Attribute-Based Signatures

The security properties required from a DTABS scheme are: correctness, anonymity, full unforgeability, and traceability. In defining those requirements we use a set of experiments in which the adversary has access to a set of oracles. The following global lists are maintained: HSL is a list of honest signers' attributes and has entries of the form (sid, a); HAL is a list of honest attribute authorities; BSL is a list of bad signers' attributes whose secret keys have been revealed to the adversary with entries of the form (sid, a); BAL is a list of bad attribute authorities whose secret keys have been learned by the adversary; CAL is a list of corrupt attribute authorities whose keys have been chosen by the adversary; SL is a list of signatures obtained from the Sign oracle; CL is a list of challenge signatures obtained from the challenge oracle in the anonymity game.

The details of the following oracles are given in Fig. 1.

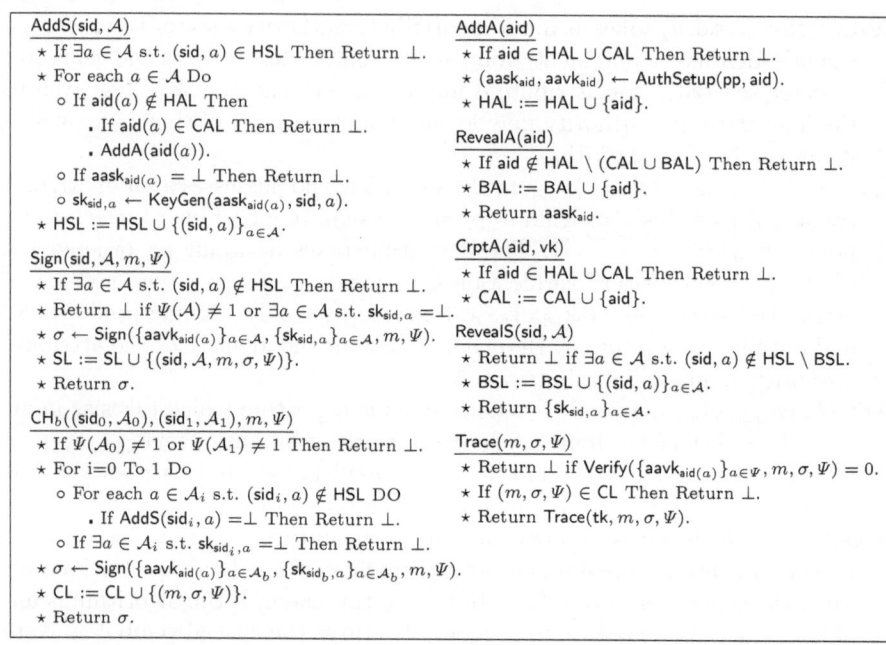

Fig. 1. Oracles used in the security games for DTABS

AddS(sid, $\mathcal{A}$) adds honest attributes $\mathcal{A} \subseteq \mathbb{A}$ for signer sid. It can be called multiple times to add more attributes.

AddA(aid) adds an honest attribute authority with identity aid.

CrptA(aid, vk) adds a corrupt attribute authority whose keys are chosen by the adversary.

RevealS(sid, $\mathcal{A}$) returns the secret keys $\{\mathsf{sk}_{\mathsf{sid},a}\}_{a \in \mathcal{A}}$ corresponding to the subset of attributes $\mathcal{A} \subseteq \mathbb{A}$ owned by signer sid. It can be called multiple times.

RevealA(aid) returns the secret key $\mathsf{aask}_{\mathsf{aid}}$ of the honest attribute authority aid.

Sign(sid, $\mathcal{A}$, m, Ψ) returns a signature σ on m using the key $\{\mathsf{sk}_{\mathsf{sid},a}\}_{a \in \mathcal{A}}$ belonging to signer sid where $\Psi(\mathcal{A}) = 1$.

$\mathsf{CH}_b((\mathsf{sid}_0, \mathcal{A}_0), (\mathsf{sid}_1, \mathcal{A}_1), m, \Psi)$ is a left-right oracle for defining anonymity. On input $(\mathsf{sid}_0, \mathcal{A}_0)$, $(\mathsf{sid}_1, \mathcal{A}_1)$, a message m and a signing policy Ψ, it returns a signature on m using $\{\mathsf{sk}_{\mathsf{sid}_b,a}\}_{a \in \mathcal{A}_b}$ for $b \leftarrow \{0,1\}$ if $\Psi(\mathcal{A}_0) = \Psi(\mathcal{A}_1) = 1$.

Trace(m, σ, Ψ) allows the adversary to ask for signatures to be traced.

The security requirements are defined by the games in Fig. 2.

Correctness. This demands that signatures produced by honest signers are accepted by the Verify algorithm and open to the signer who produced them. Moreover, the Judge algorithm accepts the proof produced by the Trace algorithm. Formally, a DTABS scheme is correct if for all $\lambda \in \mathbb{N}$, all PPT adversaries $\mathcal{F}$ have a negligible advantage $\mathsf{Adv}^{\mathsf{Corr}}_{\mathsf{DTABS},\mathcal{F}}(\lambda) := \Pr[\mathsf{Exp}^{\mathsf{Corr}}_{\mathsf{DTABS},\mathcal{F}}(\lambda) = 1]$.

Experiment: $\mathsf{Exp}_{\mathsf{DTABS},\mathcal{F}}^{\mathsf{Corr}}(\lambda)$

---
* $(\mathsf{pp}, \mathsf{tk}) \leftarrow \mathsf{Setup}(1^\lambda)$.
* $\mathsf{HSL} := \emptyset$.
* $(\mathsf{sid}, \mathcal{A}, m, \Psi) \leftarrow \mathcal{F}(\mathsf{pp} : \mathsf{AddS}(\cdot, \cdot), \mathsf{AddA}(\cdot))$.
* If $\Psi(\mathcal{A}) \neq 1$ or $\mathcal{A} \not\subseteq \mathbb{A}$ Then Return 0.
* If $\exists a \in \mathcal{A}$ s.t. $(\mathsf{sid}, a) \notin \mathsf{HSL}$ or $\mathsf{sk}_{\mathsf{sid}, a} = \perp$ or $\mathsf{aid}(a) \notin \mathsf{HAL}$ Then Return 0.
* $\sigma \leftarrow \mathsf{Sign}(\{\mathsf{aavk}_{\mathsf{sid}(a)}\}_{a \in \mathcal{A}}, \{\mathsf{sk}_{\mathsf{sid}, a}\}_{a \in \mathcal{A}}, m, \Psi)$.
* If $\mathsf{Verify}(\{\mathsf{aavk}_{\mathsf{sid}(a)}\}_{a \in \Psi}, m, \sigma, \Psi) = 0$ Then Return 1.
* $(\mathsf{sid}', \pi) \leftarrow \mathsf{Trace}(\mathsf{tk}, m, \sigma, \Psi)$.
* If $\mathsf{sid}' \neq \mathsf{sid}$ or $\mathsf{Judge}(\{\mathsf{aavk}_{\mathsf{sid}(a)}\}_{a \in \Psi}, m, \sigma, \Psi, \mathsf{sid}, \pi) = 0$ Then Return 1 Else Return 0.

Experiment: $\mathsf{Exp}_{\mathsf{DTABS},\mathcal{F}}^{\mathsf{Anon}\text{-}b}(\lambda)$

---
* $(\mathsf{pp}, \mathsf{tk}) \leftarrow \mathsf{Setup}(1^\lambda)$.
* $\mathsf{CAL}, \mathsf{HSL}, \mathsf{HAL}, \mathsf{BSL}, \mathsf{BAL}, \mathsf{CL} := \emptyset$.
* $b^* \leftarrow \mathcal{F}(\mathsf{pp} : \mathsf{AddS}(\cdot, \cdot), \mathsf{AddA}(\cdot), \mathsf{CrptA}(\cdot, \cdot), \mathsf{RevealS}(\cdot, \cdot), \mathsf{RevealA}(\cdot), \mathsf{CH}_b((\cdot, \cdot), (\cdot, \cdot), \cdot, \cdot), \mathsf{Trace}(\cdot, \cdot, \cdot))$.
* Return b^*.

Experiment: $\mathsf{Exp}_{\mathsf{DTABS},\mathcal{F}}^{\mathsf{F\text{-}Unforge}}(\lambda)$

---
* $(\mathsf{pp}, \mathsf{tk}) \leftarrow \mathsf{Setup}(1^\lambda)$.
* $\mathsf{CAL}, \mathsf{HSL}, \mathsf{HAL}, \mathsf{BSL}, \mathsf{BAL}, \mathsf{SL} := \emptyset$.
* $(m^*, \sigma^*, \Psi^*, \mathsf{sid}^*, \pi^*) \leftarrow \mathcal{F}(\mathsf{pp}, \mathsf{tk} : \mathsf{AddS}(\cdot, \cdot), \mathsf{AddA}(\cdot), \mathsf{CrptA}(\cdot, \cdot), \mathsf{RevealS}(\cdot, \cdot), \mathsf{RevealA}(\cdot), \mathsf{Sign}(\cdot, \cdot, \cdot, \cdot))$.
* If $\mathsf{Verify}(\{\mathsf{aavk}_{\mathsf{sid}(a)}\}_{a \in \Psi^*}, m^*, \sigma^*, \Psi^*) = 0$ Then Return 0.
* If $\mathsf{Judge}(\{\mathsf{aavk}_{\mathsf{sid}(a)}\}_{a \in \Psi^*}, m^*, \sigma^*, \Psi^*, \mathsf{sid}^*, \pi^*) = 0$ Then Return 0.
* Let $\mathcal{A}_{\mathsf{sid}^*}$ be the attributes of sid^* managed by dishonest (i.e. $\in \mathsf{CAL} \cup \mathsf{BAL}$) attribute authorities.
* If $\exists \mathcal{A}$ s.t. $\{(\mathsf{sid}^*, a)\}_{a \in \mathcal{A}} \subseteq \mathsf{BSL}$ and $\Psi^*(\mathcal{A} \cup \mathcal{A}_{\mathsf{sid}^*}) = 1$ Then Return 0.
* If $\exists (\mathsf{sid}^*, \cdot, m^*, \sigma^*, \Psi^*) \in \mathsf{SL}$ Then Return 0 Else Return 1.

Experiment: $\mathsf{Exp}_{\mathsf{DTABS},\mathcal{F}}^{\mathsf{Trace}}(\lambda)$

---
* $(\mathsf{pp}, \mathsf{tk}) \leftarrow \mathsf{Setup}(1^\lambda)$.
* $\mathsf{CAL}, \mathsf{HSL}, \mathsf{HAL}, \mathsf{BSL}, \mathsf{BAL}, \mathsf{SL} := \emptyset$.
* $(m^*, \sigma^*, \Psi^*) \leftarrow \mathcal{F}(\mathsf{pp}, \mathsf{tk} : \mathsf{AddS}(\cdot, \cdot), \mathsf{AddA}(\cdot), \mathsf{RevealS}(\cdot, \cdot), \mathsf{Sign}(\cdot, \cdot, \cdot, \cdot))$.
* If $\mathsf{Verify}(\{\mathsf{aavk}_{\mathsf{sid}(a)}\}_{a \in \Psi^*}, m^*, \sigma^*, \Psi^*) = 0$ Then Return 0.
* $(\mathsf{sid}^*, \pi) \leftarrow \mathsf{Trace}(\mathsf{tk}, m^*, \sigma^*, \Psi^*)$.
* If $\mathsf{sid}^* = \perp$ or $\mathsf{Judge}(\{\mathsf{aavk}_{\mathsf{sid}(a)}\}_{a \in \Psi^*}, m^*, \sigma^*, \Psi^*, \mathsf{sid}^*, \pi) = 0$ or $(\mathsf{sid}, \cdot) \notin \mathsf{HSL}$ Then Return 1.
* Return 0.

Fig. 2. Security experiments for decentralized traceable attribute-based signatures

Anonymity. This requires that a signature reveals neither the identity of the signer nor the set of attributes used in the signing. This is a stronger notion than what is used in other settings, e.g. [27,31], which only require that the identity of the signer remains anonymous.

In the game, the adversary chooses a message, a signing policy and two signers with two, possibly different, sets of attributes with the condition that both sets have to satisfy the signing policy. The adversary gets a signature by either signer and wins if it correctly guesses the signer.

Our model provides the adversary with strong capabilities, for instance, it can fully corrupt the attribute authorities and can ask for signers' secret keys to be revealed including the two signers it chooses for the challenge (and thus capturing full-key exposure attacks). Note that since the adversary can sign on behalf of any signer, it is redundant to provide the adversary with a sign oracle. The only restriction we impose on the adversary is that it may not query the Trace oracle on the challenge signature.

Our focus is on the strongest variant of anonymity, i.e. CCA-Anonymity [4]. Refer to the full version for further discussion on the different variants. WLOG and in order to simplify the security proofs, we only allow the adversary a single call to the challenge oracle. We prove in the full version that this is sufficient by showing a reduction from any adversary with a polynomial number of calls to the challenge oracle to one with a single call.

Our definition captures unlinkability because the adversary has access to all signers' secret keys and hence can produce signatures on behalf of any signer.

Formally, a DTABS scheme is anonymous if for all $\lambda \in \mathbb{N}$ and all PPT adversaries $\mathcal{F}$, $\mathsf{Adv}_{\mathsf{DTABS},\mathcal{F}}^{\mathsf{Anon}}(\lambda) := \left| \Pr[\mathsf{Exp}_{\mathsf{DTABS},\mathcal{F}}^{\mathsf{Anon}\text{-}0}(\lambda) = 1] - \Pr[\mathsf{Exp}_{\mathsf{DTABS},\mathcal{F}}^{\mathsf{Anon}\text{-}1}(\lambda) = 1] \right|$ is negligible.

Full Unforgeability. This requirement captures unforgeability scenarios where the forgery opens to a particular signer. It ensures that even if signers collude and combine their attributes together, they cannot forge a signature that opens to a signer whose attributes do not satisfy the signing predicate. It also covers non-frameability and ensures that even if signers collude, they cannot frame a user who did not produce the signature.

Unlike the single attribute authority setting, here we allow the adversary to adaptively create corrupt attribute authorities and learn some of the honest authorities' secret keys as long as there is at least a single honest attribute authority managing one of the attributes required for satisfying the policy used in the forgery.

Our definition is adaptive and allows the adversary to adaptively choose the predicate and the message on which it wants to produce the forgery rather than having to select the predicate at the start of the game. Also, note that we consider the stronger (and more standard) form of unforgeability, i.e. (strong unforgeability) where the adversary wins even if it manages to produce a new signature on a message/predicate pair that was queried to the sign oracle. The definition can in a straightforward manner be adapted to work for the weaker variant used in, e.g. [4,34,11], by requiring that the forgery is not on a message/predicate pair that was queried to the sign oracle. For the latter variant which we refer to as *Weak Full Unforgeability* (WFU), we just need to replace the check $\exists(\mathsf{sid}^*, \cdot, m^*, \Psi^*, \sigma^*) \in \mathsf{SL}$ by the check $\exists(\mathsf{sid}^*, \cdot, m^*, \Psi^*, \cdot) \in \mathsf{SL}$.

Formally, a DTABS scheme is fully unforgeable if for all $\lambda \in \mathbb{N}$, all PPT adversaries $\mathcal{F}$ have a negligible advantage $\mathsf{Adv}_{\mathsf{DTABS},\mathcal{F}}^{\mathsf{F\text{-}Unforge}}(\lambda) := \Pr[\mathsf{Exp}_{\mathsf{DTABS},\mathcal{F}}^{\mathsf{F\text{-}Unforge}}(\lambda) = 1]$.

Traceability. This requirement ensures that the adversary cannot produce a signature that traces to a signer who did not run the honest KeyGen algorithm. Thus, it covers unforgeability scenarios where the forgery is untraceable. In the game, the adversary is allowed to corrupt the tracing authority and ask for the signing keys of any signer to be revealed. However, unlike in the full unforgeability game, we require that all the attribute authorities are honest as knowing a secret key of any attribute authority makes it easy to create signatures by dummy signers which are thus untraceable.

Formally, a DTABS scheme is traceable if for all $\lambda \in \mathbb{N}$, all PPT adversaries $\mathcal{F}$ have a negligible advantage $\mathsf{Adv}_{\mathsf{DTABS},\mathcal{F}}^{\mathsf{Trace}}(\lambda) := \Pr[\mathsf{Exp}_{\mathsf{DTABS},\mathcal{F}}^{\mathsf{Trace}}(\lambda) = 1]$.

4.1   On the Model of [11] for the Single Attribute Authority Setting

Specializing our model to the single attribute authority setting, we get a stronger model than the one in [11]. In particular, our model avoids some of the shortcomings inherent to [11] which we now explain. When defining non-frameability in [11], the sign oracle used by [11] does not consider the identity of the signer and hence it does not capture the following scenario: The adversary asks for two different signers sid_1 with attributes $\mathcal{A}_1$ and sid_2 with attributes $\mathcal{A}_2$ to be added. It then asks for a signature on the message m w.r.t. the signing policy Ψ by signer sid_1 (where $\Psi(\mathcal{A}_1) = 1$), and outputs as its forgery a signature σ^* on the same message m w.r.t. the same signing policy Ψ but the signature opens to sid_2 (assume here that $\Psi(\mathcal{A}_2) = 1$).

Therefore, we believe that in this context, where traceability is required, it is important that the identity of the signer is taken into account when answering signing queries. Otherwise, some of the unforgeability scenarios are not captured. This is, of course, different from standard attribute-based signatures where traceability is not required and thus there is no way for the adversary to learn who produced a particular signature.

In addition, our full unforgeability definition protects against a fully corrupt tracing authority which is stronger than the non-frameability definition in [11] which only considers a partially but not fully corrupt tracing authority.

5   Building Blocks

In this section we present the building blocks that we use in our constructions.

5.1   Tagged Signature Scheme

We define here a new variant of a signature scheme which we call a Tagged Signature (TS) scheme. A tagged signature scheme for a message space $\mathcal{M}_{\mathsf{TS}}$ and a tag space $\mathcal{T}_{\mathsf{TS}}$ is a tuple of algorithms $\mathsf{TS} := ([\mathsf{Setup}], \mathsf{KeyGen}, \mathsf{Sign}, \mathsf{Verify})$.

$\mathsf{Setup}(1^\lambda)$ this optional algorithm takes as input a security parameter and outputs common public parameters param which is an implicit input to the rest of algorithms.

$\mathsf{KeyGen}(\{\mathsf{param}|1^\lambda\})$ takes as input either public parameters (if the scheme requires a setup) or just the security parameter (if no setup is required) and outputs a pair of secret/verification keys $(\mathsf{sk}, \mathsf{vk})$.

$\mathsf{Sign}(\mathsf{sk}, \tau, m)$ takes as input a secret key sk, a tag $\tau \in \mathcal{T}_{\mathsf{TS}}$ and a message $m \in \mathcal{M}_{\mathsf{TS}}$, and outputs a signature σ.

$\mathsf{Verify}(\mathsf{vk}, \tau, m, \sigma)$ outputs 1 if σ is a signature on τ and m w.r.t. the verification key vk.

The security of a tagged signature scheme is similar to that of a traditional digital signature and consists of correctness and unforgeability:

- **Correctness:** Requires that for all $m \in \mathcal{M}_{\mathsf{TS}}$, $\tau \in \mathcal{T}_{\mathsf{TS}}$ and $(\mathsf{sk}, \mathsf{vk})$ output by KeyGen, we have $\mathsf{Verify}(\mathsf{vk}, \tau, m, \mathsf{Sign}(\mathsf{sk}, \tau, m)) = 1$.

- **(Existential) Unforgeability:** Unforgeability under adaptive chosen message and tag attack requires that any PPT adversary $\mathcal{F}$ that is given a sign oracle $\mathsf{Sign}(\mathsf{sk}, \cdot, \cdot)$ has a negligible advantage in winning the following game:
  - A key pair $(\mathsf{sk}, \mathsf{vk})$ is generated and vk is sent to $\mathcal{F}$.
  - $\mathcal{F}$ makes a polynomial number of queries to $\mathsf{Sign}(\mathsf{sk}, \cdot, \cdot)$.
  - Eventually, $\mathcal{F}$ halts by outputting a tuple (σ^*, τ^*, m^*) and wins if σ^* is valid on (τ^*, m^*) and (τ^*, m^*) was never queried to Sign.

We note here that any signature scheme that can sign a pair of messages can be used as a tagged signature scheme. However, to allow for generality and explicitly distinguish the tag space from the message space (and hence care for the case where they might be distinct), we define this notion. Note that one can always use a collision-resistant hash function to map the tag into the message space. Defining the notion also serves to simplify the description of our constructions and security proofs.

Instantiation. To construct a tagged signature, we use a variant of the automorphic scheme from [14] which was given in [15]. The original scheme given in [15] was given in the asymmetric setting. For simplicity, the variant we give here is in the symmetric setting. The tag space of the instantiation are Diffie–Hellman tuples $\mathcal{DH} := \{(G^a, G'^a) \in \mathbb{G}^2 | a \in \mathbb{Z}_p\}$, whereas the message space is $\mathbb{Z}_p$. The scheme is unforgeable under the q-ADHSDH and WFCDH assumptions in the symmetric setting (or the q-ADHSDH and AWFCDH assumptions in the asymmetric setting). The instantiation is as follows:

- $\mathsf{TS.Setup}(1^\lambda)$: Let $\mathcal{P} := (\mathbb{G}, \mathbb{G}_T, p, G, e)$ be the description of Type-1 bilinear groups. Choose $F, K, T, G', L \leftarrow \mathbb{G}$ and return $\mathsf{param} := (\mathcal{P}, F, K, T, L, G')$.
- $\mathsf{TS.KeyGen}(\mathsf{param})$: Choose $x \leftarrow \mathbb{Z}_p$ and set $(X, X') := (G^x, G'^x)$. Set $\mathsf{sk} := x$ and $\mathsf{vk} := (X, X')$.
- $\mathsf{TS.Sign}(\mathsf{sk}, (\tau, \tau'), m)$: Reject if $(\tau, \tau') \notin \mathcal{DH}$ (i.e. $e(\tau, G') \neq e(G, \tau')$). Otherwise, choose $u, v \leftarrow \mathbb{Z}_p$ and compute $\sigma := \Big(U := G^u, \quad U' := G'^u, \quad V := F^v, V' := G'^v, \quad W := (K \cdot T^u \cdot \tau \cdot L^m)^{\frac{1}{x+v}} \Big)$.
- $\mathsf{TS.Verify}(\mathsf{vk}, (\tau, \tau'), m, \sigma)$: If $e(U, G') = e(G, U')$, $e(V, G') = e(F, V')$, and $e(W, X' \cdot V') = e(T, U')e(K \cdot \tau \cdot L^m, G')$ output 1. Otherwise, output 0.

5.2 The Full Boneh-Boyen (FBB) Signature Scheme

In [6], the authors gave a signature scheme that is secure under the q-SDH assumption (cf. Section 2). The signature scheme can be instantiated in both the symmetric and asymmetric bilinear group settings. Let $\mathcal{P} := (\mathbb{G}, \mathbb{G}_T, p, G, e)$ be the description of a bilinear group. The scheme is as follows; where to aid notation all algorithms bar KeyGen are assumed to take as implicit input $\mathcal{P}$:

- $\mathsf{KeyGen}(\mathcal{P})$: Choose $x, y \leftarrow \mathbb{Z}_p$ and set $(X, Y) := (G^x, G^y)$. Set $\mathsf{sk} := (x, y)$ and $\mathsf{vk} := (X, Y)$.
- $\mathsf{Sign}(\mathsf{sk}, m)$: To sign $m \in \mathbb{Z}_p$, choose $r \leftarrow \mathbb{Z}_p$ such that $x + r \cdot y + m \neq 0$ and compute the signature $\sigma := G^{\frac{1}{x+r \cdot y+m}}$.
- $\mathsf{Verify}(\mathsf{vk}, m, \sigma)$: Output 1 if $e(\sigma, X \cdot Y^r \cdot G^m) = e(G, G)$ and 0 otherwise.

5.3 Strongly Unforgeable One-Time Signatures

A digital signature scheme is called *one-time signature* if in the unforgeability game, the adversary is restricted to a single signing query. *Strong Unforgeability* as opposed to weak unforgeability requires that the adversary cannot even forge a new signature on a message that she obtained a signature on from the signing oracle. In this paper, we will instantiate the one-time signature using the Full Boneh-Boyen signature scheme.

5.4 Simulation-Sound Non-interactive Zero-Knowledge Proofs

Let $\mathcal{R}$ be an efficiently computable relation. For pairs $(x, w) \in \mathcal{R}$, we call x the statement and w the witness. We define the language $\mathcal{L}$ as all the statements x in $\mathcal{R}$. A Simulation-Sound Non-Interactive Zero-Knowledge (SS-NIZK) proof system for $\mathcal{R}$ is defined by (Setup, Prove, Verify, Extract, SimSetup, SimProve).

Setup takes as input a security parameter 1^λ and outputs a common reference string crs and an extraction key xk which allows for witness extraction. Prove takes as input (crs, x, w) and outputs a proof π that $(x, w) \in \mathcal{R}$. Verify takes as input (crs, x, π) and outputs 1 if the proof is valid, or 0 otherwise. Extract takes as input $(\mathsf{crs}, \mathsf{xk}, x, \pi)$ and outputs a witness. SimSetup takes as input a security parameter 1^λ and outputs a simulated reference string $\mathsf{crs}_{\mathsf{Sim}}$ and a trapdoor key tr that allows for proof simulation. SimProve takes as input $(\mathsf{crs}_{\mathsf{Sim}}, \mathsf{tr}, x)$ and outputs a simulated proof π_{Sim} without a witness.

We require: completeness, soundness, zero-knowledge and simulation-soundness which are all formally defined in full paper [10].

Groth-Sahai Proofs. Groth-Sahai (GS) proofs [23] are efficient non-interactive proofs in the Common Reference String (CRS) model. The GS system can be instantiated under different intractability assumptions with the SXDH-based instantiation being the most efficient [19].

The language for the system has the form

$$\mathcal{L} := \{\mathsf{statement} \mid \exists\, \mathsf{witness} : E_1(\mathsf{statement}, \mathsf{witness}), \dots, E_n(\mathsf{statement}, \mathsf{witness})\},$$

where $E_i(\mathsf{statement}, \cdot)$ is one of the types of equation summarized in Fig. 3, where $\underline{X_1}, \dots, \underline{X_m}, \underline{Y_1}, \dots, \underline{Y_n} \in \mathbb{G}$, $\underline{x_1}, \dots, \underline{x_m}, \underline{y_1}, \dots, \underline{y_n} \in \mathbb{Z}_p$ are secret variables (hence underlined), whereas $A_i, T \in \mathbb{G}$, $a_i, b_i, k_{i,j}, t \in \mathbb{Z}_p$, $t_T \in \mathbb{G}_T$ are public constants. Note that in the asymmetric setting, there are two types of MSM equations depending on which group the elements belong to. The proof system has perfect completeness, perfect soundness, composable witness-indistinguishability/zero-knowledge. Note that the original proof system in [23] is not simulation-sound. Refer to [23] for formal definitions and more details.

5.5 CCA-Secure Public-Key Encryption Scheme

A Public-Key Encryption (PKE) scheme for a message space $\mathcal{M}_{\mathsf{PKE}}$ is a tuple of polynomial-time algorithms $\mathsf{PKE} := (\mathsf{KeyGen}, \mathsf{Enc}, \mathsf{Dec})$. $\mathsf{KeyGen}(1^\lambda)$ outputs a secret/public key pair $(\mathsf{sk}, \mathsf{pk})$; $\mathsf{Enc}(\mathsf{pk}, m)$ outputs a ciphertext C; $\mathsf{Dec}(\mathsf{sk}, C)$ outputs a message m.

- **Pairing Product Equation (PPE):** $\prod_{i=1}^{n} e(A_i, \underline{Y_i}) \cdot \prod_{i=1}^{m} \prod_{j=1}^{n} e(\underline{X_i}, \underline{Y_j})^{k_{i,j}} = t_T$.
- **Multi-Scalar Multiplication Equation (MSME):** $\prod_{i=1}^{n} A_i^{\underline{y_i}} \prod_{i=1}^{m} \underline{X_i}^{b_i} \prod_{i=1}^{m} \prod_{j=1}^{n} \underline{X_i}^{k_{i,j}\underline{y_j}} = T$.
- **Quadratic Equation (QE) in $\mathbb{Z}_p$:** $\sum_{i=1}^{n} a_i \underline{y_i} + \sum_{i=1}^{m} \underline{x_i} b_i + \sum_{i=1}^{m} \sum_{j=1}^{n} \underline{x_i} \underline{y_j} = t$.

Fig. 3. Types of equations one can use Groth-Sahai proofs for

TPKE.KeyGen(1^λ)	TPKE.Dec(sk, t, C_{tbe})
○ $(\mathbb{G}, p) \leftarrow \mathsf{GrpSetup}(1^\lambda)$.	○ If TPKE.IsValid(pk, t, C_{tbe}) = 0 Then Rreturn $\perp$.
○ $K, L \leftarrow \mathbb{G}$; $f, h \leftarrow \mathbb{Z}_p$.	○ Parse C_{tbe} as $(C_1, C_2, C_3, C_4, C_5)$.
○ $F := G^f$, $H := G^h$.	○ $M := C_3 \cdot C_1^{-1/f} C_2^{-1/h}$.
○ pk := (G, F, H, K, L); sk := (f, h).	
	TPKE.IsValid(pk, t, C_{tbe})
TPKE.Enc(pk, t, M)	○ Parse C_{tbe} as $(C_1, C_2, C_3, C_4, C_5)$.
○ $r_1, r_2 \leftarrow \mathbb{Z}_p$.	○ If $e(F, C_4) \neq e(C_1, G^t \cdot K)$ Or
○ $C_1 := F^{r_1}$; $C_2 := H^{r_2}$; $C_3 := G^{r_1+r_2} \cdot M$.	$\quad e(H, C_5) \neq e(C_2, G^t \cdot L)$ Then Return 0.
○ $C_4 := (G^t \cdot K)^{r_1}$; $C_5 := (G^t \cdot L)^{r_2}$.	○ Else Return 1.
○ $C_{\text{tbe}} := (C_1, C_2, C_3, C_4, C_5)$.	

Fig. 4. The tag-based encryption by Kiltz [29]

Besides the usual correctness requirement, we require that the scheme is indistinguishable against adaptive chosen-ciphertext attacks (IND-CCA2) whose formal definition can be found in the full version [10].

Tag-Based Encryption. A Tag-based Public-Key Encryption (TPKE) scheme [32] for a message space $\mathcal{M}_{\mathsf{TPKE}}$ and a tag space $\mathcal{T}_{\mathsf{TPKE}}$ is similar to a public-key encryption scheme with the only difference being that both Enc and Dec algorithms take as an additional input a tag t. One could optionally require an additional algorithm IsValid which on input $(\mathsf{pk}, t, C_{\text{tbe}})$ outputs 1 if C_{tbe} is a valid ciphertext under pk and the tag t.

Besides the usual correctness requirement, we require selective-tag weak indistinguishability against adaptive chosen-ciphertext attacks (ST-WIND-CCA). Informally, ST-WIND-CCA requires that an adversary cannot distinguish which message was encrypted under a challenge tag t^* even if it has access to a decryption oracle that decrypts any ciphertext under any tag different from t^*. "Selective-Tag" refers to the fact that the adversary must choose the challenge tag at the start of the game, i.e. before it gets the public key. The formal definition can be found in the full version [10].

We will use the ST-WIND-CCA tag-based encryption scheme by Kiltz [29] which is secure under the DLIN assumption. The scheme is in Fig. 4. In [26], it was shown that the tag-based scheme in Fig. 4 can be translated into both (Type-2 & Type-3) asymmetric bilinear group settings. The security of the scheme in the Type-3 setting relies on a variant of the DLIN assumption called the SDLIN assumption, in which the last element in the input tuple is provided in both groups. However, the security of this variant requires that the message space is polynomial in the security parameter so that we can efficiently search when decrypting.

6   A Generic Construction for DTABS

Here we present our generic construction.

Overview of the Construction. The tools we use in our generic construction are two NIZK proof systems $NIZK_1$ and $NIZK_2$, an IND-CCA2 secure public-key encryption scheme PKE, an existentially unforgeable tagged signature scheme TS, and an existentially unforgeable digital signature scheme DS with a message space $\mathcal{M}_{DS}$. In addition, we need a collision-resistant hash function $\mathcal{H} : \{0,1\}^* \rightarrow \mathcal{M}_{DS}$.

We require that the $NIZK_1$ proof system, which will be used in the signing, is simulation-sound [38] and a proof of knowledge [9]. In fact, it is sufficient for it to be only one-time simulation-sound. On the contrary, it suffices that $NIZK_2$ is a zero-knowledge proof system, i.e. we require neither simulation-soundness nor knowledge extractability from $NIZK_2$.

The Setup algorithm generates two separate common reference strings crs_1 and crs_2 for the NIZK systems $NIZK_1$ and $NIZK_2$, respectively. It also generates a key pair (tvk, tsk) for the digital signature scheme DS, and an encryption/decryption key pair (epk, esk) for the encryption scheme PKE. The public parameters of the system is set to $pp := (1^\lambda, crs_1, crs_2, tvk, epk, \mathbb{A}, \mathcal{H})$, where $\mathbb{A}$ is the universe of attributes and λ is the security parameter. The tracing authority's key is set to $tk := esk$.

When a new attribute authority joins the system, it creates a secret/verification key pair $(aask_{aid}, aavk_{aid})$ for the tagged signature scheme TS. To generate a signing key for attribute $a \in \mathbb{A}$ for signer sid, the managing attribute authority signs the signer identity sid (used as tag) along with the attribute a using her secret tagged signature signing key. The resulting signature is used as the secret key for that attribute by signer sid.

To sign a message m w.r.t. a signing policy Ψ, the signer first encrypts her identity sid using the encryption scheme PKE (and some randomness μ) to obtain a ciphertext C. She then computes, using the NIZK system $NIZK_1$, a proof π that she encrypted her identity correctly and that she either has a digital signature on the hash of the combination of the signing predicate, the message and the ciphertext containing her identity, i.e. $\mathcal{H}(\Psi, m, C)$, that verifies w.r.t. the verification key tvk or that she owns enough attributes to satisfy the original signing predicate Ψ in the form of tagged signatures on her identity and the attributes. For ease of composition and following [34], we refer to $\mathcal{H}(\Psi, m, C)$ as pseudo-attributes and denote them by $a_{\Psi,m,C}$. Note here that including the ciphertext as part of the encoding of the pseudo-attribute does not affect the signature size.

The extended predicate $\hat{\Psi}$ is proved via a span program (see Section 2) represented by the matrix $\mathbf{Z}$: the signer proves that she knows a secret vector $\boldsymbol{s} \in \mathbb{Z}_p^{|\hat{\Psi}|}$ s.t. $\boldsymbol{s}\mathbf{Z} = [1, 0, \ldots, 0]$. She also needs to show that she possesses a valid (tagged) signature on each attribute in the signing predicate for which the corresponding element in $\boldsymbol{s}$ is non-zero or a valid signature that verifies w.r.t tvk in the case of

---

$\underline{\text{Setup}(1^\lambda)}$

  ○ $(\text{crs}_1, \text{xk}_1) \leftarrow \text{NIZK}_1.\text{Setup}(1^\lambda)$ and $\text{crs}_2 \leftarrow \text{NIZK}_2.\text{Setup}(1^\lambda)$.

  ○ $(\text{tvk}, \text{tsk}) \leftarrow \text{DS.KeyGen}(1^\lambda)$ and $(\text{epk}, \text{esk}) \leftarrow \text{PKE.KeyGen}(1^\lambda; \rho)$.

  ○ Choose a collision-resistant hash function $\mathcal{H} : \{0,1\}^* \rightarrow \mathcal{M}_{\text{DS}}$.

  ○ Let $\text{tk} := \text{esk}$ and $\text{pp} := (1^\lambda, \text{crs}_1, \text{crs}_2, \text{tvk}, \text{epk}, \mathbb{A}, \mathcal{H})$.

  ○ Return pp.

$\underline{\text{AuthSetup}(\text{pp}, \text{aid})}$

  ○ $(\text{aavk}_{\text{aid}}, \text{aask}_{\text{aid}}) \leftarrow \text{TS.KeyGen}(1^\lambda)$.

  ○ Return $(\text{aavk}_{\text{aid}}, \text{aask}_{\text{aid}})$.

$\underline{\text{KeyGen}(\text{aask}_{\text{aid}(a)}, \text{sid}, a)}$

  ○ $\text{sk}_{\text{sid},a} \leftarrow \text{TS.Sign}(\text{aask}_{\text{aid}(a)}, \text{sid}, a)$.

  ○ Return $\text{sk}_{\text{sid},a}$.

$\underline{\text{Sign}(\{\text{aavk}_{\text{aid}(a)}\}_{a \in \mathcal{A}}, \{\text{sk}_{\text{sid},a}\}_{a \in \mathcal{A}}, m, \Psi)}$

  ○ Return $\perp$ if $\Psi(\mathcal{A}) = 0$.

  ○ $C \leftarrow \text{PKE.Enc}(\text{epk}, \text{sid}; \mu)$.

  ○ Let $\hat{\Psi} := \Psi \vee a_{\Psi,m,C}$ and $\mathbf{Z} \in \mathbb{Z}_p^{|\hat{\Psi}|,\beta}$ be the span program for $\hat{\Psi}$.

  ○ Let $\boldsymbol{a} := \{a_i\}_{i=1}^{|\hat{\Psi}|}$ denote the attributes appearing in $\hat{\Psi}$.

  ○ $\pi \leftarrow \text{NIZK}_1.\text{Prove}(\text{crs}_1, \{\text{sid}, \mu, \boldsymbol{s}, \{\sigma_{a_i}\}_{i=1}^{|\hat{\Psi}|}\} : (C, \{\text{aavk}_{\text{aid}(a_i)}\}_{i=1}^{|\hat{\Psi}|-1} \cup \text{tvk}, \boldsymbol{a}) \in \mathcal{L}_1)$.

  ○ Return $\sigma := (\pi, C)$.

$\underline{\text{Verify}(\{\text{aavk}_{\text{aid}(a)}\}_{a \in \Psi}, m, \sigma, \Psi)}$

  ○ Return $\text{NIZK}_1.\text{Verify}(\text{crs}_1, \pi)$.

$\underline{\text{Trace}(\text{tk}, m, \sigma, \Psi)}$

  ○ Return $(\perp, \perp)$ if $\text{Verify}(\{\text{aavk}_{\text{aid}(a)}\}_{a \in \Psi}, m, \sigma, \Psi) = 0$.

  ○ $\text{sid} \leftarrow \text{PKE.Dec}(\text{tk}, C)$.

  ○ $\pi_{\text{Trace}} \leftarrow \text{NIZK}_2.\text{Prove}(\text{crs}_2, \{\text{tk}, \rho\} : (C, \text{epk}, \text{sid}) \in \mathcal{L}_2)$.

  ○ Return $(\text{sid}, \pi_{\text{Trace}})$.

$\underline{\text{Judge}(\{\text{aavk}_{\text{aid}(a)}\}_{a \in \Psi}, m, \sigma, \Psi, \text{sid}, \pi_{\text{Trace}})}$

  ○ If $(\text{sid}, \pi_{\text{Trace}}) = (\perp, \perp)$ Then Return $\text{Verify}(\{\text{aavk}_{\text{aid}(a)}\}_{a \in \Psi}, m, \sigma, \Psi) = 0$.

  ○ Return $\text{NIZK}_2.\text{Verify}(\text{crs}_2, \pi_{\text{Trace}})$.

Fig. 5. The generic construction for DTABS

a pseudo-attribute. For attributes appearing in the policy that the signer does not own, she chooses random signatures.

Note that the hiding property of the NIZK_1 system ensures that the proof π does not reveal how the modified predicate $\hat{\Psi}$ was satisfied, i.e. whether the signer has a special signature on the pseudo-attribute or she owns enough attributes to satisfy the original predicate Ψ. The signature is then set to $\sigma := (\pi, C)$. To verify the signature, one just needs to verify the proof π.

The modified predicate $\hat{\Psi}$ serves to bind the signature to the message and the signing predicate. The secret signing key tsk for the digital signature scheme DS is only used as a trapdoor in the security proofs, and thus is not given to any authority. It allows its holder to simulate signatures and sign on behalf of any signer without knowing their secret keys by simply encrypting their identity and producing a signature on the pseudo-attribute associated with the message and the signing predicate. Note that even in the unlikely case that any of the pseudo-attributes happened to collide with a real attribute, this is not a problem since signatures associated with pseudo-attributes must verify w.r.t. tvk which is different from all attribute authorities' keys.

To trace a signature, the tracing authority just decrypts the ciphertext C to recover the signer's identity. It then produces a proof π_{Trace} using the NIZK system NIZK_2 to prove that the decryption was done correctly. To verify the tracing correctness, the judge just needs to verify the proof π_{Trace}.

The details of the construction are in Fig. 5, whereas the languages associated with the NIZK proofs used in the construction are as follows, where for clarity we underline the elements of the witness:

$$\mathcal{L}_1 : \Big\{ \Big((C, \mathbf{vk} := \{\mathsf{aavk}_{\mathsf{aid}(a_i)}\}_{i=1}^{|\hat{\Psi}|-1} \cup \mathsf{tvk}, \boldsymbol{a} := \{a_i\}_{i=1}^{|\hat{\Psi}|}), (\underline{\mathsf{sid}}, \underline{\mu}, \underline{\boldsymbol{s}}, \underline{\boldsymbol{\sigma}} := \{\underline{\sigma_{a_i}}\}_{i=1}^{|\hat{\Psi}|}) \Big) :$$

$$\Big(\underline{\boldsymbol{s}}\mathbf{Z} = [1, 0, \ldots, 0] \bigwedge_{i=1}^{|\hat{\Psi}|-1} \text{if } \underline{s_i} \neq 0 \Rightarrow \mathsf{TS.Verify}(\mathsf{vk}_i, \underline{\mathsf{sid}}, a_i, \underline{\sigma_{a_i}}) = 1$$

$$\wedge \text{ if } \underline{s_{|\hat{\Psi}|}} \neq 0 \Rightarrow \mathsf{DS.Verify}(\mathsf{tvk}, a_{\Psi, m, C}, \underline{\sigma_{a_{|\hat{\Psi}|}}}) = 1 \Big) \wedge \mathsf{PKE.Enc}(\mathsf{epk}, \underline{\mathsf{sid}}; \underline{\mu}) = C \Big\}.$$

The witness consists of the identity sid, the randomness μ used in encrypting sid, a vector $\boldsymbol{s} \in \mathbb{Z}_p^{|\hat{\Psi}|}$, and signatures $\{\sigma_{a_i}\}_{i=1}^{|\hat{\Psi}|}$ s.t. the span program $\mathbf{Z}$ verifies w.r.t. to $\boldsymbol{s}$ and for every $s_i \neq 0$ for $i \in \{1, \ldots |\boldsymbol{s}| - 1\}$, the tagged signature σ_{a_i} on sid (as a tag) and the attribute a_i (as a message) verifies w.r.t. the corresponding attribute authority verification key, and if $s_{|\boldsymbol{s}|} \neq 0$, the signature $\sigma_{|\hat{\Psi}|}$, i.e. the one on the pseudo-attribute verifies w.r.t. the verification key tvk of DS.

$$\mathcal{L}_2 : \Big\{ \Big((C, \mathsf{epk}, \mathsf{sid}), (\underline{\mathsf{tk}}, \underline{\rho}) \Big) : \mathsf{PKE.KeyGen}(1^\lambda; \underline{\rho}) = (\mathsf{epk}, \underline{\mathsf{tk}}) \wedge \mathsf{PKE.Dec}(\underline{\mathsf{tk}}, C) = \mathsf{sid} \Big\}.$$

The witness consists of the tracing key, i.e. the decryption key for PKE, and the randomness ρ (if any) used in the key generation of PKE s.t. the encryption/decryption key pair is correct and the ciphertext C decrypts to sid.

Note that if we encrypted the whole witness of π (rather than just the signer identity) then we could drop the requirement for NIZK_1 to be a proof of knowledge. The reason why we cannot afford to do this is two-fold: first, since the decryption key is used as a tracing key and signers do not have their own personal key pairs, this would mean that a dishonest tracing authority will be able to forge on behalf of an honest signer once it has opened a signature by them. Second, since in both the full unforgeability and traceability experiments, the adversary has access to the tracing key, it would mean that we can no longer sign using pseudo-attributes since the adversary will be able to learn what witness we used in producing a signature. Also, note that for the construction to satisfy the stronger variant of full unforgeability (i.e. SFU) rather than WFU, NIZK_1 must additionally be strongly non-malleable in the sense that it is infeasible for the adversary to even output a new proof for a statement that it received a proof for. In particular, as noted by [21] if the proof system is simulation-sound extractable [21] then it is non-malleable.

Theorem 1. *The construction in Fig. 5 is a secure DTABS if the building blocks are secure w.r.t. their security requirements.*

The full proof of this theorem can be found in the full version [10].

We note here that instantiations of all the tools we require for the generic construction exist in the literature in both the random oracle and the standard models. In particular, we note that in the random oracle model we can instantiate the proof systems required using the Fiat–Shamir heuristics [12]. Our focus is, however, on constructions which do not rely on idealized assumptions. Before we proceed we note here that the size of the signature in [11], which requires random oracles and is over the inefficient composite-order bilinear groups, is $\mathbb{G}^{|\hat{\Psi}|+\beta+7}$. Note that the size of the group order of composite-order groups is about 10 times that of their prime-order counterparts at the same security level.

In order to improve the efficiency in the standard model, we present a construction in the next section that slightly deviates from the generic framework.

7   Constructions in the Standard Model

In order to get more efficient constructions in the standard model, we slightly deviate from the generic framework by dropping the requirement that $\mathsf{NIZK_1}$ is simulation-sound. In particular, in our instantiations we will use the Groth-Sahai proof system (which is the only efficient non-interactive proof system not relying on random oracles) to instantiate both $\mathsf{NIZK_1}$ and $\mathsf{NIZK_2}$ systems. Note that Groth-Sahai proofs are malleable and therefore not simulation-sound. Although there exist transformations which make Groth-Sahai proofs simulation-sound, e.g. [21], unfortunately, all those transformations degrade the efficiency of the proofs. Also, note that the fact that one cannot efficiently extract exponents from Groth-Sahai proofs is not a problem in our case as we never need to be able to efficiently extract the exponent components of the witness.

To eliminate the need for $\mathsf{NIZK_1}$ to be simulation-sound, we apply a trick similar to that used by Groth in [22] where we sign the final signature with a strongly unforgeable one-time signature scheme OTS. We require that OTS is strongly existentially unforgeable against adaptive chosen-message attack. We replace the IND-CCA PKE encryption scheme with a selective-tag weakly IND-CCA (i.e. ST-WIND-CCA secure) tag-based encryption scheme TPKE. We encrypt the signer's identity sid using TPKE and the one-time signature verification key as a tag. To map the one-time signature verification key into the tag space of the tag-based encryption, we require another collision-resistant hash function, $\hat{\mathcal{H}} : \{0,1\}^* \rightarrow \mathcal{T}_{\mathsf{TPKE}}$. In order to further bind the signature to the one-time signature verification key (i.e. the tag used for the ciphertext), we sign the one-time signature verification key as a part of the pseudo-attribute, i.e. the pseudo-attribute now is $(\Psi, m, C_{\mathrm{tbe}}, \hat{\mathcal{H}}(\mathsf{otsvk}))$, which we denote by $a_{\Psi, m, C_{\mathrm{tbe}}, \hat{\mathcal{H}}(\mathsf{otsvk})}$. The rest of the tools are the same as in the generic construction in Section 6.

The one-time signature serves to prevent the adversary from transforming a signature that it received into another valid signature as it now must be able to forge a one-time signature in order to succeed. Moreover, the one-time signature gives us the added bonus of realizing the stronger variant of full unforgeability. The details of the general idea of this construction is given in Fig. 6, whereas the languages associated with the NIZK proofs used in the construction are as

Setup(1^λ)
- $(\text{crs}_1, \text{xk}_1) \leftarrow \text{NIZK}_1.\text{Setup}(1^\lambda)$ and $(\text{crs}_2, \text{xk}_2) \leftarrow \text{NIZK}_2.\text{Setup}(1^\lambda)$.
- $(\text{tvk}, \text{tsk}) \leftarrow \text{DS.KeyGen}(1^\lambda)$ and $(\text{epk}, \text{esk}) \leftarrow \text{TPKE.KeyGen}(1^\lambda; \rho)$.
- Choose collision-resistant hash functions $\mathcal{H} : \{0,1\}^* \to \mathcal{M}_{\text{DS}}$ and $\hat{\mathcal{H}} : \{0,1\}^* \to \mathcal{T}_{\text{TPKE}}$.
- Let $\text{tk} := \text{esk}$ and $\text{pp} := (1^\lambda, \text{crs}_1, \text{crs}_2, \text{tvk}, \text{epk}, \mathbb{A}, \mathcal{H}, \hat{\mathcal{H}})$.
- Return pp.

AuthSetup(pp, aid)
- $(\text{aavk}_{\text{aid}}, \text{aask}_{\text{aid}}) \leftarrow \text{TS.KeyGen}(1^\lambda)$. Return $(\text{aavk}_{\text{aid}}, \text{aask}_{\text{aid}})$.

KeyGen($\text{aask}_{\text{aid}(a)}$, sid, a)
- $\text{sk}_{\text{sid},a} \leftarrow \text{TS.Sign}(\text{aask}_{\text{aid}(a)}, \text{sid}, a)$. Return $\text{sk}_{\text{sid},a}$.

Sign($\{\text{aavk}_{\text{aid}(a)}\}_{a \in \mathcal{A}}, \{\text{sk}_{\text{sid},a}\}_{a \in \mathcal{A}}, m, \Psi$)
- Return $\perp$ if $\Psi(\mathcal{A}) = 0$.
- $(\text{otsvk}, \text{otssk}) \leftarrow \text{OTS.KeyGen}(1^\lambda)$.
- $C_{\text{tbe}} \leftarrow \text{TPKE.Enc}(\text{epk}, \hat{\mathcal{H}}(\text{otsvk}), \text{sid}; \mu)$.
- Let $\hat{\Psi} := \Psi \vee a_{\Psi, m, C_{\text{tbe}}, \hat{\mathcal{H}}(\text{otsvk})}$ and $\mathbf{Z} \in \mathbb{Z}_p^{|\hat{\Psi}|, \beta}$ be the span program for $\hat{\Psi}$.
- Let $\mathbf{a} := \{a_i\}_{i=1}^{|\hat{\Psi}|}$ denote the attributes appearing in $\hat{\Psi}$.
- Let $\omega := \{\text{sid}, \mu, \mathbf{s}, \{\sigma_a\}_{i=1}^{|\hat{\Psi}|}\}$ and $\chi := (\hat{\mathcal{H}}(\text{otsvk}), C_{\text{tbe}}, \{\text{aavk}_{\text{aid}(a_i)}\}_{i=1}^{|\hat{\Psi}|-1} \cup \text{tvk}, \mathbf{a})$.
- $\pi \leftarrow \text{NIZK}_1.\text{Prove}(\text{crs}_1, \omega : \chi \in \mathcal{L}'_1)$.
- $\sigma_{\text{ots}} \leftarrow \text{OTS.Sign}(\text{otssk}, (\pi, C_{\text{tbe}}, \text{otsvk}))$.
- Return $\sigma := (\sigma_{\text{ots}}, \pi, C_{\text{tbe}}, \text{otsvk})$.

Verify($\{\text{aavk}_{\text{aid}(a)}\}_{a \in \Psi}, m, \sigma, \Psi$)
- Parse σ as $(\sigma_{\text{ots}}, \pi, C_{\text{tbe}}, \text{otsvk})$.
- Return 1 if all the following hold; otherwise, return 0:
  * $\text{OTS.Verify}(\text{otsvk}, (\pi, C_{\text{tbe}}, \text{otsvk}), \sigma_{\text{ots}}) = 1$.
  * $\text{NIZK}_1.\text{Verify}(\text{crs}_1, \pi) = 1$.
  * $\text{TPKE.IsValid}(\text{epk}, \hat{\mathcal{H}}(\text{otsvk}), C_{\text{tbe}}) = 1$.

Trace(tk, m, σ, Ψ)
- Return $(\perp, \perp)$ if $\text{Verify}(\{\text{aavk}_{\text{aid}(a)}\}_{a \in \Psi}, m, \sigma, \Psi) = 0$.
- $\text{sid} \leftarrow \text{TPKE.Dec}(\text{tk}, \hat{\mathcal{H}}(\text{otsvk}), C_{\text{tbe}})$.
- $\pi_{\text{Trace}} \leftarrow \text{NIZK}_2.\text{Prove}(\text{crs}_2, \{\text{tk}, \rho\} : (\hat{\mathcal{H}}(\text{otsvk}), C_{\text{tbe}}, \text{epk}, \text{sid}) \in \mathcal{L}'_2)$.
- Return $(\text{sid}, \pi_{\text{Trace}})$.

Judge($\{\text{aavk}_{\text{aid}(a)}\}_{a \in \Psi}, m, \sigma, \Psi, \text{sid}, \pi_{\text{Trace}}$)
- If $(\text{sid}, \pi_{\text{Trace}}) = (\perp, \perp)$ Then Return $\text{Verify}(\{\text{aavk}_{\text{aid}(a)}\}_{a \in \Psi}, m, \sigma, \Psi) = 0$.
- Return $\text{NIZK}_2.\text{Verify}(\text{crs}_2, \pi_{\text{Trace}})$.

Fig. 6. Details of the second construction

follows, where again the elements of the witness are underlined:

$$\mathcal{L}'_1 : \Big\{ \Big(\big(\hat{\mathcal{H}}(\text{otsvk}), C_{\text{tbe}}, \mathbf{vk} := \{\text{aavk}_{\text{aid}(a_i)}\}_{i=1}^{|\hat{\Psi}|-1} \cup \text{tvk}, \mathbf{a} := \{a_i\}_{i=1}^{|\hat{\Psi}|} \big),$$

$$\big(\text{sid}, \mu, \mathbf{s}, \boldsymbol{\sigma} := \{\sigma_{a_i}\}_{i=1}^{|\hat{\Psi}|} \big) \Big) : \text{TPKE.Enc}(\text{epk}, \hat{\mathcal{H}}(\text{otsvk}), \underline{\text{sid}}; \underline{\mu}) = C_{\text{tbe}}$$

$$\wedge \ \Big(\underline{\mathbf{s}} \mathbf{Z} = [1, 0, \dots, 0] \bigwedge_{i=1}^{|\hat{\Psi}|-1} \text{if } \underline{s_i} \neq 0 \Rightarrow \text{TS.Verify}(\text{vk}_i, \underline{\text{sid}}, a_i, \underline{\sigma_{a_i}}) = 1$$

$$\wedge \ \text{if } \underline{s_{|\hat{\Psi}|}} \neq 0 \Rightarrow \text{DS.Verify}(\text{tvk}, a_{\Psi, m, C_{\text{tbe}}, \hat{\mathcal{H}}(\text{otsvk})}, \underline{\sigma_{a_{|\hat{\Psi}|}}}) = 1 \Big) \Big\}.$$

$$\mathcal{L}_2' : \left\{ \left((\hat{\mathcal{H}}(\mathsf{otsvk}), C_{\mathsf{tbe}}, \mathsf{epk}, \mathsf{sid}), (\mathsf{tk}, \rho) \right) : \mathsf{TPKE.KeyGen}(1^\lambda; \rho) = (\mathsf{epk}, \underline{\mathsf{tk}}) \right.$$
$$\left. \wedge\ \mathsf{TPKE.Dec}(\underline{\mathsf{tk}}, \hat{\mathcal{H}}(\mathsf{otsvk}), C_{\mathsf{tbe}}) = \mathsf{sid} \right\}.$$

We provide a proof for the following theorem in the full version [10].

Theorem 2. *The construction in Fig. 6 is a secure DTABS if the building blocks are secure w.r.t. their security requirements.*

7.1 An Instantiation in Symmetric Groups

We use the instantiation of the tagged signature scheme from Section 5.1 and instantiate the digital signature DS used for pseudo-attributes with the full Boneh-Boyen signature scheme (cf. Section 5.2) both in the symmetric setting. Thus, we assume a collision-resistant hash function $\mathcal{H} : \{0,1\}^* \to \mathbb{Z}_p$. Note that we need not hide the integer component r of the full Boneh-Boyen signature when proving π as such a signature can only be generated by the simulator running the security game and hence r does not reveal any information about the attributes involved or the identity of the signer. In other words, in both the real signature and the simulated signature cases, r is chosen uniformly at random.

We use the selective-tag weakly IND-CCA tag-based encryption scheme by Kiltz [29] as illustrated in Fig. 4 to instantiate TPKE and instantiate the one-time signature with the full Boneh-Boyen signature in the symmetric setting.

We now give the specific details of the proofs invloved. Let $\mathbf{Z} \in \mathbb{Z}_p^{|\hat{\Psi}|,\beta}$ be the span program for $\hat{\Psi} := \Psi \vee a_{\Psi,m,C_{\mathsf{tbe}},\hat{\mathcal{H}}(\mathsf{otsvk})}$. To sign, we need the following proofs:

- To prove that $s\mathbf{Z} = [1,0,\dots,0]$, we need to prove the following equations:

$$\sum_{i=1}^{|\hat{\Psi}|}(\underline{s_i}Z_{i,1}) = 1 \qquad \sum_{i=1}^{|\hat{\Psi}|}(\underline{s_i}Z_{i,j}) = 0, \text{ for } j = 2,\dots,\beta \qquad (1)$$

To prove that if $\underline{s_i} \neq 0 \Rightarrow \mathsf{TS.Verify}(\mathsf{vk}_i, \underline{\mathsf{sid}}, a_i, \underline{\sigma_{a_i}}) = 1$, one needs to raise each pairing involved in the signature verification equations to s_i. This will ensure that if $s_i \neq 0$ then the only way for the equations to verify is by having a valid signature on sid and a_i. On the other hand, if the user does not own attribute a_i then $s_i = 0$ and the equations will verify since each pairing will evaluate to 1. Based on the observation that the components U, U', V, V' of the tagged signature are independent of the signing key and hence even when the user does not have a valid signature on a_i can still choose random components of the correct form to satisfy the first two verification equations of the tagged signature. Thus, it is sufficient to use s_i only in the last equation of the tagged signature verification equations. This reduces the number of additional GS commitments and equations required and hence improves the efficiency.

For each of the first $|\hat{\Psi}| - 1$ rows in $\mathbf{Z}$, we prove:

$$\underline{\bar{T}_i} = T^{\underline{s_i}} \qquad \underline{\bar{G}_i'} = G'^{\underline{s_i}} \qquad \underline{\bar{W}_i} = W_i^{\underline{s_i}} \qquad e(\underline{U_i}, G_i') = e(G_i, \underline{U_i'})$$

$$e(\underline{V_i}, G_i') = e(F_i, \underline{V_i'}) \qquad e(\underline{\bar{W}_i}, X' \cdot \underline{V_i'}) = e(\underline{\bar{T}_i}, \underline{U_i'})e(K \cdot \underline{\text{sid}} \cdot L^{a_i}, \underline{\bar{G}_i'})$$

For the last row in $\mathbf{Z}$, i.e. the pseudo-attribute, the proofs required are:

$$\underline{\bar{\sigma}} = \sigma^{\underline{s_{|\hat{\Psi}|}}} \qquad \underline{\bar{G}} = G^{\underline{s_{|\hat{\Psi}|}}} \qquad e(\underline{\bar{\sigma}}, X \cdot Y^r \cdot G^{\mathcal{H}(\Psi, m, C_{\text{tbe}}, \hat{\mathcal{H}}(\text{otsvk}))}) e(\underline{\bar{G}}, G) = 1$$

- To prove that $\mathsf{TPKE.Enc}(\mathsf{epk}, \hat{\mathcal{H}}(\text{otsvk}), \underline{\text{sid}}; (\underline{r_1}, \underline{r_2})) = C_{\text{tbe}}$, the signer proves $(C_1, C_2, C_3, C_4, C_5) = (F^{r_1}, H^{r_2}, G^{r_1 + r_2} \cdot \text{sid}, (G^{\hat{\mathcal{H}}(\text{otsvk})} \cdot K)^{r_1}, (G^{\hat{\mathcal{H}}(\text{otsvk})} \cdot L)^{r_2})$ was computed correctly. Since the validity of the ciphertext is publicly verifiable, and for the sake of efficiency, it is sufficient to provide proofs that C_1, C_2 and C_3 were computed correctly and the rest can be verified by checking that $e(F, C_4) = e(C_1, G^{\hat{\mathcal{H}}(\text{otsvk})} \cdot K)$ and $e(H, C_5) = e(C_2, G^{\hat{\mathcal{H}}(\text{otsvk})} \cdot L)$. Thus, proving this clause requires proving the 3 following equations

$$C_1 = F^{\underline{r_1}} \qquad C_2 = H^{\underline{r_2}} \qquad C_3 = G^{\underline{r_1}} \cdot G^{\underline{r_2}} \cdot \underline{\text{sid}}$$

- Finally, the signer needs to prove that her identity is a Diffie–Hellman tuple satisfying $e(\underline{\text{sid}}, G') = e(G, \underline{\text{sid}'})$.

The total size of the signature is $\mathbb{Z}_p^{2 \cdot \beta + 1} + \mathbb{G}^{69 \cdot |\hat{\Psi}|}$. An important observation is that the verification of the signature could be made more efficient by using batch verification techniques for Groth-Sahai proofs [18,5].

Computing the proof π_{Trace} requires proving the following equations

$$G^{\underline{f}} = F \qquad G^{\underline{h}} = H \qquad C_3 \cdot C_1^{-1/\underline{f}} \cdot C_2^{-1/\underline{h}} = \text{sid}$$

The proof for the following theorem follows from that of theorem 2.

Theorem 3. *The construction is secure if the assumptions DLIN, q-SDH, q-ADHSDH, and WFCDH hold.*

7.2 An Instantiation in Asymmetric Groups

To improve efficiency, here we translate the above instantiation into the asymmetric setting (i.e. Type-3 bilinear groups) where we use the more efficient SXDH-based instantiation of Groth-Sahai proofs. We use the asymmetric variants of all the building blocks used in the symmetric instantiation. Note that the security of the asymmetric instantiation of the tag-based encryption scheme from [26] which we use here is based on the SDLIN assumption [26] (a variant of the DLIN assumption in which the last element in the input tuple is provided in both groups) requires that the message space of the encryption scheme (i.e. the number of signers' identities to be encrypted) is polynomial in the security parameter so that we can efficiently search when decrypting. Thus, this instantiation only works when traceability is defined w.r.t. registered users in the system which is polynomial in the security parameter.

The details of this instantiation can be found in the full version [10]. The signature size of this instantiation is $\mathbb{G}_1^{34 \cdot |\hat{\Psi}| - 6} + \mathbb{G}_2^{32 \cdot |\hat{\Psi}|} + \mathbb{Z}_p^{\beta + 1}$.

We end by noting (similarly to [26]) that by translating the instantiation into the Type-2 setting, we can eliminate the requirement for the signer identity space (i.e. the message space of the TPKE scheme) to be polynomial. In this setting, we can use the instantiation of Groth-Sahai proofs based on DDH in $\mathbb{G}_1$ and DLIN in $\mathbb{G}_2$ as in [19].

7.3   Other Instantiations

By replacing the tagged signature scheme used in the previous instantiation with one based on any structure-preserving signature scheme [1] that is capable of signing two messages, we get more instantiations in the standard model.

An obvious candidate for this is the signature scheme by Abe et al. [2], which can sign multiple group elements. The Abe et al. signature scheme yields signatures consisting of 7 group elements and requires 2 PPE for verification.

Acknowledgments. The second author was supported by ERC Advanced Grant ERC-2010-AdG-267188-CRIPTO and EPSRC via grant EP/H043454/1.

We thank David Bernhard, Liqun Chen, James Davenport, Nigel Smart, and Bogdan Warinschi. We also thank anonymous CT-RSA reviewers for valuable comments.

References

1. Abe, M., Fuchsbauer, G., Groth, J., Haralambiev, K., Ohkubo, M.: Structure-preserving signatures and commitments to group elements. In: Rabin, T. (ed.) CRYPTO 2010. LNCS, vol. 6223, pp. 209–236. Springer, Heidelberg (2010)
2. Abe, M., Haralambiev, K., Ohkubo, M.: Signing on Elements in Bilinear Groups for Modular Protocol Design. Cryptology ePrint Archive, Report 2010/133, http://eprint.iacr.org/2010/133
3. Bellare, M., Rogaway, P.: Random oracles are practical: A Paradigm for Designing Efficient Protocols. In: ACM-CCS 1993, pp. 62–73. ACM (1993)
4. Bellare, M., Shi, H., Zhang, C.: Foundations of group signatures: The case of dynamic groups. In: Menezes, A. (ed.) CT-RSA 2005. LNCS, vol. 3376, pp. 136–153. Springer, Heidelberg (2005)
5. Blazy, O., Fuchsbauer, G., Izabachène, M., Jambert, A., Sibert, H., Vergnaud, D.: Batch Groth–Sahai. In: Zhou, J., Yung, M. (eds.) ACNS 2010. LNCS, vol. 6123, pp. 218–235. Springer, Heidelberg (2010)
6. Boneh, D., Boyen, X.: Short Signatures Without Random Oracles. In: Cachin, C., Camenisch, J.L. (eds.) EUROCRYPT 2004. LNCS, vol. 3027, pp. 56–73. Springer, Heidelberg (2004)
7. Bobba, R., Fatemieh, O., Khan, F., Gunter, C.A., Khurana, H.: Using Attribute-Based Access Control to Enable Attribute-Based Messaging. In: ACSAC 2006, vol. 3027, pp. 403–413. IEEE Computer Society (2006)
8. Boneh, D., Boyen, X., Shacham, H.: Short Group Signatures. In: Franklin, M. (ed.) CRYPTO 2004. LNCS, vol. 3152, pp. 41–55. Springer, Heidelberg (2004)

9. De Santis, A., Persiano, G.: Zero-knowledge proofs of knowledge without interaction. In: FOCS 1992, pp. 427–436 (1992)
10. El Kaafarani, A., Ghadafi, E., Khader, D.: Decentralized Traceable Attribute-Based Signatures. In: Cryptology ePrint Archive, Report 2013/828 (2013), http://eprint.iacr.org/2013/828.pdf
11. Escala, A., Herranz, J., Morillo, P.: Revocable Attribute-Based Signatures with Adaptive Security in the Standard Model. In: Nitaj, A., Pointcheval, D. (eds.) AFRICACRYPT 2011. LNCS, vol. 6737, pp. 224–241. Springer, Heidelberg (2011)
12. Fiat, A., Shamir, A.: How to prove yourself: Practical solutions to identification. and signature problems. In: Odlyzko, A.M. (ed.) CRYPTO 1986. LNCS, vol. 263, pp. 186–194. Springer, Heidelberg (1987)
13. Frikken, K.B., Li, J., Atallah, M.J.: Trust negotiation with hidden credentials, hidden policies, and policy cycles. In: NDSS 2006, pp. 157–172. The Internet Society (2006)
14. Fuchsbauer, G.: Automorphic Signatures in Bilinear Groups and an Application to Round-Optimal Blind Signatures. In: Cryptology ePrint Archive, Report 2009/320 (2009), http://eprint.iacr.org/2009/320.pdf
15. Fuchsbauer, G.: Commuting Signatures and Verifiable Encryption. In: Paterson, K.G. (ed.) EUROCRYPT 2011. LNCS, vol. 6632, pp. 224–245. Springer, Heidelberg (2011)
16. Gagné, M., Narayan, S., Safavi-Naini, R.: Short Pairing-Efficient Threshold-Attribute-Based Signature. In: Abdalla, M., Lange, T. (eds.) Pairing 2012. LNCS, vol. 7708, pp. 295–313. Springer, Heidelberg (2013)
17. Galbraith, S., Paterson, K., Smart, N.P.: Pairings for cryptographers. Discrete Applied Mathematics 156, 3113–3121 (2008)
18. Ghadafi, E., Smart, N.P., Warinschi, B.: Practical zero-knowledge proofs for circuit evaluation. In: Parker, M.G. (ed.) Cryptography and Coding 2009. LNCS, vol. 5921, pp. 469–494. Springer, Heidelberg (2009)
19. Ghadafi, E., Smart, N.P., Warinschi, B.: Groth-Sahai proofs revisited. In: Nguyen, P.Q., Pointcheval, D. (eds.) PKC 2010. LNCS, vol. 6056, pp. 177–192. Springer, Heidelberg (2010)
20. Goyal, V., Pandey, O., Sahai, A., Waters, B.: Attribute-Based Encryption for Fine-Grained Access Control of Encrypted Data. In: CCS 2006, pp. 89–98. ACM (2006)
21. Groth, J.: Simulation-sound NIZK proofs for a practical language and constant size group signatures. In: Lai, X., Chen, K. (eds.) ASIACRYPT 2006. LNCS, vol. 4284, pp. 444–459. Springer, Heidelberg (2006)
22. Groth, J.: Fully anonymous group signatures without random oracles. In: Kurosawa, K. (ed.) ASIACRYPT 2007. LNCS, vol. 4833, pp. 164–180. Springer, Heidelberg (2007)
23. Groth, J., Sahai, A.: Efficient non-interactive proof systems for bilinear groups. SIAM Journal on Computing 41(5), 1193–1232 (2012)
24. Herranz, J., Laguillaumie, F., Libert, B., Ràfols, C.: Short Attribute-Based Signatures for Threshold Predicates. In: Dunkelman, O. (ed.) CT-RSA 2012. LNCS, vol. 7178, pp. 51–67. Springer, Heidelberg (2012)
25. Karchmer, M., Wigderson, A.: On span programs. In: 8th IEEE Structure in Complexity Theory, pp. 102–111 (1993)
26. Kakvi, S.A.: Efficient fully anonymous group signatures based on the Groth group signature scheme. Masters thesis, University College London (2010), http://www5.rz.rub.de:8032/mam/foc/content/publ/thesis_kakvi10.pdf
27. Khader, D.: Attribute Based Group Signatures with Revocation. In: Cryptology ePrint Archive, Report 2007/241 (2007), http://eprint.iacr.org/2007/241.pdf

28. Khader, D., Chen, L., Davenport, J.H.: Certificate-Free Attribute Authentication. In: Parker, M.G. (ed.) Cryptography and Coding 2009. LNCS, vol. 5921, pp. 301–325. Springer, Heidelberg (2009)
29. Kiltz, E.: Chosen-Ciphertext Security from Tag-Based Encryption. In: Halevi, S., Rabin, T. (eds.) TCC 2006. LNCS, vol. 3876, pp. 581–600. Springer, Heidelberg (2006)
30. Li, J., Au, M.H., Susilo, W., Xie, D., Ren, K.: Attribute-based signature and its applications. In: ASIACCS 2010, pp. 60–69. ACM (2010)
31. Li, J., Kim, K.: Attribute-Based Ring Signatures. In: Cryptology ePrint Archive, Report 2008/394 (2008), http://eprint.iacr.org/2008/394.pdf
32. MacKenzie, P., Reiter, M.K., Yang, K.: Alternatives to Non-malleability: Definitions, Constructions, and Applications. In: Naor, M. (ed.) TCC 2004. LNCS, vol. 2951, pp. 171–190. Springer, Heidelberg (2004)
33. Maji, H.K., Prabhakaran, M., Rosulek, M.: Attribute-Based Signatures: Achieving Attribute-Privacy and Collusion-Resistance. In: Cryptology ePrint Archive, Report 2008/328 (2008), http://eprint.iacr.org/2008/328.pdf
34. Maji, H.K., Prabhakaran, M., Rosulek, M.: Attribute-Based Signatures. In: Kiayias, A. (ed.) CT-RSA 2011. LNCS, vol. 6558, pp. 376–392. Springer, Heidelberg (2011)
35. Naor, M.: On cryptographic assumptions and challenges. In: Boneh, D. (ed.) CRYPTO 2003. LNCS, vol. 2729, pp. 96–109. Springer, Heidelberg (2003)
36. Okamoto, T., Takashima, K.: Efficient Attribute-Based Signatures for Non-monotone Predicates in the Standard Model. In: Catalano, D., Fazio, N., Gennaro, R., Nicolosi, A. (eds.) PKC 2011. LNCS, vol. 6571, pp. 35–52. Springer, Heidelberg (2011)
37. Okamoto, T., Takashima, K.: Decentralized Attribute-Based Signatures. In: Kurosawa, K., Hanaoka, G. (eds.) PKC 2013. LNCS, vol. 7778, pp. 125–142. Springer, Heidelberg (2013)
38. Sahai, A.: Non-Malleable Non-Interactive Zero Knowledge and Adaptive Chosen-Ciphertext Security. In: FOCS 1999, pp. 543–553 (1999)
39. Sahai, A., Waters, B.: Fuzzy Identity-Based Encryption. In: Cramer, R. (ed.) EUROCRYPT 2005. LNCS, vol. 3494, pp. 457–473. Springer, Heidelberg (2005)
40. Shahandashti, S.F., Safavi-Naini, R.: Threshold Attribute-Based Signatures and Their Application to Anonymous Credential Systems. In: Preneel, B. (ed.) AFRICACRYPT 2009. LNCS, vol. 5580, pp. 198–216. Springer, Heidelberg (2009)

Rethinking Verifiably Encrypted Signatures: A Gap in Functionality and Potential Solutions

Theresa Calderon[1], Sarah Meiklejohn[1],
Hovav Shacham[1], and Brent Waters[2]

[1] UC San Diego
{tcaldero,smeiklej,hovav}@cs.ucsd.edu
[2] UT Austin
bwaters@cs.utexas.edu

Abstract. Verifiably encrypted signatures were introduced by Boneh, Gentry, Lynn, and Shacham in 2003, as a non-interactive analogue to interactive protocols for verifiable encryption of signatures. As their name suggests, verifiably encrypted signatures were intended to capture a notion of encryption, and constructions in the literature use public-key encryption as a building block.

In this paper, we show that previous definitions for verifiably encrypted signatures do not capture the intuition that encryption is necessary, by presenting a generic construction of verifiably encrypted signatures from any signature scheme. We then argue that signatures extracted by the arbiter from a verifiably encrypted signature object should be distributed identically to ordinary signatures produced by the original signer, a property that we call resolution independence. Our generic construction of verifiably encrypted signatures does not satisfy resolution independence, whereas all previous constructions do. Finally, we introduce a stronger but less general version of resolution independence, which we call resolution duplication. We show that verifiably encrypted signatures that satisfy resolution duplication generically imply public-key encryption.

Keywords: Verifiably encrypted signatures, signatures, public-key encryption.

1 Introduction

Verifiably encrypted signatures were introduced by Boneh, Gentry, Lynn, and Shacham in 2003 [5] as a non-interactive analogue to interactive protocols for verifiable encryption of signatures [3,4] and of other cryptographic objects [7]. As their name suggests, verifiably encrypted signatures were intended to incorporate a notion of encryption: the signer encrypts her signature in such a way that a special trusted party, called the arbiter, can later decrypt and reveal the underlying ordinary signature. Indeed, ElGamal encryption of BLS signatures [6] was at the heart of the original verifiably encrypted signature construction.

J. Benaloh (Ed.): CT-RSA 2014, LNCS 8366, pp. 349–366, 2014.
© Springer International Publishing Switzerland 2014

In this paper, we show that this intention — incorporating a notion of encryption — is not actually achieved by the definitions given in previous papers. To demonstrate this, we first in Section 3 give a generic construction of verifiably encrypted signatures from any existentially unforgeable signature scheme. The intuition behind our construction is fairly straightforward: to form a verifiably encrypted signature, the signer includes an annotation with her signature asking users not to verify it; later, the arbiter can append to this signature another annotation, under his own key, telling users that verification is now allowed. Our generic construction satisfies both the original security model for verifiably encrypted signatures and the tweaked definitions later given by Hess [11], Rückert and Schröder [16], and Rückert, Schneider, and Schröder [15].

Given that our generic construction therefore yields a secure verifiably encrypted signature yet makes no use of encryption, thus seemingly contradicting the spirit of the primitive, we are left with a number of different ways to interpret this result. One possible interpretation is that the current definitions are fine as is, and verifiably encrypted signatures are simply misnamed. They remain equally useful as a building block in larger protocols such as optimistic fair exchange [2] whether or not they involve encryption.

A second interpretation is that previous definitions have failed to capture something fundamental about verifiably encrypted signatures. If the signer escrows her ordinary signature and the arbiter is later meant to recover that signature, then the start and end points of that process — the signer's signature, and the signature obtained by the arbiter — should look the same. Previous definitions do not model this requirement, and in fact our generic construction does not satisfy it. In Section 4, we therefore formalize this notion, which we call *resolution independence*. We then provide a "separation" of sorts between our generic construction and existing ones (which, again, do use some form of public-key encryption) by arguing that all previous constructions of verifiably encrypted signatures do satisfy it.

A third, perhaps more extreme, interpretation is that a verifiably encrypted signature should not merely be "encryption-like" in facilitating the transfer of a signature from signer to arbiter, but should actually make use of public-key encryption in a fundamental way. To this end, we introduce in Section 5 a stronger version of resolution independence that requires the signer to be able to produce a signature that is *identical* to the one that the arbiter will output. We show that verifiably encrypted signatures that satisfy this property, which we call *resolution duplication*, generically imply the existence of public-key encryption; this approach is inspired by Abdalla and Warinschi [1], who showed that group signatures generically imply public-key encryption. Although resolution duplication is a less general property than resolution independence, all previous constructions of verifiably encrypted signatures except one — that of Lu et al. [12] — satisfy resolution duplication.

2   Definitions and Notation

In this section we provide the basic definitions for verifiably encrypted signatures as defined by Boneh et al. [5] and Hess [11]. Formally, a *verifiably encrypted signature* (VES) consists of seven algorithms. The first three, KeyGen, Sign, and Verify, comprise an ordinary signature scheme. The fourth, AKeyGen, generates a keypair (apk, ask) to be used by the arbiter (previously called the adjudicator); the fifth, VESign, takes as input (sk, apk, m) and outputs a verifiable encrypted signature ω; the sixth, VEVerify, takes as input (pk, apk, ω, m) and outputs 1 if ω is a valid verifiably encrypted signature on m and 0 otherwise; and finally the seventh, Resolve, takes as input (ask, pk, ω, m) and outputs a valid regular signature σ on m under pk (i.e., a value σ such that $\mathsf{Verify}(pk, \sigma, m) = 1$).

In order to say that the scheme is complete, we would like to ensure that an honestly computed VES will indeed verify as such, and also that once this VES is honestly resolved it will produce a valid signature as desired. This can be summarized formally as follows:

Definition 2.1. [5] *A VES* (KeyGen, Sign, Verify, AKeyGen, VESign, VEVerify, Resolve) *is complete if for all* $(apk, ask) \xleftarrow{\$} \mathsf{AKeyGen}(1^k)$, $(pk, sk) \xleftarrow{\$} \mathsf{KeyGen}(1^k)$, *and* $m \in \mathcal{M}$, *for* $\omega \xleftarrow{\$} \mathsf{VESign}(sk, apk, m)$ *it holds that* $\mathsf{VEVerify}(pk, apk, \omega, m) = 1$ *and* $\mathsf{Verify}(pk, \mathsf{Resolve}(ask, pk, \omega, m), m) = 1$.

As we show in Section 3, completeness, as well as all the security properties below, can be satisfied by a construction based solely on signatures. We therefore define in Section 4 a new notion for verifiably encrypted signatures intended to capture the "verifiable encryption" functionality.

Briefly, there are three main security properties we consider for VES schemes: *unforgeability*, *opacity*, and *extractability*. The first of these says that, for a given public key pk, no one except the signer in possession of the corresponding sk should be able to form a verifiably encrypted signature under pk. We alter slightly the original definition; as completeness does not guarantee that signatures produced by Sign and Resolve look the same (although our new definition in Section 4 does), we additionally provide the adversary with access to the Sign oracle, as otherwise the underlying signature scheme could be completely broken and the VES would still be considered unforgeable.

Definition 2.2. *For a VES* (KeyGen, Sign, Verify, AKeyGen, VESign, VEVerify, Resolve) *and an adversary* $\mathcal{A}$, *define the following game:*

- *Step 1.* $(pk, sk) \xleftarrow{\$} \mathsf{KeyGen}(1^k)$, $(apk, ask) \xleftarrow{\$} \mathsf{AKeyGen}(1^k)$.
- *Step 2.* $(m, \omega) \xleftarrow{\$} \mathcal{A}^{\mathsf{Sign}(sk, \cdot), \mathsf{VESign}(sk, apk, \cdot), \mathsf{Resolve}(ask, pk, \cdot, \cdot)}(pk, apk)$.

Then the verifiably encrypted signature scheme is unforgeable *(more precisely, secure against existential forgeries) if for all PPT algorithms* $\mathcal{A}$ *there exists a negligible function* $\nu(\cdot)$ *such that the probability (taken over the choices of* KeyGen, AKeyGen, Sign, VESign, Resolve, *and* $\mathcal{A}$) *that* $\mathsf{VEVerify}(pk, apk, \omega, m) = 1$ *but* m *was not queried to any of the three oracles is at most* $\nu(k)$.

The next property, opacity, says that a user given just the verifiably encrypted signature should not be able to pull out the underlying signature without help from the arbiter.

Definition 2.3. [5] *For a VES* (KeyGen, Sign, Verify, AKeyGen, VESign, VEVerify, Resolve) *and an adversary $\mathcal{A}$, define the following game:*

- *Step 1.* $(pk, sk) \xleftarrow{\$} \mathsf{KeyGen}(1^k)$, $(apk, ask) \xleftarrow{\$} \mathsf{AKeyGen}(1^k)$.
- *Step 2.* $(m, \sigma) \xleftarrow{\$} \mathcal{A}^{\mathsf{VESign}(sk, apk, \cdot), \mathsf{Resolve}(ask, pk, \cdot, \cdot)}(pk, apk)$.

Then the verifiably encrypted signature scheme is opaque *if for all PPT algorithms $\mathcal{A}$ there exists a negligible function $\nu(\cdot)$ such that the probability (taken over the choices of* KeyGen, AKeyGen, VESign, Resolve, *and $\mathcal{A}$) that* Verify$(pk, \sigma, m) = 1$ *but $(m, \cdot)$ was not queried to the* Resolve *oracle is at most $\nu(k)$.*

While opacity promises that no user can pull out the underlying signature given just the verifiable encrypted signature, we still need to guarantee that the arbiter can in fact do just this if necessary. While such a guarantee was not defined in the original BGLS paper, this property was proposed shortly thereafter by Hess [11] (and later formalized by Rückert and Schröder [16], who called it extractability).

Definition 2.4. [11] *For a VES* (KeyGen, Sign, Verify, AKeyGen, VESign, VEVerify, Resolve) *and an adversary $\mathcal{A}$, define the following game:*

- *Step 1.* $(apk, ask) \xleftarrow{\$} \mathsf{AKeyGen}(1^k)$.
- *Step 2.* $(pk, \omega, m) \xleftarrow{\$} \mathcal{A}^{\mathsf{Resolve}(ask, \cdot, \cdot, \cdot)}(apk)$.

Then the verifiably encrypted signature scheme is extractable *if for all PPT algorithms $\mathcal{A}$ there exists a negligible function $\nu(\cdot)$ such that the probability (taken over the choices of* AKeyGen, Resolve, *and $\mathcal{A}$) that, for $\sigma \xleftarrow{\$}$ Resolve(ask, pk, ω, m),* VEVerify$(pk, apk, \omega, m) = 1$ *but* Verify$(pk, \sigma, m) = 0$ *is at most $\nu(k)$.*

In addition to these three basic properties, there is another property we might consider called *abuse freeness*, as defined by Rückert and Schröder [16]; briefly, this says that even an adversary colluding with the arbiter cannot forge verifiably encrypted signatures for another user. Although we limit our focus here and do not consider this definition formally, we note that our signature-based construction in the next section does satisfy abuse freeness.

3   A Signature-Based Verifiably Encrypted Signature

In this section, we show how to generically construct a secure verifiable encrypted signature using just an unforgeable signature scheme. As mentioned in the introduction, our scheme works intuitively as follows: to run VESign, a user will sign the message, but then stamp, or annotate, the signed message to say "Do

Not Verify." To verify that this is a valid VES, VEVerify will ensure that it is a signed message with this stamp. To resolve this VES, Resolve will simply add its own stamp "Yes Do Verify." The verification algorithm will then check for these cases: if the signed message has a "Do Not Verify" stamp then it will output 0 (i.e., it will not verify), unless the signed message also has a "Yes Do Verify" stamp, in which case it will output 1 (i.e., it will verify).

More formally, let $(\mathsf{KeyGen}', \mathsf{Sign}', \mathsf{Verify}')$ be an unforgeable (i.e., EUF-CMA secure) signature scheme with message space $\mathcal{M}'$. To construct a VES with message space $\mathcal{M}$, let T be a function that takes a tuple of four elements: a message $M \in \mathcal{M}$, an arbiter public key $apk \in \{0,1\}^*$, a bit $b \in \{0,1\}$, and a verifiably encrypted signature $\omega \in \{0,1\}^*$, and encodes it into a binary string $M' \in \mathcal{M}'$. We will use $b = 0$ to indicate "Do Not Verify" and $b = 1$ to indicate "Yes Do Verify," and will use $\perp$ to indicate that the given field is being left empty. Furthermore, to avoid possible collisions, we assume that T encodes inputs uniquely; i.e., $T(M, apk, b, \omega) \neq T(M', apk', b', \omega')$ unless all these values are equal. Then we can define our VES as follows:

- $\mathsf{KeyGen}(1^k)$: Output $(pk, sk) \xleftarrow{\$} \mathsf{KeyGen}'(1^k)$.
- $\mathsf{Sign}(sk, M)$: Output $\sigma \xleftarrow{\$} \mathsf{Sign}'(sk, T(M, \perp, \perp, \perp))$.
- $\mathsf{Verify}(pk, \sigma, M)$: If σ is of the form (apk, ω, ω') then check that $\mathsf{VEVerify}(pk, apk, \omega, M) = 1$ and $\mathsf{Verify}'(apk, \omega', T(M, apk, 1, \omega)) = 1$; output 1 if and only if both of these checks pass. Otherwise, if σ is a single element then check that $\mathsf{Verify}'(pk, \sigma, T(M, \perp, \perp, \perp)) = 1$ and output 1 if and only if this check passes; in all other cases, output 0.
- $\mathsf{AKeyGen}(1^k)$. Compute $(apk', ask') \xleftarrow{\$} \mathsf{KeyGen}'(1^k)$ and output $(apk := apk', ask := (ask', apk))$.
- $\mathsf{VESign}(sk, apk, M)$: Output $\omega \xleftarrow{\$} \mathsf{Sign}'(sk, T(M, apk, 0, \perp))$.
- $\mathsf{VEVerify}(pk, apk, \omega, M)$: Output $\mathsf{Verify}'(pk, \omega, T(M, apk, 0, \perp))$.
- $\mathsf{Resolve}(ask, pk, \omega, M)$: If $\mathsf{VEVerify}(pk, apk, \omega, M) = 0$ output $\perp$. Otherwise, compute $\omega' \xleftarrow{\$} \mathsf{Sign}'(ask, T(M, apk, 1, \omega))$ and output $\sigma := (apk, \omega, \omega')$.

Essentially then, signing the message $T(M, apk, 0, \perp)$ corresponds to signing the message and then applying the "Do Not Verify" stamp (but indicating that the arbiter corresponding to apk may resolve if necessary), while signing the message $T(M, apk, 1, \omega)$ corresponds to applying the "Yes Do Verify" stamp. To show that this is a secure VES, we first prove that it satisfies completeness.

Theorem 3.1. *If the signature scheme* $(\mathsf{KeyGen}', \mathsf{Sign}', \mathsf{Verify}')$ *is complete, then the VES construction is complete as well.*

Proof. By definition, for any $(pk, sk) \xleftarrow{\$} \mathsf{KeyGen}(1^k)$, $(apk, ask) \xleftarrow{\$} \mathsf{AKeyGen}(1^k)$, and $M \in \mathcal{M}$, an honestly computed VES ω looks like $\mathsf{Sign}'(sk, apk, T(M, apk, 0, \perp))$. As $\mathsf{VEVerify}(pk, apk, \omega, M) = \mathsf{Verify}'(pk, \omega, T(M, apk, 0, \perp))$, the completeness of the underlying signature scheme guarantees that this check will pass. As for resolution, by definition $\mathsf{Resolve}(ask, pk, \omega, M) = (apk, \omega, \omega') \xleftarrow{\$} \mathsf{Sign}'(ask,$

$T(M, apk, 1, \omega)))$, and Verify, on input (apk, ω, ω'), checks that VEVerify($pk, apk,$ $\omega, M) = 1$ and Verify'($apk, \omega', T(M, apk, 1, \omega)) = 1$. As we've already argued that this first of these checks will pass, and the second will pass again by completeness of the signature scheme, the entire check will pass and Verify($pk, (apk, \omega, \omega'), M$) $= 1$. □

We now prove that our construction also satisfies the three security properties defined in Section 2, beginning with unforgeability (as defined in Definition 2.2).

Theorem 3.2. *If the signature scheme* (KeyGen', Sign', Verify') *is EUF-CMA secure, then the VES construction is unforgeable.*

Proof. To prove this, we show that if there exists an adversary $\mathcal{A}$ that breaks the unforgeability of the VES scheme with some non-negligible probability ϵ, then there exists an adversary $\mathcal{B}$ that breaks the unforgeability of the underlying signature scheme with the same probability. To start, $\mathcal{B}$ will take as input a public key pk. It then proceeds as follows:

1. $\mathcal{B}$ generates $(apk, ask) \xleftarrow{\$} \text{AKeyGen}(1^k)$ and gives pk and apk as inputs to $\mathcal{A}$. Because apk was generated honestly and pk is assumed to be the output of KeyGen' and thus KeyGen, both of these keys will be distributed identically to what $\mathcal{A}$ expects.
2. When $\mathcal{A}$ queries its Sign oracle on a message M, $\mathcal{B}$ creates a new message $M' := T(M, \perp, \perp, \perp)$ and queries its own Sign' oracle on M' to get back a signature σ that it then returns to $\mathcal{A}$. By definition, $\sigma \xleftarrow{\$} \text{Sign}'(sk, T(M, \perp, \perp, \perp)) = \text{Sign}(sk, M)$, so the σ returned to $\mathcal{A}$ will be distributed identically to what it expects.
3. When $\mathcal{A}$ queries its VESign oracle on a message M, $\mathcal{B}$ creates a new message $M' := T(M, apk, 0, \perp)$ and queries its own Sign' oracle on M' to get back a signature σ that it then returns to $\mathcal{A}$. By definition, we have that $\sigma \xleftarrow{\$} \text{Sign}'(sk, T(M, apk, 0, \perp)) = \text{VESign}(sk, apk, M)$, so the σ returned to $\mathcal{A}$ will be distributed identically to the one that it expects.
4. When $\mathcal{A}$ queries its Resolve oracle on a message M and a verifiably encrypted signature ω, $\mathcal{B}$ will use its knowledge of ask to execute the code of Resolve honestly to obtain a tuple of the form $\sigma := (apk, \omega, \omega')$ that it returns to $\mathcal{A}$. As $\mathcal{B}$ is behaving completely honestly, this will again be distributed identically to what $\mathcal{A}$ expects.
5. At some point $\mathcal{A}$ will output a message-signature pair (M, ω) such that M was not queried to any of the oracles but VEVerify($pk, apk, \omega, M) = 1$; $\mathcal{B}$ will then output $(T(M, apk, 0, \perp), \omega)$. By definition of VEVerify, if VEVerify($pk,$ $apk, \omega, M) = 1$ then Verify'($pk, T(M, apk, 0, \perp), \omega) = 1$ and thus $\mathcal{B}$'s output will pass verification; similarly, if $\mathcal{A}$ did not query its VESign oracle on M then, by definition of $\mathcal{B}$, we know that $\mathcal{B}$ did not query $T(M, apk, 0, \perp)$ to its Sign' oracle, and its output will therefore be a valid forgery.

As $\mathcal{B}$ therefore succeeds whenever $\mathcal{A}$ does, and the interaction with $\mathcal{B}$ is furthermore identical to the interaction that $\mathcal{A}$ expects, $\mathcal{B}$ will succeed with the same non-negligible probability ϵ as $\mathcal{A}$. □

Next, we prove that our construction is opaque, as defined in Definition 2.3.

Theorem 3.3. *If the signature scheme* (KeyGen′, Sign′, Verify′) *is EUF-CMA secure, then the VES construction is opaque.*

Proof. To prove this, we show that if there exists an adversary $\mathcal{A}$ that breaks the opacity of the VES scheme with some non-negligible probability ϵ, then there exists an adversary $\mathcal{B}$ that breaks the unforgeability of the signature scheme with probability $\epsilon/2$. To start, $\mathcal{B}$ will take as input a public key pk'. It then picks a random bit $b \xleftarrow{\$} \{0,1\}$ to decide which path it thinks $\mathcal{A}$ will pursue: if $b = 0$ then it assumes $\mathcal{A}$ will produce a forgery of the form (apk, ω, ω'), and if $b = 1$ then it assumes $\mathcal{A}$ will produce a forgery of the form σ. We discuss both of these paths as follows:

1. If $b = 0$ then $\mathcal{B}$ will generate $(pk, sk) \xleftarrow{\$} \mathsf{KeyGen}(1^k)$. It will then set $apk :=$ pk' and give pk and apk to $\mathcal{A}$. As AKeyGen calls KeyGen′ and pk' is assumed to be output by KeyGen′, this will be distributed identically to what $\mathcal{A}$ expects.

   If instead $b = 1$ then $\mathcal{B}$ will generate $(apk, ask) \xleftarrow{\$} \mathsf{AKeyGen}(1^k)$. It will then set $pk := pk'$ and give pk and apk to $\mathcal{A}$. Again, as KeyGen calls KeyGen′ and pk' is assumed to be output by KeyGen′, this will be distributed identically to what $\mathcal{A}$ expects.

2. When $\mathcal{A}$ queries its VESign oracle on a message M, $\mathcal{B}$ again has two choices. If $b = 0$ then $\mathcal{B}$ can use its knowledge of the signing key sk to honestly execute the code of VESign and return the resulting ω; the distribution here is by definition identical to the one that $\mathcal{A}$ expects.

   If instead $b = 1$ then $\mathcal{B}$ sets $M' := T(M, apk, 0, \bot)$ and queries its own Sign′ oracle on M' to get back a signature σ that it then returns to $\mathcal{A}$. By definition, $\sigma \xleftarrow{\$} \mathsf{Sign}'(sk, T(M, apk, 0, \bot)) = \mathsf{VESign}(sk, apk, M)$, so the σ returned to $\mathcal{A}$ will be distributed identically to what it expects.

3. When $\mathcal{A}$ queries its Resolve oracle on a message M and a verifiably encrypted signature ω, $\mathcal{B}$ can first check that $\mathsf{VEVerify}(pk, apk, \omega, M) = 1$ and abort if not; then, it again has two choices. If $b = 0$ then it sets $M' := T(M, apk, 1, \omega)$ and queries its own Sign′ oracle on M' to get back a signature σ; it will then return (apk, ω, σ) to $\mathcal{A}$. By definition, $\sigma \xleftarrow{\$} \mathsf{Sign}'(sk, T(M, apk, 1, \omega))$ and so the resulting (apk, ω, σ) will again be distributed identically to what $\mathcal{A}$ expects.

   If instead $b = 1$ then $\mathcal{B}$ will use its knowledge of the secret key ask to execute the code of Resolve honestly and return the resulting (apk, ω, ω'); the distribution here is then by definition identical to the one that $\mathcal{A}$ expects.

4. At some point, $\mathcal{A}$ will output a message-signature pair (M, σ) such that $\mathsf{Verify}(pk, \sigma, M) = 1$ but $(M, \cdot)$ was not queried to the Resolve oracle. If $b = 0$ then $\mathcal{B}$ will check that σ is of the form (apk, ω, ω'); it it is not, then $\mathcal{B}$ must abort. If it is then, looking at the definition of Verify, we see it must be the case that $\mathsf{Verify}'(pk, \omega, T(M, apk, 0, \bot)) = 1$ and $\mathsf{Verify}'(apk, \omega', T(M, apk, 1,$

$\omega)) = 1$. As we know that $\mathcal{A}$ never queried its Resolve oracle on ω we also know that $\mathcal{B}$ never queried its Sign$'$ oracle on $T(M, apk, 1, \omega)$ and therefore $\mathcal{B}$ can output $(T(M, apk, 1, \omega), \omega')$ to win its game.

Otherwise, if $b = 1$ then $\mathcal{B}$ will once again check if σ is of the form (apk, ω, ω'). If it is, then it is once again the case that Verify$'(pk, \omega, T(M, apk, 0, \bot)) = 1$; if $\mathcal{A}$ never queried its VESign oracle on M, then $\mathcal{B}$ never queried its Sign$'$ oracle on $T(M, apk, 0, \bot)$ and it can output $(T(M, apk, 0, \bot), \omega)$ to win its game. Otherwise, it can check if σ is a single element. If it is, then $\mathcal{B}$ can output $(T(M, \bot, \bot, \bot), \sigma)$ to once again win its game.

As $\mathcal{B}$ succeeds whenever $\mathcal{A}$ does and it correctly guesses which key $\mathcal{A}$ will use (which it will with probability $1/2$, as it guesses randomly), and interactions with $\mathcal{B}$ (in either execution) are furthermore identical to those that $\mathcal{A}$ expects, $\mathcal{B}$ will succeed with probability $\epsilon/2$ in providing a forgery for the signature scheme.   □

Finally, we prove that our construction is extractable, as defined in Definition 2.4. In fact, it is not just the case that it should be hard to produce a VES that verifies but cannot be resolved to a valid signature; by how Resolve and Verify are defined, this is actually impossible.

Theorem 3.4. *The VES construction is unconditionally extractable.*

Proof. To prove this, we show that for all $(apk, ask) \xleftarrow{\$} \text{KeyGen}(1^k)$, $M \in \mathcal{M}$, ω, and pk, every time VEVerify$(pk, apk, \omega, M) = 1$ it must be the case that Verify$(pk, apk, \text{Resolve}(ask, pk, \omega, M), M) = 1$ as well; this implies that the probability that any (even unbounded) adversary $\mathcal{A}$ can output (pk, ω, M) such that VEVerify$(pk, apk, \omega, M) = 1$ but Verify$(pk, apk, \text{Resolve}(ask, pk, \omega, M), M) = 0$ is equal to 0 and thus the scheme is unconditionally extractable.

To therefore show that VEVerify$(pk, apk, \omega, M) = 1$ implies Verify$(pk, \text{Resolve}(ask, pk, \omega, M)) = 1$, define $(apk, \omega, \omega') \xleftarrow{\$} \text{Resolve}(ask, pk, \omega, M)$. Then we observe that, by the definition of the scheme, Verify$(pk, apk, (apk, \omega, \omega'), M) = $ VEVerify$(pk, apk, \omega, M) \wedge \text{Verify}'(apk, \omega', T(M, apk, 1, \omega))$. As Resolve guarantees that the second condition is satisfied (i.e., Verify$'(apk, \omega', T(M, apk, 1, \omega)) = 1$), this reduces to Verify$(pk, apk, (apk, \omega, \omega'), M) = $ VEVerify(pk, apk, ω, M) and thus the two values must always agree.   □

4   Resolution Independence

As we've demonstrated in the previous section, the existing definitions for verifiably encrypted signatures do not seem to fully capture their desired functionality, as in particular we constructed a secure VES using only signatures. Furthermore, in our scheme the signatures returned by the arbiter look completely different from the regular signatures produced by Sign. In this section, we attempt to close this functional gap by proposing a new notion, *resolution independence*, that requires that the signatures returned by the arbiter and by the signer look the same. We then prove that our signature-based construction does not satisfy resolution independence whereas, to the best of our knowledge, all previous VES constructions do.

4.1   Resolution Independence

Informally, we want that the values output by the Resolve algorithm look like regular signatures. More formally, we have the following definition:

Definition 4.1. *A   VES   (KeyGen, Sign, Verify, AKeyGen, VESign, VEVerify, Resolve) is resolution independent if for all* $(pk, sk) \xleftarrow{\$} \mathsf{KeyGen}(1^k)$, $(apk, ask) \xleftarrow{\$} \mathsf{AKeyGen}(1^k)$, *and* $m \in \mathcal{M}$, *the distributions* $\{\mathsf{Sign}(sk, m)\}$ *and* $\{\mathsf{Resolve}(ask, pk, \mathsf{VESign}(sk, apk, m), m)\}$ *are identical.*

To begin motivating why resolution independence is the "right" definition to capture the desired VES functionality, we first observe that our signature-based construction from Section 3 cannot be resolution independent, as regular signatures and signatures output by the arbiter have completely different forms.

Theorem 4.1. *The VES construction in Section 3 is not resolution independent.*

Proof. Recall that signatures output by the signer are in Σ; i.e., the space of all possible signatures. Signatures output by the arbiter, however, consist of a public key and two signatures, meaning that if the space of all possible *apk* values is A, then they are in the space (A, Σ, Σ); the distributions over the two types of signatures are therefore not identical. $\qquad\square$

4.2   Existing Schemes Satisfy Resolution Independence

In order to further separate our signature-based construction from existing VES schemes, we also demonstrate that, to the best of our knowledge, all existing VES schemes are in fact resolution independent. As there are too many VES constructions in the literature to enumerate here, we focus on three (which we picked to demonstrate different types of schemes): the original BGLS construction [5], which is based on pairings and the BLS signature scheme [6], a construction due to Lu et al. [12] that is also based on pairings but uses the Waters signature [17], and a construction due to Rückert [14] that is based on the RSA signature scheme.

BGLS [5]. The BGLS scheme works over a prime-order bilinear group G with a generator g and a hash function $H : \{0,1\}^* \to G$. The arbiter's keys are $ask = x' \xleftarrow{\$} \mathbb{F}_p$ and $apk = v' = g^{x'} \in G$, and the user's keys are $sk = x \xleftarrow{\$} \mathbb{F}_p$ and $pk = v = g^x \in G$. As we can see in the algorithm descriptions below, Sign forms a BLS signature, while VESign runs Sign and then encrypts the signature using ElGamal encryption. The Resolve algorithm then decrypts and pulls out the original signature.

- Sign(sk, M): Parse $sk = x$ and return $\sigma := H(M)^x$.
- VESign(sk, apk, M): Parse $sk = x$ and $apk = v'$ and compute $\sigma := H(M)^x$. Pick $r \xleftarrow{\$} \mathbb{F}_p$ and set $\mu := g^r$ and $\sigma' := (v')^r$. Finally, compute $\omega' := \sigma\sigma'$ and output (ω', μ).

T. Calderon et al.

- Resolve(ask, pk, ω, M): Parse $ask = x'$ and $\omega = (\omega', \mu)$ and output $\sigma := \omega/\mu^{x'}$.

To see that the signatures output by Sign and Resolve are in fact identical, we observe that

$$
\begin{aligned}
\mathsf{Resolve}(ask, pk, \mathsf{VESign}(sk, apk, M; r), M) &= \frac{\omega}{\mu^{x'}} \\
&= \frac{\sigma\sigma'}{\mu^{x'}} \\
&= \frac{H(M)^x(v')^r}{(g^r)^{x'}} \\
&= \frac{H(M)^x((g^{x'})^r)}{(g^{rx'})} \\
&= H(M)^x \\
&= \mathsf{Sign}(sk, M),
\end{aligned}
$$

and thus the scheme satisfies resolution independence.

Lu et al. [12]. The Lu et al. scheme also works in a prime-order bilinear group G with generator g. It builds off of the Waters signature [17], which we briefly recall uses a secret key $sk = \alpha \xleftarrow{\$} \mathbb{F}_p$ (corresponding to a public key $pk = A = e(g, g)^\alpha$, where e is the bilinear map) to create signatures of the form (S_1, S_2), where $S_1 := g^\alpha(u' \prod_i u_i^{b_i})^r$, $S_2 := g^r$ for $u', u_1, \ldots, u_k \xleftarrow{\$} G$, $r \xleftarrow{\$} \mathbb{F}_p$, and where b_i is the i-th bit of the message M; i.e., $M = b_1 \ldots b_k$. We denote the Waters signing algorithm as $\mathsf{WSign}(sk, M)$.

As we see in the algorithm descriptions below, Sign is equivalent to WSign. VESign will first run Sign and then blind the resulting signature; this means users' keys will just be keys for the Waters signature, and the arbiter's keys will be $sk = \beta \xleftarrow{\$} \mathbb{F}_p$ and $pk = v = g^\beta$. The Resolve algorithm first pulls out the underlying signature, and then re-randomizes it.

- Sign(sk, M): Output $(S_1, S_2) \xleftarrow{\$} \mathsf{WSign}(sk, M)$.

- VESign(sk, apk, M): Parse $apk = v$. Compute $(S_1, S_2) \xleftarrow{\$} \mathsf{WSign}(sk, M)$, pick a random $s \xleftarrow{\$} \mathbb{F}_p$, and compute $K_1 := S_1 \cdot v^s$, $K_2 := S_2$, and $K_3 := g^s$. Output (K_1, K_2, K_3).

- Resolve(ask, pk, ω, M): Parse $ask = \beta$, $\omega = (K_1, K_2, K_3)$, and $M = b_1 \ldots b_k$. Check first that ω is a valid VES on M, and then unblind the signature by computing $S_1 := K_1 K_3^{-\beta}$ and $S_2 := K_2$. Now, re-randomize the signature by picking $s \xleftarrow{\$} \mathbb{F}_p$ and computing $S_1' := S_1(u' \prod_i u_i^{b_i})^s$ and $S_2' := S_2 \cdot g^s$. Output (S_1', S_2').

To see that the outputs of Sign and Resolve are distributed identically, we observe that

$$\mathsf{Resolve}(ask, pk, \mathsf{VESign}(sk, apk, M), M) = (K_1 \cdot K_3^{-\beta} \cdot (u' \prod_i u_i^{b_i})^{r'}, \ K_2 \cdot g^{r'})$$

$$= (S_1 \cdot v^s \cdot g^{-\beta s} \cdot (u' \prod_i u_i^{b_i})^{r'}, \ S_2 \cdot g^{r'})$$

$$= (S_1 \cdot (g^{\beta s} g^{-\beta s}) \cdot (u' \prod_i u_i^{b_i})^{r'}, \ g^{r+r'})$$

$$= (g^{\alpha} \cdot (u' \prod_i u_i^{b_i})^{r} \cdot (u' \prod_i u_i^{b_i})^{r'}, \ g^{r+r'})$$

$$= (g^{\alpha} \cdot (u' \prod_i u_i^{b_i})^{r+r'}, \ g^{r+r'})$$

$$= \mathsf{WSign}(sk, M; r + r')$$

for random $r, r' \xleftarrow{\$} \mathbb{F}_p$. The signature is therefore a random signature on M and thus has the same distribution as the signature output by $\mathsf{Sign}(sk, M)$ and the scheme is resolution independent.

Rückert [14]. Rückert's construction is a stateful VES based on the RSA signature scheme, which we recall works as follows: keys are of the form $pk := (N, e)$ and $sk := (pk, d)$, where $N = pq$ and e and d are values such that $ed \equiv 1 \bmod \phi(N)$. To form a signature, RSASign computes $\sigma := H(M)^d \bmod N$, which can be verified by checking that $H(M) \equiv \sigma^e \bmod N$. Briefly, in Rückert's construction, when forming the i-th VES, the RSA signature is blinded using a secret value x_i, which is then encrypted under the arbiter's public key. To ensure that this ciphertext contains the appropriate blinding factor, the signer will form an authentication path in a particular Merkle tree. This means that the keys for the arbiter will look like $apk = (N_e, e, \mathsf{authpk})$ and $ask = (apk, d, \mathsf{authsk})$, where (N_e, e, d) are RSA keys and authpk and authsk are used for the Merkle authentication. The user's keys, on the other hand, will look like $pk = (N_u, u, \rho, \sigma_\rho)$ and $sk = (pk, v, T)$, where (N_u, u, v) are RSA keys, T is the Merkle tree (and also contains information about the blinding factors $\{x_i\}$ by providing the seed used to generate them), ρ is the root of the tree, and σ_ρ is a RSA signature on ρ.

- Sign(sk, M): Output $\sigma := \mathsf{RSASign}(sk, M)$.
- VESign(sk, apk, M): Parse $sk = (pk = (N_u, u, \rho, \sigma_\rho), v, T)$ and $apk = (N_e, e, \mathsf{authpk})$. First form the signature $\sigma := \mathsf{RSASign}(sk, M)$. Now, increment the counter i, blind the signature by forming $\alpha := \sigma x_i \bmod N_s$, and encrypt x_i by forming $\beta := x_i^e \bmod N_e$, and $\gamma := x_i^u \bmod N_u$. Finally, generate the authentication path π for x_i in the Merkle tree T, and output $\omega := (\alpha, \beta, \gamma, \pi)$.
- Resolve(ask, pk, ω, M): Parse $ask = (apk = (N_e, e, \mathsf{authpk}), d, \mathsf{authsk})$, $pk = (N_u, u, \rho, \sigma_\rho)$, and $\omega = (\alpha, \beta, \gamma, \pi)$. First check that ω is a valid VES on M, and then compute $x' := \beta^d \bmod N_e$ and output $\sigma := \alpha/x' \bmod N_u$.

To see this that the signatures output by Resolve and Sign are identical, we observe that

$$\text{Resolve}(ask, pk, \text{VESign}(sk, apk, M), M) = \alpha/x' \bmod N_u$$
$$= \alpha/\beta^d \bmod N_u$$
$$= (\sigma x_i)/(x_i^e)^d \bmod N_u$$
$$= (\sigma x_i)/x_i \bmod N_u$$
$$= \sigma \bmod N_u,$$

which is the same as the signature output by $\text{Sign}(sk, M)$ and the scheme is therefore resolution independent.

5   Resolution Duplication and Public-Key Encryption

While resolution independence, as we saw in the previous section, can be used to separate our particular signature-based VES construction from existing constructions, it still does not require that more than just signatures are required to construct a verifiably encrypted signature scheme, although the name would suggest otherwise. We therefore propose in this section a stronger notion of resolution independence, *resolution duplication*, in which the signer must be able to output a signature that is *identical* to that of the arbiter. This definition is less general than resolution independence (yet still met by some existing VES constructions), but we show that it implies the existence of public key encryption.

5.1   Resolution Duplication

In spirit, resolution independence requires a functionality similar to that of encryption: the VES ω contains a signature σ, yet should not reveal this σ to anyone in possession of just ω (by opacity). The exception to this rule is the arbiter who, according to completeness, should be able to pull out from ω a signature σ' that, according to resolution independence, has the same distribution as σ. While this comes close to encryption, the fact that σ' and σ might be identically distributed but not identical means the functionality is not exactly the same.

In Section 4.2, however, we saw that in fact two out of the three schemes presented did in fact meet this exact requirement (and this was not an accident; indeed most VES schemes meet this requirement); in particular, because both the BGLS and Rückert schemes were based on *unique signatures* [10,13], any two signatures on the same message with the same distribution must be identical. To formally capture this stronger property, we have the following definition:

Definition 5.1. *A VES* (KeyGen, Sign, Verify, AKeyGen, VESign, VEVerify, Resolve) *is resolution duplicate if (1) it is resolution independent, (2) Resolve is deterministic, and (3) there exists an additional PPT algorithm* Extract$(\cdot, \cdot, \cdot)$

such that for all $(pk, sk) \overset{\$}{\leftarrow} \text{KeyGen}(1^k)$, $(apk, ask) \overset{\$}{\leftarrow} \text{AKeyGen}(1^k)$, $m \in \mathcal{M}$, *and random tapes* $r \in \{0, 1\}^*$, *it is the case that* $\text{Extract}(sk, m, r) = \text{Resolve}(ask, pk, \text{VESign}(sk, apk, m; r), m)$.

While this strengthened definition can no longer be met by *all* existing VES constructions (e.g., any that use a randomized resolution algorithm, such as the Lu et al. one above), we will see below that any secure VES satisfying resolution duplication can be used to construct public key encryption. In this respect then, VES constructions meeting resolution duplication guarantee that some kind of encryption really is taking place, whereas we cannot make the same guarantees about ones that meet only resolution independence.

Finally, we note that the existence of Extract is not a particularly strong requirement; for a unique signature, for example, Extract can simply run Sign. Furthermore, in our usage in the next section, VESign and Extract will be run by the same party, so the randomness used in VESign can simply be remembered and given to Extract.

5.2   Constructing Public Key Encryption

Using resolution duplication, our construction of public key encryption is fairly straightforward. Recall first our intuitive outline above: the signature σ can be thought of as the plaintext and the VES ω as the ciphertext encrypted under the public key of the arbiter; running Resolve and pulling out the underlying σ is therefore how the arbiter decrypts. Because we want to encrypt arbitrary bits rather than signatures, however, we instead use the Goldreich-Levin trick [9] and the fact that ω should not reveal σ to treat $\langle \sigma, r \rangle$ as a *hard-core predicate* for VESign; i.e., given ω and r, it should be hard to predict the value of $\langle \sigma, r \rangle$ (where $r \overset{\$}{\leftarrow} \{0, 1\}^{|\sigma|}$ and $\langle \sigma, r \rangle$ denotes the inner product of σ and r modulo 2).[1] To construct our encryption scheme, we therefore prove first that this property holds:

Theorem 5.1. *Let* (KeyGen, Sign, Verify, AKeyGen, VESign, VEVerify, Resolve) *be a verifiably encrypted signature scheme, and let* $b(x, r) := \langle x, r \rangle \bmod 2$ *for any* x *and* r *such that* $|x| = |r|$. *Then, if the VES is opaque for all messages* $m \in \mathcal{M}$, $(pk, sk) \overset{\$}{\leftarrow} \text{KeyGen}(1^k)$, *and* $(apk, ask) \overset{\$}{\leftarrow} \text{AKeyGen}(1^k)$, *it is hard to compute* $b(\sigma, r)$ *given* m, apk, pk, $\omega \overset{\$}{\leftarrow} \text{VESign}(sk, apk, m)$, *and* $r \overset{\$}{\leftarrow} \{0, 1\}^{|\sigma|}$, *where* $\sigma := \text{Resolve}(ask, pk, \omega, M)$.

Our proof strategy for this theorem closely follows that of Goldreich [8]. First, we describe how an adversary $\mathcal{B}$ attempting to break opacity can, by using specific values of r, meaningfully use an adversary $\mathcal{A}$ that can predict the value of $b(\sigma, r)$ to recover the value of σ from the verifiably encrypted signature. Then, following Goldreich's exact argument, we argue how these specific values of r can

---

[1] This isn't a hard-core bit in the usual sense, since VESign is randomized and therefore not a function, but we can nevertheless argue that it should be hard to predict.

be chosen to ensure that $\mathcal{B}$'s success probability will be appropriately correlated with that of $\mathcal{A}$.

At a high level, to use $\mathcal{A}$ to recover σ, $\mathcal{B}$ will first receive as input public keys pk and apk. To now prepare an input for $\mathcal{A}$, $\mathcal{B}$ can first pick a random message $m \xleftarrow{\$} \mathcal{M}$ and query its VESign oracle on m to get back a value ω. It now picks a random value $r \xleftarrow{\$} \{0,1\}^{|\sigma|}$ (note that, while $\mathcal{B}$ does not know σ, it might still know its length, for example if σ is encrypted) and gives (ω, r) to $\mathcal{A}$; this causes $\mathcal{A}$ to return its guess b' for the bit $b(\sigma, r)$. We could then also have $\mathcal{B}$ give to $\mathcal{A}$ $(\omega, r \oplus e_i)$ for all i, where e_i has a 1 in the i-th place and a 0 everywhere else, and get back in return guess bits b_i. If $\mathcal{A}$ guesses b' and b_i correctly for each i, then $\mathcal{B}$ can recover σ as follows: first, observe that $b(x,r) \oplus b(x,s) = b(x, r \oplus s)$. Then, if $b' = b(\sigma, r)$ and $b_i = b(\sigma, r \oplus e_i)$, it must be the case that

$$b' \oplus b_i = b(\sigma, r) \oplus b(\sigma, r \oplus e_i) = b(\sigma, r \oplus (r \oplus e_i)) = b(\sigma, e_i) = \sigma_i;$$

that is, that $b' \oplus b_i$ is the i-th bit of σ. Repeating this process for each i, $\mathcal{B}$ can therefore recover $\sigma_i := b' \oplus b_i$ and $\sigma := \sigma_1 \ldots \sigma_n$.

As observed by Goldreich, however, this process of using $r \oplus e_i$ might significantly blow up $\mathcal{B}$'s error probability, to the point where we cannot argue that if $\mathcal{A}$ has some non-negligible success probability then so does $\mathcal{B}$. We therefore follow Goldreich's exact argument to pick more clever choices for the randomness r and thus guarantee a non-negligible success probability for $\mathcal{B}$.

Proof. To show this, we assume that there exists an adversary $\mathcal{A}$ that, given (pk, apk, m, ω, r) such that $\omega \xleftarrow{\$} \mathsf{VESign}(sk, apk, m)$, $\sigma := \mathsf{Resolve}(ask, pk, \omega, m)$, and $|r| = |\sigma| = n$, can predict the value of $b(\sigma, r)$ with some non-negligible advantage ϵ and use it to construct an adversary $\mathcal{B}$ that can recover the signature σ from ω (i.e., break opacity), with related non-negligible probability ϵ'. First, we observe that if ϵ is non-negligible then by definition, $\mathcal{A}$'s advantage must be $\epsilon(n) > 1/p(n)$ for some polynomial $p(\cdot)$, and that furthermore this must hold for infinitely many n (i.e., there must exist an infinite set N such that $\epsilon(n) > 1/p(n)$ for $n \in N$). We furthermore establish the following two claims, both due to Goldreich [8]:

Claim. [8] There exists a set $S_n \subseteq \{0,1\}^n$ of cardinality at least $2^n \cdot (\epsilon(n)/2)$ such that for every $\sigma \in S_n$, it holds that

$$s(x) := \Pr[\mathcal{A}(pk, apk, m, \omega, R_n) = b(\sigma, R_n)] \geq \frac{1}{2} + \frac{\epsilon(n)}{2},$$

where the probability is taken over all possible values of R_n and internal coin tosses of $\mathcal{A}$.

Claim. [8] For every $\sigma \in S_n$ and $i \in \{1, \ldots, n\}$, it holds that

$$\Pr\left[|\{J : b(x, r_J) \oplus \mathcal{A}(pk, apk, m, \omega, r_J \oplus e_i) = \sigma_i\}| > \frac{1}{2} \cdot (2^\ell - 1) \right] > 1 - \frac{1}{2n} \tag{1}$$

where $r_J := \oplus_{j \in J} s_j$ and the s_j values are chosen independently and uniformly from $\{0,1\}^n$.

To prepare inputs for $\mathcal{A}$ given pk and apk, $\mathcal{B}$ first picks a random message $m \xleftarrow{\$} \mathcal{M}$ and queries its VESign oracle on m to get back a value ω. It now sets $\ell := \lceil \log_2(2n \cdot p(n)^2 + 1) \rceil$, where we recall $n := |\sigma|$ and $p(\cdot)$ is such that $\epsilon(n) > 1/p(n)$. It now samples $s_1, \ldots, s_\ell \xleftarrow{\$} \{0,1\}^n$ and $t_1, \ldots, t_\ell \xleftarrow{\$} \{0,1\}$, where t_i acts as $\mathcal{B}$'s guess for the value $b(\sigma, s_i)$. Next, for every non-empty set $J \subseteq \{1, 2, \ldots, \ell\}$, $\mathcal{B}$ computes $r_J := \oplus_{j \in J} s_j$ and $\rho_J := \oplus_{j \in J} t_j$. $\mathcal{B}$ now gives to $\mathcal{A}$, for all $i \in \{1, \ldots, n\}$ and non-empty $J \subseteq \{1, \ldots, \ell\}$, the tuple $(apk, pk, m, \omega, r_J \oplus e_i)$, for which it will get back a guess bit b_{iJ}. $\mathcal{B}$ then sets $z_{iJ} := \rho_J \oplus b_{iJ}$; now, for every i, it sets z_i to be the majority of the z_{iJ} values, and outputs $z := z_1 \ldots z_n$.

We first observe that the $r_J \oplus e_i$ values given to $\mathcal{A}$ will be uniformly random and pairwise independent and thus distributed identically to the input that $\mathcal{A}$ expects (and, as all the other values are chosen honestly, its entire input will be identical to what it expects). To see this, we observe that the s_i values are chosen uniformly at random, and each r_J value is set as $\oplus s_j$, which will itself be uniformly random, and thus so will $r_J \oplus e_i$. Furthermore, because each subset J is distinct, the values will be pairwise independent as well.

To determine the success probability of $\mathcal{B}$, our proof now follows exactly the proof of Goldreich. In particular, we first observe that, by Claim 5.2,

$$s(x) \geq \frac{1}{2} + \frac{\epsilon(n)}{2} > \frac{1}{2} + \frac{1}{2p(n)}.$$

Furthermore, as the values s_i were chosen uniformly at random, the probability that our guesses were correct and $t_i = b(\sigma, s_i)$ for all i is

$$2^{-\ell} = \frac{1}{2n \cdot p(n)^2 + 1} = \frac{1}{\text{poly}(n)},$$

which is non-negligible. Furthermore, if our guesses are indeed correct then

$$\rho_J = \oplus_{j \in J} t_j = \oplus_{j \in J} b(\sigma, s_j) = b(\sigma, \oplus_{j \in J} s_j) = b(\sigma, r_J)$$

for all non-empty sets J. In this case, we have

$$z_{iJ} = \rho_J \oplus b_{iJ} = b(\sigma, r_J) \oplus b_{iJ},$$

which we know is equal to σ_i with probability greater than $1 - 1/2n$ by Claim 5.2, meaning the overall probability that $z = \sigma$ is at least $1/2$. Putting everything together, we therefore know that $\mathcal{B}$ will succeed with probability at least $1/4p(n)$ for $\sigma \in S_n$; recalling further by Claim 5.2 that $|S_n| > 2^n/2p(n)$, we conclude that for random σ, $\mathcal{B}$ succeeds with probability at least $1/8p(n)^2$, or $\epsilon(n)^2/8$. $\qquad \square$

Now, armed with this theorem, we can construct public key encryption. To start, assume we have a VES (KeyGen, Sign, Verify, AKeyGen, VESign, VEVerify, Resolve) with the extra algorithm Extract required by Definition 5.1. Then we can construct an IND-CPA secure public key encryption scheme (EKeyGen, Enc, Dec) as follows:

- EKeyGen(1^k): Output $(pk, sk) \xleftarrow{\$} \mathsf{AKeyGen}(1^k)$.
- Enc(pk, m): Generate signing keys $(spk, ssk) \xleftarrow{\$} \mathsf{KeyGen}(1^k)$ and set $c_1 :=$ spk. Now pick a random tape r, compute $\omega := \mathsf{VESign}(ssk, pk, 0; r)$ and set $c_2 := \omega$. Next, compute $\sigma \xleftarrow{\$} \mathsf{Extract}(sk, m, r)$; finally, pick $r_\sigma \xleftarrow{\$} \{0,1\}^{|\sigma|}$, set $c_3 := r_\sigma$, and set $c_4 := m \oplus \langle \sigma, r_\sigma \rangle$. Output $c := (c_1, c_2, c_3, c_4)$.
- Dec(sk, c): Parse $c = (c_1, c_2, c_3, c_4)$. Check first that $\mathsf{VEVerify}(c_1, pk, c_2, 0) = 1$; if this check fails then output $\bot$. Otherwise, if it passes, compute $\sigma := \mathsf{Resolve}(sk, c_1, c_2, 0)$, and output $m := c_4 \oplus \langle \sigma, c_3 \rangle$.

Theorem 5.2. *If the verifiably encrypted signature is resolution duplicate (according to Definition 5.1), the above encryption scheme is correct.*

Proof. If the ciphertext c is formed as $c \xleftarrow{\$} \mathsf{Enc}(pk, m)$, then $c_1 = spk$ and $c_2 = \omega$, which allows decryption to compute $\sigma := \mathsf{Resolve}(sk, spk, \omega, 0)$. Additionally, we have $c_3 = r_\sigma$ and $c_4 = m \oplus \langle \sigma, r_\sigma \rangle$, where by resolution duplication the σ used to form c_4 is the same as the one produced by $\mathsf{Resolve}$. We therefore have that $c_4 \oplus \langle \sigma, c_3 \rangle = (m \oplus \langle \sigma, r_\sigma \rangle) \oplus \langle \sigma, r_\sigma \rangle = m$, so decryption really will produce the message. $\square$

Theorem 5.3. *If the verifiably encrypted signature is opaque, then the above encryption scheme is IND-CPA secure.*

Proof. By Theorem 5.1, we know that if the VES is opaque then $\langle \sigma, r \rangle$ will be hard to predict given only ω; furthermore, if it is opaque for all messages then in particular this must hold for the message $m = 0$. Thus, to prove the theorem, we can show that if there exists an adversary $\mathcal{A}$ that breaks IND-CPA security with some non-negligible advantage ϵ then there exists an adversary $\mathcal{B}$ that can predict the value of $\langle \sigma, r \rangle$ for the message $m = 0$ with the same advantage.

To start, $\mathcal{B}$ will receive as input $(pk, apk, 0, \omega, r)$, where $\omega \xleftarrow{\$} \mathsf{VESign}(sk, apk, 0)$ and $r \xleftarrow{\$} \{0,1\}^{|\sigma|}$ for $\sigma := \mathsf{Resolve}(ask, pk, \omega, 0)$. $\mathcal{B}$ will now give $\mathcal{A}$ the public key apk and at some point will receive back a challenge query (m_0, m_1). To compute c^*, $\mathcal{B}$ will set $c_1^* := pk$, $c_2^* := \omega$, and $c_3^* := r$. It then picks random bits $b, b^* \xleftarrow{\$} \{0,1\}$ and sets $c_4^* := m_b \oplus b^*$, and returns $c^* := (c_1^*, c_2^*, c_3^*, c_4^*)$ to $\mathcal{A}$. When $\mathcal{A}$ outputs its guess bit b', $\mathcal{B}$ guesses b^* if $b = b'$ and $1 - b^*$ otherwise.

To see that interactions with $\mathcal{B}$ are indistinguishable from those that $\mathcal{A}$ expects, we observe that the apk given to $\mathcal{A}$ is distributed identically to what $\mathcal{A}$ expects from EKeyGen. As for c^*, all the values except c_4^* are again distributed identically to what $\mathcal{A}$ expects: c_1^* is a random user public key, c_2^* is a valid VES, and c_3^* is a random string of the same length as σ. As for c_4^*, if $\mathcal{B}$ has correctly guessed the value of b^* (i.e., $b^* = \langle \sigma, r \rangle$), then $c_4^* = m_b \oplus \langle \sigma, r \rangle$, c^* is a valid encryption of m_b, and thus $\mathcal{A}$ should behave just as it does in the honest interaction (i.e., it should guess b with its usual non-negligible advantage ϵ). In this case, if $\mathcal{A}$ guesses b correctly, then $\mathcal{B}$ will assume that it guessed b^* correctly and thus output b^*. In the other case, if $\mathcal{B}$ did not guess b^* correctly, then c_4^* is just a random bit, meaning all information about m will be obscured and $\mathcal{A}$

will have no advantage. As $\mathcal{B}$ therefore succeeds at least whenever $\mathcal{A}$ succeeds and it correctly guesses b^*, which it will with probability $1/2$, $\mathcal{B}$ will succeed in predicting the value of $\langle \sigma, r \rangle$ with overall advantage at least $\epsilon/2$.   □

Acknowledgments. The first three authors were supported by the MURI program under AFOSR Grant No. FA9550-08-1-0352. Brent Waters was supported by NSF CNS-0915361 and CNS-0952692, CNS-1228599 DARPA through the U.S. Office of Naval Research under Contract N00014-11-1-0382, DARPA N11AP20006, Google Faculty Research award, the Alfred P. Sloan Fellowship, Microsoft Faculty Fellowship, and Packard Foundation Fellowship. Any opinions, findings, and conclusions or recommendations expressed in this material are those of the author(s) and do not necessarily reflect the views of the Department of Defense or the U.S. Government.

References

1. Abdalla, M., Warinschi, B.: On the minimal assumptions of group signature schemes. In: López, J., Qing, S., Okamoto, E. (eds.) ICICS 2004. LNCS, vol. 3269, pp. 1–13. Springer, Heidelberg (2004)
2. Asokan, N., Schunter, M., Waidner, M.: Optimistic protocols for fair exchange. In: Gong, L., Neuman, C. (eds.) Proceedings of CCS 1997, pp. 7–17. ACM Press (April 1997)
3. Asokan, N., Shoup, V., Waidner, M.: Optimistic fair exchange of digital signatures. IEEE Journal on Selected Areas in Communications 18(4), 593–610 (2000)
4. Ateniese, G.: Verifiable encryption of digital signatures and applications. Journal of Cryptology 7(1), 1–20 (2004)
5. Boneh, D., Gentry, C., Lynn, B., Shacham, H.: Aggregate and verifiably encrypted signatures from bilinear maps. In: Biham, E. (ed.) EUROCRYPT 2003. LNCS, vol. 2656, pp. 416–432. Springer, Heidelberg (2003)
6. Boneh, D., Lynn, B., Shacham, H.: Short signatures from the Weil pairing. In: Boyd, C. (ed.) ASIACRYPT 2001. LNCS, vol. 2248, pp. 514–532. Springer, Heidelberg (2001)
7. Camenisch, J., Shoup, V.: Practical verifiable encryption and decryption of discrete logarithms. In: Boneh, D. (ed.) CRYPTO 2003. LNCS, vol. 2729, pp. 126–144. Springer, Heidelberg (2003)
8. Goldreich, O.: Three XOR-lemmas – an exposition (1991), http://www.wisdom.weizmann.ac.il/~oded/COL/xor.pdf
9. Goldreich, O., Levin, L.: A hard-core predicate for all one-way functions. In: Proceedings of STOC 1989, pp. 25–32 (1989)
10. Goldwasser, S., Ostrovsky, R.: Invariant signatures and non-interactive zero-knowledge proofs are equivalent. In: Brickell, E.F. (ed.) CRYPTO 1992. LNCS, vol. 740, pp. 228–245. Springer, Heidelberg (1993)
11. Hess, F.: On the security of the verifiably-encrypted signature scheme of Boneh, Gentry, Lynn, and Shacham. Information Processing Letters 89(3), 111–114 (2004)
12. Lu, S., Ostrovsky, R., Sahai, A., Shacham, H., Waters, B.: Sequential aggregate signatures and multisignatures without random oracles. Journal of Cryptology (2012)

13. Lysyanskaya, A.: Unique signatures and verifiable random functions from the DH-DDH separation. In: Yung, M. (ed.) CRYPTO 2002. LNCS, vol. 2442, pp. 597–612. Springer, Heidelberg (2002)
14. Rückert, M.: Verifiably encrypted signatures from RSA without NIZKs. In: Roy, B., Sendrier, N. (eds.) INDOCRYPT 2009. LNCS, vol. 5922, pp. 363–377. Springer, Heidelberg (2009)
15. Rückert, M., Schneider, M., Schröder, D.: Generic constructions for verifiably encrypted signatures without random oracles or NIZKs. In: Zhou, J., Yung, M. (eds.) ACNS 2010. LNCS, vol. 6123, pp. 69–86. Springer, Heidelberg (2010)
16. Rückert, M., Schröder, D.: Security of verifiably encrypted signatures and a construction without random oracles. In: Shacham, H., Waters, B. (eds.) Pairing 2009. LNCS, vol. 5671, pp. 17–34. Springer, Heidelberg (2009)
17. Waters, B.: Efficient identity-based encryption without random oracles. In: Cramer, R. (ed.) EUROCRYPT 2005. LNCS, vol. 3494, pp. 114–127. Springer, Heidelberg (2005)

P²OFE: Privacy-Preserving Optimistic Fair Exchange of Digital Signatures

Qiong Huang[1], Duncan S. Wong[2], and Willy Susilo[3]

[1] South China Agricultural University, Guangzhou 510642, China
[2] City University of Hong Kong, Hong Kong S.A.R., China
[3] University of Wollongong, Wollongong, NSW 2522, Australia
csqhuang@alumni.cityu.edu.hk, duncan@cityu.edu.hk, wsusilo@uow.edu.au

Abstract. How to sign an electronic contract online between two parties (say Alice and Bob) in a fair manner is an interesting problem, and has been studied for a long time. Optimistic Fair Exchange (OFE) is an efficient solution to this problem, in which a semi-trusted third party named *arbitrator* is called in to resolve a dispute if there is one during an exchange between Alice and Bob. Recently, several extensions of OFE, such as Ambiguous OFE (AOFE) and Perfect AOFE (PAOFE), have been proposed to protect the privacy of the exchanging parties. These variants prevent any outsider including the arbitrator from telling which parties are involved in the exchange of signatures before the exchange completes.

However, in PAOFE, AOFE, and all the current work on OFE, the arbitrator can always learn the signer's signature at (or before) the end of a resolution, which is undesirable in some important applications, for example, signing a contract between two parties which do not wish others to find out even when there is a dispute that needs a resolution by the arbitrator. In this work, we introduce a new notion called *Privacy-Preserving Optimistic Fair Exchange* (P²OFE), in which other than Alice and Bob, no one else, including the arbitrator, can collect any evidence about an exchange between them even after the resolution of a dispute. We formally define P²OFE and propose a security model. We also propose a concrete and efficient construction of P²OFE, and prove its security based on the Strong Diffie-Helllman and Decision Linear assumptions in the standard model.

Keywords: optimistic fair exchange, signature, ambiguity, privacy preserving.

1 Introduction

The fair exchange problem is about constructing a protocol for two parties, Alice and Bob, that allow them to exchange items in an all-or-nothing (fair) manner, that is, after the protocol, either both parties obtain the other's item or none of them does. There are two major approaches to do fair exchange. The first one is to have the parties release their secrets 'gradually', e.g. bit by bit, in multiple

J. Benaloh (Ed.): CT-RSA 2014, LNCS 8366, pp. 367–384, 2014.

rounds. Besides, it is assumed that both of them have comparable computation power. Thus, this approach may not be appropriate for practical use.

Another approach is to have a third party called *arbitrator* employed. The arbitrator is semi-trusted by the two parties, and is usually offline. The arbitrator only gets involved when there is a dispute. Asokan *et al.* proposed this notion called *Optimistic Fair Exchange* (OFE) [1], and later extended it to support the exchange of digital signatures [2]. In OFE, Alice prepares an 'encapsulated' version of her signature, called *partial signature* σ_A, and sends it to Bob. If σ_A is valid, Bob returns his *full signature* ζ_B to Alice. In the third move, Alice tells Bob how to open σ_A or directly sends her full signature ζ_A to Bob if she believes ζ_B is valid. Figure 1 shows a normal execution. If Alice refuses or fails to return ζ_A, Bob resorts to the arbitrator for resolving σ_A. After checking the fulfillment of Bob's obligation, the arbitrator extracts ζ_A from σ_A, and sends it to Bob. Figure 2 shows the case in which there is a dispute.

Fig. 1. OFE: Normal Execution   **Fig. 2.** OFE: Resolution

Due to the simple and elegant framework, and the low level of trust required on the third party, OFE has many useful applications. One of them is to sign contracts between two online parties. For example, Alice wants to buy a software from Bob's online shop. She generates a partial signature on a message "Bob can withdraw \$100 from my bank account". Bob then gives Alice his full signature on message "Alice can get a copy of Windows 13 from my shop". If everything goes well, Alice gets the software and Bob gets the money from Alice's bank account. If Bob does not get the full signature from Alice subsequently, Bob asks the arbitrator for resolving Alice's partial signature and gets Alice's full signature.

(*On the Privacy of OFE and its Variants*). In conventional OFE, Alice's partial signature σ_A already reveals her will/intention to do exchange with Bob, from which Bob may take advantage of, and could be unfair to Alice. In [13,19], the notion of *Ambiguous* Optimistic Fair Exchange (AOFE)[1] was introduced to solve this problem. In AOFE, Bob is endowed with the ability of producing partial signatures computationally indistinguishable from those of Alice. Recently, Wang *et al.* [30] proposed an enhanced version of AOFE, named *Perfect* AOFE

---

[1] It is named *abuse-free contract signing* in [13] and *ambiguous optimistic fair exchange* in [19]. Hereafter we call it ambiguous optimistic fair exchange (AOFE), for the sake of the ease of presentation.

(PAOFE), in which a partial signature leaks no information about the actual signer or the intended verifier. This is useful for applications where the involved parties of an exchange wish to further protect their privacy on whether they are indeed involved in an exchange or not. For instance, when Alice and Bob sign a business contract (e.g. a procurement deal) online while revealing and confirming who is involved in the process may potentially be harmful to (for example, the image of) Alice and/or Bob. No one including the arbitrator can tell who and what exchange has taken place from the transcript of a normal execution of PAOFE.

Although the privacy is ensured in a normal execution of PAOFE, this is not the case if a dispute occurs and a resolution is solicited. At the end of a resolution protocol run in PAOFE, the arbitrator gets the full signature ζ_A of Alice. (Note that the resolution is an algorithm run by the arbitrator in (A)OFE while it is a protocol in PAOFE.) Hence the arbitrator can confirm whether a particular party, say Alice, is involved in an exchange of signatures. Note that this is always the case in (A)OFE as the resolution algorithm outputs ζ_A. Whereas there are applications in which the parties do not want anyone including the arbitrator to confirm and especially, convince others their involvement even when there is a dispute that needs the arbitrator to resolve. Even in the example above, revealing and confirming who is involved in the business contract to the arbitrator during a dispute may potentially hurt (the image of) Alice and/or Bob. We stress here that revealing the contract (i.e. the message) itself (*without the signatures*) does not entail any concern on revealing, or letting outsiders or the arbitrator to confirm the involvement of a particular party in an exchange. This is because such a contract/message can be made up by anyone. Only the signed contract can be used to confirm a party's involvement. In this scenario, PAOFE would not help because the arbitrator learns the final signature ζ_A at the end of the resolution and hence can confirm the involvement of Alice. The arbitrator can even convince others about Alice's involvement by making use of ζ_A.

Our Contributions. In this paper we contribute to the study of fair exchange in the following aspects:

1. We introduce the notion of *Privacy-Preserving* OFE (P²OFE). The new notion differs from PAOFE mainly in that P²OFE explicitly requires that even the arbitrator cannot learn the signer's full signature. The resolution in P²OFE is a protocol between the verifier and the arbitrator, and consists of two algorithms, Res^A and Res^V. Briefly, After receiving a partial signature σ for resolution, the arbitrator runs Res^A to convert it to an intermediate value θ, and gives to the verifier, who then runs Res^V to extract the signer's full signature ζ from θ. It is required that without the intended verifier's secret key, anyone cannot recover ζ from the intermediate value.
2. We present the security models of P²OFE to capture our intuition that even the arbitrator is unable to recover the signer's full signature after the resolution. As in [16,18] we consider the certified-key model in this paper, which is slightly weaker than the chosen-key model considered in [20,30]. However, the perfect ambiguity in our model is stronger in the sense that we allow the

adversary to interact with the intended verifier for resolution, which is not allowed in [30].

3. We also propose a concrete and efficient P²OFE protocol, the security of which is based on Strong Diffie-Hellman assumption [7] and Decision Linear assumption [8] without random oracles. Roughly, our protocol follows the sign-then-encrypt paradigm (which is common in the construction of designated confirmer signatures [9,18]). A full signature is simply a Boneh-Boyen short signature [7], while a partial signature is a 'twisted' double encryption of the full signature. Please refer to Sec. 5 for the detailed construction.

2   Related Works

Since the introduction, OFE has attracted a lot of attention, e.g. [3,10,11,15–22,28,29]. In [10], Dodis *et al.* showed a gap between the security of OFE in single-user setting (where there are one signer and one verifier) and that in multi-user setting (where there are multiple signers and verifiers). Using random oracle heuristic, they proposed a OFE secure in the multi-user setting and registered-key model [5]. Huang *et al.* [21] proposed a generic construction of OFE from time capsule signature [12], based on their observation on the similarity between the two primitives. The resulting protocol is secure in the multi-user setting and certified-key model without random oracles. Huang *et al.* [20] further strengthened Dodis *et al.*'s result by relaxing the restriction on using a public key. They demonstrated that there is a gap between the security of OFE in chosen-key model [27] (in which an adversary can use any public key) and that in registered-key model. A generic construction using a standard signature and a two-user ring signature was also proposed and proven secure in the multi-user setting and chosen-key model.

In traditional OFE, Alice's partial signature is generally self-authenticating and indicates her commitment to some message already. This may allow Bob to take advantage of it. Garay *et al.* [13] and Huang *et al.* [19] addressed this problem and proposed notions of *abuse-free* OFE and *ambiguous* OFE, respectively. In both notions, Alice and Bob should be able to produce indistinguishable partial signatures so that given a valid partial signature from Alice, Bob cannot transfer the conviction to others. In this paper we universally call them as AOFE. Garay *et al.* constructed an efficient AOFE from a type of signatures called private contract signatures (PCS). Their PCS scheme is built from designated-verifier signature [23], and is secure in the registered-key model with random oracles. Huang *et al.* [19] proposed another efficient construction of AOFE using Groth-Sahai non-interactive proofs [14]. The scheme is secure based on Strong Diffie-Hellman assumption [7] and Decision Linear assumption [8] in the chosen-key model without random oracles. However, the scheme suffers from long signatures, which consist of more than 40 group elements.

Huang *et al.* [15, 16] proposed a new approach to constructing *interactive* AOFE, in which the signer interacts with the verifier to produce the partial signature. Their construction applies to a specific class of designated confirmer signature (DCS) [9] schemes, in which anyone is able to sample confirmer signatures from the signer's signature space efficiently, e.g. in polynomial time. However, not many DCS schemes enjoy this property, and thus limiting the application of Huang *et al.*'s construction. The authors improved the result by proposing another construction of AOFE from standard DCS [18]. They also proposed an efficient DCS construction, which follows the sign-then-encrypt paradigm. By applying their construction, they obtained an AOFE protocol which has short partial signature and the shortest full signature, and is secure based on SDH and DLIN assumptions without random oracles.

Huang *et al.* also introduced another variant of AOFE, called *group-oriented optimistic fair exchange* (GOFE) [17]. In GOFE, two users exchange signatures on behalf of their respective groups in a fair and anonymous manner so that either each group receives the other group's signature or none of them does, and in the meanwhile the users' identities are kept secret to others except their respective group managers.

Wang *et al.* proposed the notion of *perfect ambiguous optimistic fair exchange* (PAOFE) [30], in which only the intended verifier is able to tell which parties are involved in the exchange. They proposed a generic PAOFE construction by combining an AOFE protocol and a public key encryption scheme with *key privacy* (no one is able to tell whom a ciphertext is intended for). However, no concrete implementation of PAOFE is provided in [30].

In terms of the arbitrator not learning the exchanged material even in case of a dispute, there are also some other works in the non-signature exchange fields. For example, Belenkiy *et al.* [6] and Küpçü *et al.* [25] studied the privacy in optimistic fair exchange of files, where the arbitrator could not learn the full files. Avoine *et al.* [4] proposed to distribute the arbitrator so that no single arbitrator may learn the full signature. Similar idea has been used in [26] in the exchange of files.

3   Privacy-Preserving OFE

3.1   Definition

A Privacy-Preserving Optimistic Fair Exchange protocol (P²OFE) 'blinds' the arbitrator so that the arbitrator is unable to recover a full signature. Similar to PAOFE, the resolution in the definition of P²OFE below is a protocol rather than an algorithm in a conventional (A)OFE.

Definition 1. *A Privacy-Preserving Optimistic Fair Exchange protocol (P²OFE) involves the users (signers and verifiers) and the arbitrator, and consists of the following probabilistic polynomial-time (p.p.t. for short) algorithms and protocols:*

PMG. *It takes 1^k as input where k is the security parameter and outputs the system parameter* PM.

Akg. *It takes as input* PM *and outputs a key pair for the arbitrator. We denote it by* $(\mathsf{Apk}, \mathsf{Ask}) \leftarrow \mathsf{Akg}(\mathsf{PM})$.

UKg. *It takes* PM *(and optionally* Apk*) as input and outputs a user key pair. We denote it by* $(\mathsf{Pk}, \mathsf{Sk}) \leftarrow \mathsf{Ukg}(\mathsf{PM}, \mathsf{Apk})$.

PSig. *This is the partial signature generation algorithm. It takes as input a message M, the signer's secret key Sk_i, the signer's public key Pk_i, the verifier's public key Pk_j and the arbitrator's public key Apk, and outputs a partial signature σ. We denote it by $\sigma \leftarrow \mathsf{PSig}(M, \mathrm{Sk}_i, \mathrm{Pk}_i, \mathrm{Pk}_j, \mathrm{Apk})$.*

PVer. *This is for verifying a partial signature. It can be either an algorithm or a protocol, depending on whether the verification requires the interaction between the signer U_i and the verifier U_j. If the verification is non-interactive, the algorithm takes as input $(M, \sigma, \mathrm{Pk}_i, \mathrm{Pk}_j, \mathrm{Apk}, \mathrm{Sk}_j)$ and outputs a bit b. We denote it by $b \leftarrow \mathsf{PVer}(M, \sigma, \mathrm{Pk}_i, \mathrm{Pk}_j, \mathrm{Apk}, \mathrm{Sk}_j)$. In case the verification is an interactive protocol, the common input consists of $(M, \sigma, \mathrm{Pk}_i, \mathrm{Pk}_j, \mathrm{Apk})$. The signer (acting as the prover) has private input Sk_i and the randomness r used in signature generation, while the verifier has private input Sk_j. We denote a run of the protocol by*

$$b \leftarrow \mathsf{PVer}_{\langle \mathsf{U}_i(\mathrm{Sk}_i, r), \mathsf{U}_j(\mathrm{Sk}_j) \rangle}(M, \sigma, \mathrm{Pk}_i, \mathrm{Pk}_j, \mathrm{Apk}),$$

where b is the decision bit of U_j, which is 1 for acceptance and 0 for rejection.

Sig. *This is the full signature generation algorithm. It takes as input $(M, \mathrm{Sk}_i, \mathrm{Pk}_i, \mathrm{Pk}_j, \mathrm{Apk})$ and outputs a full signature ζ. We denote it by $\zeta \leftarrow \mathsf{Sig}(M, \mathrm{Sk}_i, \mathrm{Pk}_i, \mathrm{Pk}_j, \mathrm{Apk})$.*

Ver. *This is for verifying a full signature. It takes as input $(M, \zeta, \mathrm{Pk}_i, \mathrm{Pk}_j, \mathrm{Apk})$ and outputs a bit b which is 1 if ζ is a valid full signature of Pk_i and 0 otherwise. We denote it by $b \leftarrow \mathsf{Ver}(M, \zeta, \mathrm{Pk}_i, \mathrm{Pk}_j, \mathrm{Apk})$.*

Res. *This is a protocol between verifier U_j and arbitrator A for converting a partial signature to a full one. It consists of two algorithms, Res^A and Res^V. Res^A is run by the arbitrator for resolving a partial signature. It takes as input $(M, \mathrm{Ask}, \sigma, \mathrm{Pk}_i, \mathrm{Pk}_j)$, and outputs an intermediate signature θ or $\perp$ indicating the failure of resolution. Res^V is run by the intended verifier for extracting the full signature ζ from an intermediate signature θ. It takes as input $(M, \mathrm{Sk}_j, \theta, \mathrm{Pk}_i, \mathrm{Pk}_j, \mathrm{Apk})$ and outputs a full signature ζ. We denote the two algorithms by $\theta \leftarrow \mathsf{Res}^A(M, \mathrm{Ask}, \sigma, \mathrm{Pk}_i, \mathrm{Pk}_j)$ and $\zeta \leftarrow \mathsf{Res}^V(M, \mathrm{Sk}_j, \theta, \mathrm{Pk}_i, \mathrm{Pk}_j, \mathrm{Apk})$.*

On the Resolution Protocol: To resolve a partial signature σ, V sends it to the arbitrator, which runs Res^A to convert it into an intermediate value θ and returns to V. The verifier then runs Res^V to recover the full signature ζ from θ. In this way the arbitrator does not learn the final output of the resolution. Furthermore, as in the definition of *perfect ambiguity* (Def. 3), we require that the arbitrator does not know whether the submitted partial signature contains a valid full signature on M of the signer. In Sec. 6 we explain in more details how the resolution of our proposed P²OFE protocol works in practice.

Remark. We stress that in P²OFE, giving a message/contract M itself to the arbitrator in clear does not harm the signer, since guaranteed by the perfect ambiguity, the arbitrator cannot confirm or convince others that the signer has signed M.

3.2 Security Models

We now study the security properties that a P²OFE protocol should satisfy. First of all, the correctness of P²OFE can be naturally defined, and we omit it here. A secure P²OFE protocol should satisfy the following properties: *resolution ambiguity, signer ambiguity, perfect ambiguity, security against signers* and *security against the arbitrator*. Below we introduce them individually, where for simplicity we omit the generation of system parameters PM. All the security properties of P²OFE are defined in the *certified-key* model [5, 18], in which an adversary can query an oracle O_{KR} which takes as input a key pair (Pk, Sk) and outputs 1 if it is in the range of algorithm Ukg and 0 otherwise. For simplicity we omit O_{KR} in the following experiments.

Resolution Ambiguity: The property states that full signatures output by the signer should be computationally indistinguishable from those output by the verifier at the end of the resolution protocol. Let

$$\Delta_0 \overset{\text{def}}{=} \{\zeta \leftarrow \text{Sig}(M, Sk_i, Pk_i, Pk_j, Apk)\}, \text{ and}$$

$$\Delta_1 \overset{\text{def}}{=} \{\zeta \leftarrow \text{Res}^V(M, Sk_j, \theta, Pk_i, Pk_j, Apk)\},$$

where $\theta \leftarrow \text{Res}^A(Ask, \sigma, Pk_i, Pk_j)$ and $\sigma \leftarrow \text{PSig}(M, Sk_i, Pk_i, Pk_j, Apk)$. A protocol is resolution ambiguous if Δ_0 and Δ_1 are computationally indistinguishable.

Signer Ambiguity: Before giving the definition of signer ambiguity, we describe a new p.p.t. algorithm FPSig that is run by the verifier to simulate the signer's partial signature. The algorithm is similar with PSig. It takes as input $(M, Sk_j, Pk_i, Pk_j, Apk)$ and outputs a partial signature valid under Pk_i, Pk_j and Apk. We require that there exists an algorithm FPSig such that for any p.p.t. adversary $\mathcal{A}$, which models a dishonest signer, succeeds with at most negligible advantage in the following experiment $\mathbf{Exp}_{sa}$:

$$(Apk, Ask) \leftarrow Akg(PM)$$
$$(Pk_\gamma, Sk_\gamma) \leftarrow Ukg(PM, Apk), \ \forall \gamma \in \{0, 1\}$$
$$(M^*, \Upsilon) \leftarrow \mathcal{A}^{O_{\text{Res}^A}}(\{(Pk_\gamma, Sk_\gamma)\}_{\gamma=0}^1, Apk)$$
$$b \leftarrow \{0, 1\}$$
$$\sigma^* \leftarrow \begin{cases} \text{PSig}(M^*, Sk_0, Pk_0, Pk_1, Apk) & \text{if } b = 0 \\ \text{FPSig}(M^*, Sk_1, Pk_0, Pk_1, Apk) & \text{if } b = 1 \end{cases}$$
$$b' \leftarrow \mathcal{A}^{O_{\text{Res}^A}}(\Upsilon, \sigma^*)$$
$$\text{Succ. of } \mathcal{A} := [b' = b \wedge (M^*, \sigma^*, Pk_0, Pk_1) \notin \mathcal{Q}(\mathcal{A}, O_{\text{Res}^A})$$
$$\wedge (M^*, \sigma^*, Pk_1, Pk_0) \notin \mathcal{Q}(\mathcal{A}, O_{\text{Res}^A})],$$

where

- O_{Res^A} takes as input (M, σ, Pk_i, Pk_j) and outputs the corresponding intermediate signature θ or $\bot$ indicating the failure of conversion; and

  - $\mathcal{Q}(\mathcal{A}, O_{\mathsf{Res}^A})$ is the set of queries that $\mathcal{A}$ submitted to oracle O_{Res^A}.

The advantage of $\mathcal{A}$ in the experiment is defined as $\mathrm{Adv}_{\mathsf{sa}}^{\mathcal{A}}(1^k) := |\Pr[Succ_{\mathsf{sa}}] - 1/2|$, where $Succ_{\mathsf{sa}}$ denotes the event that $\mathcal{A}$ succeeds in the experiment $\mathbf{Exp}_{\mathsf{sa}}$.

Definition 2 (Signer Ambiguity). *A P^{2}OFE protocol is* signer ambiguous *if there is no p.p.t. $\mathcal{A}$, such that $\mathrm{Adv}_{\mathsf{sa}}^{\mathcal{A}}(1^k)$ is non-negligible in the security parameter k.*

Perfect Ambiguity: It basically says that given a partial signature, even the arbitrator cannot assert which users are involved in the signature exchange. Technically, we require that the distinguisher (which could be the arbitrator) is unable to tell whether the given signature was generated honestly by signer A w.r.t. the verifier B, or randomly selected from the signature space. We need a p.p.t. algorithm Sim that is run by the public to simulate signatures of A and B. The algorithm takes as input $(\mathsf{Apk}, \mathsf{Pk}_i, \mathsf{Pk}_j)$ and outputs a simulated partial signature of the signer U_i w.r.t. the verifier U_j. Formally, we require that there exists an algorithm Sim such that for any p.p.t. adversary $\mathcal{A}$, it succeeds in the following experiment $\mathbf{Exp}_{\mathsf{pa}}$ with only negligible advantage:

$$(\mathsf{Apk}, \mathsf{Ask}) \leftarrow \mathsf{Akg}(\mathsf{PM})$$
$$(\mathsf{Pk}_\gamma, \mathsf{Sk}_\gamma) \leftarrow \mathsf{Ukg}(\mathsf{PM}, \mathsf{Apk}), \ \forall \gamma \in \{0,1\}$$
$$(M^*, \varUpsilon) \leftarrow \mathcal{A}^{O_{\mathsf{PSig}^V}, O_{\mathsf{FPSig}}, O_{\mathsf{Res}^V}}(\mathsf{Pk}_0, \mathsf{Sk}_0, \mathsf{Pk}_1, \mathsf{Apk}, \mathsf{Ask})$$
$$b \leftarrow \{0,1\}$$
$$\sigma^* \leftarrow \begin{cases} \mathsf{PSig}(M^*, \mathsf{Sk}_0, \mathsf{Pk}_0, \mathsf{Pk}_1, \mathsf{Apk}), & \text{if } b = 0 \\ \mathsf{Sim}(\mathsf{Apk}, \mathsf{Pk}_0, \mathsf{Pk}_1) & , \text{if } b = 1 \end{cases}$$
$$b' \leftarrow \mathcal{A}^{O_{\mathsf{PSig}^V}, O_{\mathsf{FPSig}}, O_{\mathsf{Res}^V}}(\varUpsilon, \sigma^*)$$
$$\theta^* \leftarrow \mathsf{Res}^A(M^*, \mathsf{Ask}, \sigma^*, \mathsf{Pk}_0, \mathsf{Pk}_1)$$
$$\text{Succ. of } \mathcal{A} := [b' = b \land (M^*, \theta^*, \mathsf{Pk}_0) \notin \mathcal{Q}(\mathcal{A}, O_{\mathsf{Res}^V})],$$

where

  - O_{PSig^V} takes as input (M, Pk'), and outputs a partial signature $\sigma \leftarrow \mathsf{PSig}(M, \mathsf{Sk}_1, \mathsf{Pk}_1, \mathsf{Pk}', \mathsf{Apk})$;
  - O_{FPSig} takes as input (M, Pk'), and outputs a simulated partial signature, e.g. $\sigma \leftarrow \mathsf{FPSig}(M, \mathsf{Sk}_1, \mathsf{Pk}', \mathsf{Pk}_1, \mathsf{Apk})$;
  - O_{Res^V} takes as input $(M, \theta, \mathsf{Pk}')$, and outputs the full signature $\zeta \leftarrow \mathsf{Res}^V(M, \mathsf{Sk}_1, \theta, \mathsf{Pk}', \mathsf{Pk}_1, \mathsf{Apk})$; and
  - $\mathcal{Q}(\mathcal{A}, O_{\mathsf{Res}^V})$ is the set of queries that $\mathcal{A}$ submitted to oracle O_{Res^V}.

The advantage of $\mathcal{A}$ in the experiment is defined as $\mathrm{Adv}_{\mathsf{pa}}^{\mathcal{A}}(1^k) := |\Pr[Succ_{\mathsf{pa}}] - 1/2|$, where $Succ_{\mathsf{pa}}$ denotes the event that $\mathcal{A}$ succeeds in the experiment $\mathbf{Exp}_{\mathsf{pa}}$.

Definition 3 (Perfect Ambiguity). *A P^{2}OFE protocol is* perfect ambiguous *if there is no p.p.t. adversary $\mathcal{A}$ such that $\mathrm{Adv}_{\mathsf{pa}}^{\mathcal{A}}(1^k)$ is non-negligible in the security parameter k.*

Remark. Notice that in the experiment above we do not give the adversary access to an oracle which returns full signatures of the verifier (with public key Pk_1). The oracle can be implemented by composing O_{PSig^V} and O_{Res^V} as well as the knowledge of Ask.

The simulation algorithm Sim does not take any secret input and can be run by anyone to simulate a partial signature that looks indistinguishable from a real one. Guaranteed by the perfect ambiguity, without the knowledge of the intended verfier's secret key, no one is able to determine whether a given partial signature does come from the signer. Due to the public simulatability, even the arbitrator cannot assert and convince others that the signer indeed signed the message M. In other words, the signer could deny the generation of a partial signature.

Security against Signers: To protect the verifier from being cheated, the signer should be unable to produce a partial signature such that it can pass the partial verification, but the resolution fails to output a valid full signature. Formally, we consider the following experiment $\mathbf{Exp}_{\mathsf{sas}}$:

$$(\mathsf{Apk}, \mathsf{Ask}) \leftarrow \mathsf{Akg}(\mathsf{PM})$$
$$(\mathsf{Pk}_1, \mathsf{Sk}_1) \leftarrow \mathsf{Ukg}(\mathsf{PM}, \mathsf{Apk})$$
$$(M^*, \mathsf{Pk}_0, \sigma^*) \leftarrow \mathcal{A}^{O_{\mathsf{FPSig}}, O_{\mathsf{Res}}}(\mathsf{Pk}_1, \mathsf{Apk})$$
$$\theta^* \leftarrow \mathsf{Res}^A(M^*, \mathsf{Ask}, \sigma^*, \mathsf{Pk}_0, \mathsf{Pk}_1)$$
$$\zeta^* \leftarrow \mathsf{Res}^V(M^*, \mathsf{Sk}_1, \theta^*, \mathsf{Pk}_0, \mathsf{Pk}_1, \mathsf{Apk})$$
$$\text{Succ. of } \mathcal{A} := [\mathsf{PVer}(M^*, \sigma^*, \mathsf{Pk}_0, \mathsf{Pk}_1, \mathsf{Apk}, \mathsf{Sk}_1) = 1$$
$$\wedge \ \mathsf{Ver}(M^*, \zeta^*, \mathsf{Pk}_0, \mathsf{Pk}_1, \mathsf{Apk}) = 0$$
$$\wedge \ (M^*, \mathsf{Pk}_0) \notin \mathcal{Q}(\mathcal{A}, O_{\mathsf{FPSig}})],$$

where

- $O_{\mathsf{Res}} = \langle O_{\mathsf{Res}^A}, O_{\mathsf{Res}^V} \rangle$ takes as $(M, \sigma, \mathsf{Pk}')$, and outputs the corresponding full signature ζ (that is valid w.r.t. the signer's public key Pk', the verifier's public key Pk_1 and Apk) or $\perp$; and
- $\mathcal{Q}(\mathcal{A}, O_{\mathsf{FPSig}})$ is the set of queries that $\mathcal{A}$ submitted to the oracle O_{FPSig}.

The advantage of $\mathcal{A}$ in the experiment is defined as $\mathsf{Adv}_{\mathsf{sas}}^{\mathcal{A}}(1^k) := \Pr[Succ_{\mathsf{sas}}]$, where $Succ_{\mathsf{sas}}$ denotes the event that $\mathcal{A}$ succeeds in the experiment $\mathbf{Exp}_{\mathsf{sas}}$.

Definition 4 (Security against Signers). *A P²OFE protocol is secure against signers if there is no p.p.t. adversary $\mathcal{A}$ such that $\mathsf{Adv}_{\mathsf{pa}}^{\mathcal{A}}(1^k)$ is non-negligible in the security parameter k.*

Security against the Arbitrator: To be fair for the signer, no one but the signer, should be able to produce valid signatures on behalf of the signer. Formally, we consider the following experiment $\mathbf{Exp}_{\mathsf{saa}}$:

$$(\mathsf{Apk}, \mathsf{Ask}) \leftarrow \mathsf{Akg}(\mathsf{PM})$$

$$(\mathsf{Pk}_0, \mathsf{Sk}_0) \leftarrow \mathsf{Ukg}(\mathsf{PM}, \mathsf{Apk})$$

$$(M^*, \mathsf{Pk}_1, \zeta^*) \leftarrow \mathcal{A}^{O_{\mathsf{PSig}}}(\mathsf{Pk}_0, \mathsf{Apk}, \mathsf{Ask})$$

$$\text{Succ. of } \mathcal{A} := [\mathsf{Ver}(M^*, \zeta^*, \mathsf{Pk}_0, \mathsf{Pk}_1, \mathsf{Apk}) = 1 \land (M^*, \mathsf{Pk}_1) \notin \mathcal{Q}(\mathcal{A}, O_{\mathsf{PSig}})],$$

where

- O_{PSig} takes as input a message M and a public key Pk' and outputs $\sigma \leftarrow \mathsf{PSig}(M, \mathsf{Sk}_0, \mathsf{Pk}_0, \mathsf{Pk}', \mathsf{Apk})$; and
- $\mathcal{Q}(\mathcal{A}, O_{\mathsf{PSig}})$ is the set of queries that $\mathcal{A}$ submitted to O_{PSig}.

The advantage of $\mathcal{A}$ in the experiment is defined as $\mathbf{Adv}_{\mathsf{saa}}^{\mathcal{A}}(1^k) := \Pr[Succ_{\mathsf{saa}}]$, where $Succ_{\mathsf{saa}}$ denotes the event that $\mathcal{A}$ succeeds in $\mathbf{Exp}_{\mathsf{saa}}$.

Definition 5 (Security against the Arbitrator). *A* P^{2}OFE *protocol is secure against the arbitrator if there is no p.p.t. adversary $\mathcal{A}$ such that* $\mathbf{Adv}_{\mathsf{saa}}^{\mathcal{A}}(1^k)$ *is non-negligible in the security parameter k.*

Remark 1. Security against the arbitrator assumes the adversary (including the arbitrator) is malicious and is allowed to try all kinds of ways to forge the signer's signature. This is for protecting the signer to the maximum extent. However, the arbitrator is still assumed to function normally as prescribed in practice, i.e. to honestly resolve signatures according to the users' needs.

3.3   Differences from Other Variants of OFE

In this part we summarize the differences between P^{2}OFE and (other variants of) OFE. Table 1 shows the comparison. In the table, "Ambiguity of σ Before Resolution" (resp. "Ambiguity of σ After Resolution") refers to that given only a partial signature σ, whether anyone (including the arbitrator) could convince others before (resp. after) the resolution takes place that the signer has signed the message. We denote by "$\sqrt{2}$" that σ is ambiguous in the sense that either the signer or the verifier could generate σ, and by "$\sqrt{\infty}$" that σ is ambiguous in the sense that everyone could be the source of σ.

Table 1. Comparison with other variants of OFE

Variants	Ambiguity of σ Before Resolution	Ambiguity of σ After Resolution
OFE	$\times$	$\times$
AOFE	$\sqrt{2}$	$\times$
PAOFE	$\sqrt{\infty}$	$\times$
P^{2}OFE	$\sqrt{\infty}$	$\sqrt{\infty}$

The partial signature in traditional OFE [3, 10, 20] is publicly verifiable, and everyone is able to tell from it the fact that the signer signed the message. In the enhanced variant AOFE [15, 16, 18, 19], although the partial signature is ambiguous, however, anyone is still able to confirm that the given partial signature was generated by either the signer or the verifier. In PAOFE [30], the ambiguity is further improved. No one but the verifier is able to tell from the given partial signature who the real signer is. However, no matter the partial signature is ambiguous or not, the arbitrator in these variants has a full copy of the signer's full signature after the resolution.

In our new notion of OFE, given only the partial signature, neither the arbitrator nor the verifier is able to find out by itself who the signer is. Thus, the arbitrator could not convince others that the signer did sign the message. Furthermore, this also holds even after the resolution in P²OFE, as guaranteed by the perfect ambiguity of P²OFE.

4 Mathematical Assumptions

The P²OFE protocol is bilinear pairing based, and its security is based on the Decision Linear and Strong Diffie-Hellman assumptions, which are reviewed as follows:

Bilinear Pairing. Let $\mathbb{G}, \mathbb{G}_T$ be two cyclic groups of prime order p, and g be a random generator of $\mathbb{G}$. The map $\hat{e} : \mathbb{G} \times \mathbb{G} \to \mathbb{G}_T$ is a bilinear pairing if (1) Bilinear: $\forall u, v \in \mathbb{Z}_p$, $\hat{e}(g^u, g^v) = \hat{e}(g, g)^{uv}$; (2) Non-degenerate: $\hat{e}(g, g) \neq 1_T$, where 1_T is the identity element of group $\mathbb{G}_T$; and (3) Computable: there exists a polynomial-time algorithm for computing $\hat{e}(U, V)$ for any $U, V \in \mathbb{G}$.

Definition 6 (Decision Linear Assumption [8]). *Let $\mathbb{G}, \mathbb{G}_T$ be cyclic groups of prime order p, and g be a random generator of $\mathbb{G}$. Let $\hat{e} : \mathbb{G} \times \mathbb{G} \to \mathbb{G}_T$ be a bilinear pairing. The Decision Linear (DLIN) assumption in the context of $(\mathbb{G}, \mathbb{G}_T, \hat{e}, p, g)$ says that there is no p.p.t. algorithm $\mathcal{A}$ such that for all $F, G \leftarrow \mathbb{G}$, $s, t, z \leftarrow \mathbb{Z}_p$,*

$$\left| \Pr[\mathcal{A}(F, G, F^s, G^t, g^{s+t}) = 1] - \Pr[\mathcal{A}(F, G, F^s, G^t, g^z) = 1] \right| \leq \mathrm{negl}(k),$$

where $\mathrm{negl}(\cdot)$ is a negligible function in the security parameter k, and the probabilities are taken over the choices of $F, G \in \mathbb{G}$, $s, t, z \in \mathbb{Z}_p$ and the random bits consumed by $\mathcal{A}$.

Definition 7 (Strong Diffie-Hellman Assumption [7]). *Let $\mathbb{G}$ be a cyclic group of prime order p, and g be a random generator of it. The ℓ-Strong Diffie-Hellman (ℓ-SDH) assumption says that there is no p.p.t. algorithm $\mathcal{A}$ such that for all $x \leftarrow \mathbb{Z}_p$,*

$$\Pr\left[Z = g^{\frac{1}{x+c}} \mid (Z, c) \leftarrow \mathcal{A}(g, g^x, g^{x^2}, \cdots, g^{x^\ell}) \right] \leq \mathrm{negl}(k),$$

where $c \in \mathbb{Z}_p$, and the probability is taken over the choice of $x \in \mathbb{Z}_p$ and the random bits consumed by $\mathcal{A}$.

5 Our Protocol

In this section we present a concrete construction of P^2OFE. Before presenting the concrete protocol, we give a high level description of how our protocol works.

5.1 High Level Idea

Briefly speaking, our protocol makes use of Boneh-Boyen short signature scheme (BB signature, for short) [7] and the tag-based public key encryption scheme [24]. It essentially follows the sign-then-encrypt paradigm. To generate a full signature ζ on message M, the signer simply runs the corresponding algorithm of BB signature scheme. To partially sign M, the signer first generates a BB signature $\zeta = (S, r)$ and encrypts ζ w.r.t. the arbitrator's public key using the tag-based encryption scheme while keeping r public. Let the ciphertext be e. Then the signer encrypts (part of) e under the intended verifier's public key again and obtains a new ciphertext c. The two encryptions are twisted together so that the arbitrator and the intended verifier can perform their own decryption, but cannot recover the signer's full signature alone. To prevent the adversary from making use of the resolution oracle to break the security of the protocol, we use a strong one-time signature scheme to sign the whole ciphertext and use the fresh one-time verification key as the tag in the tag-based encryption. To convince the verifier the validity of σ, the signer needs carry out a proof with the verifier.

In order to resolve a partial signature σ to a full one, the verifier sends σ to the arbitrator. The latter uses its secret key to do the first level decryption and returns the resulting value, which is a ciphertext of ζ. The verifier then extracts the full signature by performing another decryption using its own secret key.

5.2 The Protocol

Let $\mathbb{G}, \mathbb{G}_T$ be two cyclic multiplicative groups of prime order p, g a random generator of $\mathbb{G}$, and $\hat{e} : \mathbb{G} \times \mathbb{G} \to \mathbb{G}_T$ be a bilinear pairing. Let OTS be a strong one-time signature scheme and $\mathcal{VK}$ be the space of one-time verification keys. Let $H : \mathbb{G}^5 \times \mathcal{VK} \to \mathbb{Z}_p$ be a collision-resistant hash function. Our P^2OFE protocol works as follows. In the protocol we assume the message space is $\mathbb{Z}_p$, which can be easily extended to $\{0,1\}^*$ by applying a collision-resistant hash function onto the message.

Akg. The arbitrator chooses at random $\xi_1, \xi_2 \leftarrow \mathbb{Z}_p$, $K, L \in \mathbb{G}$, and computes $F = g^{1/\xi_1}$, $G = g^{1/\xi_2}$. It sets $\mathtt{Apk} = (F, G, K, L)$ and $\mathtt{Ask} = (\xi_1, \xi_2)$.

UKg. The user U_i chooses at random $x_i, y_i, \xi_{i1}, \xi_{i2} \in \mathbb{Z}_p$ and computes $X_i = g^{x_i}$, $Y_i = g^{y_i}$, $F_i = g^{1/\xi_{i1}}$ and $G_i = g^{1/\xi_{i2}}$. The user sets $\mathtt{Pk}_i = (X_i, Y_i, F_i, G_i, K_i, L_i)$ and $\mathtt{Sk}_i = (x_i, y_i, \xi_{i1}, \xi_{i2})$.

PSig. Given a message M, the signer U_i generates its partial signature for the verifier U_j as follows.

1. Select at random $r, s, t, s', t' \in \mathbb{Z}_p$.
2. Run $\mathsf{OTS.Kg}(1^k)$ to generate a one-time key pair $(\mathsf{otvk}, \mathsf{otsk})$.

3. Compute

$$c_1 = F_j^{s'}, \quad c_2 = G_j^{t'}, \quad S = g^{1/(x_i+M+y_i \cdot r)},$$

$$e_1 = F^s, \quad e_2 = G^t, \quad e_3 = Sg^{s+t}g^{s'+t'}, \quad \alpha = \mathtt{H}(c_1, c_2, e_1, e_2, e_3, \mathsf{otvk}),$$

$$c_4 = (g^\alpha K_j)^{s'}, \quad c_5 = (g^\alpha L_j)^{t'}, \quad e_4 = (g^\alpha K)^s, \quad e_5 = (g^\alpha L)^t,$$

$$\delta = \mathsf{OTS.Sig}(\mathsf{otsk}, M\|\mathsf{Pk}_i\|\mathsf{Pk}_j\|c\|e\|r),$$

where $e = (e_1, e_2, e_3, e_4, e_5)$ and $c = (c_1, c_2, c_4, c_5)$.
If $x_i + M + y_i r = 0 \bmod p$, the signer chooses another r and repeats the process. Its partial signature on M is $\sigma = (c, e, r, \mathsf{otvk}, \delta)$.

PVer. Given a partial signature $\sigma = (c, e, r, \mathsf{otvk}, \delta)$, U_i and U_j check the well-formedness of the signature locally, and do nothing if either of the following does not hold:

$$\hat{e}(e_4, F) = \hat{e}(e_1, g^\alpha K), \tag{1}$$

$$\hat{e}(e_5, G) = \hat{e}(e_2, g^\alpha L), \tag{2}$$

$$\hat{e}(c_4, F_j) = \hat{e}(c_1, g^\alpha K_j), \tag{3}$$

$$\hat{e}(c_5, G_j) = \hat{e}(c_2, g^\alpha L_j), \tag{4}$$

$$\mathsf{OTS.Sig}(M\|\mathsf{Pk}_i\|\mathsf{Pk}_j\|c\|e\|r, \mathsf{otvk}, \delta) = 1, \tag{5}$$

where $\alpha = \mathtt{H}(c_1, c_2, e_1, e_2, e_3, \mathsf{otvk})$. Then they carry out the following witness-indistinguishable proof to show that σ contains a valid BB signature of either U_i or U_j:

$$\Pi \stackrel{\text{def}}{=} PK\Big\{(s, t, s', t') : c_1 = F_j^{s'} \wedge c_2 = G_j^{t'} \wedge e_1 = F^s \wedge e_2 = G^t$$

$$\wedge \left(\hat{e}(e_3 \cdot g^{-s-t-s'-t'}, X_i g^M Y_i^r) = \hat{e}(g, g)\right)$$

$$\vee \hat{e}(e_3 \cdot g^{-s-t-s'-t'}, X_j g^M Y_j^r) = \hat{e}(g, g))\Big\}. \tag{6}$$

Sig. To generate a full signature on message M for the verifier U_j, the signer U_i randomly selects $r \in \mathbb{Z}_p$, and computes

$$S = g^{1/(x_i+M+y_i \cdot r)}.$$

Again, in case that $x_i + M + y_i r = 0 \bmod p$, it chooses another r and repeats the computation. Its full signature on M is $\zeta = (S, r)$.

Ver. Given (M, ζ) where $\zeta = (S, r)$, the verifier checks if

$$\hat{e}(S, X_i g^M Y_i^r) = \hat{e}(g, g). \tag{7}$$

It outputs 1 if the equation holds, and 0 otherwise.

Res^A. Given $(M, \sigma, \mathsf{Pk}_i, \mathsf{Pk}_j)$ where $\sigma = (c, e, r, \mathsf{otvk}, \delta)$, the arbitrator returns $\perp$ if either Eq. (1), (2), (3), (4) or (5) fails to hold; otherwise, it computes

$$c_3 = e_3 e_1^{-\xi_1} e_2^{-\xi_2}, \tag{8}$$

and returns $\theta = (c_1, c_2, c_3, c_4, c_5, e_3, r, \mathsf{otvk})$.

Res^V. Given $(M, \theta, \mathsf{Pk}_i, \mathsf{Pk}_j)$, where $\theta = (c_1, c_2, c_3, c_4, c_5, e_3, r, \mathsf{otvk})$, the verifier outputs $\bot$ if either Eq. (3) or (4) fails to hold; otherwise, it computes

$$S = c_3 c_1^{-\xi_{j1}} c_2^{-\xi_{j2}}. \tag{9}$$

It outputs $\zeta = (S, r)$ if Eq. (7) holds, and $\bot$ otherwise.

5.3 Security

Below we show the security of our $\mathsf{P^2OFE}$ protocol based on the assumptions described in Sec. 4.

Theorem 1. *Our* $\mathsf{P^2OFE}$ *protocol is resolution ambiguous.*

Proof. Notice that the full signature output by the signer and that output by the resolution protocol are of the form $\zeta = (S, r)$, which is a Boneh-Boyen signature on the message M. Therefore, our $\mathsf{P^2OFE}$ protocol is perfectly resolution ambiguous. □

Theorem 2. *Our* $\mathsf{P^2OFE}$ *protocol is signer ambiguous if DLIN assumption holds,* H *is collision-resistant and* OTS *is a strong one-time signature scheme.*

Theorem 3. *Our* $\mathsf{P^2OFE}$ *protocol is perfect ambiguous, if DLIN assumption holds,* H *is collision resistant and* OTS *is a strong one-time signature scheme.*

Theorem 4. *Our* $\mathsf{P^2OFE}$ *protocol is secure against signers, if SDH assumption holds, and* Π *is sound and witness-indistinguishable.*

Theorem 5. *Our* $\mathsf{P^2OFE}$ *protocol is secure against the arbitrator if SDH assumption holds.*

Due to the page limit we defer the proofs to the full version.

6 Resolution in Practice

In this section we describe one of the ways on how $\mathsf{P^2OFE}$ runs in practice. Suppose the electronic contract that Alice and Bob want to secretly sign is M, and their semi-trusted third party is Ted. Recall that the contract M itself does not need to be secret, as anyone can prepare such a contract. Instead, signatures of Alice and Bob should be kept secret from others. Without their signatures, no one can confirm whether they have signed the contract or have really performed such a business deal.

Following the framework of optimistic fair exchange, Alice and Bob exchange their signatures on M. If everything goes well, they will receive the counterpart's full signature. Due to that a party might refuse to continue the run of the exchange protocol, or that the internet connection might become down, there are two cases in which a dispute will occur between the two parties, as below:

1. after sending out the first-move message, which is Alice's partial signature σ_A on M, Alice receives nothing;
2. after sending out the second-move message, which is Bob's full signature ζ_B on M, Bob receives nothing.

Let us focus on the latter case first. In this case, Bob can resort to the arbitrator, Ted, for converting σ_A to the full signature of Alice. Before the conversion, Bob has to show the fulfillment of his obligation. Traditionally, this can be done by sending his full signature ζ_B to the arbitrator, the validity of which can be verified publicly. However, this will let the arbitrator confirm, and even show to others the involvement of Bob as ζ_B shows that Bob indeed signed M. This is undesired in some sensitive applications. To avoid this problem, Bob instead sends his partial signature σ_B on M to Ted, and carries out a *zero-knowledge* (or *designated-verifier* [23]) proof of knowledge to convince Ted that σ_B does encapsulate his full signature on M. If he accepts the proof, Ted runs Res^A on input σ_A (as well as M) to obtain the intermediate value θ_A and sends it to Bob. In the meanwhile, he also runs Res^A on input σ_B to obtain Bob's intermediate value θ_B and sends it to Alice, in order to avoid the case in which Bob tried to cheat at the end of the first move and did not ever send his full signature to Alice. Figure 3 shows how the resolution of P²OFE works in practice, where Π_B is the proof run by B to show the fulfillment of his obligation.

Now let us go back to the former case. If Bob does not try to cheat and simply aborts the protocol, guaranteed by the signer ambiguity, Bob does not learn anything from Alice partial signature, as long as Ted does not collude with Bob. In this case, neither Alice nor Bob obtains their counterpart's (full) signature. However, if Bob tries to cheat and asks Ted for the resolution, according to the aforementioned resolution procedure, Bob still needs to provide his partial signature and a proof to support the validity of his signature.

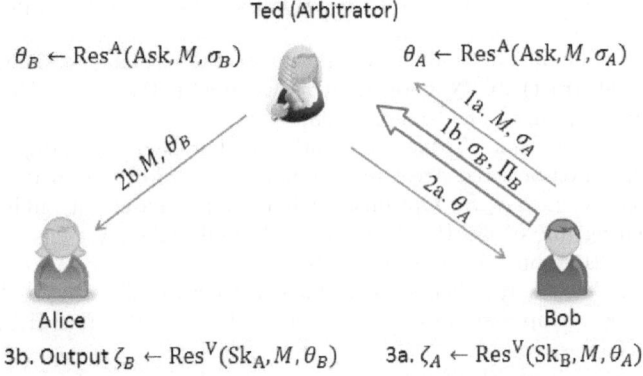

Ted (Arbitrator)

$\theta_B \leftarrow \mathsf{Res}^A(\mathsf{Ask}, M, \sigma_B)$ $\theta_A \leftarrow \mathsf{Res}^A(\mathsf{Ask}, M, \sigma_A)$

2b. M, θ_B 1a. M, σ_A

1b. σ_B, Π_B

2a. θ_A

Alice   Bob

3b. Output $\zeta_B \leftarrow \mathsf{Res}^V(\mathsf{Sk}_A, M, \theta_B)$ 3a. $\zeta_A \leftarrow \mathsf{Res}^V(\mathsf{Sk}_B, M, \theta_A)$

Fig. 3. P²OFE: Resolution in Practice

It should be noticed that the message signed by Alice and that signed by Bob are not required to be the same, depending on the applications. In applications where they need sign different messages, it suffices that Alice (resp. Bob) runs algorithms PSig, Sig on input M_A (resp. M_B) and runs PVer, Ver, Res^V on input M_B (resp. M_A).

7   Conclusion

We introduced the notion P^{2}OFE for achieving the privacy preserving property not just against a semi-trusted honest-but-curious arbitrator, but also against a completely malicious arbitrator. This is the first time in the context of OFE that signer privacy can be ensured even *after* the resolution. We also proposed an efficient concrete construction of P^{2}OFE with each of its full signatures being as simple as a Boneh-Boyen short signature. Based on SDH and DLIN assumptions, we also showed its security under the security model we defined without random oracles. As of practical interest, we further demonstrated how the resolution can actually work in practice.

Acknowledgements. We'd like to thank the anonymous reviewers for their invaluable comments. This work is supported by the National Natural Science Foundation of China (No. 61103232), the Guangdong Natural Science Foundation (No. S2013010011859), the Research Fund for the Doctoral Program of Higher Education of China (No. 20114404120027), and the Foundation for Distinguished Young Talents in Higher Education of Guangdong, China (No. LYM11033). D. S. Wong is supported by a grant from the RGC of the HKSAR, China (Project No. CityU 121512). W. Susilo is supported by ARC Future Fellowship FT0991397.

References

1. Asokan, N., Schunter, M., Waidner, M.: Optimistic protocols for fair exchange. In: ACM Conference on Computer and Communications Security, pp. 7–17. ACM (1997)
2. Asokan, N., Shoup, V., Waidner, M.: Optimistic fair exchange of digital signatures (extended abstract). In: Nyberg, K. (ed.) EUROCRYPT 1998. LNCS, vol. 1403, pp. 591–606. Springer, Heidelberg (1998)
3. Asokan, N., Shoup, V., Waidner, M.: Optimistic fair exchange of digital signatures. IEEE Journal on Selected Areas in Communication 18(4), 593–610 (2000)
4. Avoine, G., Vaudenay, S.: Optimistic fair exchange based on publicly verifiable secret sharing. In: Wang, H., Pieprzyk, J., Varadharajan, V. (eds.) ACISP 2004. LNCS, vol. 3108, pp. 74–85. Springer, Heidelberg (2004)
5. Barak, B., Canetti, R., Nielsen, J.B., Pass, R.: Universally composable protocols with relaxed set-up assumptions. In: FOCS 2004, pp. 186–195. IEEE Computer Society (2004)
6. Belenkiy, M., Chase, M., Erway, C.C., Jannotti, J., Küpçü, A., Lysyanskaya, A., Rachlin, E.: Making p2p accountable without losing privacy. In: WPES, pp. 31–40. ACM (2007)

7. Boneh, D., Boyen, X.: Short signatures without random oracles. In: Cachin, C., Camenisch, J.L. (eds.) EUROCRYPT 2004. LNCS, vol. 3027, pp. 56–73. Springer, Heidelberg (2004)
8. Boneh, D., Boyen, X., Shacham, H.: Short group signatures. In: Franklin, M. (ed.) CRYPTO 2004. LNCS, vol. 3152, pp. 41–55. Springer, Heidelberg (2004)
9. Chaum, D.: Designated confirmer signatures. In: De Santis, A. (ed.) EUROCRYPT 1994. LNCS, vol. 950, pp. 86–91. Springer, Heidelberg (1995)
10. Dodis, Y., Lee, P.J., Yum, D.H.: Optimistic fair exchange in a multi-user setting. In: Okamoto, T., Wang, X. (eds.) PKC 2007. LNCS, vol. 4450, pp. 118–133. Springer, Heidelberg (2007)
11. Dodis, Y., Reyzin, L.: Breaking and repairing optimistic fair exchange from PODC 2003. In: ACM Workshop on Digital Rights Management, DRM 2003, pp. 47–54. ACM (2003)
12. Dodis, Y., Yum, D.H.: Time capsule signature. In: Patrick, A.S., Yung, M. (eds.) FC 2005. LNCS, vol. 3570, pp. 57–71. Springer, Heidelberg (2005)
13. Garay, J.A., Jakobsson, M., MacKenzie, P.: Abuse-free optimistic contract signing. In: Wiener, M. (ed.) CRYPTO 1999. LNCS, vol. 1666, pp. 449–466. Springer, Heidelberg (1999)
14. Groth, J., Sahai, A.: Efficient non-interactive proof systems for bilinear groups. In: Smart, N.P. (ed.) EUROCRYPT 2008. LNCS, vol. 4965, pp. 415–432. Springer, Heidelberg (2008)
15. Huang, Q., Wong, D.S., Susilo, W.: A new construction of designated confirmer signature and its application to optimistic fair exchange - (extended abstract). In: Joye, M., Miyaji, A., Otsuka, A. (eds.) Pairing 2010. LNCS, vol. 6487, pp. 41–61. Springer, Heidelberg (2010)
16. Huang, Q., Wong, D.S., Susilo, W.: Efficient designated confirmer signature and DCS-based ambiguous optimistic fair exchange. IEEE Transactions on Information Forensics and Security 6(4), 1233–1247 (2011)
17. Huang, Q., Wong, D.S., Susilo, W.: Group-oriented fair exchange of signatures. Information Sciences 181(16), 3267–3283 (2011)
18. Huang, Q., Wong, D.S., Susilo, W.: The construction of ambiguous optimistic fair exchange from designated confirmer signature without random oracles. In: Fischlin, M., Buchmann, J., Manulis, M. (eds.) PKC 2012. LNCS, vol. 7293, pp. 120–137. Springer, Heidelberg (2012)
19. Huang, Q., Yang, G., Wong, D.S., Susilo, W.: Ambiguous optimistic fair exchange. In: Pieprzyk, J. (ed.) ASIACRYPT 2008. LNCS, vol. 5350, pp. 74–89. Springer, Heidelberg (2008)
20. Huang, Q., Yang, G., Wong, D.S., Susilo, W.: Efficient optimistic fair exchange secure in the multi-user setting and chosen-key model without random oracles. In: Malkin, T. (ed.) CT-RSA 2008. LNCS, vol. 4964, pp. 106–120. Springer, Heidelberg (2008)
21. Huang, Q., Yang, G., Wong, D.S., Susilo, W.: A new efficient optimistic fair exchange protocol without random oracles. International Journal of Information Security 11(1), 53–63 (2012)
22. Huang, X., Mu, Y., Susilo, W., Wu, W., Zhou, J., Deng, R.H.: Preserving transparency and accountability in optimistic fair exchange of digital signatures. IEEE Transactions on Information Forensics and Security 6(2), 498–512 (2011)
23. Jakobsson, M., Sako, K., Impagliazzo, R.: Designated verifier proofs and their applications. In: Maurer, U.M. (ed.) EUROCRYPT 1996. LNCS, vol. 1070, pp. 143–154. Springer, Heidelberg (1996)

24. Kiltz, E.: Chosen-ciphertext security from tag-based encryption. In: Halevi, S., Rabin, T. (eds.) TCC 2006. LNCS, vol. 3876, pp. 581–600. Springer, Heidelberg (2006)
25. Küpçü, A., Lysyanskaya, A.: Optimistic fair exchange with multiple arbiters. In: Gritzalis, D., Preneel, B., Theoharidou, M. (eds.) ESORICS 2010. LNCS, vol. 6345, pp. 488–507. Springer, Heidelberg (2010)
26. Küpçü, A., Lysyanskaya, A.: Usable optimistic fair exchange. Computer Networks 56(1), 50–63 (2012)
27. Lysyanskaya, A., Micali, S., Reyzin, L., Shacham, H.: Sequential aggregate signatures from trapdoor permutations. In: Cachin, C., Camenisch, J.L. (eds.) EUROCRYPT 2004. LNCS, vol. 3027, pp. 74–90. Springer, Heidelberg (2004)
28. Park, J.M., Chong, E.K., Siegel, H.J.: Constructing fair-exchange protocols for e-commerce via distributed computation of RSA signatures. In: PODC 2003, pp. 172–181. ACM (2003)
29. Wang, G.: An abuse-free fair contract signing protocol based on the RSA signature. IEEE Transactions on Information Forensics and Security 5(1), 158–168 (2010)
30. Wang, Y., Au, M.H., Susilo, W.: Perfect ambiguous optimistic fair exchange. In: Chim, T.W., Yuen, T.H. (eds.) ICICS 2012. LNCS, vol. 7618, pp. 142–153. Springer, Heidelberg (2012)

2-Pass Key Exchange Protocols
from CPA-Secure KEM

Kaoru Kurosawa[1] and Jun Furukawa[2]

[1] Ibaraki University, Japan
kurosawa@mx.ibaraki.ac.jp
[2] NEC Corporation, Japan
j-furukawa@ay.jp.nec.com

Abstract. In this paper, we show three generic constructions of 2-pass key exchange (KE) protocols which satisfy weak perfect forward secrecy (wPFS) under a sole assumption that there exists a CPA-secure KEM. Our first construction is CK-secure, the second one is eCK-secure, and the last one is both CK-secure and eCK-secure.

Keywords: key exchange protocol, KEM, CK-secure, eCK-secure.

1 Introduction

A key exchange (KE) protocol is one of the most fundamental cryptographic primitives that allows two parties to generate a common secret key in a network even when all the communication in the network is controlled by an adversary. Most of the provably secure KE protocols known so far are based on the DDH assumption or the CDH assumption [4,10,3,15,19,16,20].

Boyd et al. [2], on the other hand, showed a generic construction of 1-round (one message per party, sent simultaneously) KE protocols from an ID-based CCA-secure KEM and a pseudorandom function in the Canetti-Krawczyk (CK) model. This construction, however, does not satisfy weak perfect forward secrecy (wPFS) [16]. (They showed another construction which satisfies wPFS under the DDH assumption. It is, however, not generic because it is based on the DDH assumption.)

Fujioka et al. [14] extended the above construction in such a way that wPFS is also satisfied in the CK$^+$ model. Their construction uses a CCA-secure KEM, a CPA-secure KEM and a pseudorandom function as building blocks. Their protocol is 2-pass (one message per party, but sent sequentially).

In this paper, we study this problem one step further. From a view point of security models, we present three generic constructions of 2-pass KE protocols with wPFS such as follows.

- Protocol 2-PASS-CK in the CK-model.
- Protocol 2-PASS-ECK in the eCK-model.
- Protocol 2-PASS-BOTH which is both CK-secure and eCK-secure.

J. Benaloh (Ed.): CT-RSA 2014, LNCS 8366, pp. 385–401, 2014.
© Springer International Publishing Switzerland 2014

We also show that 2-PASS-CK is not eCK-secure, and 2-PASS-ECK is not CK-secure. (Therefore our results make it clear that there exists a clear separation between CK-security and eCK-security.)

From a view point of the assumptions, each of our construction uses only a CPA-secure KEM, a digital signature scheme and a pseudorandom function. Theoretically, digital signature schemes and pseudorandom functions can be constructed from one-way functions. Further a CPA secure KEM implies a one-way function because the key generation algorithm is a one-way function from a random string to a public-key. Therefore our minimum assumption is that there exists a CPA-secure KEM alone.

On the other hand, we cannot construct a CCA-secure KEM from a CPA-secure KEM in the plain model. (A CCA-secure KEM can be constructed from a CPA-secure KEM and a (simulation-sound) non-interactive zero-knowledge (NIZK) proof via the Naor-Yung or Dolev-Dwork-Naor transforms. However, NIZK proofs require a common reference string.) Therefore in the plain model,

- The construction of Fujioka et al. [14] needs a CCA-secure KEM as the minimum assumption.
- Each of our constructions needs only a CPA-secure KEM as the minimum assumption.

To summarize, we show three generic constructions of 2-pass key exchange (KE) protocols which satisfy weak perfect forward secrecy (wPFS) under a sole assumption that there exists a CPA-secure KEM. See Table 1 for the comparison with Fujioka et al. [14]. [1]

Table 1. 2-pass KE protocol with wPFS

	building blocks	minimum assumption	security
Fujioka et al. [14]	CCA-KEM, CPA-KEM, PRF	CCA-KEM	CK^+-secure
Proposed (1)	CPA-KEM, signature, PRF	CPA-KEM	CK-secure
Proposed (2)	CPA-KEM, signature, PRF	CPA-KEM	eCK-secure
Proposed (3)	CPA-KEM, signature, PRF	CPA-KEM	CK-secure and eCK-secure

For our generic constructions to be CK/eCK-secure, we consider to use the twisted PRF trick. The twisted PRF trick is an interesting cryptographic primitive introduced by Fujioka et al. [14] to construct their KE protocols. However, their proof is not complete. We consider it is extremely hard to prove its pseudorandomness —the property that it is required to satisfy— even if it would be. We therefore start from formulating the notion of twisted PRF rigorously, and then give a new construction which satisfies our definition. This may be another interest of our paper. We note that our design principle is totally different from [2,14] (despite of using twisted PRF.)

---

[1] See [14, Table 2] for the difference between CK^+-security and eCK-security.

(Related work) There are a variety of security models for KE protocols, the Bellare & Rogaway model [5,7], the Bellare, Pointcheval, & Rogaway model [4] and the Canetti & Krawczyk (CK) model [10]. In the original CK model, the session identifier (SID) is given by an adversary. Choo et al. [8] showed that, if the CK model is modified so as SID is defined to be the concatenation of messages exchanged during the protocol run, then this modified model offers the strongest definition of security among the above models.

LaMacchia et al. extended CK model [20] to consider stronger adversaries (in some sense) who attack even ephemeral secret keys. This model is called extended Canetti-Krawczyk (eCK) model.

In this paper, we consider CK model and eCK model such that SID is defined as the concatenation of messages exchanged.

2 Preliminaries

When X is a set, we let $x \leftarrow X$ denote that x is randomly chosen from X. When A is a probabilistic algorithm, we let $y \leftarrow A(x_1, \cdots, x_n; R)$ denote the operation of running A on inputs $x_1, \cdots, x_n$ and coins R that eventually outputs y. We let $y \leftarrow A(x_1, \cdots, x_n)$ denote the operation of $y \leftarrow A(x_1, \cdots, x_n; R)$ with R chosen at random. $\mathsf{PRF}_s(\cdot)$ denotes a pseudorandom function with key s. PPT means probabilistic polynomial time and $\parallel$ means concatenation.

2.1 Key-Exchange (KE) Protocol

A key-exchange (KE) protocol is run among interconnected parties, where each party is activated by an adversary to run an instance of the protocol. Such an instance is called a session. A party can run multiple sessions concurrently, and each session has its own session state. When a party receives an incoming message, he either (1) returns an outgoing message and updates the session state, or (2) outputs an *session key K* and completes the session by deleting the session state. A party that first sends a message is called an *initiator* and, a party that first receive a message is called a *responder*.

Each session is associated with its holder or owner P (the party which runs the session), a *peer* P' (the party with which the session key is intended to be established), and a session identifier. The session identifier *sid* of P is a tuple (Out, In), where Out is the concatenation of outgoing messages from this session, and In is the concatenation of the incoming messages into this session. Since we consider only 2-pass protocols in this paper, a session identifier is of the form (X, Y), where X is the outgoing message and Y is the incoming message. The session $(Out, In) = (X, Y)$ (if it exists) whose owner and peer are P and P' respectively, is said to be a *matching* session of the session (Y', X') whose owner and peer are P' and P respectively, if either $(X, Y) = (X', Y')$ or $((X = X') \wedge (Y = \emptyset))$.

2.2   Canetti-Krawczyk (CK) Model [10,16]

Canetti and Krawczyk [10] formulated the security model of KE protocols, which is called the CK model. In the CK model, an adversary $\mathcal{M}$ is an active "man in the middle" adversary with full control of the communication links between parties. $\mathcal{M}$ schedules all activations of parties and message delivery. Initially and upon the completion of each activation, $\mathcal{M}$ decides which party to activate next; $\mathcal{M}$ also decides which incoming message or external request the activated party is to receive. In addition to these ability, $\mathcal{M}$ can issue the following oracle queries:

- A state-reveal query is directed at a session which is still incomplete (i.e., before outputting the session key) and the oracle returns the corresponding session state (which does not include the long-term private key). [2]
- A session-key query is directed at a completed session and the oracle returns the corresponding session-key.
- A corrupt query is directed at an individual party and the oracle returns all information in the memory of that party (including the long-term private key of the party as well all session states and session keys stored at the party). We say the party is corrupted thereafter.
- A session expire query is directed at a completed session within a party P and its result is that the session key is erased from P's memory. We say the session expired thereafter.

The session expire query is used to formulate the notion of forward secrecy (FS). The FS means that "compromise of long-term keys does not compromise past session keys". Two types of FS are considered in CK-model, perfect forward secrecy (PFS) and weak perfect forward secrecy (wPFS).

Definition 1. *A session sid within a party P is called* locally exposed *if the adversary issues any of the following queries:*

1. *a* session-state reveal *query directed to sid,*
2. *a* session-key *query directed to sid,*
3. *a* corrupt *query directed to P before sid expires.*

A session sid := (Out, In) within a party P is called exposed *if*

1. *it is locally exposed, or*
2. *it has a matching session that is locally exposed, or*
3. *it does not have a matching session and its peer P' is corrupted before P outputs the session key.*

A session which is not exposed is called unexposed.

---

[2] While the long-term private key is stored and operated in a protected area in many cases, each session state may be operated in a non-protected area by an application that responds to a huge number of users concurrently. Therefore the session state tends to be more vulnerable.

At some point, the adversary $\mathcal{M}$ chooses a test-session sid^* among the sessions that are completed and unexposed at the time. We chooses a random bit b. If $b = 0$, $\mathcal{M}$ is given the session key K^* of sid^*. If $b = 1$, $\mathcal{M}$ is given a randomly chosen session key K from the distribution over the session key space. $\mathcal{M}$ finally outputs a bit b'. The advantage of $\mathcal{M}$ is defined as

$$Adv(\mathcal{M}) = 2 \times |\Pr(b' = b) - 1/2| \tag{1}$$
$$= |\Pr(b' = 1 \mid b = 0) - \Pr(b' = 1 \mid b = 1)| \tag{2}$$

Definition 2. *A KE protocol is CK-secure with perfect forward secrecy (PFS) if*

1. *If two uncorrupted parties complete sessions which are matching to each other, then they output the same session key except for a negligible probability.*
2. *$Adv(\mathcal{M})$ is negligible for any PPT adversary $\mathcal{M}$.*

An unexposed session sid is called strongly unexposed if sid has a matching session, or its peer P' is never corrupted.

Definition 3. *A KE protocol is CK-secure with weak PFS (wPFS) if the test session is required to be strongly unexposed in Definition 2.*

Suppose that the test session does not have a matching session. Then in Def. 2 (that defines PFS), an adversary $\mathcal{M}$ is allowed to corrupt the peer of the test session after the test session completes. On the other hand, in the definition of *weak* PFS, $\mathcal{M}$ is not allowed to do that.

2.3 Extended Canetti-Krawczyk (eCK) Model [20]

The extended Canetti-Krawczyk (eCK) model was given by LaMacchia et al. [20]. It is the same as the CK model except for the following.

- A session-state reveal query is replaced with a ephemeral secret key reveal query which reveals the ephemeral secret key of that party, where the ephemeral secret key of a session is defined as all random coins used by the party in that session.
- A corrupt query is replaced with a long-term key reveal query which reveals the long-term key of that party.

Let sid be a session completed by P_α, and sid' denote the matching session to sid, supposedly executed by P_β (sid' may not exist). Let lsk_α and lsk_β, respectively, denote long-term secret keys of P_α and P_β. Let esk_α and esk_β, respectively, denote ephemeral secret keys used by P_α and P_β in sid and sid' (the latter is defined only if sid' exists). Then a session sid is called **exposed** in eCK model if

- The matching session sid' exists, and the adversary $\mathcal{M}$ obtains both lsk_α and esk_α, or both lsk_β and esk_β.

- Or the matching session sid' does not exist, and $\mathcal{M}$ obtains either lsk_β (at any time), or both lsk_α and esk_α.
- Or $\mathcal{M}$ obtains the session key of sid or sid' (if the latter exists).

Definition 4. *A KE protocol is called eCK-secure if the conditions of Def.2 are satisfied in the eCK model.*

2.4   KEM

A key encapsulation mechanism $\mathsf{KEM} = (Gen, Enc, Dec)$ consists of three polynomial-time algorithms:

- $(pk, sk) \leftarrow Gen(1^\lambda)$ returns a public key pk and the secret key sk, where λ is the security parameter.
- $(c, K) \leftarrow Enc(pk)$ outputs a ciphertext c and the key $K \in \mathcal{K}$, where the key space $\mathcal{K}$ is defined by pk.
- $K = Dec(sk, c)$ outputs the key K corresponding to the ciphertext c.

For a PPT adversary A, consider the following experiment.

$$(pk, sk) \leftarrow Gen(1^\lambda), (c, K_0) \leftarrow Enc(pk), K_1 \leftarrow \mathcal{K}, b \leftarrow \{0, 1\}, b' \leftarrow A(pk, c, K_b).$$

We say that a KEM is CPA-secure if $|\Pr(b' = b) - 1/2|$ is negligible for any PPT adversary A.

3   Our Basic KE Protocol Based on KEM

Our basic KE protocol can be considered as a natural generalization of Diffie-Hellman protocol. Let $\mathsf{KEM} = (Gen, Enc, Dec)$ be a CPA-secure KEM.

(Protocol 2-PASS-AM)

step 1. P_α generates $(pk, sk) \leftarrow Gen(1^\lambda)$, and sends $X = (P_\alpha, pk)$ to P_β.
step 2. P_β computes $(c, K) \leftarrow Enc(pk)$, and sends $Y = (P_\beta, c)$ and X to P_α.
   It then outputs the session key K.
step 3. P_α computes $K = Dec(sk, c)$, and outputs the session key K.

If we use Elgamal KEM, then P_α sends $pk = g^x$, P_β returns $c = g^r$, and the session key is $K = c^x = g^{xr}$. Thus it coincides with Diffie-Hellman protocol.

The above protocol is still not CK-secure nor eCK-secure as the DH protocol is not. But by applying the compiler of [10] to the above protocol, we can obtain a 3-pass KE protocol.

Now a challenge is to construct a 2-pass KE protocol which is CK-secure (with wPFS). Also we want to construct a 2-pass eCK-secure one. In the rest of this paper, we will show such KE protocols.

4   Twisted PRF Trick

4.1   Toward eCK Security

Boyd et al. [2, Sec.3.1] suggested the following method to transform a CK-secure protocol to a eCK-secure protocol. If r is the random input used by a session and s is the long term key of the party, the protocol first computes $r' = \mathsf{PRF}_s(r)$, and uses r' instead of r. This way, even though r is available to the adversary through ephemeral secret key reveal, r' remains protected.

However, this method does not work (in the standard model). In the eCK model, an adversary $\mathcal{M}$ can obtain either s or r. Suppose that $\mathcal{M}$ obtain s, and r is unknown. Then we cannot say that r' is pseudorandom even if r is random. This is because the definition of pseudorandom functions says nothing about this.

4.2   Original Twisted PRF Trick

To overcome the above problem and then to achieve eCK-security, Fujioka et al. [14] introduced the twisted PRF trick. In their method, a random coin R of a probabilistic algorithm A is replaced with

$$F(k, (a, a')) = \mathsf{PRF}_k(a) \oplus \mathsf{PRF}'_{a'}(k). \tag{3}$$

where k is the long-term key of a party P_i and (a, a') are random coins (i.e. the ephemeral secret key). Namely P_i invokes $A(x_1, \cdots, x_n; F(s_i, (a, a')))$ instead of $A(x_1, \cdots, x_n; R)$.

They claimed that: If (a, a') is leaked, $\mathsf{PRF}_k(a)$ cannot be computed without knowing k. Similarly, if k is leaked, $\mathsf{PRF}'_{a'}(k)$ cannot be computed without knowing a'.

Although this is true, it is not sufficient enough. $F(k, (a, a'))$ must look *random* (even if either k or (a, a') is leaked) because it is substituted to the random coin R. However, we cannot prove this pseudorandomness. The reason is as follows.

Suppose that (a, a') is leaked in $F(k, (a, a'))$ of eq.(3). Then we must prove that $((a, a'), F(k, (a, a')))$ and $((a, a'), R)$ are indistinguishable, where $(a, a'), k$, and R are all random.

The proof would proceed as follows. Suppose that there exists a distinguisher D_0 which can distinguish $((a, a'), F(k, (a, a')))$ from $((a, a'), R)$. Then we will construct a distinguisher D_1 which can distinguish the underlying PRF from random functions.

D_1 has access to an oracle $\mathcal{O}$, where $\mathcal{O}$ is PRF_k or a random function. D_1 first chooses (a, a') randomly. and queries (a, a') to $\mathcal{O}$ which returns r. Then D_1 computes

$$z = r \oplus \mathsf{PRF}_{a'}(k) \tag{4}$$

and gives $((a, a'), z)$ to D_0. If $\mathcal{O}$ is PRF_k, then $z = F(k, (a, a'))$, and if $\mathcal{O}$ is a random function, then z is a random string R. Therefore D_1 can distinguish

PRF_k from a random function if D_0 can distinguish $((a, a'), F(k, (a, a')))$ from $((a, a'), R)$.

However, in eq.(4), D_1 cannot compute $PRF_{a'}(k)$ because D_1 does not know k ! Thus we cannot prove that $F(k, (a, a'))$ of eq.(3) satisfies the desired property.

5   Improved Twisted PRF

In this section, we formulate the notion of twisted pseudorandom functions (tPRFs), and present its correct construction.

Definition 5. *We say that a function $F : \{0,1\}^\lambda \times \{0,1\}^\ell \to \{0,1\}^\ell$ is a twisted pseudorandom function (tPRF) if*

- *$[(x_1, F(K, x_1)), \cdots, (x_q, F(K, x_q))]$ and $[(x_1, R_1), \cdots, (x_q, R_q)]$ are indistinguishable for any polynomial $q(\lambda)$, where $K, x_1, \cdots, x_q, R_1, \cdots, R_q$ are randomly chosen, and*
- *$[K, F(K, x)]$ and $[K, R]$ are indistinguishable, where K, x, R are randomly chosen.*

We next show a correct construction of tPRF. (Here, $\lambda = \ell = 2L$.) Define F as follows.

$$F((k, k'), (a, a')) = PRF_k(a) \oplus PRF_{a'}(k').$$

Theorem 1. *The above F is a tPRF if PRF is a pseudorandom function.*

Proof. (1) For randomly chosen $K = (k, k')$ and $x_i = (a_i, a'_i)$, let $y_i = F(K, r_i)$, where $i = 1, \cdots, q$. Let R_i be a random string for $i = 1, \cdots, q$.

Suppose that there exists a distinguisher D_0 which can distinguish between

$$A = [(x_1, y_1), \cdots, (x_q, y_q)] \text{ and } B = [(x_1, R_1), \cdots, (x_q, R_q)].$$

We show a distinguisher D_1 which can distinguish the underlying PRF from random functions. D_1 has access to an oracle $\mathcal{O}$, where $\mathcal{O}$ is PRF_k or a random function. D_1 first chooses k' randomly. Next for $i = 1, \cdots, q$, D_1 chooses $x_i = (a_i, a'_i)$ randomly, and queries a_i to $\mathcal{O}$ which returns r_i. Then D_1 computes

$$z_i = r_i \oplus PRF_{a'_i}(k')$$

for $i = 1, \cdots, q$, and gives $\gamma = [(x_1, z_1), \cdots, (x_q, z_q)]$ to D_0. It is easy to see that

$$\gamma = \begin{cases} A \text{ if } \mathcal{O} \text{ is } PRF_k \\ B \text{ if } \mathcal{O} \text{ is a random function} \end{cases}$$

D_0 finally outputs a bit b. Then D_1 outputs the same b. In this way, D_1 can distinguish the PRF from a random function. However, this is a contradiction. Therefore D_0 cannot distinguish between A and B.

(2) For randomly chosen $K = (k, k')$ and $x = (a, a')$, let $y = F(K, x)$. Let R be a random string. Suppose that there exists a distinguisher D_0 which can distinguish between (K, y) and (K, R). We show a distinguisher D_1 which can distinguish the PRF from random functions.

D_1 has access to an oracle $\mathcal{O}$, where $\mathcal{O}$ is $\mathsf{PRF}_{a'}$ or a random function. D_1 chooses a and $K = (k, k')$ randomly. Then D_1 queries k' to $\mathcal{O}$ which returns r. Then D_1 computes

$$z = r \oplus \mathsf{PRF}_k(a),$$

and gives (K, Z) to D_0. It is easy to see that

$$(K, z) = \begin{cases} (K, y) \ if \ \mathcal{O} \ is \ \mathsf{PRF}_{a'} \\ (K, R) \ if \ \mathcal{O} \ is \ a \ random \ function \end{cases}$$

D_0 finally outputs a bit b. Then D_1 outputs the same b. In this way, D_1 can distinguish the PRF from a random function. However, this is a contradiction. Therefore D_0 cannot distinguish between (K, y) and (K, R).   □

6   Our 2-Pass Protocol in the CK Model

In this section, we construct a 2-pass KE protocol which satisfies CK-security with wPFS by extending Protocol 2-PASS-AM.

Let $\mathsf{KEM} = (Gen, Enc, Dec)$ be a CPA-secure KEM, and $\mathsf{SIG} = (\mathsf{G}, \mathsf{Sign}, \mathsf{Verify})$ be a signature scheme. We assume that each P_i publishes a verification key vk_i and keeps a signing key sgn_i secret, where $(vk_i, sgn_i) \leftarrow \mathsf{G}(1^\lambda)$.

6.1   Naive Approach

In a naive approach, each P_i has a long term secret key sgn_i.

(Protocol NAIVE)

step 1. P_α generates $(pk, \boxed{sk}) \leftarrow Gen(1^\lambda)$ and sends $X = (P_\alpha, pk)$ to P_β.
 P_α also sends its signature $\sigma_X = \mathsf{Sign}(sgn_\alpha; X)$ to P_β.
step 2. If σ_X is invalid, then P_β aborts. Otherwise
 P_β computes $(c, K) \leftarrow Enc(pk)$, and sends $Y = (P_\beta, c)$ and X to P_α.
 P_β also sends its signature $\sigma_{YX} = \mathsf{Sign}(sgn_\beta; (Y, X))$ to P_α.
 It then outputs the session key K.
step 3. If σ_{YX} is invalid, then P_α aborts. Otherwise
 P_α computes $K = Dec(sk, c)$, and outputs the session key K.

However, this protocol is broken by an adversary $\mathcal{M}$ such as follows.

1. $\mathcal{M}$ asks P_α to start a session (Session 1) with P_β, and receives (X, σ_X).
2. $\mathcal{M}$ issues a session-state reveal query to P_α, and obtains sk.
3. $\mathcal{M}$ sends (X, σ_X) to P_β, receives (Y, X, σ_{YX}) from P_β, and relays it to P_α.
4. $\mathcal{M}$ sends (X, σ_X) to P_β again as a new session (Session 2), and receives $(Y', X, \sigma'_{Y'X})$ from P_β.

At the end of step 4, P_β has an unexposed session $sid^* = ((Y', X, \sigma'_{Y'X}), (X, \sigma_X))$. $\mathcal{M}$ can now compute the session key K^* of sid^* in the same way as P_α because $\mathcal{M}$ knows sk. (Note that sk is not a long term key, and sid^* does not have a matching session.)

It is quite surprising that the naive approach does not work well. And it is quite surprising again that this flaw can be fixed, as done in the next sub-section, within two pass protocols.

(Remark) Session 2 is not *matching* to Session 1. Therefore Session 2 is unexposed.

6.2 Our Protocol

We resolve the above problem by by using the improved twisted PRF trick. Our 2-pass KE protocol is given as follows. Each P_i publishes vk_i, and has a long term secret key (sgn_i, s_i), where s_i is a key of tPRF which is denoted by F. The boxed statements are the differences from Protocol NAIVE.

(Protocol 2-PASS-CK)

step 1. $\boxed{P_\alpha \text{ chooses } r \text{ randomly and computes } R = F(s_\alpha, r).}$

P_α generates $(pk, sk) \leftarrow Gen(1^\lambda; R)$ by using the above R as random coin. P_α sends $X = (P_\alpha, pk)$ and its signature $\sigma_X = \mathsf{Sign}(sgn_\alpha; X)$ to P_β.

$\boxed{P_\alpha \text{ then erase all state except } r \text{ and } X.}$

step 2. If σ_X is invalid, then P_β aborts. Otherwise
P_β computes $(c, K) \leftarrow Enc(pk)$, and sends $Y = (P_\beta, c)$ and X [3] to P_α.
P_β also sends its signature $\sigma_{YX} = \mathsf{Sign}(sgn_\beta; (Y, X))$ to P_α.
It then outputs the session key K.

step 3. If σ_{YX} is invalid, then P_α aborts. Otherwise

$\boxed{P_\alpha \text{ computes } R = F(s_\alpha, r), \text{ and reconstructs } (pk, sk) \leftarrow Gen(1^\lambda; R).}$

P_α then computes $K = Dec(sk, c)$, and outputs the session key K.

Theorem 2. *The above protocol is secure in the CK model (with wPFS) if the KEM is CPA-secure, the signature scheme is unforgeable against chosen message attack and F is a tPRF.*

Proof. It is easy to see that the first requirement of Def.2 is satisfied. We will show that the second requirement of Def.2 is also satisfied. Suppose that an adversary $\mathcal{M}$ chooses

$$sid^* = ((X^*, \sigma_{X^*}), (Y^*, X^*, \sigma_{Y^*X^*})) \text{ or } ((Y^*, X^*, \sigma_{Y^*X^*}), (X^*, \sigma_{X^*}))$$

as the test session, where $X^* = (P_\alpha, pk^*)$ and $Y^* = (P_\beta, c^*)$.

---

[3] P_α can run several sessions with P_β concurrently. For example, P_α sends (X, σ_X) and $(X', \sigma_{X'})$ to P_β. If P_β returns only Y, P_α cannot tell if Y is a response to (X, σ_X) or $(X', \sigma_{X'})$.

P_α keeps (sgn_α, s_α) secret. P_β keeps (sgn_β, s_β) secret.

$\boxed{r \leftarrow random, R \leftarrow F(s_\alpha, r)}$

$(pk, sk) \leftarrow Gen(1^\lambda; R)$

$X \leftarrow (P_\alpha, pk), \sigma_X \leftarrow \mathsf{Sign}(sgn_\alpha, X)$

$\boxed{\text{Erase all state except } (r, X)}$ $X = (P_\alpha, pk), \sigma_X \longrightarrow$

                                                    If σ_X is invalid, then abort.
                                                    Else $(c, K) \leftarrow Enc(pk)$,
                                                         $Y \leftarrow (P_\beta, c)$,
                                                         $\sigma_{YX} \leftarrow \mathsf{Sign}(sgn_\beta, (Y, X))$.

                        $\longleftarrow Y = (P_\beta, c), X, \sigma_{YX}$

If σ_{YX} is invalid, then abort.

Else $\boxed{R \leftarrow F(s_\alpha, x)}$

     $\boxed{(pk, sk) \leftarrow Gen(1^\lambda; R)}$

     $K \leftarrow Dec(sk, c)$.

Fig. 1. Protocol 2-PASS-CK

We assume that

(A1) $\mathcal{M}$ activates at most n players $P_1, \cdots, P_n$, and
(A2) $\mathcal{M}$ activates P_α as the initiator at most N times. In the ith activation, P_α chooses r_i randomly, and computes $R_i = F(s_\alpha, r_i)$.

We consider a series of games $\mathsf{Game}_0, \mathsf{Game}_1, \cdots$. In each game, a random bit b is chosen for the test session, and $\mathcal{M}$ outputs a bit b' at the end of the game. Define

$$p_i = \Pr(b' = b \text{ in } \mathsf{Game}_i) \text{ and } q_i = 2|p_i - 1/2|.$$

- Game_0 is the original attack game.
- Game_1 is the same as Game_0 except for the following. Choose $\alpha' \in \{1, \cdots, n\}$ and $\beta' \in \{1, \cdots, n\}$ randomly. Let E_1 be the event that $\alpha' = \alpha$ and $\beta' = \beta$. If E_1 does not occur, then $\mathcal{M}$ chooses a bit b' randomly. E_1 happens with probability $1/n^2$. Therefore from the last equation of [12], we have $q_1 = (1/n^2)q_0$.

In what follows, we use the last equation of [12] in this way.

- Game_2 is the same as Game_1 except for the following. Let E_2 be the event that $\mathcal{M}$ forges σ_X^* or σ_{YX}^* successfully. If E_2 occurs, then $\mathcal{M}$ chooses a bit b' randomly.

We claim that $\mathcal{M}$ does not have $sign_\alpha$ when he outputs σ_X^*, and $\mathcal{M}$ does not have $sign_\beta$ when he outputs σ_{YX}^*. Suppose that the owner of sid^* is P_α. Then $\mathcal{M}$ cannot obtain $sign_\alpha$ before sid^* expires. If the matching session sid' exists, then $\mathcal{M}$ cannot obtain $sign_\beta$ before sid' expires. If the matching session does not exist, then $\mathcal{M}$ can never obtain $sign_\beta$ from the definition of wPFS. The same thing holds for the other case (the owner of sid^* is P_β).

Therefore E_2 happens with negligible probability ϵ (because $\mathcal{M}$ does not have the signing keys). [4] We then have $q_2 = (1 - \epsilon)q_1$.

---

[4] We can construct a forger $\mathcal{F}$ by using $\mathcal{M}$ as a subroutine.

Suppose that E_2 does not occur. Then $(X^* = (P_\alpha, pk^*), \sigma_X^*)$ must be computed by P_α (not by $\mathcal{M}$), say, in the i^*th activation for some $i^* \in \{1, \cdots, N\}$.

- Game$_3$ is the same as Game$_2$ except for the following. Choose $i \in \{1, \cdots, N\}$ randomly. Let E_3 be the event that $i = i^*$. If E_3 does not occur, then $\mathcal{M}$ chooses a bit b' randomly. Since E_3 happens with probability $1/N$, we have $q_3 = 1/N \times q_2$.

If the owner of sid^* is P_α, then $\mathcal{M}$ is not allowed to obtain the session state r_{i^*}. (See (A2) for r_i.) Suppose that the owner of sid^* is P_β. If sid^* has the matching session, then $\mathcal{M}$ is not allowed to obtain r_{i^*} because the matching session must be locally unexposed too.

Otherwise the owner of sid^* is P_β, and sid^* does not have the matching session. In this case, $\mathcal{M}$ is never allowed to obtain the long-term key s_α of P_α from the definition of wPFS. Let

$$\tau = \begin{cases} 0 & \text{if the owner of } sid^* \text{ is } P_\alpha \text{ or } sid^* \text{ has the matching session,} \\ 1 & \text{otherwise .} \end{cases}$$

If $\tau = 0$, $\mathcal{M}$ may obtain s_α (after sid^* or sid' expires) but not r_{i^*}. If $\tau = 1$, $\mathcal{M}$ may obtain r_{i^*}, but not s_α.

- Game$_4$ is the same as Game$_3$ except for the following. At the beginning of the game, $\tau' \in \{0, 1\}$ is randomly chosen. Let E_4 be the event that $\tau' = \tau$. If E_4 does not occur, then $\mathcal{M}$ chooses a bit b' randomly. Since E_4 happens with probability $1/2$, we have $q_4 = 1/2 \times q_3$.
- Game$_5$ is the same as Game$_4$ except for the following.

1. If $\tau = \tau' = 0$, then $F(s_\alpha, r_{i^*})$ is replaced with a random string R.
   In this case, $(s_\alpha, F(s_\alpha, r_{i^*}))$ and (s_α, R) are indistinguishable from Def. 5.
2. If $\tau = \tau' = 1$, then all the values of $F(s_\alpha, r_i)$ are replaced with random strings R_i. In this case, $[(r_1, F(s_\alpha, r_1)), \cdots, [(r_N, F(s_\alpha, r_N))]$ and $[(r_1, R_1), \cdots, [(r_N, R_N)]$ are indistinguishable from Def. 5.

Therefore $|p_5 - p_4|$ is negligible. Hence $|q_5 - q_4|$ is also negligible.

In Game$_5$, pk^* is randomly generated by Gen from a view point of $\mathcal{M}$ because the random input to Gen is a random string R (instead of $F(s_\alpha, r_{i^*})$). Further if E_2 does not occur, then $(Y^* = (P_\beta, c^*), \sigma_{Y^*X^*})$ is computed honestly by P_β. This means that $(c^*, K^*) \leftarrow Enc(pk^*)$ is randomly generated.

Therefore we can show that q_5 is negligible because the KEM is CPA-secure. Consequently we can see that q_0 is negligible. This completes the proof. □

7   Other 2-Pass KE Protocols

7.1   2-Pass Protocol in the eCK Model

If we apply the improved twisted PRF trick to all probabilistic algorithms of Protocol NAIVE, then we can obtain a 2-pass eCK-secure protocol.

That is, let F be a tPRF and assume that each player P_i has a long-term secret-key (sgn_i, s_i), where s_i is a key of F. Then replace each probabilistic algorithm $A(x_1, \cdots, x_n; R)$ of Protocol NAIVE with $A(x_1, \cdots, x_n; F(s_i, r))$, where r is randomly chosen by P_i. We call the resultant protocol Protocol 2-PASS-ECK. (See Appendix A.)

Theorem 3. *Protocol* 2-PASS-ECK *is eCK-secure if the KEM is CPA-secure and the signature scheme is unforgeable against chosen message attack.*

The proof is given in Appendix C.

7.2   Both CK-Secure and eCK-Secure Protocol

Modify the above Protocol 2-PASS-ECK in such a way that all state is erased except (r, X) at the end of step 1 (as in Protocol 2-PASS-CK). Then this 2-pass protocol is both CK-secure and eCK-secure. (See Appendix B.) The details will be given in the final paper.

8   Separation

Protocol 2-PASS-CK is not eCK-secure because an adversary $\mathcal{M}$ can issue ephemeral secret key reveal queries in the eCK model even for the test session sid^*. In particular, $\mathcal{M}$ can reveal the random coin R_B of $(c^*, K^*) \leftarrow Enc(pk^*; R_B)$ by issuing the ephemeral secret key reveal query to P_β. Then it can compute K^*. (Further suppose that SIG is Schnorr signature scheme. Then $\mathcal{M}$ can compute the sign-key sgn_α from a (message, signature) pair and the randomness used.)

Protocol 2-PASS-ECK is not CK-secure because the attack shown in Sec.6.1 holds. (Note that in the protocol, nothing is erased at the end of step 1.) Hence

- Protocol 2-PASS-ECK is eCK-secure, but not CK-secure.
- Protocol 2-PASS-CK is CK-secure, but not eCK-secure.

References

1. Bellare, M., Canetti, R., Krawczyk, H.: A Modular Approach to the Design and Analysis of Authentication and Key Exchange Protocols (Extended Abstract). In: STOC 1998, pp. 419–428 (1998)
2. Boyd, C., Cliff, Y., Nieto, J.M.G., Paterson, K.G.: One-round key exchange in the standard model. IJACT 1(3), 181–199 (2009)
3. Boyd, C., Nieto, J.M.G.: Round-Optimal Contributory Conference Key Agreement. In: Desmedt, Y.G. (ed.) PKC 2003. LNCS, vol. 2567, pp. 161–174. Springer, Heidelberg (2003)
4. Bellare, M., Pointcheval, D., Rogaway, P.: Authenticated Key Exchange Secure against Dictionary Attacks. In: Preneel, B. (ed.) EUROCRYPT 2000. LNCS, vol. 1807, pp. 139–155. Springer, Heidelberg (2000)
5. Bellare, M., Rogaway, P.: Entity Authentication and Key Distribution. In: Stinson, D.R. (ed.) CRYPTO 1993. LNCS, vol. 773, pp. 232–249. Springer, Heidelberg (1994)

6. Bellare, M., Rogaway, P.: Random Oracles are Practical: A Paradigm for Designing Efficient Protocols. In: ACM Conference on Computer and Communications Security, pp. 62–73 (1993)
7. Bellare, M., Rogaway, P.: Provably Secure Session Key Distribution: The Three Party Case. In: STOC 1995, pp. 57–66 (1995)
8. Choo, K.-K.R., Boyd, C., Hitchcock, Y.: Examining Indistinguishability-Based Proof Models for Key Establishment Protocols. In: Roy, B. (ed.) ASIACRYPT 2005. LNCS, vol. 3788, pp. 585–604. Springer, Heidelberg (2005)
9. Cash, D., Hofheinz, D., Kiltz, E., Peikert, C.: Bonsai Trees, or How to Delegate a Lattice Basis. In: Gilbert, H. (ed.) EUROCRYPT 2010. LNCS, vol. 6110, pp. 523–552. Springer, Heidelberg (2010)
10. Canetti, R., Krawczyk, H.: Analysis of Key-Exchange Protocols and Their Use for Building Secure Channels. In: Pfitzmann, B. (ed.) EUROCRYPT 2001. LNCS, vol. 2045, pp. 453–474. Springer, Heidelberg (2001)
11. Shoup, V., Cramer, R.: Design and analysis of practical public-key encryption schemes secure against adaptive chosen ciphertext attack. SIAM Journal of Computing 33, 167–226 (2003)
12. Dent, A.W.: A note on game-hopping proofs. Cryptology ePrint Archive, Report 2006/260 (2006)
13. Dowsley, R., Müller-Quade, J., Nascimento, A.C.A.: A CCA2 Secure Public Key Encryption Scheme Based on the McEliece Assumptions in the Standard Model. In: Fischlin, M. (ed.) CT-RSA 2009. LNCS, vol. 5473, pp. 240–251. Springer, Heidelberg (2009)
14. Fujioka, A., Suzuki, K., Xagawa, K., Yoneyama, K.: Strongly Secure Authenticated Key Exchange from Factoring, Codes, and Lattices. In: Fischlin, M., Buchmann, J., Manulis, M. (eds.) PKC 2012. LNCS, vol. 7293, pp. 467–484. Springer, Heidelberg (2012)
15. Krawczyk, H.: SIGMA: The 'SIGn-and-MAc' Approach to Authenticated Diffie-Hellman and Its Use in the IKE Protocols. In: Boneh, D. (ed.) CRYPTO 2003. LNCS, vol. 2729, pp. 400–425. Springer, Heidelberg (2003)
16. Krawczyk, H.: HMQV: A High-Performance Secure Diffie-Hellman Protocol. In: Shoup, V. (ed.) CRYPTO 2005. LNCS, vol. 3621, pp. 546–566. Springer, Heidelberg (2005)
17. Hofheinz, D., Kiltz, E.: Practical Chosen Ciphertext Secure Encryption from Factoring. In: Joux, A. (ed.) EUROCRYPT 2009. LNCS, vol. 5479, pp. 313–332. Springer, Heidelberg (2009)
18. Hohenberger, S., Waters, B.: Short and Stateless Signatures from the RSA Assumption. In: Halevi, S. (ed.) CRYPTO 2009. LNCS, vol. 5677, pp. 654–670. Springer, Heidelberg (2009)
19. Jeong, I.R., Katz, J., Lee, D.H.: One-Round Protocols for Two-Party Authenticated Key Exchange. In: Jakobsson, M., Yung, M., Zhou, J. (eds.) ACNS 2004. LNCS, vol. 3089, pp. 220–232. Springer, Heidelberg (2004)
20. LaMacchia, B.A., Lauter, K., Mityagin, A.: Stronger Security of Authenticated Key Exchange. In: Susilo, W., Liu, J.K., Mu, Y. (eds.) ProvSec 2007. LNCS, vol. 4784, pp. 1–16. Springer, Heidelberg (2007)
21. McEliece, R.J.: A Public-Key Cryptosystem Based on Algebraic Coding Theory. Deep Space Network progress Report (1978)
22. Peikert, C.: Public-key cryptosystems from the worst-case shortest vector problem: extended abstract. In: STOC 2009, pp. 333–342 (2009)
23. Peikert, C., Waters, B.: Lossy Trapdoor Functions and Their Applications. In: STOC 2008, pp. 187–196 (2008)

24. Rabin, M.O.: Digitalized signatures and public-key functions as intractable as factorization, Technical report, MIT (1979) Technical Report, MIT/LCS/TR-212
25. Stern, J.: A new paradigm for public key identification. IEEE Transactions on Information Theory 42(6), 1757–1768 (1996)

A   Protocol 2-PASS-ECK

step 1. P_α chooses r_1, r_2 randomly and computes $R_1 = F(s_\alpha, r_1)$ and $R_2 = F(s_\alpha, r_2)$.
P_α generates $(pk, sk) \leftarrow Gen(1^\lambda; R_1)$.
P_α sends $X = (P_\alpha, pk)$ and its signature $\sigma_X = \text{Sign}(sgn_\alpha, X; R_2)$ to P_β.
step 2. If σ_X is invalid, then P_β aborts. Otherwise
P_α chooses r_3, r_4 randomly and computes $R_3 = F(s_\alpha, r_3)$ and $R_4 = F(s_\alpha, r_4)$.
P_β computes $(c, K) \leftarrow Enc(pk; R_3)$, and sends $Y = (P_\beta, c)$ and X to P_α.
P_α also sends its signature $\sigma_{YX} = \text{Sign}(sgn_\beta, (Y, X); R_4)$ to P_α.
It then outputs the session key K.
step 3. If σ_{YX} is invalid, then P_α aborts. Otherwise
P_α computes $K = Dec(sk, c)$, and outputs the session key K.

B   CK-Secure and eCK-Secure 2-Pass Protocol

step 1. P_α chooses r_1, r_2 randomly and computes $R_1 = F(s_\alpha, r_1)$ and $R_2 = F(s_\alpha, r_2)$.
P_α generates $(pk, sk) \leftarrow Gen(1^\lambda; R_1)$.
P_α sends $X = (P_\alpha, pk)$ and its signature $\sigma_X = \text{Sign}(sgn_\alpha, X; R_2)$ to P_β.
P_α then erase all state except r_1 and X.
step 2. If σ_X is invalid, then P_β aborts. Otherwise
P_α chooses r_3, r_4 randomly and computes $R_3 = F(s_\alpha, r_3)$ and $R_4 = F(s_\alpha, r_4)$.
P_β computes $(c, K) \leftarrow Enc(pk; R_3)$, and sends $Y = (P_\beta, c)$ and X to P_α.
P_α also sends its signature $\sigma_{YX} = \text{Sign}(sgn_\beta, (Y, X); R_4)$ to P_α.
It then outputs the session key K.
step 3. If σ_{YX} is invalid, then P_α aborts. Otherwise
P_α computes $R_1 = F(s_\alpha, r_1)$, and reconstructs $(pk, sk) \leftarrow Gen(1^\lambda; R_1)$.
P_α then computes $K = Dec(sk, c)$, and outputs the session key K.

C   Proof of Theorem 3

It is easy to see that the first requirement of Def. 2, which is inherited to Def.4, is satisfied. We will show that the rest of requirement of Def. 4 is also satisfied. Let the session that the adversary $\mathcal{M}$ tests is

$$sid^* = ((X^*, \sigma_{X^*}), (Y^*, X^*, \sigma_{Y^*X^*})) \text{ or } ((Y^*, X^*, \sigma_{Y^*X^*}), (X^*, \sigma_{X^*}))$$

where $X^* = (P_\alpha, pk^*)$ and $Y^* = (P_\beta, c^*)$. We assume that

- $\mathcal{M}$ activates at most n players $P_1, \cdots, P_n$, and
- $\mathcal{M}$ activates P_α as an initiator at most N times. In the ith activation, P_α chooses $r_{i,1}, r_{i,2}$ randomly, and computes $R_{i,1} = F(s_\alpha, r_{i,1}), R_{i,2} = F(s_\alpha, r_{i,2})$.
- $\mathcal{M}$ activates P_β as a responder at most N times. In the ith activation, P_β chooses $r_{j,3}, r_{j,4}$ randomly, and computes $R_{j,3} = F(s_\beta, r_{j,3}), R_{j,4} = F(s_\beta, r_{j,4})$.

We consider a series of games $\mathsf{Game}_0, \mathsf{Game}_1, \cdots$. In each game, a random bit b is chosen for the test session, and $\mathcal{M}$ outputs a bit b' at the end of the game. Define

$$p_i = \Pr(b' = b \text{ in } \mathsf{Game}_i) \text{ and } q_i = 2|p_i - 1/2|.$$

- Game_0 is the original attack game.
- Game_1 is the same as Game_0 except for the following. Choose $\alpha' \in \{1, \cdots, n\}$ and $\beta' \in \{1, \cdots, n\}$ randomly. Let E_1 be the event that $\alpha' = \alpha$ and $\beta' = \beta$. If E_1 does not occur, then $\mathcal{M}$ chooses a bit b' randomly. E_1 happens with probability $1/n^2$. Therefore from the last equation of [12], we have $q_1 = (1/n^2)q_0$.

In what follows, we use the last equation of [12] in this way.

- Game_2 is the same as Game_1 except for the following. Let E_2 be the event that $\mathcal{M}$ generates σ_X^* or σ_{YX}^*. If E_2 occurs, then $\mathcal{M}$ chooses a bit b' randomly. Let ϵ be the probability that E_2 happens. Then $q_2 = (1 - \epsilon)q_1$.
  We show that E_2 happens with negligible probability ϵ. Suppose that $\mathcal{M}$ generate either of these signatures without obtaining the corresponding long-term secret, then unforgeability of signature scheme guarantees ϵ be negligible. The case when $\mathcal{M}$ generate either of these signatures with the corresponding long-term secret does not happen, because such cases implies that $\mathcal{M}$ must have corrupted the corresponding party and sid^* has no matching session. But such case is considered to be exposed. Hence, unless ϵ us negligible, we can construct an effective forger $\mathcal{F}$ by using $\mathcal{M}$ as a subroutine.

Suppose that E_2 does not occur. Then $(X^* = (P_\alpha, pk^*), \sigma_X^*)$ must be computed by P_α (not by $\mathcal{M}$), say, in the i^*th activation for some $i^* \in \{1, \cdots, N\}$. Also $(Y^* = (P_\beta, c^*), \sigma_{Y^*X^*})$ must be computed by P_β (not by $\mathcal{M}$), say, in the j^*th activation for some $j^* \in \{1, \cdots, N\}$.

- Game_3 is the same as Game_2 except for the following. Choose $i, j \in \{1, \cdots, N\}$ randomly. Let E_3 be the event that $i = i^*$ and $j = j^*$. If E_3 does not occur, then $\mathcal{M}$ chooses a bit b' randomly. Since E_3 happens with probability $1/N^2$, we have $q_3 = 1/N^2 \times q_2$.

The following 4 cases can happen.

- The owner of sid^* is an initiator P_α and has a matching session $\widetilde{sid}^*$. In this case, that sid^* is unexposed allows neither of the followings happens.
  - $\mathcal{M}$ obtains both the ephemeral secret key $r_{i^*} = \{r_{i^*,1}, r_{i^*,2}\}$ and the long-term secret sgn_α.

- $\mathcal{M}$ obtains both the ephemeral secret key $r_{j^*} = \{r_{j^*,3}, r_{j^*,4}\}$ of the matching session and the long-term secret sgn_β.
- The owner of sid^* is an initiator P_α and has no matching sessions. In this case, that sid^* is unexposed allows neither of the followings happens.
  - $\mathcal{M}$ obtains both the ephemeral secret key $r_{i^*} = \{r_{i^*,1}, r_{i^*,2}\}$ and the long-term secret sgn_α.
  - $\mathcal{M}$ obtains the long-term secret sgn_β of P_β.
- The owner of sid^* is a responder P_β, and sid^* has the matching session $\widetilde{sid}^*$. In this case, that sid^* is unexposed allows neither of the followings happens.
  - $\mathcal{M}$ obtains both the ephemeral secret key $r_{i^*} = \{r_{i^*,1}, r_{i^*,2}\}$ and the long-term secret sgn_α.
  - $\mathcal{M}$ obtains both the ephemeral secret key $r_{j^*} = \{r_{j^*,3}, r_{j^*,4}\}$ of the matching session and the long-term secret sgn_β.
- The owner of sid^* is a responder P_β and has neither matching session nor pseudo-matching session. In this case, that sid^* is unexposed allows neither of the followings happens.
  - $\mathcal{M}$ obtains both the ephemeral secret key $r_{j^*} = \{r_{j^*,1}, r_{j^*,2}\}$ and the long-term secret sgn_β.
  - $\mathcal{M}$ obtains the long-term secret sgn_α of P_α.

In any of the above cases, events are classified by two parameters τ and ρ as followings: Let

$$\tau = \begin{cases} 0 & \mathcal{M} \text{ may obtain } s_\alpha, \text{ but not } r_{i^*} \\ 1 & \mathcal{M} \text{ may obtain } r_{i^*}, \text{ but not } s_\alpha \end{cases}$$

$$\rho = \begin{cases} 0 & \mathcal{M} \text{ may obtain } s_\beta, \text{ but not } r_{j^*} \\ 1 & \mathcal{M} \text{ may obtain } r_{j^*}, \text{ but not } s_\beta \end{cases}$$

- Game_4 is the same as Game_3 except for the following. At the beginning of the game, $\tau', \rho' \in \{0, 1\}$ is randomly chosen. Let E_4 be the event that $\tau' = \tau$ and $\rho' = \rho$.
  If E_4 does not occur, then $\mathcal{M}$ chooses a bit b' randomly. Since E_4 happens with probability $1/4$, we have $q_4 = 1/4 \times q_3$.
- Game_5 is the same as Game_4 except for the following.
  If $\tau' = 0$, then $F(s_\alpha, r_{i^*})$ is replaced with a random string. If $\tau' = 1$, then all the values of $F(s_\alpha, r_i)$ are replaced with random strings. If $\rho' = 0$, then $F(s_\beta, r_{j^*})$ is replaced with a random string. If $\rho' = 1$, then all the values of $F(s_\beta, r_j)$ are replaced with random strings.
  Then we can show that $|p_5 - p_4|$ is negligible because F is a tPRF. [5] Hence $|q_5 - q_4|$ is also negligible.

In Game_5, pk^* is correctly generated by Gen because the random input to Gen is a random string (instead of $F(s_\alpha, r_{i^*})$). Further if E_2 does not occur, then $(Y^* = (P_\beta, c^*), \sigma_{Y^*X^*})$ is computed honestly by P_β. This means that $(c^*, K^*) \leftarrow Enc(pk^*)$ for some K^*.

Therefore we can show that q_5 is negligible because the KEM is CPA-secure. [6] Consequently we can see that q_0 is negligible. This completes the proof. Q.E.D.

---

[5] We can construct a distinguisher D by using $\mathcal{M}$ as a subroutine.
[6] We can construct an adversary on KEM by using $\mathcal{M}$ as a subroutine.

Analysis of BLAKE2

Jian Guo[1], Pierre Karpman[1,2], Ivica Nikolić[1], Lei Wang[1], and Shuang Wu[1]

[1] Nanyang Technological University, Singapore
[2] École normale supérieure de Rennes, France
{ntu.guo,pierre.karpman,wushuang83}@gmail.com,
{inikolic,Wang.Lei}@ntu.edu.sg

Abstract. We present a thorough security analysis of the hash function family BLAKE2, a recently proposed and already in use tweaked version of the SHA-3 finalist BLAKE. We study how existing attacks on BLAKE apply to BLAKE2 and to what extent the modifications impact the attacks. We design and run two improved searches for (impossible) differential attacks — the outcomes suggest higher number of attacked rounds in the case of impossible differentials (in fact we improve the best results for BLAKE as well), and slightly higher for the differential attacks on the hash/compression function (which gives an insight into the quality of the tweaks). We emphasize the importance of each of the modifications, in particular we show that an improper initialization could lead to collisions and near-collisions for the full-round compression function. We analyze the permutation of the new hash function and give rotational attacks and internal differentials for the whole design. We conclude that the tweaks in BLAKE2 were chosen properly and, despite having weaknesses in the theoretical attack frameworks of permutations and of fully-chosen state input compression functions, the hash function of BLAKE2 has only slightly lower (in terms of attacked rounds) security margin than BLAKE.

Keywords: BLAKE2, BLAKE, hash function, rotational cryptanalysis, impossible differential cryptanalysis, differential cryptanalysis, internal differential, iterative differential.

1 Introduction

The BLAKE hash function [2], a variant improving from its broken predecessor LAKE [3,11], was one of the five finalists of the SHA-3 competition [14] that ended in November 2012, with Keccak [9] becoming the new SHA-3 standard. Along with the other finalists, BLAKE is assumed to be a very strong hash function [14]. Even though it was not selected as the winner, it enjoys a large security margin, very good performance in software, and has attracted a considerable amount of cryptanalysis. BLAKE uses addition, rotation, and XOR as building blocks for the compression function and has an iteration mode based on HAIFA [10]. Thus it supports salt, and uses an expanding to double-pipe internal state which makes meet-in-the-middle attacks unfeasible. The compression function applies only word permutations for the message schedule, thus making it very simple, elegant and more importantly efficient.

J. Benaloh (Ed.): CT-RSA 2014, LNCS 8366, pp. 402–423, 2014.

BLAKE2 [5,4,6] is a new family of hash functions based on BLAKE. Despite being a new design, BLAKE2 has already been adopted by several software packages — for instance, it is implemented in the CyaSSL library, and is supported in the RAR 5.0 archive format [6]. This surprisingly quick adoption of a new hash function is most likely due to the popularity and qualities of its predecessor BLAKE. The main objective of the new BLAKE2 is to provide a number of parameters for use in applications without the need of additional constructions and modes (e.g., it supports parallelism, tree-hashing and prefix-MAC), and also to speed-up even further the hash function to reach a level of compression rate close to MD5 [5]. The designers have achieved this goal by slightly altering the original BLAKE; in particular they have modified the initial setup of the compression function, changed the rotation constants to be optimal for software performance, excluded constants from the round functions, etc. To implement these tweaks only a small change in the code of BLAKE is required.

While the efficiency argument of the new BLAKE2 is undoubtedly correct and can be confirmed by a mere comparison of the speed of software implementations of BLAKE2 and BLAKE (or MD5), the security of the new function is unclear. The designers claim security levels similar to that of BLAKE, due to the similarity of the two designs. However they do not provide a strict analysis. Note that no universal method nor theory exists that can transitively prove the security of a symmetric primitive A obtained by modifying a primitive B, excluding of course trivial modifications such as increasing the number of rounds[1]. Moreover, the fact that BLAKE2 now omits constants in its round function is a major tweak that might lead to exploits, as the rounds now only differ by the order in which they process the message words.

Our Contribution. In this paper we give a thorough security analysis of this new hash function. Our main objective is to find out if the security level of BLAKE2 has dropped due to the tweaks. We try to exploit each tweak separately, as well as in combination with the others, in order to mount attacks on as many rounds as possible. The starting point of our analysis in the framework of permutations and compression function with chosen IV are three promising techniques that can be highly successful against primitives that employ low usage of constants (i.e. no addition of constants to the message words): rotational cryptanalysis [22], internal differentials [24] (more precisely the squeeze attack [15,16]) and iterative differentials based on rotational trails. We show that in these frameworks, the attacker can penetrate through all 12 rounds of BLAKE2b. Further, we focus on the previous attacks on the original design, in particular the differential and impossible differential attacks [1]. We improve the previous results and approaches and along the way show the impact of the new initialization used in the compression function. We develop more advanced techniques to search for differentials — in particular, we implement a search for the best differential characteristics from a certain subspace which is much larger compared to all the previously analyzed ones. We show that due to the new

---

[1] On the condition that e.g. slide attacks are prevented by the design.

Table 1. Summary of the analysis of BLAKE and BLAKE2

Framework[a]	Type	# Rounds[b]	Complexity	Reference
BLAKE-256 perm.	imp. diff.	5	—	[1]
		6.5	—	§5
	differential	6	2^{486}	[17]
	boomerang	8	2^{232}	[12]
BLAKE-512 perm.	imp. diff.	5[c]	—	[1]
		6.5	—	§5
BLAKE-256 cf.	boomerang	7	2^{242}	[12]
	near collision	4	2^{56}	[1]
BLAKE-256	collision	2.5	2^{112}	[23]
	preimage	2.5	2^{241}	[23]
BLAKE-512	collision	2.5	2^{224}	[23]
	preimage	2.5	2^{481}	[23]
BLAKE2s perm.	imp. diff.	6.5	—	§5
	rotational	7	2^{511}	§3
BLAKE2b perm.	imp. diff.	6.5	—	§5
	rotational	12	2^{876}	§3
	differential	5.5	2^{928}	§6
BLAKE2s cf. ch. IV	collision	10	2^{64}	§3
BLAKE2b cf. ch. IV	partial collision	12	2^{61}	§4
	2^{64} weak preimages	12	1	§4
BLAKE2b cf.	differential	4.5	2^{495}	§6
BLAKE2b	differential	3.5	2^{480}	§6

[a] The notations 'perm.' and 'cf.' stand for the permutation and compression function of the associated hash function; 'ch. IV' and 'imp. diff.' stand for *chosen IV* and *impossible differential*

[b] The total number of rounds in BLAKE-256, BLAKE-512, BLAKE2s, and BLAKE2b is 14,16,10, and 12 rounds, respectively.

[c] The initial analysis claimed a 6-rounds attack, but it was shown to be incorrect.

rotations, the best result is now a 3.5-round differential distinguisher for the hash function of BLAKE2b, while a 4.5-round differential exists for the compression function. In the impossible differential analysis, we are able both to find and confirm theoretically probability-one characteristics. In the previously published analysis the search of characteristics was mostly experimental, and in the case of longer characteristics was actually incorrect. Our analysis is valid for BLAKE as well, *i.e.* we improve the best known results for impossible differentials for the original design. We summarize the result of our analysis of BLAKE2 and the best existing attacks on BLAKE in Tbl. 1.

This paper is organized as follows. In § 2, we give a brief description of the BLAKE2 hash function family. In §§ 3, 4, 5, 6, we describe our rotational, fixed points, impossible differential, and differential analyses of BLAKE2, respectively. We conclude in § 7.

2   Description of BLAKE2

As a successor of the BLAKE family, the BLAKE2 hash functions share many similarities with the original design. However differences occur at every level: internal permutation, compression function, and hash function construction. In this section we give a brief specification of BLAKE2 and highlight the differences with BLAKE. We use notations similar to [5], in particular: '$\leftarrow$' denotes variable assignment; '+' (resp. '−') denotes addition (resp. subtraction) in $\mathbb{Z}_{2^{32}}$ or in $\mathbb{Z}_{2^{64}}$ (modular addition (resp. subtraction)); '$\oplus$' denotes addition in $\mathbb{Z}_2^{32}$ or in $\mathbb{Z}_2^{64}$ (bitwise exclusive or); '$\lll r$' (resp. '$\ggg r$') denotes rotation of r bits towards the most (resp. least) significant bit; if not specified otherwise, numbers written in typewriter font are in base 16, e.g. f is the number 15.

The internal state of the BLAKE2 compression function is composed of 16 words of size 64 bits for BLAKE2b, and 32 bits for BLAKE2s. The compression function takes as input an 8-word chaining value $h_0, \ldots, h_7$, 8 constant initialization vectors $IV_0, \ldots, IV_7$, a 2-word counter $t_0 t_1$ that counts the number of *bytes* hashed so far, and two finalization flags f_0 and f_1. The flag f_0 is set to ff...ff when the current message block is the last, and to 00...00 otherwise; the f_1 counter plays a similar role in tree-hashing (and is not detailed here). The input to the compression function is initialized as (we follow the notations of the design paper here):

$$
\begin{pmatrix}
v_0 & v_1 & v_2 & v_3 \\
v_4 & v_5 & v_6 & v_7 \\
v_8 & v_9 & v_{10} & v_{11} \\
v_{12} & v_{13} & v_{14} & v_{15}
\end{pmatrix}
\leftarrow
\begin{pmatrix}
h_0 & h_1 & h_2 & h_3 \\
h_4 & h_5 & h_6 & h_7 \\
IV_0 & IV_1 & IV_2 & IV_3 \\
t_0 \oplus IV_4 & t_1 \oplus IV_5 & f_0 \oplus IV_6 & f_1 \oplus IV_7
\end{pmatrix}.
$$

The main differences between BLAKE2 and BLAKE at this stage are the removal of the optional salt value, the addition of the finalization flags instead of the repeated counter words, and the fact that the counter now counts a number of bytes rather than bits.

The initial state of BLAKE2s (resp. BLAKE2b) is then processed by 10 (resp. 12) rounds of a column and diagonal application of a 'G' function. In comparison, BLAKE-256 and BLAKE-512 functions have 14 and 16 rounds. The G functions take four state words (a, b, c, d) and two message words m_i, m_j as input. The latter are defined by a position index i of the function: at round r, m_i is given by $\sigma_{r \bmod 10}(2i)$ and m_j by $\sigma_{r \bmod 10}(2i + 1)$, where $\sigma_{r \bmod 10}$ is one of 10 permutations. Because of space constraints, we leave the description of the 'G' functions (and of their inverses) and of the σ permutations to the BLAKE2 specification document [5] (or to the full version of this paper [18]). Note however that the differences between the G functions of BLAKE2 and BLAKE are the omission in BLAKE2 of an '$\oplus$' addition between the message words and round constants, and modified rotation constants for BLAKE2b.

A column step of BLAKE2 computes $G_0(v_0, v_4, v_8, v_{12})$, $G_1(v_1, v_5, v_9, v_{13})$, $G_2(v_2, v_6, v_{10}, v_{14})$, $G_3(v_3, v_7, v_{11}, v_{15})$; and a diagonal step computes $G_4(v_0, v_5, v_{10}, v_{15})$, $G_5(v_1, v_6, v_{11}, v_{12})$, $G_6(v_2, v_7, v_8, v_{13})$, $G_7(v_3, v_4, v_9, v_{14})$.

Finally, the output of the compression function $h'_0, \ldots, h'_7$ combines the input chaining value and the final state $v_0, \ldots, v_{15}$ by computing

$$
\begin{aligned}
h'_0 &\leftarrow h_0 \oplus v_0 \oplus v_8 & \quad h'_4 &\leftarrow h_4 \oplus v_4 \oplus v_{12} \\
h'_1 &\leftarrow h_1 \oplus v_1 \oplus v_9 & \quad h'_5 &\leftarrow h_5 \oplus v_5 \oplus v_{13} \\
h'_2 &\leftarrow h_2 \oplus v_2 \oplus v_{10} & \quad h'_6 &\leftarrow h_6 \oplus v_6 \oplus v_{14} \\
h'_3 &\leftarrow h_3 \oplus v_3 \oplus v_{11} & \quad h'_7 &\leftarrow h_7 \oplus v_7 \oplus v_{15}
\end{aligned}
$$

The only difference between BLAKE2 and BLAKE in this step is again the omission of the optional salt value.

The BLAKE2 hash function is defined in a straightforward way from the above compression function. We give a high-level overview of this process here, and refer to [5] for more details.

1. A 'parameter block' (described below) is added ($\oplus$) with the same initialization vectors used in the compression function, and the result is used as the first input chaining value to the compression function.
2. The message is padded with null bytes if and only if necessary to make it a multiple of a block length (*i.e.* 512 bits for BLAKE2s and 1024 bits for BLAKE2b).
3. The compression function is iterated on the padded message, and its (possibly truncated) final output is taken as the hash value.

The 'parameter block' mentioned above encodes various parameters that specify an instance of the BLAKE2 hash function. General parameters are the digest length, the optional key length, an optional salt, and a personalization string. Additional parameters are defined for tree hashing. Again, we refer to [5] for the full specifications. The main differences with BLAKE in this respect is the simplified padding and the inclusion of a parameter block. Some of the optional functionalities of BLAKE (*e.g.* the salt) have been moved from the compression function to the parameter block.

Current State of Security of BLAKE2. In the submission document, the designers state that BLAKE2 inherits the security level of its predecessor BLAKE-256/512. In particular, they expect that the number of attacked rounds in BLAKE2 and BLAKE should be the same (possibly with slightly different complexities) with regards to the published analysis. For BLAKE the designers single out three attacks that penetrate the most number of rounds:

1. The 2.5-round preimage attack for the hash function by Ji and Liangyu [23].
2. The 6-round distinguisher for the permutation of BLAKE-256 proposed by Dunkelman and Khovratovich [17].
3. The 8-round boomerang distinguisher for the permutation of BLAKE-256, and the 7-round boomerang distinguisher for the compression function of BLAKE-256 by Biryukov *et al.* [12].

However, it seems the designers have overlooked the fact that the setup of the initial state of BLAKE2, $i.e.$ the initialization, gives less degrees of freedom to the attacker and more importantly fixes completely the values of six state words $v_8, v_9, v_{10}, v_{11}, v_{14}, v_{15}$. Hence the boomerangs for the compression function of BLAKE cannot be trivially extended to BLAKE2. In particular, as the 3-round characteristic used at the top of the 6-round boomerang of BLAKE has differences in the words of the third row, it cannot be applied to BLAKE2s. After a careful examination of all the characteristics given in [12], and under the assumption that characteristics with similar probabilities can be found in BLAKE2, boomerangs could be launched for 5 rounds $(2 + 3$ rounds$)$ of BLAKE2s, and 5.5 rounds $(2 + 3.5)$ of BLAKE2b.

Our Attack Frameworks. The previous published analysis of BLAKE target the keyed permutation[2], the compression function, and the hash function of BLAKE. In this paper we show attacks on round-reduced versions of all of these three primitives. We assume a standard generic security level for them, for example the cipher BLAKE2s is a 512-bit block cipher with 512-bit key, thus an exhaustive key recovery attack requires 2^{512} encryptions.

In the hash function framework we assume that the initial state is fixed, i.e. $v_0, v_1, \ldots, v_{15}$ are some predefined constants. The compression function framework is similar, but this time we allow freedom in $v_0, v_1, \ldots, v_7, v_{12}, v_{13}$, while $v_8, \ldots, v_{11}, v_{14}, v_{15}$ remain fixed (as they correspond to $IV_0, IV_1, IV_2, IV_3, IV_6, IV_7$), $i.e.$ we assume the attacker can control the chaining value and the counters t_0, t_1. We also analyze the case when the attacker can control the IV — the so called chosen IV model. Finally, in the framework of permutations, we assume we can fully control the plaintext, thus all v_i can be chosen, however the key (the message) is unknown. The reader should be aware that the importance of the attacks drops as one goes from the framework of hash functions to the one of permutations.

3   Rotational Analysis and Internal Differentials

BLAKE2 is an ARX primitive, $i.e.$ the only operations used are modular and bitwise addition, as well as bitwise rotations on various amounts. Moreover, due to the absence of constants in the G function (which were present in BLAKE), it is a good target for rotational attacks. Recall that in such attacks, one starts with rotational pairs of inputs $(x, x \lll r)$, and checks if the output of the primitive F is also rotational, $i.e.$ if $F(x) \lll r = F(x \lll r)$. In [22] it was shown that the probability of a rotational output for ARX primitive (i.e. the probability that the previous expression holds for a random input x) depends only on the number of modular additions used in F.

---

[2] Obviously, the keyed permutation is a block cipher. Further we use the terms (keyed) permutation and block cipher interchangeably, when we want to refer to analysis in the secret key model.

The function G in BLAKE2 has 6 additions. To maximize the probability we fix the rotation amount to 1, thus the rotational probability of modular addition becomes around $2^{-1.4}$. Hence, for the whole G function we obtain $2^{6 \cdot (-1.4)} \approx 2^{-8.4}$. Experiments show that the actual probability is slightly lower, *i.e.* around $2^{-9.1}$. As one round of BLAKE2 has eight G function, the rotational probability of a round is $2^{8 \cdot (-9.1)} \approx 2^{-73}$.

The permutation of BLAKE2b has 12 rounds, thus the rotational probability for the whole permutation[3] is $2^{12 \cdot (-73)} = 2^{-876}$. Hence in a related-key framework, where the second key is a rotation by 1 of the first key, we can distinguish the permutation. Similarly, for the 10-round permutation of BLAKE2s we can attack 7 rounds with a complexity slightly faster than the exhaustive search of a 512-bit key. Converting the distinguisher into a key-recovery attacks is possible as well. We can use the knowledge of the plaintext and ciphertext, to recover $4 \cdot 1.4 \approx 6$ bits at the top and the same amount at the bottom, thus from a rotational pair of plaintext/ciphertext we can reduce the entropy of the key by 12 bits.

Let us try to apply to above distinguisher to the compression function of BLAKE2. Note that the constants $IV_0, \ldots, IV_3$ used in the initialization are non-rotational[4]. To overcome this issue, we can try to obtain rotational pairs after the first half round of BLAKE2, and use the message freedom of the second half round to probabilistically satisfy the rest of the rotational trail on t rounds. The first half round is composed of four applications of the function G with independent inputs that can be rotational for three of the four arguments. That is, for each input IV_i, we have to find a pair of triplets $(a_1, b_1, d_1), (a_2, b_2, d_2)$ such that

$$G(a_1, b_1, IV_i, d_1, m_1, m_2) \lll 1 = G(a_2, b_2, IV_i, d_2, m_1 \lll 1, m_2 \lll 1). \quad (1)$$

In total, we have 8 words of freedom to satisfy a 4-words equation, thus it seems that a solution should exist. Surprisingly, this is not the case for a randomly chosen value of IV_i. A simple analysis shows that the above problem (1) can be reduced to the problem of finding solution to the equation

$$(X + Y + IV_i) \lll 1 = X \lll 1 + Y \lll 1 + IV_i \quad (2)$$

Hence, IV_i needs to be highly structured, *i.e.* it has to be the sum of a fully rotational word and two rotational errors. Thus we obtain a rather strange fact, that *the simplicity of the function G[5] prevents straightforward application of rotational distinguishers.* We note that one can try to obtain rotational pairs after the first full round of BLAKE2, but then the problem becomes much more complex, while the message freedom drops.

The absence of constants in the function G can also be used to launch a distinguisher on the permutation of BLAKE2 based on internal differentials introduced by Peyrin [24]. More precisely, we use the 'squeeze attack' variant from Dinur *et al.*, that was recently used to attack Keccak [15]. We note that a similar

---

[3] Note that this keyed permutation has a 1024-bit key and 1024-bit state.

[4] A constant C is rotational (with respect to r), if $C \lll r = C$.

[5] If G were a random function, the solution would exist for any IV_i.

distinguisher was already applied to the permutations of Salsa and ChaCha [7,8] — two ciphers that inspired the design of BLAKE.

Let the four columns at the input of the permutation of BLAKE2 be equal, *i.e.* $(v_0, v_4, v_8, v_{12}) = (v_1, v_5, v_8, v_{13}) = (v_2, v_6, v_{10}, v_{14}) = (v_3, v_7, v_{11}, v_{15})$, and let all the message words (the words of the key) be the same. Then after the column step, all columns remain equal. Moreover, in the diagonal step, the first input is always taken from the top row (with all elements the same), the second from the second row, etc., thus after the diagonal step, all the columns remain identical. Hence, a round of BLAKE2 preserves this property of the state. We can use the above property to launch a distinguishing attack for the permutation of BLAKE2. We need only a single query to the permutation, then for a plaintext composed of four identical columns, we check if the ciphertext has four such columns as well. Thus for a version of the permutation with w-bit words, there are 2^w keys (one key word is arbitrarily chosen, the rest are equal) for the BLAKE2 permutation that can be distinguished with only one chosen plaintext. If all the inputs to the compression function could be chosen then the above approach could be used to produce collisions using the squeeze attack: 1) fix all the message words to some arbitrary value; 2) compress 2^{2w} different inputs, with the first column arbitrarily chosen, and the remaining three columns equal to the first. If there is a collision in one of the columns at the output, then the rest of the columns have to collide. As a column has $4w$ bits, 2^{2w} trials should be sufficient to produce collisions for the compression function — this is equivalent to 2^{128} calls for BLAKE2b, and 2^{64} for BLAKE2s. Similarly, it is possible to speed-up the search for preimages of a weak class of digests which are produced from the symmetric states — the size of the class is 2^{2w}. Again, the freedom in the input state and the message words is sufficient for the attacker to target digests from this class by only considering symmetric preimages, in time 2^{2w}. We would like to emphasize that in BLAKE2 the initialization once again prohibits this type of trivial attacks as $IV_0 \neq IV_1 \neq IV_2 \neq IV_3$, thus the above attack is not applicable to the compression/hash function of BLAKE2.

4   Fixed Points and Iterative Rotational Differentials for Search of Collisions and Preimages

The approach of § 3 can be enhanced further with the use of fixed points and iterative one-round differential characteristics[6]. Assume P is a fixed point for the round function of BLAKE2b when all the message words are equal. Then, as there are no constants in the function G, and the message permutation for each round produces the same set of message words, P is a fixed point for any number of rounds of BLAKE2b. Further, let $\Delta \to \Delta$ be a one-round iterative characteristic with a low hamming weight difference. If for the pair of states $(P, P \oplus \Delta)$ the one round differential holds, *i.e.* $\text{BLAKE2b}_{1\text{ round}}(P) \oplus \text{BLAKE2b}_{1\text{ round}}(P \oplus \Delta) = \Delta$,

---

[6] An attack exploiting fixed points in simplified version of BLAKE (without message permutations and constants) was given in [25] – that analysis is not applicable to unmodified version of BLAKE2.

then the differential would hold for any number of rounds. Hence at the output we will end up with a low hamming weight difference in the states and thus a partial-collision. To apply this technique to BLAKE2b we have to be able to: 1) find an iterative one-round characteristic with probability $2^{-p}, p < 256$, and, 2) find 2^p fixed points. However, as all the message words are identical, we have only 2^{64} different permutations and approximately the same number of fixed points, hence we must have $p < 64$.

First, let us show how to find fixed points for one round of BLAKE2b. We can accomplish this by finding fixed points for the function G and repeating the same value in all columns of P. In fact, this leads to a fixed point after only one half of the round, which in return results in a fixed point for the whole round. Let (a, b, c, d, m_1, m_2) be the inputs of the function G. We are looking for values such that $G(a, b, c, d, m, m) = (a, b, c, d)$ (note that we need the message words to coincide). From the definition of G (and further reduction), this is equivalent to solving the following system of equations:

$$(-d) \oplus a = d \ggg 16 \tag{3}$$
$$a + b + m + (c \oplus b \lll 1) + m = a \tag{4}$$
$$b \oplus (c - d) = (c \oplus b \lll 1) \ggg 24 \tag{5}$$
$$d \oplus (a + b + m) = (-d) \ggg 32 \tag{6}$$

With basic algebraic transformations the system can be reduced to:

$$a = d \ggg 16 \oplus (-d) \tag{7}$$
$$b + 2m = -(c \oplus b \lll 1) \tag{8}$$
$$b \oplus (c - d) = (c \oplus b \lll 1) \ggg 24 \tag{9}$$
$$b + m = [(-d) \ggg 32 \oplus d] - a \tag{10}$$

Let $V = [(-d) \ggg 32 \oplus d] - a$. Then we get:

$$a = d \ggg 16 \oplus (-d) \tag{11}$$
$$c = (b - 2V) \oplus b \lll 1 \tag{12}$$
$$b \oplus (c - d) = (c \oplus b \lll 1) \ggg 24 \tag{13}$$
$$m = V - b \tag{14}$$

If in (13) we replace the value of c from (12), we obtain

$$b \oplus [((b - 2V) \oplus b \lll 1) - d] = (b - 2V) \ggg 24 \tag{15}$$

Lemma 1. *The solution for the equation*

$$X \oplus [((X + A) \oplus X \lll 1) + B] = (X + A) \ggg 24 \tag{16}$$

where X is unknown, and A, B are constant 64-bit words, can be found on average in 2^{25} time.

Proof. The proof is given in the full version of the paper [18].

We can now present the algorithm for solving the system:

1. Fix a random value for d. Compute a from (11), and the value of V according to the above formula.
2. Compute the value of b from (15).
3. Compute the value of c from (12).
4. Compute the value of m from (14).

Thus we can find one fixed point with around 2^{25} computations. Note that d can take any 64-bit value, thus the number of fixed points is around 2^{64}. For each of these inputs, the 12-round compression function of BLAKE2b (*with modified IV*) has the form:

$$\begin{pmatrix} a\ a\ a\ a \\ b\ b\ b\ b \\ c\ c\ c\ c \\ d\ d\ d\ d \end{pmatrix} \xrightarrow{12\ \text{rounds}} \begin{pmatrix} a\ a\ a\ a \\ b\ b\ b\ b \\ c\ c\ c\ c \\ d\ d\ d\ d \end{pmatrix} \xrightarrow{\text{feedforward}} \begin{pmatrix} c\ c\ c\ c \\ d\ d\ d\ d \end{pmatrix}. \tag{17}$$

Next, let us focus on finding iterative one-round characteristics — a problem that has already been discussed for BLAKE-256 in the work of Dunkelman and Khovratovich [17]. The new rotation constants in BLAKE2b allow to apply their analysis without any significant modifications. However, straightforward use of their one-round characteristic based on two characteristics (with probabilities $2^{-12}, 2^{-21}$) for the function G is impossible. The problem lies in the condition $p < 64$:

- If we use the two characteristics and take four different values for columns in the state (fixed point) P then the probability of the first half round would be $2^{-2 \cdot 12 - 2 \cdot 21} = 2^{-66} < 2^{-64}$.
- If we take only two different column values, then the probability of the first half round is $2^{-12-21} = 2^{-33}$, and the same for the second half round. One can reduce the probability of the second half only with a special type of fixed points — instead of independent fixed points for each column (each function G) in the first half, one needs to deal with values that somehow depend on each other, but it is not clear if such values exist at all.
- If we take the same value for all four columns, then we get a contradiction from the characteristics — in the first half round there is one characteristic while in the second another. No value can satisfy both characteristics as in the first modular addition $(a+b+m)$, we want 4 and 8 to cancel in the first characteristic (thus 4 should produce carries), while we want to stay at 4 in the second (no carries).

Hence we need to find a high probability one-round differential characteristic that can be used in combination with fixed points. We have implemented our own search based on the analysis of the above authors, and found that none of these type of characteristics are compatible — there is no iterative characteristic $\Delta \rightarrow$

Δ for G, and all two round characteristics $\Delta_1 \rightarrow \Delta_2, \Delta_2 \rightarrow \Delta_1$ are incompatible, *i.e.* they do not hold for the same value of the input (and we want the value to be the same as we work with fixed points).

We can nonetheless produce iterative differentials but based on the rotational property of the function G. Assume (P_1, P_2) is a rotational input pair for G producing the rotational output pair (Q_1, Q_2), *i.e.* $P_2 = P_1 \lll 1, Q_2 = Q_1 \lll 1$. If P_1 is a fixed point for G, then for the second pair of input-output we get: $P_2 = P_1 \lll 1, Q_2 = Q_1 \lll 1 = P_1 \lll 1 = P_2$, *i.e.* the second input is also a fixed point. Therefore for these fixed points the iterative differential has the input (as well as the output) difference $P_1 \oplus P_2 = P_1 \oplus P_1 \lll 1$. Now recall that we want to minimize the hamming weight of this difference in order to produce partial-collisions on as many bits as possible. In fact from (17) it is clear that we want to minimize only the hamming weight of the difference in c and d. As we work with rotation on 1 to the left, it follows that if the value of c (or d) has zeroes in t most significant bits then $c \oplus c \lll 1$ has zeroes in at least $t-1$ most significant bits. This gives a hint of how to choose the fixed point P_1 using the above algorithm for finding fixed points:

1. Choose an arbitrary value of d that has zeroes in 27 MSBs.
2. Compute the values of a, b, c, d, m using the algorithm.
3. Check if c has zeroes in 27 MSBs.
4. If not, go to step 1.
5. Check if the input $(a \lll 1, b \lll 1, c \lll 1, d \lll 1, m \lll 1)$ is a fixed points.
6. If not, go to step 1.

The correct value of c at step 3 will be found after around 2^{27} different trials of d. As the rotational probability of the G function is $2^{-9.1}$, after $2^{9.1}$ good values of c one can find the second fixed point. Step 1 will be repeated $2^{27+9.1} \approx 2^{36}$ times, hence we have enough degrees of freedom in d (there are $2^{64-27} = 2^{37}$ possible values). The total complexity of the algorithm is $2^{25} \cdot 2^{27} \cdot 2^{9.1} \approx 2^{61}$. The hamming weight of the differences in both c and d will be at most 26 bits, and hence we can produce partial-collisions[7] on $8 \cdot 26 = 208$ bits. However this is *with chosen IV*. That is, we can produce the collisions only when the values of the IV correspond to our discovered values for fixed points. Note as the original IV used in BLAKE2b do not coincide, *our approach cannot be applied to the compression function of* BLAKE2b . Nonetheless, this shows that the choice of IV is sensitive to certain attacks.

A similar strategy can be applied for search of preimages for a special type of digests with $h'_0 = h'_1 = h'_2 = h'_3 = H_1$ and $h_4 = h_5 = h_6 = h_7 = H_2$. Let us assume that (h_0, h_1, H_1, H_2) is a fixed point (along with some message word m) for the function G. Then the full 12-round compression function of BLAKE2b (with modified IV) can be described as:

---
[7] Lately, collisions on some particular bits have been called partial-collisions.

$$\begin{pmatrix} h_0 & h_0 & h_0 & h_0 \\ h_1 & h_1 & h_1 & h_1 \\ H_1 & H_1 & H_1 & H_1 \\ H_2 & H_2 & H_2 & H_2 \end{pmatrix} \xrightarrow{12 \text{ r.}} \begin{pmatrix} h_0 & h_0 & h_0 & h_0 \\ h_1 & h_1 & h_1 & h_1 \\ H_1 & H_1 & H_1 & H_1 \\ H_2 & H_2 & H_2 & H_2 \end{pmatrix} \xrightarrow{\text{feedforward}} \begin{pmatrix} H_1 & H_1 & H_1 & H_1 \\ H_2 & H_2 & H_2 & H_2 \end{pmatrix}.$$

Hence, if we can find the corresponding h_0, h_1, m, we will be able to recover the preimage of the target digest. For this purpose, we use the system (7) – (10):

1. Set $c = H_1$ and $d = H_2$.
2. Compute the value of a from (7).
3. Compute the value of b from (9) — it is a system of linear equations.
4. Compute the value of m^a from (8), and m^b from (10).
5. If $m^a = m^b$ then $h_0 = a, h_1 = b, m = m^a$ is the preimage.

The condition $m^a = m^b$ holds with probability 2^{-64} and therefore among all the possible 2^{128} digests from the class (recall that $|H_1| = |H_2| = 64$), preimage based on a fixed point can be found for $2^{128-64} = 2^{64}$ of them with a negligible effort.

5   Impossible Differential Analysis

In this section we perform an impossible differential (ID) analysis for the permutation of all members of the BLAKE and BLAKE2 families. A similar analysis was done for the original BLAKE by Aumasson *et al.* at FSE 2010 [1], where the authors claimed a 5-round ID for BLAKE-256 and a 6-round ID for BLAKE-512. However these IDs were mainly found experimentally, and some of the presented characteristics had probabilities less than 1. Hence the analysis from [1] does not seem to cover more than five rounds for both BLAKE-256 and BLAKE-512.

We carry a similar analysis on the four permutations of BLAKE-256, BLAKE-512, BLAKE2s and BLAKE2b. Note that in contrast to the rotational analysis, the bit-wise addition of constants plays no role in these impossible differentials, while the value of the rotation amounts is of importance. Hence the analysis of BLAKE-256 and BLAKE2s is identical as their respective permutations only differ in constant addition. On the other hand, the analysis must be performed independently for BLAKE-512 and BLAKE2b. Our result is a 6.5-round impossible differential for all the four permutations of BLAKE and BLAKE2. As we need to insert differences in the message words, which play the role of the key when the permutations are seen as block ciphers, the analysis is performed in the related-key framework. The IDs are found by using the miss-in-the-middle technique that connects a forward and a backward characteristic with incompatible probability-one differences. The forward characteristic is on 2.5 rounds and it can be extended for an additional half round, while the backward characteristic is on 3.5 rounds. As in the original analysis, our approach heavily relies on the good (from an attacker point of view) properties of the different σ_r message words permutations, which allow to delay the propagation of differences for 1.5 rounds in both forward and backward directions.

The analysis in this paper is innovative in the way it uses additive differences to cancel a difference in the message word of G^{-1} with probability one. Besides being an interesting result on the G^{-1} function itself, this is an important part of extending the ID to more rounds. Moreover, we also formally checked the validity of our probability-one characteristics and we were able to prove they are correct — this was not fully done in [1] and was a cause of invalid IDs. This check was performed by a simple (although rather verbose and a bit tedious) manual computation that propagates the probability-one differences through the whole differential paths, as done similarly in [20].

We now detail the probability-one differential characteristics used in the ID. Differences are expressed with generalized constraints [13], in particular we use: '-' to denote that two bits are equal; '0' to denote that two bits are identical and equal to zero ('1' is defined similarly); 'x' to denote that two bits are different; 'n' (resp. 'u') to denote that two bits are different, and the first bit is zero (resp. one); '?' to denote that both bits can take an arbitrary value; we refer to this one as a 'trivial' difference.

5.1 Forward Characteristic on 2.5 Rounds

The forward characteristic starts at round 3[8] and is based on the fact that the message word m_{13} is used in the first half of a column-step call in round 3, and is not used again before the second half of a diagonal step in round 4. Consequently, we can introduce a difference in m_{13} and cancel it immediately with a difference in v_2; no difference will be introduced again for 1.5 rounds.

If we note MSB an 'x' difference in the most significant bit, the initial differences in this characteristic are then MSB for m_{13} and v_2, and no difference in any other state or message word.

In the diagonal step of round 4, a difference is introduced in the state by the difference in m_{13}. This difference quickly propagates to every state word, but some non-trivial differences occur with probability one. After the column step of round 5, *i.e.* at round 5.5, the state words for which there are non-trivial probability-one differences are listed below along with their differences (in the following, the leftmost constraint is for the MSB).

For BLAKE2b we have:

```
v0:  ?????????????????????????????????????????????????????????????????x------
v3:  ?????????????????????????????????????????????????x---------------------
v7:  ?????????????????????????????????????????????????????????????????x-------?
v11: ?????????????????????????????????????????????????????????????????x-------
v12: ????????x-------?????????????????????????????????????????????????????????
v15: ---------------?????????????????????????????????????????????????x-------
```

For BLAKE-512 we have:

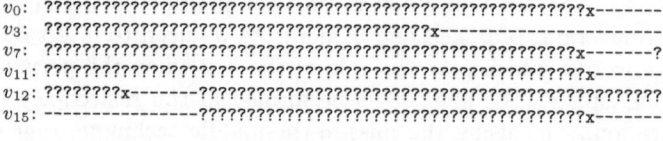

```
v0:  ?????????????????????????????????????????????????????????????????x------
v3:  ?????????????????????????????????????????????x----------------------
v7:  ????x------??????????????????????????????????????????????????????????????
v11: ?????????????????????????????????????????????????????????????????x------
v12: ?????????x-----?????????????????????????????????????????????????????????
v15: ---------------?????????????????????????????????????????????????x-----
```

---

[8] We start indexing the rounds from 0, so as to match the indexing of the σ permutations.

For BLAKE2s and BLAKE-256 we have:

```
v0:  ?????????????????????????????x---
v3:  ????????????????????x-----------
v7:  ???x---??????????????????????????
v11: ?????????????????????????????x---
v12: ????x---??????????????????????????
v15: --------??????????????????????x---
```

5.2   Backward Characteristic on 3.5 Rounds

The backward differential characteristic starts in the diagonal step of round 8. As we want to use this characteristic to mount a miss-in-the-middle with the previous forward characteristic, we need to use differences in the message words consistent with the ones used in the latter. Hence we use a single difference in the MSB of m_{13}. This message word is used in the second half of a G^{-1} call in the inverse of the diagonal step of round 8, and is not used again before the second half of a G^{-1} call in the inverse of a column step in round 7.

In order to delay the propagation of differences as much as possible, we want to proceed as for the forward characteristic and cancel the difference introduced by the message at round 8 by specifying an appropriate state difference. It is again possible to do so with probability one; in this case however, the difference will be somewhat more complex.

For BLAKE2b, we do so by using the following initial differences in the state at the beginning of the *inverse* of round 8:

```
v4  (a in G⁻¹): x--------------------------0-----------------------n-------
v9  (b in G⁻¹): -------x-------x----------------x---------------x-------n--------
v14 (c in G⁻¹): --------n-------n---------------n1---------------n------0-------
v3  (d in G⁻¹): --------n-------n---------------00---------------n---------------
```

One should note two things about this input difference. The first one is that the signed differences 'n' can all be replaced together with a signed difference 'u' of opposite sign: the only important fact is that all differences are signed similarly. Moreover, some '0' and '1'constraints in the difference for v_3 and v_{14} are here to avoid a carry propagation in the update of c in G^{-1}, which is $c \leftarrow c - d$. However, this is a sufficient condition only, and the same result can be achieved by specifying alternative differences. In other words, these differences only make a subset of the state difference we were looking for. We do not specify the whole set in here, as the existence of a subset already serves our purpose.

Similarly, for BLAKE-512, we use the following state difference:

```
v4  (a in G⁻¹): x--------------------------0-----------------------n------
v9  (b in G⁻¹): ----n---------------x------x----------------x----------------x----
v14 (c in G⁻¹): --------n------n---------------n1-------------n---------0------
v3  (d in G⁻¹): --------n------n---------------00-------------n---------------
```

Finally, for BLAKE2s and BLAKE-256 we use:

```
v4  (a in G⁻¹): x---------------0-----------n---
v9  (b in G⁻¹): ---n-------x---x-------x-------x
v14 (c in G⁻¹): ----n---n-------n1------n---0---
v3  (d in G⁻¹): ----n---n-------00------n-------
```

As for the forward characteristic, the difference in m_{13} again introduces a difference that propagates to the rest of the state. However, due to the slower diffusion of G^{-1} with respect to G, it is possible to keep non-trivial differences of probability one for more rounds. We then get the following differences after the inverse of the diagonal step of round 5, *i.e.* at round 5.5 (only the differences occurring on state words for which there were non-trivial differences after the forward characteristic are listed, but note that there were additional ones which are omitted here).

For BLAKE2b we have:

```
v0:  ?????????????????????????????????????????????????x---------------
v3:  ----------------?????????????????????????????????x---------------
v7:  ?????????????????????????????????????????????????x---------------
v12: ?????????????????????????????????????????????????x---------------
v15: -----------------------------------------------------------------
```

In this case, the differences for BLAKE-512 are actually identical. Similarly, for BLAKE2s and BLAKE-256, we have:

```
v0:  ?????????????????????????x-------
v3:  --------?????????????????x-------
v7:  ?????????????????????????x-------
v12: ?????????????????????????x-------
v15: ---------------------------------
```

5.3   Mounting the Miss-in-the-Middle

Now that we have established probability-one differences obtained at round 5.5 from two different characteristics, we show that these characteristics are incompatible. The result is immediate, when noticing that the differences on state words v_0, v_3, and v_{15} are incompatible for all four permutations of BLAKE2b, BLAKE-512, BLAKE2s, and BLAKE-256, and the differences on word v_7 are further incompatible for BLAKE2b.

As one characteristic goes in the forward direction and one in the backward, inverse direction, this incompatibility consists in effect in a miss-in-the-middle which gives a 6-rounds impossible differential. This family of ID goes from round 3 to round 8, and is specified by the differences in the message word m_{13} and in the state v_2 (at round 3), and v_3, v_4, v_9 and v_{14} (at round 8), from the two families of characteristics presented above.

5.4   Extending by One More Half-Round

The 2.5-rounds forward characteristic used in the above can easily be extended for one more half-round for all the permutations of BLAKE2 and BLAKE, thereby increasing the number of rounds reached by the ID to 6.5. The extension works as follow.

First note that the message word m_{13} is not used in the diagonal step of round 2. Thus no difference will be introduced by the message words in that step. Second, we use one of the probability-one differential characteristics for G mentioned in [1]. This characteristic has no differences in the message word, and simply maps through G the state input difference (MSB, 0, MSB, MSB ⊕ (MSB ≪ r), 0, 0) to the state output difference (MSB, 0, 0, 0). It is straightforward to check that this happens with probability one, where r is 32 for BLAKE2b and BLAKE-512, and 16 for BLAKE2s and BLAKE-256. As the output difference of this characteristic is precisely the input difference of the forward characteristic used in the ID, it is therefore possible to join the two characteristics together. The initial differences of this new forward characteristic starting at round 2.5 are then MSB for m_{13}, v_2, and v_8, and MSB ⊕ (MSB ≪ r) for v_{13}, with all other words having no differences.

6 Differential Analysis

In this section we show differential attacks on BLAKE2. The target of our attacks are be the compression function and the hash function BLAKE2b only — the analysis applies to BLAKE2s as well, but the number of attacked rounds is lower. To build high probability differential characteristics we expand the analysis of Guo and Matusiewicz [19] (see also [1]) and Dunkelman and Khovratovich [17] of BLAKE-256. In both of these papers, the difference is of a special rotational type and is chosen to cancel the effects of the rotations on 16, 12, 8, and 7 bits in the function G of BLAKE-256. The first authors note that among the four rotations in G, only the last one (on 7 bits) is not divisible by 4. Thus they choose to work with the difference 88888888 and analyze only the characteristics where before the last rotation the difference in b is 0. They linearize G, assume each modular addition involving differences has a probability of 2^{-7} (the difference in MSB saves one 2^{-1}), and with a computer search find that the best characteristic is on 4 rounds. Although their characteristic has rather high probability of 2^{-56}, they could not go more as no characteristics exist on higher number of rounds due to the condition that no difference enters the rotation on 7. The authors argue that one can consider the special case of a difference entering this rotation resulting in twice difference (i.e. 11111111) at the output, and then canceling it in the next G function, but state that their experiments show that in this case the probability of the characteristics drops significantly. Dunkelman and Khovratovich choose to work with the difference 04040404 (the probability of modular addition increases to around 2^{-4}) and consider characteristics where no difference enters the rotation on 12 bits[9]. Moreover, they consider two additional type of differences obtained by multiplying the initial difference by 2 and 3 — this way they can allow difference in rotation on 7. The authors run a full search of round-reduced characteristics with all possible configurations for the difference in the state (*i.e.* in each of the 16 words, the difference can be 0, 04040404, 08080808, 0c0c0c0c), and *no difference in the message words*. The characteristics they find are on more rounds, but have lower probability.

The new rotation amounts of 32,24,16 and 63 bits in the function G of BLAKE2b are very similar to the rotations from BLAKE-256. Hence we can apply the

---

[9] This type of characteristics were mentioned by Guo and Matusiewicz, but no detailed analysis was provided in [19].

technique of finding round-reduced characteristics from the previous two papers by considering the 64-bit differences 0404040404040404 and 0004000400040004. We also use the following improvements for the search methods:

1. In the first search we work with $\delta = $ 0404040404040404 and with two additional differences 0808080808080808, 0c0c0c0c0c0c0c0c, that is the difference in the words can be $0, \delta, 2 \times \delta$, and $3 \times \delta$. This helps us to overcome the rotation on 63, *i.e.* instead of the condition that no difference enters $\ggg$ 63 now we can allow δ to be at the input of this rotation which results in $2 \times \delta$ at the output.

2. In the second search we work with $\nabla = $ 0004000400040004 and again with two additional differences $2 \times \nabla, 3 \times \nabla$. As in the analysis of Dunkelman and Khovratovich, we require no difference at the input of rotation on 24 bits, but improve their search by considering two possibilities for the difference in each of the message words (instead of one: no difference).

The choice of 4 differences (instead of only 2) leads to the situation where in the modular addition, for the same input there are possibly several outputs. For example, $\delta + const$ can give both δ and $3 \times \delta$. Hence after the linearization, for fixed input differences to G, this function can produce several output differences. Dunkelman and Khovratovich note[10] that they get 276 possible differentials for G when the differences in a, b, c, d are one of the four $(0, 2 \times \nabla, 3 \times \nabla)$, and there is no difference in the message words. As we allow the differences $0, \delta$ (or $0, \nabla$) in the messages (see below), in the first search we end up with 4531 differentials for G, and with 1192 in the second. There are 1024 possible input differences (each of a, b, c, d can take 4 different values, while the message words can take 2), hence on average in the first search, we have 4 outputs per single input, while only one in the second. In theory (without taking into account the probabilities) this results in around $2^{2 \cdot 8} = 2^{16}$ outputs for the whole round that can be obtained from a single input in the first search, while in the second this number is 1. Thus to keep the first search practical we cannot have too many input differences. We note that the probabilities of the differentials[11] range from 2^{-8} to 2^{-75} in the first search, and 2^{-4} to 2^{-36} in the second.

In both of our searches we try to maximize the number of starting differences in the state and in the message words. We can do this up to a certain extent. For example, there are 16 message words, thus if we want to try all four possible starting differences, we will end up with $2^{16 \cdot 2} = 2^{32}$ starting points (without considering any difference in the state). To make the searches feasible, in certain cases we restrict the differences to only $0, \delta$ (or $0, \nabla$). Note that the initializations in BLAKE2 differs from BLAKE, and in particular no difference can be introduced in $v_8, v_9, v_{10}, v_{11}, v_{14}, v_{15}$. We follow strictly the definition of BLAKE2 and do not allow starting differences in any of these six words[12]. As we will see further, this

---

[10] Guo and Matusiewicz work with only 2 difference, 0 and δ, thus modular additions in G are uniquely determined and for each input they get a single output.

[11] The probability of the trivial differential with zero input-output difference is 1.

[12] We have seen in the previous sections that when the attacker can fully control the input state, then attacks on the full-round BLAKE2 are possible.

has a major impact on the maximal number of rounds the best characteristics can cover in the case of compression functions.

One final note on the message modification. In our searches we assume the attacker can always pass for free the modular additions that involve the message words in the function G, of the first round only. This is reasonable as he always controls the message and to pass these additions he needs to fix only a small amount of bits in the message words per active bit, and can use the remaining degrees of freedom in the message to go through the rest of the rounds probabilistically. Recall that in the first round all the message words are independent. More advanced message modification techniques might be available, however, as we do not know in advance the best characteristic, it is hard to predict which of the remaining modular additions in the first round can be passed for free. Using message modification anywhere but in the first round is very hard due to the condition on the fixed IV, *i.e.* once a state has been fixed in some middle round, the attacker should be sure that after going backwards the resulting initial state complies with the initialization, *i.e.* has correct values for $v_8, v_9, v_{10}, v_{11}, v_{14}, v_{15}$.

We have run the second search (with the main difference $\nabla = 00040004$ 00040004) and obtained the following results:

- For the hash function of BLAKE2b, when the difference in the message words can take any of the values $0, \nabla, 2 \times \nabla, 3 \times \nabla$ (in total $2^{16 \cdot 2} = 2^{32}$ starting differences), the best characteristic is only on 2 rounds and holds with probability 2^{-198}.
- For the compression function of BLAKE2b, when the difference in the chaining values and the counters can take $0, \nabla, 2 \times \nabla, 3 \times \nabla$, and the difference in the message words is 0 or ∇ (in total $2^{10 \cdot 2 + 16 \cdot 1} = 2^{36}$ starting differences), the best characteristics is on 3 rounds with probability 2^{-336}.

The first search (with the main difference $\delta = 0404040404040404$) requires much more computational power as we are dealing with average forking on 4, *i.e.* for each input of G there are 4 outputs. We had to optimize the code significantly in order to try all possible inputs. The outcome of this search is as follow:

- For the hash function of BLAKE2b, when the difference in the message words can take any of the values 0 or δ (in total 2^{16} starting differences), the best characteristic is on 3 rounds and holds with probability 2^{-344}.
- For the compression function of BLAKE2b, when the difference in the chaining values, the counters, and the message words can take $0, \delta$ (in total $2^{10 \cdot 1 + 16 \cdot 1} = 2^{26}$ starting differences), the best characteristics is on 4 rounds with probability $2^{-366.5}$.

Note that in both of the cases (hash and compression), the first search produced better characteristics. Moreover, note that although we have matched the number of attacked rounds in the case of compression function (both BLAKE2 and BLAKE have differentials on 4 rounds), the probability of the characteristic of BLAKE2 is only $2^{-366.5}$ whereas the best known characteristics for BLAKE hash function is of 2.5 rounds with probability 2^{-56}. Therefore, despite launching a search with much higher number of starting differences, *the new initialization used in* BLAKE2 *significantly limits the freedom*[13] *of the attacker against this type of differentials attacks.* Thus the tweaked initialization seems to have much better security properties.

We are able to extend for one half round each of the differentials for the compression and the hash function. In the case of former, we allow any difference in the last rotation on 63 bits (our search prohibits this, thus it was not able to find it). We end up with a differential characteristic on 4.5 rounds for the compression function of BLAKE2b that holds with probability $2^{-494.5}$ — see the full version for the details [18]. Similarly, we can go for an additional half round for the hash function BLAKE2b. We get low probability characteristic, however by using neutral bits we should be able to find a pair of messages that conform to the differential with a complexity of around 2^{480} hash function calls (details are again left to the full version [18]). Without the initialization limitations, we extend similar characteristics search to the permutation and obtain a result on 5.5 round with probability 2^{-928}; such a characteristic is given in the full version [18].

Table 2. Comparison of the attacks on BLAKE2 and BLAKE

Attack	BLAKE2			BLAKE		
	perm.	cf.	chosen IV	perm.	cf.	ch. IV
Rotational	12	-	7	-	-	-
Collision with internal diff.	12	-	12	-	-	-
Near-Collision	-	3	12	4	4	4
Weak class of keys/preimages	12	-	12	-	-	-
Impossible differential	6.5	-	-	6.5	-	-
Boomerang	5.5	5.5	5.5	8	7	8
Differential	5.5	4.5	12	4	4	4-6
Hash function differential	3.5			2.5		

7   Conclusion

A comparison of the security of BLAKE2 and BLAKE against the attacks we have examined in this paper is given in Tbl. 2. Based on our findings we can deduce several important facts about the impact of the tweaks in BLAKE2:

1. The absence of constants in the function G has a major impact on the basic building block, *i.e.* the keyed permutation of BLAKE2, and this cipher can be fully attacked. We can launch a key recovery rotational attack on all 12 rounds of the permutation BLAKE2b with a high complexity, and a distinguisher based on internal differentials that holds for 2^{64} keys of BLAKE2b

---

[13] No difference can be introduced in $v_8, v_9, v_{10}, v_{11}, v_{14}, v_{15}$.

(2^{32} for BLAKE2s) based on a single query. Thus one should be careful when using this permutation in applications. Note that neither of these attacks is applicable to BLAKE.

2. The change of rotation amounts in BLAKE2b does matter against certain types of attacks. The differentials we have presented in § 6 are based in particular on the fact that all rotations are either divisible by 8 or are close to being divisible by 8 (*e.g.* 63). In fact, the same search of differential characteristics applies to BLAKE2b and BLAKE-256, however the latter is a 256-bit function while the former is 512-bit, and thus permits characteristics with lower probabilities.

3. In the initialization, omitting the double use of the counter, as well as *introducing constants IV* reduces the number of attacked rounds, *i.e.* increases the security of the compression function. Note that in the differential attacks, we were able to match (and advance more) the number of rounds as in BLAKE only because we used a much more complex search of differential characteristics and we were dealing with 512-bit hash. For instance, if the initialization in BLAKE2 were the same as in BLAKE, most likely we could penetrate more rounds in the differential attack (we could not run the search for this version as it requires significant amount of computations). In fact, the new initialization is crucial as if one used the same as in BLAKE, then collisions (respectively partial-collisions) could be produced with only 2^{128} (respectively 2^{61}) compression function calls.

4. The complete absence of constants in G makes the security of the compression function highly dependent on the right choice of IV (this is not the case of BLAKE). That is, even with the new initialization but different IV, one could still launch attacks — see §§ 3 and 4. The 'weak' IV on the other hand are highly structured (either rotational, all equal, or some particular values). The random choice of IV as in BLAKE2 makes these weaknesses impossible to exploit.

To summarize, *based on our results*, we have shown that the tweaks introduced by BLAKE2, if analyzed separately, reduce the security of the version in certain theoretical attack frameworks as our analysis suggests existence of several efficient attacks on the basic building block of BLAKE2. However, taken together the tweaks do not have a significant impact on the security of the hash/compression function, aside from the one round increase (resulting in a 3.5 round attack) against the hash function and a half round in the case of compression function. Thus BLAKE2, similarly to its predecessor BLAKE, has a very high security margin against all known attacks even after reducing the number of rounds by four.

Acknowledgments. The work in this paper was partially supported by the Singapore National Research Foundation Fellowship 2012 (NRF-NRFF2012-06). We would also like to thank the anonymous reviewers from SAC 2013 and CT-RSA 2014 for their helpful comments.

References

1. Aumasson, J.P., Guo, J., Knellwolf, S., Matusiewicz, K., Meier, W.: Differential and Invertibility Properties of BLAKE. In: [21], pp. 318–332
2. Aumasson, J.P., Henzen, L., Meier, W., Phan, R.C.W.: SHA-3 proposal BLAKE, version 1.3 (2008), https://131002.net/blake/
3. Aumasson, J.-P., Meier, W., Phan, R.C.-W.: The Hash Function Family LAKE. In: Nyberg, K. (ed.) FSE 2008. LNCS, vol. 5086, pp. 36–53. Springer, Heidelberg (2008)
4. Aumasson, J.-P., Neves, S., Wilcox-O'Hearn, Z., Winnerlein, C.: BLAKE2: Simpler, Smaller, Fast as MD5. In: Jacobson, M., Locasto, M., Mohassel, P., Safavi-Naini, R. (eds.) ACNS 2013. LNCS, vol. 7954, pp. 119–135. Springer, Heidelberg (2013)
5. Aumasson, J.P., Neves, S., Wilcox-O'Hearn, Z., Winnerlein, C.: BLAKE2: simpler, smaller, fast as MD5 — version 2013.01.29 (2013), https://blake2.net/
6. Aumasson, J.P., Neves, S., Wilcox-O'Hearn, Z., Winnerlein, C.: The BLAKE2 website (May 2013), https://blake2.net
7. Bernstein, D.J.: ChaCha, a variant of Salsa20 (2008), http://cr.yp.to/chacha.html.
8. Bernstein, D.J.: The Salsa20 Family of Stream Ciphers. In: Robshaw, M., Billet, O. (eds.) New Stream Cipher Designs. LNCS, vol. 4986, pp. 84–97. Springer, Heidelberg (2008), http://cr.yp.to/snuffle.html
9. Bertoni, G., Daemen, J., Peeters, M., Assche, G.V.: The KCECCAK reference (January 2011), http://keccak.noekeon.org/
10. Biham, E., Dunkelman, O.: A Framework for Iterative Hash Functions - HAIFA. IACR Cryptology ePrint Archive 2007, 278 (2007)
11. Biryukov, A., et al.: Cryptanalysis of the LAKE Hash Family. In: Dunkelman, O. (ed.) FSE 2009. LNCS, vol. 5665, pp. 156–179. Springer, Heidelberg (2009)
12. Biryukov, A., Nikolić, I., Roy, A.: Boomerang Attacks on BLAKE-32. In: Joux, A. (ed.) FSE 2011. LNCS, vol. 6733, pp. 218–237. Springer, Heidelberg (2011)
13. De Cannière, C., Rechberger, C.: Finding SHA-1 Characteristics: General Results and Applications. In: Lai, X., Chen, K. (eds.) ASIACRYPT 2006. LNCS, vol. 4284, pp. 1–20. Springer, Heidelberg (2006)
14. Chang, S.J., Perlner, R., Burr, W.E., Turan, M.S., Kelsey, J.M., Paul, S., Bassham, L.E.: Third-Round Report of the SHA-3 Cryptographic Hash Algorithm Competition. NIST Interagency Report 7896 (2012)
15. Dinur, I., Dunkelman, O., Shamir, A.: Self-Differential Cryptanalysis of Up to 5 Rounds of SHA-3. IACR Cryptology ePrint Archive 2012, 672 (2012)
16. Dinur, I., Dunkelman, O., Shamir, A.: Collision Attacks on Up to 5 Rounds of SHA-3 Using Generalized Internal Differentials. In: FSE (2013)
17. Dunkelman, O., Khovratovich, D.: Iterative Differentials, Symmetries, and Message Modification in BLAKE-256. In: ECRYPT2 Hash Workshop (2011)
18. Guo, J., Karpman, P., Nikolić, I., Wang, L., Wu, S.: Analysis of BLAKE2. IACR Cryptology ePrint Archive 2013, 467 (2013)
19. Guo, J., Matusiewicz, K.: Round-reduced near-collisions of BLAKE-32. In: WEWoRC (2009), http://guo.crypto.sg/blake-col.pdf
20. Guo, J., Thomsen, S.S.: Deterministic Differential Properties of the Compression Function of BMW. In: Biryukov, A., Gong, G., Stinson, D.R. (eds.) SAC 2010. LNCS, vol. 6544, pp. 338–350. Springer, Heidelberg (2011)
21. Hong, S., Iwata, T. (eds.) FSE 2010. LNCS, vol. 6147. Springer, Heidelberg (2010)

22. Khovratovich, D., Nikolić, I.: Rotational Cryptanalysis of ARX. In: [21], pp. 333–346
23. Li, J., Xu, L.: Attacks on Round-Reduced BLAKE. IACR Cryptology ePrint Archive 2009, 238 (2009), https://eprint.iacr.org/2009/238
24. Peyrin, T.: Improved Differential Attacks for ECHO and Grøstl. In: Rabin, T. (ed.) CRYPTO 2010. LNCS, vol. 6223, pp. 370–392. Springer, Heidelberg (2010)
25. Vidali, J., Nose, P., Pasalic, E.: Collisions for variants of the BLAKE hash function. Inf. Process. Lett. 110(14-15), 585–590 (2010)

An Automated Evaluation Tool for Improved Rebound Attack: New Distinguishers and Proposals of ShiftBytes Parameters for Grøstl

Yu Sasaki[1], Yuuki Tokushige[2], Lei Wang[3], Mitsugu Iwamoto[2], and Kazuo Ohta[2]

[1] NTT Secure Platform Laboratories
sasaki.yu@lab.ntt.co.jp
[2] The University of Electro-Communications
{yuuki.tokushige,mitsugu,kazuo.ohta}@uec.ac.jp
[3] Nanyang Technological University
Wang.Lei@ntu.edu.sg

Abstract. In this paper, we study the security of AES-like permutations against the improved rebound attack proposed by Jean *et al.* at FSE 2012 which covers three full-active rounds in the inbound phase. The attack is very complicated and hard to verify its optimality when the state size is large and rectangle, namely the numbers of rows and columns are different. In the inbound phase of the improved rebound attack, several SuperSBoxes are generated for each of forward analysis and backward analysis. The attack searches for paired values that are consistent with all SuperSBoxes. The attack complexity depends on the order of the SuperSBoxes to be analyzed, and detecting the best order is hard. In this paper, we develop an automated complexity evaluation tool with several fast implementation techniques. The tool enables us to examine all the possible orders of the SuperSBoxes, and provides the best analysis order and complexity. We apply the tool to large block Rijndael in the known-key setting and the Grøstl-512 permutation. As a result, we obtain the first 9-round distinguisher for Rijndael-192 and Rijndael-224. It also shows the impossibility of the improved rebound attack against 9-round Rijndael-160 and 10-round Rijndael-256, and the optimality of the previous distinguisher against the 10-round Grøstl-512 permutation. Moreover, the efficiency of the improved rebound attack depends on the parameter of the ShiftRows operation. Our tool can exhaustively examine all the possible ShiftRows parameters to search for the ones that can resist the attack. We show new parameters for the Grøstl-512 permutation obtained by our tool, which can resist a 10-round improved rebound attack while the specification parameter cannot resist it.

Keywords: Rijndael, Grøstl, rebound attack, ShiftRows, ShiftBytes.

1 Introduction

Rijndael [1] is one of the most successful block ciphers which was later adopted as Advanced Encryption Standard (AES). Since then, many primitives have been

J. Benaloh (Ed.): CT-RSA 2014, LNCS 8366, pp. 424–443, 2014.

designed based on AES. Security analysis against AES and AES-like structures has been discussed actively. One approach is the known-key distinguisher [2], which aims to distinguish a randomly instantiated AES-like permutation from an ideal 128-bit permutation.

The rebound attack is a strong distinguishing attack against AES-like hash functions presented by Mendel *et al.* [3]. It was then applied to the known-key distinguisher on 7-round AES [4]. This was extended to 8-round AES with *SuperSBox* technique by Gilbert and Peyrin [5].[1] After that, the rebound attack was applied to many other AES-like primitives with several technical improvements. Showing references of all previous rebound attacks is very hard. Several examples are [7,8,9,10]. Since the publication of the 8-round distinguisher by [5], extending it to 9-round AES-like permutations had been a big challenge for a few years. At FSE 2012, Jean *et al.* [11] finally solved this problem with presenting a 9-round distinguisher against AES-like permutations with $r \geq 8$, where r represents the number of rows and columns in a state.[2] The technique in [11] was not given a specific name by the authors. In this paper, we call their technique *improved rebound attack* according to their paper title. In short, the attack generates r SuperSBoxes for the forward computation and r SuperSBoxes for the backward computation, and searches for the match efficiently at some middle state by determining the values for each SuperSBox one by one.

Jean *et al.* also applied the improved rebound attack to the 1024-bit permutation used in the hash function Grøstl-512 [13], which is based on an AES-like permutation with 8 rows and 16 columns. However, for a rectangle state size, the attack becomes complicated. The attack generates 16 SuperSBoxes for each of the forward and backward computations. The attack complexity depends on the order that these SuperSBoxes are analyzed, and detecting the best analysis order is hard. Indeed, in [11], the reason for choosing their analysis order and its optimality are not discussed at all.

Although the attack in [11] can work, its ambiguity raises several questions.

- Is the procedure, *i.e.*, the order of analyzing columns and rows in [11] the best? Is there any other choice to achieve a better complexity?
- How can we apply the improved rebound attack to other AES-like permutations with different state sizes? For example, can it be applied to Rijndael with the large block sizes (160, 192, 224, and 256 bits)? Note that it cannot be applied to the square-state Rijndael (AES).
- The attack procedure is heavily dependent on the parameter of ShiftRows, which is one of the AES-round operations. Can it be used to distinguish different ShiftRows parameters for AES-like permutation designs? In particular, are there any ShiftRows parameter stronger than others with respect to the resistance to the improved rebound attack?

---

[1] The similar technique was independently proposed by [6].

[2] A 9-round known-key distinguisher on AES ($r = 4$) is still an open problem. A 9-round chosen-key distinguisher has recently been found by Fouque *et al.* [12].

Table 1. Summary of Known-key Distinguishers. The fifth and sixth columns show the evaluation for different ShiftRows parameters. N/A represents that new attacks or improved attacks are not obtained.

Target	Previous Results (rounds,time,ref.)	Rounds	Our Results Original SR	Different SR weakest	strongest	Generic attack
Rijndael-160	$(7, 2^{40}, [14]^{\dagger})$	9	N/A	2^{112}	2^{112}	2^{96}
Rijndael-192	$(8, 2^{48}, [15])$	9	2^{112}	2^{112}	2^{112}	2^{128}
Rijndael-224	$(8, 2^{72}, [14])$	9	2^{120}	2^{104}	2^{120}	2^{160}
Rijndael-256	$(9, 2^{48}, [15])$	10	N/A	2^{128}	2^{128}	2^{96}
Grøstl-512	$(10, 2^{392}, [11])$	10	N/A	2^{336}	2^{464}	2^{448}

†Though [15] did not mention anything, we found that the approach of [15] can be applied to 8 rounds trivially with the complexity of 2^{48}.

1.1   Our Contributions

We answer the above problems by developing a tool to evaluate the best complexity of the improved rebound attack. Recall that the attack complexity depends on the state size and the parameter for the ShiftRows operation. Our tool takes the state size and the ShiftRows parameter as input, and produces the minimum complexity to apply the improved rebound attack. Our contributions can be summarized as follows. The results are also summarized in Table 1.

1. For a given state size and ShiftRows parameter, the attack complexity depends on which order we analyze forward SuperSBoxes and backward SuperSBoxes. We firstly make an algorithm when the order of the SuperSBoxes to be analyzed is fixed. We then develop a tool which automatically returns the complexity of that algorithm. Finally, by exhaustively trying all possible orders of the SuperSBoxes to be analyzed, we obtain the minimum attack complexity. Note that the state size of the Grøstl-512 permutation is too large to examine exhaustively in a trivial way. We avoid this problem by proposing several implementation techniques.

2. We apply our tool to large-block Rijndael in the known-key setting and the 1024-bit permutation of Grøstl-512. As a result, we find that the improved rebound attack can be applied to 9 rounds of Rijndael-192 and Rijndael-224. We also find that the improved rebound attack cannot be applied to 9 rounds of Rijndael-160 and 10 rounds of Rijndael-256. For Grøstl-512, we find that the previous attack achieved the best complexity. As far as we know, our results on Rijndael-192 and -224 are the best distinguishers in terms of the number of rounds.

3. We apply our tool for all possible ShiftRows parameters of each state size in order to check if there exists stronger ShiftRows parameter than the one in the specification. As a result, we find stronger ShiftRows parameters of the Grøstl-512 permutation, which can resist the 10-round distinguisher.

1.2   Paper Outline

The paper is organized as follows. Specifications and previous work are introduced in Sect. 2. The new tool is explained in Sect. 3. Distinguishers obtained by the tool are explained in Sect. 4. New ShiftRows parameters are discussed in Sect. 5. Finally, we conclude this paper in Sect. 6.

2   Preliminaries

2.1   Specification of Large Block Rijndael

The block cipher Rijndael was designed by Daemen and Rijmen in 1998 and was selected as Advanced Encryption Standard (AES) in 2000 [16,17]. The updated version of Rijndael supports five block sizes; 128, 160, 192, 224, 256 bits and three different key sizes; 128, 192, 256 bits. The number of rounds, N_b, is dependent on the block size and key size, which is defined in Table 2.

In the key schedule function, round keys are generated from the original secret key. Because round keys are regarded as given constant numbers in the known-key setting, the key-schedule function does not have any impact. Hence, we omit its description.

The internal states for 128-, 160-, 192-, 224-, and 256-bit blocks are represented by $4 \times 4, 4 \times 5, 4 \times 6, 4 \times 7$ and 4×8 byte-arrays, respectively. The number of columns is represented by a variable N_c, i.e., $N_c = 4, 5, 6, 7$, and 8 for 128-, 160-, 192-, 224-, and 256-bit blocks, respectively. First of all, the key is XORed to the plaintext. Then, a round operation consisting of the following four operations is iteratively applied to update the state N_b times.

- SubBytes(SB): substitute each byte according to an S-box.
- ShiftRows(SR): apply the s_j-byte left rotation to each byte at row $j, (j = 0, 1, 2, 3)$ of the state, where s_j is defined as (0,1,2,3), (0,1,2,3), (0,1,2,3), (0,1,2,4), and (0,1,3,4) for 128-, 160-, 192-, 224-, and 256-bit blocks, respectively.
- MixColumns(MC): multiply each column by a maximum-distance separable (MDS) matrix.
- AddRoundKey(AR): apply XOR with a round key. Throughout this paper, key values are randomly generated constants.

Table 2. Number of Rounds, N_b, for Large-Block Rijndael

Key size	Block size				
	128	160	192	224	256
128	10	11	12	13	14
192	12	12	12	13	14
256	14	14	14	14	14

The MixColumns operation is not computed at the last round. According to the designers [1], the parameter of ShiftRows was determined to satisfy the following aspects.

1. The four offsets are different and the parameter for the first row is 0;
2. Resistance against attacks using truncated differentials;
3. Resistance against the integral attack;
4. Simplicity.

2.2 Specification of Grøstl-512 Permutation

Grøstl [13] was designed by Gauravaram *et al.*, and was one of the finalists in the SHA-3 competition [18]. Grøstl-512, which is the 512-bit digest version, adopts two 1024-bit AES-like permutations called P_{1024} and Q_{1024}. The internal state is represented by an 8×16 byte-array. The number of rounds is 14. The round operation consists of the following four computations.

- AddRoundConstant(AR): apply XOR with a round constant.
- SubBytes(SB): substitute each byte with the S-box, which is the same as the one for Rijndael.
- ShfitBytes(SR): apply the s_j-byte left rotation to each byte at row j of the state where, s_j are $(0, 1, 2, 3, 4, 5, 6, 11)$ and $(1, 3, 5, 11, 0, 2, 4, 6)$ for P_{1024} and Q_{1024}, respectively.
- MixBytes(MC): multiply each column by an MDS matrix.

Although the operation names are different between Rijndael and Grøstl, the effect is the same especially for the rebound attack. Hence, we unify the abbreviations AR, SB, SR, MC. According to the designers [13], the parameter of ShfitBytes was determined to satisfy that *each byte of the state affects each column in at least two distinct ways after three rounds.*

2.3 Notations

The round function of Rijndael can be viewed as AR, SB, SR, MC in this order, and the last round is AR, SB, SR, AR. We use this view to unify the representation with Grøstl.

We denote the initial state for round x by $\#Sx^I$. Then, states immediately after AR, SB, SR and MC in round x are denoted by $\#Sx^{AR}, \#Sx^{SB}, \#Sx^{SR}$ and $\#Sx^{MC}$, respectively.

2.4 Rebound Attack

Rebound attack was developed by Mendel *et al.* [3], which is a distinguishing attack particularly useful for evaluating AES-like structures. It produces a pair of plaintexts satisfying some types of truncated differential characteristics for AES-like permutations. It firstly determines a characteristic and divides it into the inbound part and the outbound part. Let $\mathcal{C}$ and $\mathcal{D}$ be the differential forms where one column and one diagonal of the state is active, respectively. Also, let $\mathcal{F}$ be the full active state. With the rebound attack, a 2-round differential transition $\mathcal{C} \rightarrow \mathcal{F} \rightarrow \mathcal{D}$ can be satisfied only with 2^8 computations and 2^8 memory. The solutions of the inbound part are later used to satisfy the outbound part probabilistically. The attack becomes a valid distinguisher if a solution for the entire characteristic is found faster than that for the ideal case.

The SuperSBox technique for the rebound attack was independently proposed by Lamberger et al. [6] and Gilbert and Peyrin [5]. It satisfies a 3-round differential transition $\mathcal{C} \rightarrow \mathcal{F} \rightarrow \mathcal{F} \rightarrow \mathcal{D}$ with 2^{8r} computations and 2^{8r} memory, where r is the number of bytes in a single column. The technique exploits the fact that the non-linear part inside two rounds, AR, SB, SR, MC, AR, SB can be computed independently for each column with 2^{8r} computations. Therefore, by making a look-up table with 2^{8r} entries for each column, the rebound attack can be extended to cover 1 more full active state. These look-up tables with the size of 2^{8r} data are called SuperSBoxes.

Improved Rebound Attack with Three Full Active Rounds. Jean et al. presented a further extension of the rebound attack, which can satisfy a 4-round differential transition $\mathcal{C} \rightarrow \mathcal{F} \rightarrow \mathcal{F} \rightarrow \mathcal{F} \rightarrow \mathcal{D}$ [11]. Because this paper is heavily dependent on [11], we explain it in details.

If the attack is applied to a square state, i.e., the sizes of rows and columns are identical, the attack is relatively simple. The attack generates $2r$ SuperSBoxes, r are from the forward computation labeled as $L_1, \ldots, L_r$ and r are from the backward computation labeled as $L'_1, \ldots, L'_r$. These tables match at some state. An example for $r = 8$ is shown in Fig. 1. For the first step, the values of four SuperSBoxes from the backward, L'_1, L'_2, L'_3, L'_4 are chosen. This fixes both the values and differences of four bytes in each diagonal. In other words, each diagonal has a 64-bit constraint. For the second step, the values of eight SuperSBoxes from the forward computation are chosen so that the constrained four bytes are satisfied. Because the size of the constraint is 64 bits, and each SuperSBox has 64-bit freedom degrees, each SuperSBox returns a single result on average. At this stage, both of values and differences are fixed for all bytes. For the third step, the values of four SuperSBoxes L'_5, L'_6, L'_7, L'_8 are chosen. Each column has a 128-bit constraint and each SuperSBox has only 64-bit freedom degrees. Hence, the probability that each column has a solution is 2^{-64}, and the probability is 2^{-256} for four SuperSBoxes. By iterating the first step 2^{256} times, the attack can obtain a solution. In the end, the 4-round differential transition is satisfied with a complexity of 2^{256}. In general, the cost to satisfy the above 3-round transition can be expressed as $2^{8r \cdot r/2} = 2^{4r^2}$. This technique can be a valid distinguisher only if $r \geq 8$, which implies that the attack cannot be applied to the square state Rijndael ($r = 4$), or AES.

Jean et al. also applied the technique to the 1024-bit permutation of Grøstl-512. Then, the attack becomes very complicated because each SuperSBox does not have interaction with all SuperSBoxes from the opposite direction. Let us discuss the case where the state consists of r rows and $2r$ columns. An example for $r = 8$ is shown in Fig. 2. The attack prepares $4r$ SuperSBoxes, $2r$ are from

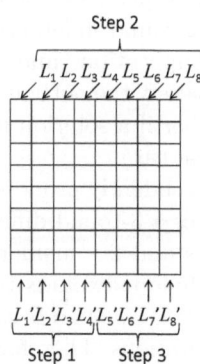

Fig. 1. Improved Rebound Attack for Square State. L_i and L_i' denote SuperSBoxes for the forward computation and the backward computation, respectively.

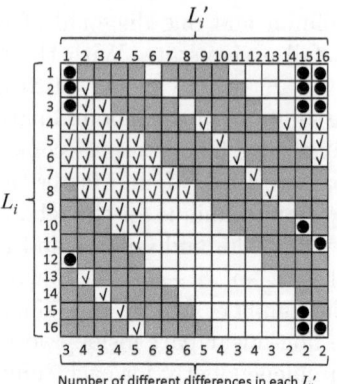

Fig. 2. Improved Rebound Attack for Non-square State. White cells denote that two SuperSBoxes interact each other and black cells denote that no interaction exists. '$\sqrt{}$' denotes a byte with a fixed value and difference. '•' denotes a byte with a fixed difference, but the value is not fixed. 'Number of different differences' shows the maximum number of differences for each column.

the forward computation and $2r$ are from the backward computation. The attack first analyzes which SuperSBoxes interact each other. In Fig. 2, white cells denote that there exists the interaction and black cells denote that no interaction exists. The matched state will be passed to the MixColumns operation, and then the number of active bytes for each column needs to be reduced accordingly to the truncated differential characteristic. For example, in Fig. 2, the number of active bytes in the left most column needs to be reduced to 3 after the next MixColumns operation, which means that the number of possible differences for the left most column is at most $2^{8 \times 3}$. In [11], this type of constraint is called the maximum number of different differences (NDD), and NDD is given at the bottom of Fig. 2. Then, the confirming pairs are searched for with a guess-and-determine approach. At the first step, the values and difference for L_2', L_3', L_4', L_5' are chosen. '$\sqrt{}$' denotes the byte with a fixed value and difference. Then, L_5, L_6, L_7, L_8 have a 64-bit constraint and thus these SuperSBoxes are fixed uniquely. The analysis further continues and L_1' and L_{16}' reaches NDD, which fixes the difference of L_1' and L_{16}'. '•' denotes the byte with a fixed difference, but the value is not fixed. Similarly, the value and difference of L_4 is fixed, and then the difference of L_{15}' is fixed, and all information in Fig. 2 is obtained. The analysis will continue by newly guessing the elements in L_6'. We omit the remaining attack procedure. As a result, the desired pair is obtained with 2^{280} computations.

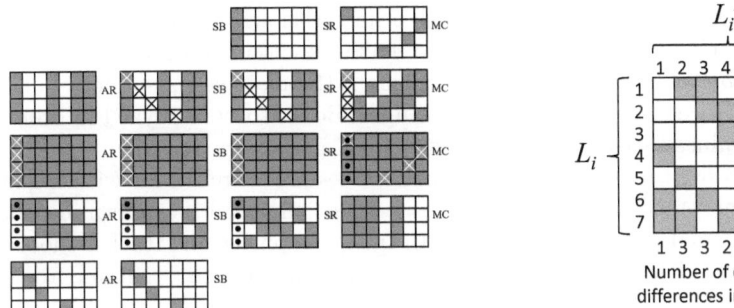

Fig. 3. Inbound Characteristics for Rijndael-224   **Fig. 4.** Intersection Table for Rijndael-224

Although the attack in [11] can work correctly, it raises several open problems.

- Is the procedure, *i.e.*, the order of guessing columns and rows in [11] best? For example, for the first step, is there other choice instead of L'_2, L'_3, L'_4, L'_5 to achieve a better complexity?
- How can we apply the technique to other AES-like permutations with different state size?
- How can we apply the technique to other ShiftRows parameters? Moreover, are there any ShiftRows parameters which can resist this attack?

3   An Evaluation Tool for Improved Rebound Attack

We develop an automated complexity evaluation tool for the improved rebound attack which works for any state size and ShiftRows parameter. Our tool returns the minimum attack complexity to bypass four-round inbound phase. The entire differential characteristic must be fixed in advance. For AES-like permutations, the best differential characteristic can be almost uniquely obtained. In this paper, we analyze the following characteristic for the inbound phase.

$$\mathcal{C} \to 4\mathcal{C} \to \mathcal{F} \to 4\mathcal{D} \to \mathcal{D} \text{ for large-block Rijndael,}$$

$$\mathcal{C} \to 8\mathcal{C} \to \mathcal{F} \to 8\mathcal{D} \to \mathcal{D} \text{ for the Grøstl-512 permutation,}$$

where $r\mathcal{C}$ and $r\mathcal{D}$ represents that r columns and r diagonals are active, respectively. We fix the active position to the left most column and diagonals. An example for Rijndael-224 is shown in Fig. 3. Active bytes are colored in grey. Cross lines ($\times$) and black circles ($\bullet$) represent a single SuperSBox for the forward computation (L_1) and backward computation (L'_1), respectively. The SuperSBoxes from two directions match right after SR in the third inbound round.

3.1   Overview

Our tool takes the state size, the ShiftRows parameter and the inbound differential characteristic as input. The first step is making a table like Fig. 2 in order to analyze which SuperSBoxes interact each other. Although the authors of [11] did not give a specific name for this table, to make the discussion easier, we name it an *intersection table*. The second step, which is the main step, is identifying the best attack procedure, *i.e.* the order of SuperSBoxes to be analyzed in order to find paired values satisfying the inbound differential characteristic.

In the improved rebound attack, paired values are searched for with a guess-and-determine procedure, which iterates a guess phase and a determine phase until all freedom degrees are consumed. In the guess phase, an attacker chooses a SuperSBox in which freedom degrees still remain, and for each remaining freedom degrees, the attacker fixes pairs (value and difference) for that SuperSBox. The fixed bytes become constraints for other SuperSBoxes. In the determine phase, for all SuperSBoxes, the attacker discards the pairs which do not satisfy the constraints. Therefore, the remaining freedom degrees are reduced. If the number of constraints are bigger than or equal to the remaining freedom degrees for some SuperSBox, the SuperSBox is fully fixed and this increases constraints for other SuperSBoxes. The determine phase is iterated until no information is updated without new guess. The search procedure can be summarized as follows.

1. generate the intersection table
2. UNTIL all freedom degrees are consumed
3.   run the guess phase (choose a SuperSBox with freedom degrees and fix pairs)
4.   UNTIL no information is updated without a new guess
5.   run the determine procedure (reduce remaining freedom degrees)
6.   end of UNTIL
7. end of UNTIL

In short, the guess phase increases the number of candidates for value and difference, and the determine phase fixes as much state information as possible by consuming the generated number of candidates. The final attack complexity is the largest number of candidates during the entire guess-and-determine phase.

The attack complexity depends on the order of SuperSBoxes we run the guess phase at Step 3. We exhaustively try all possible orders of SuperSBoxes to be analyzed, and detect the best analysis order and evaluate the attack complexity.

3.2   Generating Intersection Table

Under the fixed characteristic, the intersection table can be generated only with the state size and the ShiftRows parameter. The first task is determining black and white cells of the intersection table. In Fig. 3, L_1 and L'_1 share one byte, and thus they interact each other. Similarly, L_1 interacts with L'_4, L'_6 and L'_7. These cells become white, and intersections with L'_2, L'_3 and L'_5 are filled with black. We call the intersection between L_1 and L'_i for all i *rowmodel*. The other rows of the intersection table can be derived with rotating the rowmodel by $y-1$ positions to right for the y-th row.

Another task is counting NDD in each L'_i. This can be done easily if the differential characteristic is fixed. With the example in Fig. 3, the match of the

SuperSBoxes is done in the third inbound round after the ShiftRows operation. This state is fully active, however, the difference of each column cannot take all values. For the first column, the difference after the next MixColumns operation can only have 1 active byte. Thus, freedom degrees of the difference of the first column is only 1 byte. The result for Rijndael-224 is shown in Fig. 4.

3.3 Complexity Evaluation of Guess-and-Determine Phase

We exhaustively try all possible orders of rows and columns. Here we describe the procedure for the fixed order. It basically iterates the guess phase and the determine phase. The determine phase also consists of the iterative analysis of rows and columns until no more information is added without further guesses.

Guess Phase. During the attack, in the guess phase, the value and difference of the target row or column are exhaustively guessed. The correctness of each guess must be later checked with processing the search procedure. In our tool, we store the current number of guesses to be checked and the current complexity. Therefore every time the guess is done, our tool increases the current number of candidates and the current complexity by a factor of the remaining freedom degrees for that row or column. After each guess, the value and difference of the target row or column are fully fixed. Hence, the tool erases the remaining freedom degrees for the target row or column, and passes the state information to the next determine procedure. In summary, the guess phase performs the following three operations for the target row or column.

1. increase the current number of candidates by a factor of the remaining freedom degrees
2. update the current complexity if the current number of candidates is greater than the current complexity
3. erase the freedom degrees of the target row or column

The guess phase is the only one which increases the attack complexity. Note that in the guess phase, the value and difference are always fixed simultaneously.

Determine Phase. In the determine phase, for each row or column, we compare the sizes of the newly generated constraint and the remaining freedom degrees. If the new constraint is bigger than the freedom degrees, the valid value and difference are expected only with a probability less than 1. This implies that the number of candidates to pass the determine phase is reduced and thus the complexity for the following search procedure is reduced by the same factor. Therefore, in our tool, we reduce the current number of candidates and make the target row or column fully fixed. If the constraint and the freedom degrees are the same size, one value and difference is expected. Thus our tool simply eliminates the freedom degrees and makes the target row or column fully fixed. If the constraint is smaller than the freedom degrees, the tool reduces the remaining freedom degrees by a factor of the new constraint.

For the row information, which is the SuperSBoxes for the forward computation, we always consider the value and difference at the same time. This is because that the forward SuperSBoxes cover two SubBytes layers and we cannot argue difference and value independently. While, the backward SuperSBoxes only cover one SubBytes layer, and thus we can argue the difference without determining values. Therefore, for the column information, we firstly compare the constraints and remaining freedom degrees only for the difference. We call them *differential constraints* and *remaining differential freedom degrees*, respectively. For example, at the beginning, the remaining differential freedom degrees for each column are determined by NDD of that column. If one byte of the column is fixed, the remaining differential freedom degrees become NDD − 1 bytes.

The determine phase iteratively applies the above operation to all rows and columns. Newly fixed bytes during the determine phase become constrains to other rows and columns immediately. Therefore, the determine phase is iterated until no information is updated without a new guess. In summary, the determine phase performs the following operation.

1. UNTIL no information is updated without a new guess
2.   FOR all columns and rows, do as follows
3.   IF (new differential constraints) ≥ (remaining differential freedom degrees) THEN
4.   reduce the number of candidates by a factor of (new differential constraints)/(remaining differential freedom degrees)
5.   erase the remaining differential freedom degrees
6.   ELSE
7.   reduce remaining freedom degrees and remaining differential freedom degrees by a factor of new differential constraints
8.   end of IF
9.   IF (new constraints) ≥ (remaining freedom degrees) THEN
10.   reduce the number of candidates by a factor of (new constraints)/(remaining freedom degrees)
11.   erase remaining freedom degrees
12.   erase remaining differential freedom degrees
13.   ELSE
14.   reduce remaining freedom degrees by a factor of new constraints
15.   end of IF
16.   end of FOR
17. end of UNTIL

3.4   Fast Implementation Techniques

In our tool, we exhaustively try all orders of SuperSBoxes. The number of possible patterns with a straight-forward method is $(2N_c)!$ for large-block Rijndael, which is about 2^{44} patterns with $N_c = 8$, and $(2 * 16)! \approx 2^{118}$ patterns for the Grøstl-512 permutation. In our tool, the number of examined patterns is significantly smaller than those numbers because freedom degrees of several rows and columns are reduced by the determine phase without being guessed. However, even with the efficient determine phase, our tool takes very long to finish for the Grøstl-512 permutation. In this section we introduce two implementation techniques to keep the running time of our tool feasible. These will be useful in future for testing various larger state sizes.

Early Abort with Complexity. During the search procedure, we store the currently found best attack complexity. When we examine different row and column orders, we always compare the current attack complexity to the best attack complexity. The search is stopped as soon as the current attack complexity reaches the best attack complexity.

Early Abort with State Information. For more efficiency, we store intermediate state of the intersection table for every determine phase, together with the complexity at that stage. Every time we carry out the determine phase, we check the match between the current state and previously stored states. If a match is found, we compare the current complexity with the stored one. If the current complexity is bigger than the previous one, we stop the search immediately. If the complexity is smaller than the previous one, we update the stored results, and continue the search procedure.

Let us count the number of possible intermediate states of the intersection table. Each white cell has three kinds of state; the difference is fixed, both of the difference and value are fixed, and unfixed. The intersection table for the Grøstl-512 permutation consists of $(16 \times 16)/2 = 128$ white cells as shown in Fig 2. Thus the number of possible intermediate states is 3^{128}, which is infeasible to store. Here, we exploit the property that the intersection table is always operated in column-wise or row-wise, hence we can store the state information only in column-wise and row-wise. Moreover, we do not have to store the state where only the difference is fixed. This is because such a state can always be recovered by the previous state with both of the value and difference are fixed. In the end, the number of intermediate states can be $2^{16} \cdot 2^{16} \approx 2^{32}$. Finally, we can implement this technique, and can perform the test for the Grøstl-512 permutation. In practice, with our experiment, we only used about 2^{24} memory. There are several reasons why 2^{32} states did not appear. One is due to the early abort. Another is that the determine phase avoids extremely inefficient situations, e.g., all rows are fixed but no information is fixed for columns.

Code of the Proposed Tool

The code of the implemented tool is available in [19].

4   Distinguishers on Rijndael and Grøstl-512 Permutation

In this section, we apply our tool to the large-block Rijndael and the 1024-bit permutation used in Grøstl-512. We find that the improved rebound attack can

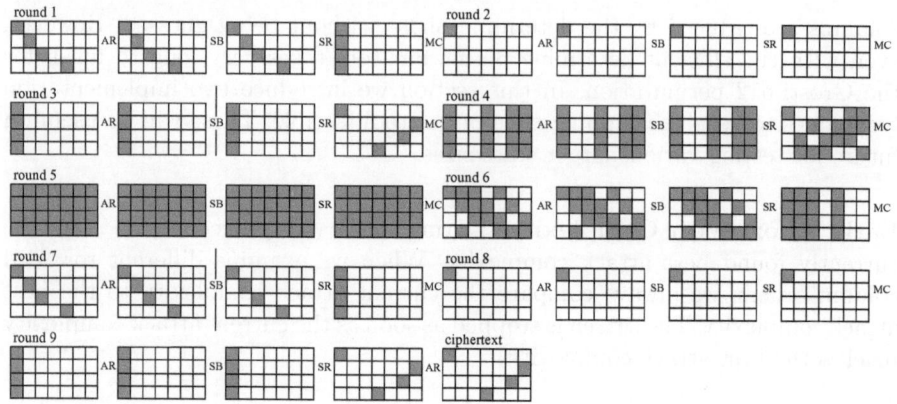

Fig. 5. Differential Characteristic for 9-round Rijndael-224

be applied to 9 rounds of Rijndael-192 and Rijndael-224. We also find that the improved rebound attack cannot be applied to Rijndael-160 and Rijndael-256, and the previous distinguisher on the Grøstl-512 permutation is the best. As an example of the application of our tool, we explain the new distinguisher on Rijndael-224 in Sect. 4.1. For the other targets, we summarize the results in Sect. 4.2.

4.1   A New Distinguisher on Rijndael-224

Overview. We use the following 9-round differential characteristic.

$$4 \to 1 \to 4 \to 16 \to 28 \to 16 \to 4 \to 1 \to 4 \to 4. \tag{1}$$

The characteristic is depicted in Fig. 5. The inbound phase is the middle four rounds. The outbound phase is the first two rounds and the last three rounds, which are satisfied with probability 2^{-24} each. In Fig. 5, the borders between inbound and outbound phases are drawn in round 3 and round 7. Our distinguisher finds each solution of the inbound phase with 2^{72} computations, and up to 2^{64} solutions can be generated in maximum. Hence, by iterating the inbound phase 2^{48} times, we can find the pair which satisfies the entire differential characteristic. The overall complexity is $2^{72+48} = 2^{120}$, while the generic attack proven to be optimal [20] to satisfy the same input and output differential forms for a 224-bit permutation requires 2^{161} queries.

Inbound Phase. First of all, we fix the 4-byte difference of $\#S3^{SB}$ and the 4-byte difference of $\#S7^{AR}$, and then generate seven SuperSBoxes for each of the forward and backward computations. This requires $14 \cdot 2^{32}$ 1-round computations, which is negligible compared to the merging phase. Note that for any difference of $\#S3^{SB}$ and $\#S7^{AR}$, we can find 1 solution on average.

Recall Fig. 3, which shows the inbound part for Rijndael-224. The intersection table for Rijndael-224 is also available in Fig. 4. Here, we show how the guess-and-determine is processed on the intersection table. We iterate the guess phase and the determine phase three times. The detailed explanation is as follows. See its illustration for Fig. 6. In Fig. 6. the first, second, third and fourth figures represent the state after the second guess phase, after the second determine phase, after the third guess phase, and after the third determine phase, respectively. The arrow lines represent which rows and columns are analyzed to achieve the state, and numbers with parenthesis represent the order that we analyze the rows and columns.

Guess 1. Guess the difference and value of L_2'. Because no constraint exists, we have 2^{32} choices.

Determine 1. No column and row can be uniquely fixed. Move to the next phase immediately.

Guess 2. Guess both the difference and value of L_3'. Because no constraint exists, we have 2^{32} choices. The current attack complexity becomes $2^{32} \cdot 2^{32} = 2^{64}$ computations.

Determine 2. For the third row and fourth row, the constraints are two-byte values and two-byte differences, in total four bytes. Therefore, the SuperS-Boxes of L_3 and L_4 can be fixed uniquely. This also generates the 1-byte constraint on the difference of the first column. Because NDD for the first column is 1, the difference for the first column is fixed. No more information can be generated at this stage. Then, we move to the next guess phase.

Guess 3. We guess the remaining freedom degrees for the second row. It has 3-byte constraints in total; 1 is from • and 2 are from $\sqrt{}$, thus the remaining freedom degrees is 2^8. This increases the current complexity by a factor of 2^8, which is $2^{64} \cdot 2^8 = 2^{72}$ computations.

Determine 3. Finally, the values and differences can be fixed for all bytes. The analysis order is shown in Fig. 6. For each of the fully fixed information, we examine the correctness of the guess. The expected number of solutions is 1. We will find it after iterating 2^{72} guesses.

The above analysis indicates that guessing 2^{72} values and differences in the above order is enough to examine the all possible differences and values to satisfy the inbound characteristic with given differences of $\#S3^{SB}$ and $\#S7^{AR}$. The procedure is the depth first search, hence the amount of required memory is much less than $14 \cdot 2^{32}$ which is required to make SuperSBoxes.

Each of $\#S3^{SB}$ and $\#S7^{AR}$ can take 2^{32} differences in maximum. Therefore, we can iterate the inbound phase 2^{64} times in maximum with spending 2^{72} cost for each difference. The outbound characteristic is satisfied with probability 2^{-48}, thus we need to produce 2^{48} solutions of the inbound phase. The total complexity to satisfy the entire characteristic is $2^{48} \cdot 2^{72} = 2^{120}$.

For the ideal 224-bit permutation, the best attack to satisfy the pair which has the same input and output differences is the limited-birthday distinguisher [5]. Let I and O be the size of the difference for the input state and the output state, respectively. The complexity is known as $\max\{\min\{2^{(n+1-I)/2},$

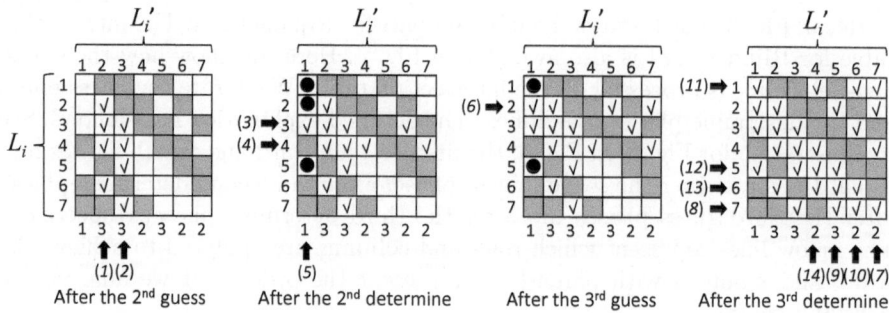

Fig. 6. Procedure for the Inbound Phase of Rijndael-224

$2^{(n+1-O)/2}\}, 2^{n+1-I-O}\}$. For our case with $I = 32, O = 32$ and $n = 224$, the complexity is $2^{224+1-32-32} = 2^{161}$. Hence, our distinguisher is valid. As far as we know, this is the first distinguisher on 9-round Rijndael-224.

4.2   Summary of Other Results

Similarly to Rijndael-224, we applied our tool to evaluate the attack complexity for Rijndael-160, -192, -256, and the Grøstl-512 permutation. For the Rijndael-160, -192, and -256, the known best results reach 8 rounds, 8 rounds, and 9 rounds, respectively. Hence, we evaluated the complexity for 9 rounds, 9 rounds, and 10 rounds, respectively.

For Rijndael-160, the obtained best attack complexity requires 2^{112} computations, while the limited birthday distinguisher on an ideal 160-bit permutation requires 2^{97} queries. Therefore, the improved rebound attack cannot be applied.

For Rijndael-192, the obtained best attack complexity requires 2^{112} computations, while the limited birthday distinguisher on an ideal 192-bit permutation requires 2^{129} queries. Therefore, we obtain a valid distinguisher. As far as we know this is the first distinguisher on 9-round Rijndael-192.

For Rijndael-256, the obtained best attack complexity requires 2^{128} computations, while the limited birthday distinguisher on an ideal 256-bit permutation requires 2^{96} queries. Therefore, the improved rebound attack cannot be applied.

For the Grøstl-512 permutation, the authors of [11] already achieved a valid distinguisher on 10 rounds. We examined if there exist other row/column orders which have a lower attack complexity. As a result, we found that the best complexity is the same as the one in [11], however we found many different row/column orders that achieve the same complexity as [11].

5   Searching for Stronger ShiftRows Parameters

The efficiency of the improved rebound attack depends on the ShiftRows parameter. In this section, we exhaustively examine all the possible ShiftRows parameters when the state size is given, and search for the strongest parameters against the improved rebound attack.

We choose the parameters under the following rules; the first parameter is 0 and all of eight parameters are different in the ascendant order. With these rules, the number of possible patterns is $\binom{15}{7} = 6435$. However, several choices produce exactly the same results, $i.e.$, there exist equivalent classes. We found that two intersection tables satisfying the following two conditions are equivalent.

- Two `rowmodels` can be identical by applying the rotation.
- Two NDDs can be identical by applying the rotation.

We need to consider only one parameter in the same equivalent classes, and the number of equivalent classes is about 600. Compared to the original 6435 patterns, the search space becomes about 1/10.

At the first glance, the active byte position of the differential characteristic appears to affect the attack complexity. However, it actually does not affect. Changing the active byte position results in the rotated NDD. The original and rotated NDDs belong to the same equivalent class and result in the same complexity. Hence, our tool covers any active byte positions.

Evaluation Results. Regarding Rijndael-160, Rijndael-192 and Rijndael-256, the best attack complexity is always the same for all possible parameters. In other words, all ShiftRows parameters have the same strength against the improved rebound attack.

Regarding Rijndael-224, the weakest parameters allow the distinguisher with 2^{104} computations, while the strongest parameters can ensure at least 2^{120} computations to be distinguished. The Rijndael-224 specification uses one of the strongest parameters. Although the best complexity changes, it is the same for all parameters that the distinguisher can work up to 9 rounds.

The results on the Grøstl-512 permutation are the most interesting. Weak parameters can be distinguished up to 10 rounds, while the strong parameters can ensure the complexity which is more than the generic attack. Therefore, the 10-round distinguisher can be prevented by adopting strong parameters. In details, the weakest parameters allow the distinguisher with 2^{336} computations while the generic attack complexity is 2^{449}. The strongest parameters can ensure 2^{464} computations. Note that the specified parameters of the Grøstl-512 permutation (identical for P_{1024} and Q_{1024}) are distinguished with 2^{392} computations. Examples of the strongest parameters are $(0, 1, 2, 3, 4, 7, 9, 12)$, and all the other parameters ensuring the complexity of 2^{464} are listed in Appendix. Note that all of them satisfy the design criteria in the Grøstl specification [13].

6 Concluding Remarks

In this paper, we developed the automated evaluation tool for the improved rebound attack against AES-like permutations with several fast implementation techniques. The tool evaluates all possible analytic orders and derives the best attack complexity when the state size and the ShiftRows parameters are given. We applied the tool to large block Rijndael and the Grøstl-512 permutation to find that the attack can be applied to 9 rounds of Rijndael-192 and Rijndael-224. These are the first distinguishing attacks for 9 rounds. It also shows the impossibility of the improved rebound attack against 9-round Rijndael-160 and 10-round Rijndael-256, and optimality of the previous attack against the Grøstl-512 permutation. Finally, we used the tool to test all possible ShiftRows parameters. We found several new parameters for the Grøstl-512 permutation that can prevent the 10-round attack.

An interesting open problem is detecting the relationship between the number of classes of ShiftRows parameters and the state size. For example, for Rijndael-160, Rijndael-192 and Rijndael-256, the best attack complexity is always the same for all possible parameters, but we obtained different attack complexity for Rijndael-224 and Grøstl-512 permutation. Finding some systematic relationship and theoretical reasoning seems hard but interesting as a future research direction. It is also an interesting future work to see if the obtained new parameters are better in terms of other cryptanalytic techniques.

Acknowledgements. We appreciate the anonymous reviewers for their helpful comments. Lei Wang is supported by the Singapore National Research Foundation Fellowship 2012 (NRF-NRFF2012-06). Mitsugu Iwamoto is supported by JSPS KAKENHI Grant No. 23760330.

References

1. Daemen, J., Rijmen, V.: AES Proposal: Rijndael (1998)
2. Knudsen, L.R., Rijmen, V.: Known-key distinguishers for some block ciphers. In: Kurosawa, K. (ed.) ASIACRYPT 2007. LNCS, vol. 4833, pp. 315–324. Springer, Heidelberg (2007)
3. Mendel, F., Rechberger, C., Schläffer, M., Thomsen, S.S.: The rebound attack: Cryptanalysis of reduced Whirlpool and Grøstl. In: Dunkelman, O. (ed.) FSE 2009. LNCS, vol. 5665, pp. 260–276. Springer, Heidelberg (2009)
4. Mendel, F., Peyrin, T., Rechberger, C., Schläffer, M.: Improved cryptanalysis of the reduced Grøstl compression function, ECHO permutation and AES block cipher. In: Jacobson Jr., M.J., Rijmen, V., Safavi-Naini, R. (eds.) SAC 2009. LNCS, vol. 5867, pp. 16–35. Springer, Heidelberg (2009)
5. Gilbert, H., Peyrin, T.: Super-sbox cryptanalysis: Improved attacks for AES-like permutations. In: Hong, S., Iwata, T. (eds.) FSE 2010. LNCS, vol. 6147, pp. 365–383. Springer, Heidelberg (2010)
6. Lamberger, M., Mendel, F., Rechberger, C., Rijmen, V., Schläffer, M.: Rebound distinguishers: Results on the full Whirlpool compression function. In: Matsui, M. (ed.) ASIACRYPT 2009. LNCS, vol. 5912, pp. 126–143. Springer, Heidelberg (2009)
7. Matusiewicz, K., Naya-Plasencia, M., Nikolić, I., Sasaki, Y., Schläffer, M.: Rebound attack on the full LANE compression function. In: Matsui, M. (ed.) ASIACRYPT 2009. LNCS, vol. 5912, pp. 106–125. Springer, Heidelberg (2009)

8. Peyrin, T.: Improved differential attacks for ECHO and Grøstl. In: Rabin, T. (ed.) CRYPTO 2010. LNCS, vol. 6223, pp. 370–392. Springer, Heidelberg (2010)
9. Sasaki, Y., Li, Y., Wang, L., Sakiyama, K., Ohta, K.: Non-full-active super-sbox analysis: Applications to ECHO and Grøstl. In: Abe, M. (ed.) ASIACRYPT 2010. LNCS, vol. 6477, pp. 38–55. Springer, Heidelberg (2010)
10. Naya-Plasencia, M.: How to improve rebound attacks. In: Rogaway, P. (ed.) CRYPTO 2011. LNCS, vol. 6841, pp. 188–205. Springer, Heidelberg (2011)
11. Jean, J., Naya-Plasencia, M., Peyrin, T.: Improved rebound attack on the finalist Grøstl. In: Canteaut, A. (ed.) FSE 2012. LNCS, vol. 7549, pp. 110–126. Springer, Heidelberg (2012)
12. Fouque, P.-A., Jean, J., Peyrin, T.: Structural evaluation of AES and chosen-key distinguisher of 9-round AES-128. In: Canetti, R., Garay, J.A. (eds.) CRYPTO 2013, Part I. LNCS, vol. 8042, pp. 183–203. Springer, Heidelberg (2013)
13. Gauravaram, P., Knudsen, L.R., Matusiewicz, K., Mendel, F., Rechberger, C., Schläffer, M., Thomsen, S.S.: Grøstl addendum. Submission to NIST (2009) (updated)
14. Minier, M., Phan, R.C.-W., Pousse, B.: Distinguishers for ciphers and known key attack against rijndael with large blocks. In: Preneel, B. (ed.) AFRICACRYPT 2009. LNCS, vol. 5580, pp. 60–76. Springer, Heidelberg (2009)
15. Sasaki, Y.: Known-key attacks on rijndael with large blocks and strengthening shiftRow parameter. In: Echizen, I., Kunihiro, N., Sasaki, R. (eds.) IWSEC 2010. LNCS, vol. 6434, pp. 301–315. Springer, Heidelberg (2010)
16. Daemen, J., Rijmen, V.: The design of Rijndeal: AES – the Advanced Encryption Standard (AES). Springer, Heidelberg (2002)
17. U.S. Department of Commerce, National Institute of Standards and Technology: Specification for the ADVANCED ENCRYPTION STANDARD (AES) (Federal Information Processing Standards Publication 197) (2001)
18. U.S. Department of Commerce, National Institute of Standards and Technology: Federal Register /Vol. 72, No. 212/Friday, November 2, 2007/Notices (2007) http://csrc.nist.gov/groups/ST/hash/documents/FR_Notice_Nov07.pdf.
19. Tokushige, Y.: Implemented tool of the improved rebound attack. Contact to the authors if the link is closed (2013), http://ohta-lab.jp/member/yuuki-tokushige/an-automated-evaluation-tool-for-improved-rebound-attack/
20. Iwamoto, M., Peyrin, T., Sasaki, Y.: Limited-birthday distinguishers for hash functions: Collisions beyond the birthday bound can be meaningful. In: Sako, K., Sarkar, P. (eds.) ASIACRYPT 2013, Part II. LNCS, vol. 8270, pp. 504–523. Springer, Heidelberg (2013)
21. Nakasone, T., Li, Y., Sasaki, Y., Iwamoto, M., Ohta, K., Sakiyama, K.: Key-dependent weakness of AES-based ciphers under clockwise collision distinguisher. In: Kwon, T., Lee, M.-K., Kwon, D. (eds.) ICISC 2012. LNCS, vol. 7839, pp. 395–409. Springer, Heidelberg (2013)

A   Experiment on New ShiftBytes for Grøstl-512

By applying our tool for all possible ShiftBytes parameters of the Grøstl-512 permutation, we found that the parameters can be classified into 14 classes. Note that the improved rebound attack distinguishes a problem on which the complexity for an ideal case is 2^{441}. The weakest class, which contains 32 parameters, allows the improved rebound attack with a complexity of 2^{336} computations, while the strongest class, which contains 128 parameters, can ensure that the optimal complexity of the improved rebound attack is 2^{464} computations. The second strongest, which contains 256 parameters, class can also ensure the optimal complexity of 2^{456} computations. The results are shown in Table 3.

In Table 4, we list all 128 parameters ensuring the complexity of 2^{464} against the improved rebound attack. We found 16 equivalent classes, and each class contains 8 different parameters.

There are several previous researches studying good ShiftRows parameters [21,15]. Nakasone *et al.* pointed out that including 0 in the ShiftRows parameter causes an efficient side-channel analysis exploiting the clock-wise collision. If an AES-like structure should be designed by taking into account the clock-wise collision, the parameters in Table 4 can be rotated so that 0 is not included in the parameter. For example, the first parameter in Class 1 can be rotated by 1, which results in $(1, 2, 3, 4, 5, 8, 10, 13)$.

Table 3. Number of Parameters in Each Class. The attack for an ideal case costs 2^{441}.

Attack Complexity (in logarithm)	#parameters	Remarks
336	32	
360	128	
376	64	
384	320	
392	320	the original parameters belong to this class
400	192	
408	352	
416	480	
424	928	
432	1000	
440	736	
448	512	
456	256	resist the 10-round distinguisher
464	128	resist the 10-round distinguisher

Table 4. 128 New ShiftBytes Parameters for the Grøstl-512 Permutation

Class 1
(0 , 1 , 2 , 3 , 4 , 7 , 9 ,12)
(0 , 1 , 2 , 3 , 6 , 8 ,11 ,15)
(0 , 1 , 2 , 5 , 7 ,10 ,14 ,15)
(0 , 1 , 4 , 6 , 9 ,13 ,14 ,15)
(0 , 2 , 5 , 9 ,10 ,11 ,12 ,13)
(0 , 3 , 5 , 8 ,12 ,13 ,14 ,15)
(0 , 3 , 7 , 8 , 9 ,10 ,11 ,14)
(0 , 4 , 5 , 6 , 7 , 8 ,11 ,13)

Class 2
(0 , 1 , 2 , 3 , 4 , 8 ,11 ,13)
(0 , 1 , 2 , 3 , 7 ,10 ,12 ,15)
(0 , 1 , 2 , 6 , 9 ,11 ,14 ,15)
(0 , 1 , 5 , 8 ,10 ,13 ,14 ,15)
(0 , 2 , 5 , 6 , 7 , 8 , 9 ,13)
(0 , 3 , 4 , 5 , 6 , 7 ,11 ,14)
(0 , 3 , 5 , 8 , 9 ,10 ,11 ,12)
(0 , 4 , 7 , 9 ,12 ,13 ,14 ,15)

Class 3
(0 , 1 , 2 , 3 , 5 , 8 , 9 ,14)
(0 , 1 , 2 , 4 , 7 , 8 ,13 ,15)
(0 , 1 , 3 , 6 , 7 ,12 ,14 ,15)
(0 , 1 , 6 , 8 , 9 ,10 ,11 ,13)
(0 , 2 , 3 , 4 , 5 , 7 ,10 ,11)
(0 , 2 , 5 , 6 ,11 ,13 ,14 ,15)
(0 , 3 , 4 , 9 ,11 ,12 ,13 ,14)
(0 , 5 , 7 , 8 , 9 ,10 ,12 ,15)

Class 4
(0 , 1 , 2 , 3 , 5 , 8 ,11 ,12)
(0 , 1 , 2 , 4 , 7 ,10 ,11 ,15)
(0 , 1 , 3 , 6 , 9 ,10 ,14 ,15)
(0 , 1 , 5 , 6 , 7 , 8 ,10 ,13)
(0 , 2 , 5 , 8 , 9 ,13 ,14 ,15)
(0 , 3 , 4 , 8 , 9 ,10 ,11 ,13)
(0 , 3 , 6 , 7 ,11 ,12 ,13 ,14)
(0 , 4 , 5 , 6 , 7 , 9 ,12 ,15)

Class 5
(0 , 1 , 2 , 3 , 5 ,10 ,11 ,14)
(0 , 1 , 2 , 4 , 9 ,10 ,13 ,15)
(0 , 1 , 3 , 8 , 9 ,12 ,14 ,15)
(0 , 1 , 4 , 6 , 7 , 8 , 9 ,11)
(0 , 2 , 3 , 4 , 5 , 7 ,12 ,13)
(0 , 2 , 7 , 8 ,11 ,13 ,14 ,15)
(0 , 3 , 5 , 6 , 7 , 8 ,10 ,15)
(0 , 5 , 6 , 9 ,11 ,12 ,13 ,14)

Class 6
(0 , 1 , 2 , 3 , 5 ,10 ,12 ,13)
(0 , 1 , 2 , 4 , 9 ,11 ,12 ,15)
(0 , 1 , 3 , 8 ,10 ,11 ,14 ,15)
(0 , 1 , 4 , 5 , 6 , 7 , 9 ,14)
(0 , 2 , 3 , 6 , 7 , 8 , 9 ,11)
(0 , 2 , 7 , 9 ,10 ,13 ,14 ,15)
(0 , 3 , 4 , 5 , 6 , 8 ,13 ,15)
(0 , 5 , 7 , 8 ,11 ,12 ,13 ,14)

Class 7
(0 , 1 , 2 , 3 , 6 , 7 , 9 ,14)
(0 , 1 , 2 , 5 , 6 , 8 ,13 ,15)
(0 , 1 , 3 , 8 ,10 ,11 ,12 ,13)
(0 , 1 , 4 , 5 , 7 ,12 ,14 ,15)
(0 , 2 , 3 , 4 , 5 , 8 , 9 ,11)
(0 , 2 , 7 , 9 ,10 ,11 ,12 ,15)
(0 , 3 , 4 , 6 ,11 ,13 ,14 ,15)
(0 , 5 , 7 , 8 , 9 ,10 ,13 ,14)

Class 8
(0 , 1 , 2 , 3 , 6 , 8 , 9 ,13)
(0 , 1 , 2 , 5 , 7 , 8 ,12 ,15)
(0 , 1 , 4 , 6 , 7 ,11 ,14 ,15)
(0 , 1 , 5 , 8 , 9 ,10 ,11 ,14)
(0 , 2 , 3 , 7 ,10 ,11 ,12 ,13)
(0 , 3 , 4 , 5 , 6 , 9 ,11 ,12)
(0 , 3 , 5 , 6 ,10 ,13 ,14 ,15)
(0 , 4 , 7 , 8 , 9 ,10 ,13 ,15)

Class 9
(0 , 1 , 2 , 3 , 6 ,10 ,11 ,13)
(0 , 1 , 2 , 5 , 9 ,10 ,12 ,15)
(0 , 1 , 3 , 6 , 7 , 8 , 9 ,12)
(0 , 1 , 4 , 8 , 9 ,11 ,14 ,15)
(0 , 2 , 5 , 6 , 7 , 8 ,11 ,15)
(0 , 3 , 4 , 5 , 6 , 9 ,13 ,14)
(0 , 3 , 7 , 8 ,10 ,13 ,14 ,15)
(0 , 4 , 5 , 7 ,10 ,11 ,12 ,13)

Class 10
(0 , 1 , 2 , 3 , 7 , 8 ,11 ,14)
(0 , 1 , 2 , 6 , 7 ,10 ,13 ,15)
(0 , 1 , 4 , 7 , 9 ,10 ,11 ,12)
(0 , 1 , 5 , 6 , 9 ,12 ,14 ,15)
(0 , 2 , 3 , 4 , 5 , 9 ,10 ,13)
(0 , 3 , 5 , 6 , 7 , 8 ,12 ,13)
(0 , 3 , 6 , 8 , 9 ,10 ,11 ,15)
(0 , 4 , 5 , 8 ,11 ,13 ,14 ,15)

Class 11
(0 , 1 , 2 , 4 , 5 , 7 , 9 ,10)
(0 , 1 , 3 , 4 , 6 , 8 , 9 ,15)
(0 , 1 , 3 , 5 , 6 ,12 ,13 ,14)
(0 , 1 , 7 , 8 , 9 ,11 ,12 ,14)
(0 , 2 , 3 , 5 , 7 , 8 ,14 ,15)
(0 , 2 , 3 , 9 ,10 ,11 ,13 ,14)
(0 , 2 , 4 , 5 ,11 ,12 ,13 ,15)
(0 , 6 , 7 , 8 ,10 ,11 ,13 ,15)

Class 12
(0 , 1 , 2 , 4 , 5 ,10 ,11 ,13)
(0 , 1 , 3 , 4 , 9 ,10 ,12 ,15)
(0 , 1 , 3 , 6 , 7 , 8 ,10 ,11)
(0 , 1 , 6 , 7 , 9 ,12 ,13 ,14)
(0 , 2 , 3 , 8 , 9 ,11 ,14 ,15)
(0 , 2 , 5 , 6 , 7 , 9 ,10 ,15)
(0 , 3 , 4 , 5 , 7 , 8 ,13 ,14)
(0 , 5 , 6 , 8 ,11 ,12 ,13 ,15)

Class 13
(0 , 1 , 2 , 5 , 6 , 8 , 9 ,11)
(0 , 1 , 3 , 4 , 6 ,11 ,12 ,13)
(0 , 1 , 3 , 8 , 9 ,10 ,13 ,14)
(0 , 1 , 4 , 5 , 7 , 8 ,10 ,15)
(0 , 2 , 3 , 5 ,10 ,11 ,12 ,15)
(0 , 2 , 7 , 8 , 9 ,12 ,13 ,15)
(0 , 3 , 4 , 6 , 7 , 9 ,14 ,15)
(0 , 5 , 6 , 7 ,10 ,11 ,13 ,14)

Class 14
(0 , 1 , 2 , 5 , 7 , 8 ,13 ,14)
(0 , 1 , 3 , 4 , 5 , 8 ,10 ,11)
(0 , 1 , 4 , 6 , 7 ,12 ,13 ,15)
(0 , 1 , 6 , 7 , 9 ,10 ,11 ,14)
(0 , 2 , 3 , 4 , 7 , 9 ,10 ,15)
(0 , 2 , 3 , 8 , 9 ,11 ,12 ,13)
(0 , 3 , 5 , 6 ,11 ,12 ,14 ,15)
(0 , 5 , 6 , 8 , 9 ,10 ,13 ,15)

Class 15
(0 , 1 , 2 , 7 , 9 ,10 ,12 ,13)
(0 , 1 , 3 , 4 , 7 , 8 , 9 ,14)
(0 , 1 , 4 , 5 , 6 ,11 ,13 ,14)
(0 , 1 , 6 , 8 , 9 ,11 ,12 ,15)
(0 , 2 , 3 , 5 , 6 , 9 ,10 ,11)
(0 , 2 , 6 , 7 , 8 ,13 ,15)
(0 , 3 , 4 , 5 ,10 ,12 ,13 ,15)
(0 , 5 , 7 , 8 ,10 ,11 ,14 ,15)

Class 16
(0 , 1 , 2 , 8 , 9 ,11 ,13 ,14)
(0 , 1 , 3 , 4 , 5 ,11 ,12 ,14)
(0 , 1 , 3 , 5 , 6 , 8 , 9 ,10)
(0 , 1 , 7 , 8 ,10 ,12 ,13 ,15)
(0 , 2 , 3 , 4 ,10 ,11 ,13 ,15)
(0 , 2 , 3 , 5 , 6 , 7 ,13 ,14)
(0 , 2 , 4 , 5 , 7 , 8 , 9 ,15)
(0 , 6 , 7 , 9 ,11 ,12 ,14 ,15)

Practical Collision Attack on 40-Step RIPEMD-128

Gaoli Wang[1,2]

[1] Donghua University
School of Computer Science and Technology, Shanghai, China
[2] State Key Laboratory of Information Security Institute of Information Engineering,
Chinese Academy of Sciences, Beijing, China
wanggaoli@dhu.edu.cn

Abstract. RIPEMD-128 is an ISO/IEC standard cryptographic hash function proposed in 1996 by Dobbertin, Bosselaers and Preneel. The compression function of RIPEMD-128 consists of two different and independent parallel lines denoted by *line*1 operation and *line*2 operation. The initial values and the output values of the last step of the two operations are combined, resulting in the final value of one iteration. In this paper, we present collision differential characteristics for both *line*1 operation and *line*2 operation by choosing a proper message difference. By using message modification technique seriously, we improve the probabilities of the differential characteristics so that we can give a collision attack on 40-step RIPEMD-128 with a complexity of 2^{35} computations.

Keywords: Hash function, collisions, RIPEMD-128, differential characteristic, message modification.

1 Introduction

The cryptographic hash function RIPEMD-128 [1] was proposed in 1996 by Hans Dobbertin, Antoon Bosselaers and Bart Preneel. It was standardized by ISO/IEC [2] and was used in HMAC in RFC [3]. The design philosophy of RIPEMD-128 adopts the experience gained by evaluating MD4 [9], MD5 [10], and RIPEMD [8] etc.. RIPEMD-128 is a double-branch hash function, where the compression function consists of two parallel operations denoted by *line*1 operation and *line*2 operation, respectively. The combination of H_{i-1}, $line1(H_{i-1}, M_{i-1})$ and $line2(H_{i-1}, M_{i-1})$ generates the output H_i, where H_{i-1} is the standard initial value or the output of the message block M_{i-2}.

As far as we know, the published cryptanalysis of (reduced) RIPEMD-128 includes collision attacks [5,6,12], (semi-)free-start collision attacks [4,5], near collision attack [5], (second) preimage attacks [7,13] and distinguishing attack [11]. As for the practical collision attacks on step reduced RIPEMD-128, Wang et al. presented an example of collision on 32-step RIPEMD-128 in 2008 [12], Mendel et al. presented an example of collision on 38-step RIPEMD-128 in 2012 [5]. In the work [5], finding differential characteristic and performing message modification in the first round are achieved by an automatic search tool.

It is widely believed that it is difficult to construct a differential characteristic including the first round of line1 operation because the absorption property of the

J. Benaloh (Ed.): CT-RSA 2014, LNCS 8366, pp. 444–460, 2014.

boolean function $X \oplus Y \oplus Z$ does not hold. Thus, in the collision attack on 32-step RIPEMD-128 [12], the difference of messages is chosen as $\Delta m_{14} \neq 0, \Delta m_i = 0 (0 \leq i \leq 15, i \neq 14)$ such that the differential characteristic of line1 operation almost keeps away from the boolean function $X \oplus Y \oplus Z$. Inspired by Mendel's work [5], we were motivated to find a differential characteristic of line1 operation, which takes advantage of the property of the boolean function $X \oplus Y \oplus Z$. By choosing a different message difference than in [5], the number of the attacked steps can be increased by two.

In this paper, we use the bit tracing method to propose a collision attack on 40-step RIPEMD-128 with a complexity of 2^{35}. The bit tracing method is proposed by Wang and formalized in [15,16]. It is very powerful to break most of the dedicated hash functions such as MD4 [15,20], RIPEMD [15], HAVAL [14,19], MD5 [16], SHA-0 [17] and SHA-1 [18]. However, in the double-branch hash functions, two state words are updated using a single message word. Therefore, the application of bit tracing method to RIPEMD-128 is far from being trivial. In this paper, constructing differential characteristic, deducing the sufficient conditions and performing message modification are all fulfilled by hand. The previous results and our results are summarized in Table 1.

Table 1. Summary of the Attacks on RIPEMD-128

Attack	Steps	Generic	Complexity	Reference
collision	32	2^{64}	2^{28}	[12]
collision	38	2^{64}	2^{14}	[5]
collision	40	2^{64}	2^{35}	Ours
near collision	44	$2^{47.8}$	2^{32}	[5]
free-start collision	48	2^{64}	2^{40}	[5]
preimage	33	2^{128}	$2^{124.5}$	[7]
preimage	35*	2^{128}	2^{121}	[7]
preimage	36*	2^{128}	$2^{126.5}$	[13]
distinguishing	48	2^{76}	2^{70}	[5]
distinguishing	45	2^{42}	2^{27}	[11]
distinguishing	47	2^{42}	2^{39}	[11]
distinguishing	48	$-$	2^{53}	[11]
distinguishing	52	$-$	2^{107}	[11]
distinguishing	64	2^{128}	$2^{105.4}$	[4]
semi-free-start collision	64	2^{64}	$2^{61.57}$	[4]

* The attack starts from an intermediate step.

The rest of the paper is organized as follows: In Section 2, we describe the RIPEMD-128 algorithm. In Section 3, we introduce some useful properties of the nonlinear functions in RIPEMD-128 and some notations. Section 4 will show the detailed descriptions of the attack on RIPEMD-128. Finally, we summarize the paper in Section 5.

2 Description of RIPEMD-128

The hash function RIPEMD-128 compresses any arbitrary length message into a message with length of 128 bit. Firstly the algorithm pads any given message into a message with length of 512 bit multiple. For the description of the padding method we refer to [1]. Then, for each 512-bit message block, RIPEMD-128 compresses it into a 128-bit hash value by a compression function, which is composed of two parallel operations: *line*1 and *line*2. Each operation has four rounds, and each round has 16 steps. The initial value is $(a, b, c, d) = (0x67452301, 0xefcdab89, 0x98badcfe, 0x10325476)$. The nonlinear functions in each round are as follows:

$$F(X, Y, Z) = X \oplus Y \oplus Z,$$
$$G(X, Y, Z) = (X \wedge Y) \vee (\neg X \wedge Z),$$
$$H(X, Y, Z) = (X \vee \neg Y) \oplus Z,$$
$$I(X, Y, Z) = (X \wedge Z) \vee (Y \wedge \neg Z).$$

Here X, Y, Z are 32-bit words. The four boolean functions are all bitwise operations. $\neg$ represents the bitwise complement of X. $\wedge$, $\oplus$ and $\vee$ are bitwise AND, XOR and OR respectively. In each step of both *line*1 operation and *line*2 operation, one the four chaining variables a, b, c, d is updated.

$$\phi_0(a, b, c, d, x, s) = (a + F(b, c, d) + x) \lll s,$$
$$\phi_1(a, b, c, d, x, s) = (a + G(b, c, d) + x + 0x5a827999) \lll s,$$
$$\phi_2(a, b, c, d, x, s) = (a + H(b, c, d) + x + 0x6ed9eba1) \lll s,$$
$$\phi_3(a, b, c, d, x, s) = (a + I(b, c, d) + x + 0x8f1bbcdc) \lll s,$$
$$\psi_0(a, b, c, d, x, s) = (a + I(b, c, d) + x + 0x50a28be6) \lll s,$$
$$\psi_1(a, b, c, d, x, s) = (a + H(b, c, d) + x + 0x5c4dd124) \lll s,$$
$$\psi_2(a, b, c, d, x, s) = (a + G(b, c, d) + x + 0x6d703ef3) \lll s,$$
$$\psi_3(a, b, c, d, x, s) = (a + F(b, c, d) + x) \lll s.$$

$\lll s$ represents the circular shift s bit positions to the left. + denotes addition modulo 2^{32}.

line1 operation. For a 512-bit block $M = (m_0, m_1, \ldots, m_{15})$, *line*1 operation is as follows:

1. Let $(a, b, c, d) = (a_0, b_0, c_0, d_0)$ be the input of *line*1 operation for M. If M is the first block to be hashed, (a_0, b_0, c_0, d_0) is the initial value. Otherwise it is the output of compressing the previous block.
2. Perform the following 64 steps (four rounds):
   For $j = 0, 1, 2, 3$,
   For $i = 0, 1, 2, 3$,
   $a = \phi_j(a, b, c, d, m_{ord1(j,16j+4i+1)}, s1_{j,16j+4i+1}),$
   $d = \phi_j(d, a, b, c, m_{ord1(j,16j+4i+2)}, s1_{j,16j+4i+2}),$
   $c = \phi_j(c, d, a, b, m_{ord1(j,16j+4i+3)}, s1_{j,16j+4i+3}),$
   $b = \phi_j(b, c, d, a, m_{ord1(j,16j+4i+4)}, s1_{j,16j+4i+4}).$

line2 operation. For a 512-bit block $M = (m_0, m_1, \ldots, m_{15})$, *line2* operation is as follows:

1. Let $(aa, bb, cc, dd) = (a_0, b_0, c_0, d_0)$ be the input of *line2* operation for M. If M is the first block to be hashed, (a_0, b_0, c_0, d_0) is the initial value. Otherwise it is the output of compressing the previous block.
2. Perform the following 64 steps (four rounds):
   For $j = 0, 1, 2, 3$,
   For $i = 0, 1, 2, 3$,
   $$aa = \psi_j(aa, bb, cc, dd, m_{ord2(j,16j+4i+1)}, s2_{j,16j+4i+1}),$$
   $$dd = \psi_j(dd, aa, bb, cc, m_{ord2(j,16j+4i+2)}, s2_{j,16j+4i+2}),$$
   $$cc = \psi_j(cc, dd, aa, bb, m_{ord2(j,16j+4i+3)}, s2_{j,16j+4i+3}),$$
   $$bb = \psi_j(bb, cc, dd, aa, m_{ord2(j,16j+4i+4)}, s2_{j,16j+4i+4}).$$

The output of compressing the block M is obtained by combining the initial value with the outputs of *line1* and *line2* operations: $a = b_0 + c + dd$, $b = c_0 + d + aa$, $c = d_0 + a + bb$, $d = a_0 + b + cc$. If M is the last message block, then $a \parallel b \parallel c \parallel d$ is the hash value, where $\parallel$ denotes the bit concatenation. Otherwise repeat the compression process for the next 512-bit message. The order of message words and the details of the shift positions can be seen in Table 2.

Table 2. Order of the Message Words and Shift Positions in RIPEMD-128

	Step i	1	2	3	4	5	6	7	8	9	10	11	12	13	14	15	16
	$ord1(0, i)$	0	1	2	3	4	5	6	7	8	9	10	11	12	13	14	15
line1	$s1_{0,i}$	11	14	15	12	5	8	7	9	11	13	14	15	6	7	9	8
	$ord2(0, i)$	5	14	7	0	9	2	11	4	13	6	15	8	1	10	3	12
line2	$s2_{0,i}$	8	9	9	11	13	15	15	5	7	7	8	11	14	14	12	6
	Step i	17	18	19	20	21	22	23	24	25	26	27	28	29	30	31	32
	$ord1(1, i)$	7	4	13	1	10	6	15	3	12	0	9	5	2	14	11	8
line1	$s1_{1,i}$	7	6	8	13	11	9	7	15	7	12	15	9	11	7	13	12
	$ord2(1, i)$	6	11	3	7	0	13	5	10	14	15	8	12	4	9	1	2
line2	$s2_{1,i}$	9	13	15	7	12	8	9	11	7	7	12	7	6	15	13	11
	Step i	33	34	35	36	37	38	39	40	41	42	43	44	45	46	47	48
	$ord1(2, i)$	3	10	14	4	9	15	8	1	2	7	0	6	13	11	5	12
line1	$s1_{2,i}$	11	13	6	7	14	9	13	15	14	8	13	6	5	12	7	5
	$ord2(2, i)$	15	5	1	3	7	14	6	9	11	8	12	2	10	0	4	13
line2	$s2_{2,i}$	9	7	15	11	8	6	6	14	12	13	5	14	13	13	7	5
	Step i	49	50	51	52	53	54	55	56	57	58	59	60	61	62	63	64
	$ord1(3, i)$	1	9	11	10	0	8	12	4	13	3	7	15	14	5	6	2
line1	$s1_{3,i}$	11	12	14	15	14	15	9	8	9	14	5	6	8	6	5	12
	$ord2(3, i)$	8	6	4	1	3	11	15	0	5	12	2	13	9	7	10	14
line2	$s2_{3,i}$	15	5	8	11	14	14	6	14	6	9	12	9	12	5	15	8

3   Some Basic Conclusions and Notations

In this section we will recall some properties of the four nonlinear functions in our attack.

Proposition 1. For the nonlinear function $F(x, y, z) = x \oplus y \oplus z$, there are the following properties:

1. $F(0, y, z) = 0$ and $F(1, y, z) = 1 \Longleftrightarrow y = z$.
   $F(0, y, z) = 1$ and $F(1, y, z) = 0 \Longleftrightarrow y \neq z$.
   $F(x, 0, z) = 0$ and $F(x, 1, z) = 1 \Longleftrightarrow x = z$.
   $F(x, 0, z) = 1$ and $F(x, 1, z) = 0 \Longleftrightarrow x \neq z$.
   $F(x, y, 0) = 0$ and $F(x, y, 1) = 1 \Longleftrightarrow x = y$.
   $F(x, y, 0) = 1$ and $F(x, y, 1) = 0 \Longleftrightarrow x \neq y$.
2. $F(x, y, z) = F(\neg x, \neg y, z) = F(x, \neg y, \neg z) = F(\neg x, y, \neg z)$.

Proposition 2. For the nonlinear function $G(x, y, z) = (x \wedge y) \vee (\neg x \wedge z)$, there are the following properties:

1. $G(x, y, z) = G(\neg x, y, z) \Longleftrightarrow y = z$.
   $G(0, y, z) = 0$ and $G(1, y, z) = 1 \Longleftrightarrow y = 1$ and $z = 0$.
   $G(0, y, z) = 1$ and $G(1, y, z) = 0 \Longleftrightarrow y = 0$ and $z = 1$.

2. $G(x, y, z) = G(x, \neg y, z) \Longleftrightarrow x = 0$.
   $G(x, 0, z) = 0$ and $G(x, 1, z) = 1 \Longleftrightarrow x = 1$.

3. $G(x, y, z) = G(x, y, \neg z) \Longleftrightarrow x = 1$.
   $G(x, y, 0) = 0$ and $G(x, y, 1) = 1 \Longleftrightarrow x = 0$.

Proposition 3. For the nonlinear function $H(x, y, z) = (x \vee \neg y) \oplus z$, there are the following properties:

1. $H(x, y, z) = H(\neg x, y, z) \Longleftrightarrow y = 0$.
   $H(0, y, z) = 0$ and $H(1, y, z) = 1 \Longleftrightarrow y = 1$ and $z = 0$.
   $H(0, y, z) = 1$ and $H(1, y, z) = 0 \Longleftrightarrow y = 1$ and $z = 1$.

2. $H(x, y, z) = H(x, \neg y, z) \Longleftrightarrow x = 1$.
   $H(x, 0, z) = 0$ and $H(x, 1, z) = 1 \Longleftrightarrow x = 0$ and $z = 1$.
   $H(x, 0, z) = 1$ and $H(x, 1, z) = 0 \Longleftrightarrow x = 0$ and $z = 0$.

3. $H(x, y, 0) = 0$ and $H(x, y, 1) = 1 \Longleftrightarrow x = 0$ and $y = 1$.
   $H(x, y, 0) = 1$ and $H(x, y, 1) = 0 \Longleftrightarrow x = 1$ or $y = 0$.

Proposition 4. For the nonlinear function $I(x, y, z) = (x \wedge z) \vee (y \wedge \neg z)$, there are the following properties:

1. $I(x, y, z) = I(\neg x, y, z) \Longleftrightarrow z = 0$.
   $I(0, y, z) = 0$ and $I(1, y, z) = 1 \Longleftrightarrow z = 1$.

2. $I(x, y, z) = I(x, \neg y, z) \Longleftrightarrow z = 1$.
$I(x, 0, z) = 0$ and $I(x, 1, z) = 1 \Longleftrightarrow z = 0$.

3. $I(x, y, z) = I(x, y, \neg z) \Longleftrightarrow x = y$.
$I(x, y, 0) = 0$ and $I(x, y, 1) = 1 \Longleftrightarrow x = 1$ and $y = 0$.
$I(x, y, 0) = 1$ and $I(x, y, 1) = 0 \Longleftrightarrow x = 0$ and $y = 1$.

Notations. In order to describe our attack conveniently, we define some notations in the following.

1. $M = (m_0, m_1, ..., m_{15})$ and $M' = (m'_0, m'_1, ..., m'_{15})$ represent two 512-bit messages.
2. a_i, d_i, c_i, b_i respectively denote the outputs of the $(4i - 3)$-th, $(4i - 2)$-th, $(4i - 1)$-th and $4i$-th steps for compressing M in *line*1 operation, where $1 \leq i \leq 16$.
3. aa_i, dd_i, cc_i, bb_i respectively denote the outputs of the $(4i-3)$-th, $(4i-2)$-th, $(4i-1)$-th and $4i$-th steps for compressing M in *line*2 operation, where $1 \leq i \leq 16$.
4. a'_i, d'_i, c'_i, b'_i respectively denote the outputs of the $(4i - 3)$-th, $(4i - 2)$-th, $(4i - 1)$-th and $4i$-th steps for compressing M' in *line*1 operation.
5. $aa'_i, dd'_i, cc'_i, bb'_i$ respectively denote the outputs of the $(4i - 3)$-th, $(4i - 2)$-th, $(4i - 1)$-th and $4i$-th steps for compressing M' in *line*2 operation.
6. $\Delta m_i = m'_i - m_i$ denotes the difference of two words m_i and m'_i. It is noted that Δm_i is a modular difference and not a XOR difference.
7. $x_{i,j}$ represent the j-th bit of x_i, where the least significant bit is the 1-st bit, and the most significant bit is 32-nd bit.
8. $x_i[j]$, $x_i[-j]$ are the resulting values by only changing the j-th bit of the word x_i. $x_i[j]$ is obtained by changing the j-th bit of x_i from 0 to 1. $x_i[-j]$ is obtained by changing the j-th bit of x_i from 1 to 0.
9. $x_i[\pm j_1, \pm j_2, ..., \pm j_l]$ is the value by change j_1-th, j_2-th, ..., j_l-th bits of x_i. The "+" sign means that the bit is changed from 0 to 1, and the "-" sign means that the bit is changed from 1 to 0.

4   The Collision Attack against 40-Step RIPEMD-128

The collision consists of a pair of two 512-bit blocks $(N \parallel M, N \parallel M')$. Let (a_0, b_0, c_0, d_0) denote the input chaining value of the message block M. As stated below, in order to implement the message modification, we have to add some conditions on b_0, which leads the hash value of the first block N to satisfy $b_{0,i} = 1$ ($i = 1, 2, 3, 27$) and $b_{0,i} = 0$ ($i = 7, ..., 10, 13, ..., 24$). We search the second block M in the following three parts:

1. Choose proper differences of message words and find two concrete differential characteristics for *line*1 and *line*2 operations respectively in which M and M' produces a collision. The differential characteristics without round 1 must hold with high probability.
2. Derive two sets of sufficient conditions which ensure the two differential characteristics hold, respectively.
3. Modify the message to fulfill most of the conditions on chaining variables.

4.1 Differential Characteristics for 40-Step RIPEMD-128

Choosing proper differences of message words plays an important role in constructing differential characteristics which contain as many steps as possible and hold with high probabilities after message modification. Let $M = (m_0, m_1, \ldots, m_{15})$, we select $\Delta M = M' - M$ as follows: $\Delta m_i = 0$ $(0 \le i \le 15, i \ne 2, 12)$, $\Delta m_2 = 2^8$ and $\Delta m_{12} = -2$. It forms a local collision from step 25 to step 29 in $line1$ operation. Although in the same round, there are the same circular shift values corresponding to the same message words between $line1$ operation and $line2$ operation, e.g. in step 25 (29) of $line1$ operation, the shift value is 7 (11) corresponding to the message word m_{12} (m_2), and in step 28 (32) of $line2$ operation, the shift value is also 7 (11) corresponding to the message word m_{12} (m_2), it can not form a local collision from step 28 to step 32 in $line2$ operation. The reason is that the property of the boolean function $(X \vee \neg Y) \oplus Z$ make it need at least three message words to form a local collision. Therefore, the differential characteristic of $line2$ operation consists of one long local collision between step 6 to step 32. In round 3, the message differences first appear at step 41 of $line1$ operation and at step 43 of $line2$ operation. Thus, we can get a collision attack on 40-step RIPEMD-128 by using this message differences.

The boolean function $X \oplus Y \oplus Z$ make it more difficult to construct a differential characteristic in $line1$ operation. Hence, the differential characteristic of $line1$ operation we presented in Table 8 is dense. The differential characteristic for $line2$ operation is presented in Table 9, which makes the probability after round 1 hold as high as possible.

4.2 Deriving Conditions on Chaining Variables of *line1* and *line2* Operations

In this section, we derive two sets of sufficient conditions presented in Table 10 and Table 11, which ensure the differential characteristics in Table 8 and Table 9 hold, respectively. We describe how to derive a set of sufficient conditions that guarantee the difference in steps 3-7 of table 8 hold. Other conditions can be derived similarly.

1. In step 3, the message difference $\Delta m_2 = 2^8$ produces $c_1[-1, -2, 3, -24, \ldots, -32]$.
2. In step 4, $(b_0, a_1, d_1, c_1[-1, -2, 3, -24, \ldots, -32])$
   $\implies (a_1, d_1, c_1[-1, -2, 3, -24, \ldots, -32], b_1[4, \ldots, 10, -11, 12, -13, \ldots, -22, 23])$.
   According to Proposition 1, the conditions $d_{1,i} = a_{1,i}$ $(i = 1, 2, 3, 31)$ ensure that the change of $c_{1,i}$ $(i = 1, 2, 3, 31)$ results in $\Delta b_1 = -2^{12} - 2^{13} + 2^{14} - 2^{10}$. Meanwhile, the conditions $d_{1,i} \ne a_{1,i}$ $(i = 24, \ldots, 30, 32)$ ensure that the change of $c_{1,i}$ $(i = 24, \ldots, 30, 32)$ results in $\Delta b_1 = 2^3 + \ldots + 2^9 + 2^{11}$. Combined with the conditions $b_{1,i} = 0$ $(i = 4, \ldots, 10, 12, 23)$ and $b_{1,i} = 1$ $(i = 11, 13, \ldots, 22)$, we can get $b'_1 = b_1[4, \ldots, 10, -11, 12, -13, \ldots, -22, 23]$.
3. In step 5, $(a_1, d_1, c_1[-1, -2, 3, -24, \ldots, -32], b_1[4, \ldots, 10, -11, 12, -13, \ldots, -22, 23])$
   $\implies (d_1, c_1[-1, -2, 3, -24, \ldots, -32], b_1[4, \ldots, 10, -11, 12, -13, \ldots, -22, 23], a_2[1, -2, \ldots, -11, 12, \ldots, 21, -22, \ldots, -32])$.
   From Proposition 1, the conditions $b_{1,i} = d_{1,i}$ $(i = 1, 2, 24, \ldots, 27, 29, \ldots, 32)$ and $b_{1,i} \ne d_{1,i}$ $(i = 3, 28)$ ensure that the change of c_1 results in $\Delta a_2 = 1 - 2 - 2^2 - \ldots - 2^7 - 2^{28} - \ldots - 2^{31}$. Meanwhile, the conditions $c_{1,i} = d_{1,i}$ $(i = 7, \ldots, 10, 12, 17, \ldots, 22)$ and $c_{1,i} \ne d_{1,i}$ $(i = 4, 5, 6, 11, 13, \ldots, 16, 23)$ ensure that the change of b_1 results in

$\Delta a_2 = -2^8 - 2^9 - 2^{10} + 2^{11} + \ldots + 2^{20} - 2^{21} - \ldots - 2^{27}$. Combined with the conditions $a_{2,i} = 0$ ($i = 1, 12, \ldots, 21$) and $a_{2,i} = 1$ ($i = 2, \ldots, 11, 22, \ldots, 32$), we can obtain $a'_2 = a_2[1, -2, \ldots, -11, 12, \ldots, 21, -22, \ldots, -32]$.

4. In step 6, $(d_1, c_1[-1, -2, 3, -24, \ldots, -32], b_1[4, \ldots, 10, -11, 12, -13, \ldots, -22, 23], a_2[1, -2, \ldots, -11, 12, \ldots, 21, -22, \ldots, -32]) \implies (c_1[-1, -2, 3, -24, \ldots, -32], b_1[4, \ldots, 10, -11, 12, -13, \ldots, -22, 23], a_2[1, -2, \ldots, -11, 12, \ldots, 21, -22, \ldots, -32], d_2)$.

   From Proposition 1, it is easy to get $a'_2 = a_2$ without no condition.

5. In step 7, $(c_1[-1, -2, 3, -24, \ldots, -32], b_1[4, \ldots, 10, -11, 12, -13, \ldots, -22, 23], a_2[1, -2, \ldots, -11, 12, \ldots, 21, -22, \ldots, -32], d_2) \implies (b_1[4, \ldots, 10, -11, 12, -13, \ldots, -22, 23], a_2[1, -2, \ldots, -11, 12, \ldots, 21, -22, \ldots, -32], d_2, c_2)$.

   From Proposition 1, the conditions $d_{2,i} = b_{1,i}$ ($i = 1, 3$) and $d_{2,i} \neq b_{1,i}$ ($i = 2, 24, \ldots, 32$) result in $F(d'_2, a'_2, b'_1) - F(d_2, a_2, b_1) = 1 + 2 - 2^2 + 2^{23} + \ldots + 2^{31}$. Combined with $c'_1 = c_1[-1, -2, 3, -24, \ldots, -32]$, we can get $c'_2 = c_2$.

4.3 Message Modification

As demonstrated in Table 10 of *line*1 operation, there is no constraint on the message words m_i ($i = 0, 9, 11, \ldots, 15$), and there is some freedom on the message words m_i ($i = 1, 5, 7, 8, 10$). Thus, all the freedom of these message words can be utilized to fulfill the conditions in Table 11, which are imposed by the differential characteristic of *line*2 operation.

We modify M so that all the conditions in the first round of Table 10 and most of the conditions in Table 11 hold. The outline of the modification is described as follows. Taking into consideration the fact that in Table 11 of *line*2 operation, the conditions first appear in the chaining variable bb_1, and the message words m_5, m_{14}, m_7 are involved in steps 1-3, we first modify m_i ($i = 1, \ldots, 7$) such that all the conditions of d_1, c_1, b_1, a_2, d_2, c_2 and b_2 in Table 10 are satisfied. Then we correct the conditions of bb_1 in Table 11. The message word involved in bb_1 is m_0, which is also involved in the first step of *line*1 operation. Therefore, if the conditions of bb_1 are corrected by m_0, it will probably lead to the correction of d_1, c_1, b_1, a_2, d_2, c_2, b_2 being invalid. As stated below, only the condition $bb_{1,4} = 0$ is corrected by m_0, and all the other conditions of bb_1 are corrected by the change of dd_1. For example, if the condition $bb_{1,24} = 0$ does not hold, we flip the bit $dd_{1,13}$ by changing m_{14}. However, we need to add the condition $b_{0,13} = 0$ such that the change of $dd_{1,13}$ does not disturb cc_1. Meanwhile, we also need to add the condition $aa_{1,13} = 0$ such that the change of $dd_{1,13}$ will invert $bb_{1,24}$. Similarly, we need to add some other conditions on the chaining variables of *line*2 operation, especially on the chaining variables aa_1, dd_1 and cc_1 in order to correct some conditions in Table 10 and Table 11. (It is noted that these extra added conditions are not presented in Table 11.) Furthermore, we also need to add some conditions on b_0 such that $b_{0,i} = 1$ ($i = 1, 2, 3, 27$) and $b_{0,i} = 0$ ($i = 7, \ldots, 10, 13, \ldots, 24$) in order to implement the message modification. (These conditions can be easily satisfied by exhaustively searching the first message block N.) Hence, we correct the conditions of *line*2 operation from aa_1, and the process of modification is as follows. It is noted that in most cases, the conditions are corrected from low bit to high bit. Sometimes, the order of correction is adjusted.

1. Modify m_i ($i = 1, 2, 3, 4$) such that the conditions of d_1, c_1, b_1 and a_2 in Table 10 hold, respectively.

2. Firstly, modify m_5 such that the conditions of d_2 in Table 10 hold. Secondly, if there is no overlap between the conditions on d_2 in Table 10 and aa_1 in Table 11, i.e., the conditions on aa_1 lies in $aa_{1,i}$ ($i \neq 1, 2, 3, 24, ..., 32$), then it is easy to correct them. For example, if the condition $aa_{1,13} = 0$ does not hold, we flip the bit $d_{2,13}$ by changing m_5, then $aa_{1,13}$ is inverted, i.e., $aa_{1,13} = 0$ is satisfied. Thirdly, if the conditions on aa_1 lies in $aa_{1,i}$ ($i = 1, 2, 3, 24, ..., 32$), we present an example below to illustrate how to correct them. For example, if the condition $aa_{1,1} = 0$ does not hold, we correct it by changing m_5, which will also flip the bit $d_{2,1}$. In order to fulfill the condition $d_{2,1} = b_{1,1}$, $b_{1,1}$ is flipped by changing m_3. Similarly, m_0, m_1 and m_4 are modified in order to ensure the conditions on d_1, c_1, b_1 and a_2, especially, $b_{1,1} = d_{1,1}$ and $d_{1,1} = a_{1,1}$ hold. The modification of m_0, m_1, m_3 and m_4 ensures that the differential characteristic of *line*1 operation is not disturbed by the change of m_5. The detail of correcting the condition $aa_{1,1} = 0$ is described in the following steps and illustrated in Table 3.

   (a) Modify m_0 such that $a_{1,1}$ in Table 10 is flipped and all the other bits of a_1 are unchanged. Without loss of generality, we suppose $aa_{1,1} = 0$, then a_1 becomes $a_1[1]$ after flipping $a_{1,1}$.

   (b) Modify m_1 such that $d_{1,1}$ in Table 10 is flipped and all the other bits of d_1 are unchanged, which ensures the condition $d_{1,1} = a_{1,1}$ in Table 10 hold.

   (c) The change of $a_{1,1}$ and $d_{1,1}$ does not disturb c_1 according to Proposition 1.

   (d) Modify m_3 such that $b_{1,1}$ in Table 10 is flipped and all the other bits of b_1 are unchanged, which ensures the condition $b_{1,1} = d_{1,1}$ in Table 10 hold.

   (e) Modify m_4 such that a_2 in Table 10 is unchanged.

   (f) Modify m_5 such that $d_{2,1}$ in Table 10 is flipped and all the other bits of d_2 are unchanged, which ensures the condition $d_{2,1} = b_{1,1}$ hold. Meanwhile, $aa_{1,1}$ is flipped by the change of m_5 and the condition $aa_{1,1} = 0$ is satisfied.

   It is noted that combined with the conditions $c_{1,1} = 1$ and $a_{2,1} = 0$, we can get that the flips of $d_{1,1}$ and $b_{1,1}$ have no impact on d_2. Hence, the modification of m_5 does not need to offset the flips of $d_{1,1}$ and $b_{1,1}$, and only flips $d_{2,1}$. Consequently, the change of m_5 is only likely to flip $aa_{1,1}$ and $aa_{1,i}$ ($i = 2, ..., 8$) by carry. Since the conditions of aa_1 are corrected from low bit to high bit, i.e., the order of modification is 9,...,32,1,...,8, then the correction of $aa_{1,1}$ does not disturb the conditions which have been corrected. Therefore, the condition $aa_{1,1} = 0$ is corrected successfully with probability 1.

3. Modify m_{14} and m_6 such that the conditions on dd_1 in Table 11 and c_2 in Table 10 hold, respectively.

4. Firstly, modify m_7 such that the conditions on b_2 in Table 10 hold. Secondly, similar to the modification of $aa_{1,i}$ ($i \neq 1, 2, 3, 24, ..., 32$), the conditions on $cc_{1,i}$ ($i \neq 2, ..., 12$) can be corrected by the change of m_7. Thirdly, the other conditions on cc_1 are corrected by the change of dd_1. For example, if the condition $cc_{1,10} = 0$ does not hold, we flip $dd_{1,1}$ by changing m_{14}. Then $cc_{1,10}$ is flipped if the extra condition $b_{0,1} = 1$ is added according to Proposition 4. The detail of correcting the condition $cc_{1,10} = 0$ is illustrated in Table 4.

Table 3. Message Modification for Correcting $aa_{1,1}$

	step	m_i	Shift	Modify m_i	Chaining values before modifying m_i	Chaining values after modifying m_i
*line*1	1	m_0	11	Modify m_0	a_1	$a_1[1]$
*line*1	2	m_1	14	Modify m_1	d_1	$d_1[1]$
*line*1	3	m_2	15		c_1	c_1
*line*1	4	m_3	12	Modify m_3	b_1	$b_1[1]$
*line*1	5	m_4	5	Modify m_4	a_2	a_2
*line*1	6	m_5	8	Modify m_5	d_2	$d_2[1]$
*line*2	1	m_5	8	Modify m_5	aa_1	$aa_{1,1}$ is flipped

Table 4. Message Modification for Correcting $cc_{1,10}$

step	m_i	Shift	Modify m_i	flipped bit	additional condition
2	m_{14}	9	Modify m_{14}	$dd_{1,1}$	
3	m_7	9		$cc_{1,10}$	$b_{0,1} = 1$

5. Firstly, the condition $bb_{1,4} = 0$ is corrected by the change of m_0. If $bb_{1,4} = 0$ does not hold, we flip $bb_{1,4}$ by modifying m_0, which will change a_1 in Table 10. On one hand, there is no constraint on a_1, so the change of a_1 does not disturb the differential characteristic. On the other hand, d_1, c_1, b_1 and a_2 are unchanged by modifying m_1, m_2, m_3 and m_4 respectively. Therefore, the change of m_0 does not disturb the differential characteristic of *line*1 operation. The procedure of correcting $bb_{1,4} = 0$ is illustrated in Table 5. Secondly, all the other conditions on bb_1 are corrected by the change of dd_1. For example, if the condition $bb_{1,24} = 0$ does not hold, we flip $dd_{1,13}$ by changing m_{14}. Then cc_1 is unchanged if the extra condition $b_{0,13} = 0$ is added, and $bb_{1,24}$ is flipped if the extra condition $aa_{1,13} = 0$ is added according to Proposition 4.

Table 5. Message Modification for Correcting $bb_{1,4}$

	step	m_i	Shift	Modify m_i	Chaining values before modifying m_i	Chaining values after modifying m_i
*line*2	4	m_0	11	Modify m_0	bb_1	$bb_{1,4}$ is flipped
*line*1	1	m_0	11	Modify m_0	a_1	a_1 is changed
*line*1	2	m_1	14	Modify m_1	d_1	d_1
*line*1	3	m_2	15	Modify m_2	c_1	c_1
*line*1	4	m_3	12	Modify m_3	b_1	b_1
*line*1	5	m_4	5	Modify m_4	a_2	a_2

6. Modify m_9 such that the conditions on aa_2 in Table 11 hold.

7. The conditions on dd_2 in Table 11 are corrected through the following four approaches. All the conditions on dd_2 are fulfilled after message modification except $dd_{2,29} = 1$. We present examples to illustrate the approaches of modification.

   (a) The condition $dd_{2,16} = 0$ is corrected by the change of m_7. In order not to disturb the condition $b_{2,2} = 0$ which has been corrected, we modify m_7 such that only $b_{2,1}$ is flipped and the other bits of b_2 are unchanged. The modification of m_7 flips $cc_{1,1}$ definitely, and is likely to flip $cc_{1,i}$ ($i = 2, ..., 9$) by carry. Hence, according to Proposition 4, bb_1 in all probability is unchanged if the extra conditions $aa_{1,1} = 0$ and $aa_{1,2} = 0$ are added, and $dd_{2,16}$ is flipped because the condition $aa_{2,1} \neq bb_{1,1}$ is hold yet. Furthermore, aa_2 is unchanged by modifying m_9. The success probability of correcting $dd_{2,16} = 0$, i.e., the probability that $dd_{2,16} = 0$ is satisfied and all the other conditions which have been corrected are not disturbed, is very close to 1.

   (b) The condition $dd_{2,24} = 1$ is corrected by the change of m_{14}. Firstly, m_{14} is changed such that $dd_{1,9}$ is flipped and all the other bits of dd_1 are unchanged. Then, according to Proposition 4, cc_1 will remain unchanged if the extra condition $b_{0,9} = 0$ is added, and bb_1 will be unchanged if the extra condition $aa_{1,9} = 1$ is added. Furthermore, aa_2 remains unchanged by modifying m_9, and $dd_{2,24}$ is flipped by the change of $dd_{1,9}$.

   (c) The condition $dd_{2,26} = 1$ is corrected by the change of m_9. Furthermore, m_9 is changed such that only $aa_{2,11}$ is flipped and the other bits of aa_2 are unchanged, which does not make the differential characteristic invalid because there is no constraint on $aa_{2,11}$. The change of $aa_{2,11}$ will flip $dd_{2,26}$ if the extra condition $cc_{1,11} = 1$ is added.

   (d) The condition $dd_{2,19} = 1$ is corrected by the change of m_2. However, the change of m_2 disturbs the conditions on c_1, which is compensated by modifying m_1 and m_6. Firstly, we modify m_1 such that $d_{1,19}$ is flipped and all the other bits of d_1 are unchanged. Then we modify m_2 such that $c_{1,19}$ is flipped and all the other bits of c_1 are unchanged. According to Proposition 1, we can get b_1 and a_2 are unchanged, meanwhile, d_2 is also unchanged because of the conditions $c_{1,19} = d_{1,19}$, $b_{1,19} = 1$ and $a_{2,19} = 0$. Thirdly, we modify m_6 such that c_2 is unchanged. Therefore, b_1, a_2, d_2 and c_2 are unchanged, and all the conditions in Table 10 are not disturbed. Obviously, the change of m_2 will flip $dd_{2,19}$, however, it is also likely to change $dd_{2,2}$. Fortunately, the conditions on dd_2 are corrected from low bit to high bit and $dd_{2,2} = 1$ is not corrected yet. So the success probability of correcting $dd_{2,19} = 1$ is 1. The procedure of correction $dd_{2,19}$ is illustrated in Table 6.

8. Modify m_{11} to correct the conditions of cc_2 in Table 11.

9. Similar to the procedure of modification above, the conditions of $bb_{2,i}$ ($i \neq 1, 4, 8,$ $16, 23, 24, 25, 26, 29, 31, 32$) in Table 11 are corrected by changing cc_2 or aa_2, corresponding to changing m_{11} or m_9, respectively.

10. Modify m_{13} to correct the conditions of aa_3.

11. Similar to the procedure of modification above, the conditions of $dd_{3,i}$ ($i \neq 2, 5, 7,$ $23, 25, 26, 30, 31, 32$) in Table 11 are corrected by changing aa_3, corresponding to changing m_{13}.

Table 6. Message Modification for Correcting $dd_{2,19}$

	step	m_i	Shift	Modify m_i	Chaining values before modifying m_i	Chaining values after modifying m_i	Conditions
line1	2	m_1	14	Modify m_1	d_1	$d_1[19]$	
line1	3	m_2	15	Modify m_2	c_1	$c_1[19]$	$c_{1,19} = d_{1,19}$
line1	4	m_3	12		b_1	b_1	$b_{1,19} = 1$
line1	5	m_4	5		a_2	a_2	$a_{2,19} = 0$
line1	6	m_5	8		d_2	d_2	
line1	7	m_6	7	Modify m_6	c_2	c_2	$c_{2,19} = d_{2,19}$
line2	6	m_2	15	Modify m_2	dd_2	$dd_{2,19}$ is flipped	$dd_{2,19} = 1$

12. Modify m_{15} to correct the conditions of cc_3.

13. Firstly, modify m_8 such that the conditions on a_3 in Table 10 and $bb_{3,i}$ ($i = 23, ..., 32$) in Table 11 hold. Secondly, the condition $bb_{3,12} = 1$ in Table 11 is corrected by flipping $cc_{3,1}$ combined with the condition $aa_{3,1} = 1$ according to Proposition 4. Thirdly, if the condition $bb_{3,2} = 0$ does not hold, we flip $cc_{3,22}$, then $bb_{3,1}$ is flipped if the extra condition $aa_{3,22} = 1$ (which is satisfied in step 10) is added according to Proposition 4. Meanwhile, if $bb_{3,1} \neq cc_{3,22}$, then the change of $bb_{3,1}$ will result in the change of $bb_{3,2}$ by bit carry. Furthermore, the condition $bb_{3,1} \neq cc_{3,22}$ can be corrected by modifying m_8.

14. Firstly, the condition on $aa_{4,5}$ can be corrected by the change of $cc_{3,23}$ and $bb_{3,23}$. Similarly, the condition on $aa_{4,9}$ can be corrected by the change of $cc_{3,27}$ and $bb_{3,27}$. Secondly, the condition $aa_{4,25} = 1$ in Table 11 is corrected by flipping $cc_{3,11}$. Then bb_3 is unchanged if the extra condition $aa_{3,11} = 0$ is added, and $aa_{4,25}$ is changed if the extra condition $dd_{3,11} = 0$ is added according to Proposition 4. The condition $aa_{3,11} = dd_{3,11}$ is already corrected in step 11, thus, the extra conditions $aa_{3,11} = 0$ and $dd_{3,11} = 0$ hold with a probability of 2^{-1}. Therefore, the success probability of correcting the condition on $aa_{4,25}$ is about $2^{-1} + 2^{-1} \times 2^{-1} = 3/4$. Thirdly, if the condition $aa_{4,7} = 0$ does not hold, we flip $cc_{3,24}$, then bb_3 is unchanged if the extra condition $aa_{3,24} = 0$ is added, and $aa_{4,6}$ is changed if the extra condition $dd_{3,24} = 0$ is added according to Proposition 4. Furthermore, if $aa_{4,6} \neq cc_{3,24}$, then the change of $aa_{4,6}$ will lead to the change of $aa_{4,7}$ by carry. The condition $aa_{3,24} = dd_{3,24}$ is already corrected in step 11, thus, the extra conditions $aa_{3,24} = 0$ and $dd_{3,24} = 0$ hold with a probability of 2^{-1}. Meanwhile, the condition $aa_{4,6} \neq cc_{3,24}$ holds with a probability of 2^{-1}. Therefore, the success probability of correcting the condition on $aa_{4,7}$ is about $2^{-1} + 2^{-1} \times 2^{-1} \times 2^{-1} = 5/8$.

15. The condition $dd_{4,9} = 1$ is corrected by flipping $cc_{3,13}$. Then bb_3 is unchanged if the extra condition $aa_{3,13} = 0$ is added, and $aa_{4,27}$ is flipped if the extra condition $dd_{3,13} = 0$ is added. The change of $aa_{4,27}$ will result in the change of $dd_{4,9}$ if the extra condition $cc_{3,27} = 1$ is added. The condition $cc_{3,27} = 1$ has been corrected in step 12. The condition $dd_{3,13} = aa_{3,13}$ has been corrected in step 11, thus, the extra conditions $aa_{3,13} = 0$ and $dd_{3,13} = 0$ hold with a probability of 2^{-1}. Therefore, the success probability of correcting the condition on $dd_{4,9}$ is about $2^{-1} + 2^{-1} \times 2^{-1} = 3/4$.

Table 7. Collision for 40-step of RIPEMD-128

N	664504b6	d6e949ba	2176407d	85426fc1	5ec28995	c3d318b	787db431	ae2c13fb
	cee9d90	c5078e4b	84bae5bc	99f3f4ae	d7403dc6	917fa14c	85155db5	fd9311e6
M	a7e4a89f	6278156c	2a535118	90eba965	670841b2	ea6f8dcb	800766d9	d0bfa5c6
	ffe74d8e	6df2c5f7	a3ffdbfd	53e156d4	54f75d	f0d3a13f	7eef12b9	ef317f76
M'	a7e4a89f	6278156c	2a535218	90eba965	670841b2	ea6f8dcb	800766d9	d0bfa5c6
	ffe74d8e	6df2c5f7	a3ffdbfd	53e156d4	54f75b	f0d3a13f	7eef12b9	ef317f76
H	a76df6ab	43ae1a6e	171d9fda	da03925e				

Table 8. Differential Characteristic for $line1$ Operation

Step	Message M	$Shift$	Δm_i	The output for M'
1	m_0	11		a_1
2	m_1	14		d_1
3	m_2	15	2^8	$c_1[-1, -2, 3, -24, ..., -32]$
4	m_3	12		$b_1[4, ..., 10, -11, 12, -13, ..., -22, 23]$
5	m_4	5		$a_2[1, -2, ..., -11, 12, ..., 21, -22, ..., -32]$
6	m_5	8		d_2
7	m_6	7		c_2
8	m_7	9		$b_2[2, ..., 10, -11, -12]$
9	m_8	11		$a_3[-2, ..., -11, 12]$
10	m_9	13		d_3
11	m_{10}	14		c_3
12	m_{11}	15		b_3
13	m_{12}	6	-2	a_4
...	...	...	...	...
25	m_{12}	7	-2	$a_7[-9]$
26	m_0	12		d_7
27	m_9	15		c_7
28	m_5	9		b_7
29	m_2	11	2^8	a_8
...	...	...	...	...
40	m_1	15		b_{10}

16. The conditions on $cc_{4,i}$ ($i = 7, 9, 12$) are corrected by the change of $dd_{4,i}$ ($i = 27, 29, 32$) respectively with probability 1. The condition $cc_{4,5} = 1$ is corrected by flipping $dd_{4,24}$ if the extra condition $cc_{4,4} \neq dd_{4,24}$ is added, which holds with a probability of 2^{-1}. Therefore, the success probability of correcting the condition on $cc_{4,5}$ is about $2^{-1} + 2^{-1} \times 2^{-1} = 3/4$.

It is noted that the conditions which are corrected in the first 12 steps hold with a probability of about 2^{-3} after message modification by experiment. Meanwhile, after message modification, in the first round of $line2$ operation in Table 11, there are 29 conditions which are not corrected, 3 conditions which hold with a probability of 3/4 respectively, and 1 condition which holds with a probability of 5/8. Therefore, all the conditions in steps 2-11 of Table 10 and in steps 4-15 of Table 11 hold with a probability of about 2^{-35} after message modification.

Table 9. Differential Characteristic for *line*2 Operation

Step	Message M	Shift	Δm_i	The output for M'
1	m_5	8		aa_1
2	m_{14}	9		dd_1
3	m_7	9		cc_1
4	m_0	11		bb_1
5	m_9	13		aa_2
6	m_2	15	2^8	$dd_2[-1, -2, -3, 4, -24, ..., -32]$
7	m_{11}	15		$cc_2[17, 18 - 19]$
8	m_4	5		$bb_2[8, ..., 15, -16, -24]$
9	m_{13}	7		$aa_3[-31]$
10	m_6	7		$dd_3[8, -23, 26, ..., 31, -32]$
11	m_{15}	8		$cc_3[7, 8, -25]$
12	m_8	11		$bb_3[2, 5]$
13	m_1	14		$aa_4[7, -9, -12]$
14	m_{10}	14		$dd_4[-5, 7, -9]$
15	m_3	12		$cc_4[-5]$
16	m_{12}	6	-2	bb_4
17	m_6	9		$aa_5[-21]$
18	m_{11}	13		$dd_5[-20, -21]$
19	m_3	15		$cc_5[-20]$
20	m_7	7		bb_5
21	m_0	12		aa_6
22	m_{13}	8		$dd_6[-29]$
23	m_5	9		$cc_6[-29]$
24	m_{10}	11		bb_6
25	m_{14}	7		aa_7
26	m_{15}	7		dd_7
27	m_8	12		$cc_7[-9]$
28	m_{12}	7	-2	$bb_7[-9]$
29	m_4	6		aa_8
30	m_9	15		dd_8
31	m_1	13		cc_8
32	m_2	11	2^8	bb_8
...	...	...	...	...
40	m_9	14		bb_{10}

Table 10. A Set of Sufficient Conditions for the Differential Characteristic in Table 8

Step	Chaining Variable	Conditions on the Chaining Variable
2	d_1	$d_{1,i} = a_{1,i}(i = 1, 2, 3, 31), d_{1,i} \neq a_{1,i}(i = 24, ..., 30, 32)$
3	c_1	$c_{1,3} = 0, c_{1,i} = 1(i = 1, 2, 24, ..., 32), c_{1,i} = d_{1,i}(i = 7, ..., 10, 12, 17, ..., 22),$ $c_{1,i} \neq d_{1,i}(i = 4, 5, 6, 11, 13, ..., 16, 23)$
4	b_1	$b_{1,i} = 0(i = 4, ..., 10, 12, 23), b_{1,i} = 1(i = 11, 13, ..., 22),$ $b_{1,i} = d_{1,i}(i = 1, 2, 24, ..., 27, 29, ..., 32), b_{1,i} \neq d_{1,i}(i = 3, 28)$
5	a_2	$a_{2,i} = 0(i = 1, 12, ..., 21), a_{2,i} = 1(i = 2, ..., 11, 22, ..., 32)$
6	d_2	$d_{2,i} = b_{1,i}(i = 1, 3), d_{2,i} \neq b_{1,i}(i = 2, 24, ..., 32)$
7	c_2	$c_{2,i} = d_{2,i}(i = 1, ..., 10, 13, ..., 21, 24), c_{2,i} \neq d_{2,i}(i = 11, 12, 22, 23, 25, ..., 32)$
8	b_2	$b_{2,i} = 0(i = 2, ..., 10), b_{2,i} = 1(i = 11, 12)$
9	a_3	$a_{3,12} = 0, a_{3,i} = 1(i = 2, ..., 11)$
11	c_3	$c_{3,i} = d_{3,i}(i = 2, ..., 10, 12), c_{3,11} \neq d_{3,11}$
24	b_6	$b_{6,9} = c_{6,9}$
25	a_7	$a_{7,9} = 1$
26	d_7	$d_{7,9} = 0$
27	c_7	$c_{7,9} = 1$

Table 11. A Set of Sufficient Conditions for the Differential Characteristic in Table 9

Step	Chaining Variable	Conditions on the Chaining Variable
4	bb_1	$bb_{1,i} = 0(i = 1, 3, 4, 24, ..., 32), bb_{1,2} = 1$
5	aa_2	$aa_{2,i} = 0(i = 3, 17, 18), aa_{2,i} = 1(i = 1, 2, 4, 19, 24, ..., 32)$
6	dd_2	$dd_{2,i} = 0(i = 4, 8, ..., 16), dd_{2,i} = 1(i = 1, 2, 3, 17, 18, 19, 24, ..., 32)$
7	cc_2	$cc_{2,i} = 0(i = 16, 17, 18, 24, 26, ..., 32), cc_{2,i} = 1(i = 8, ..., 15, 19)$
8	bb_2	$bb_{2,i} = 0(i = 8, ..., 15, 19, 23, 26, ..., 32), bb_{2,i} = 1(i = 16, 24), bb_{2,i} = cc_{2,i}(i = 1, 2, 3, 4, 25)$
9	aa_3	$aa_{3,i} = 0(i = 7, 23, 27), aa_{3,i} = 1(i = 8, 19, 25, 26, 28, ..., 32), aa_{3,i} = bb_{2,i}(i = 17, 18)$
10	dd_3	$dd_{3,i} = 0(i = 2, 5, 8, 25, ..., 31), dd_{3,i} = 1(i = 7, 23, 32), dd_{3,i} = aa_{3,i}(i = 9, ..., 16, 24)$
11	cc_3	$cc_{3,i} = 0(i = 7, 8, 12), cc_{3,i} = 1(i = 2, 5, 9, 25, 26, 30, 31)$
12	bb_3	$bb_{3,i} = 0(i = 2, 5, 8, 25, 26, 30, 31), bb_{3,i} = 1(i = 7, 12), bb_{3,i} = cc_{3,i}(i = 23, 27, 28, 29), bb_{3,32} \neq cc_{3,32}$
13	aa_4	$aa_{4,i} = 0(i = 5, 7), aa_{4,i} = 1(i = 8, 9, 12, 25)$
14	dd_4	$dd_{4,7} = 0, dd_{4,i} = 1(i = 5, 9), dd_{4,2} = aa_{4,2}$
15	cc_4	$cc_{4,i} = 0(i = 7, 9), cc_{4,5} = 1, cc_{4,12} = dd_{4,12}$
16	bb_4	$bb_{4,i} = 0(i = 5, 21)$
17	aa_5	$aa_{5,20} = 0, aa_{5,21} = 1$
18	dd_5	$dd_{5,i} = 1(i = 20, 21)$
19	cc_5	$cc_{5,21} = 0, cc_{5,20} = 1$
20	bb_5	$bb_{5,20} = 0$
21	aa_6	$aa_{6,29} = 0$
22	dd_6	$dd_{6,29} = 1$
23	cc_6	$cc_{6,29} = 1$
24	bb_6	$bb_{6,29} = 0$
26	dd_7	$dd_{7,9} = 0$
27	cc_7	$cc_{7,9} = 1$
28	bb_7	$bb_{7,9} = 1$
29	aa_8	$aa_{8,9} = 0$

There are 4 conditions in steps 24-27 of Table 10 and 17 conditions in steps 16-29 of Table 11. These 21 conditions can be easily satisfied by exhaustively searching m_{12}.

4.4 Collision Search Algorithm

From the above technique details, we present an overview of the collision search algorithm to get two 512-bit blocks $N \parallel M$, where the second block $M = m_0 \parallel m_1 \parallel ... \parallel m_{15}$.

1. Exhaustively search the first block N such that the hash value of N satisfies $b_{0,i} = 1$ ($i = 1, 2, 3, 27$) and $b_{0,i} = 0$ ($i = 7, ..., 10, 13, ..., 24$).
2. Randomly choose m_i ($0 \leq i \leq 15, i \neq 12$), and modify them by the above message modification techniques such that all the conditions in steps 2-11 of Table 10 are satisfied and all the conditions in steps 4-15 of Table 11 hold with a probability of 2^{-35}.
3. If all the conditions in steps 4-15 of Table 11 are satisfied, then goto Step 4. Otherwise, go to Step 2.
4. Randomly choose m_{12} and compute the hash values of M and M' under 40-step RIPEMD-128. If the two hash values are equal, then output M and M'. Otherwise, goto Step 1.

There are total 21 conditions in steps 24-27 of Table 10 and steps 16-29 of Table 11. By our experiment, it is easy to make the 21 conditions hold by exhaustively search m_{12} when the other conditions of Table 10 and Table 11 hold. Therefore, the time complexity of the collision attack is about $2^{35} + 2^{21}$ 40-step RIPEMD-128 computations. We give an example in Table 7.

5   Conclusions

In this paper, we propose a practical collision attack for 40-step RIPEMD-128 by using bit tracing method [15,16] and present a true collision instance. Firstly, we find two differential characteristics for *line*1 operation and *line*2 operation respectively. Then, by correcting most of the sufficient conditions that ensure the collision characteristics hold, we can improve the probabilities of the characteristics. Finding high-probability characteristics as well as implementing message modifications is nontrivial, because the compression function of RIPEMD-128 consists of two parallel and independent operations.

Acknowledgment. The author would like to thank Hongbo Yu for her helpful comments. The author also thanks the anonymous reviewers for their valuable suggestions and remarks. This work is supported by the National Natural Science Foundation of China (No. 61103238, 61373142), the Fundamental Research Funds for the Central Universities and DHU Distinguished Young Professor Program, and the Opening Project of State Key Laboratory of Information Security (Institute of Information Engineering, Chinese Academy of Sciences).

References

1. Dobbertin, H., Bosselaers, A., Preneel, B.: RIPEMD-160: A Strengthened Version of RIPEMD. In: Gollmann, D. (ed.) FSE 1996. LNCS, vol. 1039, pp. 71–82. Springer, Heidelberg (1996)
2. International Organization for Standardization: ISO/IEC 10118-3:2004, Informa- tion technology-Security techniques-Hash-functions-Part 3: Dedicated hash functions (2004)
3. Kap, J.: Test Cases for HMAC-RIPEMD160 and HMAC-RIPEMD128. Internet Engineering Task Force (IETF), RFC 2286 (1998), http://www.ietf.org/rfc/rfc2286.txt
4. Landelle, F., Peyrin, T.: Cryptanalysis of Full RIPEMD-128. In: Johansson, T., Nguyen, P.Q. (eds.) EUROCRYPT 2013. LNCS, vol. 7881, pp. 228–244. Springer, Heidelberg (2013)
5. Mendel, F., Nad, T., Schläffer, M.: Collision Attacks on the Reduced Dual-Stream Hash Function RIPEMD-128. In: Canteaut, A. (ed.) FSE 2012. LNCS, vol. 7549, pp. 226–243. Springer, Heidelberg (2012)
6. Mendel, F., Pramstaller, N., Rechberger, C., Rijmen, V.: On the Collision Resistance of RIPEMD-160. In: Katsikas, S.K., López, J., Backes, M., Gritzalis, S., Preneel, B. (eds.) ISC 2006. LNCS, vol. 4176, pp. 101–116. Springer, Heidelberg (2006)
7. Ohtahara, C., Sasaki, Y., Shimoyama, T.: Preimage Attacks on Step-Reduced RIPEMD-128 and RIPEMD-160. In: Lai, X., Yung, M., Lin, D. (eds.) Inscrypt 2010. LNCS, vol. 6584, pp. 169–186. Springer, Heidelberg (2011)
8. Bosselaers, A., Preneel, B. (eds.): RIPE 1992. LNCS, vol. 1007. Springer, Heidelberg (1995)
9. Rivest, R.L.: The MD4 message digest algorithm. In: Menezes, A., Vanstone, S.A. (eds.) CRYPTO 1990. LNCS, vol. 537, pp. 303–311. Springer, Heidelberg (1991)
10. Rivest, R.: The MD5 message-digest algorithm, Request for Comments(RFC 1320), Internet Activities Board, Internet Privacy Task Force (1992)
11. Sasaki, Y., Wang, L.: Distinguishers beyond Three Rounds of the RIPEMD-128/-160 Com- pression Functions. In: Bao, F., Samarati, P., Zhou, J. (eds.) ACNS 2012. LNCS, vol. 7341, pp. 275–292. Springer, Heidelberg (2012)
12. Wang, G., Wang, M.: Cryptanalysis of Reduced RIPEMD-128. Ruanjianxuebao/Journal of Software in Chinese 19(9), 2442–2448 (2008)
13. Wang, L., Sasaki, Y., Komatsubara, W., Ohta, K., Sakiyama, K.: (Second) Preimage At- tacks on Step-Reduced RIPEMD/RIPEMD-128 with a New Local-Collision Approach. In: Kiayias, A. (ed.) CT-RSA 2011. LNCS, vol. 6558, pp. 197–212. Springer, Heidelberg (2011)
14. Wang, X., Feng, D., Yu, X.: An attack on HAVAL function HAVAL-128. Science in China Ser. F Information Sciences 48(5), 1–12 (2005)
15. Wang, X., Lai, X., Feng, D., Chen, H., Yu, X.: Cryptanalysis of the Hash Functions MD4 and RIPEMD. In: Cramer, R. (ed.) EUROCRYPT 2005. LNCS, vol. 3494, pp. 1–18. Springer, Heidelberg (2005)
16. Wang, X., Yu, H.: How to Break MD5 and Other Hash Functions. In: Cramer, R. (ed.) EUROCRYPT 2005. LNCS, vol. 3494, pp. 19–35. Springer, Heidelberg (2005)
17. Wang, X., Yu, H., Yin, Y.L.: Efficient Collision Search Attacks on SHA-0. In: Shoup, V. (ed.) CRYPTO 2005. LNCS, vol. 3621, pp. 1–16. Springer, Heidelberg (2005)
18. Wang, X., Yin, Y.L., Yu, H.: Finding Collisions in the Full SHA-1. In: Shoup, V. (ed.) CRYPTO 2005. LNCS, vol. 3621, pp. 17–36. Springer, Heidelberg (2005)
19. Yu, H., Wang, X., Yun, A., Park, S.: Cryptanalysis of the full HAVAL with 4 and 5 passes. In: Robshaw, M. (ed.) FSE 2006. LNCS, vol. 4047, pp. 89–110. Springer, Heidelberg (2006)
20. Yu, H., Wang, G., Zhang, G., Wang, X.: The Second-Preimage Attack on MD4. In: Desmedt, Y.G., Wang, H., Mu, Y., Li, Y. (eds.) CANS 2005. LNCS, vol. 3810, pp. 1–12. Springer, Heidelberg (2005)

KDM Security in the Hybrid Framework

Gareth T. Davies and Martijn Stam

University of Bristol, UK
{gareth.davies,martijn.stam}@bristol.ac.uk

Abstract. We study the natural question of how well suited the hybrid encryption paradigm is in the context of key-dependent message (KDM) attacks. We prove that if a key derivation function (KDF) is used in between the public (KEM) and symmetric (DEM) part of the hybrid scheme and this KDF is modelled as a random oracle, then one-wayness of the KEM and indistinguishability of the DEM together suffice for KDM security of the resulting hybrid scheme. We consider the most general scenario, namely CCA attacks and KDM functions that can call the random oracle. Although the result itself is not entirely unsuspected—it does solve an open problem from Black, Rogaway, and Shrimpton (SAC 2002)—proving it is considerably less straightforward; we develop some proof techniques that might be applicable in a wider context.

Keywords: KDM Security, Hybrid Encryption, KEM/DEM, Public Key Encryption.

1 Introduction

When performing public key encryption (PKE) for large messages, it is often desirable to separate the encryption into two parts: public key techniques to encrypt a one-time symmetric key, and symmetric key techniques to encrypt the message. This type of encryption is commonly referred to as hybrid encryption. Hybrid encryption can be found in abundance in practice as it combines the benefits of flexible key management possible in the public key setting with the efficiency of symmetric encryption. Cramer and Shoup [22] were the first to capture hybrid encryption in a formal framework and their terminology is now commonly accepted: the public part of the algorithm is known as the key encapsulation mechanism (KEM), while the symmetric part, where the message is actually encrypted, is known as the data encapsulation mechanism (DEM). The main theorem of Cramer and Shoup (regarding hybrid encryption) is that the security properties of the KEM and the DEM can be regarded independently of each other. Loosely speaking, if any secure KEM is combined with any secure DEM, then the resulting public key encryption scheme is automatically secure. This theorem comes in two flavours, one for IND-CPA and one for IND-CCA2 security. Later works [30, 29, 2] looked at rebalancing the security properties of the KEM and the DEM such that the composition still guarantees IND-CCA2 security.

While, for good reasons, IND-CCA2 security has become the *de facto* security notion for public key encryption (so much so that we do not feel the need to

J. Benaloh (Ed.): CT-RSA 2014, LNCS 8366, pp. 461–480, 2014.

elaborate on its definition here), there are situations where even this strongest of notions [11] is too weak. Particularly problematic is a situation where private keys themselves end up being encrypted. This is far from an academic question and the problem of secure encryption in the presence of key-dependent messages is becoming increasingly relevant. Applications of KDM security arise in disk encryption systems such as BitLocker [16], axiomatic security proofs [1, 4] and anonymous credential systems [20].

Encryption that is secure against key-dependent inputs was first studied by Abadi and Rogaway [1], who studied security proofs for protocols and showed how security is given by a reduction if no key-cycles exist in the protocol. Circular security was defined by Camenisch and Lysyanskaya [20] in the context of anonymous credentials. A more thorough treatment of key-dependent message (KDM) security was given by Black, Rogaway, and Shrimpton [15], who provided definitions of KDM security for both the public key and symmetric key setting. They proved that in the symmetric setting it is easy to achieve IND-KDM-CPA security in the random oracle model. For the public key setting they recall a simple scheme in the random oracle model [13], which they conjecture to be KDM secure but to the best of our knowledge, no proof of this has appeared in the literature. The scheme neatly fits the hybrid encryption framework, where the key encapsulation takes a random protokey r and applies a trapdoor one-way permutation to encapsulate it. At the same time, r is hashed (giving an ephemeral key) and XORed with the message (so the DEM is a one-time pad).[1] Thus a natural question arises: how well suited is the hybrid encryption paradigm in the context of key-dependent message attacks?

Our Contribution. Although many efforts have been made to study the security of PKE schemes under key-dependent messages, we provide the first treatment of hybrid encryption in this context. Before describing our result in detail, let us take a step back and look at the problem of KDM-secure hybrid encryption from a general perspective. For the standard (IND-CPA and IND-CCA) definitions it was possible to separate the security concerns of the KEM and the DEM. In a KDM setting it will be (a function of) the private key of the KEM that is encapsulated by the DEM using an ephemeral symmetric key. Intuitively, this can mean two things: either the appearance of the KEM's private key as input to the DEM ruins the normal separation of concerns, or the use of a freshly generated ephemeral key magically nullifies the key dependency. In the full version we show how the counterexamples [3, 21] that KDM security does not follow from standard security definitions, can be cast within a KEM-DEM framework.

Our main result is presented in Section 3, where we consider the security of hybrid encryption schemes against key-dependent message attacks in the random oracle model. We show that if the key derivation function KDF is modelled as a

---

[1] Note that Black et al. assume that the random oracle returns as many bits as the message is long, which would require a slight modification to the original KEM-DEM framework.

random oracle, then a one-way secure (μOW-CCA) KEM and an indistinguishable (IND-CCA) DEM combine to form a PKE scheme that is (IND-KDM-CCA) secure against key-dependent message attacks, provided that the key-dependency does not involve the message length (this is a standard assumption). For our result, we make a distinction between KEMs for which there exists an efficient key-encapsulation–encapsulated-key checking oracle or not. Somewhat surprisingly, the former category gives a significantly tighter reduction, even though it means the KEM is weaker in some sense (in particular, it cannot be IND-CPA secure).

Although intuitively the random oracle would serve as a formidable barrier between the KEM and the DEM, removing any correlation, the proof turns out more involved than one might at first expect. To give a taster of the challenges, when reducing to a KEM security property, the simulation of valid DEM ciphertexts can be problematic without knowing the underlying message. If the DEM ciphertexts are uniformly distributed (over the randomness of the key) regardless of the message, simulation is easy (in particular, this observation suffices to prove the Black et al. scheme passively KDM secure). However, for arbitrary DEMs such simulation is not guaranteed and requires another game hop (to where a fixed message is encrypted). Luckily this does not lead to a circularity (where a DEM hop requires a KEM hop to set up, which itself requires a DEM hop to go through etc.).

Indeed, in our proof, we use the well-known identical-until-bad technique in a way similar to Dent's analysis of IND-CCA secure KEMs in the random oracle model [23]. However, a crucial innovation in our proof is a novel use of the "deferred analysis" technique of Gennaro and Shoup [24] to analyse the bad event: it turns out that we need to bound the events in two different games, but in one of these, the key-dependency hinders the usual approaches. Our solution is to move the analysis of the bad event to the other game, where the analysis is considerably easier. In contrast with the original deferred analysis, the probability of the events changes, so we need to account for this game-hop separately.

Technically even more challenging is the reduction to the DEM's indistinguishability, since the key dependency function needs to be mapped to a message for the DEM. A complication arises in that an adversary making multiple challenge queries could let the message to-be-encrypted by the DEM depend on prior, ephemeral DEM keys. We introduce a new security notion for the DEM that captures this type of key dependency (namely on past keys only) and show that is equivalent to standard IND-CCA. Moreover, we show how to map key dependency functions in the PKE world to this restricted set of key dependency functions in the DEM world by modelling the random oracle as a pseudorandom function. Thus, rather bizarrely, our security bound for KDM security of hybrid encryption includes a PRF term, despite there not being a PRF in the construction itself.

Related Work. Efforts in the area of KDM security have focused on either positive results giving circular secure schemes, or negative impossibility results. On the positive side, Boneh et al. [16] gave a KDM-CPA scheme secure under the Decisional Diffie-Hellman assumption, a result strengthened by Camenisch et al. [19] to a KDM-CCA scheme. Many other positive results have also been presented [31, 4, 28, 7, 8, 32]. Many public key schemes have been proposed of a number theoretical nature, where the class of functions for which KDM security can be proven is related, typically in some algebraic sense, to the scheme itself (see [9, 17, 5] and the references contained therein).

There have also been negative results, and in particular Haitner and Holenstein [27] showed the impossibility of obtaining KDM security based on standard assumptions and using standard techniques, and also separation results of Acar et al. [3] and Cash et al. [21]. Applebaum et al. [6] give a comparatively efficient scheme based on the LWE/LPN problems. The development of fully homomorphic encryption by Gentry [25] utilises encryption of the secret key under the corresponding public key, and recent work of Brakerski and Vaikuntanathan has looked at KDM security with FHE in more detail [18]. In the symmetric setting, recent work has focused on authenticated encryption [12], and Bellare et al. [10] describe ciphers that can securely encipher their own keys.

2   Preliminaries

Notation. If x is a string then $|x|$ denotes the length of x, and $x||y$ denotes the concatenation of strings x and y. If S is a finite set then $|S|$ is its cardinality and $s \xleftarrow{\$} S$ denotes picking s uniformly at random from S. A property of a boolean variable, which we will call a *flag*, is that once `true` it stays `true`. Boolean flags are assumed initialized to `false`. The adversary, which we regard as code of a program, makes calls to the oracles, taking as input values from some finite domain associated to each oracle.

Definition 1 (Pseudorandom functions). *Let $F : \mathcal{I} \times \mathcal{D} \to \mathcal{R}$ be a family of functions from domain $\mathcal{D}$ to range $\mathcal{R}$ indexed by seeds $\mathcal{I}$. For $x \in \mathcal{I}$ we let $F_x(y) : \mathcal{D} \to \mathcal{R}$ be defined by $F_x(y) = F(x, y) \ \forall y \in \mathcal{D}$. Let $Fun[\mathcal{D}, \mathcal{R}]$ be the set of all functions from $\mathcal{D}$ to $\mathcal{R}$. Set $\mathcal{D} = \{0,1\}^\lambda$ for some security parameter λ. Then the PRF advantage of an adversary $\mathcal{A}$ attacking F is given by*

$$\mathbf{Adv}^{\mathrm{PRF}}_{F, \mathcal{A}}(\lambda) \overset{def}{=} \mathbf{Pr}\left[x \xleftarrow{\$} \mathcal{I} : \mathcal{A}^{F_x(\cdot)} = 1 \right] - \mathbf{Pr}\left[g \xleftarrow{\$} Fun[\{0,1\}^\lambda, \mathcal{R}] : \mathcal{A}^{g(\cdot)} = 1 \right].$$

2.1   Public Key and Hybrid Encryption

We briefly recall the syntax of a public key encryption scheme PKE, consisting of four algorithms Pg, Kg, Enc, and Dec. Parameter generation Pg takes as input a security parameter λ and outputs a set of parameters common among multiple keypairs (e.g. the description of an elliptic curve); key generation Kg takes the parameters and outputs a public–private key pair (pk, sk); encryption Enc takes as input the public key and a message from $\{0,1\}^*$ (or some other message space with a well-defined length measure) and outputs a ciphertext; decryption Dec takes as input the private key and a purported ciphertext and returns a

$\text{Hyb.Pg}(1^\lambda)$

$\text{pars}_{\text{KEM}} \leftarrow \text{KEM.Pg}(1^\lambda)$
$\text{pars}_{\text{DEM}} \leftarrow \text{DEM.Pg}(1^\lambda)$
return $(\text{pars}_{\text{KEM}}, \text{pars}_{\text{DEM}})$

$\text{Hyb.Enc}(\text{pars}, \text{pk}, m)$

$(K, C) \leftarrow \text{KEM.encap}_{\text{pk}}()$
$h_K \leftarrow \text{KDF}_{\text{pars}, \text{pk}}(K)$
$\psi \leftarrow \text{DEM.Enc}_{h_K}(m)$
return (C, ψ)

$\text{Hyb.Dec}(\text{pars}, \text{sk}, C, \psi)$

$K \leftarrow \text{KEM.decap}_{sk}(C)$
$h_K \leftarrow \text{KDF}_{\text{pars}, \text{pk}}(K)$
$m \leftarrow \text{DEM.Dec}_{h_K}(\psi)$
return m

$\text{Hyb.Kg}(\text{pars})$

$(\text{pk}, \text{sk}) \leftarrow \text{KEM.Kg}(\text{pars}_{\text{KEM}})$
return (pk, sk)

Fig. 1. Construction of a hybrid cryptosystem Hyb

message in $\{0, 1\}^*$ or some designated error symbol $\perp$. The standard security notions for public key encryption are indistinguishability (IND) under chosen plaintext attacks (CPA), respectively chosen ciphertext attacks (CCA). We refer to e.g. Bellare et al. [11] for formal definitions.

A popular way of constructing public key schemes is to use hybrid encryption, consisting of a method of transporting the symmetric key called the key encapsulation mechanism KEM = (KEM.Pg, KEM.Kg, KEM.encap, KEM.decap), a data encapsulation mechanism (DEM) DEM = (DEM.Pg, DEM.Enc, DEM.Dec), and often a key derivation function KDF as a compatibility layer in between, as depicted in Fig. 1. We use the term *protokey* to describe the input to the KDF (above denoted K). The individual components have the following properties.

- The KEM's parameter and key generation work as for a public key encryption scheme. Key encapsulation KEM.encap takes a public key and returns both a key $K \in \mathcal{K}_{\text{KEM}}$ and an encapsulation C thereof. Key decapsulation KEM.decap takes as input a private key and a purported key encapsulation and returns a key in $\mathcal{K}_{\text{KEM}}$ or some designated error symbol $\perp$.
- Data encapsulation DEM.Enc takes a message $m \in \{0, 1\}^*$ and a symmetric key in $\mathcal{K}_{\text{DEM}}$ and outputs an encryption ψ. A data decapsulation DEM.Dec takes a message encapsulation ψ and a symmetric key in $\mathcal{K}_{\text{DEM}}$ and outputs the message m or error symbol $\perp$.
- A key derivation function KDF is a deterministic algorithm implementing a mapping from $\mathcal{K}_{\text{KEM}}$ to $\mathcal{K}_{\text{DEM}}$. Note that in addition to some key K the algorithm takes as input KEM.pk and DEM.pars (in order to determine $\mathcal{K}_{\text{KEM}}$ and $\mathcal{K}_{\text{DEM}}$).

As a notational convention, we omit parameters and implicitly assume that they are fed to every algorithm, and we write key inputs as subscripts except in cases where the operation really is on the key. In the single user setting, we often write $(\text{pk}, \text{sk}) \leftarrow \text{Gen}(1^\lambda)$ as shorthand for running parameter and key generation in one go.

While hybrid encryption has been in widespread use ever since the advent of public key cryptosystems, the first formalisation of the paradigm was given by Cramer and Shoup [22]. They gave security definitions of IND-CPA and IND-CCA security for both the KEM and the DEM part and proved that in the standard model, where the key derivation function only needs to be (close to) balanced, the public key cryptosystem inherits security from its constituent parts, e.g. IND-CCA security for both the KEM and the DEM part is a sufficient condition to obtain an

IND-CCA secure hybrid PKE scheme. Since then efforts have been made [30, 29, 2] to investigate how weakening the individual security notions impacts on the security of the PKE scheme. We refer to the above-mentioned articles for general security notions for KEMs and DEMs; we will be particularly concerned with μOW-CCA for KEMs (where the μ indicates there can be multiple key pairs in the game and the adversary can make multiple encapsulation queries for each public key) and IND-CCA for DEMs.

Dent [23] looked at various constructions of KEMs from one-way secure public key cryptosystems (operating on a restricted message space). He modelled the key derivation function as a random oracle and considered it as part of the KEM. A typical example of such a construction is the use of a trapdoor function to encapsulate a protokey r that is subsequently hashed to yield a derived key $H(r)$ (this is the same KEM as mentioned in the introduction). He shows several elegant, generic KEM constructions that are IND-CCA secure based on fairly minimal assumptions on the encryption scheme used to encrypt the protokey. For instance, in the example above security is attained if the trapdoor function is one-way secure even in the presence of an oracle that checks whether a ciphertext is a valid ciphertext or not (i.e., the actual range of the trapdoor function is easily recognizable by the adversary), which Dent calls OW-CPA+ security. If the KEM is constructed from a *randomized* public key cryptosystem, security based on one-wayness is proven, provided that there is an efficient plaintext-ciphertext checking oracle, that, when given a message and ciphertext pair, correctly determines whether the ciphertext is an encryption of the message or not.

Our results are reminiscent of that of Dent, however whereas he exploits Cramer–Shoup's composition theorem and only explicitly considered the construction of secure KEMs that incorporate the KDF, we (necessarily) look at hybrid encryption as a whole and our emphasis will be on constructing secure hybrid cryptosystems from a KEM treating the KDF separately. Thus where Dent used a public key encryption scheme to arrive at a protokey, we use a proper key encapsulation mechanism. As a consequence, our framework is on the one hand more general than Dent's (e.g. we can deal with Diffie–Hellman type KEMs more easily), yet on the other we are likely to run into similar technicalities. In particular, we see a dichotomy in the KEMs depending on the availability of a key-encapsulation–encapsulated-key checking oracle $\mathsf{KEM.Check}_{pk}(C, K)$ that, on input a key encapsulation C and purported encapsulated (proto) key K decides whether $\mathsf{KEM.decap}_{sk}(C) = K$ or not. This leads to the following two types of KEMs; each type will give a different reduction in the security analysis later on:

- In TYPE-1 KEMs there is an efficient checking oracle $\mathsf{KEM.Check}_{pk}(C, K)$. This class encompasses all schemes that determine the encapsulation C deterministically based on the key K, including the usual schemes based on trapdoor permutations/functions. Diffie–Hellman type KEMs in a pairing-based setting (where DDH is easy) can also be part of this class. (Looking ahead, in the security proof when an adversary makes a query $H(K)$ to its random oracle, the checking oracle allows the reduction to determine whether this K corresponds to some challenge encapsulation C.)

- In TYPE-2 KEMs there is no efficient checking oracle. This class contains all IND-CPA secure KEMs. (The lack of a checking oracle means that the reduction will need to guess whether a query $H(K)$ corresponds to a challenge ciphertext or not, leading to a less tight reduction.)

The event $\mathsf{Coll}_{\mathsf{KEM}}(q_{\mathsf{LR}}, \lambda)$, paramaterized by the number of oracle queries the adversary makes and the security parameter, implies a collision in the ephemeral key output by the KEM, which is extremely unlikely to occur (if it were, this would also adversely affect the KEM's one-wayness).

2.2 Key Dependent Message (KDM) Security

The first formal definition of KDM security was given by Black et al. [15]. They define a KDM analogue IND-KDM-CPA of the established IND-CPA security notion. Simply put, an adversary submits as challenge a function φ and receives either an encryption of $\varphi(\mathsf{sk})$ or of a dummy message $0^{|\varphi(\mathsf{sk})|}$. Camenisch et al. [19] introduced the "active" version IND-KDM-CCA security as a natural blend between IND-CCA and IND-KDM-CPA, and this is the version we will focus on. There can be multiple keys in the system and, contrary to standard IND-CPA security, for the IND-KDM security notions it is not possible to reduce (e.g. by hybrid argument) to a single key or single query.

The IND-KDM notions are relative to a function class Φ, which stipulates that the adversary is bound to asking only queries $\varphi \in \Phi$. For instance, if Φ corresponds to the set of all constant functions, notions equivalent to IND-CPA and IND-CCA emerge. The challenge is to devise schemes that can be proven secure for an as large as possible class Φ. Black et al. formally regarded φ modelled as an algorithm in some fixed RAM model; furthermore they imposed length-regularity of φ in the sense that $|\varphi(\mathsf{sk})|$ does not depend on the value sk. Following e.g. Malkin et al. [32], we will instead regard φ as an arithmetic or Boolean circuit, which will imply that the output length of φ is fixed (and automatically independent of its input).

Our syntax also differs from that of Black et al. as we make a distinction between parameter and key generation, which is not uncommon in multi-user settings. Since φ implements a function from a Cartesian product of secret key spaces to the message space and these spaces can depend on the parameter

$\mathbf{Exp}_{\mathsf{PKE},\,\mathcal{A}}^{\mathsf{IND\text{-}KDM\text{-}CCA}[\varPhi]\text{-}b}(\lambda):$	New():	$\mathsf{LR}_b(\varphi, i):$	$\mathsf{Dec}(C, i):$
pars $\leftarrow \mathsf{Pg}(1^\lambda)$	$t \leftarrow t + 1$	if $\varphi \notin \Phi(\mathsf{pars}, \mathbf{pk}, i)$ then	if $(C, i) \in \mathsf{FL}$ then
$t \leftarrow 0$	$(\mathsf{pk}_t, \mathsf{sk}_t) \leftarrow \mathsf{Kg}(\mathsf{pars})$	return $\lightning$	return $\lightning$
$\mathsf{FL} \leftarrow \emptyset$	Append sk_t to $\mathbf{sk}$	$m_1 \leftarrow \varphi(\mathbf{sk})$	$m \leftarrow \mathsf{Dec}_{\mathsf{sk}_i}(C)$
$\mathbf{sk} \leftarrow ()$	return pk_t	$m_0 \leftarrow 0^{|m_1|}$	return m
$b' \leftarrow \mathcal{A}^{\mathsf{New},\mathsf{LR}_b,\mathsf{Dec}}(\mathsf{pars})$		$\tilde{C}_b \leftarrow \mathsf{Enc}_{\mathsf{pk}_i}(m_b)$	
return b'		$\mathsf{FL} \leftarrow \mathsf{FL} \cup \{(\tilde{C}_b, i)\}$	
		return $\tilde{C}_b$	

Fig. 2. The general IND-KDM-CCA experiment for public key encryption. The bit b is hard-wired into the Left-or-Right oracle LR_b and determines whether a key-dependent message or a dummy is encrypted and returned to $\mathcal{A}$. Removing oracle Dec yields the IND-KDM-CPA experiment.

$\mathbf{Exp}_{\mathsf{Hyb},\,\mathcal{A}}^{\mathsf{IND\text{-}KDM\text{-}CCA}\text{-}b}(\lambda)$:
  pars $\leftarrow$ Pg(1^λ)
  $t \leftarrow 0$
  $\mathbf{sk} \leftarrow ()$
  $\mathsf{H}_{\mathsf{LIST}} \leftarrow \emptyset$
  $\mathsf{FL} \leftarrow \emptyset$
  $b' \leftarrow \mathcal{A}^{\mathsf{New},\mathsf{H},\mathsf{LR}_b^{\mathsf{H}},\mathsf{Dec}^{\mathsf{H}}}$ (pars)
  return b'

New():
  $t \leftarrow t + 1$
  $(\mathsf{pk}_t, \mathsf{sk}_t) \leftarrow$ Kg(pars)
  Append sk_t to $\mathbf{sk}$
  return pk_t

H:
  On query K:
  if $(K, h_K) \in \mathsf{H}_{\mathsf{LIST}}$
    return h_K
  else
    $h_K \xleftarrow{\$} \{0,1\}^\lambda$
    $\mathsf{H}_{\mathsf{LIST}} \leftarrow \mathsf{H}_{\mathsf{LIST}} \cup \{(K, h_K)\}$
    return h_K

$\mathsf{LR}_b^{\mathsf{H}}(\varphi, i)$:
  if $\varphi \notin \Phi(\mathsf{pars}, \mathbf{pk}, i)$ then
    return $\frac{\ell}{}$
  $m_1 \leftarrow \varphi^{\mathsf{H}}(\mathbf{sk})$
  $m_0 \leftarrow 0^{|m_1|}$
  $(C, K) \leftarrow$ KEM.encap$_{\mathsf{pk}_i}()$
  $h_K \leftarrow \mathsf{H}(K)$
  $\psi_b \leftarrow$ DEM.Enc$_{h_K}(m_b)$
  $\mathsf{FL} \leftarrow \mathsf{FL} \cup \{(C, \psi_b, i)\}$
  return (C, ψ_b)

$\mathsf{Dec}^{\mathsf{H}}(C, \psi, i)$:
  if $(C, \psi, i) \in \mathsf{FL}$ then
    return $\frac{\ell}{}$
  $K \leftarrow$ KEM.decap$_{\mathsf{sk}_i}(C)$
  if $K = \perp$ then
    return $\perp_{\mathsf{KEM}}$
  $h_K \leftarrow \mathsf{H}(K)$
  $m \leftarrow$ DEM.Dec$_{h_K}(\psi)$
  if $m = \perp$ then
    return $\perp_{\mathsf{DEM}}$
  return m

Fig. 3. The IND-KDM-CCA indistinguishability experiment made explicit for multi-key hybrid encryption in the random oracle model. The adversary is allowed to query decryptions of the challenge ciphertexts under different public keys than the ones generated by LR_b, and this restriction is dealt with by the list FL.

generation (e.g. which cyclic group is used for DLP based systems), the security experiment incorporates a check that φ is syntactically valid (however we will henceforth drop explicit mention of it).

Definition 2. *Let* PKE $=$ (Gen, Enc, Dec) *be a public key encryption scheme (with security parameter λ). Let Φ be a collection of circuits that map a (number of) secret key(s) to an element in the message space. Then the* IND-KDM-atk$[\Phi]$ *advantage of an adversary $\mathcal{A}$ against* PKE *relative to key-dependent message attacks for circuit class Φ and* atk $\in \{$CPA, CCA$\}$ *is defined by*

$$\mathbf{Adv}_{\mathsf{PKE},\,\mathcal{A}}^{\mathsf{IND\text{-}KDM\text{-}atk}[\Phi]}(\lambda) \overset{def}{=} \left| \sum_{b \in \{0,1\}} (-1)^b \cdot \mathbf{Pr}\left[\mathbf{Exp}_{\mathsf{PKE},\,\mathcal{A}}^{\mathsf{IND\text{-}KDM\text{-}atk}[\Phi]\text{-}b}(\lambda) = 1\right] \right|$$

where the experiment $\mathbf{Exp}_{\mathsf{PKE},\,\mathcal{A}}^{\mathsf{IND\text{-}KDM\text{-}CCA}[\Phi]\text{-}b}(\lambda)$ *is given in Fig. 2, and removing the decryption oracle yields experiment* $\mathbf{Exp}_{\mathsf{PKE},\,\mathcal{A}}^{\mathsf{IND\text{-}KDM\text{-}CPA}[\Phi]\text{-}b}(\lambda)$.

3   IND-KDM-CCA Security of Hybrid Encryption

3.1   Restricted KDM Security of the DEM

We introduce a security notion for DEMs called IND-PKDM-CCA ('Prior-KDM'), where an adversary's KDM capability is restricted to (encryptions of) functions of all 'past' DEM keys in the system. The formal security game for IND-PKDM-CCA is depicted in Fig. 4. Our reductions for KDM security of hybrid encryption will use this IND-PKDM-CCA security notion for the DEM. However, by a hybrid argument one can show that this restricted form of KDM attacks is not all that useful to an attacker—the notion is in fact equivalent

$\mathbf{Exp}^{\text{IND-PKDM-CCA-}b}_{\text{DEM, }\mathcal{A}}(\lambda)$:	New():	$LR_b(j, \vartheta)$:	$Dec(j, \psi)$:
pars $\leftarrow$ DEM.Pg(1^λ)	$i \leftarrow i + 1$	if $j \not\subseteq [i]$ then	if $(j, \psi) \in$ FL then
$i \leftarrow 0$	$K_i \leftarrow$ DEM.Kg(pars)	return $\frac{j}{2}$	return $\frac{j}{2}$
FL $\leftarrow \emptyset$	return i	$m_1 \leftarrow \vartheta(K^{j-1})$	$m \leftarrow$ DEM.Dec$_{K_j}(\psi)$
$b' \leftarrow \mathcal{A}^{\text{New,LR}_b,\text{Dec}}$(pars)		$m_0 \leftarrow 0^{\|m_1\|}$	return m
return b'		$\psi \leftarrow$ DEM.Enc$_{K_j}(m_b)$	
		FL $\leftarrow$ FL $\cup \{(j, \psi)\}$	
		return ψ	

Fig. 4. The IND-PKDM-CCA security experiment for data encapsulation mechanism DEM. Here $\vartheta(K^{i-1})$ indicates the function ϑ can depend on all keys in range $\{K_0, ..., K_{i-1}\}$.

to IND-CCA security. That IND-PKDM-CCA security implies IND-CCA security follows from standard relations between different formulations of IND-CCA security, plus the fact that a non-key dependent message can be queried (in the KDM world) by using a constant function. See the full version for proof of the reverse direction (Theorem 3), namely that IND-CCA security for DEMs implies the IND-PKDM-CCA notion.

Theorem 3. *Let* DEM *be a data encapsulation mechanism. Then for adversary* $\mathcal{A}_1$, *there exists an algorithm* $\mathcal{A}_2$ *of comparable computational complexity such that*

$$\mathbf{Adv}^{\text{IND-PKDM-CCA}}_{\text{DEM, }\mathcal{A}_1}(\lambda) \leq n \cdot \mathbf{Adv}^{\text{IND-CCA}}_{\text{DEM, }\mathcal{A}_2}(\lambda) .$$

3.2 Hybrid Encryption Is IND-KDM-CCA Secure (in the ROM)

Let Hyb = (Hyb.Gen, Hyb.Enc, Hyb.Enc) be a hybrid encryption scheme and let $\mathcal{A}$ be an adversary. In the hybrid setting there are two types of keys present: the private key of the KEM and the ephemeral key for the DEM, where knowledge of the private KEM key leads to immediate recovery of the ephemeral key. When we regard Hyb as a public key encryption scheme in the context of key-dependent messages, it follows from Fig. 1 that it is on the private key of the *KEM* that key-dependent messages (that are input to the *DEM*) will depend. For concreteness, in Fig. 3 we have expanded Fig. 2 in the context of hybrid encryption where the key derivation function is modelled as a random oracle. The forbidden list FL ensures that the adversary cannot trivially win.

We show that any KEM/DEM system that has a TYPE-1 μOW-CCA KEM and an IND-CCA DEM gives a IND-KDM-CCA[Φ] secure hybrid encryption scheme provided that the key derivation function KDF is modelled as a random oracle, and the functions in Φ can call the random oracle. By this we mean that when modelled as circuits, $\varphi \in \Phi$ can have gates that explicitly call the random oracle. Here, the μ indicates that there is a choice of multiple targets to invert. Recall that our modelling of functions in $\varphi \in \Phi$ as circuits implicitly implies that φ is length-regular, meaning that given pk and φ, one can uniquely determine the length of $\varphi(\text{sk})$ (this is the same restriction as made by Black et al. [15] and Backes et al. [7]). This result is formalized in Theorem 4. In the full version we provide an analogous, but significantly less tight result for TYPE-2 KEMs.

Proof intuition. In our proof we make use of the game-playing technique [35, 14] and introduce a sequence of games, as described in Fig. 5, and the games themselves are specified in Fig. 6. Apart from the simple, syntactical transitions (1) and (2), there are five game-hops to bound $\mathcal{A}$'s advantage distinguishing $\mathbf{Exp}_{\mathsf{Hyb},\ \mathcal{A}}^{\mathsf{IND\text{-}KDM\text{-}CCA\text{-}1}}(\lambda)$ and $\mathbf{Exp}_{\mathsf{Hyb},\ \mathcal{A}}^{\mathsf{IND\text{-}KDM\text{-}CCA\text{-}0}}(\lambda)$. These are denoted with solid lines. Here (3) and (4) are identical-until-bad hops. The 'Forbidden List' FL ensures that the adversary cannot win trivially. We define bad to be the event that the adversary queries the random oracle on a protokey K previously used by the left-or-right oracle.

So far, this is all standard fare: use the security of the KEM to decouple the key encapsulated by the KEM and the one used by the DEM (where Dent [23] used the same bad event in his analysis of IND-CCA secure KEMs), followed by a straightforward indistinguishability hop to the DEM. Unfortunately, with the introduction of key-dependent messages the latter hop has become quite a bit more burdensome; moreover bounding the bad event in the presence of key-dependent messages is somewhat troublesome. To overcome these challenges, our proof uses a number of techniques. To invoke the DEM's indistinguishability, the standard reduction would pick all the KEM keypairs and use these to simulate the KEM part of the hybrid encryption scheme (to run the adversary against the entire PKE). Since the reduction itself is playing the DEM indistinguishability game, it can use its DEM oracles to complete the DEM part (as the protokey encapsulated by the KEM and the ephemeral key used by the DEM are decoupled at this point). However if an adversary (against the PKE) may make queries with KDM functions that call the random oracle, it could in principle submit functions that decrypt past key encapsulations and, with the help of the random oracle, turn them in past DEM keys (effectively, the KDM function can cause the event that would normally have triggered bad). Since the reduction does not know the actual DEM keys being used, it suddenly finds itself in a tight spot and a direct hybrid argument (to get rid of past DEM keys) does not seem to work.

Our solution is to leverage the newly introduced IND-PKDM-CCA notion. Since we model the KDM functions as circuits, it turns out to be possible to describe a compiler that turns a KDM function against the PKE into one against the DEM. There is however one further complication. For the public key scheme, we model the hash function as a random oracle and *the KDM function has access to the random oracle*. Yet, for the DEM scheme there is no random oracle present, which would suggest that the KDM function in the DEM world should not depend on one either. Moreover, it is not possible to predict on which values the KDM function would call the random oracle. Thus, when the random oracle is implemented by the reduction using lazy sampling, though it could hard-code the hash list so far into the circuit, the simulation might fail once fresh values are requested. To handle this, we (partly) model the random oracle as a pseudorandom function (rather than using lazy sampling). This provides the reduction a succinct description of the *entire* random oracle and it can safely embed the key to the pseudorandom function in the circuit used in the IND-PKDM-CCA game. The introduction of a PRF requires two additional hops (5) and (7).

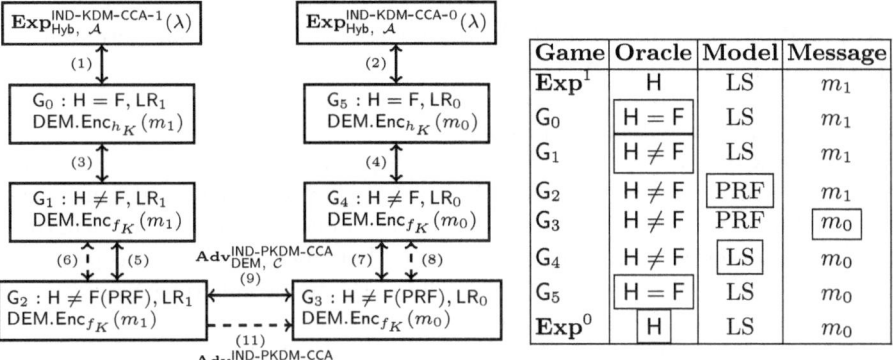

Fig. 5. Diagrammatic overview of the game hopping structure of proof that an μOW-CCA TYPE-1 secure KEM and an IND-CCA secure DEM yield a IND-KDM-CCA secure hybrid scheme in the random oracle model. The games are defined formally in Fig. 6, here the boxes indicate the game G_i and which oracles comprise the game. The transitions are labelled by the equations in the proof. The table on the right indicates which oracle is used to handle $\mathcal{A}$'s calls, how we model the random oracle (LS denotes lazy sampling) and which message is encrypted. The boxed items indicate where a change occurs in the hop from one game to another.

The bounding of event bad is relatively easy on the m_0-side of the diagram, as one does not need to know the KEM's private key sk in order to simulate the data encapsulations: bad is bounded in G_3 by $\mathbf{Adv}^{\mu\text{OW-CCA}}_{\text{KEM}, \mathcal{B}}$. However, on the m_1-side of the diagram it is less obvious how to bound the bad event, since it is not possible to simulate the key-dependent values. The solution is to move the bad event from the m_1-side to the m_0-side using the separate hop (11), which bounds the difference between $\mathbf{Pr}\,[\text{bad}]$ in games G_2 and G_3. This incurs a second $\mathbf{Adv}^{\text{IND-PKDM-CCA}}_{\text{DEM}, \mathcal{C}}$ term to the bound.

Bounding of the bad event breaks down if distinct queries to the LR oracle made identical KDF queries. We bound this event by the separate quantity $\mathsf{Coll}_{\text{KEM}}(q_{\text{LR}}, \lambda)$. It might be possible to avoid this technicality by changing the scheme so it hashes $\mathsf{H}(C, K)$ instead of just $\mathsf{H}(K)$.

Interpretation. When it comes to hybrid schemes, our result is very general. Indeed, it even generalizes the work by Dent [23] (restricted to IND-CPA-security) as we can deal with key encapsulation schemes where the protokey is derived from the randomness in a hard-to-invert fashion. For instance, if $\mathbb{G}_p$ is a cyclic group of order p with generator g, an obvious Diffie–Hellman inspired KEM would pick private key $x \in \mathbb{Z}_p^*$, set public key g^x and compute a key encapsulation by generating a random $r \in \mathbb{Z}_p^*$, releasing g^r as the encapsulation of $K = g^{rx}$. Our theorems can deal with this situation (where the KEM is TYPE-1 iff DDH is easy in $\mathbb{G}_p$), but it is not covered by the KEMs given by Dent.

Black et al. [15] suggest the use of a variant of TDP-KEM combined with a one-time pad as a KDM-secure public key scheme in the random oracle model. Here TDP-KEM is shorthand for trapdoor-permutation-KEM, where the public and private key of the KEM match that of the trapdoor permutation and key encapsulation takes a random K in the domain of the trapdoor permutation, applies the permutation to encapsulate and outputs $H(K)$ as ephemeral key, or, in the hybrid model with explicit key derivation function (Fig. 3) the KEM would output K as ephemeral protokey.

As a result of our theorem, if we restrict this scheme to any fixed-size message length, security is guaranteed. Strictly speaking, for arbitrary length messages, we would need to allow signalling of (an upper bound on) the message length to the random oracle so it can output the required number of bits. This is primarily a syntactical issue that we did not feel sufficiently important to incorporate into our main framework. Since TDP-KEM has an obvious checking oracle, we regard our Theorem 4 settling the problem left open by Black et al.

Theorem 4. *Let* Hyb *be a hybrid PKE scheme (Fig. 1) with a* TYPE-1 *KEM, with the key derivation function modelled by a random oracle. Let Φ be any set of functions, including those which have random oracle access. Let F be a family of pseudorandom functions. Then for any adversary $\mathcal{A}$ calling* LR *at most q_{LR} times, there exists algorithms $\mathcal{B}$ and $\mathcal{C}$ (of comparable computational complexity) such that*

$$\mathbf{Adv}_{\mathsf{Hyb},\ \mathcal{A}}^{\mathsf{IND\text{-}KDM\text{-}CCA}[\Phi]}(\lambda) \leq 2\mathbf{Adv}_{\mathsf{KEM},\ \mathcal{B}}^{\mu\mathsf{OW\text{-}CCA}}(\lambda) + 2\mathbf{Adv}_{\mathsf{DEM},\ \mathcal{C}}^{\mathsf{IND\text{-}PKDM\text{-}CCA}}(\lambda)$$
$$+ 2\mathsf{Coll}_{\mathsf{KEM}}(q_{\mathsf{LR}}, \lambda) + 4\mathbf{Adv}_{F,\ \mathcal{A}}^{\mathsf{PRF}}(\lambda) .$$

This theorem, combined with Theorem 3, yields the following corollary relating to standard definitions.

Corollary 5. *As above, and let n be the number of DEM keys in the system, then:*

$$\mathbf{Adv}_{\mathsf{Hyb},\ \mathcal{A}}^{\mathsf{IND\text{-}KDM\text{-}CCA}[\Phi]}(\lambda) \leq 2\mathbf{Adv}_{\mathsf{KEM},\ \mathcal{B}}^{\mu\mathsf{OW\text{-}CCA}}(\lambda) + 2n \cdot \mathbf{Adv}_{\mathsf{DEM},\ \mathcal{C}}^{\mathsf{IND\text{-}CCA}}(\lambda)$$
$$+ 2\mathsf{Coll}_{\mathsf{KEM}}(q_{\mathsf{LR}}, \lambda) + 4\mathbf{Adv}_{F,\ \mathcal{A}}^{\mathsf{PRF}}(\lambda) .$$

Proof. [of Theorem 4]

Fig. 3 contains a description of the security games $\mathbf{Exp}_{\mathsf{Hyb},\ \mathcal{A}}^{\mathsf{IND\text{-}KDM\text{-}CCA}\text{-}b}(\lambda)$ that are obtained by specifying the general PKE IND-KDM-CCA games for hybrid encryption where the key derivation function is modelled by a random oracle H. (For simplicity, we omit explicit mention of the class Φ in the description of the security experiments.) As is customary, we use lazy sampling to define H's behaviour, maintaining a list $\mathsf{H}_{\mathsf{LIST}}$ of query pairs (K, h_K) produced by H so far.

In the game there are four distinct places where queries to H could be made. Firstly, the adversary $\mathcal{A}$ can make direct H queries; any query to the oracle LR_b will require one 'direct' call to H for the key derivation and may include a number of indirect calls as part of the specified function φ; and finally as a decryption query for key derivation. For the purpose of our game-hopping approach, we need to be able to make a clear distinction between these cases. To this end, we introduce two additional oracles: F and HF. We make a syntactical change so

$\mathbf{Exp}_{\mathsf{PKE},\,\mathcal{A}}^{\text{IND-KDM-CCA}[\Phi]\text{-}b}(\lambda):$
pars $\leftarrow$ Pg(1^λ)
$t \leftarrow 0$
$\mathbf{sk} \leftarrow ()$
$\mathsf{H}_{\mathsf{LIST}}, \mathsf{F}_{\mathsf{LIST}}, \mathsf{FL} \leftarrow \emptyset$
$b' \leftarrow \mathcal{A}^{\mathsf{New},\mathsf{H},\mathsf{LR}_b,\mathsf{Dec}}(\text{pars})$
return b'

$\mathsf{LR}_b(\varphi^{\mathsf{H}}, i):$
if $\varphi^{\mathsf{H}} \not\subseteq \Phi(\text{pars}, \mathbf{pk}, i)$ then
   return $\frac{1}{2}$
$m_1 \leftarrow \varphi(\mathbf{sk})$
$m_0 \leftarrow 0^{|m_1|}$
$(C, K) \leftarrow \mathsf{KEM.encap}_{\mathbf{pk}_i}()$
$h_K \leftarrow \mathsf{F}(K)$
$\psi_b \leftarrow \mathsf{DEM.Enc}_{h_K}(m_b)$
$\mathsf{FL} \leftarrow \mathsf{FL} \cup \{(C, \psi_b, i)\}$
return (C, ψ_b)

New():
$t \leftarrow t + 1$
$(\mathbf{pk}_t, \mathbf{sk}_t) \leftarrow \mathsf{Kg}(\text{pars})$
Append $\mathbf{sk}_t$ to $\mathbf{sk}$
return $\mathbf{pk}_t$

H(K):
if $(K, h_K) \in \mathsf{H}_{\mathsf{LIST}}$
   return h_K
if $(K, h_K) \in \mathsf{F}_{\mathsf{LIST}}$
   set bad $\leftarrow$ true
   $\boxed{\text{return } h_K}$
$h_K \xleftarrow{\$} \{0,1\}^\lambda$
$\mathsf{H}_{\mathsf{LIST}} \leftarrow \mathsf{H}_{\mathsf{LIST}} \cup \{(K, h_K)\}$
return h_K

F(K):
if $(K, h_K) \in \mathsf{F}_{\mathsf{LIST}}$
   return h_K
if $(K, h_K) \in \mathsf{H}_{\mathsf{LIST}}$
   set bad $\leftarrow$ true
   $\boxed{\text{return } h_K}$
$h_K \xleftarrow{\$} \{0,1\}^\lambda$
$\mathsf{F}_{\mathsf{LIST}} \leftarrow \mathsf{F}_{\mathsf{LIST}} \cup \{(K, h_K)\}$
return h_K

HF(K):
if $(K, h_K) \in \mathsf{F}_{\mathsf{LIST}}$
   return h_K
if $(K, h_K) \in \mathsf{H}_{\mathsf{LIST}}$
   return h_K
$h_K \xleftarrow{\$} \{0,1\}^\lambda$
$\mathsf{H}_{\mathsf{LIST}} \leftarrow \mathsf{H}_{\mathsf{LIST}} \cup \{(K, h_K)\}$
return h_K

Dec(C, ψ, i):
if $(C, \psi, i) \in \mathsf{FL}$ then
   return $\frac{1}{2}$
call $K \leftarrow \mathsf{Decap}(C, i)$
if $K = \bot$ then
   return $\bot_{\mathsf{KEM}}$
$h_K \leftarrow \mathsf{HF}(K)$
$m \leftarrow \mathsf{DEM.Dec}_{h_K}(\psi)$
if $m = \bot$ then
   return $\bot_{\mathsf{DEM}}$
return m

$\mathbf{Exp}_{\mathsf{PKE},\,\mathcal{A}}^{\text{IND-KDM-CCA}[\Phi]\text{-}b}(\lambda):$
pars $\leftarrow$ Pg(1^λ)
$t \leftarrow 0$
$x \xleftarrow{\$} \{0,1\}^\lambda$
$\mathbf{sk} \leftarrow ()$
$\mathsf{H}_{\mathsf{LIST}}, \mathsf{F}_{\mathsf{LIST}}, \mathsf{FL} \leftarrow \emptyset$
$b' \leftarrow \mathcal{A}^{\mathsf{New},\mathsf{H},\mathsf{LR}_b,\mathsf{Dec}}(\text{pars})$
return b'

H(K):
if $(K, h_K) \in \mathsf{H}_{\mathsf{LIST}}$
   return h_K
if $(K, h_K) \in \mathsf{F}_{\mathsf{LIST}}$
   set bad $\leftarrow$ true
$h_K \leftarrow \mathsf{PRF}_x(K)$
$\mathsf{F}_{\mathsf{LIST}} \leftarrow \mathsf{F}_{\mathsf{LIST}} \cup \{(K, h_K)\}$
return h_K

HF(K):
if $(K, h_K) \in \mathsf{F}_{\mathsf{LIST}}$
   return h_K
if $(K, h_K) \in \mathsf{H}_{\mathsf{LIST}}$
   return h_K
$h_K \leftarrow \mathsf{PRF}_x(K)$
$\mathsf{H}_{\mathsf{LIST}} \leftarrow \mathsf{H}_{\mathsf{LIST}} \cup \{(K, h_K)\}$
return h_K

Fig. 6. Security games used for proof Theorem 4. Games G_2 and G_3 are described below the line, with all items the same as above apart from these changes. Games G_0 and G_5 correspond to the code including the boxed lines, implying that $\mathsf{H} = \mathsf{F}$ (as far as I/O behaviour is concerned). Games $\mathsf{G}_1 - \mathsf{G}_4$ have $\mathsf{H} \neq \mathsf{F}$ as two independently sampled random oracles. Games G_2 and G_3 model the random oracle as a PRF, rather than using lazy sampling. Games G_0, G_1 and G_2 correspond to $b = 1$, whereas Games G_3, G_4 and G_5 correspond to $b = 0$.

that LR_b always uses F for its key derivation, and Dec always uses HF. Oracle HF synchronises with items that are added to lists for both H and F. By ensuring that F, H and HF implement the same random oracle (i.e. are functionally equivalent, exhibiting exactly the same input/output behaviour), the changed games are equivalent to the original security experiments.

In Fig. 6, G_0 corresponds to such a modified, yet equivalent game, in this case for $b = 1$. The $b = 0$ sibling game is called G_5. In both these games the oracles H and F each maintain their own list, $\mathsf{H}_{\mathsf{LIST}}$, respectively $\mathsf{F}_{\mathsf{LIST}}$, yet control code ensures *(a)* that these two lists can not contain K overlap in the sense that no triple (K, h_K, h'_K) can exist for which both $(K, h_K) \in \mathsf{H}_{\mathsf{LIST}}$ and $(K, h'_K) \in \mathsf{F}_{\mathsf{LIST}}$ and *(b)* that the oracles H and F will look up elements from the other oracle's list, thus ensuring synchronisation. As a result of this design, F and H are functionally equivalent to each other in the games G_0 and G_5, implying that from an adversary's point of view G_0 is equivalent to $\mathbf{Exp}_{\mathsf{Hyb},\,\mathcal{A}}^{\mathsf{IND\text{-}KDM\text{-}CCA\text{-}1}}(\lambda)$, or

$$\mathbf{Pr}\left[{G_0}^{\mathcal{A}}=1\right]=\mathbf{Pr}\left[\mathbf{Exp}_{\mathsf{Hyb},\,\mathcal{A}}^{\mathsf{IND\text{-}KDM\text{-}CCA\text{-}1}}(\lambda)=1\right].\tag{1}$$

Similarly we claim that G_5 is equivalent to $\mathbf{Exp}_{\mathsf{Hyb},\,\mathcal{A}}^{\mathsf{IND\text{-}KDM\text{-}CCA\text{-}0}}(\lambda)$, so

$$\mathbf{Pr}\left[{G_5}^{\mathcal{A}}=1\right]=\mathbf{Pr}\left[\mathbf{Exp}_{\mathsf{Hyb},\,\mathcal{A}}^{\mathsf{IND\text{-}KDM\text{-}CCA\text{-}0}}(\lambda)=1\right].\tag{2}$$

We proceed by a more interesting hop, where we make F and H independent. The oracles F and H are modified such that when a query is made to one oracle (say H) that has previously been queried to the other (F) then a fresh value is still created (and added to H_{LIST}). Moreover, in this case the flag bad is set to true first. This is described in Fig. 6, where the new G_1 corresponds to the $b=1$ case and G_4 to the $b=0$ case. By syntactical inspection, G_0 and G_1 are identical up to the point at which the flag is set, enabling application of the fundamental lemma of game-hopping [14]:

$$\left|\mathbf{Pr}\left[{G_0}^{\mathcal{A}}=1\right]-\mathbf{Pr}\left[{G_1}^{\mathcal{A}}=1\right]\right|\le\mathbf{Pr}\left[\mathcal{A}\text{ sets bad in }G_1\right]\tag{3}$$

and in a similar vein G_4 and G_5 are identical until bad, so

$$\left|\mathbf{Pr}\left[{G_4}^{\mathcal{A}}=1\right]-\mathbf{Pr}\left[{G_5}^{\mathcal{A}}=1\right]\right|\le\mathbf{Pr}\left[\mathcal{A}\text{ sets bad in }G_4\right].\tag{4}$$

(To bound the difference between games G_4 and G_5 a standard hop involving the KEM's IND-CCA advantage is an alternative.)

The hop between the key-dependent scenario and the non-key-dependent world will be problematic later on due to the fact that if φ calls the random oracle, the simulation cannot correctly answer these queries since it does not know the values of the DEM keys in the system, only their indices. To counter this we add two additional hops in which we use a PRF rather than lazy sampling to model our random oracle. We regard the φ that acts on $\mathbf{sk}$ (of the KEM) as a circuit, with some gates that call the RO. Thus there is a (one-to-one) mapping from φ circuits (which act on $\mathbf{sk}$) to ϑ circuits (that act on the DEM keys). We assume that there is some kind of 'safe storage' of all DEM keys. In this manner it is possible to track the past RO queries that are made by these ϑ functions. These H gates will have some inputs, and will check if the input string corresponds to some H_{LIST} entry, or an F_{LIST} entry. If it is an F query, then assign a K_i to some of the output wires (since the game does not know the K_i but it can use them). The issue, however, is that if $\mathcal{A}$ gives a circuit φ that makes an H query in a gate, and subsequently makes another H query then the H_{LIST} lists will not be synchronised.

To counter this, consider H as a pseudorandom function PRF : $\{0,1\}^\lambda\times\mathcal{K}_{\mathsf{DEM}}\to\{0,1\}^\lambda$ chosen from some PRF-secure function family F, parameterized by some seed $x\in\{0,1\}^\lambda$, rather than using lazy sampling. Denote $\mathsf{PRF}_x(K)$ as being the PRF applied to input K and seed x. The gates for H now store the F_{LIST}, and when calls to F are made we can wire up the corresponding K_i values. When the function makes H calls, we simply implement the PRF on the given input. To make this subtle change, we need to implement another two (symmetrical) game hops in which we change the way we model the random oracle from lazy sampling (LS) to using a PRF. The difference between $\mathcal{A}$'s advantage against G_1 and its advantage against G_2 is bounded by $\mathcal{A}$'s advantage in breaking the PRF:[2]

$$\mathbf{Pr}\left[G_1{}^{\mathcal{A}} = 1\right] - \mathbf{Pr}\left[G_2{}^{\mathcal{A}} = 1\right] \leq \mathbf{Adv}^{\text{PRF}}_{F,\,\mathcal{A}}(\lambda) \qquad (5)$$

$$\mathbf{Pr}\left[\mathcal{A} \text{ sets bad in } G_1\right] - \mathbf{Pr}\left[\mathcal{A} \text{ sets bad in } G_2\right] \leq \mathbf{Adv}^{\text{PRF}}_{F,\,\mathcal{A}}(\lambda) \qquad (6)$$

and likewise the difference between $\mathcal{A}$'s advantage against G_3 and its advantage against G_4 is bounded by the PRF advantage:

$$\mathbf{Pr}\left[G_3{}^{\mathcal{A}} = 1\right] - \mathbf{Pr}\left[G_4{}^{\mathcal{A}} = 1\right] \leq \mathbf{Adv}^{\text{PRF}}_{F,\,\mathcal{A}}(\lambda) \qquad (7)$$

$$\mathbf{Pr}\left[\mathcal{A} \text{ sets bad in } G_4\right] - \mathbf{Pr}\left[\mathcal{A} \text{ sets bad in } G_3\right] \leq \mathbf{Adv}^{\text{PRF}}_{F,\,\mathcal{A}}(\lambda) \qquad (8)$$

Now we are in a position to consider the hop between games G_2 and G_3. In game G_2 the response from the Left-or-Right oracle is given to the adversary by LR_1, resulting to an encryption of $m_1 = \varphi(\mathbf{sk})$ in $\mathbf{Exp}^{\text{IND-KDM-CCA-1}}_{\text{Hyb},\,\mathcal{A}}(\lambda)$, whereas in game G_3, the Left-or-Right oracle is implemented by LR_0, leading to an encryption of $m_0 = 0^{|\varphi(\mathbf{sk})|}$ (as in $\mathbf{Exp}^{\text{IND-KDM-CCA-0}}_{\text{Hyb},\,\mathcal{A}}(\lambda)$). To show that games G_2 and G_3 are distinguishable only with small probability we introduce an adversary $\mathcal{C}$ that attacks the IND-PKDM-CCA property of the DEM, and show that as long as the DEM is secure in this respect, then the output of the games is indistinguishable. More precisely,

$$\mathbf{Pr}\left[G_2{}^{\mathcal{A}} = 1\right] - \mathbf{Pr}\left[G_3{}^{\mathcal{A}} = 1\right] \leq \mathbf{Adv}^{\text{IND-PKDM-CCA}}_{\text{DEM},\,\mathcal{C}}(\lambda) \qquad (9)$$

The consequence of F and H being independently sampled oracles is that in games G_2 and G_3 the encapsulated key and the key used for the DEM are effectively decoupled (as the adversary has no direct access to F). This decoupling allows us to use a DEM hop to prove equation (9), please see full version for details of this reduction. In the game that $\mathcal{C}$ plays, it runs $\mathcal{A}$ as a black-box that returns a valid φ, then $\mathcal{C}$ creates messages m_0 and m_1 in the same way that the LR_b oracle does in the other games. However, where in the games G_2 and G_3 there was an explicit oracle F that provided linkage between a key K output by the KEM and its corresponding key h_K actually used by the DEM, in the simulation $\mathcal{C}$ uses its own oracles to create the keys h_K in the IND-PKDM-CCA experiment it itself is playing. To do this, we need to move the function φ that acts on the KEM secret

---

[2] The more usual hop in a proof would be to replace a pseudorandom function by a perfectly random function, whereas here the perfect object is substituted by a computational approximation—for bounding the difference between the two worlds the 'direction' is irrelevant.

keys to the function ϑ, that acts upon DEM keys. The set K_ϑ contains all the DEM keys that are currently in the system. To simulate the DEM hop we need to make sure that the ϑ circuit in the IND-PKDM-CCA game is consistent with the circuit that acts on all of the DEM keys in the system in the PKE game. Every time $\mathcal{A}$ makes an F query in its PKE game we need to add that key to the set of keys that ϑ can act upon.

In this decoupled scenario, reduction $\mathcal{C}$ generates the (pk, sk) pairs itself. The seed of the PRF is then 'hardwired' into the gates of ϑ so when $\mathcal{A}$'s KDM function makes a RO call, it is dealt with by this setup. This allows the simulation to go through without $\mathcal{C}$ actually knowing which values K_i are queried to the RO. The messages m_1 and m_0 are then 'created' just as they are in $\mathcal{A}$'s LR queries. Now $\mathcal{D}$ calls its own oracles LR, New and Dec (in the IND-PKDM-CCA game) and returns a pair (C, ψ_b) as $\mathcal{A}$ would have expected.

The LR oracle in the simulation translates the φ into a ϑ. If this function makes an oracle call K_i, the simulation checks $\mathsf{H_{LIST}}$ for an entry containing K_i, and if present returns the corresponding h_K. If the value is on $\mathsf{F_{LIST}}$ then the simulation will know the index of the key but not the value itself, and thus a PRF gate can be called to retrieve the corresponding h_K. If it is on neither list, simply initiate PRF on K_i.

Since the adversary $\mathcal{A}$ has no direct access to F this indirect simulation of F is perfect. As a result, if $\mathcal{C}$ is in $\mathbf{Exp}_{\mathsf{DEM},\ \mathcal{C}}^{\mathsf{IND\text{-}PKDM\text{-}CCA\text{-}1}}(\lambda)$ then $\mathcal{A}$ will behave towards $\mathcal{C}$ exactly as it would do in $\mathsf{G_2}$, and similarly if $\mathcal{C}$ is in $\mathbf{Exp}_{\mathsf{DEM},\ \mathcal{C}}^{\mathsf{IND\text{-}PKDM\text{-}CCA\text{-}0}}(\lambda)$ then $\mathcal{A}$ will behave as in $\mathsf{G_3}$, proving (9).

All that remains is bounding the probability of the bad event in games $\mathsf{G_2}$ and $\mathsf{G_3}$, followed by a collection of the various terms into a single bound on the advantage.

The analysis of the bad event in game $\mathsf{G_3}$ is easiest, as here the adversary is given an encryption of a zero string which is clearly not key-dependent (since the adversary directly specifies its length). By simple code-inspection, it emerges that $\mathcal{A}$ can set the flag bad to true in two places in $\mathsf{G_3}$: either in a direct oracle query to H on a K that has already been queried to F by $\mathsf{LR_0}$; or if $\mathsf{LR_0}$ calls F on a K that has previously been queried to H directly by $\mathcal{A}$. Intuitively, the former constitutes a break against the one-wayness of the KEM, and the latter should just be very unlikely (although we actually bound it by a break as well to avoid the need for an additional assumption on the way K as output by KEM is distributed). Please refer to the full version for full details of reduction $\mathcal{B}$, for which

$$\mathbf{Pr}\left[\mathcal{A} \text{ sets bad in } \mathsf{G_3}\right] \leq \mathbf{Adv}_{\mathsf{KEM},\ \mathcal{B}}^{\mu\mathsf{OW\text{-}CCA}}(\lambda) + \mathsf{Coll}_{\mathsf{KEM}}(q_{\mathsf{LR}}, \lambda) \tag{10}$$

First we observe that if Enc (internally) creates a pair (C, K) and (C', K') satisfying $K = K'$ yet $C \neq C'$ the simulation will with high probability produce $\mathsf{F}(K) \neq \mathsf{F}(K')$, indicating that in that case it is not perfect. However, the event that such a pair is created by a KEM ought to be small. We define $\mathsf{Coll}_{\mathsf{KEM}}(q, \lambda)$ as the probability this happens in q queries to the encapsulation oracle.

In order to simulate correctly, we require that the reductions can make as many New calls as $\mathcal{A}$ can. To do this we can simply set an upper bound on the number of New calls that $\mathcal{A}$ makes, and then restrict the number of calls the reductions can make by this figure.

If a collision as above does not happen then $\mathcal{B}$ creates a perfect simulation of G_3 as long as bad is not set. Moreover, at the very point a query is made that would have caused bad to be set in G_3, the reduction $\mathcal{B}$ uses its KEM-checking oracle KEM.Check to detect that bad was set and retrieves the corresponding key K, plus the index of the Enc query this key belongs to.

As a technical aside, to simulate G_3 the reduction needs to answer the adversary $\mathcal{A}$'s LR_0 queries. Since $\mathcal{A}$ gives out φ and expects an encryption of $0^{|\varphi(\mathbf{sk})|}$, it is necessary (in order to simulate correctly) for $\mathcal{B}$ to learn $|\varphi(\mathbf{sk})|$ without knowing $\mathbf{sk}$. Here the length regularity condition is required: given $\mathbf{pk}$ and φ, we can determine $|\varphi(\mathbf{sk})|$ and thus simulate LR_0.

The analysis of the bad event in G_2 is more problematic and a direct approach (as done for G_3) does not work. Instead, we take inspiration from the "deferred analysis" technique of Gennaro and Shoup [24]. Rather than analysing the bad events in G_2, we will defer the analysis to G_3 (for which we already have a bound). However, it is not at all evident that in the hop G_2 to G_3 the probability the bad flag is set stays the same (as was the case for the deferred analysis by Gennaro and Shoup). Indeed, it is unlikely to be the case, however we are able to show that the difference between the two bad events from occurring is bound by IND-PKDM-CCA advantage of an adversary $\mathcal{D}$ (as described in Fig. 7) against the DEM, or

$$\mathbf{Pr}\left[\mathcal{A} \text{ sets bad in } G_2\right] - \mathbf{Pr}\left[\mathcal{A} \text{ sets bad in } G_3\right] \leq \mathbf{Adv}_{\text{DEM}, \mathcal{D}}^{\text{IND-PKDM-CCA}}(\lambda) . \quad (11)$$

Similarly to the analysis of (9), it is necessary to translate the function φ into a ϑ, and align the simulated queries correctly. We set this up so that the bad event in the security games corresponds to $\mathcal{D}$ causing an ABORT in the reduction.

1. If $\mathcal{D}$ is in game IND-PKDM-CCA-1 then, unless ABORT occurs, this is a perfect simulation of G_2 for $\mathcal{A}$.
2. If $\mathcal{D}$ is in game IND-PKDM-CCA-0 then, unless ABORT occurs, this is a perfect simulation of G_3 for $\mathcal{A}$.
3. $\mathcal{D}$ will ABORT iff the event bad occurs in (either) G_2 (or G_3).

Consequently we have

$$\mathbf{Pr}\left[\mathcal{A} \text{ sets bad in } G_2\right] = \mathbf{Pr}\left[\mathcal{D} \text{ sees ABORT in } \mathbf{Exp}^{\text{IND-PKDM-CCA-1}}\right]$$

$$\mathbf{Pr}\left[\mathcal{A} \text{ sets bad in } G_3\right] = \mathbf{Pr}\left[\mathcal{D} \text{ sees ABORT in } \mathbf{Exp}^{\text{IND-PKDM-CCA-0}}\right] .$$

Since by construction (and definition) we also have

$$\mathbf{Pr}\left[\mathcal{D} \text{ sees ABORT in } \mathbf{Exp}^{\text{IND-PKDM-CCA-}b}\right] = \mathbf{Pr}\left[\mathbf{Exp}^{\text{IND-PKDM-CCA-}b} = 1\right]$$

and so our claim (11) follows. Finally we put all of the above together and arrive at the claimed bound.

$\mathcal{D}$ playing $\mathbf{Exp}_{\mathsf{DEM},\,\mathcal{D}}^{\mathsf{IND\text{-}PKDM\text{-}CCA}\text{-}b}(\lambda)$:
  pars $\leftarrow$ Pg(1^λ)
  $t \leftarrow 0$
  $\mathbf{sk} \leftarrow ()$
  $\mathsf{H}_{\mathsf{LIST}}, \mathsf{F}_{\mathsf{LIST}}, \mathsf{FL} \leftarrow \emptyset$
  $x \xleftarrow{\$} \{0,1\}^\lambda$
  $b' \leftarrow \mathcal{A}^{\mathsf{New},\mathsf{H},\mathsf{LR}_b,\mathsf{Dec}}(\mathrm{pk})$
  if an ABORT occurs then
    return 1
  return 0

$\mathsf{H}(K)$:
  if $(K, h_K) \in \mathsf{H}_{\mathsf{LIST}}$ then
    return h_K
  if $(K, *) \in \mathsf{F}_{\mathsf{LIST}}$ then
    ABORT
  $h_K \leftarrow \mathsf{PRF}_x(K)$
  $\mathsf{H}_{\mathsf{LIST}} \leftarrow \mathsf{H}_{\mathsf{LIST}} \cup \{(K, h_K)\}$
  return h_K

$\mathsf{LR}_b(\varphi^{\mathsf{H}}, n)$:
  $\varphi^{\mathsf{H}} \to \vartheta$
  if φ^{H} makes RO call K_i then
    $h_K \leftarrow \mathsf{PRF}_x(K)$
    $K_\vartheta \leftarrow K_\vartheta \cup K_i$
  $m_1 \leftarrow \vartheta(K_\vartheta)$
  $m_0 \leftarrow 0^{|m_1|}$
  $(C, K) \leftarrow \mathsf{KEM.encap}_{\mathrm{pk}_n}()$
  if $(K, h_K) \in \mathsf{H}_{\mathsf{LIST}}$ then
    ABORT
  if $(K, j) \in \mathsf{F}_{\mathsf{LIST}}$ then
    call $\psi_b \leftarrow \mathsf{LR}(j, \vartheta)$
  else
    call $j \leftarrow \mathsf{New}()$
    $\mathsf{F}_{\mathsf{LIST}} \leftarrow \mathsf{F}_{\mathsf{LIST}} \cup \{(K, j)\}$
    call $\psi_b \leftarrow \mathsf{LR}(j, \vartheta)$
  $\mathsf{FL} \leftarrow \mathsf{FL} \cup \{(j, \psi)\}$
  return (C, ψ_b)

$\mathsf{New}()$:
  $t \leftarrow t + 1$
  $(\mathrm{pk}_t, \mathrm{sk}_t) \leftarrow \mathsf{Kg}(\mathrm{pars})$
  Append sk_t to $\mathbf{sk}$
  return pk_t

$\mathsf{Dec}(j, \psi)$:
  call $m \leftarrow \mathsf{Dec}(j, \psi)$
  return m

Fig. 7. Description of reduction $\mathcal{D}$ used to prove (11). When $\mathcal{D}$ runs $\mathcal{A}$, it needs to create an environment $\mathbf{Exp}_{\mathsf{Hyb},\,\mathcal{A}}^{\mathsf{IND\text{-}KDM\text{-}CCA}}$. The messages m_0 and m_1 and also C and K are 'created' just as they are in normal LR_b, whereas h_K is virtually set to whatever value is used in the game $\mathcal{D}$ itself is playing by $\mathcal{D}$'s calls to New, LR and Dec (from $\mathbf{Exp}_{\mathsf{DEM},\,\mathcal{D}}^{\mathsf{IND\text{-}PKDM\text{-}CCA}}$). The number of keypairs $\mathcal{D}$ can ask for is upper-bounded by the number of New queries $\mathcal{A}$ makes. Note that $\mathcal{D}$ need not know h_K for this simulation.

3.3 Conclusions and Open Problems

As stated, our result is very general as it incorporates active attacks, and allows KDM functions that call the random oracle. The proof method incorporates the use of a PRF and the non-standard IND-PKDM-CCA notion of security on the DEM (notably, a notion equivalent to IND-CCA). In the scenario where the adversary's KDM functions *cannot* call the random oracle, direct reductions to IND-CCA security of the DEM are possible, however there is an additional bad event caused when there exists (C, i) and (C', i') such that $\mathsf{KEM.decap}_{\mathrm{sk}_i}(C) = \mathsf{KEM.decap}_{\mathrm{sk}_{i'}}(C') = K$ and the adversary manages to decapsulate to a previously seen protokey, without triggering the forbidden list FL. It is consequently possible to bound both of the bad events together.

Once we move to the scenario where functions can call the random oracle however, an issue arises. First of all the adversary makes an arbitrary LR query, receiving an encryption under some protokey K_1 encapsulated in C_1. It then makes another LR query, this time submitting a function that depends on the K_1 used in its previous query, receiving (C_2, ψ_2). Then a decryption query of the form $m' \leftarrow \mathsf{Dec}(C_1, \psi_2)$ does not fall on the forbidden list and could yield information about m' to the attacker. From this perspective it is a challenge to negotiate the simulation of keys in the DEM hop without using a PRF, and to realise direct reductions to a standard notion such as IND-CCA.

Acknowledgments. We would like to thank Pooya Farshim for his contribution to initial discussions, and Bogdan Warinschi for ideas and input throughout. We would also like to thank the anonymous conference reviewers for their comments and suggestions.

References

[1] Abadi, M., Rogaway, P.: Reconciling two views of Cryptography (the Computational Soundness of Formal Encryption). Journal of Cryptology 15(2), 103–127 (2002)

[2] Abe, M., Gennaro, R., Kurosawa, K., Shoup, V.: Tag-KEM/DEM: A new Framework for Hybrid Encryption and a new Analysis of Kurosawa-Desmedt KEM. In: Cramer, R. (ed.) EUROCRYPT 2005. LNCS, vol. 3494, pp. 128–146. Springer, Heidelberg (2005)

[3] Acar, T., Belenkiy, M., Bellare, M., Cash, D.: Cryptographic Agility and its Relation to Circular Encryption. In: Gilbert [26], pp. 403–422

[4] Adão, P., Bana, G., Herzog, J., Scedrov, A.: Soundness of Formal Encryption in the Presence of Key-Cycles. In: di Vimercati, S.d.C., Syverson, P.F., Gollmann, D. (eds.) ESORICS 2005. LNCS, vol. 3679, pp. 374–396. Springer, Heidelberg (2005)

[5] Applebaum, B.: Key-Dependent Message Security: Generic Amplification and Completeness. In: Paterson [33], pp. 527–546

[6] Applebaum, B., Cash, D., Peikert, C., Sahai, A.: Fast Cryptographic Primitives and Circular-Secure Encryption based on Hard Learning Problems. In: Halevi, S. (ed.) CRYPTO 2009. LNCS, vol. 5677, pp. 595–618. Springer, Heidelberg (2009)

[7] Backes, M., Dürmuth, M., Unruh, D.: OAEP is secure under Key-Dependent Messages. In: Pieprzyk, J. (ed.) ASIACRYPT 2008. LNCS, vol. 5350, pp. 506–523. Springer, Heidelberg (2008)

[8] Backes, M., Pfitzmann, B., Scedrov, A.: Key-Dependent Message Security under active attacks - BRSIM/UC-Soundness of Symbolic Encryption with Key Cycles. In: CSF 2007, pp. 112–124. IEEE Computer Society (2007)

[9] Barak, B., Haitner, I., Hofheinz, D., Ishai, Y.: Bounded Key-Dependent Message Security. In: Gilbert [26], pp. 423–444

[10] Bellare, M., Cash, D., Keelveedhi, S.: Ciphers that securely encipher their own keys. In: Chen, Y., Danezis, G., Shmatikov, V. (eds.) ACM CCS 2011, pp. 423–432. ACM (2011)

[11] Bellare, M., Desai, A., Pointcheval, D., Rogaway, P.: Relations among notions of security for Public-Key Encryption schemes. In: Krawczyk, H. (ed.) CRYPTO 1998. LNCS, vol. 1462, pp. 26–45. Springer, Heidelberg (1998)

[12] Bellare, M., Keelveedhi, S.: Authenticated and Misuse-Resistant Encryption of Key-Dependent Data. In: Rogaway [34], pp. 610–629

[13] Bellare, M., Rogaway, P.: Random oracles are practical: A paradigm for designing efficient protocols. In: Denning, D.E., Pyle, R., Ganesan, R., Sandhu, R.S., Ashby, V. (eds.) ACM CCS 1993, pp. 62–73. ACM (1993)

[14] Bellare, M., Rogaway, P.: The security of triple encryption and a framework for code-based game-playing proofs. In: Vaudenay, S. (ed.) EUROCRYPT 2006. LNCS, vol. 4004, pp. 409–426. Springer, Heidelberg (2006)

[15] Black, J., Rogaway, P., Shrimpton, T.: Encryption-scheme security in the presence of Key-Dependent Messages. In: Nyberg, K., Heys, H.M. (eds.) SAC 2002. LNCS, vol. 2595, pp. 62–75. Springer, Heidelberg (2003)

[16] Boneh, D., Halevi, S., Hamburg, M., Ostrovsky, R.: Circular-Secure Encryption from Decision Diffie-Hellman. In: Wagner, D. (ed.) CRYPTO 2008. LNCS, vol. 5157, pp. 108–125. Springer, Heidelberg (2008)

[17] Brakerski, Z., Goldwasser, S.: Circular and Leakage Resilient Public-Key Encryption under Subgroup Indistinguishability - (or: Quadratic Residuosity strikes back). In: Rabin, T. (ed.) CRYPTO 2010. LNCS, vol. 6223, pp. 1–20. Springer, Heidelberg (2010)

[18] Brakerski, Z., Vaikuntanathan, V.: Fully Homomorphic Encryption from Ring-LWE and security for Key Dependent Messages. In: Rogaway [34], pp. 505–524

[19] Camenisch, J., Chandran, N., Shoup, V.: A Public Key Encryption scheme secure against Key Dependent chosen plaintext and adaptive chosen ciphertext attacks. In: Joux, A. (ed.) EUROCRYPT 2009. LNCS, vol. 5479, pp. 351–368. Springer, Heidelberg (2009)

[20] Camenisch, J., Lysyanskaya, A.: An efficient system for non-transferable anonymous credentials with optional anonymity revocation. In: Pfitzmann, B. (ed.) EUROCRYPT 2001. LNCS, vol. 2045, pp. 93–118. Springer, Heidelberg (2001)

[21] Cash, D., Green, M., Hohenberger, S.: New definitions and separations for Circular Security. In: Fischlin, M., Buchmann, J., Manulis, M. (eds.) PKC 2012. LNCS, vol. 7293, pp. 540–557. Springer, Heidelberg (2012)

[22] Cramer, R., Shoup, V.: Design and analysis of practical Public-Key Encryption schemes secure against adaptive chosen ciphertext attack. IACR Cryptology ePrint Archive 2001, 108 (2001)

[23] Dent, A.W.: A designer's guide to kEMs. In: Paterson, K.G. (ed.) Cryptography and Coding 2003. LNCS, vol. 2898, pp. 133–151. Springer, Heidelberg (2003)

[24] Gennaro, R., Shoup, V.: A note on an encryption scheme of Kurosawa and Desmedt. IACR Cryptology ePrint Archive 2004, 194 (2004)

[25] Gentry, C.: Fully Homomorphic Encryption using ideal lattices. In: Mitzenmacher, M. (ed.) STOC 2009, pp. 169–178. ACM (2009)

[26] Gilbert, H. (ed.): EUROCRYPT 2010. LNCS, vol. 6110. Springer, Heidelberg (2010)

[27] Haitner, I., Holenstein, T.: On the (im)possibility of Key Dependent Encryption. In: Reingold, O. (ed.) TCC 2009. LNCS, vol. 5444, pp. 202–219. Springer, Heidelberg (2009)

[28] Halevi, S., Krawczyk, H.: Security under Key-Dependent Inputs. In: Ning, P., di Vimercati, S.D.C., Syverson, P.F. (eds.) ACM CCS 2007, pp. 466–475. ACM (2007)

[29] Hofheinz, D., Kiltz, E.: Secure hybrid encryption from weakened key encapsulation. In: Menezes, A. (ed.) CRYPTO 2007. LNCS, vol. 4622, pp. 553–571. Springer, Heidelberg (2007)

[30] Kurosawa, K., Desmedt, Y.: A new Paradigm of Hybrid Encryption scheme. In: Franklin, M. (ed.) CRYPTO 2004. LNCS, vol. 3152, pp. 426–442. Springer, Heidelberg (2004)

[31] Laud, P., Corin, R.: Sound computational interpretation of formal encryption with composed keys. In: Lim, J.-I., Lee, D.-H. (eds.) ICISC 2003. LNCS, vol. 2971, pp. 55–66. Springer, Heidelberg (2004)

[32] Malkin, T., Teranishi, I., Yung, M.: Efficient circuit-size independent Public Key Encryption with KDM Security. In: Paterson, [33], pp. 507–526

[33] Paterson, K.G. (ed.): EUROCRYPT 2011. LNCS, vol. 6632. Springer, Heidelberg (2011)

[34] Rogaway, P. (ed.): CRYPTO 2011. LNCS, vol. 6841. Springer, Heidelberg (2011)

[35] Shoup, V.: Sequences of games: a tool for taming complexity in security proofs. IACR Cryptology ePrint Archive 2004, 332 (2004)

Key Wrapping with a Fixed Permutation

Dmitry Khovratovich

University of Luxembourg

Abstract. We present an efficient key wrapping scheme that uses a single public permutation as the basic element. As the scheme does not rely on block ciphers, it can be used on a resource-constrained device where such a permutation comes from an implemented hash function, regular (SHA-3/Keccak) or lightweight one (Quark, Photon). The scheme is capable of wrapping keys up to 1400 bits long and processing arbitrarily long headers. Our scheme easily delivers the security level of 128 bits or higher with the master key of the same length.

We use the security notion from the concept of Deterministic Authenticated Encryption (DAE) introduced by Rogaway and Shrimpton. Though the permutation is inevitably modeled as a random permutation, the resulting proof of security is short and easy to verify and hence provide a reasonable alternative to authentication modes based on block ciphers.

Keywords: Key wrapping, DAE, sponge, Keccak.

1 Introduction

Key wrapping schemes address the problem of key management in distributed systems. Security architects often limit the lifespan of keys in order to reduce the risk of the key compromise and lessen the amount of data encrypted on a single key. Hence keys are regularly updated, and an update protocol using an insecure channel must be carefully designed. Ideally, it should be simple and efficient. Practical constraints also limit, if not forbid the use of additional mechanisms such as nonce or random number generation.

Since the early years of digital cryptography, new keys are encrypted on (*wrapped with*) a long-term (*master*) key shared between a sender and a receiver. Confidentiality of the new key must be ensured and its integrity must be protected. A key might be bounded to a header, which is not encrypted (e.g., for routing purposes) but authenticated. Therefore, the key wrapping scheme is a special case of authenticated encryption with associated data (AEAD) schemes [23], where nonces and random numbers are avoided. Such a scheme may serve not only for key update, but also for a robust and misuse-resistant general purpose encryption [25].

Traditional AEAD schemes provide confidentiality (e.g., ciphertexts are indistinguishable from random strings) and data authenticity (ciphertexts constructed by an adversary must decrypt to invalid). They employ randomness or

J. Benaloh (Ed.): CT-RSA 2014, LNCS 8366, pp. 481–499, 2014.

nonces and can be almost as efficient as regular encryption modes [20]. It has been clear that a deterministic scheme would require at least two passes over data to make each output bit depend on each input bit.

When the NIST addressed the key wrapping schemes in the series of recommendations (since at least 2001), its designs, later called AES-KW and AKW [21], were highly inefficient. Moreover, those schemes carried no formal security claims or proofs. This was natural, as the first formal treatment of this problem appeared only in 2006 [25] as the concept of the Deterministic Authenticated Encryption (DAE). Still, only a few key wrapping schemes have been proposed so far in DAE or similar frameworks: SIV [25], HBS [19], BTM [18], Hash-then-Encrypt [15, 22].

None of these proposals are universal solutions. AES-KW requires 12-fold as many operations as to encrypt the same amount of data, SIV needs two keys and is not parallelizable, and the Hash-then-Encrypt template can not be scaled to a general-purpose encryption mode. Third-party analysis of these constructions is often difficult because of lengthy and complicated proofs of security. The recently found flaw in the security proof of GCM [17] emphasizes the need for clarity and extensive third-party verification of provably secure schemes.

All these designs employ a block cipher, and the natural choice of AES limits their security level to 64 bits[1]. To obtain the 128-bit security or higher, one would need a block cipher with a 256-bit block or larger. Except for Threefish, a component of the Skein hash function [14], no other 256-bit blockcipher enjoyed significant attention from cryptanalysts.

However, block ciphers are not the only source of good permutations. Quite recently, the hash function Keccak [5], which employs a 1600-bit permutation, has been selected as the new standard SHA-3. We expect that it will be widely deployed in the near future, and hence its building block will be readily accessible to other cryptographic applications. On resource-constrained devices, where the space is limited, it would be very tempting to use a single cryptographic primitive, such as the Keccak permutation, for many purposes. Whenever Keccak or AES are considered too expensive for a device, some lightweight hash functions like Spongent [9] and Quark [2] are also based on a single permutation and may offer it for other schemes.

This idea also fits the recent paradigm of the *permutation-based cryptography* [11] as opposed to the blockcipher-based cryptography. From the practical point of view, it would allow to have a single permutation for all purposes, whereas it would simplify the analysis as a target for a cryptanalyst would be much simpler. Permutation-based modes of operation draw attention after the selection of Keccak, as indicated by two recent proposals for the authenticated encryption: APE(X) [8] and PPAE [7].

If the Keccak permutation is selected, the available 1600 bits are often sufficient to carry the master key, the new key, and the associated data. Hence for the

---

[1] Here the key size of AES, which can be 128, 192, or 256, does not play a significant role: many modes of operation can not be proven secure as long as inputs to the blockcipher start colliding.

design of a key wrapping scheme we could restrict the use of a permutation to a single call and obtain a scheme with a reasonably short proof of security. The security model, however, would be different from the one used in blockcipher-based schemes. Since we use a single permutation, the most natural is to model it as randomly drawn and hence prove the security in the random-oracle model. An alternative approach, the Even-Mansour construction, would provide the security proof in the standard model but with weaker bounds (see the further text). Though the random-permutation model is clearly more demanding to the primitive we use, we argue that a shorter and simpler security proof and increased security level would compensate the weakening of the model.

Our proposal. We present a new key wrapping scheme with a variable security level and a proof of security that is easy to verify. We call it KWF, as it is based not on a block cipher but on a fixed permutation such as those used in sponge hash functions (SHA-3/Keccak, Quark).

A wide permutation (up to 1600 bits in Keccak) easily delivers the security level of 128 bits or higher when using the key of the same length. Associated data (header) is processed with an unkeyed cryptographic hash function, possibly the same from which the permutation comes. Apart from the header processing, the scheme has no overhead over a single permutation call. We limit the message length to at max 1411 bits, but this must be sufficient for wrapping all symmetric keys and many asymmetric private keys (e.g., elliptic curve keys).

Our scheme is about as efficient as the hash function from which the permutation comes. If the associated data H is processed with the same hash function, wrapping H and M takes roughly the same time as hashing $H\|M$. We recommend using a narrow-block permutation for shorter inputs. We also note that the key length can be freely chosen.

Our scheme, as well as other DAE-conformant designs, is also fine for general-purpose encryption and authenticated encryption of short inputs (though we avoid explicitly offering the scheme for general use because of length constraints). To emphasize this opportunity, we use the notion *message* for keys and other inputs that are encrypted by our scheme.

Security proof and random oracles. We accompany our design with a proof of security in the DAE framework, where we additionally allow the an adversary to query the randomly drawn permutation. Here we follow the strategy of proving the indistinguishability of the generalized Even-Mansour scheme from the random permutation [10]. Our assumption establishes the security of our scheme as long as the permutation we eventually fix has no untrivial properties (which so far holds for Keccak and other sponge functions). We tried to make our proof as simple as possible to encourage its third-party verification.

We note that there are two possible approaches to constructing and proving the security of symmetric schemes:

- Use a blockcipher as a primitive and prove the security assuming that it is a secure PRP;

– Use a concrete hash function or a public permutation as a primitive and prove the security assuming it is randomly drawn.

It is customary to consider the former approach more reliable as it is less demanding to the primitive and hence withstands a larger set of attacks against the primitive. Hence the scheme secure in the standard model is considered better than the one assuming a random oracle. However, the latter approach is arguably better from designer's point of view. One may go further and argue that, it should be easier to construct a single "good" permutation and use it, e.g., for a hash function, than to construct a family of them for a blockcipher, where a key selects a particular permutation, and all these permutations should be significantly different.

A part of our research is to investigate whether a single permutation gives an elegant scheme with a short security proof in the area of authenticated encryption. If we succeed, this would benefit the permutation-based cryptography and eventually the cryptographic community by giving various schemes with verifiable proofs.

Related work. We already mentioned other designs that aim for key wrapping and deterministic authenticated encryption. NIST has published its first key wrapping scheme around 2001 (see description in [21]). AES-KW is a sort of generalized Feistel scheme, where the key to and the header are divided into 64-bit blocks, and the round function is the AES applied to two leftmost blocks. No analysis of this scheme has been published, though it is believed [25] that the security level is somewhere between 64 and 128 bits. There are several modifications to this scheme, known as KW and KWP, and a special version that uses Triple-DES.

Rogaway and Shrimpton proposed the scheme SIV, which computes MAC of the message and header with a PRF under key K_1 and uses it as the IV in an IV-based encryption scheme with key K_2 [25]. The concrete proposal invokes CMAC and CTR. The scheme SIV is provably secure in the strongest model — DAE — where the adversary can choose plaintexts and ciphertexts but is unable to distinguish the pair of encryption and decryption oracles from the pair of "random-bits" and "always invalid" oracles. Scheme HBS [19] and its refinement BTM [18] by Iwata and Yasuda use polynomial hash functions for MAC and a modified CTR mode. Similarly to CMAC, secondary keys are derived out of a single key by encrypting constants. HBS and BTM are provably secure in the DAE setting.

Gennaro and Halevi proposed the general template of Hash-then-Encrypt [15], which may be viewed as weakening of SIV. Here a PRF is replaced with a hash function, which might not even be collision resistant. for instance, they showed that a composition of universal hashing and CTR mode is secure. However, the performance is gained at the cost of weakening the model. Confidentiality is achieved in the assumption of random plaintexts (RPA), where the adversary obtains two plaintexts (out of his control) and one of corresponding ciphertexts, and he has to guess which one. This "left-or-right" setting is provably weaker than DAE, but is still sufficient for key wrapping schemes where inputs have enough entropy. Osaki and Iwata [22] continued work in this direction and introduced a special class of universal hash functions which are fine to use with ECB or CBC.

The Keccak team presented an authenticated encryption mode SpongeWrap, which under certain circumstances and proper formatting of plaintext and headers may serve for the key wrapping [4]. However, the paper [4] is quite vague on this topic, and it was later confirmed [1] that the key wrapping was not among the main applications of SpongeWrap. Quite recently, a misuse-resistant authenticated encryption scheme APE(X) has been presented [8], but the paper was not available to the author at the time of submission.

On Even-Mansour ciphers. Our construction may resemble a variant of the Even-Mansour cipher [13], where a single permutation $\mathcal{F}$ is turned to a block-cipher $\mathcal{E}_K(X) = K \oplus \mathcal{F}(\mathcal{X} \oplus \mathcal{K})$. The resulting cipher is provably secure up to $2^{n/2}$ queries to both blockcipher and permutation [12] when the key is as wide as the permutation. It may be tempting to construct a key wrapping scheme by taking a wide permutation and a short key, and encrypt a plaintext with some redundancy. This would reduce the security of the whole scheme to the PRP security of the Even-Mansour cipher and hence provide a desirable proof in the standard model.

However, this approach is dangerous, as reducing the key length also reduces the overall security. Indeed, when the key length $k < n$, one may ask to encrypt $2^{k/2}$ plaintexts which are constant in the bytes not touched by the key. In the offline stage, an adversary also applies the permutation to these inputs and searches for a collision between two groups of outputs in the last $n - k$ bits. This allows to recover the key with complexity $2^{k/2}$ whereas our construction does not have a security loss up to 2^k operations. Therefore, an Even-Mansour cipher can not be used as is, and a more sophisticated PRP candidate would be needed to get a scheme provably secure in the standard model.

Outline of the paper. We recall the syntax of key wrapping schemes and relevant security definitions in Section 2. Then we describe our proposal KWF in Section 3 and also recommend a set of permutations for various security levels. We immediately proceed with the security proof of KWF in Section 4. We survey the existing key wrapping schemes in the Conclusion.

2   Syntax and Security of Key Wrapping Schemes

2.1   Syntax

A *key wrapping scheme* Π is a symmetric authenticated encryption scheme and is defined as a pair of functions $\mathcal{E}$ and $\mathcal{D}$, which provide encryption and decryption, respectively. The secret key K, shared between parties, belongs to the key space $\mathcal{K}$. The encryption function takes the key to be wrapped from the message space $\mathcal{M}$ and encrypts it to a ciphertext $C \in \mathcal{C}$. If the scheme is able to authenticate some data without encrypting it, it is called the associated data (AD). The associated data space is denoted by $\mathcal{H}$, hence

$$\mathcal{E} : \mathcal{K} \times \mathcal{H} \times \mathcal{M} \to \mathcal{C}.$$

The decryption function takes a key, a ciphertext, and possibly associated data as input and returns either a plaintext (wrapped key) from the message space or the invalid message $\perp$:

$$\mathcal{D} : \mathcal{K} \times \mathcal{H} \times \mathcal{C} \to \mathcal{M} \cup \{\perp\}.$$

The key wrapping scheme differs from the probabilistic (regular) authenticated encryption schemes as it does not use any random numbers or nonces.

Clearly, the produced ciphertext decrypts back to the plaintext if the same associated data is used:

$$\mathcal{D}(K, H, (\mathcal{E}(K, H, M))) = M.$$

The purpose of a key wrapping scheme, as well as of a regular authenticated encryption scheme, is to achieve:

- Privacy by making all the ciphertexts "look randomly".
- Data authenticity by making all the ciphertexts not produced by the key owner "decrypt to invalid".

Hence the receiver may verify that the unwrapped key is authentic as otherwise the ciphertext would decrypt to invalid. Let us introduce these notions formally.

2.2 Security

Rogaway and Shrimpton [25] were the first who introduced a single notion that amalgamates both privacy and authenticity properties of a key wrapping scheme. They called it Deterministic Authenticated Encryption (DAE). Gennaro and Halevi proposed a weaker notion of security (RPA+INT), where the plaintexts are randomly chosen and are out of adversary's control. We prove the security of KWF in a strengthened version of DAE, so our scheme is secure for general-purpose encryption where the adversary may control the plaintexts.

The security of a DAE scheme is defined as the inability to distinguish between the two worlds, where an adversary has access to two oracles [25]. One world consists of the encryption oracle $\mathcal{E}(\cdot, \cdot)$ and decryption oracle $\mathcal{D}(\cdot, \cdot)$, where the secret key is randomly chosen. The second world consists of the "random-bits" oracle $\$(\cdot, \cdot)$ and the "always-invalid" oracle $\perp (\cdot, \cdot)$ (Figure 1).

This setting serves well for encryption schemes based on secure PRPs and authentication schemes based on secure PRFs. We only have to make a couple of refinements. As we work with a single permutation, we have to additionally allow the adversary to access it. Moreover, we have to model it as randomly drawn [3,6], which in turn requires us to assume that the permutation has no nontrivial properties.

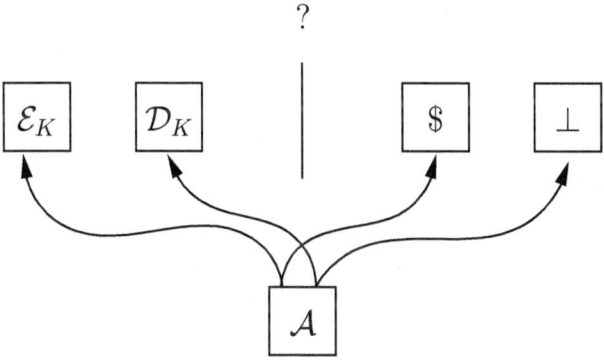

Fig. 1. Indistinguishability setting for DAE

We also slightly refine the definition of the "random-bit" oracle $\$(\cdot,\cdot)$ with the following motivation. Since the encryption is invertible, an ideal encryption scheme with a fixed key and associated data should be a permutation. Hence it is natural to model the oracle $\$(\cdot,\cdot)$ as an ideal cipher — a set of randomly chosen permutations indexed by a key. Here the associated data serves as a key. This model allows for an increased security level and a tighter bound, since a traditional proof of security for an encryption mode invokes a PRF and then applies the PRF-to-PRP switching lemma. This lemma limits the security level with the birthday bound, which we would like to avoid.

Definition 1. *Let* $\Pi = (\mathcal{K}, \mathcal{E}[\mathcal{F}], \mathcal{D}[\mathcal{F}])$ *be a DAE scheme based on permutation* $\mathcal{F}$. *Let the adversary A have the access to* $\mathcal{F}$. *The* DAE *advantage of A in breaking* Π *is computed as follows:*

$$\mathbf{Adv}_{\Pi}^{\mathrm{dae}}(A) = \Pr\left[K \xleftarrow{\$} \mathcal{K}, \mathcal{F}(\cdot) \xleftarrow{\$} \mathrm{Perm}(n) : A^{\mathcal{E}_K[\mathcal{F}](\cdot,\cdot), \mathcal{D}_K[\mathcal{F}](\cdot,\cdot)} \Rightarrow 1\right] -$$
$$- \Pr\left[\mathcal{F}(\cdot) \xleftarrow{\$} \mathrm{Perm}(n) : A^{\$(\cdot,\cdot), \perp(\cdot,\cdot)} \Rightarrow 1\right].$$

On query (H, X) the oracle $\$(\cdot,\cdot)$ returns a random string of length n so that it is a permutation (bijective function) for every H. The set of all permutations over $\{0,1\}^n$ is denoted by $\mathrm{Perm}(n)$. The $\perp(\cdot,\cdot)$ oracle always returns $\perp$ (invalid). We exclude trivial wins: the adversary shall not ask (H, Y) of its right oracle if some previous left oracle query of (H, X) returned Y and vice versa. Without loss of generality, the adversary does not repeat a query and does not ask left queries outside of $\mathcal{H} \times \mathcal{M}$. Here and in the further text we implicitly assume that $\mathcal{F}^{-1}$ is available together with $\mathcal{F}$.

The maximum advantage as a function of the number of allowed queries is the natural quantitative measure of the security of a key wrapping schemes:

$$\mathbf{Adv}_{\Pi}^{\mathrm{dae}}(q) \stackrel{\mathrm{def}}{=} \max_A \mathbf{Adv}_{\Pi}^{\mathrm{dae}}(A),$$

where we take maximum over all adversaries asking at maximum q queries to all oracles.

3   Our Proposal: KWF

3.1   Notation

For two bit strings X and Y of the same length, $X \oplus Y$ is their xor. For an integer $n \geq 1$, $\{0,1\}^n$ is the set of all bit strings of n bits, and $\{0,1\}^{m..n}$ is the set of strings of m to n bits long. Also $X_{m..n}$ denotes the substring of X containing bits with indices from m to n, where the first index is 1. We write $X \xleftarrow{\$} \mathcal{X}$ for sampling an element from the set $\mathcal{X}$ uniformly at random.

3.2   Description of KWF

Our scheme provides an authenticated encryption of short messages and is based on a fixed n-bit permutation $\mathcal{F}$. Of the n-bit input, k bits are devoted to the key K, l bits to the associated data H, and $n - k - l$ to the message M. As the associated data needs only authentication, we map a possibly long string H to an l-bit value with a cryptographic hash function $\mathcal{G}$. $\mathcal{G}$ should be collision-resistant, and it should return some valid output on empty input (if it requires redefinition of $\mathcal{G}$, the new function shall still be collision-resistant).

We define scheme KWF formally as $\Pi = (\mathcal{K}, \mathcal{E}[\mathcal{F}], \mathcal{D}[\mathcal{F}])$, where:

1.
$\mathcal{K} = \{0,1\}^k$ — the key space;
$\mathcal{H} = \{0,1\}^{0..t}$ — the associated data (AD) space;
$\mathcal{M} = \{0,1\}^{1..(n-k-l-1)}$ — the message space;
$\mathcal{C} = \{0,1\}^n$ — the ciphertext space.

2. $\mathcal{G} : \{0,1\}^{0..t} \longrightarrow \{0,1\}^l$ — hash function for the associated data;
    $\text{pad} : \{0,1\}^{1..(n-k-l-1)} \longrightarrow \{0,1\}^{n-k-l}$ — invertible padding function;
    $\mathcal{F} : \{0,1\}^n \longrightarrow \{0,1\}^n$ — fixed permutation.

3. $\mathcal{E}[\mathcal{F}] : \mathcal{K} \times \mathcal{H} \times \mathcal{M} \longrightarrow \mathcal{C}$ — encryption function (Figure 2):

$$\left\{ \mathcal{E}_K[\mathcal{F}](H, M) = \mathcal{F}\left(K \| \mathcal{G}(H) \| pad[M]\right) \oplus \left(K \| 0^{n-k}\right). \right.$$

4. $\mathcal{D}[\mathcal{F}] : \mathcal{K} \times \mathcal{H} \times \{0,1\}^n \longrightarrow \mathcal{M} \cup \{\bot\}$ — decryption function. The output $\mathcal{D}_K[\mathcal{F}](H, C)$ is computed as follows:
    (a) $X \leftarrow \mathcal{F}^{-1}(C \oplus (K \| 0^{n-k}))$.
    (b) If $X_{1..k} \neq K$, return $\bot$.
    (c) If $X_{k+1..k+l} \neq \mathcal{G}(H)$ return $\bot$.
    (d) Return $pad^{-1}(X_{k+l+1..n})$.

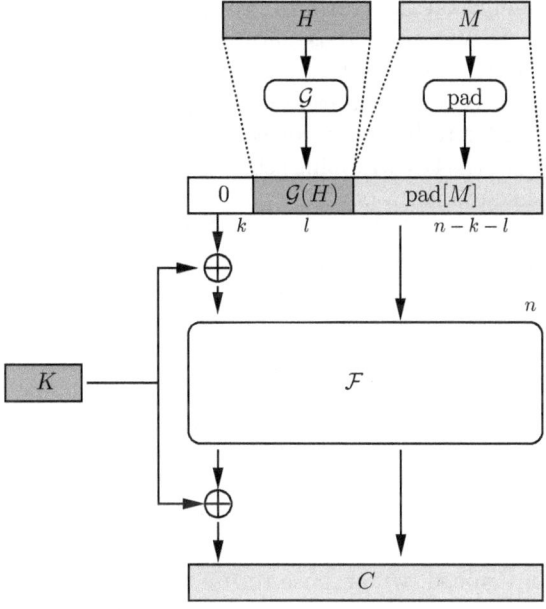

Fig. 2. Our proposal: KWF

3.3 Recommended Parameters

In Section 4 we prove that the adversary asking at most q encryption and decryption queries has the maximum advantage of

$$2\mathbf{Adv}_{\mathcal{G}}^{\mathrm{coll}}(q) + \frac{2.5q}{2^k} + \frac{8.5q^2}{2^{n-k}},$$

where $\mathbf{Adv}_{\mathcal{G}}^{\mathrm{coll}}(q)$ is the maximum advantage of the adversary trying to violate the collision resistance of $\mathcal{G}$ after making q queries to $\mathcal{G}$ (a more rigorous reduction to collision resistance is presented in Section B. We assume that for a collision-resistant hash function:

$$\mathbf{Adv}_{\mathcal{G}}^{\mathrm{coll}}(q) \leq \frac{q^2}{2^l}.$$

Then to get the security level of S bits, the following constraints are sufficient:

$$k \geq S, \quad l \geq 2S, \quad n \geq 2S + k.$$

Therefore, for 80-bit master keys and 80-bit (padded) plaintexts we need $n \geq 320$, and for 128-bit keys and plaintexts — $n \geq 512$.

There are several families of sponge hash functions that provide suitable permutations for KWF. The Keccak family [5] uses permutations of width $n = 25 \cdot 2^l$, $l = 0..6$, with $n = 1600$ chosen for SHA-3. Keccak permutations are reasonably efficient in software and hardware, and are natural choice whenever

SHA-3 is implemented on the platform. We propose to use $n = 400, 800, 1600$ and denote them as Keccak-n. It is natural to use the Keccak hash function also for the associated data. By Keccak/t we denote the sponge hash function using the 1600-bit Keccak permutation with capacity $2t$ and rate $1600 - 2t$. The function Keccak/256 is to be standardized as SHA-3-256.

As far as we know, the key wrapping schemes are also deployed on smart cards. Hence we would like to offer a portfolio of permutations for KWF that are suitable for resource-constrained platforms. Quark [2], Photon [16], and Spongent [9] are recently proposed families of lightweight hash functions based on the sponge construction. They use permutations from 88 to 768 bits wide and were not shown any internal weaknesses. Depending on the message length and the security level, permutations from 256 to 768 bits can be recommended for KWF. Some more details are given in Appendix A and the summary in Table 2.

Whenever SHA-2 is implemented on the platform, it also can be used as the hash function for the associated data. The most suitable for KWF are SHA-224 and SHA-256.

Some permutations are significantly faster than their inverses, e.g., the Keccak permutations. Assuming that the receiver in the key wrapping scheme is more resource-constrained, we propose to use the inverse of such permutation for encryption, and hence the forward call for the decryption.

4   Security of KWF

Our main result states that if an adversary can not violate the collision resistance of G and makes fewer than $\min(2^{(n-k)/2}, 2^k)$ queries, she is unlikely to violate the security of KWF as a DAE scheme. The term $\mathbf{Adv}_G^{\text{coll}}(q)$ in our bound quantifies the ability of the adversary making at most q queries to G to find a colliding pair. A more rigorous formulation of our results can be found in Appendix.

Theorem 1. *The DAE advantage of an adversary attacking KWF and asking the total of at most q queries to all oracles and $\mathcal{F}$ is bounded as follows:*

$$\mathbf{Adv}_\Pi^{\text{dae}}(q) \leq 2\mathbf{Adv}_G^{\text{coll}}(q) + \frac{2.5q}{2^k} + \frac{8.5q^2}{2^{n-k}}.$$

Proof. We split this expression in two following the approach in [25]:

$$\Pr\left[K \overset{\$}{\leftarrow} \mathcal{K}, \mathcal{F}(\cdot) \overset{\$}{\leftarrow} \text{Perm}(n) : A^{\mathcal{E}_K[\mathcal{F}], \mathcal{D}_K[\mathcal{F}]} \Rightarrow 1\right] -$$

$$- \Pr\left[\mathcal{F}(\cdot) \overset{\$}{\leftarrow} \text{Perm}(n) : A^{\$, \perp} \Rightarrow 1\right] =$$

$$= \underbrace{\Pr\left[A^{\mathcal{E}_K[\mathcal{F}], \mathcal{D}_K[\mathcal{F}]} \Rightarrow 1\right] - \Pr\left[A^{\mathcal{E}_K[\mathcal{F}], \perp} \Rightarrow 1\right]}_{p_1} +$$

$$+ \underbrace{\Pr\left[A^{\mathcal{E}_K[\mathcal{F}], \perp} \Rightarrow 1\right] - \Pr\left[A^{\$, \perp} \Rightarrow 1\right]}_{p_2}.$$

4.1   Bounding p_1 (Authenticity Proof)

Consider

$$p_1 = \Pr\left[A^{\mathcal{E}_K[\mathcal{F}], \mathcal{D}_K[\mathcal{F}]} \Rightarrow 1\right] - \Pr\left[A^{\mathcal{E}_K[\mathcal{F}], \perp} \Rightarrow 1\right],$$

where K and $\mathcal{F}$ are randomly chosen.

We assume without loss of generality that A halts and outputs 1 whenever the right oracle returns $M \neq \perp$. Prior to this event, both oracle pairs behave identically as $(\mathcal{E}_K[\mathcal{F}], \perp)$. Therefore, p_1 is bounded by the probability that A asks a right-oracle query (H, Y) so that $\mathcal{D}_K(H, Y) \neq \perp$.

Let us denote the set of ciphertexts obtained prior to this query by $\overline{C}$, the set of $\mathcal{F}$ responses and $\mathcal{F}^{-1}$ queries by $\mathcal{F}_o$, and of $\mathcal{F}$ queries and $\mathcal{F}^{-1}$ responses by $\mathcal{F}_i$.

By definition, the adversary is unable to use a pair (H, Y) where Y has been a response $Y = \mathcal{E}_K(H, X)$ for some X. Hence either $Y \notin \overline{C}$, or $Y = \mathcal{E}_K(H', X), H' \neq H$. In the latter case the ciphertext decrypts to $\mathcal{G}(H')\|X$, so the decryption returns $\perp$ unless H and H' form a collision pair for $\mathcal{G}$. Here the success rate of the collision search for $\mathcal{G}$ is bounded by $\mathbf{Adv}_{\mathcal{G}}^{\mathrm{coll}}(q)$.

If $Y \notin \overline{C}$, then

$$\Pr\left[\mathcal{D}_K(H, Y) \neq \perp\right] \leq \Pr\left[\mathcal{D}_K(H, Y) \neq \perp \mid (Y \oplus K) \notin \mathcal{F}_o\right] +$$
$$+ \Pr\left[\mathcal{D}_K(H, Y) \neq \perp \mid (Y \oplus K) \in \mathcal{F}_o\right].$$

Let us now estimate both addends of the right side.

- $(Y \oplus K) \notin \mathcal{F}_o$ (here and further we shortly write $Y \oplus K$ instead of $Y \oplus (K\|0^{n-k})$). Then the permutation $\mathcal{F}^{-1}$ is asked with a fresh query, so its output is uniformly distributed along previously unallocated values. The decryption returns invalid if

$$F^{-1}(Y \oplus K)_{1..k+l} \neq K\|\mathcal{G}(H).$$

Hence at maximum 2^{n-k-l} values pass this condition. As at minimum $2^n - q$ values remain unassigned, we obtain

$$\Pr\left[\mathcal{D}_K(H, Y) \neq \perp \mid (Y \oplus K) \notin \mathcal{F}_o\right] \leq \frac{2^{n-k-l}}{2^n - q}. \tag{1}$$

- $(Y \oplus K) \in \mathcal{F}_o$. Hence the decryption oracle ask the permutation with a query that is not fresh. Then the decryption returns $\perp$ if

$$\mathcal{F}^{-1}(Y \oplus K) \neq K\|Z$$

for any Z. We say that the *input clash* (IC) occurs, if $(K\|Z) \in \mathcal{F}_i$ for some Z. Hence without the input clash the decryption error is guaranteed:

$$\Pr\left[\mathcal{D}_K(H, Y) \neq \perp \mid (Y \oplus K) \in \mathcal{F}_o, \text{ no IC occurred}\right] = 0.$$

Finally,

$$\Pr\left[\mathcal{D}_K(H,Y) \neq \perp \mid \text{no IC occurred}\right] \leq \frac{2^{n-k-l}}{2^n - q}.$$

and

$$p_1 = \mathbf{Adv}_{\mathcal{G}}^{\text{coll}}(q) + \left[1 - \left(1 - \frac{2^{n-k-l}}{2^n - q}\right)^q\right] + \Pr(IC; q) \leq$$

$$\leq \mathbf{Adv}_{\mathcal{G}}^{\text{coll}}(q) + \frac{2q}{2^{k+l}} + \Pr(IC; q).$$

It remains to bound the probability $\Pr(IC; q)$ of getting the input clash after q queries. Here either the adversary tries to guess the key in $\mathcal{F}$ queries or hopes to obtain it as a prefix in $\mathcal{F}^{-1}$ responses. In the worst case, when all the q prefixes are different, the probability of having K among them is bounded by $q/2^k$, so we have the following bound on the input clash:

$$\Pr(IC; q) \leq \frac{q}{2^k}. \tag{2}$$

This gives the final bound on p_1:

$$p_1 \leq \mathbf{Adv}_{\mathcal{G}}^{\text{coll}}(q) + \frac{2q}{2^{k+l}} + \frac{q}{2^k}. \tag{3}$$

4.2   Bounding p_2 (Privacy Proof)

Recall that

$$p_2 = \Pr\left[A^{\mathcal{E}_K[\mathcal{F}], \perp} \Rightarrow 1\right] - \Pr\left[A^{\$, \perp} \Rightarrow 1\right],$$

where K and $\mathcal{F}$ are chosen randomly.

We can drop the oracle $\perp$ simply by considering the adversary B that has access to the left oracle only and runs A. She transfers queries of A directly to the oracles and returns $\perp$ to all queries by A to the right oracle. Hence

$$p_2 \leq \Pr\left[B^{\mathcal{E}_K[\mathcal{F}]} \Rightarrow 1\right] - \Pr\left[B^{\$} \Rightarrow 1\right].$$

In the further text we show that in the absence of two events, so called the output clash and the oracle repetition, oracles $\mathcal{E}_K[\mathcal{F}]$ and \$ produce identically distributed results and hence are indistinguishable. The clashes and some remarks on how they can be exploited are depicted in Figure 3.

Let us go to the details. Consider the query (H, X) to the encryption oracle $\mathcal{E}$ or \$. Denote by $\overline{C}$ the set of encryption oracle responses obtained beforehand. We are also interested in the last $(n - k)$ bits of ciphertext, which are unaffected by the key addition. We denote $C|_{k+1..n}$ by $\widehat{C}$ and use the same notation for $(n - k)$-bit suffixes of $\mathcal{F}_o$ denoted by $\widehat{\mathcal{F}_o}$.

Let us say that the encryption oracle response $C = \mathcal{E}_K(H, X)$ causes the *output clash* if $\widehat{C} \in \widehat{\mathcal{F}_o}$, i.e. the ciphertext collides with one of stored permutation

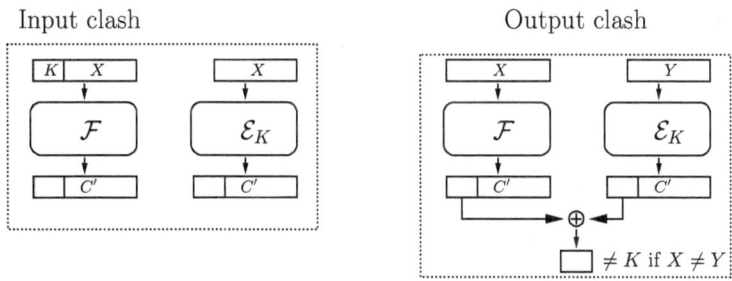

Fig. 3. Detection and exploit of the clashes. In case of input clash we encrypt $(n-k)$-bit suffix X of the permutation query $K||X$ and detect suffix collision in outputs. In case of output clash some ciphertext prefixes are forbidden, which allow to distinguish the encryption from the ideal cipher.

outputs on the last $n-k$ bits. Let $\mathcal{V}$ be the set of the ciphertexts that did not occur in previous responses and do not cause the output clash:

$$\mathcal{V} \overset{\text{def}}{=} \left[\{0,1\}^k \times \left(\{0,1\}^{n-k} \setminus \widehat{\mathcal{F}_o}\right)\right] \setminus \overline{E}.$$

Lemma 1. *If the input clash did not occur and $\mathcal{G}(H)$ does not collide with any previous such value, then all responses $\mathcal{E}_K(H, X) \in \mathcal{V}$ are equiprobable.*

Proof. Since there was no input clash and no collision, the input $K||\mathcal{G}(H)||pad[X]$ has not been queried to the permutation. Hence, it is fresh, and its output is uniformly taken from $\{0,1\}^n \setminus \overline{C}$. It remains to remove from this set the values that cause the output clash, i.e. the set $\{0,1\}^k \times \left(\{0,1\}^{n-k} \setminus \widehat{\mathcal{F}_o}\right)$. This concludes the proof.

The ideal cipher has a different distribution, as its outputs may collide for distinct H. Let us say that the *oracle repetition* (OR) occurs if $\$(H,X) = \$(H', X')$ for some previously queried (H', X'). If we exclude the oracle repetition and output clash events, the distribution will be the same:

$$\$(H,X) \xleftarrow{\ \$\,|\,\text{no OR, no OC, no Coll}\ } \mathcal{V}.$$

Combining with Lemma 1, we conclude that if no input clash, no output clash, and no oracle repetition occurs, the encryption oracles produce identically distributed responses and are indistinguishable. Therefore,

$$p_2 \leq \Pr(IC; q) + \Pr(OC \text{ for } \mathcal{E} \mid \text{no } IC; q) + \Pr(OC \text{ for } \$(\cdot, \cdot); q) +$$
$$+ \Pr(OR) + \mathbf{Adv}_{\mathcal{G}}^{\text{coll}}(q). \quad (4)$$

Output clash bound. Provided no input clash and no collision in $\mathcal{G}$, a query $\mathcal{E}(H, X)$ yields a fresh query to $\mathcal{F}$. Hence the output is uniformly distributed among at least $2^n - q$ previously unassigned values, of which at maximum $q \times 2^k$ cause the output clash. Therefore, assuming $q \leq 2^k$

$$\Pr\left(\mathcal{E}(\widehat{H}, X) \in \widehat{\mathcal{F}_o}\right) \leq \frac{q2^k}{2^n - q} \leq \frac{2q}{2^{n-k}}.$$

Thus we have the following bound:

$$\Pr(\text{OC for } \mathcal{E} \mid \text{no IC}; q) \leq 1 - \left(1 - \frac{2q}{2^{n-k}}\right)^q \leq \frac{4q^2}{2^{n-k}}. \tag{5}$$

The bound for the ideal cipher is the same:

$$\Pr\left(\$(\widehat{H}, X) \in \widehat{\mathcal{F}_o}\right) \leq \frac{q \cdot 2^k}{2^n - q} \implies \Pr(\text{OC for } \$(\cdot, \cdot); q) \leq \frac{4q^2}{2^{n-k}}. \tag{6}$$

Oracle repetition bound. We calculate the probability of the event that during q queries to the PRP-oracle $\$$ there is no collision in outputs. Consider i-th query. The oracle chooses its output uniformly out of at least $(2^n - q)$ possibilities, of which at maximum q cause a collision. Hence

$$\Pr(OR; q) = 1 - \prod_{i=1}^{q}\left(\frac{2^n - 2q}{2^n - q}\right) = 1 - \left(1 - \frac{q}{2^n - q}\right)^q \leq 1 - e^{-\frac{2q^2}{2^n}} \leq \frac{3q^2}{2^n}. \tag{7}$$

We substitute Equations (2), (5), (6), and (7) to Equation (8) and obtain the final bound

$$p_2 \leq \frac{q}{2^k} + \frac{8q^2}{2^{n-k}} + \frac{3q^2}{2^n} + \mathbf{Adv}_{\mathcal{G}}^{\text{coll}}(q). \tag{8}$$

Then we sum Equations (3) and (8) and get:

$$\mathbf{Adv}_{\Pi}^{\text{dae}}(q) \leq \mathbf{Adv}_{\mathcal{G}}^{\text{coll}}(q) + \frac{2q}{2^{k+l}} + \frac{q}{2^k} + \frac{q}{2^k} + \frac{8q^2}{2^{n-k}} + \frac{3q^2}{2^n} + \mathbf{Adv}_{\mathcal{G}}^{\text{coll}}(q) \leq$$

$$\leq 2\mathbf{Adv}_{\mathcal{G}}^{\text{coll}}(q) + \frac{2.5q}{2^k} + \frac{8.5q^2}{2^{n-k}}.$$

This concludes the proof of Theorem 1.

5   Conclusion

We have described a new key wrapping scheme — KWF. It is based on a single fixed permutation, with a lot of candidate permutations available in sponge designs: Keccak/SHA-3, Quark, Spongent, Photon. Though keys to be wrapped are limited to the length of 1411 bits, our scheme still provides a simple and efficient key update protocol for most of symmetric and several asymmetric cryptosystems. It can also bind the associated data to the message, and is able to preprocess it without the master key. The ciphertext length is equal to the permutation width n, while the master key length k can vary.

Table 1. KWF and other key wrapping schemes

	KWF	HBS	AES-KW	SIV	Hash-then-E
Message length	0..1411	Arbitrary			
Overhead	1.2–1.5	2	12	2	$1+\varepsilon$
Expansion	192–384	128	$\|H\| + 64$	128	128
Security model	DAE	DAE	No	DAE	RPA
Security proof	RP	PRP,PRF	No	PRP, PRF	PRP
Block cipher	No	Yes	Yes	Yes	Yes
Hash function	Yes	Maybe	No	Yes	Yes
Preprocess header	Yes	No	No	Yes	Yes
128-bit security	Yes	Not with AES	No	Not with AES	

We recalled several alternative schemes and concluded that KWF is a viable alternative when a user wants to achieve 128-bit security within a simple design. Though the security of KWF is proven in the random-permutation model, we showed that no similar schemes secure in the standard model have the same features, and the Even-Mansour construction needs a careful amplification to suit the 128-bit security requirement.

The scheme is provably secure in the refined concept of DAE, where we add the adversarial access to the permutation. Assuming no weakness in the permutation and a collision resistant hash function for the associated data, the violation of DAE property is unlikely for the number of queries $q \leq 2^k$. Hence the security level of 128 bits is easy to deliver, which is not the case for other key wrapping schemes using AES.

A scalable version of our scheme, which would process arbitrarily long messages and remain simple and secure, is an object for the future work.

We believe that there are numerous different applications where DAE schemes can be used. Whereas one might need 128-bit security level at first, another would want to process arbitrary long messages. We have constructed a comparative table to demonstrate that KWF may find its own niche (Table 1). The overhead is here defined as the ratio of extra blockcipher calls compared to the sole encryption of the same data; we simply divide the permutation width by the message length. The expansion is the the number of extra bits compared to the ciphertext of the same data. We also compare the need of block cipher or a hash function, the ability to preprocess the header in advance, and the ability to deliver 128-bit security with recommended parameters (usually AES for other schemes).

Acknowledgements. The author thanks Alex Biryukov, Jean-Sébastien Coron, Joan Daemen, and Gilles Van Assche for valuable comments on the paper.

References

1. Van Assche, G.: Private communication (August 2013)
2. Aumasson, J.-P., Henzen, L., Meier, W., Naya-Plasencia, M.: QUARK: A lightweight hash. In: Mangard, S., Standaert, F.-X. (eds.) CHES 2010. LNCS, vol. 6225, pp. 1–15. Springer, Heidelberg (2010), https://131002.net/quark/quark_full.pdf
3. Bertoni, G., Daemen, J., Peeters, M., Van Assche, G.: On the indifferentiability of the sponge construction. In: Smart, N.P. (ed.) EUROCRYPT 2008. LNCS, vol. 4965, pp. 181–197. Springer, Heidelberg (2008)
4. Bertoni, G., Daemen, J., Peeters, M., Van Assche, G.: Duplexing the sponge: Single-pass authenticated encryption and other applications. In: Miri, A., Vaudenay, S. (eds.) SAC 2011. LNCS, vol. 7118, pp. 320–337. Springer, Heidelberg (2012)
5. Bertoni, G., Daemen, J., Peeters, M., Van Assche, G.: The Keccak reference, version 3.0 (2011), http://keccak.noekeon.org/Keccak-reference-3.0.pdf
6. Bhattacharyya, R., Mandal, A., Nandi, M.: Security analysis of the mode of JH hash function. In: Hong, S., Iwata, T. (eds.) FSE 2010. LNCS, vol. 6147, pp. 168–191. Springer, Heidelberg (2010)
7. Biryukov, A., Khovratovich, D.: PPAE: Parallelizable permutation-based authenticated encryption, presented at DIAC (2013), http://2013.diac.cr.yp.to/slides/khovratovich.pdf
8. Bogdanov, A., Andreeva, E., Mennink, B., Mouha, N., Luykx, A., Yasuda, K.: APE(X): Authenticated permutation-based encryption with extended misuse resistance, presented at DIAC (2013), http://2013.diac.cr.yp.to/slides/luykx.pdf
9. Bogdanov, A., Knežević, M., Leander, G., Toz, D., Varıcı, K., Verbauwhede, I.: SPONGENT: A lightweight hash function. In: Preneel, B., Takagi, T. (eds.) CHES 2011. LNCS, vol. 6917, pp. 312–325. Springer, Heidelberg (2011)
10. Bogdanov, A., Knudsen, L.R., Leander, G., Standaert, F.-X., Steinberger, J., Tischhauser, E.: Key-alternating ciphers in a provable setting: Encryption using a small number of public permutations. In: Pointcheval, D., Johansson, T. (eds.) EUROCRYPT 2012. LNCS, vol. 7237, pp. 45–62. Springer, Heidelberg (2012)
11. Daemen, J.: Permutation-based symmetric cryptography and Keccak. Technical report, Ecrypt II, Crypto for 2020 Invited Talk (2013), https://www.cosic.esat.kuleuven.be/ecrypt/cryptofor2020
12. Dunkelman, O., Keller, N., Shamir, A.: Minimalism in cryptography: The Even-Mansour scheme revisited. In: Pointcheval, D., Johansson, T. (eds.) EUROCRYPT 2012. LNCS, vol. 7237, pp. 336–354. Springer, Heidelberg (2012)
13. Even, S., Mansour, Y.: A construction of a cipher from a single pseudorandom permutation. In: Matsumoto, T., Imai, H., Rivest, R.L. (eds.) ASIACRYPT 1991. LNCS, vol. 739, pp. 210–224. Springer, Heidelberg (1993)
14. Ferguson, N., Lucks, S., Schneier, B., Whiting, D., Bellare, M., Kohno, T., Callas, J., Walker, J.: The Skein hash function family (2010), http://www.skein-hash.info/sites/default/files/skein1.3.pdf (Submission to NIST (Round 3))
15. Gennaro, R., Halevi, S.: More on key wrapping. In: Jacobson Jr., M.J., Rijmen, V., Safavi-Naini, R. (eds.) SAC 2009. LNCS, vol. 5867, pp. 53–70. Springer, Heidelberg (2009)
16. Guo, J., Peyrin, T., Poschmann, A.: The PHOTON family of lightweight hash function. In: Rogaway, P. (ed.) CRYPTO 2011. LNCS, vol. 6841, pp. 222–239. Springer, Heidelberg (2011), https://sites.google.com/site/photonhashfunction

17. Iwata, T., Ohashi, K., Minematsu, K.: Breaking and repairing GCM security proofs. In: Safavi-Naini, R., Canetti, R. (eds.) CRYPTO 2012. LNCS, vol. 7417, pp. 31–49. Springer, Heidelberg (2012)
18. Iwata, T., Yasuda, K.: BTM: A single-key, inverse-cipher-free mode for deterministic authenticated encryption. In: Jacobson Jr., M.J., Rijmen, V., Safavi-Naini, R. (eds.) SAC 2009. LNCS, vol. 5867, pp. 313–330. Springer, Heidelberg (2009)
19. Iwata, T., Yasuda, K.: HBS: A single-key mode of operation for deterministic authenticated encryption. In: Dunkelman, O. (ed.) FSE 2009. LNCS, vol. 5665, pp. 394–415. Springer, Heidelberg (2009)
20. Krovetz, T., Rogaway, P.: The software performance of authenticated-encryption modes. In: Joux, A. (ed.) FSE 2011. LNCS, vol. 6733, pp. 306–327. Springer, Heidelberg (2011)
21. NIST. Special publication 800-38f: Recommendation for block cipher modes of operation: Methods for key wrapping (2008), http://csrc.nist.gov/publications/drafts/800-38F
22. Osaki, Y., Iwata, T.: Further more on key wrapping. IEICE Transactions 95-A(1), 8–20 (2012), http://skew2011.mat.dtu.dk (Also published at SKEW 2011)
23. Rogaway, P.: Authenticated-encryption with associated-data. In: ACM Conference on Computer and Communications Security 2002, pp. 98–107 (2002)
24. Rogaway, P.: Formalizing human ignorance. In: Nguyên, P.Q. (ed.) VIETCRYPT 2006. LNCS, vol. 4341, pp. 211–228. Springer, Heidelberg (2006)
25. Rogaway, P., Shrimpton, T.: A provable-security treatment of the key-wrap problem. In: Vaudenay, S. (ed.) EUROCRYPT 2006. LNCS, vol. 4004, pp. 373–390. Springer, Heidelberg (2006)

A   Lightweight Permutations for KWF

Here we recommend for KWF some particular permutations taken from the lightweight hash function families: Quark, Photon, Spongent.

The Quark family [2] offers compact and low-power hash functions best suitable for RFID technology and other resource-constrained platforms. It uses permutations of width $n = 136, 176, 256$. Here $n = 256$ (s-Quark) is a good candidate for KWF operating on 64-bit keys and plaintexts, and u- and d-Quark ($n = 136, 176$) can be chosen as the hash function $\mathcal{G}$ with the 64-bit and 80-bit level of collision resistance, respectively. We denote Quark permutations of width n by Quark-n.

The Photon family [16] is an AES-based lightweight hash function design with permutations of width 100, 144, 196, 256, 288. We denote its permutations of width n by Photon-n and recommend using Photon-288 for applications with 64-bit level security. The hash functions Photon/n offer $n/2$-bit of security for collision resistance and are suitable for processing associated data.

The Spongent family [9] is another lightweight hash function design with permutations of width from 88 to 768 bits, with all widths multiple of 4 bits available. Its permutations Spongent-n can be used for all security levels, with a particular choice optimized for the input length.

Table 2. Recommended parameters for scheme KWF. All the numbers are bit lengths.

Hash function for AD	Message length	Permutation
Security level and key length: 64		
Keccak/128, u-Quark, Photon/128	0..63	Keccak-400, Quark-256, Photon-288, Spongent-256
Keccak/128, u-Quark, Photon/128	64..212	Keccak-400, Spongent-400
Keccak/128, u-Quark, Photon/128	213..612	Keccak-800
Keccak/128, u-Quark, Photon/128	613..1412	Keccak-1600
Security level and key length: 80		
Keccak/160, d-Quark, Photon/160	0..160	Keccak-400, Spongent-400
Keccak/160, d-Quark, Photon/160	161..560	Keccak-800
Keccak/160, d-Quark, Photon/160	561..1360	Keccak-1600
Security level and key length: 112		
SHA-224, Keccak/224, s-Quark	0..464	Keccak-800
SHA-224, Keccak/224, s-Quark	465..1264	Keccak-1600
Security level and key length: 128		
SHA-256, Keccak/256	0..415	Keccak-800
SHA-256, Keccak/256	416..1215	Keccak-1600

B   Security of KWF via the Concept of Human Ignorance

Now we attempt to deal more rigorously with the collision resistance of the hash function $\mathcal{G}$ that processes the header.

We can do this by following the "human ignorance" concept introduced by Rogaway [24]. First, we introduce the variant of our scheme called KWF'. Then we show that for any adversary A breaking KWF we can explicitly construct an adversary C violating the collision resistance of $\mathcal{G}$ and an adversary B violating the DAE security of KWF' so that their total advantage exceeds the advantage of A. Then we bound the advantage of B.

Let KWF' be the version of KWF, where the headers are l-bit long and the function G is an identity function. Hence $\mathcal{G}(H)$ can be simply replaced by H.

Lemma 2. *The DAE advantage of an adversary attacking instantiation Π' of KWF' and asking the total of at most q queries to all oracles and $\mathcal{F}$ is bounded as follows:*

$$Adv_{\Pi'}^{dae}(q) \leq \frac{2.5q}{2^k} + \frac{8.5q^2}{2^{n-k}}.$$

Proof. The proof of this lemma repeats the proof of Theorem 1 with a small refinement: $\mathcal{G}(H)$ is everywhere replaced with H, so distinct H always yield distinct inputs to $\mathcal{E}$ and $\mathcal{F}$. Hence the overall bound remains the same with the collision search term removed.

Lemma 3. *There exist (and are explicitly constructed in the proof) the adversary B attacking Π' and the adversary C attacking the collision resistance of a hash function such that for any $\mathcal{G}$ and any adversary A attacking instantiation Π of KWF*

$$\boldsymbol{Adv}_{\Pi}^{dae}(A) \leq \boldsymbol{Adv}_{\Pi'}^{dae}(B^{A,\mathcal{G}}) + \boldsymbol{Adv}_{\mathcal{G}}^{coll}(C^{A,\mathcal{G}}).$$

Adversary B asks the same number of queries as A to his oracles, and adversary C asks at maximum the same number of queries to $\mathcal{G}$ as A asks to his oracles.

Proof. The proof is very similar to the security proof of the hash-then-PRF folklore algorithm, which extends the domain of a PRF by hashing the input, in [24]. Adversary B is constructed as follows. He has access to A and $\mathcal{G}$, runs A as an oracle, and forwards all his requests to oracles $\mathcal{E}$ and $\mathcal{D}$ to his own instantiations of them for KWF'. Whenever A halts, B outputs the same bit.

Adversary C also runs A as an oracle and emulates the oracle pair $(\$, \perp)$ for him. In addition he computes and stores $\mathcal{G}(H)$ for each H queried by A. Whenever a collision is found, C halts and outputs it.

Then we try to bound $\boldsymbol{Adv}_{\Pi}^{dae}(A) - \boldsymbol{Adv}_{\Pi'}^{dae}(B^{A,\mathcal{G}})$. Since B and A behave identically when their worlds consist of real encryption/decryption oracles, we obtain that

$$\boldsymbol{Adv}_{\Pi}^{dae}(A) - \boldsymbol{Adv}_{\Pi'}^{dae}(B^{A,\mathcal{G}}) = \Pr\left[B^{A,\mathcal{G}}[\$, \perp]\right] - \Pr\left[A[\$, \perp]\right] \leq$$
$$\leq \Pr\left[A \text{ makes queries colliding in } \mathcal{G}\right] = \boldsymbol{Adv}_{\mathcal{G}}^{coll}(C^{A,\mathcal{G}}),$$

where the last equation follows from the definition of C and the inequality comes from the fact that A and B may behave differently only if A makes queries which contain colliding H.

The next theorem immediately follows from these two lemmas and is a more rigorous version of Theorem 1.

Theorem 2. *There exist (and are explicitly constructed in the proof) the adversary B attacking KWF' and the adversary C attacking the collision resistance of a hash function such that for any $\mathcal{G}$ and any adversary A attacking KWF*

$$\boldsymbol{Adv}_{\Pi}^{dae}(A) \leq \frac{2.5q}{2^k} + \frac{8.5q^2}{2^{n-k}} + \boldsymbol{Adv}_{\mathcal{G}}^{coll}(C).$$

Author Index